Built Up uncovers the roots of the global real estate industry in the machinations of a patron of Shakespeare, the merged lineages of business savvy women and men, startlingly innovative collaborations with the first English architect, and the radical explorations of other denizens of early modern London – and what those colorful origins mean for the practice of property development today.

Uniting insights from the author's career as an internationally recognized developer with meticulous archival research, this resource for scholars and professionals synthesizes economic history and the latest planning and finance literature. The result is an unprecedented effort to codify the principles and activities of real estate development as a foundation for future academic research and practical innovation.

By tracing the evolution of property development to its earliest days, *Built Up* establishes the theoretical groundwork for the next phase in the transformation of the urban environment.

With over fifteen years of real estate experience, **Patrice Derrington** is currently the Holliday Associate Professor and Director of the Real Estate Development program at Columbia University. Patrice's academic credentials include a Ph.D. from U.C. Berkeley, Harvard MBA, and B. Arch, University of Queensland, in addition to teaching awards, publications, and notable contributions to research. In her industry experience on Wall Street, she worked as an investment banker, advisor, and fund manager to major individual and institutional clients such as David Rockefeller, Keybank, and the Lower Manhattan Development Corporation. She is also a registered architect and has led numerous urban development projects in the USA and Australia.

"*Built Up* reminds the real estate industry that the foundations of its private development activities were very concerned with creating public space and amenities for the benefit of the communities as well as the financial success of their buildings. I know our young professionals in Project Destined will be inspired and encouraged in achieving more equitable outcomes."

–Cedric Bobo, Co-Founder, Project Destined

"Real estate development, we like to believe, is a greedy affair. Patrice Derrington argues that it doesn't have to be that way, proposing a model that takes into account values beyond the immediate financial gains. *Built Up* is an indispensable book for anyone interested in what drives the production of our built environment and a much-needed theoretical framework to overturn 'business as usual.'"

–Reinier de Graaf, Partner, Office for Metropolitan Architecture

"*Built Up* has given me a lot of inspiration for my upcoming projects."

–Daryl Ng, Deputy Chairman, Sino Group

"We shape our built environment, and it then shapes us. Shaping our built environment is the work of real estate developers. Great spaces are not defined by ordinary folk. Patrice Derrington tells many vivid tales as she helps us understand our cities and ourselves. This is the rare book that is both deeply incisive and great fun."

–Larry Summers, President Emeritus, Harvard University

"Twenty-first-century real estate development often devolves into a painful clash of wills between entrepreneurs and the public realm. In her magnum opus, *Built Up*, Patrice Derrington gives this vital sector a history, starting with the ancient Greeks and proceeding in depth through the origins of speculative development in seventeenth-century England. Even in distant times, real estate developers were colorful characters. With this sure to be influential text, current land use struggles are reframed and alternatives for re-imagining them posited. Derrington shows us how the practice of real estate in the past can point to new approaches going forward."

–Mary Ann Tighe, CEO, NY Tri-State Region CBRE

BUILT UP

An Historical Perspective on the Contemporary Principles and Practices of Real Estate Development

Patrice Derrington

Routledge
Taylor & Francis Group

NEW YORK AND LONDON

First published 2021

by Routledge

605 Third Avenue, New York, NY 10158

and by Routledge

2 Park Square, Milton Park, Abingdon, Oxon OX14 4RN

Routledge is an imprint of the Taylor & Francis Group, an informa business

Library of Congress Cataloging-in-Publication Data

Names: Derrington, Patrice, author.

Title: Built up: an historical perspective on the contemporary principles and practices of real estate development / Patrice Derrington.

Description: New York, NY: Routledge, 2021. |

Includes bibliographical references and index.

Identifiers: LCCN 2020049667 (print) | LCCN 2020049668 (ebook) |

ISBN 9780367699949 (hardback) | ISBN 9781003144151 (ebook)

Subjects: LCSH: Real estate business–England–London–History. |

Read estate business. | Real estate development–England–London–History. |

Real estate development–History.

Classification: LCC HD610.L6 D47 2021 (print) |

LCC HD610.L6 (ebook) | DDC 333.3309421–dc23

LC record available at https://lccn.loc.gov/2020049667

LC ebook record available at https://lccn.loc.gov/2020049668

ISBN: 9780367699949 (hbk)

ISBN: 9780367699963 (pbk)

ISBN: 9781003144151 (ebk)

Typeset in Zurich

by Newgen Publishing UK

For my parents, Desmond and Patricia, of course.

Contents

Figures

List of Figures

Preface

Speculative private development is now responsible for delivering the larger proportion of the global urban built environment, even within state-ruled countries. But, unchecked, it is also held to be responsible for the tragic displacement of communities, unaffordability of housing, controversial additions to city typography and the increasing inequality of society. Private developers are typecast as brutal and greedy.

How does such a criticized and disparaged activity persist as the most compelling force in the formation of our increasingly popular urban environments?

To answer this question, this book undertakes a rigorous interrogation of the private urban development process, as it is practiced globally since its codified method is employed within a variety of politico-economic conditions. The study's objective is to search beyond the common superficial description of its methods and the continued litany of what is done badly, and reveal the inner workings of the real estate development activity: what the essential actions and most critical decisions are, why they are performed in that way, and where exactly within this process does its mechanism fail to deliver the best outcome for so many who are impacted.

An example requiring this examination is the common practice of maximizing site coverage with "salable" square footage while neglecting the provision of public space or amenities, even though the project relies on the desirability of its neighborhood for success. This decision is taken as a matter of course, and yet it consistently results in urban projects that are detrimental to communities. James Graaskamp importantly commenced an evaluation of these typical decisions and, by this, presented a modification of the "highest and best use" analysis to that of "most fitting and most probable use" (Graaskamp 1981, 10). More of this improvement to the practice is needed.

To continue the examination, I identify the protocols for the essential decisions and actions of the development activity and question their structure. In this it follows Clark's (2000, 6) goal regarding the pension fund industry: "to formalize through a set of general terms and concepts the actions and decisions that are otherwise hidden in the play of customary context practice." These exposed features are analyzed to understand why they are as they are and what influenced their formation, and then to question if they can be done differently to achieve a better outcome. This is a self-examination of real estate development practice in order to better know itself, improve itself, and produce the best professionals for it.

This investigation is not about the commercial activity of investing in or financing real estate, nor about pricing, buying, and selling existing properties, all of which have received the attention of excellent scholarship within mainstream economics. Nor is it an evaluation of physical and social outcomes, nor a discussion of urban plans and policies, since these have also incurred wide analysis by architects, planners, and urbanists. Rather, it is about the process by which individual private development projects are produced: land is located and purchased, the building envisioned and designed, the economics calculated and funding obtained, the erection of the structure managed, and finally the marketing, leasing, and selling of the completed project effected. It is a process of creation, planning, and production, of finance and business, and of impacting the urban context in which it occurs. Although it has hitherto been broadly described in terms of action steps and decision-making, and sometimes analyzed in part with respect to some selected detail such as stakeholders, until now there has been little research or discussion on the comprehensive process and how its inherent inner workings enable it to be the dominant process of private production of the urban fabric, that it has plainly become.

Complex as the activity is today and given its want of an existing critical framework, in order to investigate its details effectively it is useful to examine the origins of the process. In this approach, it follows that of William Goetzmann (2016, 1) in his extensive explanation of finance, which he describes as "the story of a technology: a way of doing things." Similar examinations of society's "way of doing things," specifically within its economic dimension, have been provided by Alfred D. Chandler (1962) in elucidating the American industrial corporation, and joins the company of *Progressive Business: An Intellectual History of the Role of Business in American Society*, by C.O. Christiansen, *Firms, Networks and Business Values: The British and American Cotton Industries since 1750*, by Mary B. Rose, and *VC* by Tom Nicholas. The stated purpose of such explorations was "to demonstrate the need for greater recognition of path dependence and historical evolution in the modern theory of finance" (Baskin and Miranti 1997, 3). It may similarly be said of private real estate development, practiced as it is with the uncritical repetition of steps and decisions, that knowing the historical evolution of these would provide an understanding that informs critical analysis and the formulation of needed theory.

The process of private urban development came into existence as Goetzmann (ibid.) similarly describes of finance: "Like other technologies, it developed through innovations that improved efficiency." The story therefore begins when the first private developers were envisioning and delivering the first truly speculative urban schemes of some scale, that responded more efficiently to the needs of a rapidly expanding community. It was different in kind from the small-scale "cottage industry" undertakings that had occurred throughout history in the form of an addition of spare space to be rented out opportunistically, or non-speculative building for one's own occupation or commercial activity, or from the government's provision of habitation for the populace, such as in Paris. It began when various new formats of land use, site layouts, property financing, project management and marketing were tested with varying degrees of success by innovative entrepreneurs. Felicitously, it was contemporaneous with a critical need for housing and the burgeoning emergence of capitalism that forced its rapid resolution of operational dynamics and economic constructs, and consolidated it as *the* model of private development for centuries to come.

In the larger context, not only was this model available as a profitable production activity for astute businesspeople but it also evolved symbiotically with the Western system of economics and governance that was rapidly colonizing much of the globe. Both at its original location in 17th-century London, and in far-distant parts, it proved to be resilient to waves of catastrophe unleashed by man and nature.

Even at the present time, the COVID-19 pandemic of 2020 challenges private development activity in all its dimensions, including its formulaic spatial arrangements, its leverage through density, its consistency of rental payments, and its interwoven capital structures. But it had already fought that battle in its infancy when in 1665 the new enthusiasm for urban living was challenged by the pandemic Great Plague that Bell (1924, vii) suggests "was responsible for fully 100,000 deaths" in London. That impact on one city, in raw numbers being close to 50% of the present national mortality in the United States, might, with some new accommodations, portend well for the survival of the model beyond even this catastrophe.

Throughout its evolution, private development practice was so successfully aligned with the dominant political and social interests that its fundamental structure became deeply embedded within the urbanization of the Anglo-American world, and persisted as the prevailing method of delivering the built environment. Though continuing to be the elemental kernel, the original entrepreneurial model has been extended by substantial commercial organizations through strategic plans with sophisticated financial structures and detailed processes for resource allocation and production, and the resulting process now constitutes a large part of many macroeconomies even beyond the original socio-economic context.

This book tells how this happened by observing the earliest instances of the activity. What has been accepted as the "way of doing things" is examined to reveal the circumstances, choices and decisions, causes and actions leading to the basic formulation of the model. That formulation is evaluated in social, physical, and economic terms with respect to its outcomes then and in the growing urban environments today. And, most importantly, within this exploration is the ripping tale of the colorful, brilliant, and bold forefathers of development practice.

Acknowledgments

As with the development process it seeks to understand, this book is the result of contributions from many of the best people in the real estate industry, many of the best people in scholarship and publication, and many of the best people in my life.

It was the enthusiasm for the intellectual struggle with the topic by Routledge's editor Chloe Layman that encouraged me to compose my passionate, but potentially endless, theoretical exploration of the essence of the development process into this book, and therefore encourage a broader discussion. Her direction has been invaluable, and I am grateful for our companionship in this production. Peter Stafford's deep knowledge of English history, and of the nuances of the period, enabled me to be so much more precise in the descriptions of people and events, and I would like to thank Jenny Guildford, senior production editor, and Shannon Welch, editorial assistant, both of whom patiently but diligently maintained our production quality and schedule at Routledge. Additionally, I am very appreciative of the grammatical guidance and diligent proof-reading of Selina Cohen at Oxford Publishing Services.

There has been a long life to my curiosity as to why private real estate development is done the way it is, and has such varied results ranging from architectural masterpieces, financial windfalls, and bountiful community amenities to urban monstrosities, developer bankruptcies, and blighted communities. Along the way, incisive minds and accomplished colleagues have furthered my understanding in these differing dimensions.

In architecture, my early studies with teachers of the Architectural Association and innovative practitioners in Australia established a deep appreciation for good design and its ability to improve the human condition. Later being influenced by numerous American architects including Cedric Price, Peter Eisenman, Jeannie Gang, Gene Kohn, Jamie von Klemperer, and Rafael Vignoly as well as my colleagues at Columbia University, I came to understand how good design can successfully permeate commercial interests. More recently, I am joined and informed by scholars such as Rainier de Graaf in reframing the intersection of architecture and commerce, and my colleague Christoph Kumpusch who inspires us all with his visual representations of that initiative, including the conceptual origins of this book's cover.

There could be no better route to learning financial constructs than through Harvard's Business School, and with the challenging pedagogy of the excellent faculty, including the recent Dean, Nitin Noria, and legendary real estate professor William Poorvu, I saw real estate as potentially supportive of good design, and moved beyond the commonly held perspective of their conflict. Further insight into the creative side of real estate finance and investment was gained under the demanding but untiringly informative direction of many industry leaders including Joseph DeLuca, Jon Salony, Richard Salomon, Michael Fascitelli, Richard Sheppard, John Streicker, and David Rockefeller. It was Dean Rosemary Scanlon, who hired me to teach real estate finance at New York University's Schack Institute, who spurred me to deeply critique the industry's unquestioned adoption of concepts and calculative methodologies, just as should be done when students are introduced to disciplines and professional codifications.

Understanding the tendency towards poor social performance when private urban development is undertaken was the necessary additional dimension to my exploration, if not its compelling driver. Here I am indebted to many brilliant social scientists including Gordon L. Clark, Robert Beauregard, and – sadly the late – Michael Sorkin.

Enriched with this background in scholarship and practice, I would not have ventured on this project without the intellectual context of discourse and contesting ideas at Columbia University's Graduate School of Architecture, Planning and Preservation. Solidly encouraged by Dean Amale Andraos, and with the helpful advice of my eminent colleagues Reinhold Martin, Felicity Dale Scott, and Gwendolyn Wright, it is hoped that this book makes a significant contribution to the scholarly initiatives of the School. Additionally, leading industry figures who are alumni of the School's M.Sc. Real Estate Development (MSRED) program, such as Marc Holliday, Blake Hutcheson, Stephen Glascock, and Ernst Valery, and invaluable advisors such as Mary Ann Tighe, have been both insightful regarding the topic and supportive in many practical respects. Immense logistical assistance, for which I cannot express enough gratitude, was provided by my administrative colleagues Jessica Stockton King and Rebecca Andersen Polimeda. Of inspiration have been recent students of the program since I have been its director, with their queries, challenges, and now exemplary activities in practice. And I thank the M.Sc. Real Estate Development (MSRED) Class of 2020 for their patience and understanding as I committed the necessary time to the book.

Locating material, both contemporary and historical, pertaining to the topic of this book was assisted by many learned people to whom I am most grateful. A very fruitful introduction to the early development activities in the USA was provided by Christine Riggle, Special Collections Librarian at the Harvard Business School's Baker Library. For providing critical details and clarifications of dates and activities regarding the creation of Covent Garden, I would like to thank Nicola Allen, Archivist at The Bedford Estates. Important introductions to key people at the estates of Bedford, Grosvenor, Portman, and Cadogan, as well as the locating of critical maps of the time from the archives of the London Society, were most generously provided by Nick McKeogh, Trustee of that institution and also Co-founder of New London Architecture. Further help from the latter, in pursuing the complex history of London's Great Estates, was provided by Lucie Murray, the Program Director, and her colleagues Sarah Yates, Matthew Quinn, and Lara Kinneir. Evan Jenkins and Nicholas Johannes were both very helpful in reviewing historical material when they were students in the Columbia MSRED program.

My research assistant for over two years, Brett Owen (Bo) Mcmillan II, has been invaluable in helping me with the historical investigation as well as in taking new paths when considering the social impact of urban development, and in some painstaking editing tasks.

Acknowledgments

I am also grateful for his intellectual companionship in exploring this uncharted area of urban form, and now, in turn, I shall be encouraging him in his challenging task of completing his Ph.D. dissertation.

Of course, a book is a personal creation and for any ability in this I am grateful to my family and friends for their formative influences. My dear parents have endlessly extended their nurturing and support, including long and insightful discussions with them on the topic; but I am also grateful for my mother's boundless encouragement and my father's generous dedication of many hours to proofreading drafts. My siblings, Roger and Margot, and their respective spouses, the Hon. Sarah Derrington and Christopher Blue, all lawyers, have trained me well in appreciating the legal context of all human endeavor; and Christopher, as an eminent solicitor to the real estate industry, has provided me with regular narrations and elucidations of real estate shenanigans.

I am also most grateful to friends who rallied round with encouraging words, particularly in the final phase of completion, including Shirley Clark, Odeta Stuikys Rose, competing author Patrick Monahan, and many, many much loved others.

Introduction

Private real estate development now delivers most of the world's urban built fabric, and the trend is growing. The architectural thought provocateur Reinier de Graaf (2017, 420) recently announced to his profession: "The initiative to construct the city comes to reside increasingly in the private sector." Cities and states are outsourcing the provision of social housing, social institutions such as schools, hospitals, etc., and basic utilities and infrastructure to the private sector. This is manifest in state-led countries as well as in Western capitalist economies. However, its impact on communities has resulted in substantial dissatisfaction and confrontational processes, and blame for many bad outcomes has been directly attributed to the developer. It would therefore seem that, if this municipal outsourcing is to continue, the private development processes should be rigorously examined and improved for the benefit of urban communities globally.

Further, while private property development generally produces approximately $80 billion in new real estate per annum, it has a track record of devastating financial failures with very serious repercussions for many, excessive vulnerability to economic cycles, and typically lax analytical and managerial processes which are becoming increasingly apparent. If such an extensive commercial activity is to remain so fundamental to the broader economy, it should be improved in its business practice and professional discipline.

Where does one start to improve a process so deeply embedded within the socio-economic context of our urban centers? Other such "institutionalized" processes that provide for the needs of the community, such as governance and legal structures, healthcare and educational systems, and commercial and financial exchange, are continually subjected to scrutiny, both internally by their practitioners and externally by recipients, and undergo an intellectual search for improved methods and performance. Private development, however, despite extensive criticism from many quarters, does not itself interrogate its fundamental processes or seek to improve its practice, and in this it does not qualify as an institutionalized discipline or attract scholarly and professional respect.

Evaluating the Urban Development Process
Despite being relatively unexamined, the urban production process somehow became interwoven or integral with significant physical, economic, and social outcomes described and analyzed by economists and urban scholars. Judging by the impact of development activity, it has very specific objectives, layers of decision-making, and procedural and managerial routines

but, as yet, these have not been intellectually linked to existing urban theory. Although extensively described in case studies or instructed through "how-to" books and even offering self-congratulatory tales of success, the process has not been subjected to the rigorous critique and analysis that it demands given its pervasive practice and far-reaching consequences for so many people.

Some notable theoretical foundations for the development process were provided by research in the later decades of the 20th century, and will be discussed in detail in a later chapter. A comprehensive and broadly adopted definition of the process was provided by Patsy Healey (1992, 36) as:

> the transformation of the physical form, bundle of rights, and material and symbolic value of land and buildings from one state to another, through the efforts of agents with interests and purposes in acquiring and using resources, operating rules and applying and developing ideas and values.

While such a definition is helpful in guiding practice, if there is no associated critique of how it is done and why it is done that way, or a constant evaluation of how it performs with an intent to progress towards improvement, real estate development cannot be an intellectually honed discipline, and will remain a trade. Though Goetzmann (2016, 1) similarly described finance as a technology, or "way of doing things" that was "not intrinsically good or bad," if such a way is proposed as having "improved efficiency," then satisfaction of this objective can be evaluated as done well or not. Therefore, the private development model that is used so extensively today can certainly be assessed as to whether it delivers the urban built form with "improved efficiency" compared to prior or alternative methods.

To confine an evaluation of the development process to that of producing built form more efficiently, though, would be to ignore the other impacts it has on society, all those physical, social, and economic aspects that are studied and around which criticism arises. Therefore, it is necessary not merely to know and understand the model by which private development is practiced but also to connect those details to the consequences that are apparent in the outcome. As noted earlier, those impacts are extensively described in other scholarship, but the dynamic by which they are produced by specific features of the model has not been examined. Without this, the practice cannot justifiably be modified for an improved outcome.

Critically, as the adverse impacts of poorly conceived projects become more noted, and as confrontation worsens between communities that need physical improvements and private developers who provide them, but also as educational initiatives for the better preparation of the practitioners emerge, the challenge of deeply understanding and critiquing the very ontological structure of the real estate development process achieves new importance.

Approach of this Book: Learning from History

The investigation of long-established and broadly accepted economic activities within a society is challenging. As for any intellectual investigation, it might be approached either by positing theoretical hypotheses and testing or by observing the details of the activity, gathering empirical findings, and evaluating the performance of what emerges. In a later chapter, the review of theoretical formulation around the private urban development process will indicate that the usual approaches are insufficient. While important strands of scholarship in the financial aspects and in the urban context can be collected in forming such a construct, an investigation is needed "from the inside out," or rooted in the activity itself. Such a theoretical framework for the real estate development process might be perceived to comprise a model of human activity with a production function of interrelated physical and financial dimensions that occur within a socio-economic context and, in turn, that have a substantial impact on that community.

Advances in modeling of the development process's complexity will be described and assessed, but a valid theory of the development activity also requires a recursive evaluation of social concerns contemporaneous with production optimization and capital market demands, that goes beyond the observation and modeling of current practice and seeks the first principles and essential dynamic of its formation as a socio-economic action.

To achieve such a theoretical understanding, a markedly different approach is proposed. Recently in the study of business – a field sharing much with private urban development in terms of itself being a form of economic production – there has been an "historical turn" underway in research and scholarly formulations, particularly with respect to the management and organizational fields (Novicevic et al. 2015, 157). It has been realized that "[b]usiness history is important for the insights it gives into the evolution and working of the modern economy. Synonymous with the study of change, a historical approach adds the dynamic dimension, lacking from much economic analysis" (Kirby and Rose, 1994, 1). Influential scholarship in the financial sector by this method is the work of William Goetzmann (2016), Jonathan Barron Baskin and Paul Miranti (1997), Geoffrey Jones (2002), and Mary O'Sullivan (2016).

Therefore, the selected methodology for a deeper exploration of today's manner of private urban development is to seek and observe the very earliest formation of that activity, when it emerged as an organized socio-economic process with distinct practices and identifiable practitioners. Located within the urban, social, economic, and institutional changes during the 16th and 17th centuries in the increasingly influential and growing metropolis of London are the early "sprouts" of a strategic urban development process wholly undertaken by private individuals. Then, the dynamic of rising capitalism in modern London becomes the milieu of its emergence with economic, political, and social networks being critical for its advanced formulation. Additionally, the formal and informal systems that existed between the governing institutions and emerging commerce came to tailor the expectations of both, it being well understood that "the institutional environment cannot be separated from the social fabric of both business elites and working people, whose values and behaviour both influence and are influenced by it" (Rose 2000, 3). Perhaps one of the key characteristics of urban development to emerge so early in its history is the penetrating and symbiotic economic relationship between it and municipal governance.

Central also to the historical narrative are, of course, the protagonists. As Polanyi (1957, 152) notes:

> [w]hether the source of the change be war or trade, startling interventions or shifts in natural conditions, the various sections in society will stand for different methods of adjustment (including forcible ones) and adjust their interests in a different way from those of other groups to whom they may seek to give a lead; hence only when one can point to the group or groups that effected a change is it explained *how* that change has taken place.

Introduction

By observing how the individual, private instigators of the early urban development schemes approached the challenges, resolved conflicts, created innovative versions of traditional activities, and also noting the varying success of their completed projects, some identification of the core and common actions can be achieved and a comparison made with other variant actions as to which were successful and which were not. Particularly for the early urban developers,

> [t]he history of economic development is a perpetual struggle between individual initiative and environmental limitations. Growth depends not just on a favorable *conjoncture* of economic forces, but on generations of unique individuals who have the motivation, the positive energy, the creative intelligence, the inspiration, and the talent to create and exploit opportunities. (Grassby 1994, 2)

Revealed in this presentation of the emergence of private urban development is the manner in which the actors moved outside the traditional mode by which the built environment had been delivered. While drawing on some of the other customary activities they performed, though in rural locales, and appropriating suitable parts of the vernacular mode of small-scale housing production, they responded with creativity to a compelling new need, formulated their own organizational structure and processes, worked their way around arising obstacles and proceeded to provide a solution for the dilemma of the acute housing shortage in expanding London of the 17th century.

Narrative Methodology

The purpose of using the historical narrative form in describing the actions of the earliest private developers is for the effective presentation of the unfolding, historical evolution and here it is structured by the genealogical method. This method has been described as "a 'gray, meticulous, and patiently documentary' approach to tracing historical process in terms of the dynamics to understand how concepts, practices, and actors have emerged, changed, and transformed over time" (Foucault 1977, 139, quoted in Novicevic et al. 2015, 171). This method supports the attempt to reveal and trace the early occurrence of the private urban development activities which have continued in their essential form to the present day. The historical context is described and the dynamic between that milieu and the emerging activities is presented, but also, as in accordance with the symbiotic essence of genealogy, the impact – both positive and negative – of the noted activities on the context is meticulously observed. Its purpose is not merely to record events but also to provide relevant historical information and commentary that helps explain how it was that the historical activities occurred as they did or even may have been undertaken in alternative ways. The experience is to be one of revelation and learning, not that of being merely told.

Historical Methodology

Delving into the history of early development, the challenge becomes locating material pertaining to these activities that may be spread across different disciplines, such as the architecture of the time, fascinating reports on commercial practices, imprecise and vague descriptions of properties, divergent discussions of building trades, and ideologically based social and political commentary. Additionally, there is the challenge for empirical or statistical analysis that lies in the paucity of recorded information of the time. The "fragility of statistical evidence" (Kirby and Rose 1994, 3) means that the details, pace, and performance of this emerging activity often require some conjecture in their reading, though this is restrained as much as possible.

In attempting to overlay the emerging capitalist system on the evolution of the urban topography and architectural form, it is helpful to provide a balance of historical material on both sides, though there has been more architecture and urban form preserved in place, or records maintained, than there appears to have been for keeping the business records and correspondence pertaining to its production. Additionally, business records are usually only of the final transactions, not revealing the decision-making and negotiations that occurred prior to this final resolution, and this requires some forensic speculation. Furthermore, in discussing issues of finance, and tracing the manner in which the early developers derived the important metrics guiding their decision-making, the analysis would typically enter the domain of quantitative history and empirical findings. However, many historians of this era have pointed out that it is almost impossible to extract quantitative data that would conform to today's requirements for empirical analysis (Harvey 1977, 18). The information is either missing in whole or in part, often varying in terms of measurements used, and frequently regarded as unreliable because of an underlying complex and unclear formulation. Hopefully, as the study of the private urban development activity proceeds in the future, more specific material will be found and utilized, and also the application of technology might make what is available more informative.

Of the acceptable historical methodologies, most suitable for the topic at hand is one of *triangulation*, which comprises a mixing of referenced materials, such as combining quantitative and qualitative data (Kipping et al. 2014), or, as in this case, reaching across the apposite theoretical frameworks referred to earlier. This approach is considered suitable as it "offers a postmodernist or relativist approach to historical research where authenticity of information does not rest on any single authoritarian source" (Novicevic et al. 2015, 164). Some archival material is viewed and utilized and for this the *underdeterministic* interpretation is adopted. As the archival data relevant to the subject is not extensive, nor always provided from reliable sources, and additionally, since the subject has been neglected by scholarship even since its beginnings, the material is scattered across various other categories of historical interest, such as land use and ownership, urban topology, demographics, and so forth. Therefore, an interpretation of archival data with these challenges, and often represented by incomplete fragments, requires some creative postulation about other useful materials or the reinterpretation of evidence in gaining an understanding of the subject from this new angle. For example, much urban and architectural material, while having been useful in its traditional perspective for scholarship in those fields, requires the addition of an economic consideration in viewing its place in urban development activities; and this is done.

With the intention of using historical revelation to better understand the contemporary activity of urban development, there is a conscious effort to avoid the pitfall of being "presentist" (Bedeian 1998), in failing to fully take into account the changes in time periods. It might

seem presumptuous to draw a simple genealogical line from the emerging property development activities of certain individuals in 17th-century London to that behemoth global activity
today, since the changes in the economic conditions, scale, geographies, and cultures have
surely forced modifications and aberrations. They have to a degree, but the essential details
of the innovative practice at that early time, particularly noted as being so robustly embedded in the economic, political, and social structure arising with modern capitalism at that
time, have been nurtured and consolidated as that structure prevailed and expanded to the
present day.

As the objective is to uncover and elucidate important and possibly unknown details of the
emerging activities, this exploration includes both primary sources of specific evidence and
secondary sources. These come from a wide range of perspectives that provide threads of
pertinent information to be woven into a rich description of the exciting context and turbulent
times in which real estate development practice began.

Methodology of Critique

Importantly, this exploration is to be more than a simple historical description of a certain
period in history and, although a narrative approach has been adopted, the purpose is to
learn through a critical analysis of that early urban development activity and its formulation.
When utilizing historical narratives for scholarly research, there is a common risk of overem-
phasizing the story and neglecting the formulation of the theoretical structure or meaningful
"plot" or purpose of the tale. Therefore, in this presentation of the history, use is made of the
scholarly process of *explanation dualism* that "involves the analysis of relationships between
variables" (Rowlinson et al. 2014). By this, as the evolution of the private development activity
is described, a direct evaluation is made of its emerging features in relation to the context,
and the benefit of hindsight is used to more clearly reveal the fundamental structure and
important dynamics. Though presented in summary in the final part of the book, the critical
lens is applied throughout.

In support of this approach that mixes history with critique, it has been said that "…
historical reasoning illustrates the interwoven relationship between variables in which the
positions and directions of variables change over time" (Novicevic et al. 2015, 161). Indeed,
urban development most surely exhibits a plethora of "interwoven relationships" between
its variables and stakeholders, and with that occurring under such continual dynamic
change. Furthermore, this approach not only eschews but also challenges the canonical
view of traditional structure and process as given and followed unquestioningly, and so the
persistently accepted mode of private urban development is finally interrogated. As typical
for such a critique, this exploration attempts to "reinterpret evidence, and rediscover voices
and issues" (Kilduff and Dougherty 2000, 778) that may be obfuscated or overshadowed in
the current mode of practice. In taking this approach of combining historical research with
critical evaluation, the methodology undoubtedly is more complex, and also attracts some
skepticism regarding its objectivist aspects. However, in addressing this multifaceted subject of the production of the built environment, precedent is found in the acclaimed work of
philosophers and social theorists such as Hayden White, Michel Foucault, and Max Weber
who have considered the scholarly interconnections and determined them useful and valid
for the field.

Reaching across Disciplines and Ideologies

Since, as admitted, the activity of private urban development currently lacks an intellectual construct for scholarship in the field, the exploration here must necessarily utilize other relevant theories and ideologies in examining matters that come to light and this includes the areas of design, urban planning, business, investment, and social sciences. If this exploration is to avoid missing aspects in the early formation of real estate development that may be at the heart of a particular perspective on the events, such as for example investment practices, it is necessary to be expansive, perhaps exhaustingly so, in capturing important views from many disciplines and within those disciplines the often conflicting ideologies such as the neoclassical versus Marxist approaches to urban theory.

As such, the exploration is at risk of endless discussion around the granular issues of each discipline. However, this is constrained by maintaining the objective of *knowing* the formation of the urban development process itself, not necessarily attempting to settle different ideological perspectives on that process. As said before, this "knowing" is not just a recording of an unbiased recording of what occurred, but to know requires an evaluative critique and this necessitates the borrowing of structures of critical assessment from the various disciplines. Although trying to avoid the use of the clichéd term "multidisciplinary," this exploration does engage numerous disciplines and utilize their ideological constructs for critique as needed.

Such an approach has been constructively used where an existing area of scholarship is applied to new matters. For example, Novicevic et al. (2015, 169) in their review of Weber's (1930) management history, a groundbreaking proposition for the nascent field of management theory, determined that a decentered approach "... offer[ed] a multi-viewpoint analysis of organizational phenomena. History explained or viewed from multiple observers offers a much richer explanation of a given phenomenon. In this way, the decentered theory is more like a kaleidoscope than a microscopic telling ..." In a similar manner, this analysis of the historical findings is undertaken through the kaleidoscope of various ideological viewpoints that have been applied to urban development activity.

Does this make the building of a theoretical construct for the real estate development process a phenomenon-led approach rather than one driven by a solid hypothesis requiring the collection of exogenous variables? Probably it does. Just as Ullmer (2009) discusses two significant economics thinkers of 17th century, William Petty and Nicholas Barbon, as offering theories within "a pre-paradigm condition," with respect to the formation of a discipline of macroeconomics, the urban development activity remains at such a stage of intellectual development. Theoretically it remains at an embryonic phase, such as Thomas Kuhn (1970, 15) describes, where "early fact gathering is a far more nearly random activity than the one that subsequent scientific development makes familiar"; but the primary objective is to create an intellectual forum for discussion and debate about the pervasive and impactful urban development activity and therefore launch further theoretical development leveraging other research methodologies.

Outline of this Exploration

This book is divided into three parts comprising a description of the historical preconditions for a considered new approach to building a city, the origins of private development activity and the work of its early practitioners, and a critique of that formalized practice in terms of theoretical principles. Through this, it proposes a reframing of present practices aimed at improving the urban environment.

Part I: Historical Foundations for Urban Innovation

For most innovation, the context in which it is introduced provides support, challenges, existing processes for adaptation, and a forum in which it can be adjudged to succeed, or fail. The complex process of private real estate development required an intricate and circumstantial confluence of many trends, new thinking, and dramatic social action for its birth. The details of these factors are organized around basic components of the process: land and its use, modes of commerce within capitalism's creation of real estate assets, urban demands for space in the face of constraints on form, and the structure of ownership and management of urban land and buildings.

Chapter 1. In explaining the suitable conditions in time and place for the first strategic development of private land, this chapter provides a fascinating prologue of critical activities in early England. Rapidly proceeding through the fifteen centuries from the Roman foundation of the city of London, through the dramatic changes introduced by William the Conqueror and the formulation of English property law, it describes the formation of a unique attitude to land, its distribution, its use, its value, the responsibilities of its ownership, and the conflicts arising over its control.

Chapter 2. During England's emergence from the Middle Ages and the political and economic changes during the reign of the Tudors, the concept of land was further modified from a focus on its mere physical form to include its financial dimension. In addition, the country experienced a dramatic rise in national prosperity, particularly in the port and commercial center of London. Associated with trading success and the formation of capitalist economics came methods of measuring financial results, and talented business minds applied them to a wide array of commercial activities including, relevantly, land transactions.

Chapter 3. Catalytic for real estate development activity in 17th-century London was the swelling population's demand for housing. Chaotic methods for its provision met with severe restrictions by the royal and municipal authorities. New philosophies and cultural progressions were harnessed to find solutions and improve the urban outcome, and the first architect of English birth reframed the spatial and physical nature of urban form.

Chapter 4. In the absence of the state's provision of housing, capitalism's full force directed private enterprise's solutions. Landlordism became a defined economic activity and builders rapidly threw up structures of varying quality. As the capital markets served this new business activity, it was viewed as the production of a consumable, deteriorating structure in contrast to permanently valuable land, and trading markets were established to accommodate both components.

Part II: The Birth of Modern Property Development

The new model of urban development was born in this context and impelled by these forces. Combining innovative approaches with suitable traditional methods, courageous participants undertook the first private urban development projects in the mode by which it continues to be practiced today. They made a number of notable achievements which gave momentum to the activity and its embrace by influential personages and commentators of the time.

Chapter 5. One of the first entrepreneurs, John Russell, combined a lineage of merchants with service to Henry VIII and was rewarded with the title of 1st Earl of Bedford, and the well-located lands of Covent Garden, amongst other rewards. He located his family on this estate, but it was not until the growing demand for housing was resolved with concessions for well-planned and well-designed development projects under the Stuarts that the 4th Earl innovatively conceived of a residential neighborhood complete with open piazza and parish church. His son, the 5th Earl, continued to expand the project with the addition of commercial premises, coffee shops, and theaters during the remainder of the century.

Chapter 6. Also in Henry's court was Thomas Wriothesley, an ambitious colleague of Thomas Cromwell who applied the new financial approach to land by gaining an extensive estate north of the Earl of Bedford's, called Bloomsbury. Made the 1st Earl of Southampton, he lived near, though not on, the estate, and it was his great-grandson, the 4th Earl, who followed Bedford's example and created the residential neighborhood of Bloomsbury Square. This estate was amalgamated with that of Bedford's through his daughter's marriage to an heir of that family, and it continues to be owned and managed by that aristocratic line today.

Chapter 7. Though landholding aristocrats had an advantage in their private development activities, it was a commoner, Nicholas Barbon, who advanced the trading structure of real estate such that all components, at all stages, could be financially defined. A noted commentator on economics, he provided credible arguments for the pricing of real estate, though he overlaid this with the notorious behavior of an investment promoter and personified the speculative developer that is recognized today. While his ingenious deal structures expanded the sources of capital for private development, his calculations and projects abandoned the contributions to the community made by the other practitioners.

Chapter 8. As an innovative business model, these early attempts were risky, though generally lucrative, while London's prosperity and population increased. The model of private development was adopted by other landowning aristocrats to create the city's Great Estates, but was also implemented by many builders and financially astute commoners in that and other growing urban areas of England. At the closing of the century, the codification of the process is apparent and with its solid incorporation of the economic, political, and social principles of the time, it was key to the governance of many new colonies being established then and in the following century.

Part III: Property Development Reframed: Theory, Principles, and Models

Having explored the historical formulation of the private urban development model, the insights gained are added to the understanding, discussion, and scholarship of the activity as currently undertaken. By this, its theoretical construct is reframed to include some of the fundamental principles and motivations that originally drove the innovative activity and produced an urban environment more equitable and beneficial to all.

Chapter 9. The details and dynamics elucidated in the historical narration are gathered in a comprehensive description of the activity and an identifiable business model is described. The innovations relating to the new approach to land control and use, the larger-scale production of built form, the creation of investment assets, and the complex relationship with the public realm are presented.

Chapter 10. The relatively small amount of scholarly literature specifically on the property development process is reviewed. Various models have evolved to visually represent the postulated components and dynamics and some cohered within theoretical frameworks. Those frameworks are discussed with a view to forming a platform from which a theory of real estate development can be further advanced with the addition of the new historical insights.

Chapter 11. The model of private urban development as historically revealed is then critiqued in terms of its objectives, analytics, processes, and performance. Building on emerging scholarship, the evaluative framework comprises economic, physical, and social dimensions. The examination is focused on the very processes by which the built form is produced for use by urban occupants, converted into financial assets with far-reaching appeal, and makes various impacts, positive and negative, on the surrounding community and public at large. In doing this, the evaluation is made both in terms of how it proceeded at the time, as much as the historic record can reveal, and as it currently operates with such a legacy.

The **Conclusion** brings into focus the performance of the private real estate development process as revealed and better understood by the examination of its earliest formation. The exposure of underlying principles, objectives, and procedural challenges are intended to advance a theoretical framework for the real estate development process. By this, the globally prevalent model of urban development can be subjected to more rigorous evaluation and critical scholarship, with certain analytical and managerial features modified and improved, and its integration into a mutually beneficial symbiosis with its urban communities formulated and promoted. Further, such an intellectual framework around the practice of property development supports the academic progress of the industry.

The book provides numerous illustrations, diagrams, and maps. It is a book about the production of a very physical thing, buildings, in their very physical context of the city. Providing visual support for the understanding of the topography in which the scenes take place, the notation of the ideas by which the intended forms were conceived, and the resultant buildings and settings should be helpful to the reader. A combination of historical pictures, maps, and documents are presented with some overlaid with explanatory diagrams. These are not presented as "evidence" of the ideas relayed in the text but rather are heuristic aids in support of the exploration of the emerging urban development process.

Historical Timeframe

The historical time frame is selected for a specific purpose. The common notion of providing someone else with the use of spare space in return for some benefit undoubtedly extends far back in the social activities of human beings. However, as such, the transaction was invariably informal either legally or temporally: the availability of the space, the control over its usage, and the barter value of it varied considerably for primitive man in a cave, early agrarian settlements, serfs of the feudal ages, or even many citizens of the classical civilizations. The formal concept of real property as being a stable, owned, and traded asset had not yet been formed. Furthermore, the claim on land has been intricately intertwined with power structures for many civilizations. Understandably, since land was the primary resource for producing the primary needs of food and shelter, it has been regarded as a highly desirable asset throughout the world, throughout the centuries. However, being highly coveted as such, it was invariably tightly held in the hands of a relatively few throughout the world and throughout the centuries.

That is, until the very structure of obtaining the necessary resources of living changed dramatically. Focusing in this instance on European circumstances, the feudal system, which had dominated economic and social conditions for centuries, disintegrated gradually as it was challenged by the advent and persistence of trade, mercantilism, and then industrialization. The European countries accumulated populations of workers who were not necessarily tied to the cultivation of the land, and these generally located in the urban areas where trade activities clustered and production systems were established. Additionally, the successful merchants and industrialists often sought to have a presence in cities for business efficiency, political proximity, or social advantage. By the 16th century, England had experienced the rise of numerous centers of agrarian trade in addition to utilization of the excellently constructed fortification and basic buildings of the city of London as a key port for some exotic imports, the arrival of European migrants, and the location of some small crafts and trade. Nearby, also, the royal residences in the city of Westminster grew to accommodate the purveyors of service to the Crown, the various ministers and advisors, and the social hangers-on.

The evolution during the 17th century of these two cities, and more specifically the couple of miles of land between them, has been extensively observed by numerous historians of the typography such as Stopes, Strype, and Summerson. The noted historian of the era, Vanessa Harding, observes London as going through "rapid and even revolutionary change, especially in relation to its social development" (1989, 206). The political, philosophical, economic, and social changes that accompanied that growth fostered the emergence of modern London, modern business, modern science, modern politics, modern literature, and the modern English person. Indeed, as usual with such dramatic times, the tales of the people orchestrating, manipulating, benefiting from, or falling foul of such changes have made for fascinating, and informative reading:

> The 17th century in London is a period full of significance and growth. Few pasts are more replete with interest and none can show forth such fateful events as the Civil War, the last of the great plagues, the [Great] fire and the expulsion of [King] James II ... The century found London a city of wood and left it a city of brick – 'from sticks to bricks' as King James I wittily put it. (Brett-James 1935, 15)

It was during this time that the population almost doubled, and London extended beyond its Roman walls and marched confidently west towards Westminster. The resultant housing need, the potential of well-located land, the new economic adventurism, the social vibrancy, the vacuum of municipal administration, and numerous other features of this century gave rise to a new method by which the London typography was modified and the people who did it. This is the nascent process of private development as an organized economic activity. Although the model did achieve its substantial formulation over approximately fifty years from the 1630s to the 1680s, the emergence was not revolutionary but rather gradual, similar to the gradualist interpretations of the Industrial Revolution by scholars in recent years (Crafts 1985; Feinstein 1978). The dawning of the 17th century saw its early sparks of activity and the closing saw it solidly established within the modern capitalist city of London.

Introduction

Importantly in regard to urban development today, this 17th-century formulation launched a potent multidimensional and pragmatic model by which Britain's extensive colonization, which commenced concurrently, could efficiently settle its new populations while also serving to institutionalize the politico-economic-social principles of the regime. Even through its revolution, the USA embraced, extolled, and expanded that enterprising model of private real estate development. Today it continues to build so many American cities, but also those of the burgeoning urban centers of China, India, South America, and Africa.

Objectives of the Book

The compelling purpose of this exploration is to establish a critical framework for the private real estate development activity that is so pervasive today in delivering the growing urban environments.

Though vociferously criticized and condemned, it continues to be utilized by governments of many different ideologies to meet urban needs, maintained as a fundamental component of macroeconomic systems seeking growth and prosperity, and continues as an asset of choice for global wealth and financial speculation. Despite the substantial and far-reaching roles it plays, in itself the private development undertaking is excessively vulnerable to unmanageable market conditions, pressured into poor decisions by dominating demands of political and economic institutions, and also often analytically superficial and managerially lax. It is a very important activity that impacts so many people, and yet is so broadly practiced without the self-evaluation, rigorous scholarship, and the intellectual clarity and purpose of a professional discipline.

To urgently address this situation, and noting the contributions of related scholarship on other professional and commercial practices, an effective path of investigation that breaks through the opacity, complexity, and resilience of the real estate development activity is found through a focus on its early formulation. As with other research into modern-day business activities, a more incisive understanding is gained in the embryonic phase during which financial features were more simplistic as they responded to economic needs, modes of production more basic as they sought efficiency, managerial decision-making more immediate and uncomplicated, and the instigators themselves more transparent in their motivations.

This historical exploration is taken to understand why private real estate development proceeds as it does, with its steps, decisions, and codified actions, and young professionals trained to repeat them. Though observed and criticized by many, few scholars and practitioners have questioned why things are done a certain way and not others, and does a manner in the way things are done have adverse consequences that could be avoided. This book therefore seeks to know how, in that context of emerging capitalism in 17th-century London, with an extraordinary demand for housing and no authority with the resources or mandate to provide it, the earliest property developers, as businessmen rather than as a "cottage industry," created a process for the delivery of the urban environment that had not (substantially) existed before. To view this formulation at its earliest stage, observe mistakes and alternative actions, note the decisions and the reasoning behind them, the processes and concerns that were discarded, and the actions that became fundamental and lasting is to incisively understand how private urban development is done.

It is intended that the research and examination contribute to an intellectual construct by which much needed scholarship can be undertaken on the activity, that is, of its own ontology integral with its expansive consequences. Additionally, it is intended to link more substantially the study of this private development activity with the related fields of urban planning and urban economics and finance. It is also intended to provide suggestions to remedy flaws in its practice and achieve a more comprehensive, analytical, and integrated process with much more certainty of a positive contribution to the urban community. And finally, though also very importantly, with the rapid growth of university programs for educating real estate professionals, it is intended to compel the formation of an intellectual discipline by which the industry will be more critical and self-evaluating, visionary, and socially responsible, and therefore better provide for the education of its future practitioners.

Part I
Historical Foundations for Urban Innovation

Chapter 1: Land Ownership, Control, and Use

In order to taste the full flavor of the circumstantial context which led to private real estate development, one should be aware of the confluence of relevant social, philosophical, political, and legal factors that provided the primordial soup from which the activity was born. It is necessary to retreat somewhat in history.

Private urban development began from the ground up, and of initial interest is the nature of the title to land upon which buildings would be erected and permanently affixed. The fundamental importance of this platform for human activity has long since been noted, and it was emphasized as modern urban communities were formed. Speaking of its significance, Marshall (1804, 1) said that "landed property is the basis on which every other species of material property rests; on it alone, mankind can be said to live, to move, and to have their being." Private urban development represents the highest level of complexity and utility yet encountered in this feature of human organization.

Title to land is a special form of owned, or "private," property, and in addition to its functional use, it has symbolic importance within human philosophical values, particularly with respect to legal structures, governance, and social status. Consequently, for a developer and the numerous stakeholders in a project, it must be apprehended that the economic, legal, and social dimensions of the rights of the land can be claimed and acted upon as private property. It is beneficial to this to note the distinction between land in its physical form and the concept of the property rights inherent in it.

Property developers often approach a project by pushing the boundaries of the local rules that inhibit the economic rewards of their project, rather than with any deep philosophical consideration of their site's place in the urban dynamic, and the societal ramifications of their possession of and actions within it. In this general attitude they are not particularly different from the rest of society, as the eminent chronicler of progressive property law in the 18th century William Blackstone (2016 [1807], 1–2) (Figure 1.1) wryly noted: "There is nothing which so generally strikes the imagination, and engages the affections of mankind, as the right of property ... [a]nd yet there are very few, that will give themselves the trouble to consider the original and foundation of this right." That the largest real estate corporation as yet in mankind's history has adopted the name of this oracle is probably not insignificant since it well appreciates that its whole *raison d'être* depends upon the stability of property laws and the societal implications of property.

1.1

Sir William Blackstone in 1774.

Such "affections" for the right of property, and indeed the land itself over which they were held, have been deeply ingrained within English culture. This national bonding of society and land, although not unique, has been noticed to be exceptionally strong and long-lasting. Sugarman and Warrington (1996, 111) opine: "In the strange, half-timeless world of the traditional English landed estate, feudal concepts blissfully lingered long after feudal relations had been eradicated … Land was not just the most valuable form of property; both to its owners and non-owners it was a social-political nexus, a way of life." And Offer (1981, 5) adds: "Both Roman law and English common law set land apart as a superior prototype of property, in acknowledgement of its primacy [of use] among the assets of agrarian societies."

The "original and foundation of this right" to which Justice Blackstone referred has not been broadly addressed with respect to the development of land as compared with the considerable general humanistic contemplation of society and the rights of property ownership within it. Primarily from a legal perspective, there have been some relevant starting points, particularly that of Pierson (2013). On adverting to the unwieldy extensiveness of a "history of property in all lands and all ages," he reasonably proposes to

focus on a series of perennial problems that arise for those who wish to defend (or to criticize) practices of property as these have developed broadly within the Latin West and its intellectual heirs. These questions include the following: How does private property come to exist? Does it require consent? (How) is it consistent with the living of a good life? And what are its proper limits? (Pierson 2013, 20)

This discussion of the dynamics of property use and changing rights provides a suitable perspective of the matter for developers of real estate. And the answers to these questions through history contribute an important component to a study of the theoretical framework of development activity.

Definition of Real Property and the Classical Conception of Ownership

First, it is necessary to distinguish real estate, or real property, from the legal category of personal property, or possessions other than real estate, such as movables, intellectual property or financial interests, or, for technical legal reasons, the leasehold of land. As Blackstone, in his *Commentaries on the Laws of England* knew the concept of land, it was not the physical soil, minerals, trees, etc., but the physical space *ab infero usque ad coelum*; and even that which was not owned. "Ownership of land" comprises merely a bundle of rights, an interest in it that is enforceable by law, and what are termed by the industry as improvements to it in the form of structures, buildings, infrastructure, and other alterations since all affixed property becomes part of the land. Such rights vary in extent, but there was no sovereign, or total, timeless ownership except when title in the land reverted to the Crown as the entity of the state. It is distinct from the construct by which existing things in general are owned and controlled. To define "ownership" in a way suitable for a developer's purpose, it is now generally accepted as a right defined by "real limitations on alienation" – that is, limitations on removing it from one's possession (Honoré 1961). These bundles may vary in the quantity and quality of the rights, but they mostly fell into general formulations with internal variations. For convenience, the object of the rights is sometimes loosely referred to as the property, but precision is sometimes necessary for technical discussion.

The accepted origins of the Western concept of real property are to be found in Greek civilization of about the 4th century BC, and although conceptually vague it was importantly directed to achieving a productive and sustained society. On the dynamics of society, the philosophers – Plato, Aristotle, and Pythagoras, among others – embraced and even emphasized a concept of real property which addressed its ownership, use, and distribution that would most effectively achieve a stable and good life for the citizens. "Plato and Aristotle did much in the fourth century BC to establish both the terms and terminology within which property has been discussed [in its societal purpose] in the West ever since" (Schlatter 1951, 19–20). Though their contributions to the notion of property have often been broadly differentiated, with the former favoring common ownership and the latter preferring private holdings, Pierson argues that such a glossed opinion is not valid. The modern developer works within a nuanced legacy which avoids the distinction and combines the use and development potential of both private and commonly claimed real estate.

Specifically regarding urban property, Plato said in chapter 5 of *The Republic* that his rejection of private ownership applies only to those appointed to the "golden class as overseers and guarantors of the good life of the community," that is, those governing and responsible for the state, and it was proposed "as a way of preventing them from using their privileged position to exploit the rest of the citizenry" (Pierson 2013, 25–26). That in following millennia this recommendation has been generally ignored, or even defied, by various persons in government has often led to dire consequences and loud protest, but this abuse of power for personal gain continues to be relatively unabated (Derrington 2017).

In a less specific approach, Plato conceded that communities generally function in a world of private property and private family structures. This acceptance is even more apparent in his later work, *Laws*, in which he outlined an arrangement for a "second-best" city, where land and houses are not held in common. This would mitigate problems of common ownership, including disputes over the "product," that is, what might be produced by an individual working on the land as against that resulting from the labor of others. He also adamantly required "those born and bred and educated as ours are" (Plato 1998, 740–741) to labor on the land in order to obtain its benefits, though unfortunately such activities, even metaphorically undertaken, later came to be in conflict with the proscribed lifestyle of the leisured landed classes.

Relevantly to real estate development activity, his first point anticipated later disputes regarding the use of shared land, termed "commons" by English law, in the resolutions of which private property development was to figure prominently. The second was also prescient with respect to Marx's condemnation of that *rentier* class of passive property owners, around which social debate continues in present times.

To these justifications for private property ownership, Aristotle was to add that "what is common to the greatest number gets the least amount of care" (Aristotle 1991, 1261b, 32). Or, as put in the more modern parlance of the former US Treasury Secretary Lawrence Summers, "no one ever washed a rental car" (Middendorf II 2011, 189). Such concerns about neglect contributed to the economic concept described in the eponymous book, *The Tragedy of the Commons* (Hardin 1968, 1243–1248). Thus, a lasting and relevant construct for real estate was Aristotle's postulation that "the better system is that under which property is privately owned but is put to common use" (1991, 1263a, 38). By common use, he meant a sharing of resources: "[I]n well-ordered cities … each citizen has his own property, part of which he makes available to his friends, and part of which he uses [and shares more broadly] as thought it was common property" (ibid.).

Pierson (2013) has helpfully provided extensions and qualifications which specifically addressed the benefits to society as a whole to be derived from private ownership. He expands the classical basis around two key points:

1. Pleasure and positive self-esteem are derived from private ownership because "to think of a thing as your own makes an expressible difference, as far as pleasure is concerned" (Aristotle 1991, 1263a, 41). It is necessary, however, to be wary of a time when this "slips from innocence into vice, when self-esteem and self-worth tips over into selfishness and avarice" (30).

2. "Private property is necessary for the exercise of generosity" (ibid.). This does not necessarily imply that ownership predicates generous action, but if it is read in harmony with Aristotle's insistence that owned property be "put to common use," the proposition apparently means that ownership of land imposes a responsibility for using it for some common good. Although this suggestion might be read as either commonsense or a devious justification for accumulation, if it is regarded as providing a direction for contribution to the public realm in which a property development occurs, it is an excellent premise by which urban settlements can satisfy their complex roles for both private individuals and the community.

In this abstraction of the propriety of use that comes with the ownership of real property, it is removed from the compulsion to overwhelming self-interest with which it is so often disastrously pursued. Rather, in the promotion of its effective and societally satisfying purpose, that is, its active utilization and contribution to the common good, the ancient philosophers enunciated a comprehensive utilitarian and socially responsible concept for its role. It should not be seen as promoting a purely altruistic culture, for most contributions were made also for pragmatic reasons also, but rather it established a cultural recognition of the desirability of public generosity as an inherent obligation and virtue of land ownership, though, as shall also be seen, it is not unlikely that personal satisfaction and the pleasure of a good reputation had some part in such motivation. Importantly, this had a beneficial influence on the urban development activity that was to commence in 17th-century England.

Thus, for property development, private ownership of site, or at least something legally approximating it, not only facilitates the objective of "working" the land for the betterment of the individual owner and the community but also enables the individual owner to be happier by performing acts of generosity to others through its use. Brewer and Staves (1996, 1) explained the potential for broad benefits: "The private ownership of land especially has seemed to hold out the hope of encouragement to honest labor, of high levels of productivity from which all can benefit, and – politically – of an independent and free republican citizenry." The fundamental principle that the ownership and benefits of private property were pertinent to the functioning of a community was established, and this axiom permeated much of European civilization.

Political Power, Social Symbolism, and Responsibility

That principle is also credited with directing societal structures. Pierson (2013) has pointed out that "(differential) property ownership (especially in land but also in movables) was also widely used as a mechanism for defining political classes in the political system of Athens," and under the Athenian Constitution, which is attributed to Aristotle, the citizenry was divided into four classes by an assessment of the property value, or citizen wealth (24). Plato allocated each class a quarter share in electing the 360-man governing council, and in linking voting rights to property ownership, those who were craftsmen, laborers, or women without property were denied a political voice. This alignment of political power with property, particularly landed interests, persisted for centuries to come and made equitable access to property for its functional use, such as housing, a challenge that still has a place in modern property development. Consistently with the influence of Greek political and social philosophy on English thought, universal suffrage in place of property suffrage is a relatively modern development in the English system.

These inequitable outcomes from governance based on land title are difficult to marry with the call for improved social outcomes resulting from responsible ownership and use, as posited earlier. Addressing this, Somers (1996, 83) suggests:

> It was not property that caused political rights; it was the political culture of membership that produced property, and the rights of property were expressed through the cultural capital of membership rights ... The rights of property in effect existed only within the context of institutional relationships and the political culture of which they were a part.

From this perspective, despite the attempts of the philosophers to constrain greed and excesses, property conflicts begin with societal structures that are based on competition for resources necessary for human survival, and the use of a resource by one person means restriction from its use by another. That land, and a habitation structure built on it, was therefore conceptually placed in this competitive dynamic for survival, rather than being treated as cooperatively useful, had the pragmatic consequence that its essential value or worth was potentially depleted by misuse.

From this European philosophical foundation, the various methods of societies for sustaining their members have represented distinct modifications of each individual's pursuit of their own means for their own ends, in contrast to that of the responsibility of all individuals for the benefit of each and all. The result is a conceptual structure in which private property development can become restrictive in its equitable access, or potentially a resource that contributes broadly to societal conditions. This shifting dynamic is at its heart.

Property Rights and Governance

Although to a certain degree society has sought to balance logistical issues of restrictive access, especially as urban centers were to have denser patterns of land ownership, the legal and political governing structures of land control were mostly directed at solidifying and protecting that fundamental precept of ownership. As Adam Smith observed (1994, 771): "Civil government, so far as it is instituted for the security of property, is in reality instituted for the defence of the rich against the poor, or of those who have some property against those who have none at all." This was presented as factual rather than an ideological judgment.

At the foundation of both Plato's and Aristotle's constructs and having accommodated the ownership of private property within societal dynamics to varying degrees, they incorporated its protection within their systems of law and governance. Although referring specifically to "moveable" possessions, Plato advanced the principle that "no one should touch my property or tamper with it unless I have given him some sort of permission; and if I am sensible I shall treat the property of others with the same respect" (1998, Lg. 913). This implies civil enforcement of the property right. In a close reading of Aristotle's suggested manner of defining and protecting private property, Fred Miller (1991) presents him as the architect of the citizen's rights, inclusive of property rights. Adding to his method of allocating land plots to households in his spatial layout of the "second-best" city, he insisted that "these property rights are inalienable [and] ... [t]here are complicated rules of inheritance to ensure that land stays permanently within the same family (1991, Lg. 740-1)" (Pierson 2013, 27), and thereby protecting each citizen family from deprivation of its means of sustenance. Again, the only practical means of ensuring this was by civil enforcement.

It was also in an attempt for social and economic stability that ancient laws vested the right of property in the family patriarch and established the status of land as private property. Consequent upon the recognition of the patriarchs' rights of private property, they could divide or dispose of their land or assemble it into larger estates. This enabled the development of legal and financial modes of land transactions, the use of land as security for loans (the precedent for mortgages), its division and distribution by will, and, most importantly for future commercial activity, its conversion by sale or other means into "movable" property, that is, money. Even if Aristotle's interest in the logistical maintenance of social stability through the property regime unrealistically meant that a population would need to be held more or less constant, it was particularly influential for Western civilizations and its central principles may be found in the laws of many other civilizations, such as early property laws in China.

In Rome, its codification, followed by its formal acceptance by all classes of Roman society, gave it the force of governance. The theoretical excellence of Greek civilization was taken up and put into rigorous logical order by the Roman empire, which by conquest took it to a large part of Europe including Britain, where over a long period it established a system of governance, legal and social, and was to be foundational for the formulation of the private development process. Even after the Romans had departed England, it is not surprising that the benefits of these principles and structures were recognized and retained by the indigenous people. It was this system, with modifications, which was still extant in the 17th century when Roman law was still studied by aspiring lawyers.

There was another classical tradition relating to land that would become relevant to private development. "The [Roman] Senate granted the [legal] possession of unprofitable and waste lands belonging to the State to those who undertook to clear them. This was called the property of possession, and the occupant paid to the treasury a periodic rent" (Letourneau 1896, 261). This established the principle of "ownership" by long and continuous occupation and, by evolution, title by "adverse possession" against the former owner. Although this notion of property rights arising from primacy of occupation or continual occupation, in some instances for a period of only two years (Watson 1975), may not seem appropriate to the progressive governance and settlement of London, the formal recognition of this right enabled the invading Romans to accommodate some indigenous English landowners of importance and thereby enjoy a less disruptive occupation. Though this law was later to be disputed, at the time it reinforced the use of property ownership in retaining societal stability. Indeed, it has survived through to modern times, and statutory intervention was even extended to the doctrine of adverse possession.

More specifically in the practical application or governance of real property, Roman law was very detailed: "There are rules which forbid building within two and a half feet of a neighbour's wall, measures regulating the flow of rainwater from a neighbour's roof and the right to deny light to an existing property through new building" (Pierson 2013, 79; Watson 1971, 75; Watson 1975, 157–165). Although, particularly in urban situations, the legal format changed over time to local legislation rather than central decrees broadly dictated throughout a country or empire, the attention to details regulating the external impact of a building or a property's operation on the surrounding environment and comfort of the community was impressive. Many building codes and restrictions were specifically formulated to ensure safe construction and healthy conditions for the inhabitants of the precinct, and there was a predominant concern of the law with the compatibility of a building with the context of its surrounding physical environment and broader community. This social imperative can be understood as the Romans' derivation of the principles of Plato and Aristotle which required community benefits as an offset to the right of private property. It is to be noticed, however, that over the subsequent centuries these rules became weighted towards the internal performance of the property and interests of the owner, in contrast to this early consideration of external impact.

Thus, the Roman trading outpost of *Londinium* was founded as typologically distinct within the jurisdiction of this highly developed Roman law, in marked contrast to the more tribal structures of the local indigenous communities. In combination with a democratic format of social governance, the Roman property law produced a city that was in England unique in that individual private land ownership, which was relatively equitably distributed amongst citizens, was inextricably linked with a complex but progressive recognition of individuality *within* a structured political format for the community. As it was to be so often in the future, this societal structure influenced the formation of the real estate industry and the attitudes and behavior of the citizens involved.

Modifications under Norman Rule

In 1042, many centuries after Rome had abandoned its London outpost, the reigning King Cnut (1016–1035) sought to deflect recurring Anglo-Saxon incursions by installing the exiled Saxon King Ethelred's son, Edward the Confessor, as his successor. Historians such as Sheppard (1998) have proposed that this subtly prepared England for Norman governance as Edward introduced French as the court language and commenced construction of the abbey at Westminster. Of importance for the future development of the London metropolis, Edward's location of his royal palace beside the abbey "ensur[ed] that the rich and fashionable quarters would always be on the western side of [London] town, clustered round the seat of royal power" (Sheppard 1998, 124).

In addition, Cnut and Edward attempted to establish national stability by directing governance away from feudal family holdings to contractual relationships based on land ownership and compensation for use. Cunningham (1890, 95) described the unfolding situation:

> At the earlier date society was bound together by ties of blood and personal duty, but in the eleventh century the position of every member of the community was defined in connexion with the property he held and the rights or responsibilities which it entailed. The existence of property implies the existence of proprietors; and by the time of [Edward] the Confessor the ties of blood and personal duty had been translated into other terms, and the social fabric was a system of contracts between proprietors.

This trend towards a Norman form of governance was expedited by the invasion in October 1066 when William the Conqueror (Figure 1.2) ousted the last Anglo-Saxon king,

1.2
King William I.

Harold II, who had retaken the throne earlier that year. As victor in the Battle of Hastings, William I exercised the traditional right by taking title to the lands of England, though he was compelled to grant lands to many of his relatives and fellow nobles for their financial or warrior services. Le Patourel (1976, 32) described the new allocations:

> ... it has been calculated that, in 1086, King William and his immediate family held about 20 percent of the land of England; the immigrant lay barons, including the king's two half-brothers, about 48 percent; the Church about 26 percent; and the few surviving pre-Conquest landowners, themselves not all of English origins, little more than 5 per cent.

This involved the displacement of many former landowners, and it is estimated that he removed approximately 4,000 indigenous lords from land ownership and replaced them with only 200 Norman barons and religious leaders. This consolidated Norman governance was to survive the following centuries of changing rulers.

Having held a Normandy dukedom based on feudal governance whereby land was distributed to loyal barons for their allegiance to the king of France, William adapted that system for the allocation of England's lands with himself as its monarch. He mapped a more centralized and hierarchical form of governance onto communities, and linked land ownership of his courtiers to specified allegiance, provision of armed troops when called upon, and political power and status. This served as a structural framework for the formulation and consistency of the country's constitutional rights for centuries to come. Underscoring the ancient basis of governance, it has been observed that for the English, "our whole constitutional law seems at times to be but an appendix to the law of real property" (Maitland 1913).

William modified the form of feudal governance by continuing the contractual land relationships that had been seeded by Cnut and Edward. As a result, it became a land-based composite that affirmed aristocratic title but also enabled contractual arrangements around economic use. Although the Gallic system of serfdom was adopted for manorial production, a parallel system of production by Saxon free farmers was maintained. Rigby (1995, 37–38) described the English compromises of feudal hierarchy that were to enable later fluidity of property ownership and social status thus:

> Landlords were not only feudal lords receiving rent from their tenants, they were also employers paying wages to laborers. Poorer peasants might work for part of the time as wage-laborers on the lord's *demesne* as well as having holdings of their own; peasants with larger holdings could also be employers of the labor of their fellow villagers. In other words, it would be wrong to see any particular individual as simply a member of a single economic class; rather, individuals could have multiple class locations, as both landlords and employers, as both smallholders and wage-laborers, and as peasants who themselves sublet land to other tenants.

In these ways, the land-based structure of governance and economic production varied uniquely from that of the Continental system. In the process, it established two important fundamentals regarding land. One was the codification of rights and responsibilities of aristocratic land title, wherein nobility and land ownership were symbiotic features. The other was a construct of economic payment for land use broadly exercised throughout society.

Recorded Land Economics

Intent upon a more centralized system under his control, William had consolidated land-holdings. He also sought to stabilize this arrangement and to deflect the persistent territorial disputes that destabilized the Continent by commanding a national survey of all landholdings. For each settlement or holding, it recorded the geographical description, its title, though not specifically ownership but rather control according to royal intent, and its valuation for the purposes of taxation by the Crown. This Domesday Book (Figure 1.3), as it was termed by the defeated Saxons, was completed in 1086.

1.3
The Domesday Book.

This uniquely formalized notion of property definition and control, and its irrefutable recording for perpetuity, was of substantial value to the eventual emergence of commercial activity around the development of land. Other cultures also had landed nobles, but their landholding was not so fundamentally aligned with continued social status and power. For example, the landholdings of the aristocratic class controlling the agrarian economy of 7th-century China were of little stature when trade and manufacturing became a much more profitable source of wealth and an avenue for socio-economic advancement (Carlen 2016). By contrast, commercial trade in England, when it came, was concentrated around wool production which established the economic advantage of title to sheep pastures.

The Domesday Book's recorded metric of the value of each landholding for the purposes of tax assessment was also critical in launching a conversion of the concept of land from simply a passive physical thing to that of an asset with specific value within the economic system. Agrarian production was measured and the tax, initially levied in kind, was a percentage of it. Due to variable weather conditions and disparity of capability in estate management, taxes were sometimes unpaid and much of the work of Crown's clerks, called receivers, was to travel throughout the kingdom collecting it, recording deficits, and negotiating settlements. Any serious issue would be resolved between the landowner and the king in person through a nervous visit to the court.

Because of the large portion of governmental revenues historically provided by property taxes, this direct link between maximization of taxes and maximization of property values placed real estate fully within the political dynamic. Even as taxation expanded beyond land, and taxpaying representatives included more than just landowners in more democratic times, the substantial proportion of tax revenues derived from land-based assets continues to bind governance and real estate.

Though this tax system, based on assessed underlying economic value, seems reasonable to modern payers of property dues, some historians have challenged that impression. Stenton (1908, 468) condemned the commercial overlay: "The Domesday system of assessment … was not the product of local conditions but was arbitrarily imposed from above. The *hide* was not only a measure of land, but also a fiscal term, dissociated from all necessary correspondence with [agrarian] fact" (Stenton 1908, 468). Undoubtedly, as with most property taxation assessments ever, the method would not have been economically perfect. But significant for this discussion, this multidimensional representation of land, especially with its physical and fiscal metrics included and merged in the term *hide*, established a fundamental and specific economic construct for land, and it nurtured the concept of real estate valuation which was to arise later.

Land Equity (for some) and the Magna Carta

A particularly harsh land-based tax was imposed by Richard I (1189–1199) to finance his expensive crusades to Palestine, resulting in substantial disaffection of the barons towards the monarchy. In 1215, as a means of averting the rising discontent, Richard's brother and heir, John, conceded to the landowners, but only to them, specific liberties that were set out in the Magna Carta. Although the range of its beneficiaries was very limited, it found special significance by establishing that the royal power was not absolute and arbitrary. This facilitated the mode of property development in later centuries, in that, though very powerful and therefore influential, the king was still obliged to attribute reasonable respect to the requests of his powerful courtiers.

Specifically, the Charter covered two socio-economic aspects. First, it established that "no scutage or aid is to be levied in our realm except by the common counsel of the realm" (translated citation of the *Magna Carta*), thereby requiring the consent of the affected taxpayers to the imposition of the tax. Second, and also significantly for land, John conceded that "if without lawful judgement of his peers, we have deprived anyone of lands, castles, liberties or rights, we will restore them to him at once. And if any disagreement arises on this, let it be settled by the judgement of the twenty-five barons." By this, the formal and legally secure right to land title and/or use was underscored and a secular, judicial forum for the resolution of disputes was defined, removing it from the unfettered discretion of the king and the jurisdiction of the church.

Brewer and Staves (1996, 1) go beyond the notion of mere defensive protection to posit the creation of a position of societal potency as embedded in property: "To Englishmen, *Magna Carta* gave a precious right not to have one's body or one's land taken by the king without due process, a right that in the English-speaking world exfoliated into a more general right to be secure in one's property." Though the Crown retained ultimate ownership of all land in the kingdom, this formalized structure, protecting titleholders' rights and the rights of use or tenancy of land lessees (Britnell 1993, 137), introduced a concept of "control of land" that was a critical practical precondition to the expenditure of considerable capital on its development by way of capital investment in them.

The Influence of Religion on Attitudes to Private Property

As Christendom progressed through the Middle Ages towards the formation of its "universal" church, its most highly recognized scholar on the nature and limits of private property, including land, was Thomas Aquinas. In the 13th century, he revived some basic Aristotelian notions and aligned them with the Christian religious coda:

- Private possession of property is acceptable, though with the purpose of use for living: "external things are necessary, not as belonging to the essence of happiness, but by serving as instruments to happiness" (Aquinas 1964–1980, I-II q4 a7 *responsio*).
- Property that is individually owned is more diligently maintained than that which is held in common: "a more peaceful state of things is preserved for mankind if each is contented with his own [defined property]" (Aquinas 1964–1980, II-II q66 a2 *responsio*).
- The ownership of private property is good, and it is the avarice of men that is the cause of its misuse. Aquinas qualifies this with the caveat that such ownership is limited since the ultimate owner of all is God and possessions must be used in accordance with His will (Pierson 2013, 92).

This combination of classical thinking on the governance of a peaceful society, and with deference to the Christian God, prevailed throughout Western Europe, and for the common man, either with property or without, it provided a framework for the tenet that the existing system of land allocation, with its associated responsibilities and duties should persist. But, despite this seemingly workable combination for much of the population, the practicalities of a fusion of increasingly powerful church interests with those of the existing *princeps*, or princely form of rule, had inherent conflicts, a significant one of which was land control. Characterized as the "high politics" of the Latin West and continuing from the fall of the Roman empire, "the clash of Church and State was perhaps the ubiquitous feature of political contest (at least in the later) medieval period" (Pierson 2013, 96). It was not so much a conflict but rather a matter of demarcation between God-given precedence of the "sacred" authorities and the jurisdiction of the "temporal" powers, since the secular authorities were practicing Christians.

In the result, towards the later period of the 13th and during the 14th centuries, governance protected individual subjective rights to private property, but it also adhered to the Christian God-ordained purpose that in such matters the individual should be in the service of humanity. Aquinas extended his framework for justifiable private ownership of property to its being "an addition to natural right [as by given by God] devised by human reason" (Aquinas 1964–1980 II-II q57 a2 ad2). Most importantly, he consistently insisted that this natural right was subject to a corresponding duty of natural law, that is, to respond to God's instruction that we pursue human benefits for the common good.

Some competing theories posited:

that private property was the product of king-made laws or, to the contrary, that it was the product of agreement between individuals and/or families prior to the existence of kings (in Giles and Ockham) and even (in the work of [Pope] John XXII) that property had always been private, since dominium was given by God to Adam alone. (Pierson 2013, 123)

Inherent key questions to such thinking were the validity and interpretation of the suggested social agreements and relationships, for they would become of critical concern when property owners sought to develop or change the use of their landholdings.

Despite this growing enthusiasm for endorsement of the individual's right to private property, albeit subject to an element of commonality for the purpose of God-directed social good, there was also an alternative principle, which was more amenable to those seeking the Christian "counsel of perfection," who were mostly confined to those in religious orders. Under this rubric, property was a strictly communal holding, or was even to be shunned according to the Franciscan oath of poverty. This alternative concept, particularly persisting within the influential church, was a counterweight to the increasing secular enthusiasm for property accumulation, and its application to land ownership would be referred to regularly in future conflicts, including in its absorption into Marxist doctrine.

This idea of a natural, God-given right to property, with some adjustment by human reason, was not received without substantial skepticism and considerable discussion of its consequences that still continues. Of assistance to an understanding of the general context in which new attitudes to real estate would develop is Pierson's (2013, 249) gloss on the situation:

> The crucial point is that we cannot find here an unlimited right to private property and this is because, for the most part, private property (or, indeed, a mixed regime which includes private property) is primarily to be justified because (under some circumstances) it secures the prior imperative of the (here God-given) natural law, that is to promote social peace and/or human flourishing.

Importantly, this view anticipates the danger that a powerful self-interested view of the rights of ownership could tend towards exclusive individual benefit and a negation of any purpose of community welfare.

The concept of a natural God-given right to the private property was of course favored by those who were the proprietors, who, for that reason, were usually the most powerful and influential group. It included the church.

Private Property and Secular Laws

After William's conquest of England, consequent upon the Norman tenet that stable land ownership was at the heart of governance, laws relating to its management such as transfer of its ownership, contracts for its use, and associated commercial transactions were made. These followed the Norman pattern, but they were influenced by Roman property law which had persisted within the city of London.

Inheritance and Primogeniture

An estate title was technically given by the Crown through the grant of right of tenure, and the residue of total ownership remained vested in the Crown to whom the granted rights escheated, or defaulted, on termination of the estate. The estate element referred to the temporal limitation of the grant, and tenure defined the nature of the holding, such as freehold or leasehold. Usually, a grant imposed a condition on the extent of the purposes for which the land could be used, such as agricultural, pastoral, or defensive. Stewardship of the estate's integrity was paramount for the nation's well-being, and forms of controlling the inheritance of aristocratic property emerged. The concept of "strict family settlement" focused on keeping the property's title fully within the family, and to that effect the lands of the estate were "settled" upon the patriarch for life, and after his death it usually passed to his eldest surviving son "in tail" (or entail). Absent a surviving son, if the estate grant broadly extended to heirs, it passed to the eldest surviving daughter. The terms of the grant were not rigid in this respect and could be defined by various limitations, such as grant of an estate "in tail male special," which excluded inheritance by daughters, and even by sons who did not meet the "special" description. The essence of male primogeniture was that the title to the property should pass "to the sayd Earl and his heyres males."

Along with the land rights, the inheritor gained the aristocratic title and the responsibility for preserving and improving the property through advancing its farming activities, exploiting its natural resources, and maintaining or developing its buildings, either rural or village, within its manorial boundaries. Though such a system was later to be heavily criticized by Adam Smith as an impediment to national economic prosperity, it served to preserve and enhance the productive capacity of the estates as agglomerations with unified productive capacity, accompanied by political power and responsibility. In contrast, the Continental form of division of inheritance broadly amongst all heirs resulted in a gradual fragmentation of estates, shorter terms of ownership, and lesser economic value.

In addition to the economic bonding of a family to its estate, the system also served to emphasize the symbolic connection between an aristocratic family and its defined landholdings – a very English characteristic that would later permeate through other social classes and the cultures of English colonies. The courts, particularly the Court of Chancery, a church court of conscionability where such disputes were taken, strongly favored holding the interests of the families together. Their view continued to be, as it had been by long tradition in English governance, that the stability of the landed society was vital for the stability of the country (Beckett 1986, 58–59). The extensive system of family-oriented landholdings of English aristocrats and their commitment to retaining them were to influence, and even possibly to compel, the later rise of private development.

Land Leases

Under the terms of an estate grant, a nobleman or member of the gentry was not permitted to make a permanent transfer of his landholding for that was part of the royal prerogative. Because a prescription of tenure in a grant of an estate usually mandated it, apart from urban habitation, land usage was initially focused on agricultural activity, and its grantee's financial concerns were directed to making tax contributions, which at that time were in the form of produce or service, and to meeting production and household expenses. In order to expand production of his land beyond what he had the capacity to cultivate with hired labor, he often leased out parcels to tenant farmers from the local community. To maintain his control, the lease only offered limited rights of use rather than the more expansive rights of use mostly granted to lessees today, and the economic bond of use, production, and rent was formalized. Marriott (1914, 26) described this situation which remained through the late Middle Ages: "For four centuries at least—from the eleventh century to the fourteenth—the soil of rural England was occupied by a continuous series of agricultural communities."

Other than maintaining his family and community by these agrarian activities, the land-holder had no overt concern for financial gain, and those who inherited their land-bound wealth were not generally familiar with production for trade or commerce or with increasing their financial wealth through their estate lands. Both landholder and his tenant farmer worked their lands only for the primary purpose of meeting their needs, and perhaps some financial benevolence by the lord of the manor towards his local parish, his tenants, and villagers associated with his estate. Rigby (1995, 23) commented upon the more important familial and community ties which were underscored by land ownership:

> Land was seen not simply as an economic category to be disposed of by the individual but as something 'half sacred' which was held in trust for the family as a whole. With an under-developed land market, geographical mobility was limited and members of a village lived side by side for life, the ties of kinship being augmented by a strong sense of neighbourliness and community.

In the earliest times of leasing to the community of tenant farmers, the duration of a lease was for the lifetime of the lessee, though usually with the presumption of a need for annual agreement for its continuation. Often, to maintain the livelihood of an extended family, a lease might extend for a number of lifetimes, such as three successive generations. Alternatively, to allow more flexibility, a grant might be limited to a specific number of years, sometimes by reference to the estimated lifetime of an adult male, which was approximately twenty years. At the end of that established period, the land would be leased for a newly contracted annual rent for the next nominated period, and so on.

For special circumstances, such as a lord's providing a small portion of land to establish a second son, or for use by a parish church, abbey or monastery, or even reflecting a lack of interest by the landlord, a perpetual lease would be given, and its rights continued indefinitely. However, such extensive long-term alienation of the loyal aristocrat from the land posed such dangers to stable governance that it was formally banned by King John in the 13th century, though it still crept into later informal agreements.

This English property law concept of perpetual leases, and the seemingly endless succession of lease after lease of landholdings, was appropriate to the concept of land as a non-deteriorating asset. However, as leases came to be applied to buildings, which deteriorate and did not last indefinitely, there arose the need for a more complex formulation, including inherent rights and obligations. But significantly, there steadfastly remained the view, even if mistaken, of real estate, both land and buildings, as having perpetual economic value.

Rising Commerce and Land Laws

As England emerged from the Middle Ages in the 14th and 15th centuries, it gleaned new ideas of commercialism and trade from the Dutch who were advancing towards economic leadership in Europe, and these ideas presented challenges to the traditional Norman feudal governance of landholdings. Within this rising transactional environment, interest moved in large part from matters of purely legal governance of land by the state to the importance of claims of property in general, and the principles and integrity of private real property in this new context attracted substantial attention and contention.

Early notable legal textbooks and commentaries that dealt with the question included Sir John Fortescue's *Thesis Concerning the Nature of the Law of Nature*, which was published in the later 15th century. He re-anchored a person's right to private property, which was earned by his labor, in the natural law of divine decree. However, he also compared the advantages of England's regime of *dominium politicum et regale*, the rule of the polity of the Crown, with the inadequacies of France's *dominium regale*, which afforded less qualification by the rights of the people to those of the Crown. Notably, English property law had departed from its Continental counterpart, which was much more deferential to royal power and rights. In its stead, it focused more on the welfare of the individual and their rights than those of the broader community. In this way, the seeds were sown for the individualism of the New World republics, and with that spirit further represented in their rights regarding landholdings.

By the 16th century, an additional contribution to legal learning related specifically to real property was provided by the textbook *St German's Doctor and Student* (1518, republished 1974). It postulated the basis of English law as one of reason, divided into the law of reason primary and the law of reason secondary. The former addressed laws derived by man's reason or instinct, and the latter relevantly examined the English construct of the common law whereby particular laws were judicially developed over time through particular judgments in the particular circumstances and customs relevant to the particular instances before the courts, thereby combining governance by tradition with flexibility through accepted advocacy and modification according to current social attitudes.

The stability of its historicism and the transparent context of legal determination through precedent, as opposed to arbitrary royal discretion, provided relative security for the individual and was to be critical for reducing risk in the ownership and development of property, which required large capital outlays in a permanently fixed place. Confirming the benefits of this security, in the following century William Petty (1690, 27–28) offered this conclusion on the productivity and growth of Holland:

> The Second Policy or help to Trade used by the *Hollanders* [after Liberty of Conscience], is securing the Titles to Lands and Houses; for although Lands and Houses may be called *Terra Firma* & *res immobilis*, yet the Title unto them is no more certain than it pleases the Lawyers and Authority to make them; wherefore the *Hollanders* do by Registries, and other ways of Assurance make the Title as immovable as the Lands, for there can be no encouragement to Industry, where there is no assurance of what shall be gotten by it; and where by fraud and corruption, one Man may take away with ease and by a trick, and in a moment what another has gotten by many Years extreme labor and pains.

Though it took many centuries for a land registry to be established in England because time-honored traditions contested it, its early adoption in the federal settlement of North America was based on this understanding, and the immediate prosperity realized in the new territory was indubitably based on such certainty of recorded title to land.

Meanwhile, in 16th-century England, its property laws strengthened the rights of the landholder and those who derived leaseholds from him, which not only enhanced economic expansion but also diminished the classical philosophical concepts that had been overlaid with Christian ethics as discussed above. The rising enthusiasm for surplus wealth creation and the important role that property played in the new commercial activities influenced social attitudes and, consequently, legal thought. Fortescue (1997 reprint, 52) focused on real property and observed that:

> [e]very inhabitant of that realm uses at his own pleasure the fruits which his land yields, the produce of his cattle, and all the emoluments which he gains, whether by his own industry or that of others, from land and sea, hindered by the injuries and rapine of none, without obtaining at least due amends. Hence the inhabitants of that land are rich, abounding in gold and silver and all the necessaries of life.

According to this exaltation of English law, the landowner would therefore have some notable expectations:

- That he (ownership being restricted to males) will achieve "yield" from his land, that is, he may use it actively for a financial return.
- That he might also gain by the "industry ... of others" on his land through leasing it out to others or employing others to work it.
- That he may enjoy "the fruits which his land yields" and is not required to share them, except through taxation which is inherent in his title to the land.
- That any hindrance or injury to his ability to do these things is to be compensated by "due amends," that is, by some form of financial remedy.
- That to be "rich" by the accumulation of wealth beyond just "the necessities of life" and essentially non-utilitarian "gold and silver," is condoned.

Such acceptance and even admiration of ownership, utilization, emoluments, accumulation, wealth, and enjoyment associated with realty was an expansive and supportive foundation for the innovative real estate transactional and development activities that were to appear in the succeeding century. The subtle discarding of responsibility for the betterment of the community was an unfortunate feature, and perhaps this critical modification of attitude facilitated the gradual retreat of those future development activities towards more self-serving objectives.

Mortgages and Property Rights
A section of property law relates to its use as security for a loan, part of which is the law of mortgage agreements that record the pledge of an asset as security for repayment of a loan. The agreement was controlled by the law of contract, but it was its content which made it a special kind that attracted special principles. In England, they were formulated under the common law, and on the Continent by civil law codes. They laid down the rules by which a mortgage as security and its redemption were enforced.

Once real property was conceptualized as an economic asset through the obligations for rental payments under a lease, it was extensively employed as security or collateral for loans. Although there may have been other instances earlier, the most renowned recorded system was introduced during the early 12th century by Cistercian monks, whose order stretched from Rome to Burgundy in France. They often received gifts of land from benefactors, who were hoping for divine blessings or forgiveness in return, and amassed a substantial property portfolio. However, occasionally the gift was unsuitably located at a distance from their monastery, or its use was not satisfactory for some reason, and they did not want to own it. But to perform their spiritual duty of providing funds for the donor landowner's participation in a crusade, they set up a system termed "pawning" by which the land remained under its original ownership and use but was pledged to the monastery as security for the money lent (Casson and Casson 2013, 104). This structure of lending and securing repayment through a claim on a land asset was the early form of a loan secured by a mortgage.

In England, the traditional importance of land and a broad understanding and acceptance of its economic value as officially recorded facilitated a broad adoption of this Continental financial arrangement, but subject to critical variations. Specifically, under the English arrangement: "In return for the loan, the full legal title was conveyed to the mortgagee [lender]" (Offer 1981, 137). For the advance of a loan, therefore, a property owner executed a mortgage contract by which he conveyed his full land title to the lender, though on a temporary basis, as security for repayment of the loan; and the lender would promise to reconvey the title, but conditionally upon repayment on the specified due date. The borrower's need to repay the loan in order to regain the title provided the lender with valuable assurance of recovery of the loan amount. If the borrower were to default, the lender had unencumbered title to an appreciating asset.

Technically, a delay of just one day in repayment amounted to a default that triggered forfeiture. The mortgagor would be alienated from the land with no residual claim to its title, use or other redress even if its value far exceeded the amount secured. On the other hand, if the land were worth less than the amount owed, absent any agreement to the contrary the lender could also proceed against the borrower for the difference. The drastic consequences of such a rigid system was mitigated by statutory law reform in later years, but for reasonable certainty, which is necessary for confidence and efficiency in commercial transactions, adherence to mortgage rights as modified by statute was and is still enforced with reasonable strictness.

In respect of landed wealth, the mortgage system caused difficulties in this area. Because the law of primogeniture was strict, estates were not infrequently inherited by sons of a young age. Further, the average lifespan was short by modern standards and aristocratic service to the Crown often required involvement in dangerous battles, crusades, explorations, and incursions. As a result, titled landholders were often immature or absent. If young and known to be wealthy, they were targets for fraudsters and unscrupulous financial dealers, and it was through a mortgage that financial predators regularly captured them. Because of variation from time to time in his income, such a borrower might not be sure as to when he might have funds to repay the loan and so the repayment date set by the mortgage could not readily be agreed to with an expectation of timely satisfaction. Nor could the value of the mortgaged land be easily estimated so as to be appropriate to the loan amount. As a result, there could be a significant risk that estate land would be forfeited to a lender through a brief default concerning a highly over-secured debt that resulted in an unmeritorious and unearned benefit to the mortgagee in the form of the excess in the value of the land.

In protection of the nation's welfare and certainly of the upper classes through the principle of land stability, the legal system sought to protect such heirs from loss of their inheritance through a strict enforcement of their mortgage agreements. In Tudor times, a remedy was dispensed by the Court of Chancery, a church court, which did not have jurisdiction to decide matters of law and did not purport to do so. But it was a court of conscience and exercised the power of the church to prevent a man from damning his immortal soul by unconscionable exercise of his legal rights. While it recognized those legal rights, if a miscreant did not cleanse his soul by obeying its orders as to his proper conduct in his exercise of them, it would order his incarceration until he did so and without any other temporal limitation. The equity so dispensed was a novel construct around unconscionability in the exercise of legal rights, and its administration by the Chancery Court was referred to as that of the Court of Equity.

In this context, the unfair exercise by mortgagees of their legal rights under the mortgage was an ideal subject for the court's attention. Its equitable jurisdiction tended to moderate the rigidities and formalism of the common law, particularly as it affected the landed titles and it "developed technical rules to ensure that contracts were not penal or usurious" (Sugarman and Warrington 1996, 123–124). Though Chancery had previously provided some protection to a borrower who had provided real property as security on a loan, upon Henry VIII's redistribution of many valuable estates, and the growing demand for and use of capital during the Elizabethan Golden Age, disputes regarding forfeiture for default in repayment increased. Sugarman and Warrington (1996, 114) noted that "the courts (continuing their interest in preserving the stable, estate-based, land ownership system) began to grant relief to borrowers as a matter of course, without looking for special circumstances that would have previously been necessary to activate equity's conscience."

Sugarman and Warrington (1996, 114) comment on the extent of this application: "A.W.B. Simpson suggested that the Chancery courts were prepared to relieve mortgagors [borrowers] from strict forfeiture conditions from the fifteenth century. But although there are examples to support this, these probably related to what Simpson calls 'peculiarly scandalous cases.'" The most common example of this would have been cases where the mortgagee has been entirely repaid by receiving the rents and profits of the property but still refused to reconvey the property to the mortgagor. Although this protection of borrowers against egregious actions of lenders was only occasionally provided, it was almost solely used with respect to real property, which indicates the continuing political and social influence of land ownership, despite the commercial ambience which increasingly grew around it.

This developing jurisprudence brought a new legal context for mortgages:

Dating from at least the turn of the 17th century, the courts of equity determined that the strict date for repayment was somewhat irrelevant ... Time was not to be of the essence of the agreement. Although the mortgagor's [borrower's] legal right to redeem the property was lost after the expiration of the time specified in the contract, in equity the mortgagor had an equitable right to redeem on payment within a reasonable period of the principal, interest, and costs. (Sugarman and Warrington 1996, 113)

By mid-century, two legal principles had emerged. The first, by a judgment in 1625, affirmed that a pledge of property was in substance no more than a security, and that the conveyance of its title was not the transacted item in itself. But since the title of the property was in fact conveyed to the mortgagee, this gave rise to a confusing situation. In 1654, this principle was linked, and probably made more workable, by the formulation, again in the Chancery Court, of an equity of redemption which was based on the real object of the transaction, the creation of a security for the debt as had been earlier established. This new equity entitled the mortgagor to redeem, or recover by full payment, the title to the property [from the mortgagee who had held it as security], though he had failed to repay the debt by the appointed time (Fisher and Lightwood 1977, 7, cited by Sugarman and Warrington 1996, 113).

Further, "The courts applied the equity of redemption irrespective of the terms of the agreement between the parties and their manifest intentions" (Sugarman and Warrington 1996, 111). This meant that the right of redemption would override any contractual arrangements, even with the consequence that "this might involve the courts rewriting the transactions between the parties" (ibid., 111). By this, the mortgage changed from a "dead pledge" (a literal translation of its legal Latin name) and allowed for other resolutions. Muldrew (1998, 115) describes this benefit: "The growth of the equity of redemption meant that they might extend the contract to avoid losing their land if they failed to make payment by the specified day, and instead only rental income could be seized to pay for the default."

As real property transactions became even more frequent, particularly around London and other emerging English commercial centers, and as enthusiasm for financial assets grew with the excess profits of the expanding national trade, this branch of the law further developed to define the right of the equity of redemption as a "thing," that is, conceptually, a legal object in the form of a right that could be possessed and even traded. Although the nature of the concept varied between a chattel in possession and "an estate in land" of which the person entitled to it remained its real owner, later in the 17th century under the influence of the jurist Lord Nottingham, it became accepted as a real property right in itself. Lord Nottingham was regarded as the "father of the equity of redemption" as he consolidated the legal principles around it. Offer (1981, 137) describes some details: "The borrower was entitled to repay the loan and regain his title at any time, subject to six months' notice or a fine [repayment penalty] of six months' interest in lieu."

The difficulty has now been resolved on the basis that on default the mortgagor retains an equity of redemption but if he does not exercise it, the mortgagee may, with the approval of the court, sell the property and recover from the proceeds the amount of the loan plus interest according to the mortgage agreement, and the costs of the court order and sale. Any balance of sale proceeds is then paid to the mortgagor. But the enforcement of mortgage loan terms remains more challenging than many other commercial transactions in the Anglo-American system, probably consistently with the persistent societal leverage of real estate ownership.

Land and Societal Power

Having been solidly ensconced in their landed estates by William I, the members of the aristocracy were tenacious in maintaining their power and social rank throughout succeeding centuries. Fundamental to this was the stability and symbolism of their landholdings which Beckett (1986, 2–3) described as follows:

> Entrance was available only to those who accepted the vital principles of aristocratic life. Of these, the first and most critical was property ownership. Property, in particular land, was the key to status and position in English society, underlying the subtleties of the graded hierarchy. As late as 1894 the editors of Burke's Landed Gentry could claim that land ownership was the principle 'test of rank and position.' ... However, to maintain the sanctity of the group it was crucial that the property remained firmly in the family.

Even as the middle class grew in numbers and wealth, they were generally not antagonistic towards the governing aristocracy, as it was throughout much of the Continent. Rather, its broad sentiment towards the upper levels of society was that "it was ready to leave government and high office in their hands because they had been born and bred to the work for generations" (Beckett 1986, 4). Part of the aristocratic sense of leadership and responsibility also lay in its administration of local communities associated with their estates, and as such "because landowners had a [substantial and immovable] stake in the country it was widely accepted that they had the best qualification [in terms of commitment] to govern" (Beckett 1986, 5). Due to this, England presented a uniquely symbiotic relationship whereby the gentry were firmly bound to allocated areas of the nation's land of which their good governance was paramount for social stability. They were traditionally ingrained with a sense of duty to service in government, often unpaid, and the under-classes generally believed in their capability and acceptance of their duties. It was described as "the habit of authority" by A.P. Thornton (1966) in his eponymous book, though other social scientists are less certain of the extent of social acceptance.

Within this framework of governance, there were two other notable differences between the English and the Continental aristocracies that are important to the manner in which land was controlled.

One was the ease and frequency of exit from English aristocratic ranks. Younger sons had neither land nor title, and although usually given a courtesy title of "lord," it was conferred only upon themselves and not upon their offspring (Beckett 1986, 23–24). From the estate's income, they might receive a stipend or a capital sum to establish themselves, though engaging in business was frowned upon, and it is understandable that many of them joined the church or the military. Daughters received from the estate only a dowry sufficient to enable them to obtain a socially suitable match. There was an exception when a daughter inherited the estate because of the absence of a male heir, and such a situation was to result in one of the earliest amalgamations of urban development activities in London of the later 17th century. While intermarriage between landed families led to the consolidation of rural estates even before urban formation, it also cast a number of young men into the lower rank of "gentleman," which at times proved to be a social problem because of their lack of training for work and their inclination to certain social trends of indolence and gambling. But as they were usually well educated, some could be resourceful when new thinking and new professional activities appeared. In contrast, the aristocracy of the Continent provided more equitable financial distribution to all members of a family, which often led to a division of estate lands so that over time, the estates grew smaller in size and economic contribution to the nation, and the power wielded by their owners diminished.

The second major difference was that Continental aristocratic privileges were enjoyed by all the family, whereas the English title and privileges were invested in only the eldest son. However, since younger sons, as gentlemen, could gain entry to clubs, social events, and economic activities, their status might command better social standing as an untitled second son of a wealthy and powerful English family than a weakly titled second son of a diminished Continental family. Again, this difference was to produce a cadre of untitled but influential young men who were keen to seize economic opportunities as England prospered.

The connection between land ownership and social standing stubbornly persisted in England, even while so much other wealth was created through industrialization, trade, and financial dealings. Even shortly prior to the 20th century, in 1883, the four largest land estates in England were owned by dukes, the ten estates of 60,000 acres or more belonged to peers of the realm, and of the 331 owners of land of 10,000 acres or more, there were 20 of the 21 dukes, 17 of the 19 marquesses, 74 of the 115 earls, and so on down the peerage ranks (Beckett 1986, 44). Offer (1981, 3) pointed out that ownership did not compete as an economic interest, but rather was so much more:

> ... this is not a theory, by a set of institutions and a code of practices, attitudes and habits. It was embodied in the laws of landed inheritance and transfer, and defined, interpreted and enforced by lawyers and the courts. It underlay the living culture of landed society.

Social symbolism was critical. As Polanyi (1957, 46) observed:

> The outstanding discovery of recent historical and anthropological research is that man's economy, as a rule, is submerged in his social relationships. He does not act so as to safeguard his individual interest in the possession of material goods; he acts so as to safeguard his social standing, his social claims, his social assets. He values material goods only insofar as they serve this end.

As the landed aristocrats' fortified castles had become outmoded with advances in military strategies and national defense forces, they built aesthetically considered grand homes at the center of their rural estates. Even in more recent times, it was often the case that:

> owning and improving a landed estate, when coupled to the upkeep of the requisite great country house, produced a lower return than almost any other form of property ... [T]here was clearly more at work here than purely economic considerations ... Acquiring a country house and an attendant country estate signaled an intention to belong to the landed society and enjoy its benefits. (Bujak 2007, 3)

This view of the importance of having and retaining control of land, and the implicit authority and status that goes with it, permeated all levels of society and was to be a critical socio-economic mindset in the rapidly growing population of later London.

The Threat to the Commons

Although the aristocrat firmly held title to his arable land, he allowed local farmers and common folk access, either unfettered or in accordance with an established schedule. During a season known as the Lammas, extending from April 6 to August 1, some lands were restricted for the sole use of the proprietor or a contracted tenant, typically for farming. Otherwise, these fields, referred to as "Lammas lands," were accessible as commons. As earlier described in its derivation from Roman property law, the term "commons" appears frequently in references to land access as customary practices that have existed simply since "tyme owte of mynde." Tawney and Powers (1953, 29–30) expand on the description of common rights to include the right to graze cattle, sheep, and geese, to provide foraging for pigs, to gleaning, and to gather berries and fuel (Figure 1.4). The historicity of English law, and its

1.4

The old parish church and village commons, Hampton-on-Thames, Middlesex.

use of precedents, protected lands for common use, and this custom became regarded as the "use-rights in common" of the community.

Common land, though, was not "common" in the modern sense of permitting open access to all comers. Rather, as Clark and Clark (2001, 1030–1031) described it:

> Other types of common rights—grazing rights on the arable lands after harvest, on the common meadow after mowing, and on pasture areas—were generally carefully limited and defined. Though these lands were cultivated in common for part of the year, the rights of access were tradable private rights.

Most generally, these were confined to members of the local community and excluded those with no ties through familial or leasehold relationships; and this nuanced concept of accessible, though restricted, open community space would become more contentious as urban areas formed.

Rising restrictions of access to rural land, however, were to cause social unrest earlier with the dramatic expansion of the wool industry and the modification of open fields to contain the flocks. Landlords enclosed their lands with stone walls or wooden fencing. Cunningham (1890, 469) provides an expanded description of this "enclosing" by pointing out that it can cover three different actions:

> The word really meant the fencing or planting of hedgerows round a greater or smaller area of land, and it was sometimes applied to the enclosing of a large district as one grazing farm or sheep run, and sometimes to the enclosing of an estate into many separate fields or closes.

Once enclosed, these fields were considered inaccessible to commoners for agrarian production or even recreation. Submission to this restriction of use was legally enforced and often resulted in opposition, resistance, and even bloodshed throughout England, and it was a controversial period of economic change. Polanyi (1957, 35) expressed this view of the socio-economic upheaval:

> Enclosures have appropriately been called a revolution of the rich against the poor. The lords and nobles were upsetting the social order breaking down ancient law and custom, sometimes by means of violence, often by pressure and intimidation. They were literally robbing the poor of their share in the common.

Although enclosure will later be seen as a critical precondition, though also with problematic consequences, for urban development, as a matter of national context it was one of the causes of the English Agricultural Revolution. Although this advanced English prosperity in general, it disrupted rural life for the common man. The increased productivity of enclosed pastures and competitively higher yielding crops meant that fewer farmers were needed to work the land, leaving many villagers without land or agrarian rights. For farmers who stayed, rental rates on tillable lands rose significantly. Many moved to the urban centers in search of work in the production of cloth and other goods, or in-service roles.

Finlay and Shearer (1986, 52) described this demographic shift in these terms: "It seems fairly clear that in the period between 1560 and 1650 people were pushed out of the countryside into the towns, particularly London, which had already become the principal trading centre in England."

A Changing Philosophy for Urban Land

In the 16th and 17th centuries, the rights and symbolism of land that had evolved for agrarian England were, however, challenged as townships arose. This was particularly true for the City of London which had retained its Roman form of democratic governance and broadly disbursed land ownership. Important philosophers of the time addressed this changing condition of mankind. Pierson (2013, 251) summarized it by adverting to the pronouncements of Grotius, Hobbes and Pufendorf that "the natural law [of private property] ... looms large." In this, Grotius (1925 [1625]) especially saw the right to private property to have continued under natural law with its religious foundation though he posed it as of a second order to permission to defend one's own life. Approaching it from another direction, Pufendorf (1994 [1660–1672]) put property in the service of maintaining social stability as its prime objective in natural law. However, Hobbes (1968 [1651], 190, 203) focused more on man's civic responsibilities and proposed that natural law is embodied in a "Constitution of a Civill [sic] Power," which provides for the governance of property, rather than its being administered through religious edicts.

Having made a detailed reading of these, Pierson (2013, 252) suggests

> that none of these key figures of the seventeenth century can be seen to have proposed a natural right to private property in any straightforward sense. A regime of private property [however] is to be favoured under the natural law because it promotes sociability and enhances overall social productivity.

He regards this as falling substantially short of an absolute right to private property under natural law. This represents a philosophical progression from the stronger right to private property of the late Middle Ages, Tudor, and early Stuart times, which supported the enclosure movement and the unassailability of landowners.

Following the application of property to the purpose of civic benefit expressed by Hobbes, John Locke (1632–1704) added two important conditions for its societal management: firstly that property not be wasted but rather, through human labor, it be used to create value; and secondly that the quantum of property in an individual's possession should be limited so that there would be "enough, and as good [quality]" remaining for the use of others (Shapiro 1996, 22, citing Locke 1970, 329). With his focus on the use of property, he proposed that as a reward for the human endeavor of "making" a thing the rights over it are realized through its ownership. His proposition of deriving title to property through suitable labor was strong and provocative. He conceded there are various contributions to "making" which are beyond that of the individual who may claim ownership. These inputs by others comprised the providing of natural resources, the social and legal conditions that facilitate the creation, such as the education of the maker, their access to the tools of making, the legal conditions supporting the creative act, and similar factors.

On this measure, applicable to the development of property are the ownership and condition of the land, the structures of governance and law that protect its ownership and use, and the social symbolism of building that enhances its value. The development activities of planning, funding, and construction are then the "labor" applied to achieve the benefits. If the labor and costs required to achieve a change of use approval for a site achieves a more productive outcome, then it should conform to his requirement of productive labor.

In order to moderate covertness in this process, Locke (2003, 56) held an important presumption, namely that this right is available to everyone as "the right ... to take care of and provide for their subsistence ... a right in common," and it therefore comes with the obligation under the Law of Nature for each individual to act to preserve all mankind. Inherent in this right is both the potential for an achievement of subsistence and direction of the manner in which an individual is to "provide" for or exercise it. This action is proposed as a "workmanship ideal" by which man labors in order "to subdue the earth, i.e. improve it for the benefit of life" (2003, 113–114). Of course, this did not mean that merely by working a piece of land its ownership could be claimed, though sometimes the law of long and continued adverse possession can result in such an outcome. Rather, Locke asserted that the possession of the land or other property comes with the responsibility to work it productively, and the benefits are what is produced.

By the inclusion of this obligation, he condemned the simple appropriation of land (Locke 2003, 116). If an individual owned land, enclosed or fenced it, but did not cultivate it or make it productive, he argued, such land "was still to be looked on as waste, and might be the possession of any other." In pursuing this objective of land productivity, it is not unreasonable to think that he might approve of the strategy of changing the use of land to its highest economic use, or as the real estate principle would put it, its *highest and best use*.

Locke's philosophical construct regarding property's value as intertwined with human effort and its productive use wielded significant influence in political, economic, and social determinations of the time. He admitted to limitations, such as property's main purpose being to secure social stability, which continued as the foundation of England's nationhood. Additionally, he gave substantial importance to property's service for the safety and flourishing of the community and restated the moral impetus for a landowner to provide "Surplusage" to his "needy brother" (Locke 2003, 29), noting the social consequences of a severely unequal distribution. Additionally, such concepts were inherent in much of the social and economic disruption that arose during this century. However, his association of human effort with the benefits of property, implying the usefulness of property if taken in hand, provided an intellectual construct by which the new process of urban property development was to find its place, even if all too often its moral tenets were neglected by its practitioners.

Chapter 2: Economic Concepts of Real Property and its Measurement

Although the English foundation of land as an economic construct was essentially established by William I, at that time its value was based solely on agrarian production with the objective of subsistence for the owner and community, after payment of taxes. For the early tenant farmer, the question of land's value did not have any financial metric. It was valued for the livelihood it could serve him, that is, for producing food for his family, housing them, paying his dues to his landlord, and trading some surplus for other necessary food or goods. Its utility value lay in meeting human needs, which for the farmer of that time were very basic.

Rent

Initially, rent took the form of a share of the land's produce or the provision of labor, with sometimes military service to meet his landlord's obligation to the Crown in that respect. However, the conversion to a financial metric took place when landowners, on being obliged to pay higher monetary taxes to the Crown, insisted that their tenants pay their rental in coinage, which was termed a "quitrent." Dyer (2005, 25) cited an early example of this: "… [I]n 1268–9, the hundred or so tenants of the Worcestershire manor of Fladbury were recorded paying annual rents in total of £22 to their lord." Under pressure to meet this new rent, a farmer, or an artisan who was occupying a village building, had to produce a surplus that could be traded for the necessary cash.

With this change, the nature of land moved from being merely a unit for production to meet subsistence needs to a unit for the production of an economic surplus, and it was the measurement of that surplus which gave it monetary value. That surplus, as coinage, was the rent, and as such, the use of land was transformed into a financial concept. In terms of its potential productive capacity, land itself was regarded as an economic asset of the estate, but its actual financial measurement as an annual rental payment recorded it as a component of the estate's income and not strictly a capital asset in accounting terms. Balance sheet financial recording had not yet been adopted.

The method adopted for the determination of rental rates has been examined from a number of socio-economic perspectives, ranging from its implied affirmation of ultimate ownership to its exploitation of the working class. To observe its role in the formation of private development activities, however, the application of Adam Smith's economic definition is useful: "Rent, considered as the price paid for the use of land, is naturally the highest which the tenant can afford to pay in the actual circumstances of the land" (Smith, 1994, 166).

By this calculation, the rent paid by a tenant farmer was determined by the value of the produce which was surplus to his family's needs and farming costs. This concept of economic surplus is controversial, but the move to its monetary representation in rental rates marked England's transition from the agrarian Middle Ages to the commercial European Renaissance and modern capitalism.

Leaseholds were typically attended by additional charges upon the lessee, specifically entry and exit charges, called the *"fine"* and the *"heriot,"* respectively. The *fine* had possibly commenced as a financial bond for anticipated lease payments, much as a security deposit is given today but without expectation of its return. Sometimes it was reduced or remitted if the tenant contracted to make extensive repairs to or even rebuild existing structures or infrastructure, such as barns and fences.

In early times, when land was held in feudal *villeinage*, which included the tenant's provision of additional labor for the landlord on his estate, the *fine* was held constant and calculated at just less than one year's dues, payable in cash, service, or kind. During the 15th century, the form of tenancy changed from *villeinage* to the land-lease contract, and the rental rate was adjusted to a more economic or market level, and *fines* were substantially reduced to a small fee for the registration of the tenure agreement (Harvey 1977, 271).

In contrast to modification of the *fine*, the *heriot* remained a significant amount over the long term. It was still paid at the end of the lease period, but its form changed from the tenant's "best beast" to a cash payment. It was part of the tenant's financial transfer of surplus to the landowner, in effect a form of profit-sharing of the tenant's benefit from being able to work the land. The only reduction in the *heriot* occurred when the period of the lease was for a life or similar hereditary arrangement, and then it was applied only for the last life, that is, upon the land's ultimate reversion to the landlord (Harvey 1977, 271–273).

For the landowner, this combination of annual rent, *fine*, and *heriot* established a financial division between his investment return by way of annual cash flow from the lease and his upfront provision of the property asset for use, keeping in mind its residual value at termination. In today's terms, it would be described as the difference between the annual income and the appreciation or capital gains netted from the sale price less the cost of acquisition. Even in these early times, as an asset, real property was unique in its variety of ways of extracting revenues, and with the resultant investment returns achieved through a complex combination of transactional dynamics.

Indeed, the options by which cash could be extracted on a lease facilitated many creative modifications of the rental rate. For instance, when an economic rent was difficult to determine, or was disputed, the agreed rental rate would be set at a high level but adjusted by ad hoc rebates during the term of the lease as the underlying economic factors became clear (Harvey 1977, 293). An urban site is recorded as having a very small *fine*, though its annual rent was probably higher than usual because of the tenant's potential benefit of profiting through a sublease:

> A site in the commercial western suburb of London [thought to be in Fleet Street or the Strand of today's London], described as 'a profitable little estate,' was granted to the Bishop of Worcester in return for a down-payment [fine] in silver equivalent to 300

pence and an annual rent of 12d. [shillings]. (Keene 1996, 94, citing Whitelock (1979, 529) and his review of historical documents)

This foreshadowed the behavior of a modern landlord who maintains a high listed, or nominal, rental rate but attracts tenants by lowering their effective economic cost through concessions such as periods of free rent, the build-out of the space, and similar means. This potential for modifying the rental payment stream continues to be an effective feature in the management of real estate investments today.

With this complexity of opportunity for adjustment in the negotiation of a lease's terms, which included landlords' negotiations with tenant farmers as to rights and obligations *inter se*, it is not surprising that they were not necessarily a mere passive managerial role. Rather, as Beckett (1986, 6) describes the function of the landlord's representative, it "resembled the role of director, and most played it with considerable acumen." A nobleman usually appointed an estate manager or steward to select and supervise workers needed to till the retained lands, and oversee tenant farmers, though the landlord had occasional direct inter-action with them. Further, the estate manager would often contribute to strategic decisions about rent levels, estate plans, and amenities for the communities. This structure of delega-tion, and the established capability of an estate manager, was later to be applied for the most part without modification to the management of an aristocrat's urban holdings.

The Economic Value of Land

Although for centuries after William I's recorded allocations of land there were minimal alien-ation transactions, there was occasionally need for the transfer of a lease holding. As a lease provided benefits to both parties, one of them might consider either disposing of his interest or acquiring that of the other, or a third party may wish to acquire the interest of one of them.

Establishing a suitable price for such a transaction to be achieved required an extension to the method of land valuation based on annual rental rate, since this was only the revenue received for one year's use. Though the economic benefit for the lessor was easily calculated in terms of the amount of rent received, a valuation of the right to use the land was complex and related to the specific agrarian potential. Of course, the optimizing of the rental rate between that which was financially feasible for the tenant, and the supply of tillable land by landowners, meant that the rental rate trended towards representing the economic position of both parties.

A term lease was usually for ten or twenty years, but many leases were yearly, with a general mutual expectation of renewal. For these, a twenty-year term was taken as implied if the tenancy was to be continued after the passing of ownership. Through common usage, the valuation for ownership (as leasehold) transfer was established as a multiple of the annual rent and the number of years for which this rent would be received, that is, the term or dura-tion of the lease. This assessment is represented by the following equation, and continues in use today, known as the *rent-roll multiple*:

Annual Rental Rate x Number of Years of the lease = Valuation of the lease

As a result, the value of a plot for which the rent was £2 for a term of twenty years was £40, ignoring discounting for extended payment. If a transaction occurred at some time *during* the period of a lease, its calculated transaction price was based on the rental rate for the remaining number of years on the lease.

This exchange of the ownership, as leasehold, or right of use of land for a capital sum represented a "capitalization" of its use value, again emphasizing that even for the person who was due to receive that capital sum, its quantum was fundamentally based on the land's economic use and its ability to support it in terms of duration and quality. Though this remains foundational to the economic role of real estate even today, within the context of expanding capitalism the unprecedented demand for urban housing, the increasing dominance of the role of capital, and the evolution of property's social symbolism will overlay that simplicity of perspective and calculation with need, speculation, and aspiration.

Extracting Value from Land

Although he inherited a well-stocked treasury, Henry VIII (1509–1547) set out to continue his father's policy of settled peace with foreign countries, thereby avoiding exorbitant costs in lives and money. He also scrupulously managed his estates and revenues and avoided any dependency on Parliament's authorization to raise funds by higher taxes. Like his father, he departed from the practice of engaging counselors from the aristocracy, and instead hired learned young men from the church, legal fraternity, and rural estate management. The benefit of their background of court management, removed as it was from the baronial and interwoven church hierarchy, would prove to be very advantageous in many of his decisions concerning the increasing commercial activity and the issue of real property. These were related concerns, for the free flow of commercial transactions across social levels was to be a fertile source of increased enthusiasm for property investment in the following century.

One of the young, bright and status-hungry cadre of clerks and administrators of his Treasury was Thomas Cromwell (1485–1540), a lawyer though also a commoner. From his work in the banking houses of Italy and commerce in the Low Countries he was particularly astute in matters of state revenues and the detailed accounting of assets and financial transactions. Due to the quality of his performance, he rose to the most eminent position of Chancellor in 1532. His colleagues of keen men with financial capabilities included Thomas Wriothesley and John Russell, who were later to establish a new format of real estate enterprise. Their rise within Henry's court, and their experience under Cromwell's guidance in finance, particularly in relation to landed estates, nurtured their talents for exploiting new property opportunities that were to arise.

Dissolution of the Monasteries

Henry enjoyed the pleasures of his direct landholdings and was personally involved in the details of palace building and land stewardship, but as king he was very cognizant of the power and economic potential of land ownership in his kingdom. A significant adverse force in his conflict with the Roman Church over the legitimacy of his marriage to Catherine and the consequent right of succession of her daughter, Mary, was the economic power inherent in the extensive ownership of land held by the parishes, abbeys, and monasteries, and the subversive fostering of treasonous sentiment within them because of their religious affiliation with France and Spain. This constituted a substantial threat to his rule and England's sovereignty.

The church's landholdings had grown substantially through many donations by nobles who sought spiritual redemption and gifts by various monarchs over the centuries. As John Hare (2003, 22) described it: "In 1536 the religious orders had owned about a fifth of the lands of England." Some orders were enterprising and entered into activities including coal mining and farming. Casson and Casson (2013, 74–76) claim that sometimes the management was strategic and clever, such as by rationing extraction volumes for mining activities, which extended the life of the resource and therefore its revenue stream. This is in contrast to the findings of Barbara Harvey (1977, 331), who writes that the monks had removed themselves from direct management of their lands, both agrarian and urban, by assigning their responsibility for their upkeep to master lessees, and thus had become "as landlords, not benevolent [as one might expect], but ineffectual."

Ecclesiastical lands were not taxed or subject to what Harvey (1977, 332) terms "the authority of the ordinary," that is, the monarch, but were subject, *nullo mediante* (without any intermediary), only to Rome. Nevertheless, relying heavily on many activities of governance that were performed by the parishes, monarchs provided financial support to religious organizations, usually in the form of income producing lands.

As Henry's friction with the pope increased, he demanded that the ecclesiastical entities inform him of their remittances to Rome. The revenues from those lands were of considerable interest to Thomas Cromwell, and he established a Court of Augmentations to produce a survey with the details of usage, existing rental rates, and lease tenures for all the ecclesiastical properties (Bernard 2011). To this he applied an early form of modern asset accounting, identifying a number of religious establishments, excluding parish churches, where revenues were less than £200 per annum, or where the number of monks had diminished below the required minimum of twelve and was insufficient to justify the costs of the facilities.

From 1535, he launched a strategy to dissolve the small monasteries first, that is, those failing the test of covering their costs. The Court of Augmentations, with his former assistant Richard Riche as its Chancellor, perform assessments and took control of the lands where the tests were failed, thereby directing their revenues to the Crown. It is estimated that the lands of 625 monastic communities which occupied between 35,000 and 40,000 acres, with a total annual income of approximately £150,000, were reclaimed. In the country's entire history, this was probably the largest volume of land title transfer within a decade.

Although this strategy served Henry's need, the Dissolution of the Monasteries is still condemned as hostile to the Roman Church by those who are less skeptical of it than Harvey. It has also been condemned for its broader consequences. Marx (1977, 882) has said:

> The process of forcible expropriation of the people received a new and terrible impulse in the 16th century from the Reformation, and the consequent colossal spoliation of church property. The Catholic Church was, at the time of the Reformation, the feudal proprietor of a great part of the soil of England. The dissolution of the monasteries, etc., hurled their inmates into the proletariat. The estates of the church were to a large extent given away to rapacious royal favorites or sold at a nominal price to speculating farmers and townsmen, who drove out the old-established hereditary subtenants in great numbers and threw their holdings together. The legally guaranteed property of the poorer folk in a part of the church's tithes was quietly confiscated.

These conflicting assessments of land ownership, management and responsibility indicate the changing economic context for land, and the fluid conceptions of its value, that would enable the later entrepreneurial approaches of the early developers.

Advances in the Valuation of Real Property

Of particular consequence to the imminent birth of private real estate development was that, from the mid-16th century onwards for almost a century, much land fell into the hands of those who recognized the economic potential beyond its existing or currently contracted use. Stone (1966, 43) describes it:

> This throwing of Crown and Church lands onto the market was accompanied by an equally important development which released a huge mass of private property, which had previously been tied up by legal restrictions against alienation. In the late middle ages, the entail [rules of estate inheritance] was a fairly effective barrier against the free disposition of property by the current owner; in the late seventeenth century the strict settlement served the same purpose. Between 1530 and 1660, however, there were relatively few legal obstacles to the alienation of property, and those that existed were weak. The result of this legal situation and of various economic pressures was the massive transfer of land by purchase and sale, which reached a peak in the 1610s.

It is estimated by Linklater (2013, 20) that within approximately seven years of the Dissolution, half of ecclesiastical properties had been sold, raising more than £1.4 million for the royal treasury by 1542. He also highlights the distribution of lands across social classes:

> Thus, within two generations a high proportion of England's most productive land was bought and sold twice over, and its eventual destination was not the ancient nobility, but people with cash – London merchants, careful farmers, government officials, even tenants on fixed rents – anyone looking for a secure investment.

That this result is referred to as an "investment" rather than merely a source of revenue predicates innovation, for it reveals the changing attitude towards land ownership and use.

The Valuation of Land Use

Another indication of change in land economics is manifest in the fact that the value of the church lands obtained by Henry were described in terms of its total sum, £1.4 million, representing the total value of the properties when they were sold, rather than in terms of the traditional metric of revenues per annum. Although the dynamic financial understanding and description of property continued in terms of revenues generated per annum under a lease, Cromwell's team placed substantially new emphasis on recording property economics in terms of total valuation, or land capitalization, taking into account the visibility of anticipated future payments with contractual obligations.

As Cromwell's talented accountants derived these valuations, they recorded rental rates and tenures according to existing contractual information, which highlights their cognizance of the association of value with a *committed* economic utility of the land. On this, they did not speculate as to what use a property *might otherwise* have, even with the anticipated transfer of ownership, for its lease was legally required to remain in place until its date of expiration. This both established the economic strength of real estate as a product of its lease terms and indicated where future potential, though uncertain, value might be as yet unrealized. Nor did they contemplate the possibility of changing market conditions and their subsequent impact on rental rates. These reasons for potentially increasing land valuation were left to the future developers, who did undertake land use change which enhanced value.

Net Income from Land

The valuation process adopted by Cromwell's team also achieved more economic precision than has been previously attained. Their calculation included the deduction of operating costs from rent revenues to determine the "clear annual income," by which the "value was ascertained" and recorded in the survey's twenty-two volumes, the *Valor Ecclesiasticus* (Hunter 1834, v). These operating costs included many categories which persist in valuations for either taxation or trading purposes. Perhaps surprising is their disregard of necessary capital costs for repairs, but this may have been because such costs had typically been the responsibility of a tenant.

This approach advanced the understanding that as an asset land has a financial value after the deduction of the operating costs necessary for its economic utilization, and this is known today as the net revenue or net operating income (NOI). Offer (1981, 113) describes the process of derivation of this financial measurement from land's functional use:

> [A] definition arises from function, not from legal form [though that would come later with land use laws]. It refers to the agricultural and location value of land and embodies the classical economic distinction between land and capital. The landowner farmed out economic opportunities (and risks) to agricultural and urban entrepreneurs; they provided skills, management and working capital and took their chances; the landowners took the residue.

This new approach further served to shift the calculation of land value to emphasize careful consideration and management of the operating costs and the economic production they supported, rather than just an imposed rental rate. Stone (1966, 53) suggests that establishing the price of bread required information about the expenses in sustaining the household of the baker rather than nature of the bread produced. For a landlord, this brought into consideration not only his management of usual operating costs but also his strategic management of his real estate, be it land and/or building, so that it could be offered in optimum condition for the occupants to achieve their best economic production. Although the potential benefits for themselves are often overlooked by lazy landlords, the almost ubiquitous detailed tailoring of work environments by the 21st-century technology companies indicates the revival of a more conscientious attention to the economics of proactively operating real estate.

The Potential and Residual Value of Land

Complementary to his survey, Cromwell also noted the usage of land and its buildings where applicable. Though records cannot be found revealing an explicit strategy, this information was to be useful to him in ascertaining any potential unlocked value in these properties. Part of his interest in the ecclesiastical lands had been prompted by his recognition that many were undermanaged, mostly by being left fallow or leased at a rent lower than was achievable. In taking these lands for the Crown, he would have intended to increase their revenues where possible through new leases upon the expiration of the current contracts.

This explicit understanding of a potential step up in value when a lease rent would be reset at the market rate was an advance in the conception of land as a capitalized asset. That appreciating factor was partly offset by a diminishing factor in that a new lease would need to be agreed, which constituted an adverse risk. Not only did the higher rental rate need to be captured in a new lease for the potential of market prices to be realized, but if there were no new lease it meant that the land might lie fallow and be wanting in economic value instead.

In seeking immediate capital for Henry, Cromwell sold some of the properties to courtiers and merchants. To establish their prices for such sales, the Commissioners of the Court of Augmentations were required to go beyond the recorded valuation based on existing leases and address the issue of the land's potential value within the solidifying capitalist economy. In doing this, there were particularly two aspects of that new context that required attention, namely, rapidly changing prices in response to increasing demand, and the process of attracting capital for the acquisitions from alternative investment options.

This expansion of valuation analysis called for the specific calculation of that potential value of the land, or the residual value when the unencumbered title reverted to the landlord upon the expiration of a lease. As addressed by Cromwell's Commissioners, the value would be based on any of three scenarios: the current tenant might renew the lease at the current rate, the current tenant might pay a higher rate at the level which a new tenant would pay, or the land might remain unleased. Habakkuk (1958, 365) describes the rationale that was adopted:

> [W]ith the rapid rise in general prices, the rents specified in the leases granted before the rise became a progressively inadequate guide to the true annual value of the property. So that the Commissioners, in calculating the price, had to allow for the excess of annual value over the old rent ... to make an accurate assessment of the price the Commissioners needed not only to estimate the excess of annual value over the old rent but to calculate the present capital value of this excess at some date in the future, i.e. they had to calculate the value of the reversion [to the landowner] after the expiry of the lease.

Of course, speculation about the new rate at which the land would be rented and the probability of its occurring meant that different opinions resulted in different valuations by this method, and eventually the appearance of a trading arbitrage. With the belief in the perpetuity of property value, and the insistence on assessing all usable land even if contingent upon a future lease, calculations regarding this economic event became critical, and also controversial, in real estate valuation and these uncertainties continue today.

Land Definition and Measurement

Cromwell's detailed accounting for church properties appears to have spurred advances in the legal and cartographic modes of definition of real property. Gerhold (2016, 2) describes the traditional format: "Until the 1570s the idea of an estate map for general reference, whether of urban or rural property, was unknown; that need was served by the written estate survey instead. Deeds and leases virtually never included plans, relying instead on written description." A graphic representation of a plot of land on a map or plan had been rare, since such forms of geographical reference were usually limited to nautical or military use.

As London's infrastructure of water pipes from Roman days became more complex because of the growing population, a graphic plan was adopted to record their location, and Gerhold (2016, 2) suggests that the earliest building plan in London was a depiction of its piping. Further, his review of records indicates that "[n]o more surviving plot outlines have been identified until 1534, when two were drawn of property purchased by Thomas Cromwell." Although such a transaction would not normally have included a graphic plan of the lot, the documents evidencing his acquisition included such a plan of the site (Figure 2.1)

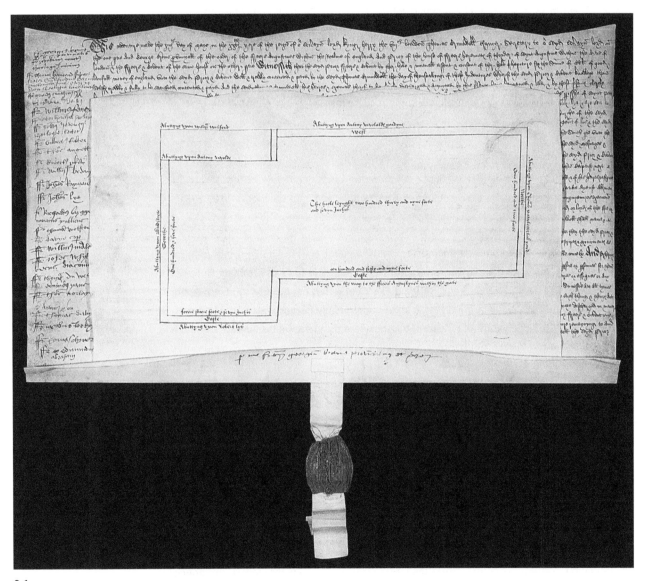

2.1

Text and graphic survey of Thomas Cromwell's property at Austin Friars at the time of its 99-year lease.

as a complement to its verbal description. This is testament to his incisive understanding of the importance of accurate property definition.

As development activity increased in the following century, plans showing intended improvements to a site became common. Gerhold (2016, 8) described its purpose: "[T]hey were either commissioned by landowners to help them decide whether or how to go ahead with building projects on their own, or they were required from the builder by a landowner who wished to understand what was proposed or to keep some control over the process."

Recovery from the Great Fire of 1666 generated a further inclination for plans, for the metes and bounds of individual lots were no longer clearly and physically delineated on the ground. The Rebuilding Act of 1667 required that foundations be staked out and plans made by the City surveyors. Subsequent transactions, including leases, employed lot outlines in the contract documents. Maps of London remained pictorial until Ogilby and Morgan's ground plan of the City in 1676, which possibly provided a legal and commercial benefit of precisely recorded individual land lots to contribute to an economic construct of the urban topography as a whole.

The rising use of plans to communicate the spatial measurement of property, especially with legal and commercial consequences, depended on an increasing presence of professionals who could perform the work accurately. Linklater (2013, 33) described this need:

[I]n a market involving buyers with no local knowledge, an objective, unchanging quality such as area allowed strangers to compare the value of different commodities. Thus, one unmistakable indicator that a true market in land had developed was the appearance of exact, invariable measurements in place of local, organic units.

In providing this, as Andrew McRae (1993, 341) explains, the rise and professionalization of the skills of the land surveyor in the early 16th century helped to establish "a social and economic order in which rights to the land can clearly and objectively be determined, in a manner which precludes competing or loosely defined customary claims." Moreover, "objective measurements afforded by geometry, therefore, further a fundamental shift in the perception of 'one's own' as 'the concept of landed property as a bundle of assorted rights over different bits of territory gave way to the idea that property lay in definable pieces of soil'" (346). In other words, the popular concept of ownership focused less on the rights and responsibilities attached to land as defined through custom, or tradition, and increasingly upon the objective measurements of surveying. Title to land is a bundle of intangible rights and responsibilities in respect of a tangible asset that must be identified and defined by physical factors, and the emphasis on the broadly accepted view of property turned to the latter. The scale of the change in ownership that followed from the transfer of the monastic properties demonstrated the high desirability, if not the necessity, of accurate delineations of land boundaries.

Capital and Land

As the wealth potential inherent in increased agrarian production during the 16th century provided a demand "pull" to real estate values as farmers bid up the rents on ground leases, a compelling supply "push" appeared in the new economic conditions of established capitalism in London. Although formal banking systems were not established until very late in the century, the funding of England's expensive wars against France and other empires and its own internal challenges to the formation of "Great Britain" necessitated intermittent Crown borrowing on a regular basis on top of its usual tax revenue. During the 12th and 13th centuries such loans were sought on the Continent, usually from Italian bankers, but in the 14th century, emerging wealthy English merchants amassed liquid capital that they could lend to the Crown. They included William de la Pole, a wool and wine merchant, Walter Chiriton, who leased all the customs of the English harbors, and Dick Whittington (of storybook legend, possibly accompanied by his cat), who apprenticed as a mercer (Casson and Casson 2013, 69–73). In providing financial support to the Crown these men of wealth leveraged their connection with it to achieve political power, often for the purpose of advancing their business interests. For example, Whittington supplied cloth and spices to the courts of Richard II, Richard III, Henry IV, and Henry V, and provided large loans to the last two. He was rewarded not only with interest and commercial profits but also appointed by Richard II as Mayor of London. In this position, though broadly benevolent, he established Blackwell Hall as a very productive cloth market for his own purposes.

With the formation of corporate entities, the dynamic continued. It has been claimed that the late 17th-century currency crisis was a consequence of depleted precious metals reserves at the Royal Mint due to its overuse by the East India Company for trading payments (Barber 1975, 9), but that company was also a regular funding source for the Crown. Naturally, a large cohort arose to participate in this boom and its benefit and influence, as Stone (1966, 28) notes: "... there was a marked influence of the merchant community over English policy—especially foreign policy—thanks to the leverage it could exercise over any government by the offer or withholding of its facilities for credit."

This early use of capital to establish high-level connections that would then benefit business activities became an inherent part of English commerce. It was to be particularly critical for real estate development, where practitioners were dependent upon authorities for direct approvals and permits, and especially for impactful decisions on land use, taxation, and the municipal economy. Though the forms of financial connections and political influence vary in the present age, such economic interdependence was fundamental from the start, and continues to remain so.

Elizabeth I Expands Trade and Commerce

While strategically retaining her sovereign control of England through governance of its lands, Queen Elizabeth I (1558–1603) also understood the new economic potential of trade, and she encouraged the advance of English mercantilism by fostering adventurers and rewarding the discovery of important trade routes.

> Francis Drake's circumnavigation of the earth between 1577 and 1580 has been regarded since the sixteenth century, and rightly so, as the most striking of the many overseas exploits of Elizabethan Englishmen ... Drake's voyage played a vital role in this awakening of the English people to the possibilities for personal and national profit in faraway lands. (Rabb 1967, 19–21)

As land trading and its operational use became part of the new economic system, the adoption of the new attitude to real estate was inherent in the settlement and exploitation of new colonies.

Further, with England's entry into the trading and commercial activities of the Continent, attitudes to agrarian production changed from seeking sustainability to maximizing commercial output. This was inherent in the choice of crop or agrarian activity, by which a change of use might potentially achieve a higher commercial output. It followed that as the land was a key resource in this production activity, its role came to be apportioned as part of the trading price of potential output and its value was a derivative of that economic result, and no longer directly related to the rental rate of its current lease, nor even to the costs of productive activity, as in the earlier example regarding the price of bread. Now, as the allocation of land use would respond to the trading price of its produce, merchant markets became a primary determinant of the highest economic use of land.

Further Economic Abstraction and "Financialization"

This trade-led derivation of land value, however, made its metrics vulnerable to production gluts or economic disruptions in the foreign markets with which England traded. Appleby (1978, 20) describes this dramatic impact in the late 16th century: "The removal of key links in production and consumption from the range of tactile experience promoted the creation of symbolic representations. Price, rate [or investment return], and credit began to stand in place of the bargain, the payment, and contract they represented."

The dynamics of these purely financial concepts of value increased in complexity as English enterprise diversified during the queen's late reign. No longer could monocausal factors, such as weather or crop disease, explain changing prices of goods, and noticeable consequences for affordability, employment, and ultimately national wealth focused the discussion of the times on macroeconomic activity. This led to the conceptualization of an abstract single market that represented the multitude of formal and informal transactions and exchanges that took place. Such a market for real estate developed in parallel with other salable items, and it was within this market that the land was "financialized" or impacted by the financial dynamics of interrelated trading systems beyond its fundamental productive use. Marx noted this binary purpose of property: "Its value thus acquires a double existence. One part of it remains attached to its use-form or bodily form belonging in the process of production. The other part detaches itself from that form in the shape of money" (Marx 1976a, 163). This extraction from its basic utility continues today with real estate firmly embedded in the global capital markets (Derrington 2019).

Although sophisticated economic thinking was to flourish later in the 17th century, leading to Adam Smith's lasting paradigms of capitalism in the 18th century, at the dawning of the century incisive economic thinking was expressed by Thomas Mun (1623). As he was involved in the East India Company, his discourse centered on the dynamics of trade and he regarded the commercial network as a coherent community of producer, trader, and consumer. In fact, Appleby (1978, 38) credits him with playing down the importance of the consumer and giving the merchant the central role of purchasing goods when pricing was suitable and sales evident. By this system, money flowed rationally and freely, and profits, which were achieved as residual benefits from trade, were larger with increased transactional volume. Further, from this perspective, assets were of less significance than the financial earnings that could be derived from their use.

Capital Markets for Real Estate

Within this increasing mercantilism, the new businessmen of London absorbed the practices and knowledge of immigrants and learned from the experiences of those countries which were already advanced. Commerce developed its sophistication, supported by an early form of banking where excess capital was distributed as loans for commercial ventures. Corporations originated as legal structures which established the legal and financial arrangement between their investors in their enterprises and, most attractively, in the event of insolvency, limited those investors' losses to the amount of their investment. This encouraged greater commercial risk-taking by the corporations and was most suited to entrepreneurship in trading and goods production and, eventually, real estate trading.

To raise capital, a corporation issued stock that allocated proportional ownership of its incorporeal legal persona to each contributing shareholder. Its value and hence the value of its stock was related to regularly paid dividends and was calculated as a multiple of its annual dividends. The value of a stock that was entitled to £1/annum, as nominated on the stock certificate, for say twenty years was £20. This method of valuation was unsurprisingly similar to the calculative method of real estate valuation. Investors therefore paid £20 upfront, in order to receive the £1 per annum for the next twenty years, often allocating such receipts to a beneficiary. Although such an investment represented simply a deferred return of capital, as an annuity it functioned as a temporal repository of wealth and an organized method for distributing it to the next generation; and, of course, there was always the speculation that the company would thrive and dividends would exceed the original coupon. When inflation was taken into account in capital markets in the late 17th century, the distribution was discounted by the opportunity cost of capital (OCC) to result in today's stock valuation method, and was similarly applied to lease valuations. Initially, these regulated corporations avoided trading and carefully arranged ownership and profit distribution while retaining control of who their economic participants would be.

In contrast, though a derivative of the corporation, joint-stock companies diluted their control by permitting stock trading. It was particularly established to fund ventures requiring large capital outlays such as shipbuilding and foreign trade. Rabb (1967, 3) describes its advantages and potential popularity:

> With its shares available [and tradeable] to any buyer, whether he [or she, since this was a form of property that a woman could own] was skilled in trade or not, the joint-stock company, from the primitive beginnings of the Muscovy Company in the 1550's to the flowering of the East India Company in the first decades of the seventeenth century, enabled merchants for the first time to attract capital from all sections of society.

The valuation of these companies for stock *trading* purposes now required two assumptions:

1. The annual dividend amount (£1) anticipated to be paid in the future for the time period (twenty years) over which the enterprise would function, which represented the *income potential* of the investment, as offered on the certificate, though it was also vulnerable to failure.
2. The enterprise's potential for growing profitability that would provide dividends beyond £1, which represented its *appreciation potential*.

Because these assumptions were based on a written, though vulnerable, offer for the former and an anticipated outcome, or speculation, for the latter, there were differences of opinion regarding a valuation due to differing views on the *risks* of the offer and the *uncertainty* of appreciation or anticipated future profitability. Further, the component of value due to appreciation, whether anticipated or even actually achieved during the holding period, would be converted into currency or its financial value crystalized only when it was sold. These speculative differences continue to be the basis for stock market activity, as well as being applied to the trading of other assets such as real property.

The extension of this energized economic vitality of trade to ordinary real estate activity was to be specifically noted later in the 17th century by a commentator on and very active participant in British commerce, Nicholas Barbon. He surmised:

Trade Raiseth the Rent of the Land, for by the Use of several sorts of Improvements, the Land Yieldeth a greater Natural Stock; by which, the Land-lord's Share is the greater: And it is the same thing, whether his Share be paid in Mony, or Goods: Mony is an Immaginary Value made by a Law, for the Conveniency of Exchange: It is the Natural Stock that is the Real Value, and the Rent of Land. (Barbon 1690, 7)

That he undertook real estate development is not surprising and his adept handling of property value was to add significantly to its new formulation.

Such an environment of commercial transactions, based on exchange valuations and facilitated by currency, was a potent context in which real property was to be transformed from its traditional purpose of function with some side benefit of social status, to that of adding financial assets to the heady mix of rising capitalism and broadening democratization of commerce. And so it was to be with real estate development.

Investment Returns on Land

As conveyances of landed interests increased, their correct valuation in that commercial context was necessary to the efficient functioning of the commerce itself. It has been explained how in these emerging capital markets, land had undergone its initial capitalization when its rental rate was employed in its valuation for the purposes of ownership or leasehold transfer, and formally established as a calculative purpose by Cromwell. A subsequent inclusion of future economic potential from rising rental rates added the residual value of land to the capitalization amount. Then, the increasing volatility in trading rural products overlaid that simple calculation with the complexity of the economic environment. Even if land were used for housing and not the direct production of tradable goods, its value as a resource in the macroeconomy was dependent upon the income its resident could earn, with the restoration of that earning capacity achieved through their habitation. In turn, the earnings of that resident were dependent upon the trading market value of the economic production in which he was engaged, and therefore the value of the real estate was derived from the broad macroeconomic context of global trading markets.

With the trading of investment assets, a further factor affecting reliable valuation was a transaction's participation in mobile capital markets. As real estate transactions typically required large amounts of capital, they needed to be particularly competitive in attracting capital to the sector. For alternative investments, the calculation was based on the relationship between the anticipated income for a given period and the investment amount. For example, if at the start of a corporate bond for twenty years at £1 per annum, the capitalized value was £20, and the yield or return in the first year was £1/£20, or 5%.

Although the economic objective of land ownership had incorporated capitalism's tenet of revenue maximization, its trading price in the capital markets alongside merchant activities and loans demanded the provision of a base or hurdle rate. Viewed within the same framework as the corporate bond above, in a commercial dealing involving land, it would be required to earn a competitive *return* on the capital outlay, such as 5%. Therefore, for a twenty-year lease with an annual rent of £1, to deliver a 5% yield its trading price would be £20.

However, the trading price of a lease at a point during the term presented a calculative conundrum. If the value at the eleventh year was calculated only on the remaining term, the yield was £1/£10 which is 10%. But this is not a useful metric since the rent and invested capital, not amortized, has remained the same. Therefore, the advance in valuation methodology to include a residual value of the land, based on a subsequent lease executed at reversion, was conceptually more suited to indicating a valid return metric as required by contemporaneous capital markets. By this approach, if a residual value were calculated on anticipated rent of £2 per annum on a subsequent lease, the capitalized value over the next twenty years would have included ten years at the new rent to give an answer of £30. The return at year eleven is therefore 3.3%. If the residual value due to a successive future lease were added, and this were done indefinitely, the annual returns would increase in response to rising rates. This calculation, with the later addition of discounting for the opportunity cost of capital (OCC) over the investment period, is the conceptual foundation for the *capitalized valuation* of property and use of a *capitalization rate* that is so widely used today.

This construct was broadly adopted during the 17th century and was fundamental to the economic rationale of urban development as a profitable venture. The dissemination of the rationale was aided by publications such as Primatt's reference book (Figure 2.2) which gives lease term tables for capital market interest rates of 5%, 6%, 8%, and 10%.

44   *The City and Countrey*

Four Tables, shewing how many Years, Months and Weeks Purchase the Lease of any Land or Houses is worth, Calculated to four several Rates of Interest, viz. at V. VI. VIII. and X. per Cent. per Annum.

Purchaser and Builder.   45

The description of the Table.

The Table consisteth of four Parts; the first is calculated to the Rate of Five *per cent.* the Second at Six *per cent.* the Third at Eight *per cent.* and the Fourth at 10 *per cent.* In the first Column of each of them you have the Number of years to be purchased from 1 year to 100. In the next Column you have how many Years, Quarters, and Weeks, any thing for so many years is worth, let the Rent be great or small.

Example I.

What is an Annuity, Lease, Rent, or Pension, of 20 *l.* a year, and to continue 17 years, worth in ready Money, at 5, 6, 8, and 10 *l. per cent. per annum?*
Look in the first Column of the Table for 17 years, and right against 17 in the Table of

		T.	Q.	W.
V	per cent.	11	1	0
VI	per cent.	10	2	0
VIII	per cent.	9	0	5
X	per cent.	8	0	0

(you shall finde)

And so many Years, Quarters, and Weeks Rent will the Purchase be worth. So that the Rent being 20 *l.* a year,

		l.	*s.*	*d.*		
11 Y. and 1 Q.	will come to	225	0	0	at	Five
10 Y. and 2 Q.		210	0	0		Six
9 Y. and 5 W.		181	18	6		Eight
8 years.		160	0	0		Ten

per cent.

And the like may be done for any other number of Years, and for any other Rent.

Example:

2.2

The *City and Country Purchaser and Builder* showing interest rate tables used in valuation.

He proposed their use for determining the value of land or buildings and also, critically, he gave the annual yield on the investment. By this method he was able to conclude that

[s]ome Houses near *London*, and in other places, that were built more for pleasure than profit, do very seldom yield the Owner or Builder above four, five, or six pounds *per cent.* when they Let or Lease the same; the Tenant that takes them not regarding what they cost building, but what is reasonably worth *per ann.* And if any Purchaser is to buy the same, he will have allowed him after the rate of eight, nine, or ten *per cent. per ann.* for his money, or more or less, as it may be valuable. (Primatt 1680, 37)

Advancing Mortgage Law

As leases were modified to better accommodate the new relations between landlords and tenants, so too did the nature of loans involving real estate evolve. In the early part of the 17th century, the tradition of the landed gentry to maintain debt within manageable levels generally continued and Beckett (1986, 300) noted that "[d]uring the 1630s, for example, only about one-fifth of the peerage were in debt to individual creditors (the Crown and family apart) for more than two years' income." But the increased opulence of the Stuart court seems to have led to some overspending and crippling levels of debt amongst the upper classes.

In this mobile economic context, the asset value of land found use in another range of financial transactions in the form of a mortgagee's rights in a mortgage transaction. He could use the mortgage, fortified as it was by his title to the mortgaged land, as an item of sale or security for a loan to himself, or he could sell it. Its increasing use expanded the possible participants in the tenurial markets, through the rights of the borrower regarding repayment defined the limits of its value. This afforded another product to be traded on the capital markets, and through its use, a lender could also potentially participate in the growing property markets. As urban land later became a rapidly appreciating investment opportunity, lenders were enticed to the asset class and real estate financing became an established part of the capital markets.

Nor was the mortgagor excluded from those markets. His equity of redemption was itself a marketable right and its value was the difference between the market price of the property and the value of the outstanding loan. Of course, in a market of falling property prices, the value of this interest might become negative, resembling the instances of negative equity in mortgaged houses after the financial crisis of 2008, which also removed the mortgagor's incentive to repay.

With this growing credit market, a flourishing trade grew, providing for the capital needs of the extensive housing development occurring in the metropolis.

Chapter 3: The Rise of London

The Evolution of English Towns

Unlike Egypt, ancient Britain functioned as a nation state, as Everitt (1966, 57) described it, a land sprinkled with villages where "the farmworking family more often remained rooted in the same district from one generation to the next, sometimes working on the same farm and passing on the same customary skills to children and grandchildren." The cultural influences of successive invading Continental tribes of Angles, Saxons, and Vikings were absorbed into these spatially dispersed, nucleated communities. It was not that the nation was unfamiliar with city formation, for the Romans had established urban centers as trading outposts which Palgrave (1831, 8) describes as "many strong cities in different parts of the island, which they surrounded by lofty ramparts. These 'colonies,' or '*municipia*,' were peopled with Roman inhabitants, who came hither from Italy, accompanied by their wives and children." As autonomous communities, they were each required to define its membership, establish spatial arrangements, and formulate methods for maintaining control of its populations and economy.

With the fall of the Roman empire, these urban centers declined and throughout the Middle Ages Western Europe became feudal in its economic, social, and spatial arrangements. However, on the Continent and then England, with the economic and social upheaval brought about by the emerging production of surplus and its trade, townships grew around marketplaces. Though their origins were fostered by the landowners, Eliassen and Ersland (1996, 8) have suggested that as an increasing number of independent citizens settled in place permanently:

> the right of usage [of the land], if not the ownership, must have been transferred from the landowner to the towns-people – either as full property rights [in contrast to feudal fee transactions] or as more or less limited rights of disposition, against the payment of a yearly rent.

Keene has proposed that the nature and form of modern property markets took shape in those times and any later changes are merely in scale, capital resources, and contractual arrangements. He noted:

> By the early twelfth century the urban property market had developed a form and a dynamic that in essence have persisted to the present. It was distinguished by the

subdivision of land and buildings, by the creation of monetary interests that could serve a wide range of purposes, by the relatively free exchange of these units, by underlying land values that reflected the demand for sites close to central areas of business, and by high investment in building (indicated by the height, density and solidity of structures, as well as by financial measures) close to those areas. (Keene 1996, 95)

In the 13th century, the use of timber for the construction of habitable buildings made a further contribution to the changing physical typology of towns. Although the use of stone for grand residences resulted in more stable and durable structures, they were inefficient in their use of land because of their thick walls and limitations in height. In contrast, for building clusters, the technology of timber structures was advanced to enable heights of two or three storeys. This new method also ushered in the growth of timber crafts, with a consequent availability of employment and an increase in tradesmen with advanced skills, especially for interior work such as cabinetry, walls, doors, and stairs. Although the broad use of timber for urban residential construction was to prove disastrous in the Great Fire of London in 1666, until then it enabled speedy construction and the provision of more floor space on the tighter and more costly urban sites (Milne 1992, 131–138).

Certainly, town dwelling increased in popularity. By the 14th century about 15% of the English population lived in towns or villages, and a century later the urban population is estimated to have grown to 20%, similar to some regions on the Continent (Dyer 1995, 24). Further, Britnell (1993, 115) observed that about one-fifth of wage earners worked in trade or crafts and resided in towns. Town dwellers began to arrange the structures of their civic organization without disturbing the goodwill of the local aristocratic landowner. Significant scholarship by Beresford (1967) reveals the formation of a sophisticated, resilient local governance that was the forerunner of today's strong municipal centers.

As townships grew, the agricultural use of fields or fallow lands was converted to residential habitation, inns for travelers, commercial activities such as the production of cloth, metalwork, and leather goods, and trading centers. The aristocratic landowner directed the layout of streets and land plots and built the parish church, and then transacted ground leases suitable for the township purposes with tenants who were capable of paying the rent. Essentially, the organization of this urban fabric represented an early property development project.

An Early English Real Estate Developer!

Despite their experience of this basic activity, there is little evidence that the general growing enthusiasm for urban living during the late Middle Ages spurred ecclesiastic or aristocratic owners of urban land to consider development schemes. As has been explained, the familiar economic model was based on agrarian production by which relatively passive rents were received from tenants who worked the land and made improvements only in the form of farm structures and sometimes their own modest abodes. Typically, a landowner's only building activity consisted of the erection of an estate house for his own residence, and perhaps a parish church and marketplace. There was no ambition to seek higher returns from his property, and any surpluses were given to charitable or religious causes in accordance with Christian thinking.

It was therefore most unusual, but possibly portentous for London six centuries later, that in about 1066, just before the Norman invasion, some enterprising Saxons had undertaken early property development in the midland town of Lincoln. Tochi, son of Outi, an extensive landowner with holdings in six midland and northern counties, noted the novel appearance of market centers, and he appropriated a "new town" scheme from what had been introduced earlier by Anglo-Saxon kings at Winchester. He laid out roads, built thirty houses for rent, and provided social infrastructure in the form of at least two parish churches. He paid taxes or dues of 1 penny *landgable* to the king, who retained the ultimate title to the land, but it is reported that he gained significant revenues above those from his project.

Nearby, another landowner, Colswein, built thirty-six houses and two churches; and in Nottingham, forty-eight houses were built and let to merchants (Keene 1996, 100). Some of these holdings functioned as mini-kingdoms and maintained social and economic stability. This was recognized by William I, and although Tochi lost his property to the conquerors, Colswein was permitted to retain his land title, and it was recorded in the Domesday Book of 1086 (1783: i, 336, 280).

Although these developments were lucrative, their wealth-creating objective was in conflict with changing social attitudes. William was introducing a principle of Christian restraint towards possessions and wealth, and while the stability of landholding was embraced, the derivation of substantial economic benefit from it was not. A restraint on rental rates was either undertaken voluntarily or imposed by statute, and this principle of socio-economic constraint has remained an objective of governing authorities ever since. Wealth amassment was dismissed from private landowners' consideration in the management of their holdings, and remained so until some centuries later when capitalism revived economic entrepreneurship in England.

The City of London

There is an historical consensus that London's birth as a city took place under the rule of Roman land laws. Although other trading ports were active along England's southern coast, London was primary in the growing commercial competition. As a port in their extensive trading system, the Roman occupiers planned its location, layout and building with an eye to the distribution and collection of rural goods, and its employment as trading markets. It was so well located on the Thames Estuary, that as Sheppard (1998, 10) has said, it may be seen as the first faint assertion of the geographical power of what was to become Britain's economic center of gravity.

Although it was more than a millennium before the appearance of private urban development, the nascent London was notable not only for its physical structure, which retains a surprising presence through to current times, but also for its variety of social, economic, political, and cultural traits. Within the walled City, its infrastructure was constructed and managed by its governing body, which resembled the product of an early form of democracy. It was invested with strict control of any development activity. The Roman officials who settled there brought their homeland's clearly established concept of legally protected private property which was divided and distributed as individually owned land parcels, even to residents who were not necessarily of high social status. Lots were allocated for businesses and housing according to an agreement as to ownership and use between the owner/occupier and the authorities. As in Rome, some wealthy citizens funded the building of structures for the use of others in return for regular payments, but not to the extensive degree that development projects were to provide in later centuries.

Governance of a Roman city extended beyond its fortified walls, and so the authority of *Londinium's* government extended beyond the City walls to a large surrounding region, known as the Liberties. Areas immediately outside the walls were established for the residence of non-citizens who would work within the City. Beyond that, a substantial area was designated and used for the production of food, and some of the City's wealthy inhabitants established country residences there (Gomme 1912). Additionally, the Roman empire had fared well through the rise of "freedmen," who were emancipated slaves and involved in artisanal or craft activities, or trade. For those who were still learning, housing was available outside the City walls until they were sufficiently trained by the industry guilds, and they were then admitted as citizens with the right to own urban property.

Despite some deterioration of London's status and activity in the 5th century after its abandonment by Rome, in the Middle Ages it continued to remain generally resilient to various invaders because of its strong fortifications. It participated in the growth of European trade by providing rural produce and urban craft goods, and through this commerce it became the most important urban center in the country.

Because of its growing strength and power as a metropolis and economic center, it attracted the king to abandon his former defensive and scattered government posts for a physical proximity to this plainly more suitable location. Green (2017, 198) has found that by the late 12th century, Westminster, complete with the new "royal residence," increasingly housed "central departments of [national] government." But it was outside London and the royal primacy lived side by side with this unusually autonomous part of the kingdom. This geographical arrangement reflected the symbiotic dependency necessary for England's growing prosperity:

> Kings needed to be sure about the security of the city and its defences; they needed financial contributions to their coffers and access to the luxury goods brought to the London wharves. The Londoners, for their part, wanted to be able to rule their own affairs, and to have favourable trading conditions in the rest of the kingdom. Their success depended on the strength of their negotiating position at any given moment. (Green 2017, 201)

While the City of London remained relatively independent in its governance, there was some overlap of jurisdictions, specifically in the geographical area between the two cities, which today is known as London's West End. Approximately 3.5 square miles, it lay officially within the Crown's Borough of Middlesex, but it was also part of the City's Liberties. This duality of legal oversight, particularly in respect of land use, was to prove a significant complication as the expansion of London moved through it. Tensions between state and municipal control of it still continue, as are often the case with large cities globally. As the conflicting systems converged, the resolution of urban governance, though often seemingly impossible, was to be a formative element in the modern development process.

Changing Economic and Topographical Features of Growing London

Following its 14th-century's population loss due to the plague, London again exploded in size in the 16th century. Finlay and Shearer (1986, 52) have summarized the driving forces for this:

> It seems fairly clear that in the period between 1560 and 1650 people were pushed out of the countryside into the towns, particularly London, which had already become the principal trading centre in England. This was due to a rising population resulting in a shortage of land and a need to use land more effectively by enclosure and conversion to grassland [grazing pastures] in order to increase productivity.

This exacerbated London's increase in population, which was already thriving, and in Henry's reign it added unemployed, unskilled, and displaced people to the growing number of courtiers, gentry, Parliamentarians, traders, and merchants who needed habitation. It is for that reason that the physical development of London is judged to have been driven as modern commerce demanded rather than by social governance.

Complementary to this spatial concentration of commercial activities, new notions of an integrated residential population were forming. Cities on the Continent had coalesced around the residence of the monarch or leader, but the development of England's land around London became divided by tensions between the commercial hub of the City and the court of the monarch who lived outside it at Westminster. Those Continental rulers who resided in their major cities instigated their development and directed substantial topographic changes to accommodate their growing economic activity and populations. In contrast, England's rulers could not enter the gates of the City of London without formal invitation and were weakened in their relations with it by their reliance on its administrators for funding, especially for war and national defense. Further, they had neither the resources nor the strategic leverage to provide the needed urban fabric for the nation's, and particularly London's, growing population. The City, on the other hand, lacking the financial resources of Continental kings, did not welcome the strain on its municipal capacity and sought to restrict access to those who were not already citizens.

Although only a few of those citizens had sufficient resources to build and lease out more residential space than they needed for their own habitation, when the population grew markedly in the 15th century, many enterprising homeowners and tenants sublet space, innkeepers established lodgings on an economical scale, and other formats for multi-family accommodation such as tenements were imported from the Continent.

Hare (2013, 485) traced the history of London's inns and observed that in the later 14th and early 15th centuries many of the landed gentry who flocked to London, did not at first establish their own town residences, but stayed at inns. These varied in status and capacity, but a well-managed establishment returned high annual revenues to its landowner through a premium on its traditional residential lease and to its tenant innkeeper through consistent occupancy. Hare (2013, 487) reported that "the rent [revenue per annum] of *The George* at £20 would have been what contemporaries ... perceived as sufficient income for a justice of the peace" and as a result "[s]uch high revenues generated heavy investment in inn building from a variety of institutional and individual lords." Moreover, particularly amongst commoners who conducted inns and restaurants, there was the opportunity to increase their revenues by adding food and personal services for their lodgers. In this way, real estate began to move from its traditionally passive holding of land and buildings to becoming an economic activity whereby space was imbued with extra value though operational expertise.

English Trade to English Business Centered on London
Despite a long antagonism between the Crown at Westminster and the City of London, Elizabeth I appreciated the efforts of her great-grandfather, Sir George Boleyn, a former Mayor of London, and she supported its growth in commerce and trade. A scholar of this divided governance, Ian Archer (2008, 158), has surmised that during the peace and prosperity of the Elizabethan reign, the relationship tended more towards a respectful "interdependence of the two: the Crown offering support for chartered trading companies and various commercial concessionary interest; the City playing an increasing role in the machinery of royal credit."

Antwerp's trading dominance declined and London, with its new Royal Exchange, was a favorable environment for merchants and financiers to converge and conduct new trading operations through new companies. As a consequence of this relocation of commerce from the Continent, and the presence of religious wars in the Low Countries, London became the preferred destination of many educated and prosperous immigrants. Religious refugees came from France and Spain, bringing with them crafts, trading alliances, and commerce. Boulton (2008) places the periods of the most substantial inflow in the 1560s, the 1570s, and in the late 17th century.

Most trading ventures were officially founded in London, where their offices, investor meetings, and promotional activities benefited from urban proximity and begat considerable excitement. Others were under a statutory obligation to establish their headquarters there. As a result,

> spurred by the propaganda for a tremendous national enterprise whenever they came
> to London, and encouraged by the example set by leading courtiers and noblemen,
> a large section of the landed classes was persuaded to invest – for the first time in
> European history – in overseas trade. (Rabb 1967, 26)

They also required residential and commercial premises in the growing capital.

London's Population Explosion of the 17th Century
As the new century dawned, the accelerating pace of England's trade and economic prosperity set underway numerous and substantial changes to English life and the City of London, and together these would compel the emergence of a new approach to creating flourishing

HOUSE OF STUART
James I 24th March 1603 — 27th March 1625
Son of Henry Stuart and Mary Queen of Scots Married Anne of Denmark
Charles I 27th March 1625 — 30th January 1649
Son of King James I and Anne of Denmark Married Henrietta Maria of France
Charles II 8th May 1660 — 6th February 1685
Son of Charles I and Henrietta Maria of France Married Catherine of Braganza
James II 6th February 1685 — 11th December 1688
Son of Charles I and Henrietta Maria of France Married 1. Anne Hyde. 2. Mary of Modena
William III and Mary II 6th February 1689 — 8th March 1702
William was the son of William of Orange and Mary, daughter of Charles I; Mary was the daughter of King James II and Anne Hyde William and Mary were married

3.1

Lineage of the Stuart monarchs.

urban centers. This century of rule by the Stuart kings (Figure 3.1) brought civic disruptions, new social philosophies, and the rise of modern capitalism, all of which were particularly pertinent to a new formulation of urban development.

As a major European center, London's prestige was rising considerably and rapidly. Boulton (2008, 315) describes this change over just one century:

> London was already a major capital city, ranking sixth in terms of size [of population] in mid-sixteenth-century Europe ... Within fifty years all this had changed. By 1600 London was ranked third in Europe after Naples and Paris ... Continued growth meant that London came second only to Paris by 1650 and by the end of the seventeenth century was the biggest European city.

Of course, the new Stuart kings of the 17th century strongly supported this one-upmanship over their Continental cousins. Wealth, size, and power were not only matters of vanity: they were a strong deterrence against attack and enabled the country to prosper in peace.

The demographic composition of this dramatic population increase was extensive and full of potential, as Harding (2007, 115) describes it:

> The capital's population more than doubled, from *c.* 200,000 in 1600 to over 500,000 in 1700, thanks largely to migration drawn from provincial England and, increasingly, from the rest of the British Isles and continental Europe. Most of the migrants were young people, male and female, seeking training or employment and yet to form families and households.

London's Commerce Arising

Within England's traditional social structure, the royal court, and the landed gentry typically were distrustful of those who engaged in commercial trade. This was not misplaced, as the proletarian uprising of the French Revolution was encouraged by this class. However, an enthusiasm for colonial expansion and the financial success of trading ventures did much to elevate the status and importance of commercial activities and the businessmen who conducted them. Stone (1966, 52) notes "the rise of the commercial and professional classes in numbers and wealth, and their consequent acquisition both of a share in political decision-making and of social recognition." That social acceptance meant that

> ... the gentry lost their earlier reluctance to put their sons into trade. By the middle third of the seventeenth century nearly half the Freemen of the Drapers' Company of Shrewsbury and nearly a fifth of the London Stationers' Company apprentices were coming from gentry stock. Thirdly, the business or professional man could acquire the title of 'Gent,' and on occasion even 'Esquire,' without having to buy an estate and cut himself off from his economic roots. (Stone 1966, 53)

The production of goods also expanded in London. Beier and Finlay (1986, 5) note this pre-industrial activity: "Massive urban growth in the absence of factory industrialization might strike an unfamiliar chord, yet by 1650 there was a largely free-market economy in London organized around small manufacturing enterprises." Craftsmen and tradesmen continued to be supported by their guilds in training, monitoring of performance and promotion of their products. And the demand for their output was strong. "The capital's inhabitants possessed exceptionally high purchasing power throughout this period [late 17th C], so that consumption of goods and services took place on an even greater scale" (Boulton 2008, 324). Housing was to gain a central role in this new consumption economy.

In this commercial climate, the attraction of and opportunity for investment crossed class boundaries. Galsworthy's (1906, 246) historical fiction most lucidly and elegantly expressed the scene, indicating the general understanding and extent of the importance of investment: "... half of England, and the better half, too, the safe half, the three per cent [loan interest rate] half, the half that counts. It's their wealth and security that makes everything possible; makes your art possible, makes literature, science, even religion possible." New and sophisticated equity investments were taken up in addition to the stable debt opportunities, so that Boulton (2008, 322) estimates that "[i]nvestment in shipping and company stocks and bonds attracted perhaps one in seven of those occupying the middle station in Restoration London."

Further, although political turmoil was to continue throughout the century, society generally embraced the commercial changes, often dramatic, resulting from the vibrant entrepreneurial activities in which so many were engaged. Polanyi (1957, 33) describes the spirit: "Fired by an emotional faith in spontaneity, the common-sense attitude toward change was discarded in favor of a mystical readiness to accept the social consequences of economic improvement, whatever they might be." This broad economic engagement and acceptance of change was a fertile context for the increasing activities of builders and private landlords, who were dramatically altering the urban socio-spatial arrangement. While this acceptance of change would enable new business models to form, a laxity of social criticism and an overt enthusiasm for financial achievements probably diminished attention to community conditions so that the direction veered towards dominance of financial considerations.

The Housing Crisis within the City

In the absence of the Continental custom of housing provision by government authorities, meeting the housing needs of London's rapidly increasing population was piecemeal and varied. Schofield (1984, 142) assessed the situation this way:

> The demand for extra housing was met in a number of ways. First, the landlords and entrepreneurs of the city soaked up many of the remaining open spaces with buildings. Gardens were built over or subdivided to form smaller patches for the expanding tenements; some old inns were turned into housing schemes. The owners of the former religious precincts were quick to profit from the rush of immigrants, though they preferred the upper-class end who could afford large new houses. Thus several of the convent sites sprouted four-storey houses, where there had been none before.

On the other hand, City authorities continued to attempt, by the use of the legal constraints established towards the end of the prior century, to restrain building. However, their capacity to enforce such regulations was limited in the face of such challenging demand, and even the condemnation of structures was not prosecuted due to the want of legal enforcement resources. Baer (2007b, 259) assesses that "[s]uch growth was a new phenomenon for which there were no guides, much less regulation. Parliament, London's Lord Mayor and Aldermen were in effect caught off guard."

Concern about habitation conditions related to two key features, the proliferation of new houses and the overcrowding of residences. This duality of the problem had been apparent early and in 1580 Elizabeth proclaimed:

> [The Crown] ... doth charge and straightly command all manner of persons, of what qualitie soever they be, to desist and forbeare from any new buildings of any house or tenement within three miles from any of the gates of the said citie of London, to serve for Habitation or Lodging for any person where no former House hath bene knowen to have bene in the memorie of such as are now living; and also to forbear from letting or setting or suffering any more families than are only to be placed or to inhabit from henceforth in any one house that heretofore hath been inhabited. (Dyson 1618, #749)

This restriction on building within three miles of the City walls encompassed the area between London and Westminster and would initially constrain the early developers of estates there, but their innovative responses would set models for new practices.

The conflict of governance between the Crown and the City was extended by this attempt to control building growth. Ward (1997, 17) provides an insight into Elizabeth's new main objective:

> In June 1583, the [Queen's] Privy Council wrote to the [city's] Lord Mayor complaining of the continued construction of new houses and the division of tenements within the City and suburbs, contrary to the Queen's proclamation, and it ordered him to proceed

against all offenders. However, it seems that the Crown itself made little attempt to enforce the restriction until the 1590s, and then its main objective was to recover financial penalties from developers rather than to prevent new building.

In turn, the municipality raised substantial revenues by imposing fines on breaches of building restrictions, but it was not inclined to prevent development absolutely, since real estate fees and taxes had become a significant source of its funding, as it continues to be today.

Within a couple of decades, however, the demand for housing was so high and supply so constrained that its price grew exorbitantly, which exacerbated the increasing socioeconomic disparity of the City dwellers, as Boulton (1987, 194) indicates: "The range of wealth in this society was reflected in a concomitant spread of housing type and quality. Even the more modest High Street housing was at least twice as costly as the 40s[hilling] or 50s[shilling] tenements within the Boroughside alleys and yards."

The population of London could no longer be contained within its City walls and the areas surrounding it, even beyond the Liberties, so it became necessary to find new locations for housing. Porter (1994, 42) reports the distribution of the resident populations to be "by Elizabeth's death in 1603, 140,000 within and without (in the liberties) its ancient walls and another 40,000 in its spreading suburbs – almost a threefold leap in a century."

The building of housing necessary to meet the growing demand was begun in the Liberties immediately outside the City walls, but as this area was quickly filled, the expansion continued into the suburbs stretching to the east, north and west, and also across the Thames to the south. These suburbs were suitable because they had a quantity of unbuilt land, often open fields generally belonging to longtime passive landowners, and also because they stood on existing highway routes, such as the Strand and Holborn, which connected them to the City. In contrast to the rigorous oversight and control of the lands within the City's governance, they were subject to only weak parish control and were often vulnerable to the loss of their publicly accessible open spaces as houses were erected. Baer (2007b, 259) reports that "[o]utside the walls and ignoring the earlier sense of compact containment within, suburban growth spilled out into the city ditch and encroached upon open fields where Londoners had once strolled and practiced archery."

Westward Migration

During the reign of Elizabeth I, royal courtiers began to locate their town houses outside the City walls and close to the Crown's presence in Westminster and at St James's Palace. They either occupied former opulent residences of English bishops or built new mansions that fronted onto the Strand, stretching westward from the City along the Thames. The most prominent of these, such as the Earls of Essex and Salisbury, resided here, and the early residence of the Russell family, prior to their move to Covent Garden, was located on the southside of the Strand, opposite that future project (Figure 3.2). Barnes (1971, 65) describes this locus of power: "From the Western limit of London proper, at Temple Bar, to the palace of Westminster, a mile of roadway, consisting of the Strand and Whitehall, connected the commercial and political capitals of England."

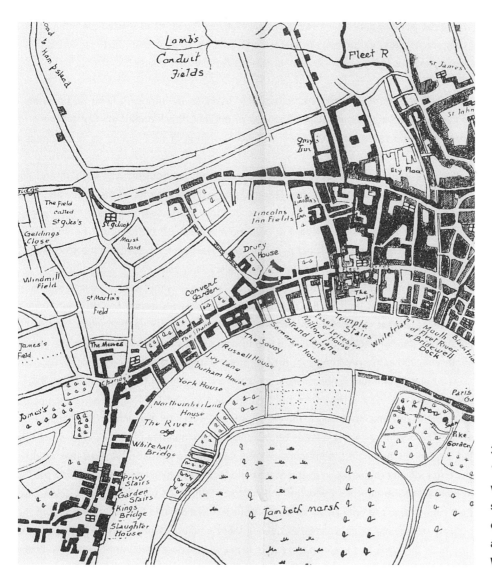

3.2
**1603 map of lands to the
west of the City of London,
showing the residences
of nobles extending
along the Strand towards
Westminster.**

At the time of James I's accession in 1603, much of the land to the north of the Strand remained rural with dairy farming and market gardening (Smuts 1991, 117). The wealthy preferred this healthier environment to the crowded conditions that harbored the plague, and to the industrial emissions, smog, and dirt of the City. It was well known that "[t]he use of coal for domestic purposes brought smog conditions for many months of the year, and encouraged London's wealthier inhabitants to move westwards, since for three-quarters of the year this was the direction of the prevailing winds" (Beckett 1986, 267). Such a locational preference by the wealthy continued in the industrial cities which grew in the following centuries, and it still prevails in urban formations.

Other gentry, courtiers, counselors, and professionals took up leased residences in Lincoln's Inn Fields, Chancery Lane, and Holborn, which also had ease of access to the City and Westminster. As much of the commercial business of both nobility and merchants was conducted in allotted rooms of their mansions, this growing area also started attracting some retail merchants whose presence continues today. Support for this new business district came with the construction of the New Exchange, a commercial trading bourse, on the Strand.

With these advantages, the demand for housing in the district grew dramatically, a call by not only aristocrats and wealthy merchants but also by others in menial trades who provided services to them. An insightful commentator of urban dynamics, the economist and scientist William Petty (1689, 22) described the mixed demographics of this new urban settlement:

> Now it is follow from hence, that the Pallaces of the greatest men will remove Westward, it will also naturally follow, that the dwellings of others who depend upon them will creep after them. This we see in *London*, where the Noblemens ancient Houses are now become Halls for Companies, or turned into Tenements, and all the Pallaces are gotten Westward ...

With their ideal location, the western suburbs of London also contained the estates which were to be developed by the Earls of Bedford and Southampton for these aristocratic and wealthy merchant families. Those perceptive pioneer developers were suitably poised to benefit from the confluence of an urban exodus due to plague epidemics, the identification of healthier urban regions in proto industrial cities, and the interweaving of the court government with rising capitalism.

Governance

There were numerous attempts to attach the growing western suburbs with either Westminster or the City, or to incorporate it as an independent entity in itself. The last-mentioned proceeded to a point, but many compromises were required along the way. For example, to diminish its independent authority, Letters Patent were issued by the Crown regarding the performance, restrictions, and freedoms of tradesmen such as carpenters, bricklayers, and tile makers, within a 3-mile radius of the City. However, the powerful City fought to preserve its dominant role in the area, and the court submitted and discarded the notion of incorporation.

(As an aside, it should be remarked that although this attempt failed, establishment of independence by incorporation for a growing community was to be very influential in the settlement of the American colonies where, seeking control of their situation prior to the formation of federal government, the early towns incorporated to protect their property from the English Crown and to enable them to gather as a congregation. Neither of these rights had ever been achieved in Britain.)

By way of counterattack, numerous planners presented physical representations of a potential integration of the growing community with the City itself, but such ideas too were never consummated. As for the control of building construction, the 1667 regulations for London's rebuilding after the Great Fire were useful in directing building format rather than restricting building itself. Many urbanists since have been disappointed in this outcome and, in his extensive and detailed presentation of the City during this century, Brett-James (1935, 245) remonstrates: "The attitude displayed by the City Corporation in the seventeenth century left a large and constantly increasing area without satisfactory government and without any connection to the City, and was largely responsible for the chaotic condition of the suburbs under the Georges."

These failed attempts to impose governance on the area provided a felicitous context for private real estate development. Though there was no absolute freedom in such an impactful activity, and the combination of royal Proclamations and City directives continued to provide relevant constraints, this freedom from stultifying bureaucratic interference in the prevailing lax regulatory context and the perfect physical location of sites provided an ideal opportunity for experimentation and entrepreneurship.

Inherent in the Crown's Proclamations and City regulations on building was the intention that only houses of quality were to be built, and only persons of substance were allowed as residents. Though this would seem to suit the more expensive developments undertaken at Covent Garden, Bloomsbury and St James's Place, astute entrepreneurs such as Bedford and Southampton strategically expanded the resident demographics for their housing, whether due to their understanding of domestic logistics, or social or market concerns, or all such factors. Fortunately, the loose public administration allowed organic urban compositions to form, and although the western suburbs were and are still known particularly for the wealth of their residents, a vibrant and prosperous social mix arose. Smuts (1991, 123–124) undertook a close reading of the urban development of that area during the Stuart reign and found that, "like most London neighborhoods, the western suburbs contained a mix of rich consumers, prosperous tradesmen, struggling manual laborers, and paupers living in close proximity to one another."

Importance of the Commons in the Metropolis

As the definition of private land became more precise spatially and in terms of its economic potential, there was a change in the general attitude to land traditionally comprising public areas known as commons. The density of urban conditions made the availability of open space more necessary for gatherings, markets, fairs, events and celebrations. Not only did the need for these spaces intensify with urban population growth, but as Wood (1997, 53) observes: "From the late sixteenth century and onwards, just as conflict over customary rights intensified, so plebeian understandings of custom underwent important change, becoming both more assertive and definitive."

Early in modern London's expansion, attention to the commons was intense. Johnson (1952) speaks of conflict during Henry VIII's reign concerning the area surrounding the City. Many landowners who had recently received distributed church lands began to enclose their property by hedges and ditches, but the parish of St Martin-in-the-Fields claimed that many of these areas were "Lammas lands" and therefore open to the public each year other than from April 6 until August. The minutes in vestry meetings for 1549 contain a list of lands claimed to have been commons since the first year of the reign of Henry VII and which therefore should have been open to all tenants of the city of Westminster and the parishioners of St Martin's. Londoners gathered to protest against the enclosures, but the king's Privy Council ordered the Mayor of the City to ensure that no such protests occur in future. Enclosure was condoned in that area.

The effects of this were enlarged because though the authorities were interested in restricting building within the City, they did not plan for designated public space. Baer (2007b, 263) describes the results in the early 17th century:

> The decree [restricting building] simultaneously created permanent open space [along with defined building]. That space also had not been planned for. It was merely the

residual vacant land after the haphazard development up to that time. There would be an open space at the irregular boundary and also towards the centre of the city where a few unbuilt parcels remained, regardless of parcel size, configuration, juxtaposition to other development and other open spaces.

This lack of municipal interest in providing open space was the result of the economic demands of managing the growing population, but its absence is important in understanding the dramatic impact of the offerings of the private developments which were then imminent.

Throughout that century, amongst those with power, the attitude of those towards the common good deteriorated. Wood (1997, 51) describes it in this way:

> The post-Restoration policies of the Crown and other major estate holders, encouraged by mercantilism and the weakening of copyhold, were markedly more hostile to customary rights than before the Revolution. This development was contemporaneous with processes of social differentiation which moved many parochial 'middling sorts' away from their earlier support for many customary entitlements. The scale was local and uneven, but in much of England by the middle of the 17th century wealthier freeholders had turned decisively against the customary rights of the poor.

In contrast, the substantial contributions to the public realm made by the new private developers at Covent Garden and Bloomsbury Square are noteworthy. Unfortunately, their efforts were not to be extensively emulated, and by the later part of the century, Wood's observations would be applicable to many urban developers.

A New Approach to Controlling Growth

Because of the increasing settlement in the western suburb verging on Westminster, in 1603 the new king, James I, viewed the situation as problematic. But, welcoming the presence of his nobles at his court, he changed his objective from restricting building in general to improving the quality of what was to be built. His first Proclamation of 1604 required that new buildings must be of brick or stone, or both, and that the façades must be uniform with all other structures on the street (Barnes 1971, 75). Baer (2007b, 267) describes the shortcomings of this approach:

> There were no general plans of course, much less zoning ordinances to say what kind of structure was allowed where; no public requirement for setbacks from property lines; no future street rights-of-way planned and mapped, save what abutting property owners worked out piecemeal for themselves – often following customary roadways and paths, or following the edge of property lines. Nevertheless, James's early requirements for brick, for some modicum of approval from an Alderman, and now for a licence to build, were forerunners of architectural controls and buildings permits.

Even in those earliest times, the court struggled with formulating legislation to achieve the desired outcomes in controlling urban building. The 1607 Proclamation reiterated Elizabeth's 1602 restrictions and James's 1604 quality proscriptions in tandem; the 1608 Proclamation explained the 1607 Proclamation; the 1610 Proclamation rescinded the previous three with the intention of combining them, though this was not achieved; the 1611 Proclamations set out new standards for building; the 1615 and 1618 Proclamations reinstated the prohibition of all new buildings, or at least placed very tight restrictions on them; and the 1619 Proclamation established "minute standards both for construction and ornamentation of new buildings," prescribing "a Palladian simplicity that clearly demonstrates the hand of Inigo Jones" (Barnes 1971, 76).

This reference to "the hand of Inigo Jones" introduces an important new player in the dynamic of urban development. He not only revised the required approach to building conditions but also personally contributed to the delivery of innovative built form and dramatically different spatial layouts, all while fostering and guiding the activities of the early real estate developers.

Inigo Jones

In 1616, Inigo Jones (Figure 3.3) was appointed to the office of King's Surveyor of the Works. Although during Elizabethan times it had a relatively modest role as caretaker of the royal properties, the Jacobean Court was much more culturally and recreationally active, and it was through his participation and his professional ambition that he was able to transform the role into one of fame and influence.

3.3
Inigo Jones, c. 1650.

Important to his career and works was his learning on the subject of neoclassical architecture that had been blossoming during the 16th century in Italy, where he traveled for an undetermined period in about 1602. While Venice seems to have impressed him, it was probably Florence that provided him with the aesthetic and professional knowledge which was the impetus for his future in the English court. In Florence, the Medici court of Ferdinand I supported a bountiful culture of patronage of the arts and the masque form of entertainment, and leading this movement was the architect, painter and sculptor Bernardo Buontalenti.

His responsibilities extended from designing the scenery and costumes of the masques to the planning of the piazza and church of Leghorn. Not only was Jones's appreciation and comprehension of this grand neoclassical format of urban revival very influential upon his future work but Buontalenti's extension of his role as masque designer to that of creator of the impressive piazza with such public impact and aesthetic admiration also inspired Jones's professional ambitions. The multiplicity of effects that he was to have on English architectural and urban design, his leading role as the first English architect, and in particular his substantial involvement in the conception and realization of the development of Covent Garden, the first private development project, makes his path to that activity notable in some detail.

Jones's Early Career

As Summerson (2000, 15) explains, " 'Architecture,' in the England of this time, was a rare word, at once invoking architectura, the Roman science of building … Nearly all the building work of James I's reign was designed by those who built it, and they were masons, bricklayers or carpenters …" But as the value of accurate measurements of land had become recognized under the Tudors, the professional surveyor had entered the activity to ensure the building's compliance with the metes and bounds of the land on which it was erected, and he was also given responsibility for the management of the construction work. This was the role to which Inigo Jones was appointed at the royal court. Despite his lack of experience in building, he expanded his responsibilities to include design, and to this end he studied the work of the Italian masters.

His occupation of the influential office concerning the royal buildings promoted an emerging sense of taste in architectural design amongst the upper levels of British society. Summerson (2003, 10), the renowned critic of English architecture, acknowledged this standard of taste, describing it as "in the exclusive, snobbish sense of recognition of certain fixed values by certain people." His flippancy aside, he also seriously recognized that the introduction of taste in architecture required "the right man and the right opportunities, and both came in 1615[/1616], the year that Inigo Jones, just back from his second visit to Italy, took up his appointment as Surveyor to the King" (ibid.). Jones's application of the Continental architectural orders to building design was novel to England, for its building activity had for so long been dominated by traditional carpenters and masons, who reliably repeated vernacular forms. Jones had successfully introduced some architectural concepts of his new mode as splendid stage sets for the court masques, but as Summerson says: "To put up a pure Italian building in such a setting [as vernacular London] was sensational … [and] it could only be done under the immediate patronage of the Court" (2003, 11).

With authority similar to that of today's municipal architect or urban planner, Jones provided the court with valuable guidance, particularly by taking responsibility for the condemnation of unwanted development within the jurisdictional area that extended for two miles beyond the periphery of the City. He also initiated projects and offered the king his design for certain outbuildings at the royal rural hunting estate in Newmarket. Although not credited with great architectural significance, they were his important early experiments in the Greek Tuscan style, a lower order used for more functional buildings in contrast to the more ornate Roman styles of grander buildings. His interest in this simpler classical tradition was at variance with the aesthetic enthusiasms on the Continent that tended towards Mannerism and Baroque. He claimed that his restrained, if jarringly novel, architectural order was more suitable for the emerging English urban form with its tradition of modest buildings. Fortunately for the developers who were to build to his designs, it was also more economical and in keeping with English taste for understatement.

The quality of his aesthetic achievement, notably under the patronage of the Crown, elevated the general architect's role as a designer to a standing superior to that of a tradesman who built in the vernacular tradition. Further enhancing the ascendancy of professional architecture, Jones innovatively extended his consultancy role outside royal patronage to private commissions. Summerson (2000, 31–32) reports that, among others, he undertook projects for Sir Fulke Greville (Lord Brooke) in Holborn, and the Duke of Lennox at Ely Place. Usually, as a commissioned professional, an architect could privately negotiate a higher remuneration than he received by patronage, which took a discount for the prestige it brought. The new form of engagement by commission for specific projects also meant that obtaining a satisfactory volume of work provided a new personal challenge to the practitioner, which continues to this day.

Jones's aesthetic tastes were not always acceptable to the average London citizen, however. The parishioners of St Michael-le-Querne, located at the western end of Little Conduit Street, protested against his proposed Continental design for the 1637 rebuilding of their early 15th-century church. After public meetings presided over by London's Archbishop Laud, and hearings before the Privy Council which Charles I himself attended, Jones's design prevailed, but, in deference to the wishes of and financial burden on the parish, he was under some restraint imposed by a budget prepared by the master bricklayer, Peter Mills (Stevenson 2013, 39–40).

This lesson of restraint on innovative design by the public's traditional taste has held true in the following centuries of urban building, with an impact, largely in the form of delay in acceptance of progressive formats in design or financial aspects, for both the architect and the developer. For environments of close personal contact such as the home or a church, ordinary people desired familiarity and tradition, even if it was of poorer quality functionally and aesthetically. At best, if they had sufficient financial resources, they tended to build replications of the country residences of landed gentry, and for this they hired building tradesmen to do so without any comprehensive assessment of the changing programmatic user needs. The dissonance between progressive architectural design and urban development solutions, such as higher density buildings, on the one hand, and, on the other, the expressed wishes of the public is still unresolved.

However, through the scholarship and disciplined application by its practitioners, by the 18th century the concept of architecture gained more acceptance and was defined in the Complete Builder's Guide (Neve 1736, 3) as being

> a Mathematical Science, which teaches the Art of Building, a Skill obtained by the Precepts of Geometry, by which it gives the Rules for designing and raising all Sorts of Structures, according to Geometry and Proportion Containing under it all those Arts that conduce any thing to the framing Houses, Temples, Etc.

This position of the architect as a key figure in the creation of built form had been established and owed much to Jones's courageous efforts to add design innovation to the building process, overriding the prior unchallenged use of an increasingly obsolete vernacular.

The Stuart Kings Prescribe Building Quality

In 1625, Charles I continued the attempt to control building growth, though his efforts were focused more on prescribing its quality rather than restricting it. As Royal Surveyor, Inigo Jones sought to define the emerging urban typology explicitly and to ensure that its aesthetic quality compared favorably with that of Paris, Vienna, and other major Continental cities.

The loss of fields and gardens for common usage was decried for reasons ranging from its disadvantage to the poor who lived in cramped conditions to its detriment to a general aesthetic vision of the city. Offenders, however, became more numerous and daring and the plodding procedures of the king's Star Chamber to prosecute and condemn it was generally ineffective and of little deterrence, with the result that ramshackle housing and overcrowded tenements mushroomed along the Strand and other routes through the western suburbs such as along the Holborn and St Martin's Lane. As the resident population in this area rapidly increased, the parishes became overburdened and did not have the resources to extend their rate and rent recording activities to the administration of building approvals or construction oversight.

Various forms of government were considered for these emerging communities, but as much of the land consisted of aristocratic estates including those of the imminent developers, Bedford and Southampton, and of land hold by powerful parish vestries, attempts by the City and the Crown to impose governance directly were successfully resisted. It is apparent that private development, in this case represented by the aristocratic estate owners and wealthy parishioners, strove to minimize legislative restrictions on land use in this highly desirable area.

In contrast to the attitude of today's urban communities was the lack of popular support for restrictions. So many were desperate to find habitation that restraints did not seem to serve them well. Barnes (1971, 70) describes the mixed reviews of restrictions at that time:

> There is no evidence that the governmental attempt to restrict building in the metropolis and, later, to establish standards of material and workmanship for new construction, was in response to any general public pressure. Few of the ambitious programs of late Tudor and early Stuart 'strict and strait governance' grew from informed public opinion or public pressure, though often such programs were in the public interest and enjoyed a modicum of popular support.

This complexity involving the objectives of municipal authorities in opposition to those of the developers, and even some of those of the public, remains a challenge for urban planning.

Another difficulty arising from these new building standards was that compliance was not economically feasible: "The early Stuarts initially imposed higher building standards than builders desired, because the finished house would cost more, requiring the rent to be set too high" (Baer 2012, 428). Many of the new residents were migrants from rural occupations or poor tradesmen who were seeking work and were temporarily without much income. The average London household typically had to keep expenditure on shelter within 15% to 20% of its income, and low incomes meant that only modest rental rates could be charged. Therefore, construction costs needed to be low, but the stricter standards initially imposed proved to be too expensive for most builders and property entrepreneurs. Here was the early conflict between the costs of meeting legislative requirements and the objectives of capital which was necessary for the production, with adverse consequences for housing supply and affordability.

At the Restoration in 1660, Charles II (1660–1685) returned to the throne from exile spent at the Court of Louis XIV. He continued the Crown's many decades of restraint on overbuilding and in 1661 issued a Proclamation restating many of the earlier regulations, but with an eye to avoiding rapid deterioration of structures and having a cultured taste for masonry architecture, he ordered that new building be made in stone or brick rather than the traditional timber. In another advance for urban environments, public concern for the aesthetics of buildings was extended to the open spaces. As Baer (2012, 428) describes,

> Just prior to the Civil War, parliament was beginning to respond to citizen complaints about new buildings' disorderly intrusions on urban life, complaints that perhaps influenced the better-planned residential squares and ensembles following the Restoration, a process also encouraged by Charles II who had made Christopher Wren his Surveyor of Works. He charged Wren with improving London's housing by checking the plans of most large developments and requiring changes when necessary *before* construction began, rather than, like James, having objectionable buildings pulled down *after* their construction.

Jones's new architectural principles and use of neoclassical orders were applied to subsequent development projects such as Newton's housing in Queen Street and Lincoln's Inn Fields. Some of these were designed by other architects, including Jones's son-in-law who had assimilated the new aesthetic approach. For others, the designs were drafted by skilled surveyors and executed by craftsmen such as the stonemason William Stone, without architects. Although there is no evidence that other early developers formally engaged architects to plan site layout or design buildings on their larger schemes, the aesthetic quality of the results indicates substantial influence. Baer (2007b, 269) finds this enthusiasm extended to development by master builders: "Builders began to sense profit from this new style for city building, so would hire only those in the building trades willing to learn how to build to the new style."

More generally, with this regulation of London's rebuilding and Charles II's interest in urban beautification, architectural standards became even more important and subject to public interest. Stevenson (2013, 4) examines the complex interactions between the king and the formation of the City and reveals "the ways that, alongside other objects like the gold boxes, buildings were made to serve as political instruments, in part by being construed as displays of authority, homage or wealth, and sometimes all three at once." This encouragement of building to high aesthetic standards was fortified by official and critical denigration of poor-quality buildings, though these were often the only option for the lower classes. The noted aesthete of the time, John Evelyn (1995b, 155), did not spare his criticism, and suggested that:

... the farther exorbitant increase of Tenements, poor and nasty Cottages near the City, be prohibited, which disgrace and take off from the sweetness and amœnity of the Environs of London, and are already become a great Eye-sore in the grounds opposite to his Majesty's Palace of White-hall ...

Evelyn's understanding, however, extended beyond the built form to include inherent economic requirements and production activities. Describing the new urban development process, he advised that

this ought to be the joint and mature contrivance of the ablest men, Merchants, Architects, and Workmen, in consort; and such as have a true idea of what proprieties, and conveniences, belong to so great a city, and which I therefore briefly, but fully, comprehend in these two transcendences, Use and Ornament. (1995c, 336)

This early vision of real estate as comprising both shelter for occupants and contribution to the public realm, and as including reference to the financial dimension, recognized the complexity of real estate development at its advent.

The Plague, the Great Fire, and Controlling Growth, Again

The plague of 1665 had widespread consequences for urban developments that were then underway, particularly those located in the loosely administered outer suburbs of London. The urgent demand for housing by less affluent migrants was met by the erection of low-quality tenements, often without approval. They were not only illegal but were also generally overcrowded and without any water supply or sewage services. As Bell (1924, 32) described it: "[A] multitude of the poorest people failed to find accommodation within the [City] walls ... [and] herded thickly in the Liberties and slums they created about the outer edge; at St Andrew Holborn, St Giles and neighbouring western parishes."

Bell continues with his description of the living conditions there: "Left and right of these [streets] the low overhanging wooden houses, ill-kept, dark and congested, covered the ground in seemingly impenetrable rookeries of filthy courts and blind alleys. Back-to-back building was customary to save cost and space" (1924, 33). Cummins et al. (2016) determined a correlation between these poor living conditions in the out-parishes and mortality rates even prior to the 1665 plague (Figure 3.4).

3.4

Ratio of child mortality to baptisms by years in intra-mural (solid line), extra-mural (dashed line), and out-parishes (dotted line) prior to the 1665 plague.

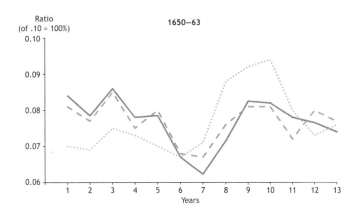

Ratio
(of .10 = 100%)

1650–63

Years

That the earliest private developments were interwoven with this hotbed of infection in St Giles's parish may have influenced some features of the evolving development model in respect of urban location and spatial arrangements. Bloomsbury, though officially in the northern reach of the parish, was still mostly pastoral and did not share the infection rate of the area south of Holborn. When housing projects were undertaken there later in the decade, the developer was able to capitalize on its salubrious ambience in healthy open fields and plan his housing around an open square and infrastructure that included wide well-kept streets.

Of serious spatial consequences, early plague infections were not monitored or addressed, since, as with building regulation, health governance of the area was outside the jurisdiction of the City and relied totally on overburdened parish officers. Their ability to provide care for the sick or protect the uninfected was by no means fore-planned (Figure 3.5). It was further reduced by the flight of many doctors and their wealthier patients to the country, though voluntary doctors, including one who was to become a noted property developer, attended to the infected poor in their assigned wards. The parish resources were further strained by the loss of tithes from rents as houses were abandoned or their tenants were left without work.

3.5
Street scene during the Great Plague of 1665 in London with a death cart and mourners.

Appreciating the need to contain the disease, "[t]he magistrates [of Middlesex county] sought to isolate it … [with] constables of the different parishes encircling St Giles's, and set warders at all roads leading thereto" (Bell, 1924, 28), though that administrative response had been slow, as Bell (ibid.) continues: "As a measure of quarantine the step was wise, and had it been taken when first the frost broke, London might have been saved much distress."

The burial of victims at St Giles required the excavation of five large pits that were filled to overflowing, and the churchyard is still among the largest in London.

The delay in the administrative response to the outbreak reflected the king's actions. Despite the growing number of deaths as June proceeded, the royal court remained at Whitehall. Parliament had risen in April, and those associated with governance, the professions, and business were leaving. Rugge (*Diurnal*, July 1665) estimated an exodus of 1,800 families during July. Nevertheless, Bell (1924, 57) noted, along with those who were required to remain in attendance at court, there was a reticence to leave on the part of "others whose mode of life required that they must themselves be wherever fashion [in the person of the king] consorted."

The poor quality of housing, and unsanitary conditions of the slums exacerbated the residents' vulnerability to the plague, though there is not much recorded information that this was fully appreciated until later centuries. Cummins et al. (2016, 16) have referred to statistical work by Monecke et al. (2009) on the survival of wealthier residents in the Saxon town of Freiberg during the 1613 plague, which killed the father and brother of the 4th Earl of Bedford. It was found that stone buildings in the wealthier parishes provided their inhabitants with greater protection from the rats and their fleas that carried the virus. In the second half of the 17th century, too, more of the wealthier London residents had masonry buildings because of the edicts of James I under the guidance of Inigo Jones.

Although the plague continued through the autumn of 1665, London's mortality rate had returned to normal levels as 1666 began, and commerce and social life recovered.

The Great Fire of 1666

Tragically, in September of that same year, another disaster struck. The Great Fire commenced as a small blaze in a bakery in the City's Pudding Lane. More than 80 churches and 11,000 houses were destroyed (Bell 1920). These were mostly within the City walls, but some damage also occurred in a few areas just outside the city limits, predominantly in the outer ward of Farringdon Without (Brett-James 1935, 301), and just beyond the western wall along the Strand towards Chancery Lane. Including the damage outside the City, Reddaway (1951, 271) provided an estimation of the value of property lost: "The houses destroyed were computed at 13,200, representing a value of about £4,000,000. Goods and commodities added another £3,650,000, and eighteenth-century historians, by including estimates for transport and the like, brought the combined figures to nearly £8,000,000."

There is substantial research with excellent commentary on the many tragedies of this event and its impact on London life and topography. For the nascent private development activity, the disrupted context and the need for radical response to the enormous building damage provided an opportunity to replace unsatisfactory traditional processes with innovations and improvements, and to consolidate its own role as central to the production of the built fabric of modern cities.

Increased Housing Demand in the Western Suburbs

Requiring the most immediate response was an overwhelming demand for new buildings. McKellar (1999, 73) surmises that "[t]o rebuild 13,000 houses in brick as the King had commanded meant an expansion in demand without precedent in the history of London." This was a second wave of critically needed housing within the century, but this time, the practice of large-scale production was explored by the master builders, such as Newton and Frith, and improvements in spatial layout and design were offered by Bedford at Covent Garden and Southampton in Bloomsbury.

Rebuilding on small lots in the City was complex, however, as Reddaway (1951, 76) explains: "There remained only ash-covered foundations, unenforceable liabilities and a tangle of conflicting claims. Freeholder, leaseholder, subtenant, and quit-rent owner – they made an unmanageable team, opposed to any concessions, concerned only for their own rights. Left to themselves they would have wasted years composing their differences." Prior to rebuilding, residents were required to have their lot surveyed by one of the four surveyors assigned to the task, and although this was a worthy exercise in better land definition, it substantially delayed the work. Nevertheless, City authorities and the Crown provided direction and support and it is reported that by 1670 much of the private rebuilding within the City was completed.

While many London residents rebuilt their homes, many others took temporary housing or relocated outside the City. Another property type was also in demand, as Brett-James (1935, 397) notes, "[m]any City merchants found it less expensive and more profitable to have businesses in the western suburbs, and their migration tended still further to mark off the City from the West End." Coupled with the return of the aristocrats and gentry to their townhouses in western London, the demand for housing of various scales and places for business and retail activities was a catalyst for the revival of the development projects that had begun some decades before.

Rebuilding Regulations

The need to rebuild the City's fabric also offered an opportunity for new controls over the quality and format of layout and structure. Brett-James (1935, 300) describes the intention of the Crown: "The King was certainly anxious that advantage should be taken of the Fire to rebuild the City 'with more decency and conveniency than formerly.'"

Despite their uneasy relationship, the king and the City authorities conferred and eventually agreed on building standards and requirements. These were promulgated in a series of legislative bills known as the Rebuilding Acts. Studied in much detail by urban planning scholars, these formalized regulations had serious implications for early developers. Reddaway (1951, 137) summarizes the intentions of the first two and most important Rebuilding Acts: "firstly to facilitate a rebuilding by private enterprise, unsubsidized and unsubjected to stringent regulations for improving both the streets and the houses which lined them, and secondly to enforce a number of public improvements applying alike to the lay-out and life of the city."

Despite seeming to give an open license to developers, the First Rebuilding Act (1667) structured its facilitation of private rebuilding by giving clear directions on construction procedure and approvals, and by extensive specification of building materials and form. Houses were to be built in brick or stone and with restrictions on the quality of timber when it was used. There were to be four types of houses of different scale and siting: the smallest was of two storeys with a garret and cellar and suited to the small streets and lanes; the slightly larger, of three storeys, was for fronting onto the larger streets or open areas such as the river; the third was a slightly more commodious version comprising four storeys; and the largest was regarded as a mansion for wealthy merchants and, though restricted to four storeys, was to include a garden set back from the street frontage.

In further stabilization of building quality, the City "appointed a committee to treat [or form agreements] with brickmakers, limeburners, and other undertakers for building materials, and it also pushed forward with a Bill for 'Regulating the Making of Bricks and Tiles'" (Reddaway 1951, 73). This served to support an efficient standardization of construction processes, materials and trade work and better ensure quality workmanship.

In May 1670, the Second Rebuilding Act set up a funding mechanism for meeting many of the civic expenses of repairing the damage from the Fire. A tax was imposed on imports of coal and the proceeds were to be applied to paying compensation for land taken for street widening within the City, repairing or rebuilding of parish churches, reconstructing ports and public places, and for the rebuilding of St Paul's Cathedral. It represented an important combination of royal power, the Parliament, and the Established Church for rebuilding the City functionally and socially. This new attention to improved infrastructure was also to influence the activities of private land development.

Building for the Public Benefit

Not only did the authorities attend to the rapid rebuilding of streets and public amenities, but they also used the situation to instill a public-mindfulness in their citizens. As often happens after substantial physical destruction, a goodwill of cooperation and care for others appears, despite that it may also be followed by some predatory behavior. In the aftermath of the Fire, the authorities extolled the felicitous combination of formal features for the new buildings as well as social guidance on the process:

> Whilst the City was carrying out the survey, a plot or model was to be made for the whole rebuilding, 'which being well examined by all those persons who have most concernment as well as experience, we make no question but all men will be pleased with it.' No private selfishness was to be allowed to operate to the public detriment. If any man presumed to erect buildings upon the pretense that the ground was his own, the City had strict instructions to pull them down. In addition, the name of the builder was to be returned to the King or to the Council, who would inflict exemplary punishment. (Reddaway 1951, 50)

When rebuilding was generally completed, the authorities continued to incorporate a civic obligation into their building legislation. Baer (2007b, 273) sees improvements in subsequent rulings during the remainder of the century:

> Now embracing the Low Countries' more recent sense that new houses had to confer a positive benefit, not just avoid being a nuisance, the proclamation required that houses be 'built Firmly and Regularly, according to such Design and Order as may best suit 'With the Public Benefit and Convenience' – broader criteria that supplemented the more specific requirements in the Rebuilding Acts.

A new public spirit was also growing around individual action. Stevenson (2013, 202) describes the promising changes in society's behavior:

> There were still plenty of rich men and women in the City after the Fire, when this old scheme of values found new and more pointed elaboration. It has long served as a kind of social cement, especially by offsetting envy and suspicion of what Evelyn sniffly called 'over growne & suddainly monied men'; now it encouraged men to accept expensive civic offices, which was especially difficult after 1666, and to contribute to the reconstruction of their charities, company halls and parish churches. Most generally, the public spirit reveals itself though individual enactments of the loving and mutually advantageous relationship between City and [C]ourt, while remaining clear on the separateness of these spheres.

Increased Funding for Real Estate

The Fire's £8 million damage, of which half was represented by the destruction of buildings, was a shocking loss for the City. Complexities arose around the responsibility for rebuilding, but the onus for it was finally imposed on the tenants. The authorities provided them with some financial assistance, but their lack of resources resulted in a takeover of many leases by those with capital who used them to build for new tenants. Landlords also bore a substantial economic burden since courts were established for tenants to have their leases legally terminated or to have their ground leases extended at current rates to provide a suitable amortization period for building costs.

For new investors in real estate, this opportunity was appealing, though the suspicion of another potential fire was a deterrent. However, the traditional desirability of property holdings persisted and "[l]and and buildings, still the most respected of all investments, backed by urgent personal appeals, were strong enough after the Fire to entice at least a part of such funds from their hiding" (Reddaway 1951, 275). Since the process of speculative building for the market rather than specific tenants had been successfully tested in housing developments earlier in the century, the practice was broadly adopted by all who could participate with capital or building skills, or even as project managers or deal creators.

Large-scale financing schemes were also proposed. Sir William Petty, an economist in Charles's Treasury, proposed a national tax for the rebuilding since the productivity of the revived city would satisfactorily repay investment and enable tax reductions in the future. And Sir Edward Ford suggested that the new adoption of traditional forms of credit, such as bills of exchange, could be used to raise capital from private sources. He proposed that they be secured by the taxes of the City and formalized by an Act of Parliament. It was an early form of municipal bond that, despite its strong economic rationale, was not pursued.

In the tumultuous religious context, a consensus also arose around the need for generosity in financial matters. Reddaway (1951, 277) describes the spiritual, civic-minded ethic proposed in the sermons of Samuel Rolle, in which: "[t]he rich were exhorted to lend, landlords to grant fair terms, workmen to labour hard, and suppliers of materials to wrong themselves rather than others. Rebuilding was extolled as a work of honour and proved to be one of profit. Litigation was deprecated, moderation advised." And so the scene was set for active urban development by private entrepreneurs that would broadly benefit the community and create an exemplary new urban fabric.

Chapter 4: Improvements to the Land: A Modern Production Activity

Growing Interest in Private Real Property

It has long been a fundamental principle of real estate investment that excessive demand spurs the opportunity for property ownership to produce rental income. So it was in London at the time as the result of population growth, plague conditions, and fire losses. Boulton (1987, 85) describes the response to increasing housing need at the level of the common man: "In rapidly expanding Stuart London one of the most important sources of supplementary income came from the heavy demand for accommodation. The large inns could not meet all this demand and therefore the taking in of lodgers was a very important by-employment" (Boulton 1987, 85).

As a culture of landlordism expanded through numerous levels of society, general attitudes towards private real estate were changing. While the new enthusiasm for accumulating wealth and possessions drove a booming commercial activity in a wide variety of goods and services, the attention of accumulators was gradually drawn towards urban land and buildings, both old and new, of the whole metropolis. The objective of property ownership was extended beyond merely the need for a subsistence income to an enthusiasm for the potential financial surplus gained from rapidly rising rental rates.

This new wealth-maximizing objective was fundamental to whom economists term *rentiers*, that is, those who seek the highest possible revenues for their property without providing any offsetting service or effort. However, in the new climate of capitalism, a more active operational role of the property owner was heralded and the prior role of the landlord as a relatively passive accommodator of tenants, in the traditional manner of the landed gentry, was disparaged. In the following century, Adam Smith (1994, 286) continued to criticize the passive property owner: "They [landlords] are the only one of the three orders whose revenue costs them neither labour nor care, but comes to them, as it were, of its own accord, and independent of any plan or project of their own."

Although actively pursuing the improved productivity of property is an admirable aspiration of a real estate owner, the increased attention to the asset management that was undertaken in London of the later 17th century was more focused on and limited to demanding higher rents from their tenants, following the example of traders who aggressively raised the prices of food products in short supply.

At first, the new capitalist merchants used their money to advance their trading businesses and showed little interest in the moderate returns of real estate. But, when they had achieved success and acquitted sufficient excess wealth, they turned their interest to the prestige, and possibly diversification, of property ownership. Tawney (1941, 18) describes this:

> The Government of the first two Stuarts continued, on a more majestic scale, the Elizabethan policy of turning Crown estates into cash. So far from deprecating the acquisition of land by the business world, it threw land at its head. It was not surprising that a successful merchant, who had made his pile in trade, should prefer to the risks of commerce the decorous stability of what was regarded as a gilt-edged investment. By the middle years of James, if not, indeed, earlier, it is difficult to find a prominent London capitalist who is not also a substantial landowner.

He adds that the increasingly wealthy professional class also took an interest: "Fortunes made in law went the same way" (Tawney 1941, 18).

As so many landlords now possessed the commercial and professional skills to strive for maximum rental rates, and even some commoners changed their attitude towards their lodgers or tenants by becoming more avaricious, it was not surprising that tensions arose between landlords and tenants. There was also an early form of pricing arbitrage with respect to leases and which became a common activity as Harding (2002, 565) describes: "Eventually, many leaseholders came to act as intermediate landlords, buying a lease for a capital sum and a moderate annual rent and subletting the property for a shorter period and at a higher rent to the person who could occupy it." This new commercial activity became an economic end in itself, eventually spawning the professional leasing agent, as "... some Londoners began to live as *rentiers*, purely from the management of property" (Schofield 1984, 140).

This overlay of a ubiquitous objective of wealth accumulation through property ownership, as it was practiced in this context of profit maximization, resulted in a distinct transformation of the early attitude to real estate that continues to be almost globally accepted. The necessary inclusion of a number of participants across the social strata continued through Victorian times when the dramatist George Bernard Shaw penned his play *Widowers' Houses* (1893), revealing the complexity of the situation and exposing the hypocrisy of general attitudes to property matters. It was, he implied, an activity requiring many to perform their allocated roles and to be acknowledged for their efforts irrespective of social standing.

The Breadth of the Entrepreneurial Spirit

This opportunity for economic optimization began to permeate through class layers and such democratization, even if limited, was to be critical to the first private undertaking of urban property development, particularly regarding the conversion of land use. Tawney (1941, 15) has pointed out the variance in investors' grasping the economic opportunity as the general commercial mindset expanded:

> There are plenty of gentry who stagnate or go down the hill. [But] it would be easy to find noble landowners who move with the times, and make the most of their properties; the sheep-farming of Lord Spencer; the enclosures of Lords Brudenell, Huntingdon and Saye and Sele; the coal-mines of the Earl of Northumberland and the Earl of Wemyss; above all the grandiose reconstruction [of the Fens] carried through by the

Russells [also to be the developer of Covent Garden], are cases in point. The smaller the part, nevertheless, played by passive property, as compared with active enterprise, the larger the opportunities of rising; and the increased rewards to be reaped by the improving landlord favoured classes still ascending the ladder compared with those already at the summit.

Also, Linklater (2013, 22) has mentioned that it was the broad adoption of the commercial spirit that drove this new approach to land: "With landlords pressing to increase rents and tenants eager to improve their [profit] margins, each individual had to find ways of making the land more profitable."

Facilitating the middle class' entry into this land-based entrepreneurship was the English tradition of ground leases. Rather than having to raise large capital amounts to purchase freehold title to land, for it could not be sold to him, the acquiring party could obtain a sufficient economic interest through the established process of leasing land. It began with the farming sector, where leases were traditional, and seen as a convenient vehicle for gaining control of a site when the entrepreneurial mind turned to other land uses such as urban development. This reduced his start-up or expansion costs to annual rental fees. Britnell (1993, 200) described the growth of this business method: "[gaining land which was] leased in parcels ... contributed to the ease with which a few tenants were able to accumulate large agglomerations of property." This efficient and cost-reducing process of scaling up land for economic production foreshadowed the dynamic by which private urban development would be approached with the benefits of scale.

Not only did the tenancy system encourage more productive, even if profit-motivated, responsibility, but there were also changes to it that supported this approach. Habakkuk (1940, 15) described the three important modifications to land control as "consolidation of holdings, enclosure, and the replacing of leases for lives by leases for a term of years." The enlargement of holdings enabled scaled production, and enclosure fenced in sheep or prevented intrusion, but the changing of lease tenure to a specific number of years enabled agrarian production to be undertaken more strategically. Greater certainty allowed for the planned amortization of improvements, and the absence of linkage to a tenant's life span facilitated the transference of leasehold rights. This form of title was sufficient for making improvements on a site, and for those participants who did not own land already, it had a distinct economic advantage and made real estate development more feasible.

Of most relevance in clearing the way for private urban development was the opportunity for maximizing a land's economic use. The conversion of ownership from passive to active to achieve its *highest and best use*, as measured by economic return, came to be fundamental to the development decision by which the large range of possible land and building uses were evaluated as urban centers grew.

Extending Investment Calculations for Development
Following Primatt's (1680) provision of interest rate tables for guiding real estate returns, further publications presented calculative methods for determining the valuation of a completed building and the rental rate necessary to fully amortize costs. For example, Hayes (1789, 69) (Figure 4.1) describes the detailed financial analysis:

16l. a year rent, valuing his money at 8 per cent. it fhews the purchafer what his annual rent ftands him in.

At 8 per cent. 100l. is worth 8   1   8½ per yr. for 61 yrs.
Multiplied by 200l. the fine,   2 hundred pounds
―――――――――
Shews the fine is worth   16   3   5 a year for 61 years
To which add the rent, viz. 16   0   0 a year
―――――――――
Shews that the tenant pays 32   3   5 a year for the leafe.

―――――――――

ANOTHER

FOR VALUING RENTS OF BUILDINGS.

THE FOREGOING EXAMPLE CONTINUED.

The builder at the year's end finifhes his work, and finds that the coft of the buildings, lofs of intereft, and the rent paid during the time, amounts to 1200l. which money he values at 8 per cent. By the fame tables he may eafily know the annual rent thefe buildings muft be valued at, to make his money again.

N. B. This valuation muft be made upon the years due in the leafe.

	l.	s.	d.	
At 8 per cent. 100l. is worth	8	1	10	per year for 60 yrs.
Multiplied by the money laid out, viz. -			12 hundred pounds	

―――――――――

Shews the building ftands in 97   2   0 per year for 60 yrs.
To which add the value of ground rent and fine, viz } 32   3   5 per year

―――――――――

Shew the rent to let at, is   129   5   5 per year to make 8 per cent.

―――――――――

A SHOPKEEPER PAYING A FINE, AND THE CHARGE OF REPAIRS.

A fhopkeeper takes a leafe of an houfe for 7, 14, or 21 years, paying 45l. a year rent, and 200l. fine, and lays out 100l. more upon fitting his fhop up, and altering conveniencies to the houfe, and would know what his rent ftands him in a year, for any of the terms of years mentioned in his leafe, he valuing his money at 10 per cent.

	l.	s.	d.	
At 10 per cent. 100l. is worth for 7 yrs.	20	10	10	per year.
Multiplied by the fine and repairs, viz.			3 hund. pds.	

Shews the money laid out in fine and repairing, is worth - - } 61   12   6 per year.
To which fum add the rent he pays, viz. - - - } 45   0   0 ditto
―――――――――
Shews if he holds his houfe no longer than 7 years, he pays - } 106   12   6 per year

---

4.1

Excerpt from _Tables and Method_ for determining the valuation of a building, inclusive of the opportunity cost of capital.

The builder at the year's end finishes his work, and finds that the cost of the building, loss of interest, and the rent paid during the time, amounts to 1200l. which money he values at 8 per cent. By the same tables he may easily know the annual rent these buildings must be valued at, to make his money again.

In this case, the addition to the calculation of the "loss of interest," as a component of the opportunity cost of capital (OCC), or "money he values at 8 per cent", fully completes the financial analysis of discounted value in real estate that has continued in use since that time.

Therefore, at this early stage of private development activity, an efficient developer, investor, builder, or landlord could calculate the valuation of a completed property with a committed lease, and also derive its investment yield. This provided a metric for comparing real estate with alternative investment opportunities, and as usual returns were in a range of 8–10%, it became very popular. Further, since the concept of real estate value is based on both the economic value of its functional purpose and returns on the capital invested, almost uniquely as an asset class, real estate performed as both a production function within the macroeconomy and as a repository of wealth, a duality which has ensured its continued popularity.

Complexity in the Value of Improvements

Although the financial concepts of valuation and investment returns were applied similarly to both land and buildings, these two physical resources were actually used very differently in man's habitation activities. This overlay of the calculative methods pertaining to land leases on transactions involving buildings must have been an expedient, organic extension of the traditional ownership and use arrangements. However, the metaphysical natures are different, and the inadequacies of the financial construct for buildings raised problems of ownership definition, funding, and use of the improvements from the outset that have yet to be rectified.

Ownership and Its Benefits

The first arises with respect to the legal ownership of the building erected on land not held in fee simple title, but rather used by right of a ground lease. Under English common law, a building that is attached to land becomes part of the land, and in the case of the erection of a structure on the leased land by its lessee, the whole reverts to the land lessor on termination of the ground lease. The benefit to a ground lessee of erecting a structure was that he could sublease it to occupants during the term of the lease of the land, which was usually long. However, it did not invest in him interest in the structure other than his rights as lessee of the land of which it had become part, despite the funding and management of its construction and continued capital expenditure on its maintenance over the life of the ground lease. This unusual allocation of rights, responsibility, and economic benefit is sometimes misunderstood or misrepresented. Nevertheless, it enabled entrepreneurs to erect structures for their subtenants without the large capital outlay required for purchase of stronger title.

The lease of a building was kept distinct from that of a ground lease to a tenant farmer, which was essentially purely for the land. In the case of a farm lease, the expectation as to the magnitude of any lessee's improvements would usually be minimal. If a building were constructed by the landowner, it would provide an additional layer of utility for the property and therefore command additional rent through a combination of rent for the land and rent for the building, though often maintained as separate leases. In a variation of that transaction, the rents due for the building and for the land might be distributed differently if an additional party stepped in to finance the building and thereby command that associated rent from the subtenant, who also paid the ground lease rent. In the case of a development lease, the developer would take a ground lease from the owner, erect the structure and sublease it to an occupant at a rent that covered his own payments for the ground lease and the amortization of his building costs.

This last situation frequently became the case as more urban development was undertaken by a broad array of practitioners and a wider source of construction funding was sought. It has continued in the real estate arrangement known as the ground lease and is used throughout the world where ownership of the land and building are different, or the land is retained by the nation or community and individual ownership is not allowed. The ground lease system of much of London today, and other cities such as Baltimore in the USA, are examples of private land ownership, and the structure used in the development of land in China is an example of absolute state ownership.

Economic Consumption

The economic construct for the improvements was also more complicated than that for land. Legally, English land was often held in different interests, and the transfer of title or lease of each interest occurred separately. A lessee could transfer or sublease his leasehold interest, and his lessor could quite separately sell or assign his reversion. Further, as part of the land, a building could be the subject of a transaction which was limited to that specific lease term without reference to the economic condition of either at reversion.

The price to be paid for land, its capitalized value, was calculated as a multiple of the annual ground rent, even if it extended indefinitely, since at any point its value was fully retained or even appreciated. In his history of the construction industry in Britain, Smyth (1985, 52) notes that "the use value of land continues in perpetuity, and is not consumed."

Unlike the land, as a building is put to its economic use it is consumed and deteriorates. Smyth (1985, 52) above calls attention to this aspect of property which is often forgotten: "Buildings as fixed capital will suffer a small amount of wear and tear [but, over the years] this will amount to a large portion of constant [in-place] capital. The use value of the building, therefore, is gradually consumed." With its gradual consumption to the point of having no value, a building required a different method of valuation. In contrast to the value preservation inherent in land, capital applied to the construction of a building gradually disintegrates and is not recovered at the end of its temporary life. Therefore, aside from the expected investment return or yield, as compensation for contributing the capital, the cash flow during the use of the building should also provide for *a return of the original construction capital* over the lifetime of the building. Hayes (1789, 69) addresses this return *of* capital requirement in his calculations, though he refers to it as enabling the builder "to make his money again."

Not only did a building gradually deteriorate but its existence and continuity of use were more at risk than land. Primatt (1680, 37), writing just fourteen years after the Great Fire, proposed that the yield derived from owning and renting a house was heavily discounted by the new cognizance of risks to it. He notes that "the ground on which the same stood, being not subject to such casualties as the Houses ... it may be the Ground-rent of such Houses was worth and would yield half the Rent or more." In the early 18th century, Phillips (1719, B4) provides a generalization that houses "are sold at 13 or 14 years purchase; whereas Land is sold at 20 years purchase." Converted into return metrics, this means that land requires a 5% return, but a house requires approximately 7.5%. While the higher latter return is justified by Phillips because of the risk of loss in a fire, what is not made explicit is that the premium on the house must also provide the return *of* the capital spent for construction in addition to a competitive investment return *on* that capital.

In the late 18th century (1776), Adam Smith confirms this complex relationship between rent and invested capital. He also went further and linked the determination of a competitive return to interest rates on a security, which though seemingly undercompensating for the more-risky building asset, appropriately aligns expected returns with the capital markets. He said:

The building rent is the interest or profit of the capital expended in building the house. In order to put the trade of a builder upon a level with other trades, it is necessary that this rent should be sufficient, first, to pay him the same interest which he would have got for his capital if he had lent it upon good security; and, secondly, to keep the house in constant repair, or, what comes to the same thing, to replace, within a certain term of years, the capital which had been employed in building it. (Smith 1994, 904)

As unmet demand intensified with population growth, rental rates often rose merely with rebuilding. For example, if before a ground lease terminated after twenty years the land had a ground rent of £3 and a rack rent, or rent of the building on it, of £7, and the existing building had fully deteriorated, demand had so increased that a new building would rent for £14, that is, a 100% increase. If a developer who constructed the new building incurred some increased costs above those of the original construction, say 50%, and the ground rent payable to the landowner increased to say £5, the rental income on the house would have increased so substantially that even after paying the increased construction costs, the developer would receive a much higher return. In this example it can be seen that although the landowner received an increase of £2, this did not reflect the proportional increase in the capitalized value of the total property, building and land, under the new lease. This situation became typical of the rapidly developing urban fabric.

In those instances when urban land and its building are combined in a single lease, the infinite life of the land component is intertwined with the limited life of the building, and when a property as a whole has appreciated in value, unless the materials or costs of construction are unusual, the appreciating value is generally inherent in the land component. The use of the building will have been reduced by wear and tear, natural aging, and its trend towards obsolescence, so unless there is significant unmet demand for the space that elevates rents beyond typical growth rates, any value appreciation in response to demand is offset by its fading ability to function as required. Adam Smith (1994, 905) specifically noted the proper attribution of value:

Whatever part of the whole rent of a house is over and above what is sufficient for affording this reasonable profit, naturally goes to the ground-rent; and where the owner of the ground and the owner of the building are two different persons, is, in most cases, completely paid to the former. This surplus rent is the price which the inhabitant of the house pays for some real or supposed advantage of the situation [site].

In this attribution of gain through appreciation to the land, he is even joined by Marx who says: "the ground-rent, and not the house ... forms the actual object of building speculation in rapidly growing cities" (Marx 1976b, 774).

Residual Value of the Improvements
With masonry components and better-quality timber construction, by the 17th century many buildings were still habitable at the lease's termination. At first, this did not lead to a change in lease tenure since property law tended to keep contracts and land usage consistent and comparable for ease of administration. However, if the improvements had been undertaken by a lessee, this altered the value of what the lessor received on reversion, specifically in respect of the residual value of the building to which he had not contributed.

This sometimes caused a further difficulty as to the amount of rent which should be agreed for a new lease. If the improvements still had a viable use but showed some deterioration, the question could arise as to the amount of refurbishment required to restore it to a condition deserving of the rent demanded. As a solution, the landowner might grant a Repairing Lease, which required the new tenant to carry out certain specified repairs and improvements; and to incorporate the inherent value of the remaining usable structure, the ground rent was increased but only on the value of the residual structure and not that of the new structure which would be partially funded by the tenant. The charge was converted to what was known as a "rack rent." Smith focused attention on an accurate determination of that rent reduction in relation to the tenant's capital expenditure, which continues to be an issue today. This calculation also continues to be fundamental to the contractual conditions of a lease as to rent offsets, or increases, in relation to capital expenditure when building out raw space to accommodate the tenant's use.

With the even more durable materials and construction methods employed in following centuries, making capital improvements to buildings to reposition them or keep them competitive and extend their life has been a strategic asset management activity in commercial real estate. Building rehabilitation came to be regarded as a better economic decision than rebuilding, according to Needleman's (1969, 198) calculation "if the cost of rehabilitation, plus the present value of the cost of rebuilding in [x] years' time, plus the present value of the difference in annual running costs and rents for [x] years, is less than the present cost of rebuilding." However, today's dramatically changing work and living styles are making some buildings obsolete for their required use even as they remain structurally solid. The presumption of the total deterioration of a building within an estimable period of time is returning to real estate analysis, echoing Hayes's incisive calculation of this at the commencement of modern real estate financial analysis.

Change of Land Use
Though in the context of a lease any appreciation in value is typically limited to the land component, in the early days of property development it was noticed that improvements to the land, usually by the erection of a building, increased even the ground rental rates if the building's usefulness attracted higher rents on the subleases than were required to amortize the construction and reward the builder to the usual extent. Constructing a building that offered a usefulness higher than that previously available for that land effectively represented a change of its use, since change of use can mean an expansion of an existing use for financial outcomes.

Since the economic value of land was based on the contractual rent paid for prescribed use, the change of use required an adjusted valuation. That difference in value is calculated by reference to the "conversion rent" which represents the step-up in revenue between the annual rent under the prior use and the annual rent under a new economic use (Offer 1981, 114). As London urban development progressed, when agricultural land was converted to urban use, the economic impact was often in the order of a multiple of 8 to 10 times, and this carried over from annual cash flow to capitalized value. Petty (1690, 2) provided an example of this economic transformation at the time: "The same Land being built upon, may centuple the Rent which it yielded as Pasture."

Apportionment of the Economic Uplift by Change of Use

The disparity in economic benefit resulting from the development activity which changed land use through the construction of buildings on ground leases threw up the question of its proper apportionment. As Smyth (1985, 34) describes its elemental factors: "This [additional ground] rent is, therefore, related to the differential output [by end users of the developed space] resulting from the additional capital investments [by the developer]." From this perspective, it was implied that the person providing the improvements, the developer, should receive all of the rental increase, to compensate him in part for his financial liability and any future uncertainty due to the ground lease (Olsen 1982, 37).

However, the improvements could not be made without the provision of the land, and its features, such as its convenient location in London's western suburbs, were critical to achieving its urban residential use. By this view, the landowner should receive the conversion rent.

The third alternative was that the conversion rent should be apportioned according to a calculation of value attribution. In the late 19th century, there are some records of the rationale behind the legislated apportionment of the improved economic value due to development. Providing testimony to the London Town Holdings Committee in 1887, Edward Ryde explained:

> The general mode of dealing with building land which is ripening up for building is for the freeholder to let it in a large block to a well-to-do builder ... and to let it at such a rent as will give the building about one third of the ground rents as profit to himself ... [S]upposing, for instance, that the ultimate ground rent to be realized would amount to £3,000, the builder only agrees to pay the ground landlord £2,000, and secures the £1,000 as a profit ground rent to himself ... [But he also is to pay for the infrastructure of the] new streets [that] have to be marked out, and not only marked out but made, sewered, and paved. (*Town Holdings*, 1886 (213) xii, 303–304)

This value to a developer derived through the rent uplift between unimproved land and a developed project was also noticed as an opportunity for investors and financial intermediaries. Often, there was an astounding number and complex relationships of financial parties involved in the early London projects, and it was speculation about this specific financial component of real estate that possibly provided the attraction of so much capital to private development activity and consolidated its business formulation.

The "Highest and Best Use" of Land

In the circumstantial context of valuation methodology and the possibilities for changing the use of land, the comparative analysis, referred to earlier and known as the *highest and best use*, directs the assessment of various land functions and the selection of that which achieves the highest economic value potential. This form of evaluation is pervasively used today in development decisions, though the concept had appeared at the genesis of 17th-century urban development. In *The Surveiors Dialogue*, Norden (1618, 192) noted that, regarding the various plots of land worked by landlords and tenants, "they have more land, than they, or you, have experience how to convert to best use, they their owne, and yon your Lords."

Converting land to its highest economic potential at that time may not necessarily comprise a definitive change of use but could involve only an improvement in it such as the draining of bogs, improvement of water supply, or upgrading to a better quality of housing. The most productive use was also required to conform to feasible or allowable uses as were either informally established by a community or formally imposed by a ruling authority.

A challenge to the use of the principle arose in the determination of what characteristics constituted the "best": to what attributes did it apply, and for whom was it to be the best? For different stakeholders, the highest use might be relegated by an alternative definition of the best economic use. Observing the impact of land use choices on the broader population of the late 17th century, Petty (1689, 30) specifically noted that:

> ... if there be ten Acres of Land, I would have it judged whether they be better for Hay or Corn ... and according to the multitudes of people living near this Land, together with the luxurious or frugal living of them; and besides all, according to the Civil, Natural, and Religious Opinions of the said people ...

He then distinguishes between the impact on the owner and that on others: "This I call a Survey or Inquisition into the former intrinsick values of Land, this latter of extrinsick or accidental follows" (Petty 1689, 31). Therefore, in the decision of highest and best use, there was from the outset the need to ascertain the "extrinsick" or impact that a development might have external to its own operation and occupants, that being on the broader community.

Many of the traditional house builders in expanding London made a financially self-oriented analysis of the highest and best use and fully built out their land lots. However, it was an innovation of the early private developers to make some land allocation to an amenity, such as a piazza (Covent Garden) or open square (Bloomsbury Square), based on the realization that the houses built in its vicinity commanded higher rent than the mere rows of houses. Such pleasant open space could also be enjoyed by the local community and therefore the project would be more successfully integrated into the neighborhood. This was a more effective application of the principle of highest and best use since the economic value of the whole development was superior as a result.

Though these steps were probably partially based on financial objectives, in providing public space these developers followed the example of municipal authorities, or heads of state, who had set aside lands for the public realm. In London, though few, these were provided by the City, where Lincoln's Inn Fields was an influential example. These were dedicated to the public good and not directly intended for economic uplift, though cities have learnt to improve their physical environment with the intent of also improving general prosperity, property values, and land taxes. Therefore, although conforming to solid economic analysis, the planning of developers and their early schemes also manifested some intention to contribute to the public good, and their squares were originally established as public places.

Investment Returns on Development Projects

In the emerging real estate development business, the return on equity investments was therefore complex, even at its beginning. It adopted formats from various other businesses, though none perfectly suited its combination of large capital sums, production processes, and its traditional determination of valuation according to trading practices. It was a milieu in which building requirements were increasing the costs of development, and yet after the Restoration the demand and ability to pay by certain segments of the market continued solidly. Nevertheless, these cost burdens significantly influenced the resulting business model. As Baer (2007b, 269) points out:

> Most importantly, costs and 'return on investment' were paramount if private individuals were to carry out the King's lofty schemes via their own money, hence builders also resorted to real estate principles for their design. Ultimately, therefore, it was the 'business' of city building that was paramount in determining London's form, not the aesthetics.

Despite the general enthusiasm for investment returns, for real estate as with many other production activities there was less focus on its percentage return and more on the absolute amount of profit. Phillips (1719, 3–4) describes contemporary investor sentiment that pressed for high legislated interest rates: "It must needs be so, because the less profits [interest rate] is allowed, the greater principal must be expended to bring in the same profit."

As a result, in the earliest real estate ventures, performance was measured by profit metrics, though the calculations did not appropriately allow a discount for the temporal difference between investments and revenues. This shortcoming seemed in ignorance of the emerging economic rationale for trading, such as was noticed by Thomas Kerridge in 1636 that "the merchant who only counts his gains without regarding the time lost will make a poor reckoning in the end" (quoted in Grassby 1994, 108). This was also in contrast to other activities oriented towards resource harvesting, which is the way in which real estate development might have been regarded because of the similar centrality of land use. Pollard (1965, 220) reports that in these other instances, the accounting for investment capital was very advanced, with the inclusion of the investor's opportunity cost of capital (OCC), the use of compounding interest rates, and the depreciation of capitalized assets. It had been particularly developed for assessing the valuation of mining activities and timber plantations.

Equity Capital for Real Estate Development

As private urban development activities became too large to be funded solely by the landowner, as had been the case for Covent Garden and Bloomsbury Square, other equity investors began to participate in real estate projects. Equity investments in real estate had not traditionally interested the new businessman since they had deployed their capital more lucratively to their own merchant or production businesses or to the early trading companies. This changed because of a continued constraint on additional trading opportunities as the monarchs granted trading monopolies to their favored courtiers and financiers, and because the increasing amount of capital resulting from flourishing commercial activities forced the commercial minds to turn to the potential of property investment. Habakkuk (1940, 11) describes this dynamic:

> It might be argued that the flow of commercial capital into land under Elizabeth and the early Stuarts was in fact a rather peculiar phenomenon, due in part to the policy

of trade monopolies which fiscal exigencies forced the Crown to adopt, to institutions of foreign trade which limited the possibilities of profitable investment and forced a surplus of commercial profit into land.

Londoners became enthusiastic investors in real estate, and as Baer (2007a, 315) observed "… *All* socioeconomic classes and both sexes joined in financing and investing in housing, thereby providing this 'lumpy,' high-cost product with some liquidity which then redounded to all – builder, owner-occupant, investor, landlord and tenant – allowing the market better to function." This relatively inclusive financial participation in real estate continues through to this day, though sometimes to the disadvantage of some, such as many homeowners in the financial crisis of 2008.

For the early investments in real estate development, investors followed the tradition of providing loans to third parties. As there was no Continental banking system in London until the end of the 17th century, these loans were often arranged by lending agents such as silversmiths, who maintained high levels of liquidity, or law clerks who were also able to produce necessary legal documentation. Equity investments were therefore structured similar to loan investments with the anticipated "profit" fixed like an interest rate. There was no consideration or reference to a total value of the project since capital was to be repaid from a variety of sources such as the sale of the lease. In effect, real estate equity was practically indiscernible from debt, though sometimes it commanded a slightly higher yield.

Towards the later part of the century, the new type of investor appeared, having the role of a passive partner but sharing in the expanding value of an enterprise that created large capital items such as ships and wharves. This source of capital expected an ongoing tally of the capital investment in relation to the accumulation of enterprise value from successful operations that would provide the return of capital and profit. For the financial management of development projects, it therefore became necessary to establish a system for accurately monitoring its accumulation of value so that its returns and profits or losses could be constantly measured. These became the standard capital accounts for real estate development and present an almost duplicative though distinct system of financial recording in addition to the statutory financial reports for corporate business undertaking development, and this duality persists.

Distribution of Investment Returns

When the value of the completed development of a house on a leased site could be established, the questions arose as to the stakeholders' (the developer and any additional equity interests) respective entitlement to the profit, and how it should be allocated. If the profits were to be apportioned according to the ratio of equity capital provided, that would be a simple *pari passu* distribution. However, as the developer would have initiated the project and managed the entire process, he often claimed a higher proportion of the profit. This dynamic, described as a promoted investment scheme, was adopted from other investment opportunities offered by entrepreneurs such as the split-stock companies engaged in global trade. The initiator, or sometimes a hired salesman, was known as the "promoter." Eventually, as it became a common structure of distribution, the additional amount of profit allotted to the promoter beyond his proportional share based on his capital contribution became known as the "promotional" distribution, or the "promote" as it continues to be called today.

Once a developer proffered a project with his receiving a "promote," the scheme's financial attractiveness determined that amount. An investor might accept the developer's receiving a reward in the form of a larger share of the profits, but contingently upon the attainment of a suitable investment return on the capital which would justify the proposed size of the promote. Accordingly, for the formulation of this business model, economic thinking was turned to determining the appropriate levels of returns for this contribution.

Adam Smith was aware of this inclusion of entrepreneurial or project management capability and responsibilities in the price determination of a product:

> As soon as stock has accumulated in the hands of particular persons, some of them will naturally employ it in setting to work industrious people, whom they will supply with materials and subsistence, in order to make a profit by the sale of their work, or by what their labour adds to the value of the materials. In exchanging the complete manufacture either for money, for labour, or for other goods, over and above what may be sufficient to pay the price of the materials, and the wages of the workmen, something must be given in this adventure. (Smith 1994, 54)

In this way he justified the financial reward to that entrepreneur who had initiated and taken control (or stock) of the project.

However, Smith (ibid.) found the valuation of those actions difficult to determine, and posited that:

> [t]he profits of stock, it may perhaps be thought, are only a different name for the wages of a particular sort of labour, the labour of inspection and direction. They are, however, altogether different, are regulated by quite sufficient principles, and bear no proportion to the quantity, the hardship, or the ingenuity of this supposed labour of inspection and direction. They are regulated altogether by the value of the stock employed, and are greater or smaller in proportion to the extent of this stock.

He does, however, align the calculation of profit from which the developer's promote is derived with the pricing achieved by the trading of the (stock or) building. For real estate, this means an alignment with price appreciation rather than income levels, and once again raises the complexities, and confusions, as to the attribution of returns on development projects.

Private Urban Development

The increased demand in London for housing not only raised rents but also ignited a demand for new buildings. In the face of scarcity of available sites, extensive restrictions and rising costs of compliant construction, as Baer (2002, 516) points out, a commercial response required a relatively new skill set:

> Accommodating the growing population required entrepreneurial vision and skill, as those undertaking the task had to acquire building sites, mobilize money and credit,

labor and materials, and frequently had to procure government license for new construction in the face of royal proclamations. Such growth also required the ability to assess investment opportunities by rules common to both buyer and seller.

The authorities also had to advance their skills in their land use planning, as to which Baer (2007b, 261) presents their new approach:

> While all building prohibitions did not even slow London's growth, they had a different and unintended outcome. The opposing parties greatly modified their ideological positions over time. The authorities came to tacitly agree that speculative building was in London to stay, indeed might be doing London and England some good. Developers, who at first defied the prohibitions and regulations as too expensive, eventually came to accept them – even harnessing them to their own ends.

Compromise was in the air.

The new urban fabric of modern London was determined through this combination of more sympathetic public oversight and progressive approaches by private developers. Retrospectively reviewing its progress during the 17th century by the application of the new science of housing economics, William Petty (1690, 98) commented:

> As for *Housing*, the Streets of *London* it self speaks it, I conceive it is double in value in that City, to what it was forty years since; and for *Housing* in the Country, they have increased … far beyond the proportion of what I can learn have dilapidated in other places. For in *Ireland* where the ruin was greatest, the *Housing* (taking all together) is now more valuable than forty years ago, nor is this to be doubted, since *Housing* is now more splendid, than in those days, and the number of Dwellers is increased, by near ⅔ part …

The Rise of the Speculative Developer

In his determination of economic value, not only did Petty consider the quality of building structure but he also explicitly included the dynamics linking population and housing:

> For if a Man would know, what any Land is worth, the true and natural Question must be, How many Men will it feed? How many Men are there to be fed? But to speak more practically, Land of the same quantity and quality in *England*, is generally worth four or five times as much as in *Ireland;* and but one quarter or third of what it is worth in *Holland*; because *England* is four or five times better Peopled than *Ireland*, and but a quarter so well as *Holland.* And moreover; where the Rent of Land is advanced by reason of Multitude of People; there the number of Years purchase, for which the Inheritance may be sold, is also advanced, though perhaps not in the very same proportion. (Petty 1690, 67–68)

Although this learned pronouncement was made later in the century, it reveals the early understanding of the potential economic uplift of land when improved. The needs of an increasing population had been met with the expanded agrarian production, and rising value of land, in the early Stuart years, and Petty's focused reference extends this to the use of land for shelter.

By this economic assessment, the building of shelter on land became recognized as more than just building a house for a certain resident but rather producing a product with an economic value which was related to the demand for it. A builder did not need to know what a particular resident would pay for his building but could determine its price, or economic value according to the demand, that is according to prices indicated by the whole trading market. Using this rationale, a speculative builder could proceed to build in advance of his identification of an occupant, tenant or purchaser, with the markets providing pricing information.

Some historians locate the speculative approach to private building activity prior to the creation of the capitalist housing market. Summerson (2003, 21) suggests that

> [s]peculative building is a very old way of making money. It must go far back into the Middle Ages and have grown up almost simultaneously with the notion of a rent roll as a source of wealth. It was familiar practice in Tudor times. As the aristocrats shifted out of the walled cities their palaces were taken over and demolished or subdivided to provide accommodation for humbler people whose rents brought an income to the new landlord.

In contrast, referring to later Victorian activities, Inwood (2005, 41) advances a definition of these new economic producers, describing them as " 'speculative' because they built without a specific client in mind." Irrespective of their exact historical birth date, these speculative builders produced building stock on plots involving the holdings of large landowners. Often a completed building was sold to a wealthy investor who would then become responsible for its maintenance and collect the rent for it from its occupants. The same reasoning applied to those investors who did not build on acquired land but speculated on its unimproved state. Numerous speculative parties emerged and participated in the increasing private production of housing.

Definition of the Activity

With such an increase in activity, these many and varied responses of builders of the early decades of the 17th century provide a rich assortment from which to attempt a broad definition of speculative development.

In the category of land speculator, which is today termed "horizontal developer," was a land merchant who bought "wholesale and sold retail" by acquiring a large block of land and subdividing it into smaller lots for individual sale. Youings (1971, 126) defines the speculator in this way: "A man who buys up a substantial block of property and then, over a period gradually sells it in portions, at a profit, may justifiably be called a speculator if, when he made his purchases, he had only a hope and not a certainty of sale." Bernard (2011, 126) too draws attention to the fundamental risk-taking aspect of this speculation: "A man who buys up a substantial block of property and then, over a period gradually sells it in portions, at a profit, may justifiably be called a speculator if, when he made his purchases, he had only a hope and not a certainty of sale." This format was derived from other contemporary trading activities. Although no substantial improvements were made to the land, this approach took on economic uncertainties pertaining solely to the trade, such as the level of the prices which would be obtained in the sales of the separate lots.

Next, Summerson (2003, 28) helpfully distinguishes two categories, "those who speculated in land *plus* houses and those who speculated only in houses. The former included financiers; the latter were principally building craftsmen." He identifies the method of the building craftsmen as taking the building leases of one or more plots and working in trade groups to construct a building of which the house lease was sold to either the resident or an investor. Baer (2007a, 309) describes the earliest of these activities: "Even before the advent of competitive bidding and general contractors, small speculative builders would undertake this risk [of taking building leases and covering costs] by investing in a building site or two strung along an 'embryo street' and constructing a house or two." And in an earlier work she had established its extensiveness: "[t]he great majority of building prior to the second half of the century was still along traditional streets, alleys, and courts, and was undertaken by the 'blue apron' classes and the 'middling sort'" (Baer 2002, 526).

The group that speculated in land for which they outsourced the construction of buildings undertook a much more complex activity because, as Summerson implies, of the complexity of the financial aspects. It necessitated acquiring, or substantially controlling, the use of land, obtaining approval to erect the structure, and then contracting with the building trades, followed by having a tenant commit to it. The earliest to take this path were those who were professionally knowledgeable of the relevant legislation, and of contracts and commercial transfers. They were often lawyers, particularly solicitors, who had been involved in the land transfers begun by Henry VIII and continued by the Stuarts. For example, during the 1630s, a solicitor, John Moore, Esq., "doubled his income by his tenement investments in and near what had once been an orchard lying between Covent Garden and the old parish church of St. Martin's-in-the-Fields" (Barnes 1971, 66). He diligently disregarded the ever-changing anti-building legislation, and despite having houses demolished and being fined due to prosecution by the Star Chamber, he still profited handsomely.

Also were those who already owned land and speculated on the improvement in economic value they could attain. Because of their significance in founding the private activity of development, these will be examined in more detail in Part II. They undertook the planning of the site, the erection of buildings, and the ongoing management of the completed project, and by that they maximized its value-creation. Not all landowners were to be so active and McKellar (1999, 39) perceives that "[t]he majority of aristocratic landowners on fairly small sites did not, it seems, become involved in the development process, preferring to sell the land off completely." For the new entrepreneurial developers, however, it was their strategic amalgamation of well-located land, their incisive perception of its economic potential as a larger scheme, and their diligence in overcoming the building restrictions that distinguished them from passive landowners, mere builders, and land speculators.

Despite this multifaceted concept of speculative land activity, the essential private urban developer is distinguished by the complexity of its functional and administrative processes.

McKellar (1999, 52) attempts to describe its extensiveness, even apart from details of the management of the building production:

> The development process relied on the skills of a variety of people: building specu-
> lators who understood the market and could raise finance; businessmen prepared to
> become part of a syndicate of investors; managers ... who could organize the opera-
> tion; lawyers who could draw up contracts and understood how to manipulate the lab-
> yrinth of seventeenth-century property legislation; and scriveners who could provide
> finance and arrange transfers of money between parties and to employees.

Further defining the activity is the multiplicity of contributions that have been noted. Baer (2007a, 312) commends its ability to meet unanticipated urban housing needs: "Speculative building's emergence is an unofficially calculated (if not 'planned') way for society to gear up quickly in the face of population and housing demand surges to provide a very expensive good so as to mitigate a looming 'housing crisis.'" Hollis (2008, 192) sees it as exercising the skills of a broad cross-section of London's commercial classes that had been acquired in other areas of business, noting that "as the market in speculative building was being invented by a new breed of businessmen, and emerging class of self-made Londoners who understood business, either as merchants or city tradesmen and invested their surplus in the speculator's promise of profits." And Summerson (2003, 21) acknowledges their contribution in creat-ing the built fabric of that important metropolis: "The speculative builder, the mainspring of London's expansion for three hundred years ..." All three aspects of it – the provision of shelter, its financial component, and its impact on the urban environment – were inherent at its origin, and continue to be critical in its ongoing formulation.

Master Builders

Although the defining developments of Covent Garden and Bloomsbury Square were to be much more significant, Baer (2012, 410–411) calls attention to the smaller, earlier builders who adopted this speculative mode of production:

> Unfortunately, historians' preoccupation with ... larger, showier developers, often
> building famous squares and other ensembles of housing for the middling sort and
> the wealthy, has perhaps left the false impression that they dominated housing pro-
> duction. They did not. Even after the Restoration, more London households of lesser
> wealth lived in lower-quality housing including tenements and dwelling sheds pro-
> duced by virtually unknown smaller-scale builders. It was these people who made
> up the great majority of *all* builders. This aspect was even truer in the first half of the
> century.

The development of rows of houses or tenements as the earliest response to London's increasing population was undertaken by building tradesmen in the centuries-old tradition of the "undertaker." Following traditional methods, they learned their trade as apprentices, and erected various structures of stone and brick for religious and institutional purposes, as well as using timber for domestic buildings. Typically, they were engaged by a landowner, institution, or intended resident under a fee-based arrangement. As urban centers grew, an entrepreneur with capital resources occasionally took a ground lease from an estate owner and then contracted for the building of rental housing. Separate trades were usually engaged in such a project, but the leading tradesman, usually from carpentry or masonry, managed the logistics of the other trades as well as performing his own work. This led to the advent of the "master builder."

McKellar (1999, 102) described his function as follows:

> The master builder took on contracts for whole houses from other developers. He then employed workmen in the different trades to carry out the work, sometimes paying them himself and sometimes letting out contracts to the separate trades. He later received either payment or building leases for the whole work from the developer. His role was as a building organizer, manager and supervisor. He undertook his work not in the manner of a clerk of works employed by somebody else, but at his own risk and with his own money.

> It must be understood that he did not take on a contract to produce the finished product but to provide the workmanship to that end.

With expanding housing demand, the activities of some master builders changed to take the major initiative. A more astute and perceptive one would realize that he could become a developer himself if he were to gain control of the site. In most cases he could not buy it outright, and he would not wish to take a long-term ground lease. Instead, he would obtain the right to make improvements on a site by taking what was known as a building lease at a cost similar to the land's annual rent. It allowed him access for the purposes of making the improvements but terminated upon their completion. Under this arrangement, he constructed a building and by way of recoupment of its costs and for a profit, he sold it to the intended resident or a third-party investor coincidently with that purchaser's taking a ground lease directly from the landowner. If he were sufficiently resourced, he would take the ground lease himself and retain the building. And if he repeated this process by offering the leased property as security for a loan, he could amass a portfolio of completed properties, the rents of which would provide the operating cash flow to meet debt obligations and possibly seed new projects.

In this manner, such operators became what might today be termed "merchant builders" since their trading activities were added to the construction activity. Their participation in the transactional dimension of housing production then thrust them into the dynamics of capitalist markets. Their business strategy and economic performance were described by Baer (2007a, 304):

> The industry was composed of small, highly flexible units – to its advantage and detriment. It adapted itself to inherent instability and building fluctuations by an immense number of organizational permutations fitting themselves to a great variety of circumstances. This very flexibility, while usually positive, also at times contributed to the industry's instability because multiple and differentiated suppliers and speculators could not coordinate supply to fit demand, often building too much.

Though the building of repetitive houses in the vernacular style does not qualify as development comprising the extensive aspects to be described in Part II, with the analogous precedents its methods influenced those later development activities, and their histories became interwoven. To the public and many practitioners, they are virtually indistinguishable, probably to the detriment of the competence of each.

Individual Leadership of the Real Estate Development Process
In other commercial activities, and as was again tried during a later period of large-scale industrial production, various functions were shared among partners, or even across members of a family, so that each performed as a department head. It is more clearly observable in the later operation of textile mills, such as that of the noted Horrocks and Strutts families, that this structure was often successful in continuing routine production, but when changes were required, differences of opinion and expertise often conflicted with economic interests, and tensions were difficult to resolve.

In response to the complexities of industrial production in the rapidly changing economic conditions of the 18th century, the method "of a single managing partner controlling lower echelons of managers, ultimately proved to be more flexible in practice and therefore more favoured by go-ahead firms" (Pollard 1965, 267). This somewhat resembled the earlier mode of leadership structure adopted by an entrepreneur, but that earlier method differed in that the owner or capital provider had appointed technically skilled staff to administer the production activity. Notably exemplifying it was the system of Benjamin Gott (1762–1840), originally a wool merchant, who proceeded in what would be called a "downstream" expansion to build a large-scale woolen cloth factory at Bean Ing in Yorkshire where he employed 761 workers. As noted in his own papers, while he retained ultimate control as owner, he realized his managerial advantage if he stepped back and "paid for the talents of others in the different branches of manufacture."

Consequent upon the delegation of managerial power in infrastructure projects such as wharves, bridges, and drainage systems as they became larger and more complex, the budding civil engineering profession devised the position of "General Agent," who was to carry the ultimate, overarching responsibility for the delivery of the completed project but would delegate duties to specialists and external contractors. In many ways, the initiator of a property development project necessarily assumed this leading responsibility, and managed the costs of production, but had added tasks, namely, to raise the capital to cover those costs and to produce an investment return on it by effecting the crystallization of the economic value of the completed project through sale or lease.

Builder-developers

William Newton: Great Queen Street
Although the impetus for master builder William Newton of Bedfordshire to commence his undertaking of the rather grand row of housing in Great Queen Street off Lincoln's Inn Fields is unknown, his work is notable in its commitment to advancing good architectural design and in quickly following the stylistic discipline of Covent Garden. Chancellor (1932, 144–145) reports that in 1635 he acquired the land on the south side of Great Queen Street from Sir

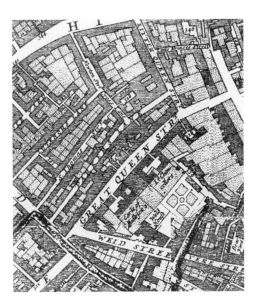

4.2
Great Queen Street, 1682.

Kenelm Digby and obtained a license to build fourteen houses, each with 40-ft frontages and "fitt for the habitation of able men" (Figure 4.2).

Built of brick and stone, they had continuous cornices and roofs with their separate entries defined by pilasters with Corinthian capitals (Figure 4.3). In this architectural uniformity they showed the influence of Inigo Jones's residential buildings at Covent Garden, though Jones more typically used the simpler Tuscan and Doric architectural orders. Although erroneously said to have been that of Jones, it is more reliably attributable to his son-in-law and pupil

4.3
William Newton's houses, south side of Great Queen Street, 1637.

John Webb. Dasent (1895, 8) describes its social recognition and alludes to the mystery of its designer:

> One of the most fashionable streets in London in the reign of Charles the First, was Great Queen Street, Lincoln's Inn Fields. Some of the houses therein are said to have been designed by Inigo Jones, but that now numbered 55 and 56 on the south side is perhaps the only remaining specimen of his work to be seen in the whole street.

Although urban buildings with neoclassical façades had become rather commonplace in European cities and countries of European colonization, for England at the time it was a radically new format, particularly for a residence. Whether rural or urban, a house was usually constructed with a gabled roof, and upper floors were functionally secondary and formed merely as a vertical extension of the ground floor, all with a familiar vernacular appearance. In the appearance of these Great Queen Street houses, Summerson (1991a, 354) sees the townhouse as having reached "a decision stage in its conversion to classicism." He describes the transformation: "The gable vanished and a classical order was applied … in a wonderfully appropriate way, the ground floor being regarded as a podium [for the more important floor above] and the order itself embracing the two upper floors without inconvenience or distortion."

Important to the progression of the urban typography as private developers became such substantial providers of the built fabric, these houses in

> Great Queen Street were reputed, in the eighteenth century, to constitute 'the first regular street in London.' They laid down the canon of street design which put an end to gabled individualism, and provided a discipline for London's streets which was accepted for more than two hundred years. (Summerson 1991b, 20)

That this precedent for urban building was achieved through a strong and collaborative approach of architect, developer, and public authority provided a strong principle of practice for the tyro developer, as well as the newly engaged architect.

Part II
Birth of the Modern Property Development Business

Chapter 5: The Modern Developer: Russell

Developers Create Buildings and Places

Although of smaller volume than the master builders' development of London's environs, but more important for the formulation of the private development activity, as it has come to be practiced, were the activities of certain owners of land in the areas accommodating the City's expansion. The history of the common individual's ability to access and control land indicates it was possibly the biggest impediment to private development. Without control of the land on which a building was to be constructed, only the foolhardy would incur the expense and effort of development. Ground leases and building leases provided temporary mechanisms for builders to gain control of land and this facilitated their early response to housing demands. The outright ownership of land, however, provided much more potential for long-term economic gains with more flexibility determining its use in whole or in part and accommodating a grander vision for the typically larger site. The land lying west of the City presented a complex mix of ownership that included the Crown, various aristocrats, some enterprising gentry and merchants and farmers. It was these fortunate landowners, ideally located in the most desirable suburb of London, who were presented with the compelling opportunity to develop their sites.

Under the long-established and strictly enforced property law of England, land ownership allowed some flexibility in the application of legal rights as Harding (2002, 556) describes:

> Property owners were able to exploit the freedom of urban tenure and devise to create a variety of rights and expectations through conditional grants, life grants with specified remainders, grants in marriage, in fee tail, and so on, restricting the long-term descent of the property that they controlled. Taken together, these practices created another class of participants in the property market at one remove: those with life interests and those with serial expectations, including distant contingent remainders. Many of these interests were legally assignable; indeed, they were transferred and resigned through the same medium as more immediate property interests. Thus were the notions of property and the ownership of space extended through time and, to some extent, into speculative situations or contingencies.

Therefore, despite the building restrictions, Beckett (1986, 263) claims that in the outer areas of metropolitan London, as in other emerging towns in the prosperous 17th century, "landowners were the vital pivot on which the course of urban development turned. An obstreperous owner could delay or even prevent improvement ... By contrast, an enthusiast would take a leading role in development." Though Summerson (2003, 23) explains certain constraints on these lands: "It must be remembered that most of the great London estates have been either entailed in a family or held in trust by a corporation. They could not, except under Act of Parliament, be sold, in whole or in part." As a result, although by a tortuous process of gaining permission they could sell the freehold to a developer, in accordance with the traditional reluctance to dispose of any family estate lands as well as the legislative hurdles, this was not the preferred option. It must be noted, though, that in lesser cities than London the eye of the court was less focused, some estates were sold to optimistic builders, and Nottingham, Hull, Portsmouth, Leeds, Leicester, and Brighton all evolved by this model.

Some of the estates to the west of the City were longtime holdings of ancient aristocratic families such as Essex, Montagu, and Arundel, while others had been granted to newly titled men with business backgrounds, such as the Earls of Bedford and Southampton. For all these landowners, the chance to benefit through the long term by retaining the lands involved a strategy of dividing the estate into smaller lots, building some houses for rent, or offering lots on long-term ground leases to residents or developers who were to construct their own buildings. Of the two choices, providing the ground lease for developers was the most common method by which they chose to participate in the growing London metropolis. It also enabled the family to maintain its duty to the governance of the local communities, which was widely regarded as important for the general stability of the country.

Given the potential long-term appreciation in the value of the land despite modest ground rents, the return on land ownership was probably less risky than that of the builder erecting the structures on the leased land. Providing a ground lease to a builder, skilled in undertaking the improvements and reliable for making the ground lease payments, if suitably priced, might have been the most beneficial strategy by a risk/return assessment. If further details could be uncovered on the performance of some of these developments, an empirical comparison of this strategy with other options might not only help understand the early development decisions but also present such alternatives for use in contemporary times.

The other possibility for a landowner in a vibrant urban location was to undertake the development activity himself. Though this course of action was not widespread, its emergence in 17th-century London was to be notable, influential, and provide the basis for the private urban development business. Historians of many aspects of this era of London's history have made related observations. In addition to Summerson's comments given earlier, Beckett (1986, 265) specifically attributed the contribution to those owning the lands: "Great landowners were heavily involved in London's development between the seventeenth and nineteenth centuries ..." They were also, though mostly during the following century, to significantly contribute to the development of provincial towns and seaside resorts. For example, an early "new town," Whitehaven, planned in 1680 by Sir John Lowther who laid down a grid pattern of streets, is still perceptible today.

From the outset, these aristocratic landowning developers showed an interest in strategically planning the site for their schemes, laying down the streets, creating infrastructure, providing amenities, and also establishing building requirements. The desire for the scheme to be as appealing and as efficient as their rural estates was not just based on an economic interest but also because its condition reflected upon their families. Pride, legacy, and local relationships were important considerations. Additionally, as McKellar (1999, 42) observed, "they found it easier to obtain a license from the Crown for building than those without connections at Court."

John Russell, 1st Earl of Bedford (1485–1555)

The Russell family began the foundation of their fortunes as merchants and traders. In 1487, William, who was to be the great-uncle of the 1st Earl of Bedford, obtained a license for exporting wool broadcloth from the port of Weymouth to Spain. His sons, Stephen and Henry, extended the burgeoning trade to France. As they amassed wealth, they also acquired country estates and the gentry status of squires. They solidly established courageous and entrepreneurial business activities for the Russell lineage, and they complemented their trading wealth through the traditional stability and status of real estate holdings.

A court presence also provided a significant advantage to the family. In 1506, John Russell (Figure 5.1) became a Member of the Privy Chamber to Henry VII and later to Henry VIII,

5.1

John Russell, 1st Earl of Bedford.

where he undoubtedly associated with the Exchequer, Thomas Cromwell, and later with Thomas Wriothesley who succeeded to that role. In his military service he was successful in various field battles, and was knighted in 1522 for bravery. In 1538, he was created Baron Russell, the first step on the aristocratic ladder, and later elevated to the high rank of Knight of the Garter. His inclusion in aristocratic circles was assured.

With Henry VIII's seizure of many ecclesiastical holdings in the area between the City of London's western wall and Westminster, in 1539 Russell was able to purchase the house of the former Bishop of Carlisle on the south side of the Strand. He established his family's town residence in this emerging area, which was convenient because of its proximity to

Westminster for his royal duties, and also valuable because it was on the main route to the vibrant commercial activity of the City.

Significantly, Henry directed that his lesser-titled, loyal and capable officials and advisors to be promoted to the level of nobles since he had felt "that the nobility of this realm was greatly decayed." Thus, after serving as an executor of Henry VIII's will, Russell was appointed to be the 1st Earl of Bedford and granted title to the former abbey and town of Tavistock. This advancement of acute businessmen to the aristocracy, together with their culmination of talents and perseverance, a substantial accumulation of land, and the circumstances affording social and economic mobility, was the primordial soup for the origins of the private real estate developer.

Russell then served as a Councilor in the minority of Edward VI, and purchased the estate of the former Woburn Abbey in Bedfordshire, which he made his official seat. He remained Lord Privy Seal until his death in 1555. The family lineage followed this 1st Earl of Bedford (Figure 5.2) through to an important merger over a century later of his estate with the valuable London lands of his court colleague Wriothesley.

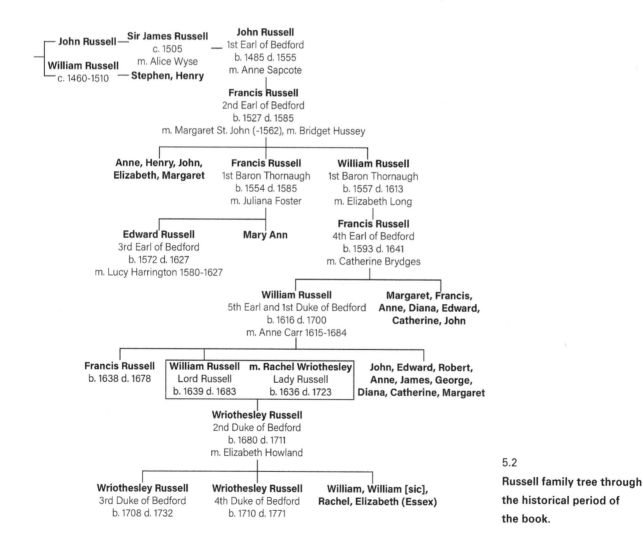

5.2

Russell family tree through the historical period of the book.

The Covent Garden Estate

In 1553, additionally for his service to Edward VI, he was granted the approximately 27-acre estate of Covent Garden which brought in a total rent estimated by Olsen (1982, 39) at £6 6s 8d. It was offered "to the sayd Earl and his heyres males ... to be held in soccage and not in capite," as recorded in the Minister's Accounts (Strype, 1720, book vi, 88). As an effective form of ownership within the tenure structures of the time, and with its inheritance included, this provided an important longevity of control.

Sheppard (1998, 173) established that by 1541 he had already obtained control by leasehold of some of this estate that remained undeveloped on the northern side of the increasingly important Strand thoroughfare. From his residence across the road, it is highly likely that he had monitored these holdings and, by this move, he employed the fundamental tenet of real estate, the importance of location, though he arrived there ahead of its popular embrace. Leveraging his leasehold, he was ready to acquire portions when they were to be sold by the King's Exchequer to raise revenues. During these years the Crown didn't formally put property on the market, and "the initiative in deciding what particular items were to be disposed of came from the prospective grantee" (Youings 1971, 118). By this strategic assemblage, Russell positioned himself to receive the large grant of the Covent Garden fields from an appreciative monarch.

Below are shown two maps for comparison of the Covent Garden grant to Bedford, with the first mapped on present-day streets (Figure 5.3). The second map by Agas in

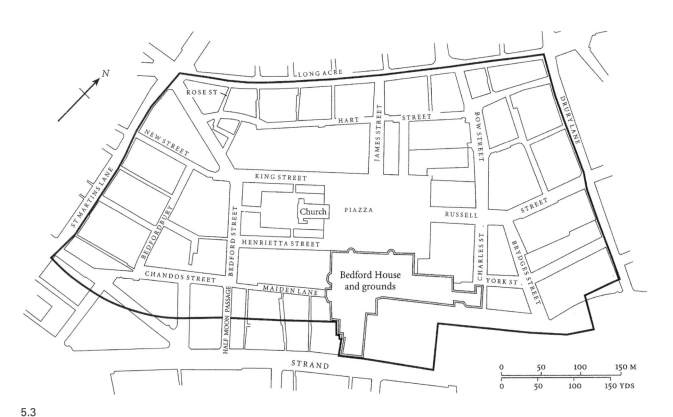

5.3

Map of Bedford's Covent Garden estate mapped on present-day streets.

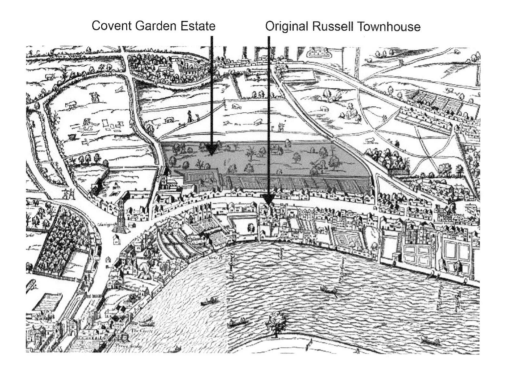

Covent Garden Estate   Original Russell Townhouse

5.4
**Covent Garden estate,
and probable location of
John Russell's town house
on the south side of the
Strand prior to the grant.**

1561 (Figure 5.4), which was close to the time of the acquisition, shows the direct routes to Westminster and St James's Palace to the left and the City to the right along the Strand.

The specific Covent Garden land, comprising approximately 20 acres of the total estate, lay in the center of the estate, and is recorded as being offered under a lease in 1559 for twenty-one years for rent of £1 16s. The other large portion, Long Acre field, in the northern region, was a 6-acre pasture bounding the street of that name. From the 14th century it was owned by the Mercers' Company and was leased to John Fortescue, who granted to the Mayor and Corporation of London an exceptionally long sublease of one hundred years, under which the City dug and broke ground, effectively using the site as a quarry (Chancellor 1930, 16). On its transfer to Russell, that activity ceased, though removal of the long subleases and associated activities would delay his control of its use for development.

Various historians have uncovered aspects of Covent Garden's complex early history. Chancellor (1930, 15) describes its origins as follows:

[T]his site was merely a garden attached to the Abbey of Westminster which owned ... the property. It seems probable that the produce of the ground was more than the Abbot and monks of Westminster were capable of consuming, and that the surplus was sold to the community at large.

Importantly for its future real estate development, the estate had substantial name recognition and was respectably endowed with historical significance.

As these lands were located just northeast of Henry VIII's new St James's Palace, the monarch was concerned with that part of Middlesex county lying between the cities of London

5.5

Location of Bedford's residence, as highlighted, between the Covent Garden estate and the Strand.

and Westminster. They were not only the source of his personal fresh water supply but also affected his physical milieu because of their potential to enhance or denigrate his new residences through local activities and appearances.

Also appreciative of the landscape and fields, Bedford relocated his London residence to the new estate (Figure 5.5). He selected the plot known as the Friars Pyes, which ran from the northern side of the Strand to the southern wall of the field of Covent Garden. This is approximately where Southampton Street enters the Strand today. In early 1553, he began construction of the house, which, though built of wood rather than masonry, was of good quality and, with various additions, survived 120 years to the early 18th century. Unfortunately, he enjoyed only a short period of residency there before his death late in 1555.

The 2nd Earl of Bedford

The Earl's son, Francis (1527–1585), succeeded to the title as 2nd Earl of Bedford and took his father's place in the House of Lords. Though imprisoned during Queen Mary's reign, he was released on Elizabeth I's ascendancy and appointed Privy Councilor. As London expanded under the latter's rule, he commenced his development activities at Covent Garden, though interestingly with a business associate involved, as continues to be the structure for many real estate investments. The Chancery Records (*Chancery Inquisitions post mortem*, ser.2, vol. 241, No. 126) reveal that on December 21, 1578 there was an agreement for the conveyance of the fee simple holding of two messuages and one tenement, leased to various occupants, to a partnership of the 2nd Earl of Bedford and Gilbert Littleton, of the gentry, of Worcester.

Bedford had four sons, but in living until the age of 58, he survived them all. On his death in 1585 the title skipped a generation and passed to Edward, the son of his third son, Francis. Chancellor (1930, 17) sees the family as by this time firmly established in this location in the area described in the parish rolls as "The Earl of Bedsford's [*sic*] – Covent Garden."

The 3rd Earl of Bedford

Despite his long tenure exceeding forty years, Edward (1572–1627), the 3rd Earl of Bedford, did not exhibit the financial acuity of his forebears, and it resulted in a deterioration of the family estates. However, he was married advantageously to Lucy Harrington, who came with an excellent dowry and extensive patronage of the arts. Part of Lucy's dowry was stock, held in her own right, in the Company of Adventurers and Planters of the City of London, which launched a settlement in Virginia in 1607, and also included as a founder John Wriothesley, 3rd Earl of Southampton, a descendant of the 1st Earl of Bedford's colleague in Henry's court. This was a second intersection of the two families that was to continue and be foundational to private development processes. Although the 3rd Earl's wife carried several pregnancies to full term, the infants did not survive and Edward died in 1627, leaving no issue.

Francis Russell, 4th Earl of Bedford (1593–1641)

In 1618, eight years prior to the 3rd Earl's death, his cousin Francis (1593–1641), son of the 2nd Earl's fourth son, William, had become the probable heir to the Bedford title. William himself, though as a fourth son and therefore of meager means, had distinguished himself in military service. He rose to serve as Lord Deputy in Ireland and also as an officer in the Low Countries (Netherlands) where he would also have known the 3rd Earl of Southampton. For his service, he had, upon the death of Elizabeth I, been made the 1st Baron Russell of Thornhaugh.

His second son, Francis (Figure 5.6), often accompanied him in his duties at court because the elder William was sickly and unable to be adequately groomed for succession. In 1613,

5.6

Francis Lord Russell of Thornbaugh, 4th Earl of Bedford, 1636.

just as he was about to achieve his majority, the young Francis inherited the baronetcy of Thornhaugh upon the tragic death of his father and brother, most likely from plague while on duty on the Continent. With his worldly experience, court training, and astute business acumen, though still second in line in the Bedford family to his cousin Edward, the 3rd Earl, and with careful deference to Edward's primacy in the peerage, Francis Russell effectively took responsibility for rescuing the Bedford holdings (Duggan 2001, 15).

Most crucially, before the death of Francis's father who was in favor with James I, the pair had petitioned to enjoin the irresponsible Edward from further alienating any of the entailed Bedford estates (Duggan 2001, 14). Astutely, they had him committed to large bonds and annuities that secured the extended family's rights to the landholdings. He was forced to undertake that "he could not sell his inheritance of Covent Garden, having bound himself under a heavy penalty [established by his family] not to impoverish further himself [and hence the family] by the sale of his property" (Russell 1610). Although the earl would live another dozen years until 1627, Francis had removed the rights to all the family estates from his control, and worked behind the scenes to improve the inheritance.

Additionally, in 1622, the 3rd Earl, probably with the direction of Francis, executed a short lease renewal on a small plot for the neighbors at Covent Garden, the Earl and Countess of Exeter, to allow them to walk in the Covent Garden pasture, probably entering through by way of the gateway in the northern boundary of their garden adjoining the eastern boundary of that of the Bedford's. Later, in 1627, the stables would be relocated from the rear of Bedford House to this edge of the Exeter Garden, thereby precluding their trespass, but allowing for and enabling the creation of a classical garden at Bedford House that would abut the southern side of the intended Covent Garden Piazza.

Francis married Katherine Brydges, the daughter of Lord Chandos of Sudeley. Instead of his main boyhood residence at Thornhaugh, he chose to make his home at Woburn Abbey. Duggan (2001) notes that such a choice was understandable since it was the most interesting historically of all the Russell properties. It had been inherited by Anne Sapcote, the 1st Countess of Bedford, heiress of the Cheney and Semark families that could be traced back to the time of the Norman invasion. Woburn, in what would become known as Bedfordshire, was also located closer to the court at Westminster and the family estate at Covent Garden in London.

There is an instructive story regarding leaseholds at Woburn. The 3rd Earl had leased the manor to Francis Randall and Thomas Cockayne, two of the trustees of the Bedford estate, and they attempted to sublease it to other parties, with probably a substantial profitable margin. Since this was in contravention of the lease terms, and although probably not noticed by Edward, his astute cousin Francis forced a reversion of the property to the family in 1619. In addition, extensive pastures of hundreds of acres of Woburn land had been leased to Edward Duncombe on a ninety-year lease, but Francis bought him out with a payment of £1,900. Though this was a considerable amount at the time, his action indicates a deep understanding of increasing the potential of land by active management rather than passive ground leases. This early strategic action of a lease buyout to produce a more valuable amalgamated property continues to be a popular device of developers to this day.

Dianne Duggan (2001) reports that by 1625, Francis had refurbished Woburn Abbey to a comfortable degree and moved there with his wife and eight children. It would be through his further renovations of this building that much of his architectural interest would be shared with the undertaking in Covent Garden. Though there is no evidence that Inigo Jones was directly engaged for this rural project, the influence of this notable architect is noted by John Summerson who sketched a façade and describes it as being "in the manner of Inigo Jones but early 1620s." Duggan says that this could be a reference to Jones's "Preliminary elevation for the east or west sides of the Queen's House, Greenwich," which was created for James I in 1616, and the importance of which Francis would have been very aware. She also suggests the actual designer may have been the surveyor Edward Carter or another water engineer, Isaac de Caus, both of whom were to work on the development at Covent Garden. There is evidence that Nicholas Stone was responsible for the house's statuary and masonry while he lived and worked at his workshop established on a Bedford plot on Long Acre adjacent to Covent Garden (Duggan 2001, 48–51). It would seem that the renovations of Woburn Abbey provided useful preliminary experience for this team of client, architect, surveyors, and stonemason that would next undertake the development of Covent Garden.

Development Activity Commences

In the early decades of the 17th century, the Covent Garden estate remained primarily as fields, gardens and orchards, and only two persons, namely the 3rd Earl of Bedford and a single tenant, John Barnard, were rated as residents in that part of St Giles parish. However, as the earl paid little attention to his tenancies, Barnard had granted a sublease to a builder, Edward Palmer, who erected "nine several Messuages or Tenements," without formal approval. These were typical of the buildings James I was attempting to restrict and would later be problematic for development approvals.

The remaining fields of Covent Garden proper buffered Bedford House and also Exeter House from the haphazard building occurring on Long Acre. Duggan (2001, 104) advances evidence that by the 1620s, Francis had been making preliminary moves to develop Covent Garden, focusing on these remaining central fields of approximately 20 acres. He undoubtedly noted the increasing demand by other peers for housing in the vicinity of these well-located holdings. To the west of Bedford House along St Martin's Lane, some mansions were being erected, causing Stow to observe (1956 [1598–1603], 290–291) "a continuall new building of divers fayre houses ... on the north side of a lane that turneth up to the parish church of St Martin's-in-the-Field." The houses of the grandest nobles were aligned along the Strand, and many landed gentry and wealthy merchants too sought new residences in this northern area, though the lack of available sites and a restriction on building provided them with little opportunity.

Appreciative of the delightful vegetation that had been cultivated for centuries in the orchards of Covent Garden, Francis eschewed the format of the merchant builders in erecting cheap tightly packed houses on narrow streets, and even Newton's better results in Great Queen Street and around Lincoln's Inn Fields. Plainly aware of the pleasant effect of open places for residences such as his own, he planned an open central garden for his new housing scheme. Such formations, called piazzas or places, had been created on the Continent during the Renaissance, and continued as a popular spatial typology. The difference was that these were created by the rulers and monarchs of wealthy kingdoms, such as Louis XIV and the Medicis, as part of their ruling public function. Because of English land ownership structures, to replicate it would have required either a complex conveyance of private space to the Crown or municipality, which would probably not want to bear the expense of maintaining such a non-productive area, or for a private landowner to provide it to the public; and Francis undertook the latter. He conceived of the idea of a central open area surrounded by prestigious residences.

An early plan of such a layout dated 1612 in the Bedford archives indicates that the family had been considering such a development even earlier than his attaining the title. The unattributed "Covent Garden ground plan" has the nomination of the titleholder, Earl of Bedford, which would have referred to the 3rd Earl, in the lower center and surrounded by typical heraldry and embellishment (Figure 5.7). Given that Francis was 19 years of age and largely managing the estate in the stead of the 3rd Earl at this time, it is probable that he, in conference with his father Baron Thornhaugh, directed the production of this plan, despite its official nomination.

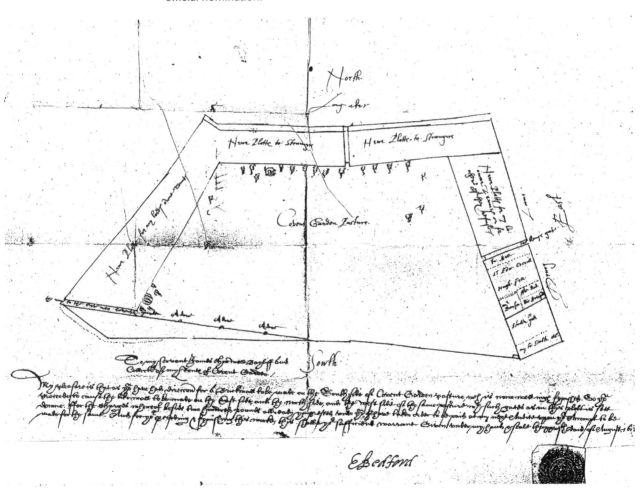

5.7

Early plan of proposed Covent Garden development, 1612.

Creatively, it presents a spatial arrangement that locates residences around three sides of a central open space, but without the strict geometry of a Continental piazza. On the fourth side, to the south, lay Bedford House and garden. In a curious detail, the wall between the development and the garden of Bedford House includes piers and/or drains, which might indicate some contribution by the hydraulic engineer/surveyor, de Casse, who was to work at Woburn soon after. Effectively the planned residences, together with the existing peer's house, formed an enclosure around the retained garden of the Covent Garden field.

Additionally notable on this plan, the involvement of other peers in its conception is indicated by their specific allocation as proposed residents of the housing scheme. Further historical research on particular connections between them and the 3rd Earl, the 1st Baron of Thornhaugh, or the young Francis Russell might indicate the extent of the respective parties' participation in this planning.

Overcoming Building Restrictions

Despite the strategic thinking and desirable urban features of the 1612 plan, there seems to have been little recorded activity towards implementation. In response to the 1614 plague which had taken his father and elder brother, many of the aristocracy abandoned infested London for the relative isolation and safety of their country homes. With the resurgence of plague to an even worse degree in 1624–1625, the demand for housing in growing London was diminished by loss of lives and the reluctance to reside there unless absolutely necessary.

As discussed earlier, James I continued to reinforce Elizabeth's building constraints with further Proclamations. Despite his economic ambitions at Covent Garden, Francis Russell was suitably deferential to royal decrees and, as Duggan (2001, 110) notes, he retained among his papers the printed copies of the 1615 and 1618 Proclamations and remained sufficiently concerned to record in one of his commonplace books a parliamentary discussion on January 27, 1618 concerning transgressions of these laws.

Though no official record is available, it is said that a first application for the development project was rejected by the Privy Council which adamantly opposed such a scale of building. Undeterred, educated, and cultured, however, Francis was aware of the rising interest of the monarch in the aesthetics of the built environment and an enthusiasm for improving London. Further, the Stuart court embraced the patrimonial style of governance of the Tudors and applied its prestige to breach tradition, as Appleby (1978, 30) saw it: "The king's approval justifies the novelty." As a result, James moved building legislation away from outright restriction to regulation more definitive of materials and architectural quality and, to envision the possibilities of a grander aesthetic purpose and implement this new approach, he had appointed the Royal Surveyor, Inigo Jones.

Architect for Covent Garden

Though James I died in 1625, just as Jones was creating the new aesthetic for London, his heir, Charles I, was even more enthusiastic in embracing the architectural sophistication of Continental Europe, and when, within a couple of years, Francis became the 4th Earl of Bedford, he was probably emboldened in his aspirations for the residential development of Covent Garden. Although there is no surviving record or signed drawing as evidence,

Duggan (2001, 111) refers to many of his documents, newly found, to postulate confidently that Bedford engaged Jones to plan the layout of the scheme and design the major buildings surrounding the central area, now designated as a "piazza." She reports that the Covent Garden project is mentioned by Jones in a contemporary notation he added to his copy of Barbaro's *Vitruvius*, the bible of neoclassical architecture. Summerson (2000, 75) too argues that Jones's role as the King's Surveyor and executive officer of the Commission on Buildings by which the "principle that [he] should exercise control would clearly apply" and he therefore might be the author of the design, not merely serving to approve it.

Although Summerson (2000, 77) also claims that "the employment of Jones was, in effect, a condition imposed on the [building] licensee," Bedford's understanding of court politics would in any case have led him to work directly with Jones, particularly as he knew of his design for Newton's houses in Great Queen Street. Accordingly, rather than being an imposition, the architect's involvement was essential to working through the constraints in order to optimize the economic conditions for the project. This close engagement of the public authority in conceiving of a development design that would be approved thus became firmly embedded within the emerging model of private urban development, and maintenance of a favorable relationship with the municipal authorities continues to be relevant to the success and smooth progress of a development.

Plan of Covent Garden

The Public Piazza

The design concept for Covent Garden is probably most authoritatively sourced from the prominent architectural critic of the late 17th century, John Evelyn. When he arrived at Leghorn in 1644, he recorded in his diary (1906, i, 139), "the piazza is very fair and commodious and, with the church, whose four columns at the portico are of black marble polished, gave the first hint to the building both of the church and piazza in Covent Garden with us, though very imperfectly pursued." As discussed earlier, Jones's education in architecture had included two visits to Italy, and specifically to Tuscany and Medici's magnificent Piazza Grande (Figure 5.8), created to transform Leghorn into a thriving international seaport.

5.8
Piazza Grande, Leghorn, c. 1800.

This extensive and impressive new urban typology, with grand neoclassical elements built by royal funding and design control, was influential throughout much of Continental Europe as the Renaissance and economic prosperity spread. Summerson (2000, 78) suggests a further linkage of influence: Ferdinando's niece, Marie, now Queen of Henri IV of France, may have been a factor in Henri's initiative in 1605 in building the Place Royale in Paris as a similar spacious public square surrounded by uniform buildings, and "Jones will have subsequently seen [it] in progress in 1609, [and it particularly] has a distinct bearing on Covent Garden."

The Place Royale, now Place des Vosges (Figure 5.9), is generally regarded as having been built as residences for French nobility, and the historian of Henri IV, Hilary Ballon (1991, 57), notes from the reportage of Lambeau (1902–36) and Dumolin (1925–26) "prominent noblemen lived at the square during the seventeenth century," and that contemporaneous situation probably suggested the use to Jones. However, regarding the arcaded lower levels

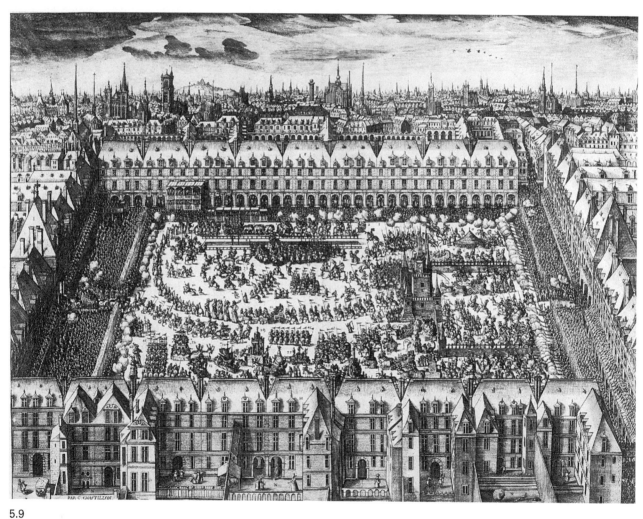

5.9

Place Royale or Place des Vosges, Paris, 1612.

of the surrounding buildings that Jones adopted for Covent Garden, such residential use was not its original intention of the Parisian design. From archival material, Ballon (1991, 58–59) discovered that "[t]he Place Royale was conceived not as an aristocratic residential square, but as a commercial square, the centrepiece of a royal campaign to stimulate French manufacturing." She maintains that when the construction of the square was announced in July 1605 it was intended that the arcaded pavilions were "intended for commercial and residential use by artisans and merchants with ground floor shops" and this commercial use of arcades was derived from the nature of medieval market squares such as that in the Pont Notre-Dame.

Additional intended uses for the Place Royale included an open public recreational area, and an area for court ceremonies and popular celebrations. In respect of this Ballon (1991, 69) surmises that "the Crown was lending its prestige to commerce, not unlike King James I was to do for the private development of Covent Garden a couple of decades later." By 1607, the commercial function of the Place Royale ceased and on the northern side the pavilion was replaced by grand free-standing residences, and other pavilions were remodeled as residences for the nobility. It was this new use as a residential neighborhood that was adopted for Covent Garden.

The economic structure by which the Place Royale was created also introduced a stage in the transformation of the Italian piazza to the London urban square. Whereas piazzas, including their surrounding buildings, such as at Vigevano and Leghorn, had been built for and continued to be owned by the very wealthy Italian nobility, by way of distinction the French kings, though owning the land, undertook urban development schemes (*lotissements*) not only to control the urban typography but additionally to raise revenues from the residents. Henri's innovation was to avoid the usual fully built-out grid of streets of medieval towns and create an open public place that was to remain Crown land. But for the surrounding buildings he had insufficient resources to construct the building himself. Ballon (1991, 70–71) reports that according to the royal edict of July 1605 he "leased the lots ... around the said square ... to those who offered to build according to our design" and that the required design details were very explicit in terms of the layout of the arcades, the materials, and the architectural symmetry. By this combination of public contribution of open space and distributed development rights, Henri was able to be a beneficent monarch while having substantial building done without a significant depletion of the royal treasury.

Although the development at Covent Garden advanced to being a completely private project, in accordance with Charles's wishes regarding urban topography, Inigo Jones integrated the influences of the Vitruvian form of the Leghorn Piazza and that of the Place Royale's functional program to envision a layout of rectangular open space presided over by the parish church and the arcaded pavilions providing entrances to the grand residences. Summerson (1991a, 124) gives credit to Bedford that he constructed "London's first formal open space and lined it on two sides (north and east) with buildings of strictly uniform and classical character." Bedford was to retain ownership of all the land, build some residences to plan, and then provide leases for the construction of other residences. Together, they were able to maintain the desired architectural uniformity by using Jones's detailed specifications and strict building requirements as conditions of the ground leases. Further, it would have been beneficial that the queen of Charles was Henrietta Maria, daughter of Queen Marie of France, because Bedford and Jones prepared the petition for royal approval with a grand and aesthetically controlled urban contribution which would have substantial similarities to the Place Royale.

Impressively, the Covent Garden project sought to replicate the grand urban visions of the Continental sovereigns, and although it directly engaged the monarch in determining urban form, it did so without royal resources, for it was a private undertaking that predicated financial viability. It marks the birth of private development in delivering to that objective: that private capitalist enterprise could also provide benefits for the public in a number of ways, even across different social levels, was a new approach to urban development.

Though there are no historical records of design concepts to indicate Jones's progress in the site layout, it did make reference to the early intent of Bedford's 1612 schematic plan, with housing surrounding a central open space. From the anonymous freehand survey carried out between 1627 and 1629 (Figure 5.10), it may be assumed that Jones directed that the central space be of a more regular geometry, in this case a rectangle typical for a piazza. The residential blocks were also distributed more broadly beyond the piazza. The larger estate was suitably broken up by streets to provide lots with a practical depth of approximately 200 ft, allowing for necessary domestic outbuildings and rear access typical of a town house of the time.

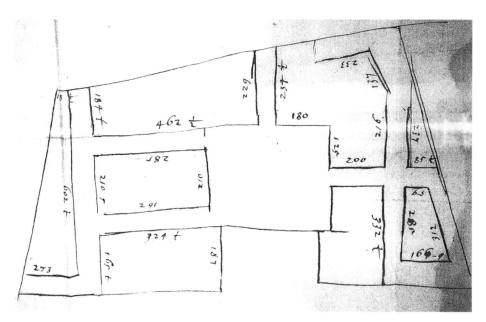

5.10
Survey ground plan Covent Garden, c. 1627–1629.

This layout of the site was later more formally presented and drawn in ink by the surveyor and project manager employed by Bedford, Isaac de Caus (Figure 5.11). This site plan was probably close to that submitted for the development's approval.

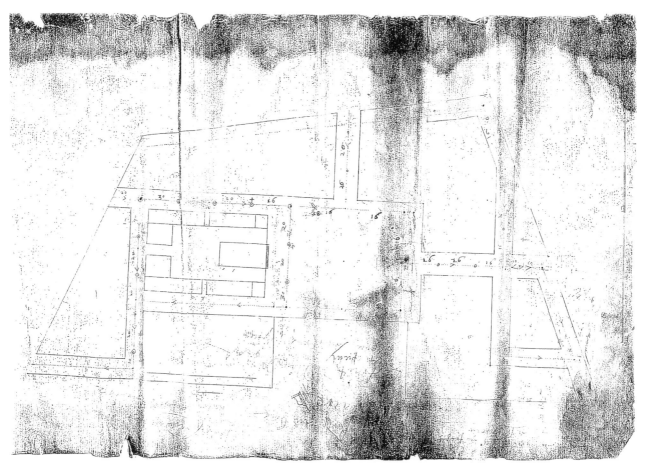

5.11
Annotated survey ground plan Covent Garden by Isaac de Caus, c. 1627–1629.

Strype (1720, Book VI, 87) describes the specifics of the development in the following terms:

About the Centre of the Ground, he caused to be set out a large square or rather oblong piece of ground, 500 foot in Length and 400 foot in Breadth, and into this Plot of ground, four large Streets of about 50 or 60 Foot Broad, have their Entrance, viz. Russell Street on the West, James Street on the North, King's Street and Henrietta Street on the East, and the South Side is taken up by the Wall of Bedford Garden.

It was this expansive open space within a collection of residences that was so novel in crowded London and readily attracted potential inhabitants. Even in historical fiction, an example is provided in George Tavener, a wealthy merchant, who

had bought the lease, only two days ago, of the house in Covent Garden, away from the foul air and dirty streets of the city. Mirjam [his wife] could walk the pleasant square and wide streets and gardens around the piazza. She would be surrounded by people of quality, and not look out any more on the poverty and squalor, taste the bad water, of the city, for it was that he had been assured by more than one physician, that prevented her from conceiving the child they both longed for. (Maclean 2015, 154–155)

Further Public Amenities to "Sweeten" the Deal

Although the beautifully designed project found the approval of King Charles, there remained an extensive objection to new building around London that led to a complex issue for the municipal leaders. The vibrancy of the Stuart court produced a discernible trend that required aristocrats to attend regularly at court, but they wished to avoid the unhealthy, crowded, and dirty conditions of the City and to locate in the salubrious emerging suburbs to the west. The parish in western Middlesex where Bedford's land was located was the old, rural and formerly small diocese of St Martin-in-the-Fields (Figure 5.12), but its virtues were attracting parishioners beyond its capacity. Despite the building restrictions of the court and City, its population had trebled within the first decades of the 17th century.

In critical need, in 1627 the parish leaders petitioned the king to procure a site in the neighborhood on which to build a new church. However, as Duggan (2001, 86) reports, as early as 1626, even before he succeeded to the title, the 4th Earl had been approached by

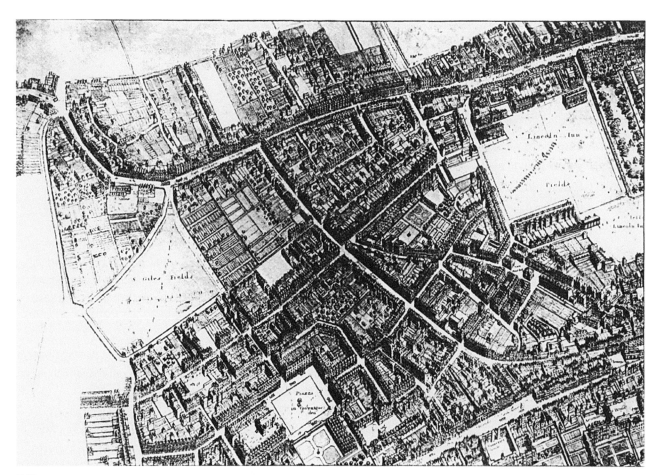

5.12

West-central London, c. 1658–1660.

neighboring residents with the request to "donate" a plot of land for "a chapel of ease" to relieve the overcrowding of the church of St Martin-in-the-Fields. Probably during 1628, seeing an opportunity to make his development proposal more attractive to the authorities and the community, Bedford approached the Bishop of London, William Laud, since St Martin-in-the-Fields, though not geographically a parish of the City, was under his jurisdiction. Their discussions included St Martin's incumbent pastor Dr. Muntford, and dealt with the feasibility of locating an additional chapel within Bedford's Covent Garden estate.

The importance of this action of public contribution in cognizance of a public need cannot be understated. As Duggan (2001, 112–113) has pointed out, a document dated May 3, 1629 was discovered, specifically highlighting the extent of the need for the new church and the benevolence of Bedford in providing for it. It stated that the church leaders

> foreseeing the mischeife that may ensue [from the overcrowding in the parish,] have desired from our right trustee the welbeloved Cosen ffrancis Earle of Bedford soe much grounde parcell of his feilde called Covent Garden … as might serve for the building of a small church or a chappell of ease.

As a further identification with the Medici's piazza at Leghorn, Jones placed the proposed church at the end of the long axis of the open space. The eastern end was not suitable since an important access to the piazza, Russell Street, was in formation with its extension through a further block to meet Drury Lane, the major north–south route to the Strand. Though this resulted in the altar being at the eastern end of the church, between the two entry doors, it complied with the ritual of the Church of England, and this western location was more convenient to the underserved growing population of St Martin-in-the-Fields.

Becoming aware of the growing costs of his Covent Garden project, Bedford indicated to Jones that he desired the design of only a modest church. As Summerson (2000, 80) recounts the prime minister, Horace Walpole, saying to Mr. Speaker Onslow:

> When the Earl of Bedford sent for Inigo he told him he wanted a chapel for the parishioners of Covent Garden, but added he would not go to any considerable expenses; 'In short,' said he, 'I would not have it much better than a barn.' 'Well! Then,' said Jones, 'You shall have the handsomest barn in England.'

Whether or not he was driven to deliver on his wry response, Jones designed the church in a simple Tuscan order, just as he had adopted for the small buildings at the Royal Lodge at Newmarket. In his doing this, historians such as Summerson who cast a detailed eye on the work, saw a deliberate use of this most primitive of the five classical orders of architecture, almost regarded as an unsophisticated vernacular style. Not recognized by some of the Italian masters of neoclassicism such as Alberti, and relegated to buildings of low importance by Vitruvius and Serlio, Palladio's application of the order for rural buildings might have recommended it to Jones as suitable for the English gentry who were relatively new to major urban buildings. Summerson (2000, 80) surmises that "[a]s such it would have classical dignity at the vernacular level: it would be the 'handsomest barn' of the anecdote."

The historian of the Russell family, Gladys Scott Thomson (1940), has suggested that such a simple design reflected the character of that "puritanically inclined grandee," the 4th Earl of Bedford. However, while admitting to those more Protestant leanings, Duggan (2001) disputes this classification, indicating that the earl could not have exerted so much influence on Jones for such a public building. Furthermore, the design bore a relationship with the newly (1627) completed Park Gate at St James's Palace, of which Charles, most definitely not Protestant in his religion or taste, was so proud.

On the other hand, Summerson (2000, 126) insinuates that the Protestant context of England at the time did influence Jones's choice of this style. He wrote,

> St Paul's was, after all, the first wholly new church to be raised in London since the Reformation. Much more than Catholic chapels for princesses, it had to harmonize style and purpose. The Vitruvian Tuscan was the furthest an architect could reach to the 'natural' beginnings of architecture, unalloyed by association with the corrupt mutations of the Roman church.

Irrespective of these possible symbolic uses, the adoption of the progressive movement in architecture of the Continent and the rigorous and exemplary application of the neoclassical order was an important advancement for English building form, and also an accomplishment for the new private mode of development of public structures. Its utilization for an entrepreneurial speculative development, which was not only intent on economic feasibility but also demonstrated its intent to balance and yet satisfy the variants in public taste and social symbolism, was a significant foundational feature of the emerging business model. Its breadth of objectives that included concerns across all social levels, and pushed both capital and architectural form to these ends, as well as meeting their own new and compelling aims, was exemplary.

As shown by the front elevation of the proposed Covent Garden church (Figure 5.13), Jones designed an elegant and beautiful building of which the earl and new parishioners were to be proud. As well, Lees-Milne (1953, 85–86) records that it was very much appreciated by the cultivated and influential group surrounding Lord Burlington who "considered it one of the few buildings produced by the moderns to bear comparison with the works of

5.13
St Paul's Covent Garden, front elevation.

the ancients." These students of the classics noted the perfect application Vitruvius's Golden Mean, or Golden Ratio, a rigorous classical geometric order related to natural beauty that was recognized in classical Greek architecture. They noted that, as an example of that stricture, the height of the Tuscan columns was classically one-third the width of the temple, their base thickness was one-seventh of the height, and the thickness at the top was three-quarters of that at the bottom. The columns of the inner rows are correctly wider than the outer ones, and the eaves of the pediment are measured to be, again classically, one-third the length of the roof. In summary, Lees-Milne (1953, 86) applauded the disciplined, fine classicism of Jones's building, stating that "his every dimension was a proper interpretation of the module," and in comparison he noted that "St Paul's church is the first building in England to have a classical portico with detached columns." Even a century later, in 1734, the architectural critic, James Ralph, described the St Paul's church as "without a rival, one of the most perfect pieces of architecture that the art of man can produce" (Lees-Milne 1953, 78).

The siting of this architectural masterpiece was very aesthetically strategic for Jones. Following the spatial topography of the Italian piazzas, he placed it such that it presided with importance at the end of the longitudinal axis. In Hollar's etching (Figure 5.14) there is a general impression that the church is located at the head of the piazza, but Downs (1967, 8) has pointed out the inaccuracies of that depiction in its longer north–south dimension of the piazza rather than the true elongated east–west format. Importantly for the best economic

5.14
Covent Garden piazza looking directly at St Paul's church.

performance of the project, the private residences were placed along the lengthy northern boundary, so that they captured the ambient southern light.

Bedford committed to paying £3,000 for the construction of the original building, though records indicate that it proved to be more expensive than he anticipated, with its final costs reported to be approaching £4,500 (Chancellor 2012, i, 176). (It seems that significantly underestimating costs was a flaw in even the earliest urban development.) Sadly, the original church was gutted by fire in 1795. Although it had been insured for £10,000 which would have substantially assisted in funding its rebuilding, the insurance policy had lapsed during the prior year. For the Bedford estate it was an expensive lesson that continues to this day.

Despite the lapse of the insurance, the church continued to be a critical amenity for the neighborhood, and it was rebuilt. In the rebuilding, the exterior was faithfully restored by the architect Thomas Hardwick, though the interior was remodeled into what Summerson (2000, 89) describes as "a neat but uninteresting Georgian box." A further restoration in Victorian times replaced the sides and rear with red brick, removing Hardwick's Portland stone that had replaced Jones's stucco finish. Also removed were the north and south walls of the portico, leaving it now open on three sides rather than just at the grand front steps (Figure 5.15). Unfortunately, the ground level has risen over the centuries to be almost level with the plinth, which diminishes the church's aboveground height.

The church's crucial role in achieving the project's approval is underscored by Duggan's (2001) recently uncovered documents concerning a Royal Warrant, dated May 3, 1629, from Bishop Laud and Dr. Muntford. After noting the urgent need, those influential prelates detailed Bedford's contribution of land and £3,000 for building costs for a new parish church and stated that, in connection with this contribution, the earl has sought their "leave and licence to build the residue of the said feild [*sic*] called Covent Garden with uniforme houses and buildings according to the forme and propor[ti]on in our said proclama[ti]on

5.15
St Paul's church, 1638.

expressed" (Alnwick archives 2, B1, E2). From a later paragraph of this document, she notes the statement that it is "our will and pleasure, that in the said building plattforme contrived by the Surveyor of our Works and presented unto us to be observed as farre forth as maybee." In this statement, the "plattforme" is the platt or plan, and it was "contrived" or designed by the Surveyor of Works, that being Inigo Jones, and it was approved as being excellent or "as farre forth as maybee." Thus Jones is identified as the author of the plan, and the church, through its officeholder, is recorded as being involved in the official approval of the design.

Now, armed with this well-regarded design which offered the king an open piazza in the Continental mode and the community a new parish church, the 4th Earl of Bedford received Letters Patent approving his scheme. Although it has long been thought that this occurred in 1630/1631, Duggan's research referred to above implies that no later than May 1629, "its conception has been clarified" (2001, 113).

This ambitious new residential precinct was ideally located, architecturally inspiring, and at the heart of a new suburban parish, as shown in a later rendering in 1722 (Figure 5.16).

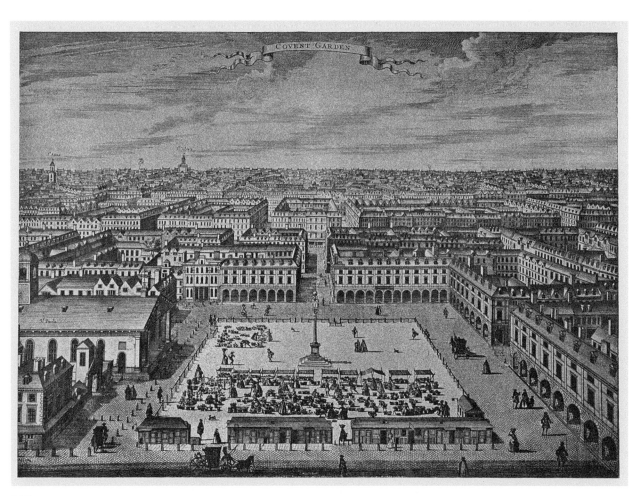

5.16
View of Covent Garden looking north, c. 1720.

It was an example where the developer produced a built environment that was well recognized for its aesthetic quality and yet also created a successful investment. The restraint of Jones with respect to the materials should not be underestimated: while he was erecting royal buildings in Portland stone, here he was pragmatic in achieving his design goals. For the church he used stone only for the columns with the walls being of brick covered with stucco which, not only being true to the original Tuscan structures, also "was more *economical* than solid stone construction" (Downs 1967, 13). Similarly for the residential buildings, rather than adorn the façade with Doric columns, Jones was able to use less expensive pilasters to achieve the effect of the classical order.

The Residential Buildings

To establish an influential example of a new urban residential form that would achieve the "Uniformitie and Decency" required by the king's Proclamation, Jones gave the designs for the residential buildings bordering the piazza considerable attention. Another motive was that it would be through the leasing of them that Bedford received a commercial return on his capital outlay, and the product's quality and appeal for his intended market would have been of critical economic concern. These buildings are not particularly notable architecturally, with the critic Summerson (2000, 86) saying: "[I]t is puzzling at first to find the main source for the houses in one of Serlio's rather naive woodcuts." But Jones referred to Serlio for "Una habitatione per far dentro alla Citta in luogo nobile," that is, a grand townhouse that would suit the intended occupants. To further conform with English taste, and probably also contain costs, he adapted the Continental design by replacing the ornate Ionic columns on pedestals with simple, and less expensive, pilasters which adjoined the eaves cornice with a form of Tuscan *mutules* or bracket. The resultant design was ideal for the new prestigious neighborhood, and the astute modification of the typically civic neoclassical style for these residential buildings was a precursor to the Georgian style that was to be exceedingly popular well into the future.

The colonnaded arcade feature, which Jones adopted from the Continental piazza format for the ground floor and entrances to the residences, was also a new architectural feature for England. Although generally arcades were used in commercial, almost civic, buildings, Jones employed their visual cohesion for the street frontage, and he recessed the entries to the houses within them. Although the colonnaded residential buildings have been demolished, an original remnant (Figure 5.17) is preserved on the lower storey of Bedford Chambers, built in 1880 on the north side of the piazza when extensive repairs and restorations were made to the Covent Garden precinct.

Above the arcade, he then pulled each house to its lot's front line, where it rose three storeys, and aligned windows and pilasters provided an elegant and relatively simple neoclassical façade (Figure 5.18).

Because of this covered entrance to the houses, the buildings were called the Portico Buildings in the building records of the time (Summerson 1964, 178). The colonnaded arcade was occasionally called "portico rooms," which the Italians termed loggia. Various plans ascribe the term "piazza" to these arcades rather than to the central open area but Summerson (2000, 40) is emphatic that such a term is incorrect. Presenting various depictions of the project in the quarter-centenary exhibition of Jones's work in 1973 at the Whitehall Banqueting Hall, the catalogue's authors, John Harris et al. (1973, 185–186), note that "the nobility and

5.17

Doorway arch from the colonnaded arcade of the Portico.

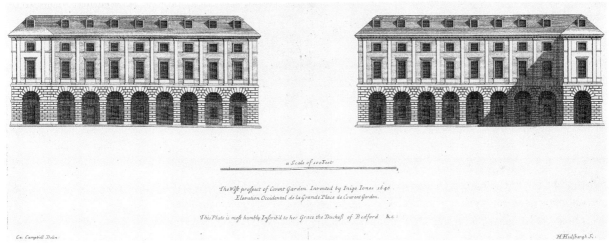

The West prospect of Covent Garden Invented by Inigo Jones 1640
Elevation Occidental de la Grande Place de Covent Garden.

This Plate is most humbly Inscrib'd to her Grace the Dutchess of Bedford &c

5.18

Elevation of the Portico Buildings.

gravity of his portico is at once apparent. It is no less neoclassical than any other archaeological reconstructions after 1760, and it would seem that in Europe only Jones could have done this at the time" (Figure 5.19).

An historian of urban life in the Stuart era, Chancellor, described the manner in which the colonnaded arcade was to be used by its occupants: "The space in front of these houses and the others adjoining was then known as the Portico Walk; and the lease gives the ground-landlord power to walk underneath the same messuage, commonly called the Portico Walk." It seems that it fell to the tenant to maintain the condition and security of this zone between the public piazza and the private dwellings (Figure 5.20), for Chancellor (1930, 40) reports that "Sir Edmund Verney [tenant of 2 houses] was to exercise the right of expelling youths who might disturb him

5.19

Portico Buildings in Covent Garden looking north, c. 1720.

5.20

Portico arcade, c. 1768.

by playing there." This conflict in the right to occupy versus the responsibility for maintenance of such transitional public–private spaces continues to be generally unresolved today.

By means of this arcade, Jones structurally and visually combined several residences into a large single building. This arrangement, rather than individually defined houses, had been employed throughout the Continent for a number of reasons. First, with the rise of the middle class in Renaissance times there was a need for good quality housing which was to be prestigious though not as expensive as the grand palaces of the ruling class. To enable these smaller units to have a grander appearance, a practice was adopted of combining them into an integrated building frontage that provided a more impressive massing and façade. This technique in the form of integrated cornices and parapets was further applied to even smaller row houses that were built in London at this time.

Jones planned for these arcaded residences to abut the piazza, except in the west where the church would stand, and in the south where the garden of Bedford House met the open space. There has arisen a misconception that he had planned for it to be surrounded on all sides with arcaded residences, much as shown in the 1720 drawing (Figure 5.20). However, Duggan (2001) and Downs (1967) both provide strong arguments that the church was integral to his original plans for the piazza.

An important commentator, and later a patron of urban development, at the time, Roger North (1981 [c. 1700s], 129–130), did not view the open colonnades so favorably, noting they were not "generally recommendable to us, because the same reasons doe not occur here, as in Italy, the climats being so vastly different with respect to weather ... the raines and snows are not so furious, frequent, and driving as here [in England]; nor is the heat so furious."

Although the colonnade was to disappear from use in residential buildings, Jones's integrated design of the façade across a number of houses was to influence the building of grand crescents and residential neighborhoods by developers in the following Georgian times. Even closer to the project in time, the noted aesthete of the second half of the 17th century, John Evelyn (1995c, 343), praised it in his instructions for rebuilding after the Great Fire, suggesting that new buildings "should exactly respect uniformity" as did those of Covent Garden.

Jones proved very adept in achieving the innovative architectural design of these residential buildings while taking into account Bedford's economic constraints. But it should be noted that this duality of objectives was not introduced by the private developer. Jones had formerly experienced significant challenges with economic constraints in his work for the monarch. He had been asked to design new buildings for the Star Chamber, but because of the lack of available funds James could not undertake the project. On another occasion, his design for the Banqueting Hall had been much more extensive but only a section, comprising the surviving building, could be afforded. So, he was able to adapt well to Bedford's specified budget limitations and only the church is reported to have exceeded it.

Model Houses

As this residential design was new in both internal configuration and façade appearance, it challenged the usual economic dynamic for house building. Under the existing general system, typically a prospective resident would select a site, commit to a house lease, and a builder would undertake the construction; or a speculative builder would construct the shell on a site and then secure a tenant before completing the interior. In both cases, the design would be traditional and the tenant would know from existing examples what could be anticipated, while the experienced builder could very closely estimate the cost by which the rent would be set. As the proposed plans for Covent Garden comprised unfamiliar designs for the residences, the two determinations essential to the transaction prior to construction, the nature of the product to be delivered, and the cost that would be amortized by rent, were unknown. Neither resident nor builder was sufficiently informed to proceed confidently.

As a further indication of Bedford's business acumen, in order to display the new houses fully to potential residents and to entice them with their well-designed features, he funded the construction of three model houses prior to any tenant commitments. While achieving a uniform frontage, variations were offered at the rear for access and service activities. Further, although the structure was expressed to be a single storey on the façade, the amended interior plans allowed for the first floor above the ground level to be divided to allow for a mezzanine floor. If structured this way, the residence contained two layers above ground level, each of 11 ft in height, thereby increasing the useful internal square footage and one of the models displayed this arrangement. Whether Bedford was inspired to produce these models by the practice of trading mercers in displaying their sample cloth, or other contemporary business practices, is not known. There are references to some master builders' use of untenanted houses to encourage prospective tenants, but this more explicit presentation was sound marketing, and the notion of a model unit by which to best present innovative design became part of the development process.

Because construction drawings were usually lacking in detail since tradesmen were already skilled in the details of execution of vernacular features, Bedford also was able to use his model houses to provide instruction to the builders and tradesmen who were to replicate this design throughout the Portico residences. Although it is fairly certain that he funded all the demised buildings for first several tenants, many of the rest were accomplished through a direct transaction between builder and resident. Irrespective of that financial arrangement, however, the project would have involved numerous builders and tradesmen, not a consistent entity or crew as occurs today, and this required an effective dissemination of building instructions. The model houses also served this purpose conveniently on site.

In meeting his obligation to conform to the design and aesthetic requirements of Jones's plans across the whole scheme, Bedford also used these model houses to set the standard against which other buildings on the site would be measured and approved for construction. Even if he were not to be involved in the building of a residence, he could include in the Articles of Agreement of the ground lease a condition that used these models as a reference to specify the details of the house which could be built on the site so that it must "observe and conforme his to those alreadie built on the East parte ... by the said Earle" (Duggan 2001, 119). By this method, and by having surveyors check the work during construction and ensuring that the standard of the models was met, he established a system of monitoring the project by way of quality control for the innovative design. Managing the execution of a large project became an important part of the development process, not only in meeting legislative requirements but also in maintaining the level of quality throughout (Figure 5.21).

5.21
Covent Garden piazza and residential buildings before 1666–1667.

Market-oriented Housing Product

In comparison with the traditional manner by which aristocrats, gentry, and the wealthy took a ground lease and paid a builder to construct their townhouse of vernacular design, Bedford's approach in pre-building residences for such potential tenants was unusual and probably considered extremely risky, but he undertook it with a solid estimate of demand and successful sales. This fabrication of a product in advance of identification of the specific end-user was an innovative feature of the forming speculative development model.

With notable business acumen, he mitigated these risks in various ways. Amongst the folios recently uncovered by Duggan (2001, 114) are lists of prospective lessees who were grouped around the piazza according to their respective allocated areas. The lists change from the original arrangement (Figure 5.7) and the measurements of some frontages are enlarged for the final design, but the continuing allocation of each proposed residence to a specific tenant indicated an attention to accomplishing full occupancy upon completion. Although he may not have finalized leases with them in the same way that developers today may attempt to do by means of pre-leases, he would not have allocated residences without some knowledge of the prospective lessees' interest and financial capacity. In this procedure, he was performing a critical pre-development activity, that is, understanding the future end-users' specific physical requirements of space and finishes, and their financial capacity, in order to deliver a satisfactory product at the affordable price level. As the list of prospective lessees became more resolved, the names listed can be compared with those of the eventual residents on leases executed between 1631 and 1637 (*Survey of London* Vol 33, 294–311), and many remained committed to the project.

Put in charge of tracking the spatial position and preparation for construction of these nominated residences was no less than Inigo Jones himself, or at least his direct supervision was required. Duggan (2001) notes the architect's handwriting of "Convent [*sic*] garden" and the date of "1629" (Figure 5.22) on the work orders (Figure 5.23) related to that schedule of residence in a document endorsed "The contents of the surveyors plott."

To understand the spatial references on this schedule, Duggan suggests that these surveyor's measurements be viewed in conjunction with an explanatory plan she provides (Figure 5.24).

The exercise reveals the very detailed and strategic approach to the layout of private urban land and the transactions to specific residents that became key concerns in the process of development. Initially, as shown in Figure 5.24, the piazza was divided into the "Great Piazza" on the northside of Russell Street and the "Little Piazza" on the southside. Though the reason is not explicitly known, and while this locational distinction was commonly used in recorded lists of leases and lease documents, for Bedford it may have served as a loose marketing strategy, with the more intimate and smaller residences located in the Little Piazza and the grander ones fronting the Great Piazza. To launch the project with prestige, he took care to place the most socially prominent tenants in the arcaded residential buildings to the north and east of the piazza with the Great Piazza Leases #1–19.

Appearing for the first time in the parish rate lists in 1632 as residing in "new built" structures were twenty ratepayers, who paid a modest rent of 4s 4d per annum. This group

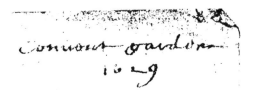

5.22
Detail of endorsement "Convent Garden 1629" on survey document.

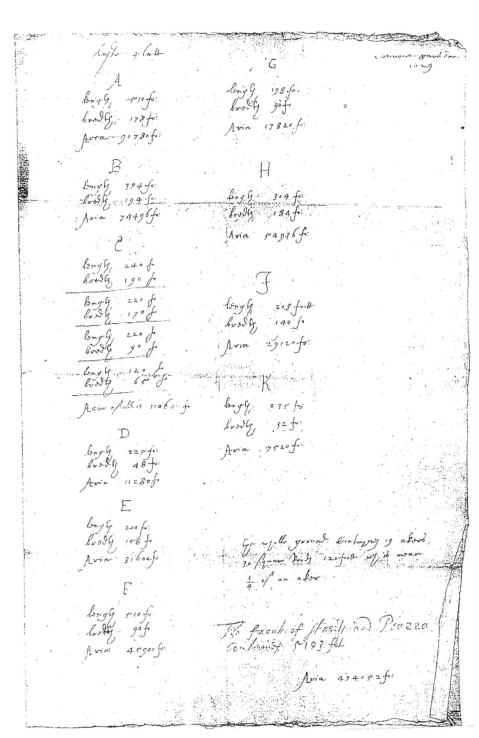

5.23
The contents of the surveyor's "plot" of the scheme showing ten lease subdivisions giving length and breadth, and total square footage of each, as tabulated by Inigo Jones, 1629.

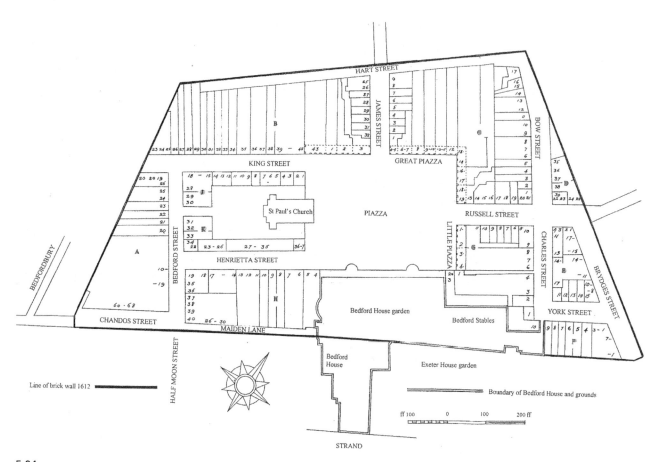

5.24

Duggan's explanatory plan of the Covent Garden project.

comprised seventeen men and three widows, and five others were located somewhere on the piazza. They included Sir Edmund Verney, who took up a double-frontage site, and his neighbor, Edward Siddenham, Esq. Verney was regarded as the epitome of aristocratic gentility at the time. This was also the first time that the square was specifically referred to in the rate list as "the piazza."

While willing to develop the combined residences with diligence to Jones's aesthetic standards, Bedford was cognizant of the need to accommodate the desires of other residents of his precinct. Some of the more wealthy or elevated aristocracy wished to have large individual houses, and so two grand houses, designed by Jones, were available on either side of the church in the west.

The combination of the church, the Portico Buildings, and various free-standing houses including the Bedford home completed the enclosure of the piazza. As indicated on a map of the area fifty years later (Figure 5.25), the residential accommodation was comfortably integrated with the amenities of church and piazza, and also well connected to the surrounding urban fabric.

In the following century, continued programmatic changes altered the typology of the residential buildings, though the overarching aesthetic composition was retained. This has

5.25
**Map showing Covent
Garden, 1682.**

led to historical controversy regarding the original design as well as occupants of various buildings. An example is the large, stand-alone mansion located at 43 King Street in the northwest corner of the piazza (Figure 5.26). The historian Chancellor (1930, 114) states that "it was doubtless one of Inigo Jones's creations, the pillars and capital and the rusticated lower portions being quite in his style, but changes in the form of the windows and so forth have helped to obliterate the essential hall-mark of that great architect." This is contested by Summerson (1991b, 18), who suggests that "[t]he Baroque house ... has nothing to do with Jones ... [being in a style that] would have made Jones shudder." Having made a very detailed review of the parish rate lists, Downs (1967, 10) surmises that this is an 18th-century building, decades after Jones's death, and in fact replaces a demolished north-west section of the Portico Buildings. Whether it was a work in the manner of Jones, or as alternatively posited, by the architect, Captain Wynde, who designed Buckingham House (Palace), it importantly represents yet another commercial engagement of the emerging architectural profession for private urban residences.

5.26

House of Lord Archer in Covent Garden.

The other historical anomalies relating to this building concern its first resident, incorrectly said to be Sir William Alexander, the Earl of Stirling. Though importantly overseeing the colonization of eastern Long Island in America (the future Hamptons) at the time, he resided more modestly in one of the Portico Buildings to the east of James Street, determined by Downs (1967, 10) to be "the second from the corner." He resided there from 1638 until his death in 1640. Correctly recorded as living at No. 43 King Street in the early 17th century was Lord Archer, so its suitability as an aristocratic residence was confirmed irrespective of the identity of its earliest occupant. With relatively modest alterations, it remains standing today and now functions as the National Sporting Club (Figure 5.27).

In addition to the aesthetic quality that architects brought to London houses, whether built by a developer or not, they also advanced the design of the new residences to have them function more suitably in accordance with the mode of living of the increasingly urban

5.27

No. 43 King Street as the National Sporting Club in 2020.

society. Though focusing in more detail on the subsequent 18th-century Georgian houses, the architectural historian Summerson (2003, 149) commends this:

> It is all devised for the conduct of an elaborate social parade – a parade which was felt to be the necessary accompaniment of active and responsible living. The houses of [the architect, Robert] Adam ... were not built for domestic but for public life – a life of continual entertaining in drawing rooms and ante-rooms and 'eating rooms' ...

Since Summerson credits Inigo Jones with launching what he terms the "proto-Georgian" house that substantially influenced Adam, it may be inferred that Jones had served Bedford well in more suitably tailoring his new residences to the changing lifestyles of his intended tenants.

He was also able to accommodate the commercial needs of his tenants by permitting the inclusion of shops in residences at ground level, just as in the historical use of the format. For example, a goldsmith, Andrew Bayley, took a house in the Little Piazza in 1651 and was able to have two shop fronts built into the Portico façade (*Survey of London, Volume 36: Covent Garden* 1970, 83).

Bedford also appreciated the economic expediency of providing lots, though not those fronting on the piazza, to other developers who would build much-needed but lesser-quality housing. In the area bounded by the western wall of the estate and Chandos Street, Bedford Street, and King Street, he granted leases on sizable lots to various builders. Downs (1967, 11) named the first as William Newton, who had been developing Great Queen Street and now took land west of Henrietta Street. Following his lead, in 1632 a consortium of John Powell, Edward Palmer, and John Borradaile took a thirty-four-year lease for a plot approximately 180 ft by 33 ft along the north of Henrietta Street and bounded in the east by the church yard and vestry site. These were sizable holdings that they divided into lots for small and often non-uniform houses which can be seen in the background of St Paul's church, and as the smaller lots on the western side of the estate shown in Crowle's Plan (Figure 5.28).

Olsen (1982) also reports that, according to a map of 1795, there were some lots that were leased in perpetuity at a "fee-farm" rent, which was similar to property rates or property taxes on freehold land. Bedfordbury Street is shown to be almost wholly held under this tenure. Whether or not Bedford was forced to make these grants in order to cope with any financial difficulties as a developer or personally, or as the legatee of the profligate disposal of lands by his predecessor, the 3rd Earl, is not known. Nevertheless, the realities of the tensions of land use and ownership associated with real estate development are apparent here and the form of resolution that he adopted provides an important lesson in accommodating such conflicts.

Resolving Further Legal Problems of Development
Of importance in Duggan's placement of the project's approval in 1629 rather than two years later is that it reveals Bedford's strategy in obtaining it prior to attending to various existing building infractions on the estate. Although the authorities continually pressed him to resolve this issue, it might be inferred from his reticence in this respect that he was unwilling to

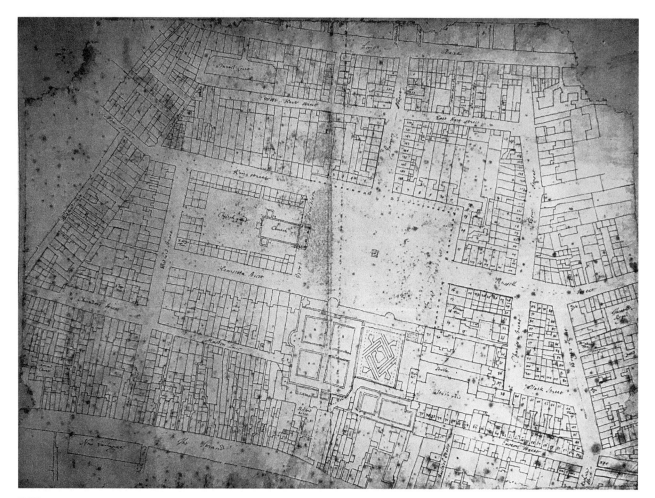

5.28
Crowle's map, c. 1690.

undertake the expense without seeing an advantage for his proposed development. Once he received approval and was ready to proceed with his project, it was opportune for him to rectify these matters. His attention to this was an important component of the emerging process of private urban development, first in avoidance of wasteful expenditure on speculative pre-development work, and secondly in eventually securing good relations with the municipal and planning authorities.

As an early lesson in landlord–tenant relations, of interest is the case of the problem of property tax equivalents that were left unpaid by the widow Dauson, the lessee for life of the Covent Garden pasture and other land along Long Acre. While her longevity had beneficially precluded the misuse of this land by the 3rd Earl, she had failed to pay the parish tithes, or annual fees of approximately 10% of the ground rent, to the parish. In 1626, Richard Pugitt had brought an action on behalf of the church for the unpaid amount. As is often the case with operating expenses such as property taxes when competent conveyancers are not engaged, the "understanding" between the landlord and the tenant as to where the liability lay was not made clear, and in this case the problem was compounded by a claim that the land had originally been granted to the 1st Earl without a tithing liability. Duggan (2001, 164, footnote 5) suggests that it may have been the commencement by the 4th Earl of discussions with the widow Dauson for her surrender of the lease that precipitated a dispute with the parish, now aware of the site's potential value, and may have triggered the discussion of the need for a new church with leverage in the hands of the parish.

Another lesson in compliance with the standards of authorities can be learnt from this nascent period. Bounded by the northern side of the Long Acre fields, a main highway called Long Acre was often taken from Westminster to and from the royal residence at Theobalds. Bedford had land that abutted it on its southern side and the Earl of Monmouth had land on its northern side. Writing of court intrigue at the time, Downs (1967, 10), with reference to Brett-James (1935, 162) reports that

> they [the Earls] had met with royal displeasure because [the highway] … was continually disrupted 'by reason of the new buildings which cast out their dust, soyle and filth' into the street. The matter had come to a head in early 1629, since it is recorded that Bedford was issued with official orders to stop damaging the important route and to demolish some houses that had been built unlawfully. Subtenants had probably erected these over the prior decades either without the landowner's approval or with tacit agreement by the 3rd Earl. The King insisted that immediate steps be taken for 'the cleansing for the same passage and the better keeping of it hereafter' and to see that it was done properly, His Majesty directed that those persons whom he had appointed 'for the surveying of ways' [Inigo Jones and his staff] were to attend upon the said Earls.

The historian puts this at early in 1630 and though there are no formal records Bedford must have attended to the matter since in a letter to Bedford's fellow peer Lord Strafford, George Garrard (1739 [1634], 263) reported that "[t]hey [the Star Chamber] are now at the *Earl of Bedford* for his Buildings in and about *Covent Garden*, notwithstanding his Licence. His Counsel pleaded hard for him before the Commissioners, but Mr. *Noy* being away, no Answer is yet given him …"

In fact, in rectifying the situation along Long Acre, Bedford took a further inspired act of land development. Given that he had worked through concepts of suitable land lot sizes in his Covent Garden plans, he realized that the inherited defined sites for lease in that northern area were too large for moderately sized houses, and since it was still rather distant from the main route of the Strand, neither were the sites attractive to persons of substantial financial means to build large houses or mansions. Additionally, because of encroaching urban activity, the market for such farming lots was also diminished and therefore the land had failed to obtain substantial leases other than for the digging of stone and clay. Bedford probably calculated that its rental rate as relatively undeveloped land provided him with insufficient income to cover the costs of maintaining the adjoining highway or removing the unlawful residents. As a solution, and something of an extension to his Covent Garden project, he proposed that, with approval, he would divide the area into smaller lots, where appropriately sized structures could be built lawfully. This would greatly improve the area and its attractiveness for the king's passage and yet generate sufficient funding for consistent and reliable road maintenance. He was apparently successful in this negotiation, and he added the smaller lot divisions along Long Acre, as shown at the top of Crowle's Plan (Figure 5.28). His resolution of the matter also indicates his continued engagement with Jones, who supervised this resolution on behalf of the king, as an extension of the development activities of Covent Garden and a constructive relationship between architect and developer.

Project Oversight

Given the extensive involvement of the king and his architect in the project's design, Bedford was obliged to ensure that the construction faithfully observed the aesthetic standards of Inigo Jones's approved plans and the requirements of various municipal authorities. Concerned with the consequence of a development scheme on such a scale, the authorities, through the office of the Attorney General, continued to be involved as construction proceeded. William Noy, who was appointed Attorney General in 1631, directed the establishment of the new church, insisting that its operation and the financial support of its rector be "completely endowed and not left to the willing contributions of his flock." He also fortified the authority of the Crown regarding conformity with the development approval by amending the building license to include "the covenant in what sort that the earl will buylde" (Duggan 2001, 117–118).

Jones's continued authority over the scheme is evidenced in Articles of Agreement binding the ground lessees with specific material requirements on the project so that "such brickes as are bespoken by Mr Surveyor for the makeing of the Peeres" (Duggan 2001, 119). To ensure adequate quality, Bedford also engaged the architect to oversee the construction of the first three model houses.

For detailed inspections of the three model houses, Bedford engaged two surveyors, Isaac de Caus and Edward Carter. Recent documents indicate that they acted as joint surveyors, the former seemingly reporting to Jones in checking the standard of building work, and the latter communicating with Bedford, probably in measuring the work and equating it with trade payments (Duggan 2001, 126).

For the residential development as a whole, it would seem that site inspections during early construction were thorough, when the work was paid for by Bedford himself. An invoice from the stonemason William Mason (Figure 5.29) lists a charge of £8 12s "For 64 ft 6 ins. of sill for these windows at 2s. 8d. per foot being altered from the first bargain ..." and that alteration could not have been directed by anyone less than the architect or his agent. It also seems that this incidence of an alteration during construction, the modern-day concept of the change order, was a regular occurrence with another item being a charge for £21 9s 4d "[o]f fascia 171 ft 9 ins. at 2s. 6d. per foot being 1 in. more in height than was agreed by the covenant which was appointed by Mr. Decuase [de Caus, the surveyor]" (LMA Box 552). As often with innovative design, details would necessarily be resolved during construction, though perhaps this early warning of the significant cost changes, and occasional disputes, associated with that practice might have led to a better form of project management from the outset.

One of the more problematic design features requiring on-site resolution was the cast iron balcony, referred to as "a pergula of Iron," intended for the Portico houses. This was an architectural feature imported from the Continent and insisted on by Jones. However, its production according to specification proved challenging and affixing it to the façade required extensive experimentation, and after a couple of successful installations it was no longer

p. 3

Mason's work done by William Mason

	£	s.	d.
In the ten several peers, 'Plints', springers and keystones 1,853 foot for stone working and setting 2s. 8d. per foot	247	0	0
Of fascia 171 ft. 9 ins. at 2s. 6d. per foot being 1 in. more in height than was agreed by covenant which was appointed by Mr. Decause	21	9	4
In the jambs and heads of the windows 432 /3 feet/ 1 in. at 2s. 8d. per foot	57	12	2
For 76 ft. 7 ins. of cornice over these windows at 5s. 2d. per foot	19	2	6
For 51 ft. 9 ins of frieze for these windows at 2s. 4d. per foot	6	0	9
For 64 ft. 6 ins. of sill for these windows at 2s. 8d. ... foot being altered from the first bargain by	8	12	0

5.29

Excerpt from transcribed invoice for (stone) mason's work at Covent Garden from William Mason.

used. Nevertheless, once in place, as an aesthetic gesture it was well received by cultured London society and gave distinction to the project. In Stow's Survey, two of the piazza houses are noted to have these "highly fashionable purgulas." The struggle with innovative features and the successful resolution of their inclusion continues to be fundamental to producing a distinct and commendable development.

Quality Control and Compliance

Of importance in meeting both the aesthetic and economic objectives of this development was quality control, comprising the maintenance of consistent quality in the structures while controlling budgets during the building process. A number of supportive factors already operated, including:

- General building requirements of the royal Proclamations.
- Conditions of the approval for the development.
- The lease conditions that required compliance with the quality demonstrated by three sample Portico houses built by him.

Bedford was careful to disseminate the first of these obligations for compliance with legislative requirements by including in his leases reference to that higher authority. For example, a lease covenant reads: "Ar:2: fo:2, front standings towards the streete of the premises to conteyne 20 foote: by this the lessees have liberty in build backward how much & in what manner the[y] please without any restraint be it never contrary to my lords promise to his Majesty" (Duggan 2001, 114).

Specific obligations that primarily bound the earl as the landowner were extended to those taking ground leases, which required compliance with the buildings' specifications in the leases. The details of these varied considerably. For those not fronting onto the piazza, the basic specifications for materials and structure were to be compliant with the royal Proclamations. But for those on the piazza, both the Great Piazza and Little Piazza, there were further detailed specifications.

An example of the latter is provided in the Articles of Agreement for the Lease to George Hulbert dated 1632. They specified the building details for two portico houses on the south-east corner, in the Little Piazza. Of the twenty-four Articles, the first ten covered the construction of the portico houses to deliver "sufficient stronge uniforme and proporcionable double buildings [of greater depth than width] and dwelling houses." The height of the façade was to be 54½ ft to the eaves and was to be divided into two-and-a-half storeys and built in brick and stone. The width was to be of 20 ft with a minimum depth of 42 ft. The portico, or arcaded walkway parallel to the façade, was to be built as 19 ft wide and 20 ft high, and the regular and aligned placement of windows and perpendicular pilasters were specified. Other Articles dealt with construction requirements such as width of walls, foundations, and chimneys.

Conscious of the appearance of success in the progress of his project, and because lease payments would not commence until building completion, Bedford included a schedule of temporal requirements in the Lease Agreements with his lessees of the first colonnaded residences. This specified that the cellars, floors, columns, walls and pilasters of the portico or ground level were to be completed within seven months of the date of the agreement, and to maintain momentum, the construction logistics for the common party walls required that the composite multi-unit building be erected somewhat synchronistically.

Other construction process requirements that Bedford established through his leases have become important for development management since. Particularly for urban developments, the funding and responsibility for party walls often raises disputes, and to manage this through arbitration Article 18 prescribes a process. Similarly seeking to protect existing building conditions, Article 23 required the preservation of any conduits or pipes uncovered during construction. Further, in the light of the consequences of improper construction of any components, it was an important contractual feature of his administration of this complex scheme to establish, with Article 21, an overarching right of access and supervision. This has continued to be a principle of project management ever since.

Slip-ups in Project Oversight

Unfortunately, after a successful early start, there appears to have been some deterioration in effective oversight, which provides a further lesson for developers.

The engagement of two quantity surveyors, one representing the architect's objectives and the other responsible to the developer for financial expenditure, was a substantial cost in the construction phase. Therefore, after completion of the model houses the range of de Caus's services was reduced. Only Bedford's advisor, Edward Carter, is recorded as the signatory to all accounts, and he was responsible for oversight of the construction of only St Paul's church. From correspondence it is evident that de Caus was given "a separate charge to act in an advisory capacity concerning the buildings outside the Piazza area" (Duggan 2001, 126), which were of less importance and generally undertaken by ground lessees who were charged for his services.

Such removal of Bedford's control of the architect's agent in supervision of the construction had what might be the expected effect of reducing adherence to quality. After completion of the model houses and the first important residences, the consequence of a lack of adequate management was soon realized in the poor performance of the numerous other builders now working on various sites. There are records in the archives of the trade guilds of such poor-quality workmanship. For example, the carpenter, Mr. Giles Whiting, was to pay a fine for "very ill" workmanship in and about Covent Garden (Guildhall MSS 4329/4, *Cost Book of Carpenters Co*. 1618–1635), though it cannot be determined whether or not the responsibility was specifically Bedford's.

Although the development scheme had the king's approval, the City of London authorities, who had not been enthusiastic, now took the opportunity to raise objections regarding the quality of work. It was then that, succumbing to public pressure, the king's Attorney General, Sir John Banks, in 1634 filed charges against Bedford in the Star Chamber. This complaint attempted to set aside the original approval for the project:

> albeit the Charter of the King tend to give you leave to erect the same yet if the thing bee to the publique nuisance of all his subjects or anie principall citty or borough such as the buildinge or over buildings at Convent-gardine [*sic*] may be interpreted to bee to London or Westminster, Then by lawe such Charter or letters patents tending to dispence with the Comon lawe may be supposed to be voyd. (Duggan 2001, 131)

The charges covered 450 houses that had been built on the estate and surrounding areas of Long Acre, Russell Street, and stretching to St Martin's Lane. It is apparent that by 1633 Bedford had concerns, and he had engaged de Caus on a specific examination of the quality of the buildings underway. The surveyor reported a lack of adherence to the building specifications as stipulated in the Articles of Agreement of the leaseholds and he particularly faulted six builders on sites beyond the piazza area where Bedford had exerted less oversight (Duggan 2001, 132). Some principal examples of poor workmanship involved brickwork of less than the required thickness, poor-quality timberwork, and the use of types of timber that had been banned by royal Proclamations.

Bedford's defense included a proposed dismissal of charges relating to houses that had been erected prior to the commencement of his project, and for which he had sought relief when applying for the project's approval. However, perhaps as an oversight, he had not been granted specific immunity for such transgressions in the approval documents, and consequently was liable for pre-existing conditions. This important step of risk mitigation with respect to a site is still an important part of the development process. Also, as part of his defense he relied on an early site visit to the project by the king that resulted in alterations to accommodate even more parishioners. Such changing programmatic requirements by users, the community or municipal authorities also continues to be a common difficulty in urban development, and managerial expertise should be adequately prepared for such possibilities.

Duggan (2001, 129) infers from the drafts of these defenses that although Bedford clearly stipulated the building requirements in the Articles of Agreement for his leases, his "employing a 'surveyor' initially to supervise his lessee-builders does not seem to have been a priority." As the Commissioners of Buildings had condemned approximately 200 structures that had been built under his license, his dereliction as to oversight was not confined to outlying areas or illegal building.

Although he cleverly bound his tenants by their leases to comply with the specified requirements, he remained guilty of the charges that he should have undertaken more supervision to ensure compliance with the conditions of approval for the scheme. Thus, his desire to diversify the risk of construction management was not successful. Nevertheless, though no record of the outcome of the Star Chamber proceeding has survived, in April and May of 1635 he made two payments totaling £2,000, probably as a fine, but he was granted a confirmation of his license in 1635 and continued with the project. He became more vigilant in his oversight and his correspondence indicates that he later avoided a lease with certain ground-tenants who consistently failed to comply with regulations.

Despite the scale of the project and the novelty of the undertaking, and the lessons learnt along the way, Bedford's commitment to the architectural plans, compliance with legislative requirements, and of course retention of the favor of the king were impressively maintained. Although the process of oversight did not constitute the more rigorous process of inspections performed today, the intended adherence to the details of the building's aesthetic standards and license requirements was an important early step in establishing an effective dynamic standard between the relevant authorities, the architect, and the private urban developer.

Project Management Skills and Structure

In addition to insufficient oversight of construction compliance, Bedford also failed to have suitable overall project management structure in place. It may have been his lack of knowledge of or familiarity with the logistics of large-scale projects that resulted in this omission. At that time, large construction activity was confined to the construction of churches, grand mansions, or royal facilities, all for the benefit of a single owner or occupier. This new project, structured as the delivery of multiple houses by multiple builders for multiple disparate lessees, posed a challenge of substantial difference in nature and degree from precedent. It is not difficult to contemplate the chaotic conditions that prevailed amongst the clashing activities of several independent builders who were responsible to various neighboring residents, all of whom were to be accommodated around the central piazza. This task was beyond even the most experienced tradesmen or master builders administering projects comprising multiple rows of houses. Despite the innovative design and the disbursed construction activities, on Bedford's site there is no record of the presence of any overarching project manager to coordinate the complex undertaking.

The earl had successfully managed building projects on the family estates and renovation of Woburn Abbey before commencing Covent Garden, but this afforded him limited experience. For instance, those rural domestic projects probably required a substantial degree of personal involvement that would not be feasible on a larger-scale urban project.

He had made a similar mistake in advancing from his success in draining the fens on his own estate to undertaking a large infrastructure project of fen drainage for the king. With the installation of appropriate pumps and drainage ditches, this area was to be drained within six years and deliver 95,000 acres of new arable land. However, from 1630, just as the Covent Garden development was getting underway, his management skills and capacity were stretched. His claim in 1637 to have successfully completed the project was contested by counselors to the king and the Crown took over the project (Darby 1940).

Presenting a lesson that is relevant today, it appears that the financial ambitions and inge-
nuity of the developer were not matched by his skills in project management, and further,
those skills were not easily scaled up across a number of projects at once nor on a project of
substantially larger scale.

Quality over the Long Term and Economic Implications
Although Bedford was concerned with the quality and longevity of the houses that he built,
he faced challenges with respect to the costs and responsibility for building maintenance.
As typical of a ground lease, upon the expiration of its term, all the buildings at Covent
Garden reverted to Bedford with the associated demand for major capital works. There
are records of some completely rebuilt residences, at full cost to the landlord, though the
use of masonry ensured that most structures continued to be habitable. Intent on retaining ownership, in contrast to speculative builders, he understood the benefit of durable
construction to minimize future maintenance costs. For the surviving structures, ideally for
Bedford, the tenant would wish to renew the lease, and having made the refurbishment,
Bedford had the tenant share its cost. This is demonstrated in archival material referring to
the re-leasing of the Chandos Street buildings where amounts of between £100 and £250
were spent on rebuilding, of which 50% was charged by way of a fine to the continuing
tenant (Figure 5.30).

5.30

**Listing of King Street
and Chandos Street
properties when leases
fell in during 1689–1691,
with some rebuilding cost
estimates shown.**

Despite his concerns for longevity, Bedford's achievements were often undermined by the tenant's responsibility for the costs of maintenance and repairs during the lease, which might include a major capital item such as replacing a substantial portion of the roof, or the whole building in the event of a conflagration. Of course, attendance to this responsibility varied amongst tenants and it was only by diligent and tenacious asset management that a consistent quality of building fabric could be maintained. This tension between upfront expenditure, the quality and longevity of a structure, and wear and tear by tenants was inherent from the start, as a result of the conjunction of legal responsibilities and building deterioration, and it continues to be problematic at times.

Importance of the Contribution to Infrastructure
Not only did Bedford regard the beautiful central piazza as central for his scheme, but he also recognized the importance of the more mundane public infrastructure that would be necessary for movement within the residential precinct and for an efficient connection with the surrounding urban district. Jurisdiction over this area remained unresolved between the City of London and the Crown at Westminster, so all infrastructure, including streets, for these new developments was to be provided by the developer, often at a substantial cost. It also required continual upgrading, and even when the municipality eventually became more involved, the landowner remained responsible for contributions to large capital expenditures.

Just as he had evaluated the best means of access to his own residence from the fashionable Strand, he turned his mind to the access of the residents on all sides of the piazza to surrounding thoroughfares.

As shown in Blome's map (Figure 5.31) and described by Strype (1720, Book VI, 87),

[a]bout the Centre of the Ground, he [Bedford] caused to be set out a large square or rather oblong piece of ground [the Piazza], 500 foot in length and 400 in Breadth, and into this Plot of ground, four large Streets of about 50 or 60 Foot Broad, have their Entrance, viz. Russell Street on the West, James Street on the North, King's Street and Henrietta Street on the East, and the South Side is taken up by the Wall of Bedford Garden.

The street infrastructure was phased with the build-out of the residential sites. In 1634, the earliest access and main entrance to the piazza was provided by way of Russell Street. For access for churchgoers and marketgoers, he provided a number of new streets to the west of St Paul's, sometimes enlarging existing laneways and paths. By 1637, he had laid out both King Street and Henrietta Street, named after Charles I and his consort respectively, both streets opening onto a wider thoroughfare, Bedford Street. The following year, James Street and Maiden Lane were built on the site of the old garden. From there, he added a number of streets connected to main thoroughfares, the Strand, St Martins, and Long Acre. To accommodate visitors to the piazza on the eastern side, he efficiently used Bow Street as the intermediate thoroughfare to distribute traffic to Drury Lane and the Strand.

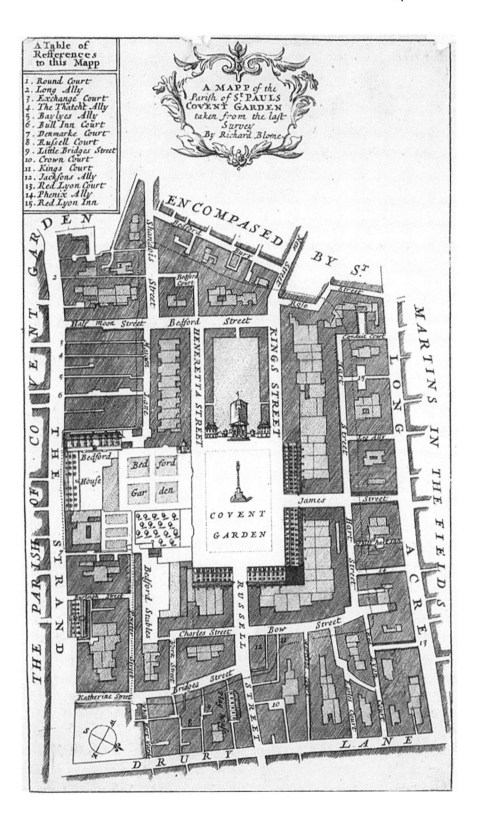

5.31

Blome's map of the Covent Garden (St Paul's) Parish, 1686.

On quality control of the improvements to the whole estate, Bedford has been criticized for his lesser concern for the buildings outside the piazza area. Although Olsen (1982, 40) praises the accomplishment of Covent Garden development, he was less laudatory concerning the other areas and said:

> The rest of the estate – although it abounded with large and expensive houses and remained fashionable until the early eighteenth century – was laid out in a fashion that was neither regular nor generous. Many of the streets were fairly wide, but behind them were narrow, mean, and unsanitary course. There were no squares apart from the main Piazza.

The wide main streets of Bedford's project are shown in stark contrast to the smaller streets and alleyways further from the piazza.

How Bedford approached the spatial layout of those backstreets is not revealed by the surviving documents, but it has been noted earlier that upon approval of the project he leased much of the lots on the western side to other developers. There is no indication that Inigo Jones was involved in their layout, though his general rules of building quality were imposed through the ground lease contracts. Most likely, in Bedford's efforts to manage the project's liquidity, as he would not receive rent from the master leases until the houses on these lots were completed and rented to residents, he may not have hesitated too long on such details, and probably acceded to some of the wishes of those developers for tighter backstreets and less refined infrastructure within their lots.

It received the attention of the harsh architectural critic of Victorian times, James Ralph (1734, 29), who wrote: "*Covent-Garden* would have been, beyond dispute, one of the finest squares in the universe, if finish'd on the plans that *Inigo Jones* first design'd for it ..." Unfortunately, the same competition of aesthetic and financial concerns remains prevalent today.

Social Infrastructure

In the schedule of development for Covent Garden project, in 1631, the church of St Paul's was the first building to be constructed in anticipation of the formation of a new parish, though it was not until 1638, some five years after its completion, that it was consecrated, and even later still, in 1645, that the new parish was established by an Act of Parliament. Its presence, however, was significant from the time of its construction. In the emerging culture of London, it was of interest to architectural critics, social commentators, and artists of life such as Hogarth, as may be seen in his portrayal (Figure 5.32).

Having built the church and piazza, Bedford addressed the challenge of maintaining these public amenities as part of his social responsibility but also for their impact on the retention of the quality and value of the residences in his development. Once consecrated, the church became part of the ecclesiastical property of the Church of England and when the parish was established, and as was typical of that time the church undertook its responsibilities and gained its revenues, which were not insubstantial in a wealthy neighborhood such as Covent Garden.

As for the maintenance of the public piazza, it can be deduced from the records of transactions between Bedford and the churchwardens that the maintenance of the piazza was to be performed by the parish church. However, continuing his commitment to the provision of this

5.32

Four Times a Day: Morning by William Hogarth, 1736, showing St Paul's church portico.

social amenity, and taking into account that his own house overlooked it and that the value of his leased residences depended on it, he established a funding source through an assignment of rental income from three residences on the piazza. This sum was reported in 1732 by the then clerk, John Stacey, to be approximately £350 per annum (Chancellor 1907, 177). Additionally, the Bedford estate continued to make capital contributions such as a donation of £20 in 1668 towards the erection of a stone column with a sundial at its center (Chancellor 1907, 39).

These social benefactions manifested an early form of public–private partnership in the provision and maintenance of the public realm, though in this case the public entity was the parish church. It continued the tradition in which aristocratic landowners provided for their communities by working with an informal and tacit understanding of the sharing of rights and responsibilities. For the landlord of buildings for which the value was strongly bound to the quality of the public realm, the economic symbiosis was explicit, and the financial contribution warranted.

However, this was the first contribution to the public realm on private urban land and, in the context of the contemporary political turmoil, it was courageous of Bedford to assume this management of such a large public portion of his new development. As this model of the residential square was emulated in following centuries in England and in other countries, any absence of a satisfactory maintenance structure, as was often the case, would diminish the benefit of the amenity.

Marketplace

As can be seen to the left of the piazza in Figure 5.31, there was a grove of trees which, although later enclosed as part of Bedford House's garden, was in the earliest days open to the piazza and became the first site of the neighborhood's revived marketplace.

The re-establishment of this long tradition of the former abbey's market garden was also commercially astute, since convenient food supplies were scarce in this still relatively undeveloped district outside the City walls. Letters Patent to hold the market in the central piazza area were not granted until 1671, but the early informal stalls provided a substantial income for Bedford and added a vitality to the neighborhood.

As a development project that produced a comprehensive urban environment of public and private places and was well integrated into the surrounding neighborhood, the Covent Garden project was enthusiastically praised and, when political stability prevailed, proved to be financially successful. As an innovative undertaking, it importantly demonstrated a viable dynamic for the private provision of contribution to the public realm that was successfully incorporated into this early private urban development model.

Financial Strategy

Bedford funded the cost of at least the initial portion of the Portico Buildings, which included walls of the garden and stables at the rear. The total budget of his undertaking may be derived from archival material where it is summarized in the "Declaration of the charge of the Portico Buildings" presenting a total cost of £4,706 0s 7d and a trades list (Figure 5.33). How this cost compares to the original budget cannot be determined, but the substantial costs for the

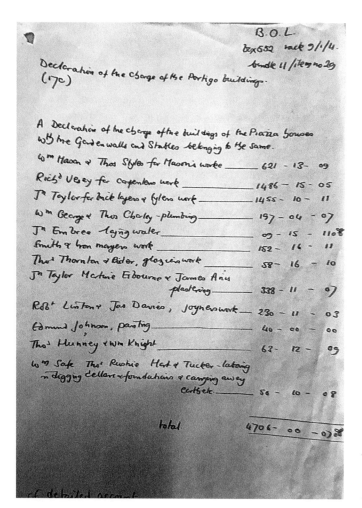

5.33

Transcribed summary of costs for trades on some "Portico buildings" and the associated garden walls and stables at the rear.

houses of Vesey and Taylor at approximately £1,486 and £1,455, respectively, indicate that Bedford assumed the responsibility, if not the final cost for the construction of these Portico houses.

Monitoring total costs on a project through a detailed account of separate trades continues to be the format of project costing today. Even the management of capability and skills of tradesmen is still separately administered by a form of guild or union, just as it was in the similarly tightly controlled building activity in the 17th century. While this training and oversight of capability is critical, its rigid categorization and fragmentation of skills might constrain building design and execution from more innovative solutions. Bedford took a substantial step beyond the traditional designs that had been repeated incessantly at the time and took on an additional supervisory burden with his model houses and dual surveyors, but few notable advances on these measures have taken place since.

A notable feature of the development was the substantial upfront funding that Bedford provided without using other capital sources. It typically commenced as an aristocrat's improvement of his estate by incrementally enhancing its topography and structures, starting with his own house and garden extensions. However, when he commenced his more ambitious scheme, because of his early need to deploy substantial capital to build the church, streets, and three model examples of the colonnaded residences, the project demanded a more dramatic strategy for investment in the potential of the land.

Although traders and merchants had adopted a growing entrepreneurial mindset of investing substantial capital to add value to or improve the productivity of their commercial activities, such as shipbuilding, dock construction, warehouses, and processing, real estate development was such a nascent business that it did not qualify for such equity participation. It was left to a few landed aristocrats, such as the 4th Earl of Bedford, to apply a strategy of investing in what could be called the capital structure, or "plant," of their property business. In the active management of his agrarian estates, Bedford would have appreciated the benefits of capital investment to improve production. And he was following the advice of contemporary economic commentators who were encouraging capital investment. He noted in his *Commonplace Book* (Bedford Archives, No. 25, 1639), "in sume cases the best thrift is to be prodigall," a justification for spending to stimulate economic prosperity. Although the costs of the enlarged development were substantial compared to the traditional expenditure on building houses, to Bedford, his making such a large investment to achieve a profitable outcome was in the manner of an astute businessman in the emerging commercial activity of 17th-century London.

Lease or Sell Housing Lots

Although his family had been part of the aristocracy for only a few generations, Bedford adopted the typical style by which landowners managed the productivity of their rural estates, that is, by leasing out farming lots to tenant farmers and even for opportunistic mining activities. In the same vein, he also intended that his urban development scheme would be similarly based on long-term leases. He was not of a mind to subdivide the area and sell lots, for that would require the reluctant approval of the Crown and would erode the land ownership which was the basis of support for his family and descendants, which he had worked to prevent at the hands of the 3rd Earl. Therefore, his strategy for Covent Garden was set: "Selling to developers reduced the family holding, but long leases represented a more socially conscious attitude, since these enabled them to try to ensure the orderly development of the site" (Beckett 1986, 7).

There was, however, a departure from common practice. While many landowning gentry, unskilled in building and tenant management, granted long-term ground leases to enterprising builders, Bedford embarked on the construction of the buildings on his subdivided land himself so that he would receive revenues from house rents as well as from the ground rents. As many Instruments of Lease for the project in the early decades have been lost, it is not possible to establish precisely how much of the residential building he funded, though he regularly stated that his capital resources were strained as the project proceeded.

Contribution of Covent Garden to the Growing Metropolis

Despite his shortcomings in the management of the project, Bedford did, within a decade, deliver the essential elements of Inigo Jones's design in the form of the much-acclaimed piazza, the stately dominance of St Paul's church, and the strong yet graceful definition of the public realm by the arcaded residential buildings on the north and eastern sides. Although probably in error in his assessment of incompletion, the noted Georgian architectural critic Noorthouck (1773, 734) describes it as

> a fine square, the area of which is the greatest market for greens, fruit, and flowers in the metropolis; a circumstance which it must be owned has more of utility than elegance in it ... Had Inigo Jones's plan been compleated, this would have been the most finished square any where to be found.

As apparent in the map by John Lacy of 1673 (Figures 5.34 and 5.35), the piazza had been completed, with a tree at its center and arcaded residences surrounding two sides to the north and east. The chapel of St Paul's had been erected at the western end of the piazza, and residences surround the churchyard along King Street, Bedford Street, and Henrietta Street. Stretching south to the Strand was Bedford House and its classical gardens. Less grand housing has been built in the streets behind in Hart Street, Bow Street, and Bridges Street.

Further, Hollar's "birds-eye view," produced in 1648 (Figure 5.36), presents the harmonious interweaving of the project into the surrounding topography, though its geometric regularity remains in contrast to the organic spatial arrangement by which this western region of London had developed.

Commendation of Covent Garden by Olsen (1982, xix) extends his praise to the developer:

> While the influence of Charles I and Inigo Jones on the conception and layout of Covent Garden is evident, equally so are the skill and imagination with which the fourth Earl of Bedford and his servants responded to the royal challenge to use the physical expansion of London as an occasion for embellishing the metropolis.

Importantly for the London metropolis, this residential development at Covent Garden and others it inspired in the later 17th century, presented an urban ambience that differed from the wealthy cities of the Continent. Porter (1994, 95) comments:

Yet the new West End did not exude imperiousness, like baroque St Petersburg or Dresden: it was *sui generis*. For it was the work not of princes or popes but of aristocratic capitalism, its driving forces noblemen building for profit and prestige ... But it was not just exclusive: it was particularly intimate and private.

In the following century, although the more desirable residential areas moved further west beyond Hyde Park as the West End became more built up, the Covent Garden neighborhood retained a distinctive reputation such as described by Edward Walford (1878, 238): "remarkable as including in its circuit more of the literary, and, indeed, of human interest, than any other spot in modern or ancient London."

The Interregnum

The Civil War adversely impacted the Covent Garden development project, though only temporarily. Since 1636, Oliver Cromwell had resided in the neighborhood on Long Acre where he is recorded as paying rent of 10s 10d. As the neighborhood's prestige rapidly grew, rental rates rose considerably, and as an indication, Cromwell's reached 14s by the time he left in 1643. By the late 1640s, however, the continuing turmoil of London resulted in vacancy rates of more than 60%.

During the crisis preceding the Civil War, the 4th Earl of Bedford was reputed to be the ringleader of a group which included eleven other peers who petitioned Charles I to dismiss his ministers and succumb to the pressures of Parliament. After the flight of the king, and the commencement of parliamentary rule in November 1640, and "during the first few months of the Long Parliament, Bedford was [its] undisputed leader" (Clarendon State Papers II, 94, 110, 115). He was appointed a Privy Councilor and Treasurer, answering to Parliament, but he contracted smallpox and died in May 1641.

Clarendon described him as "a wise man, and of too great and plentiful a fortune to wish the subversion of the government," and one of the "great contrivers and designers [politically] in the House of Lords" (Clarendon State Papers II, 25). He was survived by his wife and seven children including four sons, of which the eldest, William Russell, succeeded to the title.

William Russell, 5th Earl of Bedford (1613–1700)

After having studied at Magdalen College, Oxford, William (Figure 5.37) served as the Member of Parliament for Tavistock until inheriting his father's peerage. He continued his father's business acumen and political diplomacy. On the sequestration of various parliamentary lords, such as the Earl of Kent, and members representing Bodmin in Cornwall and Heylesbury, all of whom had refused to attend the new government's sittings, he provided a house at 12 Henrietta Street of his Covent Garden estate for their residence under guard. From this location, the errant Parliamentarians were led by the guards to attend the required sessions.

Following the family's political position, William had initially sided with Parliament but then became a "Peace Lord" in seeking a resolution with the dethroned monarch. In 1644, he withdrew with his family to his country seat and away from public life until the Restoration, and with Anne Carr, he had eleven children, of whom four sons and four daughters survived.

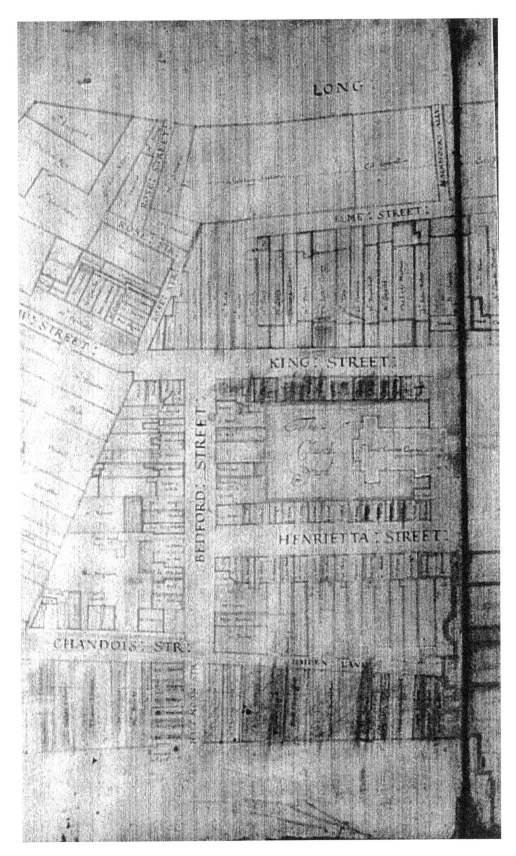

5.34
**Left side of John Lacy's
map of the parish
of St Paul, Covent
Garden, 1673.**

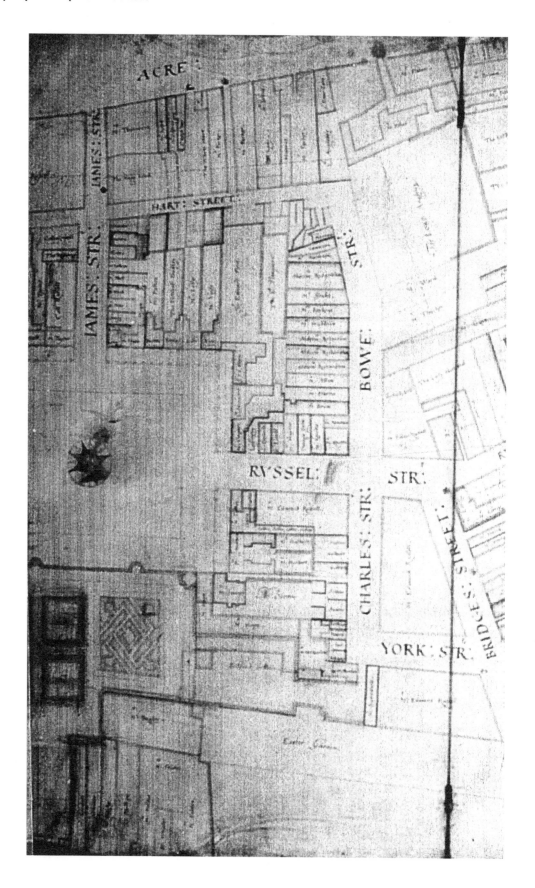

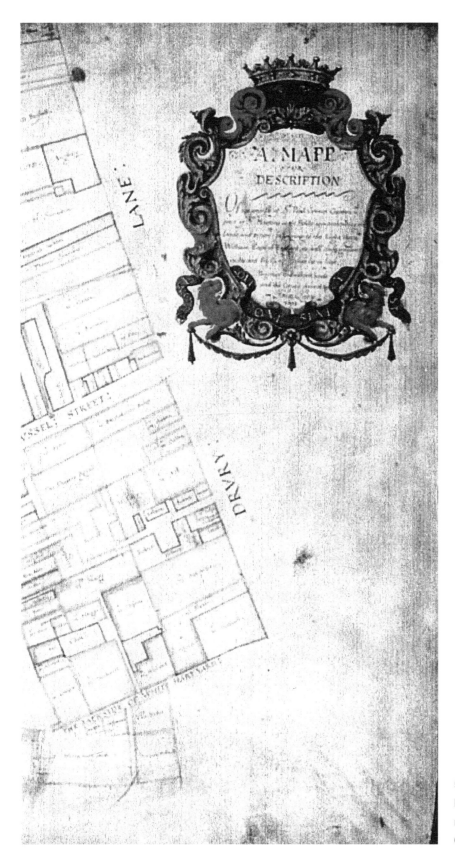

5.35
Right side of John Lacy's
map of the parish of St Paul,
Covent Garden, 1673.

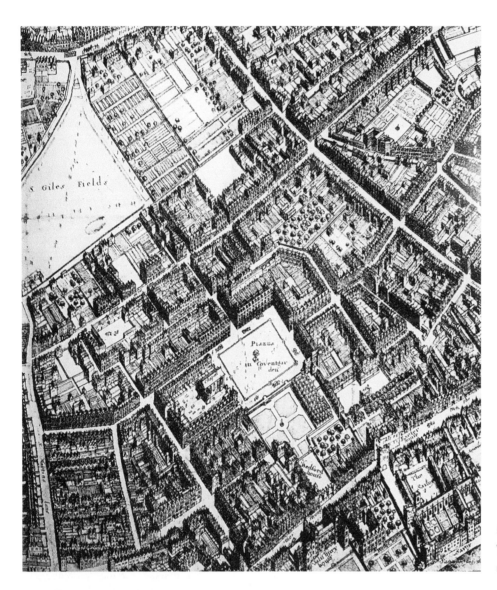

5.36
View of Covent Garden and neighborhood, c. 1658–1660.

5.37
William Russell, 5th Earl of Bedford, later the 1st Duke of Bedford.

His eldest son, Francis, was sickly, but his second son, William, was healthy and expected to succeed to the title.

Although some revenues were received by the 5th Earl in respect of services to Parliament, the demand for his higher quality townhouses fell quite dramatically as many nobles and gentry retreated to their country estates. Downs (1967, 23) has reported that prior to 1644, the parish rate listing had shown twenty houses leased, but in that year and the following, the ratepayers of record was reduced to only eleven. He has suggested that since the list for the entire row of residences to the north side, east of James Street, has no entries, it may have been undergoing renovations overseen by the 5th Earl, or unfortunately vacated by its tenants. The leasing was to be resumed however, since when the Verney's residence was again recorded on Crowle's Plan of circa 1670, it had expanded to include an additional residence, now behind seven arches rather than just five (Bruce 1853, 194–201). For Verney, the vacancies of the Interregnum had provided an opportunity to expand his holdings at Covent Garden.

The devastating effect of the troubled times on rental revenues in Covent Garden is indicated by the pleadings in a legal action in Chancery, a Court of Equity, in 1646 concerning a property on Drury Lane. The complaint alleged that ground leased from the Earl of Bedford was not worth the rent of £18 per annum, though it admitted that it was worth £28 "in poooooble times" (Chancery 7/53/9). There is not a record of the resulting settlement, but a reduction of probably around 50% in the rental rate would have been a severe financial hardship to him during already challenging times. Although during the 1650s the total ground rents improved to approximately £1,200, this was substantially below potential revenues in more settled times, such as the £5,700 obtained in 1739 (Olsen 1982, 220).

On the other hand, during the Civil War, there was a general recognition by the citizenry that the burden of the changed circumstances for residing in the London area had to be carried by all. After landlords sued their tenants for failing to pay their rent, and tenants challenged the high rates that were charged, compromise was frequent and settlements that were viable for all parties were reached. For example, the outcome of a court action by the residents of Henrietta Street was that "all or most of the Tenants of Covent Garden have agreed with their landlords for half of the former and orig[inal] rents for their houses" (Chancery C3/453/33). These rental rate cuts would have flowed through to the relevant subleases to impact upon Bedford's revenues from his ground leases. Additionally, he was not always successful in collecting the reduced rate, for it is recorded that "during the 'troubles'" little or no rent was received from the tenant at No. 34 King Street.

The Restoration

With the Restoration, the 5th Earl resumed his seat in the House of Lords and was a strong leader of the Presbyterian faction. Although he carried the royal scepter at the coronation of Charles II, he was not close to him. With the aristocracy's new enthusiasm for the many and flamboyant royal events, his houses in Covent Garden were again filled with important residents. The archives of the family reveal that by the 1660s, about half of his landed income came from the Covent Garden development and the fields of the fens, though the latter were still undergoing drainage and so probably provided little net revenue.

His second son, William, gained business experience by assisting his father in the administration of the estates. He was to add to those holdings by his marriage in 1669 to Rachel, Lady Vaughan, daughter and co-heir of Thomas Wriothesley, the recently deceased 4th Earl of Southampton, and the details of his Bloomsbury estate are presented in the following chapter. On their marriage, the formal ownership of her inherited lands would pass to William, and this future amalgamation of the properties of these two families, the Russells and Wriothesleys, and their innovative early development projects, would resonate with the coincidence of the forebears who had both been granted these lands by Henry VIII.

Rising Commercial Activity

It remained for the 5th Earl of Bedford to continue to administer his flourishing Covent Garden estate. Other urban developments, such as Lincoln's Inn Fields, Bloomsbury, and St James's Square, were predominantly occupied as residences, while there were some areas of commerce within designated rooms, but the buildings in the Covent Garden piazza gradually attracted greater commercial activity.

Specific shop fronts appeared, as was evidenced in the rate books as early as 1644, though the occupier was not specified as a commercial tenant. Downs (1967, 31–32) infers that this smallholding within the arcade was probably just a ground-floor shop of a single room. Later, as the distinctions between residential and commercial activities were more clearly identified, shops were mentioned as such in the parish rate listings, and such a description was used in 1662 for a business in Covent Garden. The tenancy type was noted separately in the estate's revenue accounts as early as 1667.

Although it was not formally licensed until 1671, the vegetable and flower market functioned on temporary stalls on certain days in the southern end of the open Small Piazza area. In an early lesson on the specialization of property management, by 1677, Bedford realized that such operational activities were beyond his capability and had given a twenty-one-year lease at a rent of £40 per annum to Adam Piggot and James Allen to hold a market every day except Sunday. Under this more focused management the market expanded and was later moved to the larger and central part of the piazza (Figure 5.38).

To accommodate the growing commerce, Piggot and Allen were allowed to build cellars and shops along the southern end of the piazza up against the garden walls of Burghley House and Bedford House. As both earls had installed in their gardens platforms from which to view the piazza, these market stalls were restricted in height to one foot below the garden walls, and their roofs were specified to be of slate and lead, and ornamental. In 1829–1830, more than a hundred years later, the present structure would be erected by the 6th Earl of Bedford and placed under the stewardship of the Beecham Estate Trust.

After the Great Fire, shops and wholesale trading operations had relocated from the City to sites along the Strand to the near south, and their activities spread to the piazza which provided easy carriage access to the arcaded Portico Buildings, which could accommodate businesses on the ground floor. As Pepys noted in his *Diary* (1668, 276), the tradesmen and the retail of their wares migrated west beyond Temple Bar to the more fashionable neighborhood of the Strand and Covent Garden. Particularly in Henrietta Street and Charles Street, many of the city shops were relocated from the city at this time.

Most prominent of these, the powerful guilds of Mercers, who dealt in silks, and Drapers, who dealt in woolens, had established Covent Garden as their trading base after the

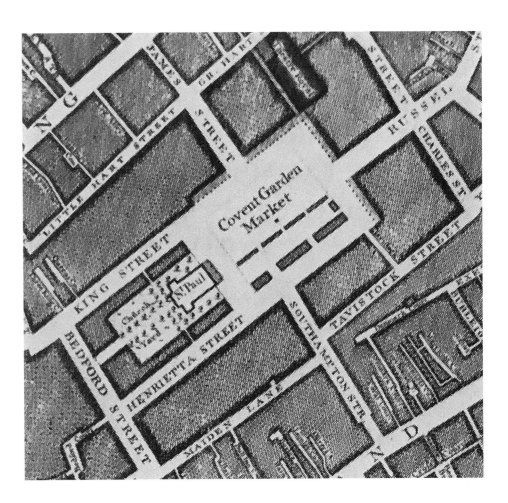

5.38
Map of Covent Garden,
c. 1746.

destruction of their Guild Hall in the City. This commercial activity, and the thriving produce stalls which now occupied much of the open space on the market days, characterized the precinct as busy and commercial, which moved some residents to leave for the calmer ambience that was being developed to the north and west. However, as the City was rebuilt after the Fire, its proximity to the wharves drew back many of the wholesale merchants and trading guilds. Defoe (1745) reported that around 1686, the Mercers had returned to the City and others soon followed. Unfortunately, having lost its prestige as a residential neighborhood, Covent Garden declined in prosperity during the late 17th century.

With the arrival of the theaters to the district, its ambience further evolved. The first of these was the Theatre Royal, which was privately built at a cost of £1,500 by Mr. Killigrew for "The King's Servants" dramatic company (Chancellor 1930, 258). He resided at Covent Garden. Later, in 1732, the Covent Garden Theatre was erected, having its main entrance through the Portico Buildings in the northeast corner.

New commercial ventures were also launched in the now affordable and well-located Covent Garden. Describing London's commercial evolution, the historian Margetson (1967, 1268) noted:

Meanwhile, outside the City, the area of Covent Garden was already a well-known center for book and fine-art auctions. A notable auction room called the Vendu was established as early as 1698 by Edward Millington. Sales were held in the winter at four o'clock in the afternoon to suit the persons of rank and fashion living in the neighborhood, who dine at three o'clock, and afterwards, if they were not inclined to visit the playhouse [also conveniently located in this area], looked in at the Vendu, where specially devised lighting enables them to view the paintings 'as if by daylight.'

Russell Street

From about the middle of the 17th century, as residents were settling into their new forms of housing, some of London's earliest coffee shops opened. Chancellor (1930, 205–206) placed the first coffee house in London at Cornhill in 1652. The coffee shops had just emerged as gathering places for the business of sampling and trading the new imports of coffee beans. They rapidly became notable places for gentlemen to gather, irrespective of their interest in transacting business in coffee, for confidential conversation away from their households and servants. Boulton (2008, 330) noted that "[t]he new Restoration coffee-houses were also vibrant places of face-to-face contact, where gossip, news and ideas circulated freely amongst an often surprisingly mixed clientele."

Regarded by Chancellor (1930) as the two most important coffee houses in Russell Street were Tom's and Button's. Captain Thomas West opened Tom's in 1700. It occupied the upper portion of the building while the bookseller and publisher T. Lewis leased the ground level. By 1764 an association, or club usually occupied by men, had formed there and consisted of over 700 members including nobility, gentry, foreign officials, and recognized men of letters, including the prominent authority of the times, Dr. Samuel Johnson (Chancellor 1930, 208).

Button's Coffee House (Figure 5.39) was opened in about 1712. It was on the south side of Russell Street in competition with Tom's on the north side. The proprietor, Button, had been in the service of Lady Warwick. Here was the famous Lion's Head, a letterbox, into which

5.39

Mr. Davies's shop, Russell Street.

intended contributors to the Guardian newspaper, founded in 1713, could place their submissions (Chancellor 1930, 213). The illustration of the head of the lion on the box is attributed to the well-known artist of the time William Hogarth, and when this coffee house closed, the box was passed around until the Duke of Bedford bought it and displayed it at Woburn Hall.

With their implicit assurance of confidentiality and trust, these coffee houses were the precursors of the private gentlemen's club which eventually proliferated nearby in St James's Place and Pall Mall. As they multiplied in St James's Street and then along Russell Street, the clientele of a particular shop tended to coalesce around a specific interest such as business, politics, or literature and arts.

Further Troubles at Court

With the rising conflict of the Third Anglo-Dutch War, Bedford was made the Governor of Plymouth in 1671. Two years later he was appointed to the office of the Joint Commissioner for the Earl Marshal and made a Knight of the Garter. However, he was and remained an ally of the 1st Earl of Shaftesbury, who opposed attempts to establish the dominance of the Anglican Church by the powerful Earl of Danby, and Bedford lost favor with the king, resulting in the cancelation of the charter of his Tavistock seat.

His son William had also been committed in his political views during the Exclusion Crisis. Although he continued to engage in the development at his wife's estate in Bloomsbury, particularly along Great Russell Street as described in the Southampton episode, he associated himself with Shaftesbury in activity against the king in the Rye House Plot and was arrested and executed for treason in 1683. Desolate at the loss of his son, and out of favor at court, the 5th Earl again withdrew from public life for almost five years until James II fled England.

Chapter 6: The Other Modern Developer: Wriothesley

The Southampton estate, which would include Bloomsbury Square, was established by Thomas Wriothesley (1505–1550). Though not of noble birth, he had been assisted in his entrance to royal service by the influential position in the court of his uncle, Sir Thomas Writh (also Writhe or Wryth) (died 1534), who held the office of Garter King of Arms.

The early, innovative development of Bloomsbury is the legacy of these two important Thomases (Figure 6.1).

Thomas Wriothesley, 1st Earl of Southampton (1505–1550)

Thomas Wriothesley (Figure 6.2) began his career in Henry VIII's court at the age of 19 and in 1532, after apparently excellent service to important administrators, he was made chief clerk

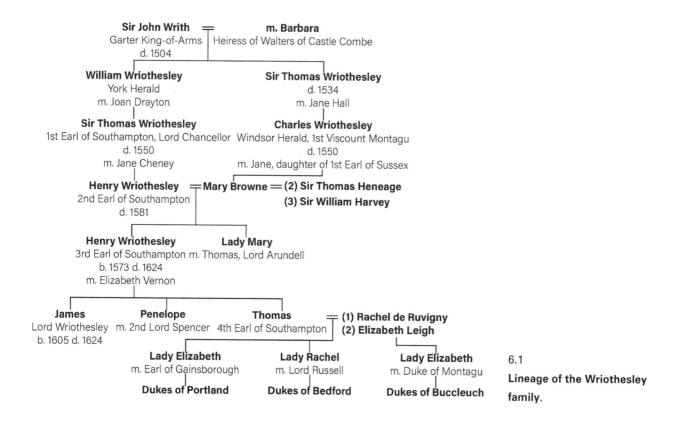

6.1

Lineage of the Wriothesley family.

6.2
**Thomas Wriothesley, 1st Earl
of Southampton.**

and personal secretary to Thomas Cromwell. In that role, he was significantly involved in the new, incisive financial assessment of England's properties and the annexation and transference of monastic lands.

In 1536, although he had a country estate at Micheldever in Hampshire for his new family, he also needed a townhouse in which to reside during his many days at court. Although the people who frequently attended the court found it convenient to locate in the area that stretched from Aldgate on the western edge of the City, along the Thames to Westminster and accessed from what is now known as the Strand, for Wriothesley the less busy and better air further north at the Holborn highway, and close to his legal associates at Gray's Inn, was more desirable. He took a townhouse in the Holborn Barre just outside the City walls.

Wriothesley's Gain: Title and Territory

Continuing his rise at court, he participated in establishing a new office of non-aristocratic governance at the highest level: "In April 1540, when Cromwell gave up the post of secretary, Wriothesley was appointed as one of the two replacement principal secretaries, with Ralph Sadler: these two men were subsequently seen as the first holders of the double office of Secretary of State" (State Papers 1540, 7). He also maintained a consistent and unsullied reputation for administrative capability and reliable diplomacy. A fellow officer of the court observed: "I knew he was an earnest follower of whatsoever he took in hand, and did very seldom miss where either wit or travail were able to bring his purposes to pass" (Morisyne 1551, cited by Rowse 1965b, 120). Though another, slightly different description presents him as: "able, enterprising, tenacious and ruthless, yet insufferably overconfident and egotistic" (Weir 2001, 390). How strikingly such characteristics were to be replicated in many property developers to come!

In 1544, he was rewarded by being made Baron Wriothesley of Titchfield in Wiltshire and was granted the lease to a large swathe of land, some of which comprised land of dissolved monasteries and other rural lands in Stratton Micheldever and outlying pastures in Wiltshire and Hampshire. Although these estates undoubtedly served him well, he positioned himself to amalgamate them with other lands in the district. He was able to pay a fee to occupy the Premonstratensian house of Titchfield near Southampton, which would locate him suitably for future roles of governance in the region. And, he had already received a 61-year lease, generously lengthy, of the Hyde Abbey parsonage of Micheldever, with its strong ground lease revenues for his appeals to Rome on behalf of the abbot of Hyde.

The death of Henry VIII in 1547 was officially announced by Wriothesley as Lord Chancellor, and he acted as one of the executors of his will, alongside John Russell. Also with Russell, he was appointed to the higher aristocracy and made the 1st Earl of Southampton.

The Bloomsbury Estate

In support of the aristocratic titles distributed by his will, Henry also granted substantial land estates, and Wriothesley received further lands in Hampshire. Most critical to the birth of the private development model, however, was his gain of land in the London environs. The historian of the Russell family, Gladys Scott Thomson (1940, 19), reports that Wriothesley was granted "the fields, crofts, gardens, and house which were included in the manor of Bloomsbury, with some outlying pieces of land, all of which had formerly been part of the possessions of the Carthusian monastery commonly known as the London Charterhouse" (Figure 6.3).

On this land, situated just to the northeast of Edward VI's stockyards and stables, Wriothesley was required to pay a capital sum of £1,666 11s 3d as just compensation for the removal of the monarch's right to pasture horses and mules on the Bloomsbury lands, as Henry had done. With acute foresight, he knew it was necessary to remove such an encumbrance and free up the potential use of those for new purposes. As a lesson in preparation for development, this step indicated a strategic intention to change the *use* of the land and

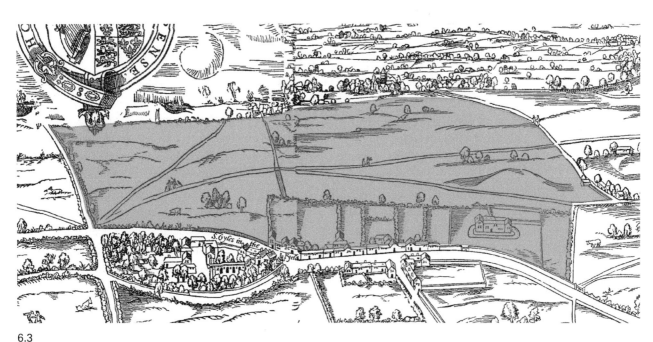

6.3

Bloomsbury estate.

more specifically in this case, to exclude anyone else's use that would adversely affect his anticipated use as a residential precinct.

Looking to expand his residence in the London metropolis to reflect his new status, though not yet interested in locating in Bloomsbury himself, Rowse (1965b, 125) noted that "Southampton made an exchange with [the Earl of] Warwick by which he got what came to be called Southampton House." This was probably the process by which he was able to obtain a fee simple title to the former Bishop of Lincoln's house, which gave its name to the adjacent Lincoln's Inn Fields. Though clear title to the specific lots is not recoverable, contemporary comments and court papers support the interpretation of Akrigg (1968, 6, Note 1), that this residence "stood south of Holborn and east of Chancery Lane, hence the name 'Southampton Buildings' for the edifice which now occupies part of this site," though the extension of land ownership to accommodate all these surviving buildings was to come later.

For his daily duties, the location was convenient. Going south on Chancery Lane was the Rolls House office where court administrators such as he often worked. Also, as he traveled west along the Holborn to his rural estates, he would have appreciated the pleasant fields and gardens of the Bloomsbury area on that highway's northern side. The 1561 Agas map (Figure 6.4) depicting the location of the Wriothesley town house and pastoral fields of Bloomsbury is probably the most common reference for spatial information of the Elizabethan period, and is one of the earliest maps made of London. However, the present-day interactive use of the map indicates Wriothesley's Southampton House as being within the Bloomsbury fields at the time of the map's drafting. But, as will be described in detail later, the relocation of that residence from Holborn Barre to Bloomsbury did not occur until almost a century later under the direction of the 4th Earl of Southampton. It is possible that Agas's grand rendering

St. James's Palace   Bloomsbury Fields   Rolls House
    Whitehall   Manor House   Wriothesley House
                              (not Southampton)

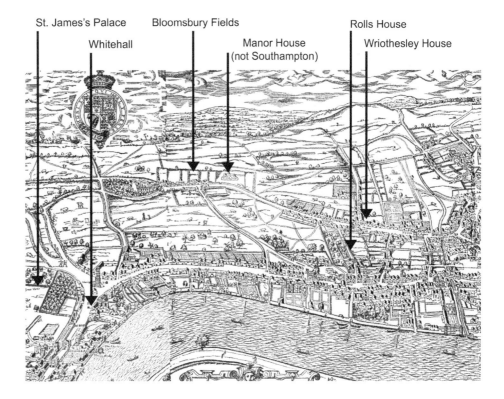

6.4

Approximate location of the first Wriothesley town house, the Bloomsbury fields, the Rolls House on Chancery Lane, and the commuter route to St James's Palace and Whitehall.

Bloomsbury Fields   Manor House   Southhampton House

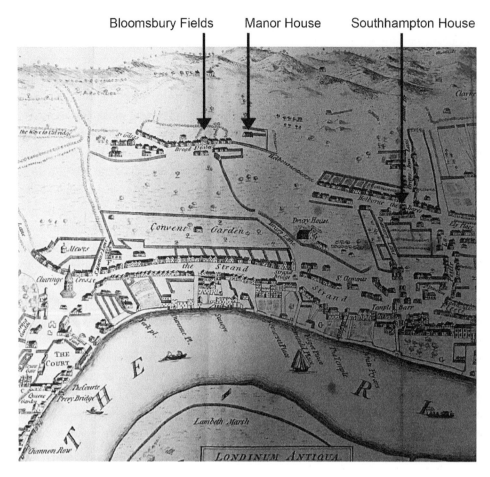

6.5

The Manor House on the Bloomsbury estate and the first Wriothesley town house, the first Southampton House, at Holborn Barre as indicated.

of a manor house is mistakenly labeled with respect to its timing, though not in its eventual location there.

A more suitable depiction of the Bloomsbury fields pastoral condition is that of the London map commissioned as Elizabeth I ascended to the throne in 1558 (Figure 6.5). Additionally, it presents the Bloomsbury fields as being particularly rural and remote and thereby emphasizing Wriothesley's astute appreciation of the area being so well positioned for the expanding market and trade activities of London.

Henry Wriothesley, 2nd Earl of Southampton (1545–1580)

During the tumultuous time following Henry VIII's death, the 1st Earl of Southampton passed away in 1550. Inheriting the earldom at the age of 5, his surviving son, Henry, was made a royal ward of the court until he came of age, as was the procedure for underage nobles.

The young earl grew up with familiarity of the court, initially under Edward VI, followed briefly by Lady Jane Grey, his godmother Queen Mary I, and finally Elizabeth I. He did not pursue a career at court but rather practiced law after admission to Lincoln's Inn in 1566. In that year, contrary to his mother's wishes since she thought it best to remain of low profile in religious matters during these times, he married Mary, the daughter of Anthony Browne, 1st Viscount Montagu, doyen of one of England's oldest and most venerable aristocratic families and who had been an unbending supporter of the Catholic Queen Mary.

At the 2nd Earl's death in 1581, a contemporary listing of the Southampton estate puts its total valuation at £1,097 6s per annum. As the 3rd Earl was a minor, that estate was distributed traditionally with a third of income to provide support for the widow, a third given to the Crown until the heir came of age, and a third used for the heir's support.

Henry Wriothesley, 3rd Earl of Southampton (1573–1624)

As for his father when he succeeded to the title, Henry (Figure 6.6) was made a ward of the court and, because of the wealth of the family though also the political mistrust aroused by his father, his wardship was taken by Lord High Treasurer and Master of the Wards himself, William Cecil, Lord Burghley. Having played a key role in Elizabeth's execution of Queen Mary, Burghley continued to hold a central role in the perilous intrigue throughout the new queen's reign.

6.6

Henry Wriothesley, 3rd Earl of Southampton in his teens, c. 1590–1593.

Coincidentally, this important courtier resided at Cecil House (sometimes referred to as Burghley House) on the northern side of the Strand contiguous to the lands of Covent Garden that had been granted to John Russell, the colleague of his grandfather. During his boyhood, Southampton spent much of his time with other young nobles at Cecil House, and in addition to the continual expansion of the stately mansion of Lord Burghley, he would have noticed the building of Bedford House next door, and also numerous other grand homes lining the Strand, though he would not have foreseen that his family's Bloomsbury estate would one day be merged with that Bedford estate of Covent Garden through the marriage of his granddaughter.

Shakespeare's Patron

Renowned for his extraordinarily elegant looks and demeanor and, given his maternal lineage and paternal wealth, the young Southampton was also at the center of the extravagant social and cultural life of London. He was enchanted by the emerging literary scene and attended the theater regularly, conversing with the players and forming artistic collaborations. It was said that "we know nothing whatever of the player-playwright's [Shakespeare's] introduction to the notice of the young Earl" (Rowse 1965a, 58), though the scholar Charlotte Stopes (1922, 40) has proposed that the "spring of 1591 best suits the lives of both peer and player." It seems that a friendship developed between them and he became Shakespeare's patron during those years; and at least two narrative poems were dedicated to him, *Venus and Adonis* and *The Rape of Lucrece*, both published in 1593.

Some studies of Shakespeare's work extend to note his commercial astuteness: the obvious financial awards delivered by his successful acting company with its royal patronage, his published playbooks, his very popular poetry books, his investment in a coat of arms, his shareholding in the development of the Globe Theatre, and acquisitions of property in Stratford. These strategic business moves had begun with the patronage of Southampton and, as the earl himself took on commercial interests, Shakespeare was most probably influenced and advised by him. With his heritage from his grandfather of an enthusiasm for investment combined with his culturally progressive support for Shakespeare and the arts, this 3rd Earl of Southampton may be seen to personify the changing ethos of the era relating to the growth of capitalism and its intertexture with culture and society.

Commencing His Business Ventures

Southampton came of age in 1594 and sought the return of his family properties from the Crown. Later that year, he was amongst a number of courtiers who invested in privateering that was part of England's many important nautical activities, including the great expeditions to Lisbon in 1589 and Cadiz in 1596 (Rowse 1965a, 68). Although his share in the galleon *Dudley*, with its capture of a ship laden with Brazilian sugar, led to a contest for the goods against the Crown in the Privy Council, his enthusiasm for commercial enterprises resulted in his continued investment in nautical ventures. He became a leader among the young aristocrats who turned to modern investment practices – "in industry, in modernizing their estates and in overseas trade and colonization" (Heinemann 1993, 139).

In 1598, Southampton quietly married Elizabeth Vernon (1572–1655), a childhood friend.

Although Southampton was arrested as a member of the Earl of Essex's 1601 plot against Elizabeth, his death sentence for treason was commuted on the serious entreaties of his longtime protector, Lord Burghley. Southampton remained a prisoner in the Tower and suffered the confiscation of all the revenues of his estates until the death of the queen in March 1603. From the parish rent rolls, it appears that the tenancies of the Bloomsbury estate had continued, though the revenues would have been directed to the Crown, while his wife and child lived very modestly on an allowance at Southampton House.

With the accession of the Scottish Protestant James I (1603–1625) to the throne, Southampton was released, his fine forgiven, his properties returned to him, and he regained a place at court. Now, by his cooperation with Burghley, who had managed the succession smoothly, he quickly returned to the inner circle of nobility, and by 1603 was elected to the order of Knights of the Garter, Europe's elite of chivalry and networked aristocracy (Figure 6.7).

Now the keen businessman applied himself to renovating his estates to be suitable for a royal visit, aware that comfort and hospitality were necessary "investments" in his relationship

6.7
**3rd Earl of Southampton,
c. 1618.**

with the king. The evolving social activity was such that "prominent in that pattern was the house party, an almost unforeseeable consequence of the building of the immense 'prodigy houses' of the sixteenth century" (Akrigg 1968, 145). At the Titchfield seat of his earldom he dispensed hospitality and "[o]n various occasions his sovereign was his guest … at Beaulieu, which the King found conveniently close to the New Forest, for centuries one of the royal game preserves" (Akrigg 1968, 144).

He also took his seat when James's Parliament opened, and

> [f]rom this time onwards we find [him] taking a very full part in all the business of the Lords, placed on numerous committees, including all the important ones and a number dealing with private matters, often named among those to confer on leading issues with the representatives of the [House of] Commons. (Rowse 1965a, 185)

The excellent relationship that he came to develop with the lower, elected House was regarded as indicative of his progressive attitudes and embrace of the new thinking that was to mark the 17th century and usher in new forms of business including private urban development.

Now staying steadfast and relatively politically neutral in matters of religion, he served in a government that saw the suppression of the Gunpowder Plot in 1605. He also played an important role in attempting to rescue the Crown's treasury. James was extravagant and "[o]f [the former monarch] Elizabeth's constant scrutiny of the whole fabric of public finance he was utterly incapable" (Willson 1956, 165). Lord Salisbury, the Crown Treasurer, sought to increase the royal revenues by taxing the ebullient import activity that was proving so prosperous for the merchants of London. However, he did so without recourse to Parliament, and though legally correct, this did not serve for harmonious relations between the Crown and the Commons. Southampton played a role in smoothing these waters, and in doing so he was also able to achieve relief from the tax for his wine import business.

His personal life also blossomed in 1605 with the birth of his son and heir, named James after the king, and for whom both the king and Robert Cecil, now Lord Cranborne, were god-fathers. A second son, Thomas, was born in 1607, and the family's succession was set with "an heir and a spare," though, as it will be seen, the "spare" proved to be more important. Southampton continued to support the theater, and also higher learning by making a grant of £100 per annum to the Bodleian Library at Oxford. His relationships at court were strong, and the young Prince Charles made visits to his estates at Carisbrooke, Titchfield, and Beaulieu.

Business Activities and Involvement in the New World
His immersion in the challenges of revenues and Crown budgets, and his comprehensive insight into London's hyperactive commercial world through his dealings with taxes and the Commons awoke in him an entrepreneurial spark. Enthusiastic about emerging industrial production, he financed the first tinplate mill in England and set up ironworks in his country seat at Titchfield. And with the rising popularity of corporate shareholding as a form of investing, he bought interests in new trading companies such as the East India Company.

Early in the 17th century, the whole country was curious about the colonization of North America, hoping to challenge Spain's increasing wealth through their expeditions to South America. In 1606, James I granted substantial lands in the new territory to the Company of Adventurers and Planters of the City of London, also named the London Company, and to the Plymouth Company. As shown in Figure 6.8, the overlapping area (yellow) was granted to

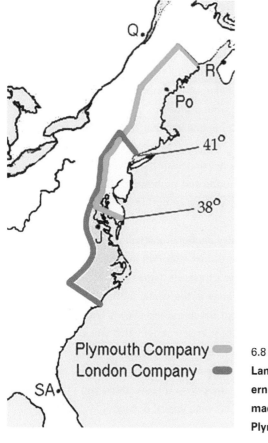

6.8

Land grants on the east-ern coast of today's USA made to the London and Plymouth companies.

both companies on the stipulation that neither founded a settlement within 100 miles of each other. In 1607, the London Company, supported by the interests of the Earl of Southampton with the Treasurer, Lord Salisbury, and other aristocrats, Suffolk and Pembroke, established a new settlement, Jamestown, as the first colony in Virginia, as the new country was then known.

The nobles and gentry exhibited a particular interest in investing in joint-stock companies in these ventures that expanded the reach of England's trade and territory. Although they shared an enthusiasm for profit with the merchant investors, the broader appeal to them was different. In promoting an expedition to Newfoundland in 1583, Sir George Peckham had noted the differences between "noblemen and gentlemen" and "merchants" and styled his promotional material accordingly.

> For the gentry he stressed the fine climate, the conditions favorable to landowners, the crops that could be produced, and the excellent hunting, include[ing] a description of a moose. For the merchants he provided a list of over 70 commodities which could bring them profit, with leopards, silkworms, pepper and rubies quite unabashedly claimed for fair Newfoundland. (Rabb 1967, 35)

This differentiation of investment objectives was an important characteristic of the rising commercial activity at the time and would resonate in the nature and motives of the early investors in the London property development projects that were just commencing.

However, in the early new settlement of Virginia the colonials struggled. The first arrivals of approximately 100 people were diminished within seven months to only 38 survivors, and their provisions were exhausted. A further series of settlers was sent but, unable to establish a satisfactory local production of food, Jamestown continued to flounder. Nevertheless, enthusiasm for the colony continued, and its success was regarded as a matter of national pride. To try to retrieve the situation, the Company was granted a new charter with extended powers to govern and create order in the colony and its membership expanded to "no less than fifty-six City companies and six hundred and fifty [individual] members" (Rowse 1965a, 238). Southampton invested another £350 in it.

The disasters for the settlement continued through a harsh winter in 1609–1610, during which only 60 of the approximately 500 settlers survived starvation. By 1616, it numbered only 350 and the funds of the company were exhausted. Even the presentation of the native "princess" Pocahontas in England failed to rally further support for the colony. It is possible that it was only the land grant policy providing 50 acres for each person settled, indicating an understanding of the economic potential for the individual that real estate provided, and the chance of a thriving crop of tobacco, that saved the colony.

The reports of Strachey, the first Secretary of Virginia, though not widely distributed, had very fully described Southampton's persistent efforts in support of the new colony: "They give a new idea of the relation of Southampton to the colonies, he being made the figurehead of the new and abiding work for the seventeenth century and Jacobean settlement" (Stopes 1922, 320). His involvement in the early days of the colony is also memorialized today in the State of Virginia's city of Hampton and its nearby harbor of Hampton Roads (Akrigg 1968, 165).

Southampton House

Although he was very involved in the newer forms of commercial enterprise such as industry, trading, and colonial settlements, Southampton also tended diligently to his London properties, particularly towards the end of his life. During his mother's life, Southampton did not reside at the family's town residence on the Holborn, nor did he yet have a claim to the Bloomsbury manor estate further west. However, with the death of Mary Browne in 1607, the former became his primary residence and that of his young family. By all accounts, he renovated it to suit his new status and also to accommodate his now thriving London business activities associated with trading and colonial settlements.

He was also able to extend the grounds of Southampton House to the south along Chancery Lane (Figure 6.9). In the State Papers of King James's court, the inclusion of this allotment is confirmed by a decree of the king to the Attorney General, Sir Henry Yelverton: "that the liberties and bounds of Southampton House in Holborne shall be extended from the Barres there to the Rolls in Chancery Lane" (D.S.S.P. James xciv. 93, Nov. to Dec. 1617).

Today, these lands are occupied by the Southampton Buildings, memorializing the town residence of the first four Earls of Southampton.

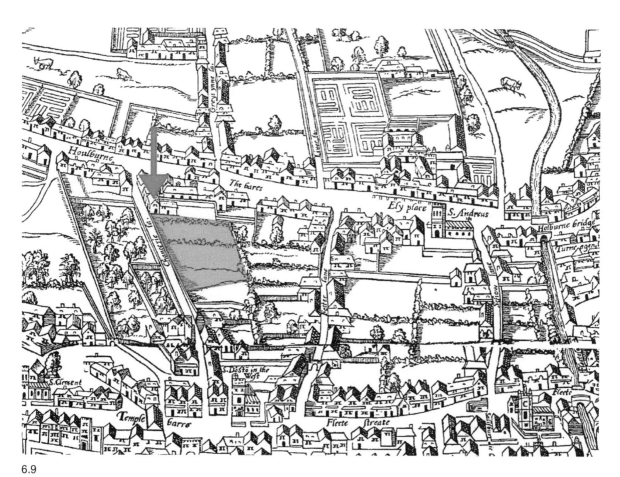

6.9

Southampton House with the acquired land on Chancery Lane.

Developing the Bloomsbury Estate

The Bloomsbury estate had continued to be occupied by tenant farmers and the manor house leased for residential use, as it had been prior to the grant to his grandfather, the 1st Earl. With the rapid expansion of London's activities to this area west of the City walls, its potential for residential use probably would have come to pique the 3rd Earl's interest, though, as it was probably encumbered by long leases, he was not at first able to alter the tenancies and there are no reports of rent roll changes.

By tradition, established landed estates were expected to expand or consolidate their estates in order to achieve more efficient utilization or to gain more political influence (Beckett 1986, 54–55), and Southampton would have noted some land acquisition opportunities. In his seniority, his relationship with the Crown was so strong that in 1616 he made an important acquisition of a piece of land for the Bloomsbury estate. Although small in size, this plot had been owned by the hospital of St Giles-in-the-Fields but had suffered a complex history of lease holding since the Dissolution (Thomson 1940, 23–24). It excluded the St Giles manor house and some other pieces under divided ownership, but significantly had frontage to the important Holborn high road (Figures 6.10 and 6.11). Strategically, it was adjacent to the Pond Piece and stretched westward between the southern boundary of the Bloomsbury fields and the Holborn highway to where Bury Street would eventually run.

The entrepreneurship of this action cannot be overstated, since it manifests a commercially progressive understanding of strategically increasing the value of a landholding. Rather than conforming to the usual motive of increasing the scale of an estate, this enlargement was not extensive but so vitally important to the access for Southampton House and to the integration of the Bloomsbury estate within future city infrastructure (Figures 6.12 and 6.13).

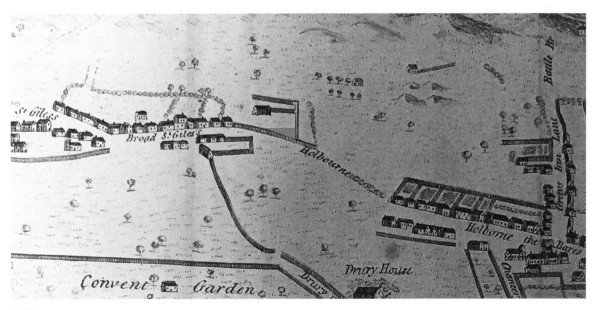

6.10

Map of 1563 prior to the acquisition of the plot on the Holborne.

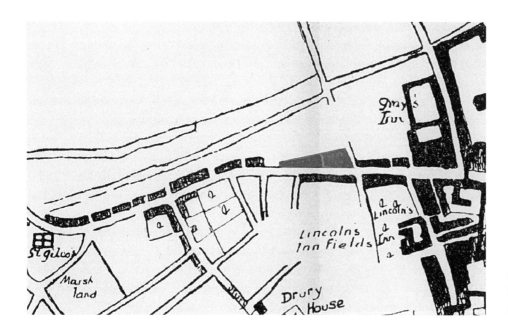

6.11

Map of 1603 with the strategic plot acquired in 1616.

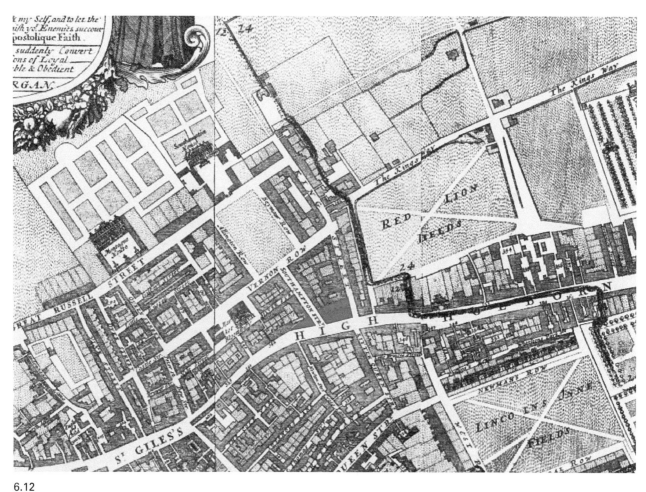

6.12

Map of 1682 showing development over the strategic plot acquired in 1616.

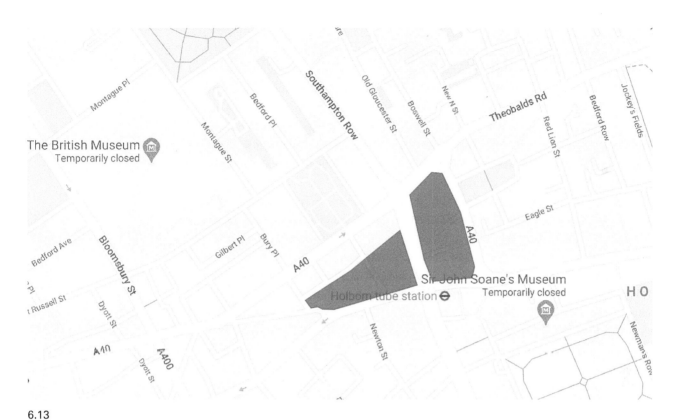

6.13

Map in 2020 showing continued development and city infrastructure over strategic plot acquired in 1616.

By 1624, when he died, not only was this Holborn highway becoming a thoroughfare, but houses were appearing at the edge of the fields on both sides. It was no longer rural countryside but had become an emerging residential area with much higher potential rental rates. When the 4th Earl was to undertake his Bloomsbury Square development, he placed the central access to the Square and also his new Southampton House through this plot, establishing Southampton Row. And by the end of the century, it was fully built out with fine residential homes as part of what would be called the Southampton Square precinct.

James's Troubles

By 1620, James's government was in turmoil. Religious conflict on the Continent had flared up again, and the early disturbances leading to the Thirty Years War were embroiling the British king and the Catholic relatives of the Stuarts. Charles had ascended to the throne in 1625, and the ceremony had included the participation of both the Earl of Southampton as cupbearer, and his son, James, now Lord Wriothesley, as one of the attending knights (Stopes 1922, 383–384).

Such political disruption resulted then, as it does today, in troubles for the economy, particularly as the kingdom's prosperity was now very dependent upon trade, and those trade routes and distant ports that were at risk. James attempted an alliance with Spain by arranging the marriage of his eldest surviving son Charles to Princess Henrietta Maria of France, though this was regarded by many as problematic to England's relationship with other important trading partners on the Continent. Probably of particular concern to Southampton would have been the threat of the inferior Spanish tobacco that would undermine the Virginia Company's monopoly on tobacco imports into Britain.

In 1622, he was more vocal than usual in opposition to the king and was "taken into custody and held in honorable confinement from mid-June to the end of July" (Rowse 1965a, 253). Although he was released and again took his place in the House of Lords, the conflict between the king and the Parliament continued. By 1624, both Houses had voted for a breach with Spain and an alliance with the Dutch, and £300,000 provided for the Anglo-Spanish War. By August, Southampton was included in the campaign, departing for Holland, where his eldest son James was serving in a regiment.

However, with winter, a plague raged through northern Europe and, in Rosendale of the Low Countries, James was dead by November 5th. While taking his son's body home, the exhausted and aging Southampton himself died on November 10th. His widow sadly received both bodies at Titchfield, where they were buried in the tomb that had been built there by his father. Remembrances of Southampton were particularly focused on his capability as a member of the House of Lords, in which role he discharged numerous duties well, and was known to be "one interested in the common cause" as evidenced by his continued constructive rapport with the members of the House of Commons. Additionally, in the management of his business interests, he was seen as honest and diligent in resolving problems: "One sees that he was a man to whom people resorted with their troubles in entire confidence in his uprightness and justice, and also that his concern in the Company's affairs was close and practical" (Rowse 1965a, 247).

His surviving son, Thomas, who had excelled in managing the family estates in the absence of his father and elder brother, was accelerated in his promotion to the title of 4th Earl of Southampton at the age of 17.

King James I survived the 3rd Earl of Southampton by less than a year, and his son, Charles I (1625–1649), ascended to the throne in 1625. Within months, fulfilling his father's plans, he married Henrietta Maria, and the newlyweds visited the country seat of the Southampton family at Titchfield for over five weeks while London suffered through its plague.

Thomas Wriothesley, 4th Earl of Southampton (1607–1667)

Although Thomas Wriothesley (Figure 6.14) inherited the title when still a minor, his well-connected mother retained his wardship, and was the administratrix of her late husband's intestate estate (Stopes 1922, 473). Following tradition, he attended St John's College Cambridge, though it is also recorded that he had studied at Oxford, though possibly at an older age than usual. This wide scope of his education may have fostered his freedom of vision and his confidence and ability to implement it.

Then, like his father he traveled abroad for eight years, importantly retaining contact with his father's friends and colleagues throughout France, Italy, and the Low Countries. There he also met his future wife, Rachel (Figure 6.15), daughter of Daniel de Massue, Seigneur de Ruvigny, a French Protestant nobleman. They married in 1634 and returned to England (Akrigg 1968, 478). They had a son who died in infancy, followed by four daughters.

He took his seat in the House of Lords and, having learnt from his father to value the mood and legislation of the House of Commons, initially supported it in upholding constitutional rights and opposing the royal prerogative that had been persistently promoted by the Tudor and Stuart kings. The Tudors had solidified their position such that, by a constitutional consent

6.14
Thomas Wriothesley, 4th Earl of Southampton.

6.15
Rachel Wriothesley dressed as Fortune, c. 1635.

of the people, the monarch ruled unfettered and, although resenting the Parliament's power over them, particularly financial resources, they had managed the delicate balance of authority. The Jacobean Court, however, was more familiar with and inclined to the absolute royal rule of the Continent and this conflict, combined with numerous other structural and personal matters, evolved into the troubled rule of James, and was exacerbated with the claims of the young, arrogant Charles I. To meet this delicate situation, Southampton managed diplomatically between his loyalty to the Crown as an aristocrat and the rising discontent with Charles's rule. Meanwhile, he diligently attended to his properties, working with the managers at the various manors to make necessary repairs, new tenancies, and pastoral changes.

In 1636, preparing for the growth of his family, he felt that their London residence, Southampton House at Holborn Bars, was being crowded by many new and badly built buildings. He would have also noticed the gentry's elegant houses that had been built by William Newton along the north of Lincoln's Inn Fields and the row of houses at Queens Way, later called Great Queen Street, nearby to the west. He therefore removed his family from the original Southampton House, which had been the family's town residence for three generations, and planned a grander residence in the new style within the delightful pastoral area of his Bloomsbury estate.

Here, the large fields to the west and on the northern side of Holborn protected his family from the noise and dust of the highway and provided a pleasant outlook to the countryside and hills. Under the care of the 3rd Earl, the estate

> had acquired a certain beauty of which the open fields and meadows had not in the earlier years been able to boast ... Bloomsbury had acquired a fringe, even a very extensive fringe, of orchards and gardens which, laid out for commercial purposes, yet shed their beauty upon the surroundings. (Thomson 1940, 27)

Most notable was a cherry orchard, often referred to as a local landmark called the Great Cherry Garden, which probably extended from the original plantation of the manor house, along the back of the Holborn buildings to the pastoral Long Field.

Additional commercial floral gardens were established at the southern end, including the Rose Field, tilled by the long-commemorated William Short of Short's Gardens in St Giles. There was also a "Licours Garden," or Liquorice Garden, where medicinal herbs were grown for commercial purposes and processed in a stillhouse nearby. Further west, a field became a bowling green, for common usage, and was attached to another inn called the Crown. Indeed, according to the memoirs of the notable gentleman Captain Awdley, the address was highly regarded and referred to as "in Bloomsbury near the great cherry garden."

The design for the new Southampton House (Figure 6.16) was elegant, and said to have been designed by Inigo Jones, though this is unconfirmed and has even been denied. However, Southampton would have noted Jones's substantial involvement in the Covent Garden development undertaken by his fellow peer the Earl of Bedford, and desired to meet these new aesthetic standards. As he would require the court's approval for his new building, he probably consulted Jones in some planning and design capacity in order to smooth its approval. He applied for the necessary Letters Patent necessary to build, and the final design adopted some of the neoclassical architectural principles and features, though the less rigorous proportional composition probably denies its direct attribution to Jones.

Having experienced the planning for the development of his new London residence, Southampton saw the opportunity to use his talent profitably in exploiting the growing housing market which he was sufficiently astute to recognize. And he had the wherewithal to do it, including particularly suitable lands and the financial resources to develop them. With the continued influx of wealthy nobles and merchants to west of the City, for an aristocratic developer, such as Southampton, it was "[t]heir personal predilection to provide housing for the most important, wealthy and influential townspeople" (Beckett 1986, 267). Accordingly, his initial developmental undertaking on the Bloomsbury estate was in response to that

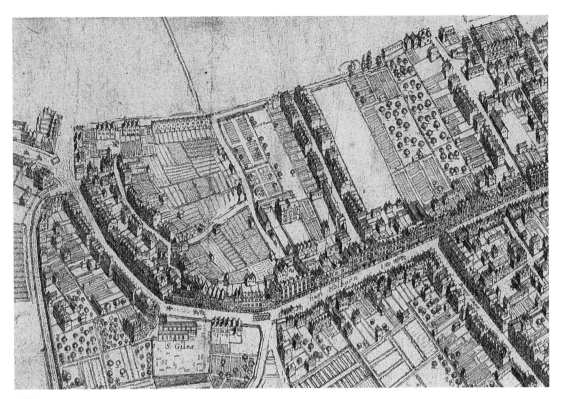

6.16

Bloomsbury estate showing the new Southampton House and the many gardens, c. 1658.

market segment, with a proposal for some free-standing houses. He planned to build four large houses with gardens on the eastern side of the Bloomsbury estate, conveniently fronting onto King's Way, for lease to gentry and merchants.

In 1636, applying for approval of this development project, he petitioned for the necessary license from the Privy Council. He was reasonably confident in his close connections at court and the king's support for his application, and he had probably been encouraged by the success of Bedford in obtaining approval for his Covent Garden project. But he was not successful, possibly because of the broader administrative restrictions on development that had re-arisen in the mid-1630s.

But, with the same tenacity as Bedford that would become so typical of the successful property developer, Southampton continued to petition for the scheme's approval, and in 1638 he received the necessary Letters Patent. He immediately commenced the construction of the houses along Kings Way (now Kingsway): "[F]our at least, described as facing on to the King's highway and having gardens behind them were of sufficient importance, as is shown by the names of the occupants, to be suitable for letting to gentry" (Thomson 1940, 26) (Figure 6.17).

On February 16, 1640, Rachel, his wife, died, and he was devastated. Their three daughters were left in the care of the aging Dowager Countess Bess, and he applied himself to his duties in the House of Lords while Charles's tumultuous reign was worsening. Despite Charles's unpopular behavior, in Southampton's opinion Parliament also behaved badly, and he finally gave his loyalty to the king. "He thought even a faulty Royalty better for the country than an unstable Republic" (Akrigg 1968, 481).

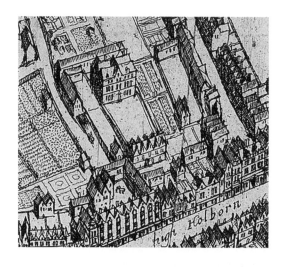

6.17

Southampton House and four houses developed on King's Way, c. 1660.

In 1641 he moved closer to the king with his appointment as one of the King's Bedchamber, the innermost circle of advisors. This was followed by his appointment to the Privy Council, the highest legal authority, and in 1642 as a High Steward of the University of Cambridge. The last may not seem to be politically important but, in fact, the intellectual discontent with the monarchy was most hotly debated in the universities of Oxford and Cambridge. Numerous proposals for peace between the Crown and Parliament emanated from them, and as High Steward, Southampton was one of the conveyors of their aspirational entreaties. In 1642 he married Elizabeth Leigh, daughter of Sir Francis, Lord Dunmore, and Earl of Chichester. By a special remainder in the Letters Patent of that Chichester's title, it was provided that, should he die without direct heirs, his title would go to his son-in-law and his estate to his daughter.

By 1642, though the new Southampton House was still not built, the small residential development which he had constructed proved to be a commercially successful subdivision in which expensive ground leases were incorporated in the rent of the buildings, testing the Bedford's new economic model at Covent Garden. In this small but important initial urban development, he changed the land's use from the agrarian activities to the more lucrative residential use, and by undertaking the building with his own funds, he received a high level of rent from the buildings as well as the ground. By retaining ownership of the buildings, rather than selling the right to a long-term lessee, he was also able to maintain those houses and gardens at a higher level. With their highly visible frontage to Kings Way and their proximity to the site of his own proposed new residence, it was important to him to retain the quality of this development.

The Interregnum

During Parliament's and Oliver Cromwell's rule, the gentry and aristocrats were heavily taxed but generally they retained ownership of their lands. It is recorded that in 1646 Southampton was fined, or taxed, a sum of £6,466, representing an estimated 10% of his estate's value (Thomson 1940, 30). He was also required to pay £250 per annum in support of the new Parliamentary government.

In 1653, his second eldest daughter, Rachel, aged 17, married Lord Vaughan. Then, in 1655, Southampton married again, this time to Frances, Lady Molyneux, a widow and the daughter of the 2nd Duke of Somerset, thereby consolidating his place among the aristocracy who were able to continue with their estate ownership under Cromwell.

By 1657, he had decided to proceed with building the Bloomsbury mansion and was able to do so by reason of the original permission of 1640. Even if the original plans had been prepared by Inigo Jones, he could not have supervised the building process as at Covent Garden since he had died in 1652. Southampton was required to conform with the given stipulations. Five acres, marked out in the southern half of Long Field, were to be enclosed by a brick wall and would contain the mansion house, outbuildings, and gardens, but leave open a grassy space between the wall and the Cherry Orchard to the south. The permit also required that the building should be carried out on "appropriate lines" to avoid conflagration, so it had to be of brick or stone, rather than wood. Further, as had been directed by the status-conscious Charles, the Privy Council's approval also required that the house should be "suitable in design and appearance for the purposes of which it was required. If anyone of the rank of the Earl of Southampton wanted to build a residence, then care must be taken that he should put up one that was in accordance with his position" (Thomson 1940, 33). In this, the 4th Earl of Southampton complied (Figure 6.18).

The building is specifically referred to by Sir Roger Pratt, the architect who was to act as Commissioner for Charles II in the rebuilding of London, as being of brick with walls approximately 40 ft in height and with foundations 3 ft thick. The main block was of three storeys

6.18

Southampton House, Bloomsbury, presenting the south façade that would be the north side of the future Southampton Square.

with wings on either side of two storeys, and entrance was gained by means of a sweeping staircase from the front courtyard. At the front of the courtyard were ornate gates of wrought iron. Later these would open onto the square which would be developed by Southampton.

The Restoration

By 1660, the year of the Restoration, Southampton's London residence in Bloomsbury was completed and given the name of Southampton House in the Fields. He was once again well placed to maintain a beneficial relationship with the new king, Charles II. Having provided substantial funds to the prince in exile, Southampton was rewarded with an appointment as Lord High Treasurer, serving from 1660 until 1667. He "was remarkable for his freedom from any taint of corruption and for his efforts in the interests of economy and financial order," a noble view of his work as the keeper of the nation's finances (Chisholm 1911). He proved to be an excellent statesman, and constantly excelled at raising funds when it was generally considered impossible. (This was to be yet another characteristic of a successful real estate developer!)

Bloomsbury Square

His enthusiasm for private urban development also returned and after considering the land proximate to the gates to his own home and gardens, he envisioned building more residences for the country aristocracy who were returning to reside in gracious homes in London to attend the extensive social and festive events of the new king. The demand for grand residences was also expanding to other markets as Schofield (1984, 5) describes in the expansion of London: "the merchants who controlled foreign commerce rose in power and tended to control the community. In London, their houses were in the same class as those of the nobility, from whom they had often been bought."

Now, like Bedford, in a high-profile position in society, Southampton also knew that he must remedy the developments on the rest of his Bloomsbury estate, to the south of his new home (Figure 6.19). They were mostly illegal improvements by his tenants. He had been notified by the authorities that they were unsatisfactory because of non-compliance with the new standards of structure and appearance, since they were of wood and often badly built. As he was now to live in close proximity to them, he was even more keen to remove them and improve the quality of the neighborhood.

Undertaking this, he strategically planned a certain portion of the site according to the principle of maximizing its potential value by obtaining legal approval for a distinct change of use from its current agrarian activities and minor housing. In this, he followed Bedford's innovative approach at Covent Garden, in contrast to the more passive aristocratic landowners. Additionally, rather than merely subdivide lots on an ad hoc basis, he viewed the site in a comprehensive way and intended to compose a balanced topology of building and landscape by also including a central open space. Even in the intervening decades, such urban layouts had not yet otherwise been adopted in London, where the distinction between private and public spaces remained more abrupt than being transferred through this intermediate open space. He even more explicitly followed Bedford by adding the prestige of his own residence to the new development.

New Southampton House

First four townhouses

Various illegal structures

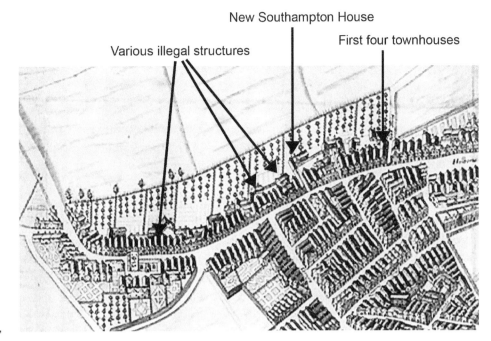

6.19

Southampton House and various illegal structures, Bloomsbury estate, c. 1661.

Through the Interregnum, however, London had evolved in a more democratic arrangement than many cities of Europe. Its various levels of society were housed cheek-by-jowl, while nobles or gentry from provincial locations were accustomed to distinct distances between their manor houses and a cluster of village homes. London's prosperity also now included wealthy merchants, who wished to be neighbors with the aristocracy. Thomson (1940, 178) noted that in respect of the Bloomsbury development the presence of the Russells, later joined by their relatives, the Montagus, "drew others thither."

For his Bloomsbury development, Southampton created an elegant square that continued the open space of his front garden and planned for the residential cluster of houses around it. With the exception of the small ancient City's public squares, Southampton Square is regarded as the oldest of the London squares as it was called a square in contrast to the Covent Garden piazza (Chancellor 2012, vol. 1, 183). The importance of its presence on the Bloomsbury estate was underscored by the commentary of urban critics of the day such as John Evelyn and Samuel Pepys (1900, vol. 4.2, 240), the latter of whom noted in his diary that it was "a very great and noble work" when he viewed in on October 2, 1664. After dining at the Southampton's home on February 9, 1665, Evelyn (1906, ii, 223) recorded his impressions:

> Dined at my Lord Treasurer's, the Earl of Southampton, in Bloomsbury, where he was building a noble square or piazza, a little town; his own house stands too low, some noble rooms, a pretty cedar chapel, a naked garden to the north, but good air. I had much discourse with his Lordship, whom I found to be a person of extraordinary parts, but a *valetudinarian* [hypochondriac].

The square deliberately did not in fact take the form of a piazza like that of Covent Garden, and E.B. Chancellor (2012, vol. 1, xxv), in the introduction to his authoritative compendium, describes its uniqueness:

> The 'Square' as we know it, that is, as a residential quarter, is essentially an English institution. It is neither exactly analogous to the French Place, the Italian Piazza, or the German Platz; nor do we find it on the Continent, to take but this quarter of the globe, any collocation of private homes, the inhabitants of which have a sort of prescriptive right over the ground on which their residences abut, as have those in the residential Square of London.

In 1703, the square was formally named Bloomsbury Square (Figure 6.20) and around that time it evolved to include a central garden. In this, the urban form was probably influenced by John Evelyn, the most distinguished of mid-17th-century gardeners. As described earlier, in 1661, he had published a scheme for London as a garden city, and though never realized, it had influenced the urban landscape and particularly the residential squares developed in

6.20

Bloomsbury Square, c. 1720–1728.

London over the following century. As the Southampton family funded the creation of the features of the square and maintained it, they varied its form from time to time, though its condition was also to vary with the fortunes of the family.

To the present day, no evidence of Southampton's specific deliberation regarding the economics of these decisions about the spatial layout and neighborhood composition of his project have been uncovered. However, given his business sense combined with his knowledge of the urban environments he would have experienced in France and Italy during his travels, it seems to have been a strategic decision. An empirical study by a rigorous comparison of the economic impact of such investment in amenities would be useful in evaluating his decision in this respect, as it would for development schemes today.

Petition for the Building License

These exciting new proposals for the estate represented modifications to the original layout that had been submitted primarily for approval of Southampton House in 1638. So in 1661, a new petition was prepared, and in November of that year, he received the permit that "enjoined" him to do things, and "permitted" him to do others. Of these there were two key items:

- Enjoined: Though no aooucation was made as to responsibility for the existing illegal and unsatisfactory structures on the estate, he was to put these buildings in proper repair, or demolish and rebuild them in stone or brick.
- Permitted: He was permitted to build on the open spaces of Pond Piece, Licours Garden, Bowling Green and the Cherry Orchard, and on the open space in front of his Southampton House.

Such a conditional approval in response to an application for an unusual urban development proposal was anticipated, and conditions attached to the plans for its implementation continue to be the format for development permission to this day.

Housing Product

However, Southampton learnt from the reaction to Covent Garden, and noting on the Restoration a rising sense of individuality and competition, instead of a monolithic arcaded residential structure Bloomsbury Square was to be bordered by distinctly distinguished, single-family houses. Running along their frontage on both the east and west sides were defined paths rather than public streets. The paths had the designations of Seymour Row and Allington Row, respectively, and they would provide a uniform line for the front of the house lots (Figure 6.21). Also having noted the potential value of smaller lots that were attractive to entrepreneurial builders in the area, he planned to divide each side of the square into housing lots of various sizes suitable for those constructions.

The total project was his astute, conscious calculation of the financial benefit to him of the more picturesque, genteel, and prestigious layout for the potential residents against the sacrifice of the valuable space for the square. Much as with any successful entrepreneur, and most certainly like the more inspired real estate developer, his continued modification and improvement of spatial format in response to an incisive understanding of nature and needs of his prospective tenants led to substantially improved financial returns.

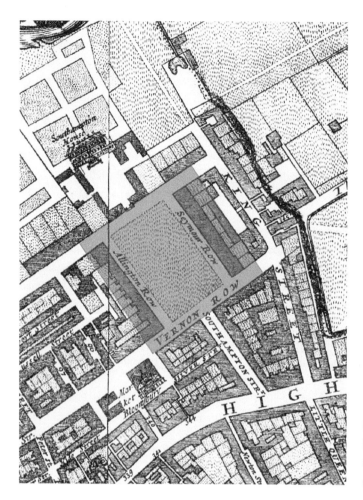

6.21

Map showing
Southampton Square
development, c. 1682.

As a man of business and financial interests, upon receipt of the approval, he immediately began to grant building leases for the planned lots, described as the demised premises standing around "the void space in front of my Lord's mansion." This language is interesting in its omission to declare the ownership of the "void," but by referring to the adjacency of the "front of my Lord's mansion," a constant vigilance towards and attention to, if not absolute control of that space is implied. This would certainly have provided some confidence in its maintenance by the lord for tenants who were located around it, though it also masked any indication of authority over it, who could make decisions about it, and who could complain, and this ambiguity as to authority and responsibility for the public realm provided by private interests continues to this day.

Despite the lease's clear definition of the central open space and the restrictions on lot configuration so that the street frontages were aligned, the size of the individual plots was not specified in the scheme plans. Thomson (1940, 178) regarded this flexibility of lot area as an astute business decision to meet the variation in potential demand of typical urban growth: "That the evolution of the district represented a natural rather than a planned growth is the more probable because it is clear that there was never any question as to the smaller sites being let alongside bigger ones even in the square itself."

The notion of uniform lots did not as of yet have a history of economic or aesthetic value. It emerged in the following century. Until that time, it had been an expeditious and logistically efficient method that was used by Newton and other merchant builders when they constructed rows of modest houses. A similarity of lot size and configuration represented a commodification of housing which both Southampton and his potential tenants would not have wished to adopt. As in other production activities, despite the arrival of industrialized methods he would have noticed the commercial importance of offering products of varying scale and potential individualization so that the plots of his development scheme would be best offered in portions of varying scale.

He might also have noticed that during the substantial rebuilding which was taking place within the City walls, the uniformity of lot sizes there posed problems to families that were growing in size and wealth and the combining of the small lots would have required a substantial approval process, and delay. On his proposed development project since he could not be certain of the exact requirements of the hoped-for residents, he innovatively incorporated flexibility in accommodating the needs of as broad a market as possible. Additionally, although the earliest developments by Bedford and Southampton were for grand houses for wealthy tenants, both projects accommodated more modest options since "their financial instincts favoured middle-class housing because it was likely to be maintained in good order, and to have a higher one-term value" (Beckett 1986, 267).

The market was certainly receptive to the scheme and tenants included fellow nobility, merchants, professionals, wealthy widows, and also "lesser folk." Examples of the variation in these leases are described by Thomson (1940, 42) as follows:

On the east side:

- First lease of 24 ft x 110 ft was to a widow, Mrs. Anne Tresham. Ground rent of £6/year.
- Four other plots of 24 ft x 110 ft configuration. Ground rent typically of £6/year.
- Lord Bellasis plot of 61 ft x 140 ft. Ground rent of £16/year.

On the west side:

- Edward Newcombe 1662 plot of 50 ft x 140 ft, to build TWO HOUSES, but they were required in the lease to be UNIFORM, and were restricted to habitation by only one family each.

On the south side:

- Seven plots cut into the Cherry Orchard of 20 ft to 44 ft frontage but only depth of 40–50 ft.

Throughout the inventory, the larger lots were leased at £12–£26/annum.

As the urban areas around London developed, various residents, either for a household of for business activities, aspired to the customization and outright ownership of their premises and, though generally claiming the use of the land through a ground lease, they funded the construction of the improvements to the site and were able to create the building they desired. In contrast to the uniform architecture continued ownership by Bedford of the residences of Covent Garden, this more independent form of development by owner-occupiers could be found in 23% of the Bloomsbury estate by the late 19th century (Offer 1981, 119).

Quality Control

Southampton's approach, therefore, tended more towards that of the traditional aristocrat's provision of ground leases for third-party improvements, though also without the control over the architectural quality achieved by Bedford. With the consideration of the topographical consequences, the historian Harding (2001, 130) notes that: "Where landlord control was weak, or local government control non-existent, the result [of development] could be chaotic." And the result of this difference in control of the development sites by the larger landlords was soon apparent in London's expanding metropolis. As Beckett (1986, 267) recorded: "The East End, where many of the landholdings were fragmented, became predominantly a lower-class housing area, but on the larger aristocratic holdings of the West End high-quality housing was erected."

However, still keen to control the resultant built form, and following an example of Bedford, Southampton included substantial restrictions on the quality and scale of building that would be permitted on the leased sites. While some of these restrictions and requirements were conditions of the development approval, Southampton also understood the need to retain control of the quality of the precinct's ambience in order to maintain its desirability and value. Thomson (1940, 52) quotes a noted doctor, Everard Maynwaringe (1628–1699), who remarked specifically with respect to this location:

And here I cannot but take notice of Bloomsbury (the Right Honourable Earl of Southampton' property and seat [*sic*]) for the best part about London both for health and pleasure exceeding other places. It is the best air and finest prospect, being of the highest ground and overlooking other parts of the city.

Development Progress

Southampton's project was successfully launched and Coulter (2016, 70) reports that "[b]uilding went on briskly throughout the 1660s. The east side was known in the early days as Seymour Row, the west as Allington Row, the south was Vernon Street and later Hart Street."

By the year 1668 the Bloomsbury estate included 146 tenants, excluding those who rented marketplace stalls. The ground rent varied widely, ranging from a moderate £2 or £3 a year to substantial levels of £20. Additionally, some land was still leased to farmers for grazing and the total rent roll probably approximated £2,000 per year. After the earl's death when William Russell relocated the young household to Southampton House, this encouraged significant new development along the road leading from the square to the thoroughfare of Tottenham Court Lane, at that time named Russell Street. Subsequently, between 1671 and 1681 at least forty new building leases were taken along that fashionable street.

Long-term Planning and Lease Tenure

In his strategic plans to retain control of the estate and to be able to reconsider future use and potential value, Southampton insisted that his consistent lease tenure was to be forty-two years (Thomson 1940, 44). This period was assessed to be adequate for the amortization of the cost of erecting a good quality masonry building, and was substantially longer than the more common twenty-two years of lesser-quality housing. By this means, though allowing flexibility in terms of lot size, he formulated the lifecycle of the development.

Appreciating that changes in urban London might present different opportunities for his estate, he arranged his leases to be co-terminal, which provided a schedule for that re-evaluation. Olsen (1982, 43) notes this planning strategy, saying:

> The Earl of Southampton provided for future redevelopment with more foresight than the Earl of Bedford had done in Covent Garden. He granted no property on fee-farm rents [that is, in perpetuity], but disposed of the whole of the building land on forty-two-year leases. When the leases fell in, the estate would be able to pull down, replan, and rebuild.

Nor did Southampton lease large swathes of land to other substantial developers, thereby maintaining a more direct link to the quality of the building and the behavior of the residents.

Role of Agent for Real Estate Business
Undertaking this new urban development, Southampton required the services of a capable "receiver-general," also known at that time as "chief agent" or "agent-in-chief." Today this is called the asset or property manager, with the responsibility to manage the lease transactions, collect the rent, and direct maintenance expenditures. It is remembered that the earl's ancestor, William Wrythe, served in this role for the Duke of Somerset.

Appreciative of the importance of this role, especially for the complex urban properties, the 4th Earl took great care in making this appointment. The role had traditionally been given to members of the country gentry, a second son, or an heir to a small estate to provide training. However, immediately with his embarking on the project in 1660, he appointed Mr. Collop. Though a son of one of his lesser tenants at the Dorset estate, he was of the new breed of educated commoners working as a professional in the thriving metropolis.

For the Bloomsbury estate, Collop introduced the practice of retaining "docketed bills," that is, the receipts of specific expenses paid. This more detailed accounting of the outgoings on the estate provided a more comprehensive economic picture of the project. Additionally, by relating expenditures to rental revenues, he revealed the detailed dynamics of net income derived from the real estate holdings, that could be compared year-to-year. Though seemingly common practice today, achieving this understanding of cost offsets to specific revenues enable important future decisions requiring a cost-benefit analysis to be informed by experience. This aspect of real estate is critical to decision-making in both asset management and development, though unfortunately even today is often inadequately performed.

This innovator was succeeded by a professional lawyer, Mr. Fox, who continued the evolution of this important role of asset manager responsible for overseeing the assets, continually extracting pertinent information, and performing rigorous financial analysis.

Infrastructure
As this square was removed from the major thoroughfare of Holborn, and involved the transformation of fields and pastures, it required the placement of streets through it and connection to existing main roads. Thomson (1940, 46) reports that by 1662, Southampton had retained the Long Field on the west side of the square for himself, but from it allocated two lots with a southern boundary as "an intended street" to lead from the Square west to Tottenham Court Lane. Completed in 1664 this substantial infrastructure was referred to as

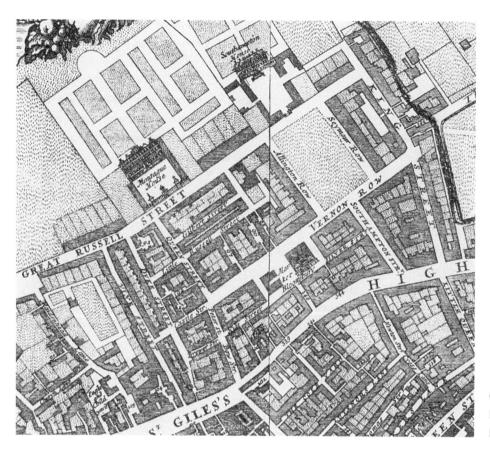

6.22

**Infrastructure of the
Bloomsbury estate, c. 1680.**

"a great street leading from Southampton House towards Tottenham Court Lane," and would later be named Great Russell Street (Figure 6.22).

Between 1661 and 1663, southern access was made to the important Holborn highway to provide Southampton and other residents attending court with ease of access to the south on their way to Westminster and St James's Palace. This important connection traversed the critical, though small, lot bordering the highway that had been strategically acquired by the 3rd Earl of Southampton, as described earlier. This became known as Southampton Street, though was not specifically mentioned in any leases at the time. By 1666, Russell Street extended eastward through the Pond Piece fields making a connection to the ancient lane of Kings Way, which was later renamed King Street.

Thomson (1937) refers to an article in a gentleman's magazine of 1755 in which the author rallied for the construction of a road from Edgeware Road in Paddington to Islington on land owned by the Duke of Grafton. Although this bypassed the Bloomsbury estate and the duke was not required to contribute land to it at all, he initially did join with some of his tenants in protesting that the dust resulting from the traffic would adversely affect the remaining pastures and fields on the estate; and perhaps he perceived that the new residential lots released by such access would diminish the level of demand for his lands. However, he soon realized the opportunity which this road, becoming Euston Road in time, might provide for his estate if he himself connected to it, thereby shortening his journey, and those of many of his tenants, to their country estates. This he did, though not without encountering the refusal of his neighbor for the use of a small segment at the intersection and resulting in the frequent the bitter dispute between landowners over easements.

Commercial Activities

While there is speculation that a small market may have existed on the Bloomsbury estate prior to the development activities that commenced in the 1660s (Thomson 1940, 48), a market was formally established in 1662. It was held on Tuesdays, Thursdays, and Saturdays, after Southampton successfully obtained the license. The process of approval for such a public undertaking included then, as now, the input of various stakeholders. The Letters Patent referred to an assessment made by gathering opinions, under oath, by lawful men of the county, that it would not damage the king or any neighboring markets. Although the produce to be traded is not nominated in this approval, its specific limitation to "fish and flesh" was established in a second permit issued in 1666. In contrast, the Covent Garden market was where fruit and vegetables were offered for sale.

The market's location was at the northern end of the small, truncated Darby Lane, which provided the necessary connection for deliveries from the Holborn. Eventually Southampton widened it to function better commercially, and lined it with housing plots; and it is now known as Lion Street. By 1663, Hyde Street was established, running westward from the southwest corner of the market, and by 1664, Hart Street ran along the north side.

Although seeming to provide a strategic amenity for the growing residential neighborhood, he was also establishing the market as a substantial commercial activity for which he received rent and tolls for access. By 1668 that enterprise was worth £340/annum. With this flourishing trading activity came the usual recreational activities of London's citizens and visitors. To accommodate visitors, more inns were built, and these usually included taverns. Scott Thomson (1940, 178) reports that by 1666, "Inns were everywhere … Several were to be found in King Street besides the first tavern which had appeared there, the Three Kings."

Social Status

Southampton intended for his neighbors to be of significant social status and for Bloomsbury Square to be the new prestigious residential precinct. The buildings of Covent Garden were aging, and after the Great Fire of 1666 many commercial activities were relocated on the Strand and around the piazza. In contrast, the Bloomsbury area was still overlooking gardens and open fields and offered sites for new houses. Williams (2001, 193) describes the advantages sought by those who could afford the better locations, and the conditions of those who could not, saying "those with the means chose residences in open, spacious, and leafy parts of town, layering environmental patterns with a social zoning whereby the poorer citizens were left in the least salubrious areas."

When potential competition arose with the proposal by the Earl of St Albans to develop St James's Square, the Earl of Southampton, as Lord Treasurer, attempted to exert his influence and have the development application refused. However, St Albans had even stronger connections at court and was able to gather support. Relating the history of that new square, Dasent (1895, 372) describes the rebuttal to Southampton's efforts: "On 25 March 1665 Lord Arlington wrote to Clarendon, then Lord Chancellor [the second most powerful role in the kingdom], urging that Lord St Albans should be granted the inheritance of the square whether the Lord Treasurer had given it his sanction or not." Undoubtedly to Southampton's chagrin, the Earl of St Albans received his approval a week later, on April 1, 1665.

Bloomsbury, however, continued to be much sought after by upper-class residents. Scott Thomson (1940, 178) describes its status:

> It was in this quarter, made up of the square, Great Russell Street, Southampton Street and King Street, with its prolongation as Southampton Row, which housed the more important residents in Bloomsbury ... The choice of the site by the Earl of Southampton for his own mansion had been a deliberate one ... The presence of the Russells and the Montagus in Bloomsbury drew others thither.

In retrospect, Southampton's plans for the Bloomsbury estate marked the beginnings of the opportunity, if not a social pressure, for the merchant, the professional, and the non-nobility who wished to reside near London, to construct a house that reflected their socio-economic position. The selection of lot, its location, its size, and its aspect became more than utilitarian, and was loaded with social significance. Southampton's use of the proximity and pleasant features of his own mansion provided such privileged sites, and he benefited financially by their rising desirability. The contemporary social commentator, Pepys, recorded in 1664 that he took a look at "Lord Southampton's new buildings in the fields" and approved.

The 4th Earl of Southampton died on May 14, 1667, having achieved the prestigious office of High Treasurer to Charles II. He had married for the third time to Frances Seymour, daughter of the politically influential William Seymour, 2nd Duke of Somerset, though they had no children. The Dowager Lady Southampton surrendered what would have naturally been her right to reside at Southampton House for the remainder of her life and lived elsewhere before remarrying in 1676.

Amalgamation of London Land Estates: Southampton and Bedford

The 4th Earl died leaving only three daughters and no male heir and therefore his aristocratic title was extinguished. However, the prudent businessman had ensured that the family properties would not be escheated to the Crown and, having successfully sought to own the lands on a fee simple basis, was able to appoint his daughters as co-heirs to those estates.

Trust Structure for Estates

A further evolution of the real estate development business model was the appearance of this specific trust structure for property ownership. It has been a long English tradition for the head of a landed aristocratic family to administer the estate personally, and for leases to be renewed by an heir if the head of the family had died. However, because of an increase in the complexity and kind of urban leases, such a system was not viable, and a system of continuous and open-ended trusts was established.

By this structure there was continuous ownership of the lands, which simplified the management of revenues and expenses and a distribution to the beneficiaries according to the annual financial support determined by the head of the family. Since by legacy this structure inherently maintained the ownership claims of the estate and the distribution of proceeds, it closely resembled the partnership equity structure that has been at the core of much real estate investing today. That this structure was appropriated from other contemporary commercial dealings by merchants, and even investors in the early insurance schemes, indicates how rapidly the perception and management of land was converted from a passive agrarian holding to an asset to be developed and actively managed according to changing real estate markets. Additionally, that trust structure has continued as a popular vehicle of property ownership and served as the forerunner of the corporate structure known in the USA as Real Estate Investment Trusts (REITS).

The process of allocating his properties amongst his three daughters was not specific, and Scott Thomson (1940) describes its resolution:

> The Earl of Southampton, in his will, had merely desired his trustees to divide the properties into three parts, one for each of his three daughters ... He had expressed no wish as to how the lands were to be divided, nor how, when divided, they should be apportioned. But someone, whether a trustee or a daughter, had a scheme. The estates being divided, according to the rentals, as equally as might be into three parts, the decision as to which part should go to which daughter had been left to the ancient biblical method of casting lots. (Thomson 1940, 16–17)

Rachel Wriothesley Inherits

The resultant distribution is revealed in a note left by the second sister, Rachel Wriothesley (1636–1723) (Figure 6.23), who grew up in the time of Charles I and the Interregnum following. Now a childless widow, she most probably played a role in the administration of the deceased's estate. She wrote:

> Valuation delivered to me by trustees 1668; the estate being at that time valued and divided into 3 parts. My sister Noel, my sister Northumberland and myself cast lots. Mine

6.23

Rachel Russell, Lady Russell (1636–1723).

was: The manors of Stratton Micheldever, etc., in Hampshire; Southampton House and the manors of Bloomsbury and St Giles in Middlesex. (Archives, Woburn Abbey)

It should be noted that while this endowment for Rachel provided her with a sizable income, she could not directly hold title to the property. Rather, it was to be held in trust for her until she married and then transferred to her husband. This did, however, make her a much more "attractive" wife than when she had married Vaughan while her father was alive, for while he lived there remained the possibility that he might have a son to whom all his property would pass. However, now that she was an heiress in possession, such a risk was removed (Beckett 1986, 56). Furthermore, there is no evidence that her inherited land was settled in such a way that, should she fail to produce an heir, it would revert to a distant male cousin. Her father obviously sought to provide well for his daughters and had confidence in their abilities to provide at least informal administration of their wealth.

Within two years, Rachel was participating in an important dynamic relationship for real estate property that continued a centuries-old aristocratic tradition but also ushered in a new process by which modern cities would be built. In a manner similar to that undertaken in maintaining the wealth of European families, Rachel's prosperous partial holdings of the former Southampton estate were to be amalgamated by marriage with those of the Bedford estate:

On 31st July 1669, at Titchfield in Hampshire, a marriage was celebrated between William Russell, second son of William, fifth Earl of Bedford, and Rachel, Lady Vaughan, daughter and co-heir of Thomas Wriothesley, fourth Earl of Southampton ... The marriage was a good match for both bridegroom and bride ... His marriage settlement gave him and his bride an allowance of two thousand pounds a year, chargeable upon the principal rentals, notably those of Covent Garden and Woburn ... William, however, had taken a wealthy bride, who, as co-heir to her father, brought him no inconsiderable inheritance. (Thomson 1940, 13–14)

A substantial component of this wealth that Rachel brought to the union was the Bloomsbury estate, which formally became part of the enduring estate of Bedford.

With the combination of the Bloomsbury estate and the Covent Garden estate, the development of a large portion of the general urban fabric of London's West End would be undertaken with a strategy of long-term ownership by a private landlord. Later, the model was adopted by other aristocratic families who owned, acquired, and amalgamated holdings, many of them in important urban areas. For example, the legacy of Rachel's sisters described earlier would produce respectively the 1st Duke of Portland, and the 5th Duke of Buccleuch, one of the largest landowners in the United Kingdom (Stopes 1922, 483).

The other Great Estates of London (Figure 6.24) were similarly formed in this manner.

The Grosvenor estate was amalgamated with the Marlborough estate. The Cadogan estate was built on the legacy of one of the oldest of families in Britain when in 1717, Charles, 2nd Baron Cadogan (1685–1776) married Elizabeth, daughter of Sir Hans Sloane (1660–1753), described by the historian of the Cadogan family, Norwich (2017, 13), as "the richest, most celebrated and by far the most eccentric doctor in London." Relating back to the Southampton

6.24

London's Great Estates today.
Key to Fig 78: 1. The
Portman Estate, 2. The
Howard de Walden Estate,
3. The Bedford Estate, 4. The
Grosvenor Estate, Mayfair,
5. The Crown Estate, Regent
Street, 6. The Grosvenor
Estate, Belgravia, 7. The
Cadogan Estate. The "new"
Great Estates, 8. King's
Cross, 9. Broadgate.

family, Sloane had established his practice at No. 3 Bloomsbury Square and from which he attended the monarchs Queen Anne, George I and George II. He would have been appreciative of the business interests of Southampton, followed by Bedford, in the development of Bloomsbury, and in 1712 he bought for £7,000 from the 2nd Viscount Newhaven the 166-acre manor of Chelsea, which with its orchards and gardens would have appeared much as those Bloomsbury fields had appeared fifty years previously. This estate was to be developed as the extensive Cadogan holdings of Chelsea that continue to this day.

As Britain settled its far-flung colonies, this model of urban development under the patronage of a wealthy owner of large landholdings was also widely used to create the built environment long before municipal authorities could be formally established to do so. As has been seen, both the Southampton and Bedford families had been involved in some expeditions and settlements in early America and the West Indies, and their established formulation of estate development was emulated by many in those new settlements.

Continued Development of Bloomsbury

Together, William and Rachel lived a delightful social life after moving into Southampton House in Bloomsbury. It was during this time that Southampton House was renamed Russell House, in accordance with the male line of the couple. William became very involved in developing that estate further, particularly since he had been extensively groomed in such matters by his father, the 5th Earl of Bedford.

From the Bloomsbury estate, they continued to receive a rent of just over £1,200 per annum, an estimated £340 per annum from the market, and other rent from the farmers on the remaining fields and pastures. Only a few vacant lots around the square remained and, although the records from 1667 until the 18th century have been lost, it would seem they were developed under William's capable direction.

Also understanding the importance of connecting such a square to the surrounding neighborhood and emulating his grandfather's attention to the Covent Garden precinct as a whole, it seems that he encouraged significant new development along the road leading from their Southampton House westwards to Tottenham Court Lane. Between 1670 and 1681, under his supervision, at least forty new building leases were taken up along this street and it was

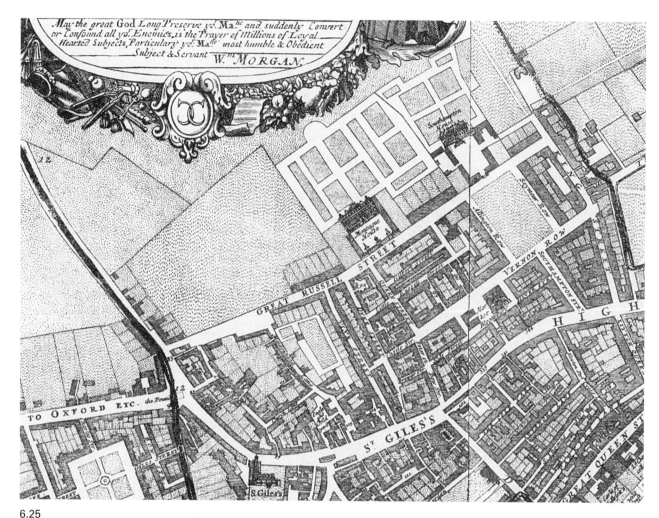

6.25

Development of the Bloomsbury estate by c. 1680.

paved and laid out with a uniform frontage. In a 1670 lease, it is referred to as "the new street called Russell Street," and, by 1674, called Great Russell Street.

In 1673, Rachel's stepsister Elizabeth made her second marriage to Ralph, who ten years later was to become the 3rd Baron Montagu of Boughton, thus reuniting his family with that of the 2nd Earl of Southampton's wife's. He had been on important missions to the Continent for the Crown and was Ambassador in Paris in 1669. Returning to England, he was made a Privy Councilor in 1672, shortly prior to his marriage.

For their town residence they leased a piece of the Bloomsbury estate located on the northern side of Great Russell Street, just to the west of Rachel and William's Southampton House (Figure 6.25). It comprised just over 7 acres and required an immediate payment of £2,610 together with a fee farm rent of £5/annum. The agreement was made in 1675 and the wall enclosure for their house and garden was erected immediately. In his *Survey of London* (1720), Strype described Montague House as being the handsomest of the houses of noblemen in Great Russell Street. Later, in 1753, the land was resumed by the Crown for the construction of the British Museum, which continues on the site today.

6.26
Nos. 89–91 Great Russell Street in 2019.

Much as had followed the residential development in Covent Garden, land lots were provided for craftsmen and traders who resided above their commercial premises on the ground level. Some of these early structures still exist and continue this mixture of uses in the streets surrounding Bloomsbury Square. Showing only minimal upgrades to its windows and parapets is a row of three such structures at Nos. 89–91 Great Russell Street, being the dark gray row with the red awning on No. 90 in the center (Figure 6.26).

As the prestige of the Bloomsbury neighborhood continued into the 18th century, more wealthy merchants and noble families established their London residences there. Generally, the north side with its prospect of the open fields at the rear was preferred. Lady Gower and Sir John Meres both had leases there as recorded in the rent book of 1729. By this time there were just over forty houses on that side, stretching from King Street to Tottenham Court Lane, and approximately thirty houses on the south side, part of which side gave onto Southampton Square. Along the east side of King Street, and in its prolongation into Southampton Row, other large houses with gardens were built, generally by the residents.

In succeeding generations, the Bloomsbury estate continued to be owned and managed by the Bedford family. Only a few parcels of land were sold, for example as the lot on which the government funded the building of St George's church in 1714, though some other sales were to occur much later under the 1976 Leasehold Reform Act. Other additions were made to the estate, such as the lot now recorded as 195 Tottenham Court Road that had been the farmhouse used by Bedford's longtime tenant farmer Christopher Clapper. This area of Cantelowe Close was not part of the fields of the Bedford estate, but had been owned by the Earl of Clare. It was purchased in 1772 to strengthen the estate strategically at that northwestern corner.

Russell Family Succession

William and Rachel had four children. The eldest, Anne, was born in 1671 but died in infancy. The two succeeding children were also girls, Rachel and Katherine, who both lived into adulthood.

In 1678, William's sickly elder brother, Francis, died and therefore provided clarity to his succession to his father's title. With further determination of the Bedford family succession, on November 1, 1680, William and Rachel had a son, Wriothesley, combining his mother's family name with his father's Russell. This would provide continuity of the Bedford lineage, now fully joined with that of the Southampton's.

Russell Executed

In the following decades, troubling times arose because of the question of succession to Charles II as he had not sired a son. The competitors included his unpopular brother, James, Duke of York, who had rekindled a strong relationship with the Church of Rome. William Russell was a member of the Protestant Whig party, which was at odds with the Tories who supported James. Plots against and in support of James were numerous, and in 1683 Russell was implicated in what became known as the Rye House Plot. In July of that year, he was beheaded in Lincoln's Inn Fields. It was said that as he was driven to the place of execution from the Tower in the east and the coach turned left into Little Queen Street, he looked further west where his beloved family were bereaved at Southampton House in the Bloomsbury estate and where he had created such an important part of modern urban London. It is said that he remarked to the Dean of Canterbury, who was attending him in his last moments: "I have often turned to the other hand [that is, to the right towards Holborn and Southampton House] with great comfort," and briefly shed his only tears during his final ordeal (Chancellor 1932, 40).

Although the Bloomsbury estate was now part of the Bedford estate and all the revenues were directed to the 5th Earl of Bedford, Rachel, as William's widow, continued to receive an annual stipend of £2,000. This was augmented by the Earl's grant in support of the young Wriothesley of a landholding valued at £8,000, though also encumbered by a mortgage with an interest rate of 5%. Rachel efficiently met this financial obligation and conducted a very careful accounting of household expenses. The historian Thomson reports that she trained her three children in the astute financial management of their gifts and spending money, and to keep account books of their financial activities.

She also carefully managed the marriages of her two daughters. In 1688, the elder, Elizabeth, married Lord William Cavendish, later Duke of Devonshire, though their union was not consummated for a number of years since the bride and groom were 14 and 16 years of age respectively at the time they were wedded. The marriage of the second daughter, Catherine, was arranged to be with Lord Roos, heir to the Earl of Rutland, in 1693 when she was 16.

The Joint Lineage

On September 7, 1700, the 5th Earl, now elevated to the title of 1st Duke, died aged 84, in residence at Bedford House in Covent Garden. He was to be succeeded by his grandson Wriothesley Russell (1680–1711), the 2nd Duke, when he came of age the following year, and this descendant of both Southampton and Bedford lineage was now head of the combined extensive western London estates of Covent Garden and Bloomsbury.

A year later, Bedford was betrothed to Elizabeth, daughter and heir to the considerable estate of John Howland, owner of the Surrey lands of Streatham and Tooting Bec. Through Giles Howland, the Howland family, though not of nobility, had established a prosperous drapery business. The family's fortune had been enhanced by John's marriage to Elizabeth, daughter of an eminent banker, Sir Joshua Childs.

The London residence of his family was moved to Southampton House, which was renamed Bedford House and the original family residence on the Strand was demolished in 1705.

When the 2nd Duke died in 1711 and his widow, Elizabeth, moved the family to Streatham House in Surrey, Lady Rachel Russell remained at Bedford House in Bloomsbury where she had been wife, widow, mother and grandmother. She lived to the age of 87 years and died in 1723. She had been a notably strong link between her father's Wriothesley heritage and that of the Bedford lineage, both of whom were significant as the first private developers of urban London. She was known for her astute mind and social qualities. Chancellor (2012, ii, 90) described her as "so well known for her charm, abilities and sad fortunes."

Olsen (1982) traced the evolution of the merged estate through the subsequent centuries and has proposed that an identifiable phase of a new strategy occurred in 1776 and was primarily concentrated on the area north of Great Russell Street where there were still undeveloped fields. These houses exhibited Bedford's increased control of architectural features, as had been established at Covent Garden (Figure 6.27).

6.27

Houses in Bedford Square, showing an architectural uniformity of façade.

Olsen further describes this advanced development formulation: "The building north of Great Russell Street, beginning with the granting of Articles of Agreement for Bedford Square in 1776, involved town planning of a most sophisticated variety, surpassed nowhere else in London" (Olsen 1982, 42). This uniform and high-quality architecture of the Bloomsbury area was also applauded for its longevity. Inwood (2005, 216) noted that other than late Victorian development in Russell Square, "[t]he other Bloomsbury squares kept their Georgian harmony for a few more years."

In 1800, Bedford House, originally the grand Southampton House built overlooking the innovative Bloomsbury Square by the 4th Earl, was demolished and new houses were built on the site in a regular and well-proportioned formation that retains its appeal to this day.

As the arcaded building of Covent Garden on the west side of James Street deteriorated badly later in the following century, the 9th Duke of Bedford rebuilt this section. The Victorian era design of Henry Clutton repeated the colonnaded arcade, but on a slightly larger scale, and with sensitive references to the original upper levels of the façade of Inigo Jones. This building, Bedford Chambers, was completed in 1778.

In 1918 the Duke of Bedford sold the Covent Garden estate to Sir Thomas Beecham, the orchestral conductor, and his company, for £2 million. In 1962, excluding the Royal Opera House, it was sold to the Covent Garden Market Authority for £4 million. When it relocated to Nine Elms in 1974, fortunately the Greater London Council, encouraged by public opinion, began a process of restoration and retrofit that continues to provide a vibrant public realm where some pertinent features of Jones's architectural vision and Bedford's innovative creation of the urban fabric remain.

Chapter 7: The Ultimate Speculative Developer: Barbon

The most substantial modifications to Bedford's model of development were made by neither an aristocrat nor a builder but rather by the financial entrepreneur Nicholas Barbon. Though without a building trade or prior estate management experience, he was intellectually adventurous and had trained in the new clinical mode of medicine in the midst of flourishing Dutch capitalism before a tragic event led him to real estate development. Summerson (2003, 29) heralds his arrival: "From among many such speculators of the time there stands out one who was a first-class financier, economist, and big businessman. His name was Nicholas Barbon and his career sums up decisively the building-economic tendencies of the Restoration period."

In casting the nomination of speculator, albeit of first-class capability, upon Barbon, however, Summerson mistakenly diminishes the innovative business practice that had importantly provided the much-needed housing for the expanding London metropolis. The emergence of the investment speculator in London was discussed earlier and its focus on financial returns was noted as fundamental to the new private urban development model. The evolving formulation of that activity, however, has been shown to comprise strategic, analytical, and socially cognizant thinking that makes it more than merely speculative. Nevertheless, a specific dimension of speculation does continue visibly within real estate activities, as will be discussed later in an evaluation of the model, and the early expansion and consolidation of that dimension is mostly due to the activities of Barbon. As Summerson (2003, 30) more precisely describes the contribution: "If Barbon was hardly the 'inventor' of a 'new method', he certainly developed existing methods on an unprecedented scale."

Further, the activities of Nicholas Barbon demonstrate the way in which strategic transactional features, such as rapid trading, reduction of financial risk, and economies of scale, can be misused to the point of being scurrilous and often detrimental to others. Unfortunately, as Barbon behaved in a deceptive and irresponsible manner in many instances, the innovative and professionally astute aspects of his approach are often tainted and the whole performance presented as definitive of the property speculator. A deeper understanding of his activities should help distinguish the valuable contributions which he made to the advancement of the business model of private development.

7.1

Nicholas Barbon.

Nicholas Barbon (1637–1698)

While various nobles built their fine developments of Covent Garden, Bloomsbury Square and St James's Place, the efforts of a common man, Nicholas Barbon (Figure 7.1), probably delivered what could be called the most purely financial format of the emerging business model of private urban development. Having neither land nor a building trade to bring to a project, his role was solely that of the "deal-maker" or "promoter" of the scheme, whose role it was to structure the financial transaction and bring all parties to the deal. A commentator of the time, Roger North noted that "[a]ll his aim was profit." Perhaps more than any of his predecessors, he realized that the highest risk in a development activity is maintaining liquidity, and his approach to this was to minimize the amount of capital captured within the project at any time.

Barbon's father, "Praise-God" Barebone (1598–1679) (Figure 7.2), a leather worker located with other artisans and trades around Fleet Street in the growing area west of the City, had been a radical Parliamentarian of note. He rose to prominence during the Interregnum, being selected in 1653 by Cromwell as one of the representatives of the City of London and played a strong role in the Puritan leanings of the government, lending his name to the period of the "Barebones" Parliament during the second half of that year.

He had named his son, "Unless-Jesus-Christ-Had-Died-For-Thee-Thou-Wouldst-Be-Damned," but the young man returned as "Nicholas" after his medical studies at the progressive Dutch university in Leiden and later at the newly founded university in Utrecht, a city at the center of European commerce and trade. It was rapidly and vibrantly expanding with the arrival of artists, skilled tradesmen and businessmen and, driven by strong civic governance, large-scale housing projects were undertaken to provide the necessary affordable accommodation.

This experience for Barbon, and the insight provided through his father of contemporary London's politics, prepared him well to participate in the flourishing urban activity upon his

7.2

"Praise-God" Barebone.

return home in 1664. However, before making a contribution in that area, his mettle was tested more urgently. He was awarded an honorary fellowship of the College of Physicians and during the 1665 plague, he is noted by an historian of the event, Walter Bell (1924, 87) as one of the "doctors [who] offered themselves for the perilous work without fee" of tending the sick: "Dr Barbone, for the parishes of St Dunstan's West, St Bride, St Martin Ludgate, and St Anne Blackfriars." Parsons (2012, 62) also mentions that this young physician tended the sick "in one of the highly dangerous pest houses that ringed the City," taking on risks similar to those of the frontline workers responding to the COVID-19 pandemic of 2020, when this book was underway.

Surviving this challenge, with his progressive Continental training, Barbon then became one of the numerous young London intellectuals who contributed significantly to political, scientific, and economic thought during the latter half of the 17th century. Others included William Petty, John Locke, Benjamin Worsley, and Hugh Chamberlen. This coincidence was noted by William Letwin (1963, 49) in his writing of the times and he posited that "[p]erhaps medicine, as it was then taught in the Lowlands [being the Dutch method of clinical studies], was one of the few academic disciplines that could appeal to energetic young men interested in the modern learning."

"Needs must" Beginnings

The devastation of the Great Fire in the following year of 1666, however, diverted Barbon from his intended career as a physician. He experienced a very personal impact when his family's home in Fetter Street and his father's leather workshop in nearby Crane Court were destroyed in the fire as it swept west along Fleet Street (Figure 7.3). Entrepreneurial in the face of this adversity, and though still young, he managed to work through the municipality's regulations for rebuilding and received permission to reconstruct the family home. As the damage had not been the result of war, in which case the landowner would have had the obligation to rebuild, the Barbon family as leaseholders had to bear the costs. Financially astute, he contested the lease's rental rate in the Fire Courts, newly established by the Crown to handle such disputes. He succeeded in obtaining judgment against the landlords, Elizabeth

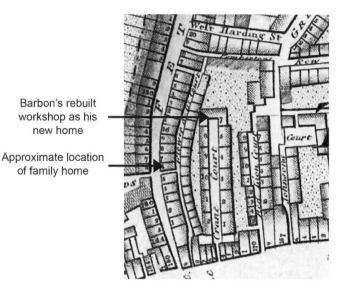

Barbon's rebuilt workshop as his new home

Approximate location of family home

7.3

Fetter Street and Crane Court: The location of Barbon's family home and father's workshop rebuilt as Barbon's residence.

Speght, a widow, and her infant son, reducing the rental rate to £25 per annum from the market rate of £40, and granting a forty-year extension of the lease.

After his success in restoring the family home and upon noting the current critical demand for housing, he turned his attention to the site of his father's former workshop. He expanded its use to include his own residence, improved its quality in layout and construction, and increased its value (or potential sublease) as a new building while keeping the ground rent at £40. Summerson (2003, 30) has reported that this was achieved by "apparently shifting [the building's] site to the far end of the court and giving the new structure a facade of some distinction. Here he lived in a lordly way."

From these projects, he realized the profits to be made by purchasing burned-out sites and rapidly rebuilding with relatively little capital outlay if occupancy were immediate and the ground sublease were sold to the new resident. In recounting the innovations in London's rebuilding, Reddaway (1951, 275) particularly noted Barbon's activity in connection with a property known as the Lock and Key in Fleet Street near his family home. This project required some capital, and the records of the Metropolitan Survey (Guildhall MSS. 2827) show that Barbon was able to borrow at an interest rate of 6%, probably from one of the guild companies.

Reddaway also estimated that the rebuilding costs £400 for the High Street and Principal Street properties, and £300 for a property on a lesser street, not an alley which would have been less. He described Barbon's method of building the higher quality properties at £400, though he would borrow at least £300, and to avoid any input of capital such as the £100 deficit by selling a 21-year lease on the completed building before they were to be paid. By these financial machinations, he shifted the objective of the development process more towards the creation of financial assets rather than the provision of buildings for residents, and his quick exit from the project often led to neglect of the quality of construction.

The Speculative Development Business

On calculating the economy of erecting several small identical houses on a subdivided site, he sought larger estates and areas of accumulated deterioration. His was the field of slum clearance, and he worked on many sites within the City and just outside its walls. Cognizant of the population movement away from the City towards the newly emerging western suburbs, he purchased the old mansions that were being deserted along the eastern end of the Strand.

Essex Street

His first substantial redevelopment involved the 1674 purchase of the Essex House estate, which fronted onto the Strand and extended to the bank of the Thames. He applied for approval to demolish the grand house, which was in disrepair, and laid a street through the site, providing for smaller building lots for houses and commercial activities. Although aristocrats' mansions along this stretch of the river running west to Westminster were losing their popularity, or were becoming too expensive for their owners, this dramatic destruction of the estate of an historically popular noble was regarded with consternation by the Crown.

Protests against his Essex development were also voiced by lawyers who resided in the adjacent Temple building; so, to gain their favor, Barbon offered to build them new lodgings, their New Court chambers. Although at the time appeasement of objectors to business ventures was becoming commonplace in London's commercial world, Barbon's approach of making a payment in kind, that is, applying his own skills and business activity, rather than a direct payment of money to improve the situation of the objectors, was innovative.

For the Essex House site, he considered the overarching scheme more than for his earlier projects, as it was necessary for the success of the project to establish internal streets and connect them to their external urban context. The neighborhood's activities were also more varied than those of his typical residential precincts, for they included expanding commercial activities of retail and professional businesses. Lawrence Stone (1966, 25) noted this new urban mix: "Though statistics are wholly lacking, it is likely that there was an equally important proliferation of secretarial and administrative jobs." Barbon's astute sense of economic markets enabled him to realize that there was demand for accommodation of all these activities, and so he built for both residential and commercial use.

When he undertook this project, urban planning was at a very embryonic stage, and most attention to that topic was given to large-scale urban schemes undertaken by monarchs of rising Continental states. As a result, the manner of his arrangement of features of the urban fabric came partly from his personal experiences in Holland, but also from the ancient spatial arrangement of the City of London and the innovative combination of residential and commercial uses in the recent Covent Garden development. Although it was plain that the Bloomsbury and St James's Square projects were established as purely residential precincts, he would have discerned that the uses of even these grand houses were changing in that many of the nobility, gentry, and businessmen conducted their business and financial activities from an allocated suite of rooms in their houses, usually on the ground floor to the left of the entrance.

Consequently, Barbon strategically accommodated mixed uses within his Essex House development by providing variations in spatial format as well as allowing for the different needs of access by land and by water (Figure 7.4). However, he adopted a mostly uniform building structure irrespective of use, by which he retained the economics of construction standardization. Apart from a small portion of the estate, the garden wall, which he sold to the neighboring Society of the Middle Temple to entice them to be a further customer, the final layout of the site encompassed Essex Street, Little Essex Street, Devereux Court, and the Watergate at the Thames embankment which served the trading activities of the wharves. Essex Street suitably debouched onto the Strand, the main thoroughfare at the north, and

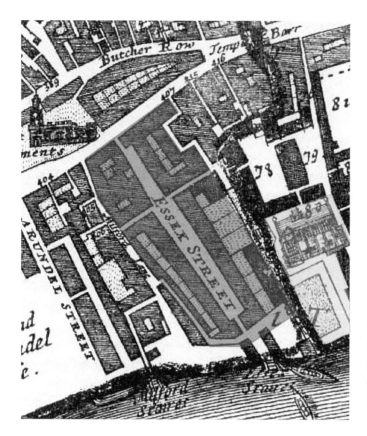

7.4

Barbon's development at Essex Street and the adjacent Temple Building.

also accessed the adjoining Temple property. Its southern exit at the Thames bank is today connected to the public Embankment pedestrian traffic.

The results were variously applauded. For a commentator on the formation of modern London in both its physical form and economic activities, Hollis, "the new designs were, in their way, revolutionary. The land had been cleverly planned to mix business and domestic use, offering a new style of urban living" (Hollis 2008, 195). Later, Strype (1720, Book IV, 117), in his topographical survey of the emerging metropolis, observed:

> Almost against St Clement's Church is an open passage into Essex Street or build-ing, being a broad clean and handsome street, especially beyond the turning into the Temple, where it crosseth Little Essex Street into Milford Lane; it consisteth of two rows of good built houses, well inhabited by gentry ...

A notable among the gentry who soon took up residence was Lord Chief Justice Scroggs of the King's Bench.

Evolving towards Inclusion of the Public Realm

Although he did not usually give much consideration to it in his projects, at Essex Street Barbon enhanced the street environment by placing an elaborate arch with Corinthian pilasters at the river end in order to mask the less attractive wharves on the river (Figure 7.5).

7.5
Surviving Temple Arch in Barbon's development of Essex Street.

This was one of the rare instances in his developments where he consciously contributed to the public realm, though his juxtaposition on the residential streetscape of the over-scaled pilasters bordering the arch does not indicate a deep sensitivity to intersection of public and private domains. Though he did not adopt the format of a central square, he produced a functionally efficient and pleasant layout of streets that gave onto the small court to the east in the middle of the block. In addition, at its southern exit to the Thames bank he contributed to the reconstruction of some of the burnt public areas by rebuilding the No.1 staircase in Pump Court that remains part of the Thames embankment today.

Temple Building

On the adjacent property, the Temple, which he had appeasingly committed to rebuilding, he proved most adept at delivering offices, or chambers as they were known, for its lawyer tenants. This was possibly one of the earliest examples of the development of a specifically commercial property. It is claimed, though not proven, that he conscientiously engaged Christopher Wren for a prestigious design, and he did formulate the detailed programmatic requirements for the new structure by having many conversations with his clients. It was here that he first became known to Roger North (1887), an eminent lawyer who had chambers there and who was to relate much of Barbon's approach as a developer: "He knew our way of disposing our rooms, what conveniences we had need of, and being a very good contriver could apply to serve not only our occasions but our fancies ..." (p. 57).

Whether by design or through gradual learning of the format by which each lawyer held a strata-title or condominium interest in his particular space, Barbon established the structure's composition, both physically and economically, by a two-step process. Initially, he proposed a very basic approach whereby the existing building would be rebuilt much as it was, and each lawyer's unit would be priced according to rank, which entitled preference in the new chambers. As might be expected, the gentlemen all overvalued their respective holdings and the matter proved impossible to resolve. His second proposal was more indicative of his business brilliance. Though "preserving the courts and gardens" (North 1887, 58), the site was to be developed more intensively than in its original configuration, providing more space for an accommodation of professional activities, and affording the occupants with the opportunity of enhancing or reducing their prior situation.

He proposed that a strict measurement of each occupant's interest in the old building be made in three dimensions (including ceiling height), and the level noted, and as the starting point each would have its equivalent in the new structure. From this he set a pricing system for the new building where he provided four floors, each of 10-ft ceiling height except for the upper level which would be 9 ft, each level divided into rooms of useful size and shape, and with the value relating to the location on a specific floor, with the value diminishing as it rose. (Stairs were regarded as disadvantageous, outweighing any benefit of views.) Associated with each choice of room was an allocation of the underlying ground. For example, chambers on the first floor attracted a total rent of £6 15s for the ground component and £13 10s for the building portion. Each occupant was able to choose his new chambers and to appropriate the value of his existing chambers to the new selection, with an additional payment or reimbursement of the difference, as the circumstances required. Most chose something very similar to their old interests and the arrangement "was the happiest resolution of a perplexed touchy affair that I have known," said North (1887, 61).

Red Lion Square

As the development of the (now) Bedford estate in Bloomsbury continued under the direction of Lady Russell after the execution of her husband, Barbon purchased the fields around the Red Lion Inn to the east of Southampton Square for a similar residential square scheme (Figure 7.6). His development activity here, and his growing status, was noted by his

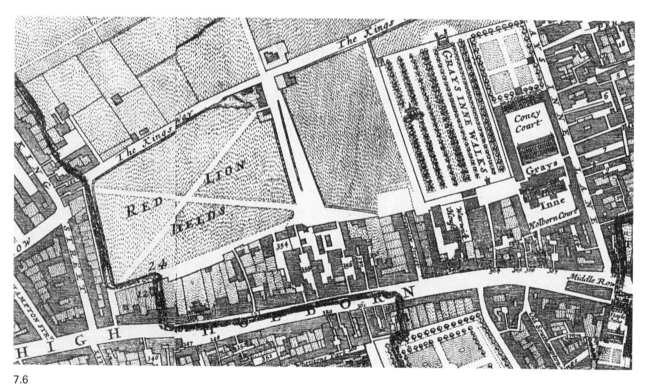

7.6

Map of Red Lion Fields, c. 1682, site of Red Lion Square.

contemporaries: "Dr. Barebone, the great builder, having sometime since bought the Red Lyon Fields, near Graies Inn walks, to build on ..." (Luttrell 1972, Diary entry: June 10, 1684).

However, his plans for the site were regarded as contrary to the wishes of Christopher Wren, the Surveyor-General, and were objected to by the lawyers of Gray's Inn, which was adjacent to the east. He fought the Crown through the court process, but also set his builders to skirmish physically with a contingent of the legal gentlemen. "Barbon's workmen [were] attacked by gentlemen (100) of Graies Inn to prevent development" reports Chancellor (2012, I, 173).

Aware of the residential square developments of Covent Garden, St James's, and Bloomsbury, he proposed the necessary infrastructure of a central square, streets, water and sewerage, though a more modest version. Chancellor (ibid.) continued by noting that "this garden is laid out somewhat in the formal style beloved by the Dutch, access to it being by two gateways" (Figure 7.7), and was probably correct in Barbon's familiarity of it from the time of his studies.

There is also evidence that he learnt from Covent Garden the economic benefit of the presence of a parish church and planned for its construction on the western side. Although it appears that he did not obtain approval for it at the outset, later in 1695, as a Member of Parliament he personally submitted a petition for the church. However, it was defeated on its

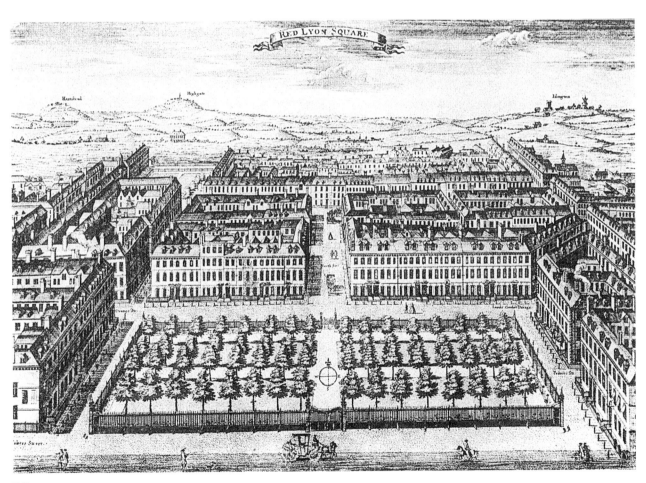

7.7

Red Lion Square, London, 18th century.

second Committee reading (Hoppit 1997, No. 31.010, dated 13.12.1695), and it was not until 1874–1878 that St John's Parish Church, designed by the celebrated John Loughborough Pearson, replaced three of his five houses on the western side (Coulter 2016, 389).

As for the development, around the central square, the intended residences on ground leases were arranged in the usual format of row houses. However, because the rental rates for land leases were based on the length of street frontage, irrespective of the size of the lot or house, he sought to fit as many house fronts as possible onto the square, which resulted in narrow but tall house forms, also probably as he had seen on the Continent, in similarly constrained urban areas. They were notable for "showing a Dutch regularity in the buildings, as well as the formal arrangement of the central garden" (Chancellor 2012, I, 183). Quickly monetizing this efficient spatial arrangement, he did not undertake the construction of the housing himself, but offered building leases or required construction by purchasers, in accordance with his usual model.

In distributing the construction work for residences, on this project he further refined his business structure. First, he specifically targeted a demand segment that had largely been ignored by the aristocratic developers, that is, the rising craftsmen, commercial traders, and increasingly wealthy lawyers and doctors. For these, who would probably have been unfamiliar with the process of specifying the amenities and details of a new residence, he established a standardized house, replete with an

> attention to details in interior decoration … to accommodate the tastes of polite society, who wished to show their new status in conspicuous consumption. There was paneling in the major rooms and the balustrades of the principal staircase were restrained and classical, prefiguring the elegant simplicity of the Georgian town house. (Hollis 2008, 249–250)

Advancing the Business Model

Barbon was recognized as a personification of the new capitalist in his business activities, and he became intellectually immersed in the exploration of the economic dynamics of production, both macroeconomic and microeconomic. His most significant influence on the innovative private development model was to demonstrate a number of commercially astute decisions. Importantly, and perhaps the reason why his modifications persisted, these insights extended across the activity ranging across discernment of a marketable product, efficient production management, operational profitability, financing, and disposition.

House Typology

The architectural historian Hollis (2008, 199–200) extended the credit he felt Barbon deserved, particularly for the row house typology of urban development, saying that "Barbon had not only identified the motivation of the new commercial city but also its form: the London terraced house … [that] would remain a template for bourgeois living for nearly three hundred years." Though the format had been created decades earlier by merchant builders such as Newton, it was Barbon who cleverly refined the details, maximizing the profit margin of such a template. Some variation in the form came with improvements in the quality and cost of glass during the middle of the 16th century, and glazed windows replaced shutters and oiled

7.8
Nos. 42–43 Bedford Row.

paper in wall openings. By the time of Barbon's construction, the form had advanced from the side-hung casement style to that of a double-hung sash window that did not project onto the street.

Summerson (2003, 34) suggests that in the development of Bedford Row, particularly in the surviving buildings from Nos. 36 and 42, "that Barbon's particular brand of terrace house can best be studied today, though the mind's eye must re-establish the wooden eaves-cornice and casement windows, which have everywhere been replaced by sashes." Sheppard (1998, 181) reports that Nos. 36, and 42–43 Bedford Row have survived (Figure 7.8).

Production Process Formulated
Barbon advanced his method of construction by appropriation of some processes of industrialization which were then just emerging in England and on the Continent. To achieve the

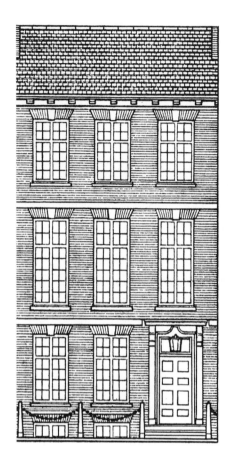
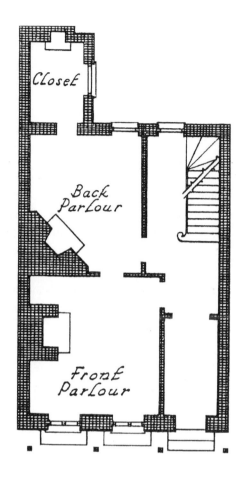

7.9

Elevation and plan of typical house built by Nicholas Barbon, 1670–1698.

fastest construction with least reliance on the skills of tradesmen, he adopted standard plans for the houses (Figure 7.9). Summerson (1991a, 29) concluded that "[h]e completely grasped the advantages accruing from standardization and mass-production in housing." Often the work was not of the highest standard but his strategy for development was to build and exit as quickly as possible, without consideration of the longevity of his projects.

He did not engage in building work himself, but he was assiduous in managing the process, and of course the cost, efficiently. Since the major component costs were labor and materials, he established control over the former through his contracts with the various trades. And discarding the usual reliance on tradesmen to procure the materials and pass on the costs to the developer, he dealt directly with the suppliers of the main materials, timber and bricks.

For timber materials, he ordered according to standardized sizes thereby reducing the amount of work on site. And because the supply of bricks was unreliable in timely delivery and consistency of quality, he established a brick kiln to accomplish what today is called the "vertical integration" of the supply chain (Baer 2007a, 302). These were strategic business actions. His use of factory production was not taken on lightly, for it required additional investment in fixed production assets, but later, when industrialization became prevalent, such approaches were more common in response to the cost of expensive materials, risks in material supplies, the need for speedy and reliable delivery, and the procurement of specialized or proprietary components (Jones 1994, 44).

His standardized production and strict management of costs delivered both an affordable product that satisfied a substantial market and a sustainable business model for the developer. With this, however, the inevitable conflict between commercially efficient production and aspirational aesthetic taste arose. It may be seen in Summerson's (1991a, 29) qualification of his accolades to Barbon's innovation: "The houses he built were all very much alike, economically planned to the point of meanness, with coarse ornaments which repeated themselves over and over again."

Ambitious for social status, Barbon also proved himself capable of producing buildings of quality and erected houses of notable architectural standards for people of high rank. For example, for a former Lord Mayor of London, Thomas Gresham, he built a beautiful home in Osterley Park, the design of which is credited to Sir Christopher Wren. And he erected an attractive house in Buckingham Street for the courtier Samuel Pepys.

Lease Innovations

Barbon made a further economic advance in the operating dimension of his Red Lion Square model by his extension on the period of its tenures of ground leases to forty, fifty, sixty, or sixty-one years. This strategy was similar to that of Henry Jermyn at St James's Square when he offered either freehold of very long-term leases to those who wished to build more expensive houses, requiring longer cost amortization periods. Barbon sought to win the same marketability by offering longer leases, though he also pressed most tenants to buy the ground lease also, which for this purpose amounted to an approximation of a freehold sale.

Further, although it is not possible to be sure of his strategic intent, he staggered the tenure of ground leases to provide a more stable stream of rental rates and ease of management in re-leasing. It also constituted a diversification that reduced the risk that all leases would mature during a particularly difficult economic period, a strategy that is still adopted in respect of multiple leases in residential and commercial buildings. It does, however, preclude any potential for substantial redevelopment of the precinct, which was anticipated by Southampton when establishing co-terminal leases for his Bloomsbury project. But that aristocratic view of continued ownership far into the future was not shared by the rising entrepreneurs and proponents of the new capitalist economic strategy such as Barbon.

Standardization of Leases

As a further step in efficiency in his business, Barbon tendered a standardized form of lease to potential tenants. Though this is common practice today, at that time scriveners and legal clerks typically drafted uniquely negotiated contracts, but with his large production volume, Barbon appreciated the risk that such a contract could well prove faulty, and he mitigated this by using a well-drafted and consistent template (Figure 7.10). As his counterparties were usually less learned in legal matters, they probably accepted this form without modifications.

Innovative Funding

Of advantage to Barbon's expansive use of the private development model was the relatively low cost required to gain site control through the traditional ground. Barbon often minimized this cost even further by contracting a lease with a residential tenant, even before

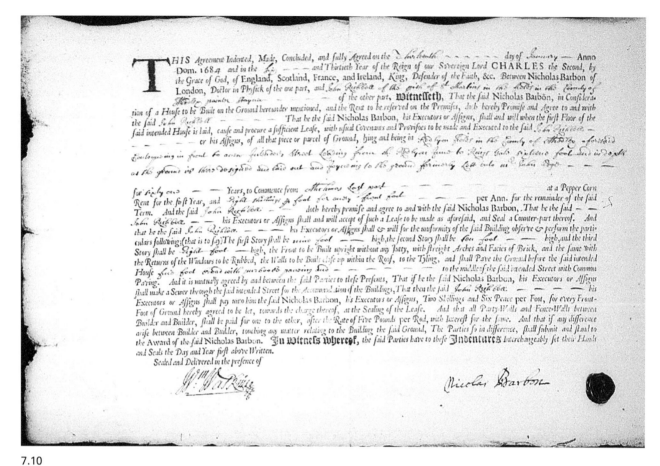

7.10

Barbon's standardized lease agreement.

commencing construction, and then selling it and the ground lease to an investor for a capital sum. The funds thus generated would pay for his outgoings on the ground lease and construction expenses on the project, so that he could avoid any expense to himself while carrying out the development and effectively capture the profit upfront.

He occasionally overreached with this tactic by failing to retain the proceeds of the lease sale to meet construction costs while relying on credit terms of three or six months from tradesmen. It can be inferred from court documents that he was not always scrupulous in meeting those terms and often delayed payment, and then took advantage of the delay in court proceedings against him before finally settling the debt. Sometimes his settlement was not in cash but by an offer to grant a ground lease on an undeveloped site. In these maneuvers, his advantage as a large-scale developer and continuous hirer of tradesmen meant that serious actions were often not taken against him by those hoping to work for him again. This aggressive form of capital management in the engagement of consultants and contractors has continued to be engaged in by some developers.

By means of these contractual processes and innovative financial structures, Barbon significantly reduced his business' economic risk. To mitigate the remaining risk during the construction activity, he structured his contracts with the tradesmen to transfer obligations as to timing and quality of work to them. Although it has often been said that his developments were "very incomplete, imperfect and unfinished, and such works as were done were so ill ... several of the piers being cracked, the floor shrunk, and the house in some places in danger of falling" (Stow 1956, 30), it was not he who was prosecuted for such failings. Court and other documents show that it was the contractors or tradesmen such as masons or carpenters who were admonished and fined in the Chancery Court or by the guilds.

Other Financial and Economic Endeavors

Although he predominantly directed his financial acumen to real estate development, Barbon's understanding and capability with broader economic matters are well known. Intellectually ambitious, he wrote a number of manuscripts which contributed to the formation of important abstractions of commercial transactions such had begun with Thomas Mun (1623) earlier that century. His most influential is *A Discourse of Trade*, an economics treatise in which he expounded the fundamental principles of trade and its structure as a business (Figure 7.11).

He called it the "Business of Trade" and identified its "chief End" as being "to make a profitable Bargain." He listed its important components in the following way: the quality and quantity of the "wares," their value or trading price, the "Money or Credit" by which the transaction is made, and, most innovatively, the "Interest that relates to the time of performing the Bargain," or effectively the amount of time for which the capital is tied up in the trade (Barbon 1690, 2). These concepts and his various applications of them were to be significant in the formulation of private development business activities.

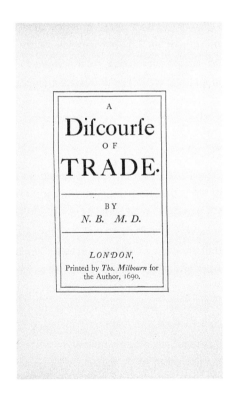

7.11

Barbon's *A Discourse of Trade*.

In addressing broad macroeconomic concerns, his interest resembled that of Sir William Petty (1623–1687), a learned man at court and a founding member of the Royal Society who was formulating the new science of statistics and, in partnership with John Grant (or Graunt), strove to make a credible estimate of the population of the metropolis by referring to the London Bills of Mortality. It is possible that through their intersecting discourse, Barbon would have discerned the importance of greater numerical precision in assessing the growing market for his houses and identifying the specific location of that demand through formatting population divisions according to parishes.

His most notorious engagement on macroeconomic matters was his confrontation with the eminent political scientist John Locke (1632–1704) over the value of coinage. Barbon regarded it as an institutional token, and Locke argued that it had intrinsic value. "In the early modern period there was no central bank and little concept of macroeconomic policy because the power of the state was still much too weak." Muldrew (1998, 99) reports on Locke's thinking: "Money, thus, had to have an 'intrinsic' value as a commodity which could be set by the market so that trust could be generated through the process of exchange, just as it was for any other form of goods."

In 1696, Barbon wrote *A Discourse Concerning Coining the New Money Lighter Debate*, which he subtitled "In Answer to Mr. Lock's [*sic*] Considerations about raising the Value of Money." It was published anonymously but attributed by Norman Brett-James to Barbon himself. In 1691, Locke had written a letter to Parliament entitled "some considerations of the consequences of the lowering of interest, and raising the value of money," which had received substantial public attention. Barbon regarded the proposal as economically dangerous, particularly with respect to payment for goods and assets, and in his conclusion he asserted: "Besides the preventing those fatal Consequences that follow the Coining the Money too weighty; As, The Loss of the Money; Decay of Trade; The Fall of Rents; And a general Poverty and Clamour all over the Nation" (Barbon 1696, 96). Although his theory's generalization of a "devaluation of currency" might be unfair exaggeration, his argument was supported by many valid and surviving assumptions, but his adherence to this position was not politically wise. He was publicly derided, and it probably adversely affected his credit standing later in life.

Advances in the Valuation of Real Property

From another perspective, particularly that of Symes (1903), Barbon was regarded as a predecessor to the Scottish economist Adam Smith. Particularly regarding the valuation of goods, in a manner similar to that of Smith, Barbon proposed that, in addition to the cost of input materials, the value of a product such as a house should include the value of the time spent on its production and the level of skill required of the workers who produced it. Symes (1903, 629) described this model as "a better analysis of the cost of production than had been made."

Specifically, in respect of building construction, however, Barbon's methodology was not necessarily better but was rather a replacement of the historical method of payment for tradesmen's work according to qualification and skill as recognized by the guilds. His attempt to allocate labor costs to the pricing of housing production more efficiently was to be underscored later by Smith (1994, 168) who noted:

Rent, it is to be observed, therefore, enters into the composition of the price of commodities in a different way from wages and profit. High or low wages and profit are the causes of high or low price; high or low rent is the effect of it. It is because high or low wages and profit must be paid, in order to bring a particular commodity to market, that its price is high or low.

Though his substantial contribution to the formulation of private development practice was the framework of market valuation and trading as suitably demonstrated by his own actions, in his *Discourse* he also emphasized the dependency of value upon use. He regarded the use value of things with respect to the extent to which they met the wants and necessities of life. He divided these wants and necessities into two general categories: one to meet the needs of the body and the other to meet the wants of the mind. For the body he considered only food to be absolutely necessary, so even the uses of clothing and habitation were enhanced by aspirations, and therefore vulnerable to changing tastes and fashions of both the individual consumer and society at large.

He conceded that valuation by price was honed in the marketplace but posited that prior to that overlay, its estimate was founded on the measured use value of a product. This was to be calculated by reference to the number of occasions of its use and the quantity of such products available at each of those occasions. Importantly, he proposed that the availability of a product beyond the timely demand of its use was superfluous and worth nothing, and the immediate application to an oversupply of housing probably provided affirmation of that theory. Williams (1944, 55) described this as "what may be called Barbon's underconsumption theory ... By not consuming there raises a 'dead stock, called Plenty,' which causes value to fall, including that of land and money." This derives from his proposition that "Prodigality is a vice that is prejudicial to the man, but not to trade ..." (Barbon 1690, 62). By this he appreciated the economic stimulus provided by production and consumption, as opposed to the hoarding of wealth. Of this, it is said to be "what Mr. Keynes is talking about when he says that abstinence of the rich, far from aiding progress, actually impedes it" (Williams 1944, 55), and its application to the production and use of buildings proposes that urban development makes a broader economic contribution to the whole community than to just the developer.

Barbon proposed that the marketplace further incorporated this value principle in that the scarcity of a product makes it worth more, but if there is plenty it will be worth less because it will not be used due to its superfluity, and its nil value will be allocated across all available goods. This dynamic was very apparent in real estate, and he noted that builders would cease producing houses if their completed ones were not leased: they would stop supply in response to a curtailment of demand. In his business practices, he strategically avoided the current problem of oversupply in the upper level housing market by producing for the less served middle market.

His principle of valuation based on use, and specifically the number of occasions of a product's use, or its longevity, encompassed another important dimension of price calculation beyond just that of supply and demand. He regarded price as presenting the "present value" of a product, embodying an estimate of when its use will occur within a future time period and a prediction of what alternative goods will then be available. Since goods age irrespective of use, inherent in this thinking is a factor for a deterioration of value over time. However, he maintained that all those estimations of value could be undertaken within a projection of the future marketplace. Though he cannot be credited with creating the discounted cash flow (DCF) model of valuation in use today, his conception of real estate valuation, particularly with respect to the constructed component and its diminishing returns over time, embodied that essential calculative methodology. In financial analysis, this was an important advance over that used by his developer predecessors, who had offset long-term annual income against capital outlays in the determination of profits, though often without allowance for building deterioration, but also almost always without anticipation of changing supply conditions.

Further, because London's broad real estate market was rapidly expanding, attracting many building tradesmen, and experiencing substantial fluctuations in land values, it was very difficult to read. As Baer (2002, 521) interpreted it:

> The market in urban properties had a number of inherent problems to overcome when ascertaining value. One obstacle was the disorganized state of the real estate market and of information about it. Houses and leases were traded in a decentralized, fragmented fashion. The housing market was, for the most part, shaped by a myriad of individuals, companies, and corporations. It was not dominated, as it later would be, by a few firms, which set the rules of property assessment and transaction procedures.

Nevertheless, Barbon sought an improved alignment of real estate principles with those of the new markets of capitalism, and thus he related the payment of interest due on the capital expended for economic production, such as of a house, to that of the article's use represented by payment of rent. In this, his contribution is applauded by Schumpeter (1954) in his history of the development of economic thought. And, in his business practices, Barbon had provided many examples of the theory's application by fluidly exchanging housing production for leases, for credit, or for investment capital, and this expansion of funding methods progressed the acceptance of real estate as a financial asset. However, his multidimensional determination of property value established a tension between its production cost, use value, and asset trading price that continues to call for rigorous resolution.

Importance of Location

As a result of real property's unique feature of fixed location, Barbon very explicitly discussed this attribute's impact on pricing of the development product:

> Houses in the middle of a Town, are more of a value than those at the out-ends; and when a Town happens to be increased by addition of New Buildings to the end of a Town, the old Houses were then at the end, become nearer to the middle of the Town, and so increase in value. (Barbon 1689, 21)

In an objective demonstration of that dynamic of urban growth he cited by way of example that the houses on Bishopsgate Street and in the Minories were made more valuable by the building of Spitalfields and Shadwell, which were further out. He contended that it was beneficial to the success of early development in London's western suburbs that the increased prices of houses in the Strand and on Charing Cross were increased by the "great addition" of buildings in St. James's (Barbon 1689, 21). This, he explained, was due to the dynamic that "… Houses are of value, as they stand in a place of Trade, and by addition of new buildings the place becomes to be a greater Thorough-fare, by the passing and repassing of Inhabitants to these new Buildings" (Barbon 1689, 22). In this, he shows a comprehension of a property's economic value due to an improved neighborhood context, though he limited that attribute to increases in passing trade.

Finally, in presenting the numerous benefits of buildings for urban prosperity, he made the case for the need for commercial buildings interspersed amongst the houses. He pointed out that these structures contribute:

> that which is the greatest advantage, they do not only provide a Livelihood to those that belong to the building and furnishing of Houses, but [also] for the Tenants of those New Houses: For the People being collected and living together in one Street, they serve and trade one with another. (Barbon 1685, 32)

He realized that commercial buildings were best located in close proximity to customers for the ease of exchanging their labor and goods.

In Support of Urban Development
Not only did Barbon see the benefits of new capitalist thinking in his development activities, but conversely he credited urban building with fueling the increasing commercial activity of London:

> They [the new buildings] are advantageous to the City, because they increase the Trade of it: The Trade of the City is either Whole-sale, or Re-tail. Now the new Buildings of Bloomsbury, Leicester-Fields, St. James's, Spittle-Fields, & c. are like so many new Towns, for the Wholesale Trader to traffic in. The Inhabitants of these places do eat, wear Clothes, and furnish their Houses, and whatsoever Commodity they use, comes first from the Merchants, or Wholesale Trader. For the City is the great Mart for Goods from whence all other places must be furnished; so that the new Buildings are beneficial to the Wholesale Trade of the City. (Barbon 1689, 22)

In *A Discourse of Trade*, he specifically set out the business principles supporting private urban development and its role in the larger social and macroeconomic systems that go beyond mere profit-taking by the developer. He proposed that:

> Building is the chiefest Promoter of Trade, it imploys a greater number of trades and People than Feeding and Cloathing: the Artificers [craftsmen] that belong to Building, such as Brick-layers, Carpenters, Plaisterers, etc. imploy many hands. Those that make the materials for Building, such as the Bricks, Lyme [for cement], Tyle, etc. imploy

many more and with those that furnish the Houses, such as Upholsterers, Pewterers, etc., they are almost Innumerable. (Barbon 1690, 68)

In making this claim he was indeed insightful as to the large role in the economy that the industry would fulfill.

For the additional benefit of government, Barbon claimed that "[t]he increasing of Buildings, and inlarging of Towns, preserveth the peace of a Nation, by rendring the People more easily governed ... [since] all Cities are more inclined to Peace, than the Country ... [since] Citizens [of the cities] being usually rich, cannot endure the hardship of War," and that "great Cities are more easily Governed, because they are under the eye of the Prince, as generally the Metropolis is" (Barbon 1685, 33–34). All this, in addition to the taxes levied upon city residents, he claimed, was due to prodigious building activity within the metropolis and would be to the great benefit of a flourishing London and the English monarch.

To counteract public opposition to expanding London's extensive building activity, he published a pamphlet fully titled *An Apology for the Builder or a Discourse shewing the Cause and Effects of the Increase of Building* (1685). In this context, Apology meant a discussion in favor of the subject rather than an expression of remorse, invoking in aid of his thesis the flourishing city's appreciation of the arts and achievements of architectural design to be found in it, where "every House is a little Book of Architecture," though he expressed a wry concern that its citizens "are angry with the builders for making her so great" (Barbon 1685, 2).

In disputing the complaint that too many houses were being built, he justified the rising demand for houses as the necessary response to the beneficial increase in London's population. In the absence of a formal census, the extent of the expansion was vehemently disputed, but he looked to the official Bills of Mortality, as recorded in the parishes, and the increasing number of trades' apprenticeships to demonstrate that London had grown substantially in recent times. He made a mathematical case that, on an estimate of eight people per house, at least 1,000 houses should be built per year to accommodate the increase indicated by "these Nine thousand Apprentices that come out of their time [of apprenticeship], and the Ten thousand Weddings to have room to breed in" (Barbon 1685, 18). This increase, he posited, would result in an increase in the availability of goods and services and in the wealth of individuals, the city and the nation, and even of the rural population, since they produced more food which they sold to those in the city.

Adverting to the basic human need for shelter and how that need could be met, he pointed out that "[w]hen Mankind is civilized, instructed with Arts, and under good Government, every man doth not dress his own meat, make his own Clothes, nor build his own House" for which the activities of building tradesmen are needed (Barbon 1685, 5). Further, he implied that not only is production skill required, but the capital costs of erecting a house cannot usually be found in the usual forms of household income. An upfront source of construction capital is necessary to meet the need of housing, and through its resolution of this difficulty is where the business of building activity was justified.

By his comprehensive reasoning, Barbon placed the production of urban shelter validly alongside the new proto-industrial structures of provision for consumption goods, but he also cleverly wove the special product of real property into the system of capital investment that was the novel compelling engine of production and consumption.

Market Analysis

While encouraging demand, Barbon advanced the business model of private development by promoting an early form of discipline with respect to its markets. He argued, reasonably, that a builder can learn from the trader, who determines the amount of goods to supply by studying the market and noting the prices paid, and by judging that there would be an unmet need if prices were increasing, or an oversupply if they were falling.

Incisively, in this production analysis he included the notion of sales pace in addition to the consequential economic multiplier effect, and described its dynamic:

> Now the Trader takes care from time to time, to provide a sufficient quantity of all sorts of Goods for mans occasions, which he finds out by the Market: That is, By the quick selling of the Commodities, that are made ready to be sold. And as there are Butchers, Brewers and Cooks, Drapers, Mercers and Taylors, and a hundred more, that furnish him with food and clothes; so there are Bricklayers, Carpenters, Playsterers, and many more Traders, that build homes for him; and they make houses of the first, second, and third rate of building, in proportion to the several degrees of men, which they find out by the Market ... (Barbon 1689, 6)

With reference to "Mr. Morgan's Map of the City" and it regular updates, he contended that there was evidence in its portrayal of the urban topography that there had not been a problem of oversupply since "there are no more Houses built every year than are occasion for; because there are Tenants for the Houses when built, and a continuance every year to build more" (Barbon, 1689, 19). Although Brett-James (1929, 132) treated this as "an unsound argument, for it does not consider the number of houses left untenanted: and we know from contemporary tracts that in 1672 and 1673 there were 3,423 houses uninhabited in the city itself," such criticism may overlook the probability that many uninhabited houses were damaged stock from the Great Fire of just six years before, and the process of rebuilding on that mass scale was protracted.

Although modifying production in response to market demand is now regarded as fundamental to commercial activity, this dynamic was part of the new capitalist economic construct that England was embracing after centuries of producing solely according to capacity. Barbon's direction of the new rationale to housing production, as quoted above, not only served to modify its supply but also logically to connect it to the broad economic system. Formerly, the construction of buildings was undertaken simply to provide necessary space for work or craft, or transactional or residential requirements. But Barbon reclassified it as an inherent part of the economy, both responding to demand for space and creating the demand for trades services and goods such as furnishings and other household items.

Further in his education of the early private development industry on the subject of markets, he indicated the need for a detailed evaluation of demand by his reference to "houses of the first, second and third rate of building, in proportion to the several degrees of man" (Barbon 1689, 6). In this, he was stressing the need for the selection of specific features for an intended development according to the differing demand at various price-points, that is, to decide upon the type of housing as high-end, middle market or affordable to a lower economic class according to the demand in the market to which it was targeted. Though the Earls of Bedford and Southampton had applied their intuition and natural business acumen to their decisions on the various types of housing for their developments, many other projects undertaken by aristocratic developers, such as Berkeley Square and Arundel Street, failed because they offered expensive housing to an already satiated market. Making the same mistake as many later developers, those developers proceeded to build according to the product they knew, gentry housing, without first checking the unmet demand for it. In contrast, for each of his projects Barbon examined the level of demand and adjusted the specific developments in response. For example, Essex Street residences were more high-end, but others were "for the middling sort," such as at Red Lion Square.

Thus, he established a fundamental principle for the private urban development model that endowed it with the economic rationale of other commercial activities. In his normative observation, he said:

… Builders do design to build no more Houses every Year than what they think there may be occasion for; and would do as other Traders, who when the Market is overstocet with their Commodities, forbear to make any more, or bring them to Market, till a new occasion requireth them,

and added that "when they find they cannot lett those already built, they will desist from building" (Barbon 1689, 19–20). Further, he also described the metrics to be observed in gauging market demand. By proposing vacancy as an indicator of slackened demand, and by using it to make a rational evaluation to constrain production levels, he established this metric as a leading indicator of market conditions, and it remains so today.

Unfortunately, his proposed analytical check was not diligently adopted, for there was often the danger for a developer of losing a crew of skilled building tradesmen if they were not put to work. This was a risk broadly inherent in the trade specialization, of all varieties, that was growing at the time. It was to become more exaggerated in the Industrial Age that followed and has continued to be a flaw in the production economy, including private development activities.

Other Credit Vehicles

Extending his commercial interests beyond real estate, Barbon introduced an additional and novel financial instrument that bought overdue payable accounts at a discount. He had drafted a submission for Parliament titled *A Proposal for Raising the Publick Credit, By Setting up an OFFICE for Transferring and Discounting TALLIES*. Although the specific date of its submission is not known, it was probably during the late 1690s since it suggests that it would be of assistance to fund the Bank of England's £2 million of needed funds, and that bank had been established in 1694.

The discounted asset acquisition process was derived from the traditional interchange of credit between wealthy persons or even operating entities, including those involved in construction. Muldrew (1998, 107–108) described the dynamic thus:

> … numerous debts, of course, had to be paid eventually, and the means by which this was done with the limited amount of cash available was to 'reckon' or compare accounts, cross out equivalent debts, and then to settle only the difference in cash or with a bond. Because credit was so common, most people eventually accumulated numerous reciprocal debts over time, and these were either remembered or recorded in account books, and then mutually cancelled, at convenient intervals. Because this was so common, interest was not charged on sales credit to account for any risk or delay, as opposed to moneylending or lending on bond, where interest was standard by the 17th century. Such 'reckoning' was a ubiquitous practice which was mentioned often by numerous contemporary diarists.

Barbon proposed that the payable accounts, or credit assets, be contributed at a discount of 5% through subscription to an established "Office," which was responsible for completing the obligations over the given terms. If such a system were established broadly it would certainly add liquidity to the economy, which would be its "Publick" contribution, and such a structure in a variety of forms has been used in both the public and private sectors since. Although he may not have been the inventor of the structure, perhaps having known of it from systems he encountered in the capital hub of Antwerp, his adaptation of it to the trading environment of London was resourceful.

Reducing Property Risk with Fire Insurance

As a response to the devastation of the Great Fire of 1666 and the dramatic loss of economic value through the destruction of housing, and appreciative of the risk being taken on by his new tenants, Barbon opened London's first fire insurance business with a ready-made market in the following year, corresponding with the production of his new buildings. He emulated the structure of Maritime insurance, which had been in existence for centuries, brought to London as a branch office of the Lombardi family business from the Mediterranean, and taken up by what became Lloyds of London from the transactions of merchants in Mr. Lloyd's Coffee House. It required payment of a premium which was a small percentage of the total value of the building for the provision of cover for a specified sum for a limited policy period, usually a year, and usually renewable. His rates were quoted at 2.5% of the annual lease payment for brick houses and 5% for timber structures (Brett-James 1929, 137–138).

After thirteen years of personally assuming the risk and of receiving the revenues of his private business, in 1680, he converted it into a limited liability corporation called the Fire Office, later the Phoenix Insurance Company, and today operating as the Royal and Sun Alliance Company. In 1681 the London City authority considered providing fire insurance directly, but found it to be disallowed by its charter, so Barbon's business escaped undercutting by the public institution. His business flourished and is reported to have insured 5,650 houses between 1686 and 1692. Then, typically adroit at reducing risk, when claims under his policies began to become troublesome, he formed a fire brigade service, the *Cohortes Vigilum*, thereby mitigating the risk of damage by conflagration.

The Promoter

Despite his intellectual contributions, Nicholas Barbon was first and foremost a successful dealmaker and presented himself in great style, continuing to live grandly in his first development at Crane Court. He was known for using charm and artifice to mollify the concerns of his creditors and investors, and has been described as "a mob manager who knew the art of leading, winding or driving mankind in herds" (Porter 1994, 99). He has been described by Letwin (1963, 48) as "the type of the late seventeenth-century 'projector'," a person who put business projects together.

As a real estate developer, he was often regarded as a bully. Perhaps to an egregious extent, he stretched the concept of trade credit from building tradesmen, or in the manipulation of complex leases, with the result that he was regularly sued or aggressively approached for payment. He astutely abused the overstretched court system to counter-sue and delay actions while he worked on a project, and settled the matter shortly before judgment was enforced against him. He viewed this as an affordable method of financing his projects, telling Roger North that while loans carry an interest rate of 10%, this process resulted in his paying an additional amount, by way of legal costs that amounted to only approximately 3–4% on the debt. For those who persevered with litigation against him, "the first thing he did was to pull down their houses about their ears, and build upon their ground, and stand it out at law till their hearts ached, and at last they would truckly and take any terms for peace and a quiet life" (North 1887, 56–57).

He was also very talented in structuring a transaction with his investors, often intricately entwining leases and mortgage loans, the two fundamental sources of cash flow, in such a way that minimized his risk but increased his total profit. For example, he created the sale-leaseback structure, by which he financed a property acquisition with a mortgage loan that could be supported by the rental payments and also provide a profitable spread for him.

Lack of Concern for Public Impact

Though he was an aggressive businessman, his conflicts with the public were complex and the blame for them was not always clear. For example, as mentioned earlier, he was said to have orchestrated physical clashes between his construction crew and objecting neighbors, such as against the lawyers of Gray's Inn when he was developing Red Lion Square. Although Brett-James (1929, 119) exonerated Barbon reporting that "[t]his seems to have been an entirely unprovoked assault on the part of the lawyers," he was prosecuted. A Middlesex Justice granted "warrants by direction of the Attorney General for the suppression of Dr. Barbon and his men from committing any insolence in their late riotous meeting in Red Lyon Fields and to prevent them from annoying his Majesty's subjects" (Privy Council Registers 1684, 2/70, 244).

Not one to back down, Barbon commenced an action against the judge, as well as the constable directed to enforce the warrant, which eventually required arbitration by the Chief Justice of the King's Bench, George Jeffreys. This jurist had been the prosecutor who in the year before had brought a charge of treason against William Russell, the young Bedford lord who had been developing Bloomsbury Square, and pressed for execution. As a judge he was reputed to be cruel and corrupt, and in 1685 he presided over the "Bloody Assizes" where he earned the title, "The Hanging Judge," so this was the juristic context for Barbon and the lawyers of Gray's Inn. A record of the outcome cannot be found, but from later records of Barbon's buildings on the site, it appears that Barbon did not back down and the controversy did not stymie his development project.

He was even more audacious in his dealing with the royal court on this project. On the northern edge of the land parcel, he was at odds with the king by disrupting the "private way on the backside of Holborn and Gray's Inn and soe through Finsbury Fields to Kingsland, for his Majesty's passage to Newmarket, which said way with the gate and bridges are maintained at his Majesty's charge" and, it was said, this was problematic for the king's "just and ancient rights in the aforesaid way" (Privy Council Registers 1684, 2/70, 208). Barbon's frequent and free use of the roadway for the delivery of his heavy construction materials and passage for his numerous workers caused deterioration of its surface. Although it is recorded that the Middlesex Justices and the King's Surveyor attempted to restrain Barbon, he proceeded with his project without regard for their efforts.

Over-extension

Although Barbon formulated and refined many of the details of the process, he also made a significant business error that has been associated with the industry ever since: he overextended in his financial obligations beyond his resources.

After many profitable projects of moderate scale, his most egregious mistake was undertaking a large and complex development project offered by the Bedford Corporation, continuing to build out the estate in Bloomsbury. The land of approximately 13 acres had been hunting fields of Sir William Harpur, but was granted to the Corporation as an endowment for the financial support of the Bedford School. In the school's listing of assets, the recorded rent from its lease rose from £12 in 1566 to £90 in 1650 as London expanded and even proximate agrarian lands were in demand. In the late 17th century, subscribing to an alternative use and potentially much higher rent, the Corporation provided a ground lease to a residential developer, Mr. Thompson, but he was not able to resolve the infrastructure challenges relating to water supply. Recognizing its potential, in 1686 Barbon promoted a development scheme to the Corporation and succeeded in taking over the ground lease. He committed himself to an annual rent of £99 for the twenty-three years remaining under the Thompson lease and £419 per annum for a further fifty-one years.

He combined it with a nearby site that had been granted to the Rugby School, intending to build a large scheme of terrace housing for the "middling class." He immediately commenced the infrastructure and it has been speculated that he laid out and paved Bedford Street, Bedford Row and Court, Princess Street, Theobald's Row, North Street, East Street, Lamb's Conduit Street, Queen Street, Eagle Street and Boswell Court (Pennant 1813, 255) (Figure 7.12).

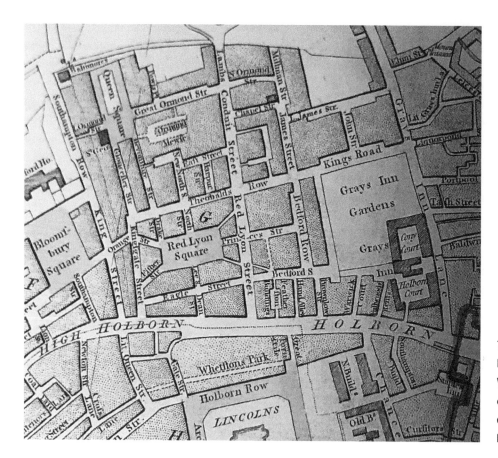

7.12

Map c. 1790 of London's West End, showing streets of the Bedford Corporation development laid out by Barbon.

Additionally, he completed the houses lining both sides of Bedford Row, which are regarded as his most resolved residential development format, and were referred to earlier as a major contribution to the typology of modern urban housing (Figure 7.13).

However, after just eighteen months he became over-extended in meeting his development costs and fell into arrears on the ground lease rent payments. For a number of years he managed to stave off the Corporation's lawyers' demands for payment, but eventually defaulted in 1690. The Chancery Court ordered him to settle his arrears with a bond, but he was unable to purchase it. Instead, he attempted a "land-swap" offering the Corporation some rural lands in exchange for the freehold interest in the project.

The Corporation's deliberations over this offer are instructive in the evolving manner in which properties were valued as long-term endowments based on ground leases. The proffered rural property provided an annual rent of £164, which initially compared favorably with the London fields at £99 and rising to £149 in 1701. The rural property, however, had numerous buildings which would require upkeep and rebuilding, in order to offer short-term leases to tenant farmers, and the rental growth was moderate if not at risk of declining. In contrast, given the potential for substantial rent increases resulting from strong demand for the housing that could be built on it, the London property might be expected to command substantial rental rate increases at its subsequent lease maturity in 1760. The Corporation's minutes indicate that the trustees estimated that its ground lease rent could range from £2,000 to £6,000 per annum. Although their forecast was overly

7.13
No. 36 Bedford Row in 2020.

optimistic, their perception of the trend was accurate since it actually achieved a rent of £3,000. Because the investment's objective was long-term, effectively in perpetuity, and its purpose was to fund the school's operations, the trustees rightly preferred the longer-term potential of the urban land over the initially attractive rural fields, and rejected Barbon's offer. He continued to develop the Rugby School property but, due to his lack of liquidity, he also defaulted on its rental payments in 1695, and the project was stalled by legal actions until his death in 1698.

A further example of his pushing the financial dimensions of his projects to risky levels was his project for developing Gresham House in Osterley Park. He had acquired the site for £9,500, but then mortgaged it for £12,000, thereby making an immediate profit of £2,500 in cash, though he failed to share it with his fellow investors. It was these whom he later frustrated by entering the Parliament where he could not be prosecuted. After three decades of success in his development projects, these later costly projects resulted in his serious financial condition at the end of 1694.

At the same time, the macroeconomic environment also deteriorated, and with continuous spending since the accession of William and Mary, the English currency had deteriorated in value and Parliament pushed for the minting of a new coinage. This topic has been discussed earlier in relation to the public debate between the political economist John Locke and Barbon. A crisis arose when in advance of the last day of the existence of the old coinage the Goldsmiths, the predominant moneylenders, gathered a substantial amount of the old currency and tendered it at the Bank of England for exchange. Without adequate resources of new currency, the Bank defaulted on its obligation to meet what was still current coinage and the price of its stock, an important buttress of its capital, declined from 110d to 83d. The impact was felt throughout the nation's capital markets and the stocks of trading companies also fell precipitously. Although England's financial condition recovered through the efforts of its capable governor, Lord Montagu, who was married to the sister of Rachel Russell, née Wriothesley, the disruption of capital markets adversely affected London real estate and these poor financial conditions were still distressing Barbon's affairs at his death (Brett-James 1929).

In the aftermath, even the management of his lifestyle can be viewed as precarious, though well interwoven with intellectual advancement. After his death, in settlement of his membership fee arrears to the Royal Society, his house at Crane Court was transferred to it at a value of £1,450 and served as its new headquarters for more than seventy years. At that time, it was under the presidency of the scientist Isaac Newton, who described the premises as "being in the middle of town, and out of noise," surely a notable quality in the bustling metropolis (Noble 1869, 123).

Personal Characteristics

Since the new mode of private property development was established by innovation and entrepreneurship, the personal nature of early individuals so involved has been historically regarded as an important component of the evolution, much as the stories and personalities of technology entrepreneurs are studied today. So although a general elucidation of a business practice would not normally dwell on the personal characteristics of one of its major practitioners, it is necessary to make an exception here, for Barbon's nature and behavioral patterns were integral to his professional actions, and they in turn strongly influenced the general mode of practice that has persisted. As with the other major protagonists of private urban development at the time he had an interest in and experience with finance and economics, though he excelled more than most in theoretical formulation and discussion. However, he also employed other attributes that may have been significant to his achievements, and that a number of these characteristics are still associated with real estate developers is either an unfortunate legacy of this early practitioner, or a key component of his method of practice. That question needs further empirical exploration for an answer, which may be pursued elsewhere.

Leading the innovative production of goods and without strategic and multi-channel marketing programs, a businessman of the time had to be a capable salesperson in order to encourage the take-up of those products, and Barbon sold not only houses but also land, leases, and financial products, such as his mortgages. With respect to North's earlier description of Barbon's development activity as "transacting with multitudes," it indicates Barbon's recognition of its magnitude that put it on a larger scale than one-off sales and called for an expansive salesperson. It is uncertain whether he meant a "multitude" of different people or the public at large, for it would seem that Barbon managed the former but probably failed with the latter since he and many of his projects were derided. Some of today's developers find themselves in the same position.

North (1887, 54) also applauded his business acumen and diligence: "He judged well of what he undertook, and had an inexpugnable pertinacity of pressing it through." Barbon demonstrated this in particular with respect to the funding structures that he built, his understanding of markets, and his formulation of an efficient, standardized construction process. On many of his projects, challenges such as gaining control of the site or resolving complex infrastructure requirements were handled with a persistence that set him apart from other developers at the time. North (1887, 54) added, "He never despaired of a design if it were sound at the bottom, but would endure repulse after repulse, and still press his point." Developers continue to require and generally exercise tenacity and persistence to accomplish their complex and often controversial projects, or they fall by the wayside.

Specifically with respect to Barbon's overlay of commercial interest in the development process, North (1887, 54–55) noted his creativity in maximizing the economic value of projects:

> He was the inventor of this new method of building by casting of ground into streets and small houses, to augment their number with as little front as possible, and selling the ground to workmen by so much per foot front ... This has made ground rents high for the sake of mortgaging, and others following his steps have refined and improved upon it.

The most successful development projects since that time have also tended to find creative and innovative solutions, rather than to repeat easy formats, a quality that sets development apart from mere building projects.

Barbon's consistent method of over-extending his financial obligations was of much interest and curiosity to North. He commented: "His fault was that he knowingly overtraded his stock, and that he could not go through with undertakings without great disappointments to those concerned, especially in point of time" (North 1887, 54). He asked Barbon why he acted in this way and recorded the response as follows:

> He said it was not worth his while to deal little; that a bricklayer could do. The gain he expected was out of great undertakings, which would rise lustily in the whole, and because this trade required a greater stock than he had, perhaps £30,000 or £40,000, he must compass his designs either by borrowed money or by credit with those he dealt with, either by fair means or foul. (North 1887, 55)

Such a predilection towards large high-profile projects, often requiring resources beyond those readily available, has become a characteristic of real estate developers, though all too often it similarly has resulted in the destruction of a formerly modestly constrained but financially sustainable business.

North (1887, 54) was also observant of Barbon's negotiating style: "He never proposed to tempt men to give way or join but by their interest, laid plainly before them ... If he could not work upon all together he would allure them singly by some advantage above the rest, and if he could not gain all, divide them." He also reported that he would stage a scene to his advantage by calling a meeting of those who were discontented with him, delaying them when they arrived, but then "he would make his entry, as fine and as richly dressed as a lord of the bedchamber on a birthday." The result would be that "these hard-headed fellows that had prepared to give him all the affronts and opposition that their brutal way suggested, truly seeing such a brave man, pulled off their hats and knew not what to think of it" (North 1887, 56).

Birth of the Modern Property Development Business

The display of personal wealth by property developers since has often been derided, though today, as in Barbon's time, it does appear to be convincing to those they wish to influence.

He was also known to use other modes of behavior, such as to remain calm and patient: "He would endure all manner of affronts and be as tame as a lamb" (North 1887, 54), or to present an air of one who was "all honey, and a real friend" (ibid., 56). In conclusion, having described a brilliant though imprudent businessman, North (ibid., 57) conceded that "had not his cash failed, which made his works often stand still, and go to ruin, and many other disadvantages grow, in all probability he might have been as rich as any in the nation."

Not only were his methods absorbed into the evolving private development practice, but his personal behavior is presented as embodying the essence of the new urban developer. Brett-James (1929, 111) said:

> With the occasion came the man, and Dr. Nicholas Barbon, the able, but unprincipled son of an eccentric father, is one of the earliest, and, for a time, one of the most successful of the great speculative builders, to whose efforts the modern development of London, for good or evil, has been largely due.

Chapter 8: Consolidating the New Private Urban Development Model

The Earl of Bedford's innovative development of Covent Garden, its financial success, and its enthusiastic approbation by the monarch and urban commentators, established it as the new model of private urban building development. This influential role related not only to the use of the residential square spatial format but also to his production of an identifiable neighborhood area. Carefully managed, this concept was an effective marketing tactic, and it also enabled him to reap the benefit of positive externalities that followed as he built the initial residences and associated amenities.

Although much building of row houses and other repetitive formats continued, other builders undertook more complex and usually larger development schemes. Major advances included new site layouts, changing the current use to a new and approved function, defining the programmatic needs of residents who were not yet specified, refinements in providing suitable amenities, infrastructure and public spaces, and achieving integrity of the physical and economic factors. It became a more comprehensive business activity, requiring the resolution of many unique factors in the context of a relatively unknown economic outcome, in contrast to traditionally commissioned small-scale production, the "cottage industry," and it was therefore called speculative development, as distinct from merchant building.

The characteristics of this emerging model and its inherent dynamic are gathered and reviewed later. At this stage of the investigation, of importance to the continuation and success of this business activity were instances where it was so manifestly attractive that it was adopted by others, successfully implemented, refinements made, and the model consolidated.

Although these subsequent schemes varied in scale, and were located in other parts of expanding London and other emerging cities in England, the most formative adoption of the new approach took place proximate to the two originals in the important area between the City of London and Westminster. Of particular interest is St James's Square, which closely followed the model in such features as its developer's socio-economic position, its physical layout, and its target market, but also subject to some instructive modifications. Further, the schemes of Nicholas Barbon, though generally conforming to the model, exhibit distinct differences in respect of the developer's situation, his developments' physical resolution, and some very specific financial formulations that he introduced.

More Aristocratic Residential Squares

Other aristocratic developers quickly followed suit. Southampton's development has been envisioned before the Interregnum, as had Salisbury's to the west of Covent Garden. With the Restoration, however, the new model was enthusiastically embraced by numerous aristocrats, particularly those with landholdings in the now prestigious West End of London. As these pursued their respective projects, unique circumstances led to some minor modifications of the urban development model, but generally it became consolidated as a process of creating the urban fabric and as the business model of rising entrepreneurs.

St James's Square

The unusual details of the development of St James's Square will be discussed as it includes features important to the future of the model.

Henry VIII had amassed what was referred to as the Bailiwick of St James, which comprised an extensive tract of meadowland bounded, in today's geography, by the Haymarket on the east, Piccadilly in the north and the Royal Parks to the west and south (Figure 8.1). He had acquired these lands, possibly before the Dissolution of the Monasteries, from the ecclesiastical entities of Westminster Abbey, the Convent of Abington, and the Hospital of

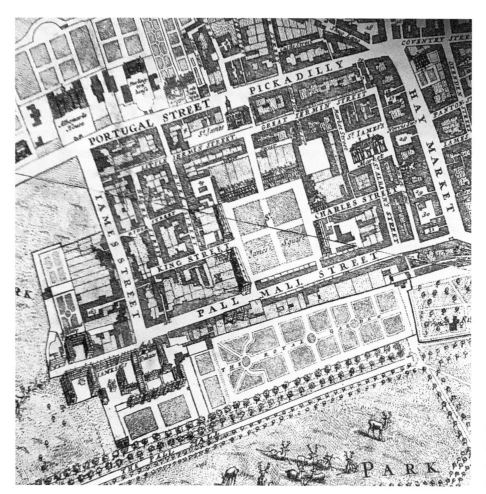

8.1

Map showing the Bailiwick of St James and St James's Square, c. 1682.

St James, in order to protect the water supply drawn from springs and conduits in the area for his new St James's Palace.

Prior to that endowment, in 1654 under the Parliamentary government, Hugh Woodward had purchased the pasture known as St James's Fields with plans to develop it as row houses. In line with common sentiment, the parishioners objected to the loss of their open space and by 1656, the development was forbidden. After the Restoration, the adjoining street, now named St James's Street, attracted the attention of Charles II, who regularly traversed it on his route to Whitehall, and he required that it be paved and kept free of waste. In addition to this improvement, as he continued to reside at St James's Palace, St James's Fields to the north became a desirable location for the houses of courtiers and aristocrats.

In 1661, Charles reclaimed these lands from the defunct Parliamentary Commission, canceled Hugh Woodward's lease to develop it as row houses, and granted a thirty-year lease of 45 acres of his mother's holdings in St James's Field to Henry Jermyn, her loyal courtier during their exile. The monarch remained personally interested in the quality of Jermyn's development of this land, particularly its aesthetic standards and appeal. The Letters Patent of the grant specified that: "His Majesty intending those Places near unto his Majesties's Pallaces of White-Hall and St James's [Palace] should be Built for the conveniency of the Nobility and Gentry who were to attend upon his Majestie's Person and in Parliament; and for the better Ornament of the Place" (*Letters Patent*, 17 May 1662).

Following the example of Covent Garden, the now Earl of St Albans planned a central square surrounded by grand houses and mansions. But despite a strong demand for prestigious sites, his estate was burdened by the short duration of its Crown lease. The usual ground lease of land for the erection of a mansion building on it was sixty years, and interested potential residents regarded St Albans' limited thirty-year tenure as an insufficient period for the economical amortization of the substantial costs of building. Although the hereditary holdings of the Earls of Bedford and Southampton also offered a limited term ground lease to the potential occupant of a building on their developments, their continued ownership of their land, in contrast to its reversion to the Crown in St Albans' case, allowed for the possibility of a renewed lease if the house remained habitable.

To enhance the marketability of his project, Jermyn made the case in a court petition "that the town was defective in point of houses fit for the dwellings of noblemen and other persons of quality." This led to a clash between an increasing protectiveness by the Crown of the value and importance of its overarching control of its landholdings around London and the growing financial sophistication of the real estate developers. But in 1665 St Albans's petition for relief was successful, and he was granted freehold title to the land for the project, comprising between 4.5 and 5 acres. It forms a square, bounded on the north by Piccadilly and on the south by Pall Mall, on the east by Haymarket and on the west by St James's Street.

In relation to authoritative hierarchy this was a notable manifestation of the Crown's dominance over the City authorities in matters of land development in this area to the west of the City walls. Many were astounded at St Albans's success, and on September 2, 1663 Pepys (1900, vol. 3.2, 251) commented that "the building of St. James's by my Lord St. Albans, which is now about [or underway] (and which the City stomach, I perceive, highly, but dare not oppose it)."

Rather than develop the estate himself as Bedford had done at Covent Garden with the consequences of huge expenditure in advance of revenues, St Albans preferred Southampton's system and disposed of sites through ground leases or, in a couple of cases, by an outright freehold sale.

In dogged disregard of Southampton's opposition to his development, he adopted his opponent's strategy of taking up residence in the square himself, and also followed, though to a less generous degree, Bedford's example by providing land for the building of St James's church, Piccadilly, which was designed by the leading arbiter of building approvals at the time, Sir Christopher Wren (Summerson 1991a, 26).

Although to all appearances this development (Figure 8.2) was a success for St Albans, its implementation had certain unusual features. First, he sold the fee simple title of the site for a sizable down payment, but also imposed a small annual ground rent in perpetuity. This followed the Scottish *feuing* system whereby the land title was sold outright, though the vendor retained the receipt of a small annual fee or feu-duty. The vendor retained no reversionary rights and did not participate in any increase in the property's value, and therefore, unlike

8.2
View of St James's Square.

long-term landowners, had no regard for balancing long-term capital gains through appreciation with short-term income capacity.

In this respect, his transactions essentially amounted to outright sales. If he had correctly determined that he could achieve a higher return on the capital so derived, he was exemplary in making this investment decision, though on limited information it would seem that the liquidated capital was placed in less remunerative investments. However, the hold or sell decision in such a situation, with viable options, was established as one of the most important strategic features of the new business model of private urban development.

Public Place

Since St Albans sold the freehold of all his estate, other than his own residence, he paid little attention to the public square. In accordance with the usual practice of residents' responsibility for the street in front of their houses, there is a record of Lord Bellasis being required to pave the piazza in front of his house, though it is suggested that he attended only to the footpath. So, like other squares that lacked maintenance by a landowner or the public authority, it was not adequately maintained and by 1726 was polluted by much waste.

In what probably established the precedent for the proper maintenance of such orphaned public squares, the residents petitioned the Parliament for a private Act that required the inhabitants of a square to pay a rate for funding to "cleanse, adorn, and beautify" and maintain it. The 1727 Act levied an annual rate at 8s per foot of frontage or £21 for a house of 52.5 ft frontage. This enabled the residents of St James's Square to raise £5,000 and purchase an annuity of thirty-two years at 7% to cover future maintenance costs. Fines were also imposed for dumping trash, encroaching on the footpath, or loitering in a carriage.

Master Builders' Urban Development Projects

To meet an increasing housing demand as London grew, many master builders erected a row of three or four identical houses by subdividing a single plot. Bedford's larger and planned development was rare, but his model was taken up by some ambitious and capable builders such William Newton, almost contemporaneously, and by Richard Frith and Thomas Neale later in the century. Their developments were located amongst those of Bedford and Southampton, and contributed various unique features to the creation of the built fabric of London's West End (Figure 8.3). The varied projects also illustrated the broad applicability of the new business model of private urban development.

William Newton's Lincoln Inn Fields

As described in London's early development, Newton had undertaken the construction of row houses in Great Queen Street, where like Bedford, he engaged architectural services to provide an integrated and aesthetically pleasing street environment, which he realized would enhance the value of the individual properties. He applied Bedford's model even more assiduously when he later acquired sites surrounding Lincoln's Inn Fields. Here, he planned for the beautification and maintenance of the existing public square at his own expense, and he sponsored residential designs that conformed to Inigo Jones's neoclassical architectural order, a notable example of which is Lindsey House (Figure 8.4), which is still admired today.

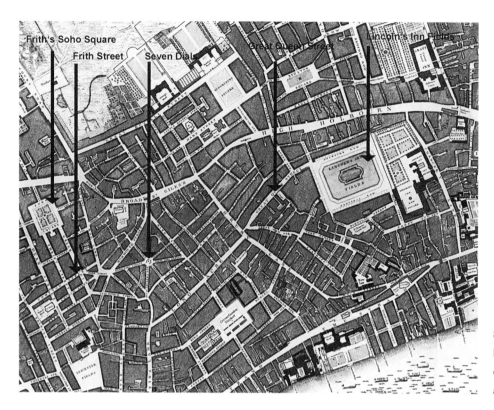

8.3

Map c. 1746 showing developments by Newton, Frith, and Neale.

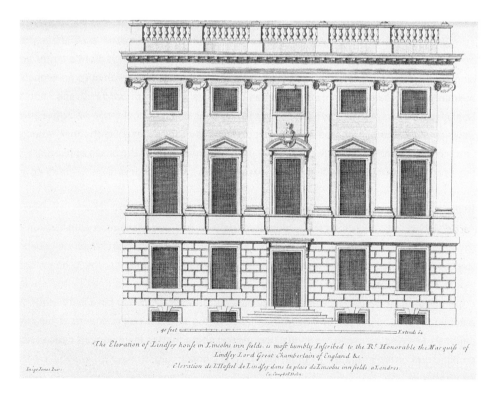

8.4

Elevation drawing of Lindsey House.

This extended adoption of the model by entrepreneurs who were without aristocratic status and its long-term land ownership, and the manner of its consolidation around certain key decisions, were critical to its progressing formulation and being so broadly applicable.

When the residents of Lincoln's Inn failed to raise the money for the beautification of the square, it was William Newton who undertook the earliest strategic improvement of the neighborhood. Brett-James (1935, 155) has suggested that in 1629 he successfully acquired the lease of Cup Field on the west side to develop fourteen large houses, probably paying a substantial fee into the hungry treasury of the profligate James I. After commencing the project, he acquired the interest of Lady Cornwallis in Purse Field (Brett-James 1935, 155) and made a subsequent application in 1638 to expand the project to thirty-two houses. Although he had no formal authority over the open space at the center, Coulter (2016, 265) suggests that Newton "... was anxious to preserve the greater part of the open space as a means of attracting builders and tenants to an estate of the highest quality." He had noted Bedford's experience that the provision of surrounding amenities raised the economic value of the houses.

Retained and embellished, this important building exemplifies the achievement of the earliest developers in balancing the physical quality of the structure with the financial imperatives of project feasibility. The success of the development in responding to the government's restrictions and requirements, as well as satisfying new aspirations of social symbolism, continue as an example of the potential of the private real estate development model even in its earliest days of application.

Richard Frith

In his discussion of London's squares, Johnson (1952, 88) described Richard Frith as a bricklayer and member of the Tylers' and Bricklayers' Guild. There was no trade known as a builder as the term is now understood, and he was also known as a mechanic, a general term, and he undertook the erection of complete buildings by subcontracting to fellow tradesmen with complementary skills. A prolific producer, he built many row houses on land to the north of St James's Palace and, in 1682, he entered into a ground lease agreement with the Earl of Leicester for a substantial residential project on the north side of Lester Fields, now Leicester Square.

Being aware of the new urban format of residential squares, he turned his hand to such a development scheme in 1667, obtaining a permit to build what was originally eponymously known as Frith Square, later renamed King Square, in honor of either King Charles II or a court herald and statistician, Gregory King, who claimed to have a hand in its planning. Coulter (2016) reports that the debate continues, but today it is known as Soho Square.

Soho Square: The Residential Square Format

Though Frith's project did not introduce any innovations, it replicated and consolidated Bedford's format for Covent Garden. Though it provided a much more modest central square, it was a well-executed example of the new topographical format. It followed the residential arrangement of Southampton Square, with a large single house along one side and several small sites on the others. He commenced by building smaller houses, and leased the first

8.5

View of Sohoe or King's Square, c. 1731.

ones in 1679. By 1683, he had completed a total of fourteen, and by 1691 there were forty-one (Coulter 2016, 448) (Figure 8.5).

Although using the physical format of Covent Garden and Southampton Square, Frith embraced the business plan of Nicholas Barbon so that he did not retain or consolidate ownership of the land. Thus, in this case the grand house was not occupied by the owner of the entire precinct, including the public space, and the neighborhood suffered some neglect which was similar to that experienced by St James's Square and Red Lion Square. Frith, however, had learnt some of Bedford's lesson regarding the public realm and, as the surrounding small houses achieved a critical mass, he included in the leases a stipulation for an annual contribution to the upkeep of the central space. Creating an attractive square while structuring the legal responsibilities for its maintenance was probably an important factor in his strategy to attract a tenant for the grand house lot still vacant on the south side.

Frith Street: Applying Inigo Jones's Urban Residence Design
Richard Frith is also notable for adopting Inigo Jones's new design for grand urban residences at Covent Garden, but he chose a less expensive variation by reducing embellishments for a

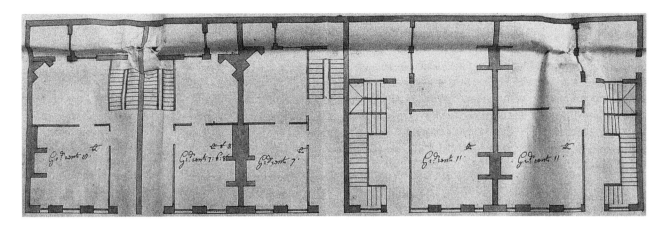

8.6

Plans for houses Nos. 6–10 Frith Street, 1712.

8.7

Elevations for houses Nos. 6–10 Frith Street, 1712.

whole street of his development known as Frith Street (Figure 8.6). Nevertheless, evident in the drawings and completed buildings that still stand today is the neoclassical order of the façade with its *piano nobile* for gracious living on the level above ground. He also engaged the desirable aesthetic integration of a number of houses with a continuous entablature, though with an interesting punctuation of pilasters stretching over three storeys (Figure 8.7).

Thomas Neale

Thomas Neale was not a builder, but rather an ambitious businessman who held the position of Master of the Mint and Groom Porter, often involved in the critical raising of funds for Charles II's court (Brett-James 1929, 136). He was broadly interested in speculative investments including mining projects and quickly noted the financially rewarding activity of private development. While pursuing some property schemes in partnership with other developers and builders, his notable contribution to the formulation of the development process was his project known as Seven Dials.

Seven Dials: A Unique Format

His reading of the market was incisive, and he identified the substantial unmet demand for housing by the growing class of professionals and clerks. He obtained a site in the Marshland Close area north of Covent Garden, and commenced laying out his scheme in 1693. However, the usual street and block arrangement such as at Covent Garden provided quite large land plots, with a frontage of approximately 21 ft and depth of 50 ft, but he sought a method for creating smaller, less expensive lots. Since a ground lease at the time was defined by its street frontage, the later solution of providing "flag" or "hatchet" lots at the rear of the housing lining the streets was not a possibility. Neale's creative solution of a radiating system of seven streets was a clever use of the geometry skills that were popular amongst the men of science, such as Newton and Halley, and with whom he was probably socially acquainted. Not able to afford the contribution of an open piazza at the center, he completed the composition with a civic feature found in the circular plazas of Europe, though his contained circle was much smaller. In October 1694 John Evelyn (1906, iii, 312) described it in his diary as "where seven streets make a star from a Doric Pillar placed in the middle of a circular area" (Figure 8.8).

Although comprising land lots of irregular shape, the project yielded the intended collection of small houses with well-paved streets of suitable scale. Summerson (1991b, 28) describes it as "that extraordinary freak of town-planning … where seven street meet at a point formally marked by a pillar-sundial, the idea perhaps being to cram as much street

8.8
Seven Dials showing Doric pillar at the intersection of the seven streets.

frontage as possible on to a restricted site." The precinct continues to present its unique shapes, unusual sightlines, and pleasant sense of neighborhood to this day.

Given his association with the royal court and probably influenced by the aristocrat developers, Neale generally exhibited a concern for the community in which he developed. This was most evident in his project in Shadwell in London's East End, and Power (1978, 41) notes that what allowed the site to take off was Neale's recognition that the layout needed to include recreational space and "civic amenities." As one of these civic amenities, Neale funded the construction of a new parish church in order to create a framework for social aid and unity in the rapidly developing suburb. He also worked with the city authorities to establish a market and improved waterworks system to serve the middle- and upper-income two-storey houses. Power (1978, 43) concludes the evaluation of changes brought to Shadwell through Neale's development: "By the end of the century, helped by an enterprising speculator, it developed into an identifiable and unified suburban centre."

Setting the Course for London's Continued Development

Following the lead of Bedford and Southampton, the additional entrepreneurial developments at Lincoln's Inn Fields and St James's Square, and the projects of Barbon, Frith, and Neale amongst others, set the format for housing of various levels of society in expanding London. Though accommodation for the poor remained unsatisfactory, the peers, businessmen, craftsmen, and professionals were well settled, some within the City walls but many in the surrounding environs. The majority of the new private development activity occurred in the area of its origin, the western suburbs. Beckett (1986, 268) describes the ensuing dynamic of that region: "By 1700 the heaviest concentration of aristocratic names was in Soho Square, south of Oxford Street, and Golden Square, north of Piccadilly ... By around 1714, another step westwards had begun, as the aristocracy moved into Hanover Square (1717–19), Cavendish Square and Grosvenor Square" (Figure 8.9).

Fluctuating economic conditions impacted the prosperity of London's residents and consequently the development activity. Habakkuk (1940, 13) reports the changed conditions at the end of the century: "Rents, which rose considerably between 1640 and 1690, hardly rose at all between 1690 and 1720. Heavily mortgaged landowners attempted to raise them, but failed; and on land let at a rack rent there was often a decrease. For this there were four main reasons." Another difficult period occurred from 1740 to 1742 when at least nine substantial development businesses failed. However, momentum increased again after the end of the Seven Years War in 1763. Particularly in 1774, with the passing of the London Building Act which was to govern metropolitan building for seventy years, private enterprise commenced several great schemes, including Manchester Square and Bedford Square, Portland Place, and Charles Cadogan's Chelsea estate.

In the next century the model was continued with the development of Regent's Park and the Grosvenors began to develop their Belgravia and Pimlico estates, proximate to Buckingham Palace, which became the residence of King George IV. Further afield, "[a] number of park-like suburban middle-class areas were laid out, including St John's Wood, Primrose Hill, Clapham Park and Highbury New Park" (Beckett 1986, 269). These typically utilized the same method of subdividing a large acreage with the Highbury project being on 100 acres

8.9

Map c. 1790 of London's West End, showing residential square developments.

developed by Henry Rydon, who also followed the examples of Bedford and Southampton and lived within the scheme himself.

While both Bedford and Southampton had attempted to control the physical quality of the buildings built, the new development model could not withstand the desire of the newly prosperous to distinguish themselves with individual features on their townhouses. Inigo Jones's plan for arcaded residences on three sides of Covent Garden was curtailed on the western end of the north Portico by the townhouse of Lord Archer. Southampton had explicitly provided flexibility in his scheme to allow for a variety of site sizes and buildings in response to market demand, although he did retain restrictions on materials and some other architectural features. As a result, although some single buildings were noted by Evelyn and others for their beauty, the physical format of the overall schemes has been described as "haphazard and was largely left to prospective inhabitants or speculative building contractors" (Beckett 1986, 270).

However, from about the middle of the 18th century, as these developers became more practiced with their business model, they realized the importance for economic value if more attention was paid to increasingly popular notions of architectural aesthetics. A leading proponent of this more refined model was Lieutenant General Sir John Russell, 4th Duke of Bedford, who was great-grandson to both of the development pioneers, the 4th Earls of Bedford and Southampton, and now applying what would today be called a deep corporate intelligence to the amalgamated estate. Planning the north side of Great Russell Street in

8.10
Uniform façades in Great Russell Street in 2019.

1776, to the west of Southampton Square, he restricted the format to a uniformity of architectural façade, dimensions, material, and quality, in addition to sizing and pricing the residences specifically for the upper-middle class (Figure 8.10). Although it took almost a century to complete, the surviving ambience of this street and its compositionally cohesive role for the Bloomsbury estate is notable.

Funding Progress

Not only was the topographical planning format of this private urban development model replicated as London grew, its economic structure and prospects also continued their appeal to the aristocracy, even when they did not themselves own urban land. Beckett (1986, 270–271) reports:

> In December 1717 Lords Dartmouth, Chando(s), Harcourt, Bingley, Bathurst and Castleton … proposed to Edward Harley, later second Earl of Oxford, the idea of developing Cavendish Square as a residential area north of Oxford Street. A plan was drawn up in 1719, as a result of which a market [demonstration] house was started in 1720 and a church in 1724. James Gibb was put in charge of architecture in the square, and Charles Bridgeman was employed to lay out the garden. The Duke of Chandos leased the whole of the north side of the square, and considered several uses for the land – including a large new house for himself …

Advances were also made in terms of the financial structure of these developments, and some changes to lease structures were instigated for the benefit of the increasingly savvy landowners. While not being the developer of Tavistock Square on the estate lands, and instead giving sponsorship to the well-known Thomas Cubitt who had built out much of Grosvenor Square, Bedford provided a ground lease that went beyond the usual set rent commitment and was both speculative and yet patient in terms of the landlord's revenues.

The ground lease rent was contracted not to exceed a set proportion of the rack rent, or rent paid by the resident to the builder, and this would allow flexibility in that intermediary's obligations when the house rent varied according to markets. However, offsetting this variability, was a clever mechanism for being rewarded for his speculative risk: he also took a share of the profit, that is the rack rent less the payments made on the loan for the building. Although he set this share relatively low in the early stages, enabling Cubitt to regain some early capital and returns, the profit share to Bedford increased to be substantial towards the end of the lease. Of course, it may have been Cubitt who proposed the idea, but the willingness of all participants to enter such arrangements, with their varying levels and timing of returns, indicated an understanding of the complexity of risks and cash flows inherent in private urban development projects.

As practiced in Cubitt's development of Tavistock Square, construction costs came to be partially funded by debt, as also continues today. These were often repaid when mortgage loans were made for completed, leased properties, as continues today. In the early part of the 17th century, the landed gentry had maintained debt within manageable levels, but the increased opulence of the Stuart court was associated with some overspending by the upper classes. With the increasing availability of capital, created from trading and merchant surpluses, borrowing also escalated and the tenure of its liability extended longer. Whereas some settlement of loans had been achieved in earlier times by the sale of non-critical lands within an estate, the new higher levels could not be met with only minimal sales, and the entail restrictions had been put in place by prudent elders to prevent more extensive diminution of holdings.

As a result, new methods for holding debt evolved and the longtime provision of property as security on loans, usually for small landowners, artisans, or merchants, was taken up by these landed nobles. Beckett (1986, 300) reports:

> The decision to switch from redeeming debts through land sales to maintaining them via mortgages is well illustrated by the activities of the second Earl of Bridgewater. In 1649 he inherited his father's estates and with them debts totalling nearly £52,000 ... Payment of the debts began in the 1650s through land sales totalling £13,470, but the second earl began to refinance repayment through mortgages. By 1662 these totalled £16,000. Over the following two decades he was able to continue relying on mortgages, and the success of his efforts at deriving the largest possible yield from the property enabled him to pay off some of the principal sum during the 1670s.

The Network for Development

Additionally with respect to the capital resources, rather than being the sole sponsor of the project, as both Bedford and Southampton had done, later developments such as St James's Square, Cavendish Square described earlier, and Berkeley Square were funded by a syndicate of peers with the addition of some wealthy merchants and lenders. Though spreading the extent of the financial resources, this structure did, however, limit the funding qualification to those with some closeness or connection to the project, in contrast to the complex and removed capital structures that Barbon had utilized.

This connectedness of the capital, and its capable application by interconnected entrepreneurs, as well as the government relationships necessary for project approvals, and the sense of community responsibility embedded in some social positions would all prove to be important features of the private urban development model. The mix of these features, that are reflected by the inherent networking dynamic of the real estate development activity, was critical for a variety of outcomes including the quality of the buildings, the provision and maintenance of amenities, the targeted residents, and often the tenacity and persistence of the sponsor.

Although requiring much further elucidation of details, the importance of the networking dynamic in producing the earliest development projects, Covent Garden and Bloomsbury Square, is represented in the double-paged diagram in Figure 8.11.

It was noted in the business activities in the early rise of capitalism and commercial investment that the "notion of duty was such that aristocrats were ready to carry on investing beyond the point at which hardnosed [sic] businessmen might well have called it a day" (Beckett 1986, 8). However, as the real estate industry grew and the size and number of development projects expanded, arranging capital that retained some form of connection, not necessarily monetary, in the projects became more challenging. Consequently, the Barbon practice of obtaining capital from the changing, anonymous marketplace became more prevalent and most certainly is the basis for funding real estate today.

The Provinces and Resorts

The model for urban development on a scale was also influential as other towns in England grew:

> Urban development in the provinces benefited from the examples set in London. Although towns were growing prior to 1750, the really significant changes got under way [sic] only in the second half of the eighteenth century. Consequently, landlords could observe what had happened in London, and weigh up the advantages of ground-rent leases, developers, and the alternative methods of building and control. (Beckett 1986, 273)

As in London, the approaches of the landowners varied. In Birmingham, two large estates totaling approximately 250 acres were leased on 99-year and 120-year leases to developers with minimal requirements in terms of the improvements. In Manchester, on the other hand, the estates of the Byron, Legh, and Mosley families were laid out by the owners, often undertaking some of the infrastructure themselves.

Liverpool was yet another approach whereby, in 1672, a corporation took 1,000 acres on a 1,000-year lease from the Molyneux estate and developed and managed most of the housing for the emerging industrial city. In contrast, however, ownership of land in the city of Bath was fragmented and, although some architecturally beautiful crescents and groupings were developed, it was thought that "this gave rise to internally coherent schemes unlinked

Southampton Family

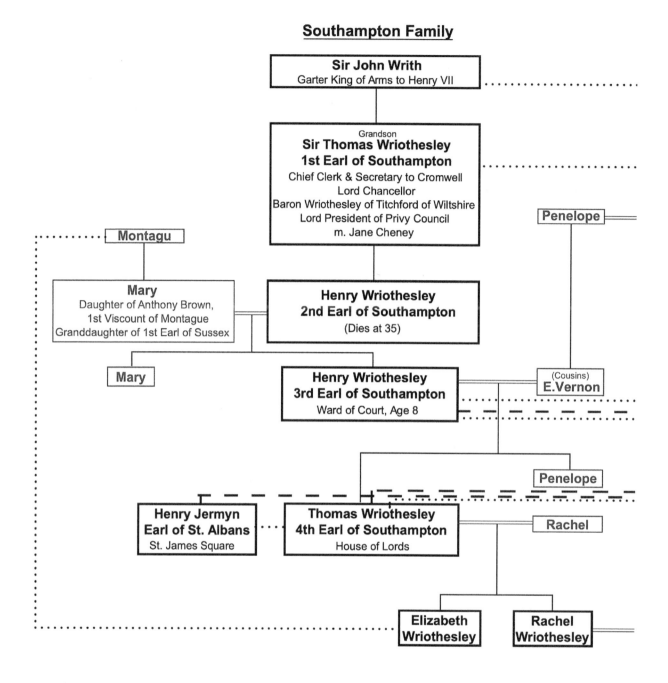

Legend of Connections

─────────── **Family**

═══════════ **Marriage**

·············· **Commercial**

━ ━ ━ **Social**

Royal Court

William the Conqueror

11th Great Grandson
King Henry VII

King Henry VIII

Bedford Family

Thomas Wolsey
Advisor

Thomas Cromwell
Chancellor

Richard Riche
Assistant
Chancellor of Court of
Augmentation

John Russell
1st Earl of Bedford
Privy Chamber to Henry VIII
Purchased Bedfordshire & granted
28 acre estate of Covent Garden
m. Anne Sapcote

Francis Russell
2nd Earl of Bedford
4 Sons (Outlives 1st & 2nd)
m. Eleanor Forster

Edward VI

Mary I

Elizabeth I
Cecil / Burleigh

Lucy
Harrington

Edward Russell
3rd Earl of Bedford
3rd Son, No Heirs

William Russell
4th Son
m. Elizabeth Long

(Closest royal relative)
James I

Charles I

Oliver Cromwell

Francis Russell
4th Earl of Bedford
m. Catherine Brydges

Charles II

James II

William & Mary

Nicholas Barbon

Royal Society
Isaac Newton

Christopher Wren

William Russell
5th Earl of Bedford
m. Anne Carp

William Russell
Lord Russell

Wriothesley Russell
2nd Duke of Bedford

8.11
Political, economic, and social network behind the earliest private development activities.

to existing developments" (Beckett 1986, 274). It is to be remembered how much importance Bedford and Southampton placed on the connections of their estates to the surrounding neighborhoods – a development principle not always followed in succeeding schemes.

Unfortunately, another key development concern of the earliest developers that was abandoned was that of providing the public realm and community amenities. The model of subdivided developments was extended to the more suburban format of individual villas set in their own large gardens, and many such schemes were done in Tunbridge Wells (Calverley Park), Cheltenham (Lansdown) and Liverpool (Sefton Park), amongst others. And, although some elegant planning included tree-lined circuses and wide boulevards, there were barely any community amenities provided with even some promised ones not being delivered. When a development did include substantial facilities, as in the case of the scheme for 787 houses in Skegness undertaken by the Earl of Scarbrough, the capital demands may have been too much since it "proved to be over-ambitious, and only the southern half of the plan ever came into existence" (Beckett 1986, 279). This neglect of the public domain and the provision of community amenities was an unfortunate evolution of the model of private urban development.

Social Acceptance of the Property Businessman

It has been noted that in English society the ownership of real property was continued amongst the aristocracy in order to maintain the stability of that society. However, as new property developers emerged, they occupied an interesting middle ground between the old landed interests and the men of commerce and money of the late 17th century. While the active modern commercial interests stood in contrast to the passive management of rural land assets, the new commercial ideology had also come to be expressed in terms of real property ownership in the growing London metropolis. The urban properties were strategically managed not only to provide a steady annual income in the traditional manner of landed interests but also to provide significant gains in wealth through developing them to higher economic uses and through opportunistic transactions that captured their appreciation in value. While commercial trading changed from merely a sector of economic activity to an inherent part of the new capitalist economy as a whole, so too some traditional assets such as real property were pulled into the new commercial zest that the English economy was experiencing.

This new parading of real property by a lower class was not without social frisson. Many of the old-line landowners continued to see themselves and their social position as integral to their property holdings, even while those mostly passive ground-lease holdings delivered only a modest cash flow. And continuing with the Protestant notion of shunning excessive wealth, these social "grandees" even prided themselves on their perceived "modest" income. However, as the recently titled and more business-minded landowners who were developing the fashionable residential precincts of the city gained more wealth, status, and political power, their activities were lauded by a society that was becoming inclusive of wealthy merchants, financiers, and professionals. During this time, in contrast to prior centuries and also more reticent future periods, the pursuit of wealth was a considered intention in itself, and the innovative model of private urban development proved to be an effective means by which many could achieve it.

That model will now be fully described and evaluated.

Part III
Property Development Reframed: Theory, Principles, and Models

Chapter 9: The Model Formulated!

"At the end of the seventeenth century no more than 16 per cent of the population lived in settlements of 5000 or more. London, already in a class of its own, had a population of around half a million" (Beckett 1986, 262).

To house such a relatively large population, private entrepreneurs creatively synthesized emerging business strategy and organization with traditional methods of land management. They made use of the abundant investment funds arriving with the launch of capitalist commerce. And they embraced the fashionable urban aesthetics promoted by the Stuart monarchs. With courage, diligence, and persistence, they provided the predominant, if not the only, solution for London's housing needs, so that by the dawn of the 18th century in London's metropolis, the business model of private real estate development had been established.

It served as an efficient production process for creating the needed urban built form, with an identifiable sequence of actions, an explicit array of decisions, and a carefully determined outcome. But also, and uniquely, this new business activity resulted in the deliberate creation of an investment asset with its own distinct and innovative analytical methodology – urban real estate. An important incidental consequence was that, despite its being undertaken by private individuals for their own economic interests rather than by a monarch or wealthy Renaissance courtier for symbolic grandeur, this commercial undertaking also delivered a substantial "public good" in an advanced urban typology, competitive with that of the Continent. In a vacuum of municipal planning, it delivered public streets; open squares, courts, and gardens; a façade onto the public realm; and numerous changes of functional use and activity for new inhabitants and an altered economic context.

Although its first recognizable attempts in the early part of the 17th century manifested varying approaches, through collective modification and refinement of methods an identifiable formulation of the business model evolved within a few decades and was emulated by most successful contemporary practitioners.

Towards a Model of Private Real Estate Development

In the context of emerging capitalism and the particular business interests of its first practitioners, it is not surprising that the format for real estate development resembled the structure of its companion commercial undertakings. It had reference to the advancing mode of mechanized production and financial arrangements that were evolving in Europe and continue at the heart of Western capitalism today. As a consequence, although variant in some details such as the general absence of uniformity of product, the tension between its consumption and asset values, and its unavoidable public impact, the private development of urban real estate took the fundamental construct of the modern business model. Therefore, to gather together the features and dynamics revealed by the historical exploration and to present this formulation of the activity, guidance is given by Haslam et al.'s (2013, 6) definition of the business model as "a loose conceptual framework [that] should provide an overarching abstraction about the real world, generate a system of classification, and reveal the specific activity characteristics."

As the specifics of the model's structure and process were hard to distinguish in its earliest appearance, given the combination of production outsourcing and ad hoc adoption of new commercial actions, a search for the specific characteristics of a real estate development model is suitably commenced with attention to its driving objectives and heralded accomplishments at the time. These were compelling and varied, though also had been regularly found in conflict. But, clearly identifying the key purposes of this nascent commercial activity, and tracing the complex dynamics between those within the rapidly changing physical, economic, and social conditions of urban London, will serve to elucidate the actual processes by which the model functioned.

This chapter presents the objectives, processes, and codified procedures inherent in the model that was formulated in 17th-century London and subsequently extended throughout the Anglo-American world, in addition to being more recently adopted globally. An assessment of the performance of the model and the private practice of urban development, with reference to existing theoretical perspectives, then follows.

Early Objectives

The first consideration for understanding a business activity or, one could say, any deliberate human activity, would be defining its objectives.

In that its most obvious manifestation took a physical form, the earliest development activity was driven by the need for urban shelter, particularly housing, which had risen to a compelling level at the time and place in which this activity is first observed. However, the early entrepreneurs in this field, the Earls of Bedford and Southampton, were businessmen and would not have ventured into it had it not offered them a financially beneficial opportunity. They were not focused on responding to a social need over and above seeking to maximize the economic value of their resources, namely the land they owned, which was most advantageously located where housing was in demand. As any businessman would have done, they assessed the value of the product they could deliver, compared it to production costs, evaluated the net result with that from other alternative uses of the asset, and proceeded if the outcome was seen to be profitable.

Mere profitability alone, though, was not the only economic objective. Unlike some other production activities, the development of urban properties required a significant amount of capital. Although the Earls of Bedford and Southampton funded their developments themselves, the attraction for capital investment by others was quickly adjusted on the basis of financial feasibility. They sought a level of investment return that was competitive with alternatives such as joint-stock trading companies and merchant partnerships. Fortunately, then as now, the perceived low risk in the security of "bricks and mortar" as collateral allowed for a more moderate acceptable return on real estate. But macroeconomic conditions often influenced the situation irrespective of asset performance, and this objective of consistently and competitively attracting capital to the asset class emerged as a primary objective of the real estate development process.

The perceived demand for the housing product did matter, however, and efficiently satisfying the critical housing need as London expanded set up the opportunity for new suppliers to this substantial market. To most satisfactorily meet the needs of intended residents, a fundamental attribute was location. A view that the earliest developers were fortunate to be endowed with well-located land may overlook that their personal residences were initially quite humble, but their carefully selected locations enabled them to recognize the potential of other sites around them. From this observation and analysis, they positioned themselves strategically to receive land with substantial economic potential.

There were impediments. Until then, these well-located lands had been put to rural use, and as with the general inclination of most authorities, that use was not freely permitted to change. Moreover, the existing residents of London and Westminster were disturbed by the crowding caused by new arrivals and opposed the construction of more housing. Regularly, opposition was shared by neighborhood communities threatened by development and further crowding. Therefore, we see immediately, and in this simple early situation, some of the complexity and contradictions of the objectives in urban development.

Key Objectives of the Model

Though often interrelated or in conflict, there were three discrete objectives of the private development activity that rapidly became apparent:

1. Profitable completion of the project with the creation of an investment asset, comprising both a land component and a built component, that may function as an equity or as a debt instrument.
2. Provision of shelter for which the occupant has a use or even multiple uses, ranging from accommodation to social symbolism.
3. Creation of built form within an urban context, with its attendant physical presence, economic consequences, and social implications.

Processes

To achieve these objectives, early developers formulated the necessary processes. These initially comprised the adaptation of traditional methods of land estate management and building construction by trades to new conditions of restricted land use, changing spatial and aesthetic requirements, expanding scale, and intensifying public interest. As they progressed on their projects, these entrepreneurs applied methods of the flourishing commercial markets such as outsourcing production, gaining economies of scale in product design and quality control, pre-contracting transactions, leveraging returns with debt, syndicating equity and applying timing discounts to the analysis of capital flows.

Thus the general sequence for the development activity evolved, and can be described as a process typically under the direction of a singular entrepreneur and managed comprehensively through to the arrival of residents. Its dynamics were centered on its basic components of **Land**, **Building**, **Capital**, and **the Public Realm**, but achieving the satisfaction of the three key objectives given above required an intertwined procedure simultaneously engaging in all these components with uncountable iterations. The attention to these components and modifications and refinements made by the early developers to achieve a satisfactory and replicable procedure are now presented comprehensively.

Land Use and Control

The importance of land in real estate development may seem obvious, but the formalization of the connection between the developer and the land is a precondition for the activity. While ownership of land has been claimed since the earliest human settlements, the impetus to strategically improve it in order to derive revenue from a third party did not occur until a developer's connection with a specific site happened to have certain features.

Land had long been held by monarchs, aristocrats, and churches, and rarely traded, and its use was usually confined to agrarian, defense, taxation, habitation, and community service purposes. That limitation of use typically remained unchanged since if a new form of use was desired, the approval of the holder of the overarching title, the Crown, was required. England was later than most in moving from an economic construct of maintaining self-sufficiency at all levels of society to an interest in increasing wealth, such as had become prevalent in the late Middle Ages commercial centers of Italy and the Netherlands. That in England this entrepreneurial spirit was first applied to trading and merchant activities, with little dependence on the use of land, indicates its traditional disinterest in any such potential for substantial economic gain from land use.

However, with the rapid growth of the production of high-value goods for trade, particularly wool, the change of rural land activity from agriculture to sheep grazing raised the country's first tensions over land use. As landowners enclosed pastures, tenant farmers were evicted, and commoners' traditional access to commons for subsistence and recreation revoked. Relevantly for real estate, this conflict over land use – between private economic interests and general public benefits – has since continued to be fundamental to development activity.

While English land use was undergoing change, its ownership under the overarching title of the Crown was most strategically and conscientiously kept stable. That static condition was a specific intention of the Norman conqueror William I when he formally designated the holdings of all English land in the Domesday Book of 1086, and that tenet guided the country's governance for many centuries. In property law, reducing the risk of a landowner's alienation from his property was so crucial that even legal mortgage foreclosures were restrained, and land was steadfastly retained under aristocratic ownership rather than be taken by lenders seeking recourse. This certainty of possession was to be a necessary precondition for developers expending large capital amounts on their building projects.

When a substantial transfer of land was effected in Henry VIII's Dissolution of the Monasteries, his Chancellor of the Exchequer, Thomas Cromwell, devised a commercially credible method of land valuation that has been applied to real estate ever since. He formalized the custom by which land was designated a value based on its annual rent (to a tenant farmer, for example), multiplied by the number of years of the lease. This seems obvious today, and its continued application is testament to its clever rationale, but it had previously been used only informally and rarely as land was not usually traded. With rental rates becoming more directly derived from production levels as commerce increased, however, the valuation method facilitated that these lands should be maximized in their economic use. The resulting concept of "highest and best use" of real estate guided the decision-making of early developers and remains a persistent tenet of development activity.

Although they accumulated some productive and prestigious rural properties, early developers' application of an economic valuation to the lands they acquired between the growing City of London and the court at Westminster undoubtedly led them to consider the potential of a change of use from agrarian to residential.

The change of use of some lands, such as those surrounding expanding urban areas, was becoming necessary in the late 16th century, and politically well-positioned men with business expertise like Thomas Wriothesley and John Russell, later to be the Earls of Southampton and Bedford respectively, became interested in its potential and adventured. Through their actions, the key principles relating to the land component of real estate development were established. These are:

- obtain control of the land component;
- calculate its value based on possible uses;
- determine its highest and best use; and
- achieve any necessary legal change of use to maximize its potential.

Control of the Land

Although control of the land is usually considered to be assured by ownership, the activities of the early developers demonstrated creative and nuanced applications of this principle.

A useful flexibility in the control of the land could be found in the contract for a ground lease. It allowed for the distribution of productive use of the land while retaining ownership in the lessor. The respective rights and obligations, which it regulated through the parties' agreement, achieved both sophistication and clarity under the law. While full ownership of some land was transferred and played a role in encouraging development, much of the activity by entrepreneurs who did not own land was undertaken through their use of a ground lease – on the one hand to obtain the security of a sufficiently lengthy leasehold title to justify the cost of construction of the development, and on the other to grant a sublease of the relevant portion of the developed land and building to a tenant. This method facilitated the construction of improvements and also reduced the initial outlay of funds.

Value of the Land and its Use

For the early developers, the demand for housing rose significantly and the construction of housing provided a higher economic use of land than its existing agrarian activities. But if that were to be maximized it required critical decisions about the nature and quality of the product and the targeted clientele. Residential market segments had to be analyzed with respect to the programmatic requirements of each. As aristocrats, both Bedford and Southampton were aware of the extent of their own social class's housing needs, its detailed and symbolic physical requirements, and the prices it could pay to achieve those ends.

Highest and Best Use

To complete their feasibility analysis of a potential development, information for sale or lease prices and construction costs to the builder would have been accessible to Bedford and Southampton. Axiomatically, while the construction of buildings of poorer quality for people of lower social classes was less costly, the rental rates of both the building and the land were less. By comparing profits, Bedford and Southampton decided that the better outcome would flow from high-end residential development, though for a suitable demographic mix in the neighborhood they also leased out smaller lots to builders for the "middling" classes.

Following this overarching decision regarding land use, considerations of layout and functional arrangement of the site were more complex and nuanced, particularly since developed property is spatially fixed and incorporates the critical features of the land's location and adjacencies. For example, Bedford made adjustments regarding the Covent Garden fields, which were located in the south-eastern part of the whole estate and closer to the Strand, the main route between the court and London City, in contrast to his plans for the land in the north at Long Acre. He placed his prestigious housing on those southern fields and leased out the larger portions to the north for other uses such as furniture workshops. Also, though at the time these western suburbs were less suitable for merchants who did business within the City, he anticipated possible interest from this market segment with his Portico Buildings that included ground-floor space for commercial activities. Only a few decades later, this planning proved prescient since the displacement resulting from the Great Fire pushed commerce out of the City and many merchants found accommodation in Covent Garden.

Also apparent in these early site-use decisions were the economic benefits to be achieved by improving the surrounding environment so that it better accommodated new uses. This included paving roads to connect with main thoroughfares, maintaining access to remaining open fields and creating other public amenities. Importantly, these improvements benefited not just the site itself but, by its "spill-over" effect, the broader neighborhood too. In managing their rural estates, these early developers were cognizant of the positive economic externality of making improvements such as draining swampland, upgrading infrastructure, or building worker housing. In the urban context, therefore, to establish the virtuous cycle of an improving proximate neighborhood, they provided substantial extraneous amenities for their intended residents and others in the community. At Covent Garden, Bedford provided a new parish church, the open public piazza, and an efficient network of streets, all of which contributed value to the development and also enhanced the economic condition of surrounding property. By his evaluation, the use of land for these community facilities resulted in the highest economic outcome for the estate as a whole.

As an ultimate contribution, both the Earls of Bedford and Southampton, and many involved in subsequent residential square projects, also lent the social importance of their own grand residences by living within their new developments. This collection of prestige and amenities enhanced the estates' reputation as parts of desirable neighborhoods and, with their contribution to the welfare of the broader community, won both public and governmental approval.

Unfortunately, the understanding of the mutual benefit achieved through designating portions of a site to these *positive economic externalities* for the community was not explicitly formulated in the financial calculations for urban development. As a result, within the analytical processes that were broadly adopted, the community contribution remained as a qualitative assessment not clearly justified by economic rationale and was therefore neglected when financial objectives later became dominant.

Consent to Change of Use

At this nascent stage of urban development activity, the true and detailed requirements of the community were complex, obscure, and often contradictory. Although Bedford had the personal support of the king for his housing scheme, there was at first some general public opposition to additional building around London, and his development proposal was then regarded as detrimental rather than beneficial to the community. The thrust of the opposition was not directed at the type of his chosen development, since housing of all types was desperately needed: it was a blanket opinion against development of any kind on the remaining open fields. He overcame this resistance by providing the new parish church to alleviate overcrowding in the St Martin-in-the-Fields parish, and although this was an expensive contribution to the community, it was also an important amenity for the residents of his piazza.

A final obstacle to the potential use of the development site was the lengthy and arduous process of obtaining the consent of relevant authorities for change in use. In this, both Bedford and Southampton were advantaged by their connections at court. They were familiar with the processes and aware of the relevant regulations, both of which assisted them in making applications that had a high probability of success. In contrast, the non-aristocratic Nicholas Barbon, who undertook a rigorous analytical process in support of his proposed development, did not meet so much success in his applications, though within the improving democratic context he was able to contest the matter in court. This legal option continues in present times.

From the origins of urban development, the complex analysis of what was necessary to gain the approval of the authorities and what features would be most compelling in support of an application – such as community contributions – was a critical part of the land use decision, and continues to be challenging. Although formal requirements are usually clearly disclosed, normative factors with an uncertain outcome, such as the interpretation of aesthetic features, community attitudes, and other fluid urban conditions, can preclude permission for a proposed use that would achieve the maximum economic benefit for the developer. As a result, the objective of gaining the highest and best use of land, regarded as at the nexus of development decision-making, is suggested by Graaskamp (1972) as modified to be the most "fitting and probable" use. In this, the decision resonates with the broader community considerations of the early developers.

Principles Regarding Land Use and Improvements

Accordingly, in applying land use principles of the real estate development model as it has evolved, the developer will usually make the following important decisions:

1. Deciding how to achieve control of the site and realize its best economic potential without restrictions but also with minimal capital commitment.
2. Identifying the use for which there is a substantial unmet need, be it for consumption, social status, or commercial benefit.

3. Selecting details of a use, or combination of uses, for maximum overall benefit.

4. Making a cost-benefit analysis to identify the highest and best use.

5. Assessing the suitability of the location of the site for the best uses.

6. Evaluating the impact of the project on the surrounding neighborhood, and through the circular effect of positive economic externalities how the affected neighborhood will influence the future of the project. (*Often neglected*)

Buildings

Having established the most fitting and probable use of their sites, the early developers proceeded to the planning and design of the project. Traditionally, the erection of a building involved a repetitive vernacular form that was constructed by guild tradesmen and arranged along the frontage of narrow streets to achieve the maximum site coverage. That Covent Garden, Bloomsbury Square and Barbon's Temple and Essex Street developments do not resemble that earlier approach is testament to the innovations in site layout, building design, and production methods made by these entrepreneurs.

Spatial Layout

The above developers' innovativeness undoubtedly made their route through this phase more complex and much more challenging as they explored new physical possibilities. Although no explicit discussion of their thought processes in this respect has been found, their approach resonated with rising enthusiasm for the customized production of many goods ranging from clothes to carriages, fueled by the increased social symbolism of material goods under the Stuart kings. The display of aesthetic taste and increasing wealth among those seeking town residences required new architectural formats and spatial arrangements that would reflect their progression from modest backgrounds to more elevated levels of class. Although there were probably some experiments that were not accepted by potential tenants, the projects of note and longevity were able to achieve higher economic returns with advanced designs and formats. As a result, in terms of both satisfaction of residents' needs and achieving financial outperformance, developer's intent to improve and advance their physical product beyond traditional or "cookie-cutter" solutions distinguished the nascent real estate development process from the simple building of preformulated structures.

Although making unprecedented and varied explorations in building form and spatial arrangements, the evolving formulation of the process presented certain key principles with respect to building production. The following details of these features serve to explain their importance in the new urban development process.

Detailed Programming Specifically for the Market

Although there was a broad need for housing, the early developers sought to maximize their investment returns by focusing on the most profitable segments of the market. However, cognizant of the requirement for proximate staff housing and support services, in addition to building housing for the very wealthy they arranged for the erection of more modest buildings, usually by other parties such as master builders.

Selecting a less wealthy but voluminous segment of the housing market, Barbon built for the middle market of professionals and small businessmen. Specific programmatic requirements were sought and defined for these selected residents and honed to the most suitable and economical spatial arrangement, interior layout, exterior appearance, amenities, and finishes.

Complex programmatic situations were also addressed. Because of Inigo Jones's design of a uniform façade across all the Covent Garden Portico houses, Bedford provided three different internal layouts to meet the varying needs of his prospective occupants. To ensure that during the planning and design stage they were able to choose those interior details for their later satisfaction, he had three model homes built. Although there is no specific evidence on the matter, it is probable that along with these demonstration models potential residents could make further refinements of design for their own individual homes. Through this, Bedford demonstrated in these early stages of the project the developer's important role of balancing the overall appearance of a suitable architectural composition and quality with variations that met the wishes of privileged residents keen to display their individuality. In successfully achieving this programmatic outcome, he was fortunate to have the creativity and practicality of an architect, Inigo Jones, who was also very familiar with the lifestyles and detailed needs of Bedford's targeted residents.

However, to underscore that these design objectives were not merely tangential to the driving economic objectives of the project, Bedford proceeded in a businesslike way to formalize the lease transactions with particular respect to the settlement of design decisions. He did not commit to customized interiors, specific to a single user's wishes, without an executed lease with the respective tenants, though the process towards agreement on these matters would have involved substantial negotiation. This method of risk mitigation strategy, by securing rental revenues as development expenditures are committed, was an early form of the pre-leasing tactics used today, and Baer (2007a) presents multiple instances of its use for housing developments, even on a small scale, at this early era. Its invention was partially due to the increasing resident desire for customization even within development projects, and pre-leasing became a very important mitigant of financial risk for developers and continues to be so.

While facilitating this opportunity for customer choice, Bedford also cleverly limited customizing by restricting those models to forms compliant with the project's development approval. Residents were also held contractually responsible for that compliance through constraints in their ground lease and therefore accepted those resolved solutions, despite some curtailing of their customization. This delicately nuanced strategy continues to be employed by many large-volume home builders today.

Responding to changes in consumer demand, however, when planning his Bloomsbury Square subdivision Southampton addressed a housing market that had become more varied socially and economically. While some landed gentry and wealthy merchants could afford large homes in the prestigious residential estates, there were also members of the aristocratic class and successful professionals who wished for more modest premises. This led to his decision to offer a variety of lot sizes and to accommodate individual designs with only minimal variations on the frontage alignment and material requirements.

Design Quality and Economic Returns

While the debate regarding appropriateness between vernacular architecture and more learned and innovative design continues to this day, in the 17th century the conversion to the neoclassical aesthetic appealed to the monarchs, the cultured gentry, and aspirational professionals and merchants. Importantly, it also established the role of the architect in creating new designs that better served the needs of the intended residents, as well as achieving the financial objectives of the developers. That the latter were not just focused on low cost solutions, but rather on the balancing of expenditure to attain the desired rental rates and the costs of construction to optimize the economic outcome, was also a feature of the developer's strategic thinking.

Thus, progressive design became a key principle of the process. Each building faces new functional demands and takes its place in a unique location, and it thereby establishes a new need for design resolution particular to that situation rather than the replication of a previous solution. Although today, as then, repetitive designs are often adopted in a frenetic activity to meet the needs of urban markets, the earliest true development projects indicated that a more rationalized design resolution could respond more thoroughly and successfully to the requirements of each site and situation. By this procedure, a project can achieve not just architectural quality but also an environment which is appropriately functional for the occupants and, in such careful satisfaction of market, can demand a higher economic return for the developer.

Urban Layout and Public Contribution

The public response to their projects was also of concern to the early aristocratic developers since the outcome reflected on themselves and their responsibility as leaders of society. They donated substantial lands within their estates to create open public areas that not only benefited the immediate residents but also attracted admiring visitors. In fact, the introduction of this community-friendly spatial format significantly influenced English urban typology. Coulter (2016) describes this impact:

> The history of the London square begins in 1631 with the great name of Inigo Jones, whose houses and church in Covent Garden were both started in that year. Lincoln's Inn Fields followed from 1638. Southampton (now Bloomsbury) Square was the first to bear that name ['Square'] formally, although it had been applied to Covent Garden as early as 1641 in a licence for Lincoln's Inn Fields. Building in front of Southampton House was begun in 1661 and the development was referred to as 'the square' from 1663. After that they came with a rush ..." (Coulter 2016, 7)

They also efficiently allocated land and arranged sites around the open areas they had established, contrived convenient means of ingress and egress, and provided streets of suitable size and an infrastructure of good quality.

This objective regarding the benefit of the broader neighborhood, however, was not always present in the activities of other developers, such as those of Barbon, who typically disregarded open spaces and public amenities. When he did broaden his concerns, however, such as providing the extravagant Essex Street arch to act as an attractive division between the residential street and the wharves beyond, he undoubtedly recognized their potential economic benefits for his scheme. On a project such as this he would have been well aware of the more discriminating standards necessary to attract the higher-paying residents.

Though the inclusion of community amenities was often employed as leverage to gain project approvals, when it was played out with a sincere interest in contributing to the quality of the neighborhood and community well-being, it proved to be a significant characteristic of the early visionary developments. Unfortunately, as commercial gains became more compelling with expanding capitalism, and developers did not retain a personal engagement with neighborhoods, the concern for the local context faded as the development business model evolved. Providing amenities, not only for the residents but also for the general public and understanding their economic potential for the whole development scheme and its future performance, appeared as an early challenge in planning and design decisions that are still with us. The model continues to contend with the issue of how much a project should be focused on maximizing internal profit to the exclusion of public concern.

Production of Buildings

Though the treatment of land and the planning and design of the improvements were innovative in the early development projects, the construction activity underwent only minor modifications of traditional methods. Since the building tradesmen of the traditional guilds were the only resource available for construction work, their craftsmanship was applied with only small modifications even to the more innovative building designs. In this way, the traditional building methods, both tradesmen and project management procedures, influenced rather than were influenced by the formation of the new model.

This was unusual in the history of innovation since it has often been technical discoveries that drove new activities, such as the arch, the steam engine, and even the Internet. However, it has been suggested that innovation in building construction methods was impeded by certain circumstances at this time, such as the restrictions on practice exerted by the trade guilds and the absence of scientific research in home-building while the physics, astronomy, and chemistry were being addressed. Although Christopher Wren, who was primarily an astronomer, worked on large royal buildings and the rebuilding of St Paul's, scientific contributions to the construction of more pedestrian buildings seems to have been neglected.

Minor Construction Advances

Notwithstanding this general state, there were some advances in the production of London housing during the 17th century: brick and stone were used for all urban construction, firstly because they were deemed necessary to the aesthetic taste of the Stuart kings and their newly appointed court architects, and secondly because it was required for safety reasons as part of the rebuilding after the Great Fire.

As the volume of work increased, some standardization of materials was introduced in order to make construction more efficient and to maintain its quality. This included specifications for bricks by the authorities. Pre-cutting of timber framing members to uniform dimensions was adopted by Barbon. House design pattern books were published and broadly used, and a clearer delineation of carpentry trade work, such as for cabinetry, appeared.

General Contractor or Project Manager

To develop complex urban sites required leadership, planning, and oversight. The earliest developers performed some of this direction and oversight themselves, at least strategically planning the production. Implementation and on-site administration were initially performed by the client's surveyor, though generally they were mostly concerned with checking compliance with material, structural and progress requirements, or measuring completed work for compensation. Gradually, surveyors expanded their skills and formal engagement on projects, and master builders sometimes assumed this role. The architect also adopted some of the responsibilities of this role with respect to monitoring the quality of production and resolving problems of design execution.

The administration of various independent builders on the site and organization of broad site logistics were without precedent and the results often problematic. The construction activities were managed by what today would be called a project or construction manager, but at the time was referred to as an "undertaker," in terms of undertaking the project. This person was traditionally allocated to a single building where he managed the process comprehensively, being responsible for scheduling the trades, paying the lead tradesmen, inspecting and measuring the work, while also generally acting as an intermediary between the trades and the owner or developer. This role was merely expanded in scale on later projects probably through a confluence of related prior activities:

1. Master builders extended the range of their work from fee-based jobs to erecting houses on their own lots for sale for profit, and thus took on a wider scope of activities that included initiating the project, obtaining control of the land and approvals to build on it, financing the materials and labor, and managing the employed trades through to completion. These new lead contractors rose from one of the traditional trades most extensively involved, such as carpentry or masonry, and took control of the project, scheduling the other trades for coordinated activity. The head tradesman of that crew acted as the project manager. As it has been observed, these trades often provided trade credit and may themselves have taken out loans to finance their contracts, so that they were usually experienced in regard to the capital markets and the timing of payments. They were fully qualified to act as project managers for the new developers.

2. Aristocratic developers usually engaged rural estate managers whose management activities included improvement projects, and it was a natural progression for their employers to seek similar expertise suitable to the urban context.

3. As more complex infrastructure projects were undertaken throughout England and the mining of tin and iron ore proliferated, often on estates of aristocrats and the landed gentry, the roles of chief engineer and mine manager became more common and their disciplines were recognized as quasi-professional, with such features as organized training, work manuals, and collective organizations. Although their engagement for urban housing was not immediate, engineers for structural and hydraulic infrastructure projects

gradually became project managers on the largest projects and have generally continued to command that role.

Building for the Life Cycle

As property development emerged as a strategically commercial business activity, it was caught in the crossflow of two differing attitudes towards the quality and longevity of a dwelling, particularly in urban locations. It was traditionally intended that a building should remain habitable for the life of the tenancy, without any aspiration for its continuity beyond the term of the ground lease, and early responses to the London housing demand continued in this mindset. However, in pursuing the construction of impressive urban forms the Stuart kings focused their preferences on masonry rather than traditional timber, and also extolled the expression of noble social status in town residences built of high-quality materials. These structures lasted much longer than the usual term of ground leases, and the additional incurred expense required longer amortization periods. When they could do so, such as in the development of St James's Square, the resident acquired freehold to remove the risk of losing the house at the end of a ground lease. This simple resolution probably led to the broader adoption of land governance through freehold in the new colonies. Otherwise, longer ground leases became the norm through negotiations between a landowner and tenants who were to build houses on leased land, and houses of suitable duration were built.

Less clear for the resolution of competing considerations was the situation in which a landowner or developer constructed and retained ownership of the leased building, and anticipated his own future rebuilding and re-leasing to residents. Here, the developer was required to balance upfront costs for a more durable product with the required maintenance expenditure for a less durable one, which is still an issue for most rental buildings. Life cycle costing was not formally undertaken in those days, but in principle the decisions and trade-offs were addressed at this stage.

A further model of private development, the most speculative version, comprised the development of buildings followed by a quick sale of the building lease, and also generally the ground lease. With this quick return of capital and realization of profit in an early exit, the developer was less concerned with the performance of the structure and its longevity. Decisions regarding form and materials were based on gaining attractive prices for the leases, and given the lack of knowledge of many residents and even investors who purchased the leases, many building failures occurred when the entrepreneur was long gone.

It was therefore almost at the outset of the private urban development activity that a bifurcation of concerns for building quality and performance emerged. There were developers who remained involved with their projects over the long term and undertook an optimizing analysis regarding upfront costs and ongoing maintenance, and even established a strategy for the property's usable life. But there were also those who built with a focus on merely achieving an investment return on price appreciation, not ongoing operations, and spent on superficial appeal with little thought given to long-term function and performance, and this distinction in approaches has continued since.

Principles Regarding Buildings

Although the practice of engaging an architect on a development project was just coming into use as these early schemes commenced, the developers themselves were very cognizant of the relationship between design quality, market appeal, and economic success and innovated accordingly. When they undertook the construction of the buildings, however, traditional methods and constraints persisted, and only minor changes were made to procedures and management. The key principles that emerged regarding the production of the buildings are:

- Formulate detailed programmatic requirements: In their choice of the abode, people have significantly varying requirements in terms of format, finishes and amenities, and details must be determined with respect to the intended occupant.
- Advance design quality: The aesthetic aspirations of the target market and surrounding community should be rigorously analyzed and incorporated into producing a better environment both internally and externally.
- Perform cost-benefit analyses to optimize design: In determining the programmatic requirements, a trade-off of the revenues to be received versus the cost of each detail reveals not the most economical outcome but the most profitable one.
- Contribute to the community and public realm through the building's interface: In gaining statutory and public approvals, determination of the most pertinent needs and concerns of the community should be undertaken early and satisfied. If the interaction with the public realm is of good quality the development is more likely accepted in the neighborhood and more successful in its occupancy.
- Continue traditional methods but make minor modifications to realize new designs.
- Standardize the production or preparation of materials to improve efficiency and quality.
- An overarching project or construction manager is necessary to oversee the complex logistics of the larger schemes, including the responsibility for construction costs.

Funding the Project and Creating Financial Products

In the excited capitalist context in which private development was born, the contribution of capital to real estate soon diversified from merely loans, with fixed interest rates and contractual obligation for the return of capital, to equity investments, which by way of compensation allowed an open-ended expectation of higher returns. This appealed to some of the wealthy who were given to gambling and risk-taking speculators. Functioning within volatile markets, investment in real estate had this attractive element of contingency while remaining lawful, and the development activity, at the nexus of demand and supply, presented a most risky and yet potentially profitable part of real estate. Its formation of various methods of funding was impressively innovative while cleverly building on established commercial concepts and historical methods of analysis and evaluation.

Building Leases for Development Activity

While retaining ownership, a landowner sometimes granted a long-term lease on land for a modest rent to a developer who funded and constructed the improvements and collected the rents from the building's occupants. However, when a builder did not have the financial capacity to commit to the ground lease for the usual long tenure, a new form of lease, called a building lease, allowed the builder to have access to the site for the construction of improvements. Upon completion, the occupant of the new building would pay housing rent to the builder or other funder of the construction and took the ground lease directly from the landowner. Its validity was supported by advances in the legal concept of *property use* to include the use as a site for erecting a building. Though this arrangement fell somewhat into desuetude as developers of buildings became able to purchase the underlying land, in countries where the ownership of land remains with the state or ultimate power, variations of this contractual form are extensively used.

Debt for Development

As real estate was initiated into the capital markets of the 17th century, mortgage loans for operating properties gained popularity. However, then as today, unless there was provision for deferment of interest charges and capital amortization payments, debt incurred under a mortgage loan was not suited to the one-way flow of development costs during the construction phase when there were no revenues from the property to service the loan. Loans for the construction work were taken on personally by the developer, typically to be repaid when the intended resident, or an intermediary investor, or eventual landlord, paid a lump sum for the lease or ownership of the building.

Master builders, who maintained professional relationships with debt providers, worked on traditional arrangements which combined trade credit that was redeemed through the regular receipt of payments from the intended resident or a financial intermediary.

The under-resourced Nicholas Barbon leased development sites and used trade credit as his capital management strategy. Although in principle it was an astute application of the financing model used in other commercial activities, his use of it intruded on established understandings within the formalized building industry. He was fortunate in that the increased work available attracted tradesmen who were not affiliated with the City guilds and who were willing to work outside traditional arrangements. Unfortunately, it is reported that his trade credit arrangements were regularly deceptive and often destructive to small tradesmen. He treated his development activity more as a trading asset, with little interest in long-term industry relationships that are usually important to continuous sources of funding.

Equity for Development

In the early stages of capital market formation in England, equity contributions to sustain businesses functioned more as debt capital since the partners withdrew only a portion of the net revenues according to an agreed return rate and the remainder was treated as retained earnings. As development projects conducted by persons other than those with family estates were generally one-off, the dynamics of equity investments differed in that the revenues after debt repayment were fully returned to the equity investors, and each new project required new capital sources.

With the riskier investments in foreign trading activities including funding the large capital needs of building the ships and establishing trading posts, the notion of an equity investor's receiving a variable share of the profits rather than a set return on capital was offered to encourage speculators. It was established in the joint-stock scheme structure which was the precedent of the stock corporation, and was also inherent in the rudimentary co-operative insurance arrangement conducted in such places as Lloyd's coffee shop, where the underwriters would share in the financial benefits of a covered cargo that arrived safely. In other words, the concept was not alien in business circles. But, because of its complex formation, the need for registration as a stock company, and an intention of longevity, this financial structure was not suitable for short-term real estate development schemes.

The financially innovative and aggressive Barbon did create a variation of the joint-stock company structure on a small scale, though usually confined it to a single development project even if comprising a number of houses. He omitted to formalize it by registration but arranged for a group of investors to contribute to a syndicated form of partnership in which they were not active partners but received a distribution of all profits in proportion to their respective contributions. This was an early and informal equity syndicate, and its structure has continued to be used extensively in real estate development.

Of course, there were some failures of this development funding that emphatically demonstrated the risk of a development's stopping before completion with the result that there was no value in what remained despite all that had been done. Often the ground lease for the land would have been sold to another investor, so the equity investor did not even have recourse to that asset. Reasons for failure ranged from exhaustion of capital necessary to pay for materials and labor, to disputes over the property rights on the land, and to the developer's abandoning the project through diversion to other interests. In such cases, equity investors experienced the complete loss of capital, and some cases in the Chancery courts show their failed attempts to claim on the development because of the lack of value in the half-finished project. These risks have continued.

Developer's Promote

As the question of risks and proportional distribution of profits among participants arose, the structuring of equity investment for real estate adopted another feature of the joint-stock companies that has remained, the origination of the "promote."

Given the risk and large amounts of capital to be raised for those companies, it was considered justifiable to direct a share of profits to the "promoter" of the deal. This person was often the initiator of the venture, though it was also extended to a salesman of the investment opportunity, and they touted its potential profit across all levels of society. He received a share of the profits that reflected the success of his efforts and often that compensation was in the form of a part interest in the investment, though without a proportional personal capital contribution. The attractiveness of the investment would generate a higher interest in the "promote," and large profits on the investment would produce consequential benefit to the promoter.

Nicholas Barbon was an exemplar of this role, though he fashioned his "promote" structures in a way that was so complex that a typical investor would find it difficult to determine how much Barbon had directed to himself. A review of the scant references available indicates that he probably profited more from this position than from any capital he contributed as equity. Real estate investments, and particularly development projects, continue to provide this incentive to the originator of a deal, or the developer, as a means of maximizing the investment's returns.

Development Budget Methodology

Though real estate construction funding was challenging, the completed product was quickly embraced as an attractive financial asset for London's flourishing investment activities in the 17th century. For equity investment in these built properties, their trading price was determined by capitalization of the rental rate according to the lease tenure. This information in the marketplace then informed the valuation of potential development projects. For a completed development, the valuation was crystallized upon execution of a resident's lease. This calculative advancement, which moved from the prior valuation of a project as the summation of its construction costs to a determination based on market conditions for the completed product as indicated by rental rates, reframed the economics of the development activity.

Given the market valuation, after deducting compensation for capital contributions and the development effort, a maximum cost was calculated for the project and established the development budget, comprising building components and land whether acquired freehold or through a ground lease.

In keeping to these market-determined cost constraints on Covent Garden, it was notable that the developer was assisted greatly by the architect. The restraint of Inigo Jones with respect to the materials should not be underestimated: while he was erecting royal buildings in Portland stone, here he was pragmatic in achieving his design goals. For the church he used stone only for the columns with the walls being of brick covered with stucco which, not only being true to the original Tuscan structures, also "was more *economical* than solid stone construction" (Downs 1967, 13). Similarly for the residential buildings, rather than adorn the façade with Doric columns, Jones was able to use the less expensive pilasters to achieve the effect of the classical order. It was an example where the developer produced a built environment that was appropriately recognized for its aesthetic quality and yet also created a successful economic asset.

Investment Returns

The market-led concept of real estate valuation laid the foundation of other economic features and metrics for real estate investment analysis.

Although an increase in the value of goods, described as price appreciation or price inflation, had been experienced in times of shortages in respect of food, clothing, and other consumables, it was a relatively new feature of durable assets such as the rural lands, precious metals and stones, and developed urban property. Asset appreciation and also asset losses were a new experience for investors in joint-stock companies, but in this commercial atmosphere, the opportunity for asset appreciation of even traditional investments became accepted and even strongly sought.

As an examination of its evolution reveals, however, improved real property – that is, land with a habitable building on it – is an unusual product of components with strikingly different life cycles. It combines the durable asset of land, which theoretically lasts forever and requires only relatively small maintenance costs and taxes, with a wasting building component that is consumed through use and deteriorates to negligible value, though its utility might be extended by the expenditure of large sums in upgrades. In the traditional management of the physical property, there was complete rebuilding at the beginning of each new ground lease, which meant that while the ground retained the value of the capital invested in it, the building lost all its value over the lease term. The calculation of an improved property's value was fractured in that the value of the land was based on its continued utility and represented by a capitalization of its ground rent for infinity, but the value of the house, also based on capitalized rent, was limited to the finite term of its viable use.

This variance in value retention of the land in contrast to the building necessitated their consideration as distinct investments, and their respective investment capital structures, the returns on capital and the returns of capital were different. Often in the times of the earliest development projects, various investors held an interest in one or other of these separate assets discreetly. Because land is a lasting asset, the capital invested to acquire it was expected to be recouped when its ownership was discontinued through a sale, or not at all while it was retained for future generations.

During the period of ownership, if the land is not used by its owner, its economic utility is reflected in the rental price paid for that use. If the market is balanced, that revenue provides a suitable return on the commitment of the capital. But as its value at a given time is based on what someone would pay to use it, this might result in an appreciation in its value, or there may be a loss if that site is no longer in demand. Apart from market influences, a rent is usually set to compensate the landowner as capital provider for the land, much in the same way as when capital is provided as a loan. However, any appreciation in land is speculative and uncertain and less related to its economic use than to market demand.

The capital provided for improvements was for a production process involving materials and building trade workers. Its return and compensation for its use was paid through a sale upon completion, or as more typically at that time, by a series of annual rental payments for the occupancy of the building. By the end of the housing lease term, usually established as equivalent to the ground lease term, it was expected that the building had fully deteriorated, and therefore had no residual value at all. That the rent level was sufficient to repay the capital and compensation for the use of that capital was the hurdle for the investor. If the rental revenues were higher in response to competitive demand, and, on top of the repayment of the invested capital and its cost, the investor received additional return on capital that represented a profit over and above the capital cost. However, even if achieving a higher investment return *of* capital, and *on* capital, because of the increased rental revenues, the investor still did not participate in any asset appreciation since the asset had fully deteriorated by the end of the lease.

As materials and construction methods improved, however, and a building outlasted its ground lease, there was an opportunity to make major additional capital improvements, rather than rebuild completely, to maintain its habitability under a new ground lease. In this case the building could be regarded as salvageable at the end of the lease, and either the original builder or a subsequent investor undertook to restore it for a new tenant, though sometimes the tenants undertook the work themselves, with an offset against the future rental rate. Later, and in other jurisdictions, as tenants took leases combining land and building, or made a freehold purchase of the composite property, the residual value of the structure became intertwined with that of the land, and the notion of residual value used in property calculations today represents a melding of both.

In 17th-century London, if a site underwent a change of use, such as from pasture to housing, the determination of the amount of a new suitable rent was difficult, for changes in land ownership were infrequent and provided no pricing information. Additionally, in a strong market, the rack rent of a new or renovated building would be adjusted upward at lease renewal, but it was uncertain what portion of that should be directed to an increase in the ground rent. Parish rolls indicate that generally the increased rental revenues were apportioned between the landlord of the building and the landowner, though without any pattern being discerned (as yet in the historical material available). While landowners were often passive and slow to increase ground rents, and the new urban developers were reaping most of the gains through rising building rental rates in the strong markets, the outcome was probably most dependent on the respective negotiating strengths of the individuals involved.

As the demand for new urban developments in London increased, and struggling supply resulted in rising values of both land and surviving buildings, recouping the construction capital became expected upon a sale event, rather than achieving its full amortization during the holding period. Unfortunately, this strategy for return of capital was inadequate during times of falling asset values, but the industry mindset remains less cognizant of this shortcoming and typical practice continues to combine potential appreciation (though realizable only upon sale) with annual cash flow in its measurement of investment returns as the capitalization rate or cap rate. An important principle of real estate development is to ensure the full return *of* the capital provided for the project, but the protracted nature of operating property cash flow, and the duality of investment returns through income and price appreciation, have enabled this objective to be compromised with the pursuit of returns *on* capital.

Return on Capital
The formulated model of private urban development offered two distinct strategies for enhancing a project's profitability or return on capital:

1. *The development activity is undertaken with a transactional focus*: the costs of obtaining some title to the land and effecting improvements are quickly covered upon or even in advance of completion by capitalizing the project through a sale. This capital event may be either an outright sale of the freehold title land and building, sale of the ground lease for a lump sum, sale of the building lease for a lump sum, or a combination of these last two. The amount of capital used for the land and improvements and its cost are paid from the proceeds of sale, and any profit is then realized. With this focus, the financial rewards for the developer and equity investors are consummated within a few large capital transactions, and the return of capital, compensation for the cost of capital, and any additional profit are received with desirable expedition, though perhaps less quantum. The focus is upon the capitalized value of the completed asset as a tradable product. As such, its value at the time of exchange will, during the period of development, be speculative since it is based on an anticipated future revenue stream and its value in the marketplace at the time of sale. This model provides a quick recycling of capital for the capital provider and the developers.

2. *The development activity is undertaken with an investment focus*: costs are incurred to produce assets which will deliver a regular revenue stream over the length of the leases of the completed buildings, and over time that revenue will repay the capital, and provide a competitive compensation to the investor for the use of the capital. However,

the capital contributions and receipts are unevenly timed. Upfront costs requiring capital are incurred within a relatively short period, the development phase, but the capital is returned and rewarded over the longer term of the holding period. The economic focus is on the rental performance of the property to deliver long-term, stable, and reliable revenues with an appropriate compensation for the protracted return of capital. This strategy is also speculative in that future rental payments may not be forthcoming or grow as anticipated, though actual cash flows will often attenuate that speculative factor over time. Any impact on revenues by changing market conditions will be spread over the term of the lease and not just realized at the time of sale, so some of the speculative dimension is abated.

Speculation on Rising Prices

In the evolution of the new real estate markets, the continual rising rental rates for houses and land often meant that investors were rewarded with returns beyond their anticipated compensation for use of their capital. When transactions crystallized this increasing cash flow in asset prices, the portion of the investment return due to the rising values was recognized as asset appreciation or a capital gain for the vendor. The anticipated extent of this gain became a matter of speculation, since the future rental rates of building or ground, on which the higher prices would be based, were not yet contracted. But, in the second half of the 17th century, the persistent experience of these rising prices being particularly lucrative shifted the focus of real estate investment returns from its yield derived from income to value appreciation. It encouraged more trading, and thence more speculation, and embedded a fundamental error in real estate investing that continues.

Despite this questionable focus on appreciation, the results of this evolution in return analytics continue to provide the main principles of real estate returns on capital invested as comprising both an annual yield, related to economic use, and asset appreciation, based on market speculation. This determination of the total return on invested capital is a fundamental calculation of real estate development, and its maximization is a primary principle of the activity. Not to be overlooked is the importance of a reliable strategy for the return of capital to investors as a priority over those investment returns.

Principles for Funding Decisions

The complex and variable financial structures that have remained inherent in the private urban development model were formulated with surprising rapidity. They covered the various phases of the capital needs and applied to the different available sources of equity and debt, and through trial and error the efficient principles were fashioned. These are:

Equity
*   Equity is required in the early stages of a project when many aspects have not yet been resolved and a rigorous risk/reward analysis is not possible.
*   Equity contributions from parties who are not active in the project may be structured as an equity syndication or a partnership in which they are limited partners. They are not typically entitled to a specific rate of return on their capital but share in the distribution of profits.

- Equity holders expect the return of their capital, though it is subordinate to the claims of creditors for payment of the debts, and they do not usually have collateral security for this return of capital.
- Equity technically receives its return of capital through both some of the annual net income, after returns on capital are deducted, and the proceeds of a sale at the end of the holding period, though a mistaken perception places complete reliance on the sale transaction to meet this objective.
- Achieving a return of equity capital from the development as early as possible enhances investment return rates, though not necessarily the quantum.
- Equity investors apply the early modern commercial practices of profit incentives to development projects by offering a "promote" fee as compensation to the developer as deal originator, leader, and manager. The amount of its benefit is usually in the form of a larger profit than that which is determined by proportional contribution of the equity capital.

Debt

- Debt obtained for the construction of the project usually does not have the security of a mortgage, and the borrower often personally bears the obligation for its repayment.
- Historically, debt tenure was co-terminus with the term of the ground lease as the building was to be fully depreciated in that time. The loan amount was determined by the payment of interest and amortization of capital that could be made from the net income over the term. This derivation of the amortizing loan amount according to the debt service capacity of the property's cash flows continues to be used despite the lasting habitability of the buildings beyond the tenure of ground leases or loans.
- Debt for a building with expected habitability at the end of the ground lease term, or investment holding period, has evolved to achieve repayment through a combination of annual net income and proceeds from the sale of the residual term of the lease of the land, or freehold land, plus the surviving building.

Calculative Methods

Sources of capital for operating real estate, both equity and debt, base the quantum of their contribution on two main economic features of the real estate:

1. The annual net cash flow after rental revenues are offset by operating expenses.
2. The value of the property as determined by the anticipated net cash flow annually and from its sale at the conclusion of the holding period.

Valuation

The calculative method of real estate valuation evolved from its origins as an addition of contractual rent revenues over a lease term to the adoption of the neoclassical economic model of discounted cash flow applied to commercial production and investment, which continues to be in industry use. Fundamental principles for this calculation are:

- In theory, land typically retains some value forever. It may enter negative value if its costs in taxes, security, and preservation have a prospective duration that together exceed its potential worth.

- The change of use of land that can be achieved with built improvements results in a change in the value of the land.

- Persistent strong market demand for real estate adds the dimension of potential appreciation in land value, originally realized through increased ground rent on subsequent leases, but now generally through the sale of land and building together.

- Price appreciation or valuation increases are dependent on future changes to two key economic factors:

  - Increases in net cash flow achieved by rising rental revenues, decreasing operating expenses, or both.

  - The reduction of the cost of capital funding the real estate, either of equity, debt, or both.

Appreciation in value is monetized only upon sale or other form of equity extraction.

- Buildings deteriorate and their production costs were originally amortized over the length of the underlying ground lease. With the longevity of buildings, this capital strategy is replaced by financial planning for building maintenance and replacement.

- In respect of the residual value of the comprehensive property, that is, land and building, the appreciation due to market demand and change of use are predominantly contained within the value of the land. This is the basis for the calculation of "highest and best" use, as commonly applied in the choice of property type for development.

Capital Management and Business Liquidity

The capital management of both current projects and a continuing development business required an estimation and pre-arrangement of present and future capital needs. Early aristocratic developers were mostly able to self-fund their activities, but for those who did not have that resource the capital markets were unpredictable, and even Bedford's and Southampton's projects were adjusted due to capital constraints. Further, their business model of developing for long-term ownership over generations meant that the large capital amounts expended in development took a long time to be replenished.

On the other hand, developers with a more transactional focus such as Barbon, Neale, and even the aristocrat St Albans, received their return of capital and recovery of capital costs promptly. Their timely sales of completed projects is the continuing model for a real estate business.

The simultaneous formation of these two approaches towards the financial rewards of development, and the fact that a consensus did not form around one or the other are instructive of the quality of the business model. Most other business' financial structures move towards a common approach, as has been extensively described by the business historian Chandler (1977). That real estate development did not do this indicates either weakness in its model or strength in its flexibility of options, given that many developers vary their choices between both, according to the exigencies of the circumstances.

Contributing to the Public Realm

Although the new model of real estate development notably achieved innovations in the private production of much needed housing and the creation of new financial products for capitalist investors, their activities were integrated with public authorities and the public realm. Their method of engagement with the legislative leaders was courageous and cleverly strategized, and the synergy between politics and real estate was a core dynamic of the business model from the outset. In its early formulation, this private commercial activity was also involved with the populace at the grassroots level and was notable in making significant contributions to the surrounding community and to public amenities such as open squares, churches, and paved streets.

Engagement with Government

Land has been a fundamental concern of many rulers, particularly the English monarchs, and for real estate development to be even credibly considered their involvement was necessary. Further, not only were the prevailing principles of property law critical to the control of land for development, but legislation and the sentiment of community leaders had a substantial impact on options for land use, and were extended to defining building standards, construction processes, and the management of tenants. The earliest developers were confronted with substantial restrictions by the authorities, but it may have been their capability and advanced methods of handling such a dynamic that enabled them to take the first daring steps with urban development schemes. The earls were all members of the royal court, and Southampton and Barbon had involvements with the House of Commons and connections with municipal leaders, both of which provided the knowledge of necessary approval procedures. Real estate developers since that time have realized the benefits of civic engagement for the smooth progression and success of their projects.

Connections with the authorities were necessary to gain their formal approval, but a social and sometimes a financial engagement with the monarch and municipal leaders was also helpful to the success of the very earliest ventures. Bedford engaged the King's Surveyor, Inigo Jones, to ensure that his plans for Covent Garden met the king's aesthetic aspirations, and to overcome community opposition to the increased housing of his project he made an offer to the powerful Bishop of London to construct a new parish church. Similarly, through his close relationship with James I, Southampton secured a crucial site connecting his Bloomsbury estate with the busy Holborn thoroughfare. And St Albans's closeness to the court of Charles II undoubtedly served him well in gaining the very rare grant of freehold for his St James's scheme.

Public Square and Urban Topography

The 4th Earl of Bedford solidly exhibited a concern for the community in his Covent Garden project. As well as carefully calibrating its amenities and design to an aesthetic and cultural level necessary to the project's approval and the desired housing standard of his intended tenants, he placed significant importance on his provision of the novel open piazza for residential ambience and the benefit of the neighboring community. There were earlier squares within the City walls, but they were not on private land.

The combined benefit for the public was described by Strype (1720) in his survey (Vol. II, Book VII, 87/9): "[I]ts open and large Piazza or Garden, so delightful to walk in. It may deservedly be reckoned for one of the best Parishes in the Cities of London and Westminster, or Parts adjacent." A further important contribution of the piazza was its ability to cohere a specific locality, or rather, to give an identifiable definition to a neighborhood. Chancellor (1930, 30) claims that, along with St James's Square developed later, "isolated houses of importance already stood ... but it was the systematic laying out of a large space ... that consolidated the neighbourhood into one of special importance and gave [it] ... a special and homogeneous character."

Not only was Bedford's attention to this contribution to the public realm an innovation, but the architecture, particularly that of St Paul's church, was conceived with its civic role in mind. Though partially required to obtain the project's statutory approval, Bedford himself understood the importance of a new church to the burgeoning parish and collaborated with church leaders to provide it. He conceded to the authority of Inigo Jones for the design and, with a sensitivity to the neighborhood, that architect noted in his own copy of the "bible" of classical architecture, *Palladio*: "The Greek architecture is fitter for us than that of the Romans; for their buildings were for use, and not so profuse." This is reported and interpreted by Downs (1967) to mean that "the more primitive orders, perhaps specifically the Tuscan, were more suitable for public architecture than those more lavishly ornamented." He concluded that "Here Jones shows his sensitivity to the symbolic quality of the orders. His own ideas of the general rightness of a simple order for public architecture" (Downs 1967, 13). Particularly in this emerging suburb located between the City of London and royal residences of Westminster, the modest, accessible structure, though with its inherent classical aesthetic proportions, was appropriate.

His attention to the reception of his project across many levels of stakeholders was an inspired act of community understanding and neighborhood analysis. Despite his target of wealthy aristocrats and merchants to reside in the housing he erected, Bedford was aware of the heterogeneous social composition and encouraged its continuance. In the early days of its completion, at least sixteen tradesmen are recorded as living in the new St Paul's parish (*Survey of London, Volume 36: Covent Garden* 1970, 159). Although he attended to the construction of the housing for the wealthy, he accommodated the diverse socio-economic demographic by leasing ground to the west of the piazza to developers who produced modest housing. All of these residents strolled in the piazza, attended the church, and made use of the markets. His foresight in commencing the development with the construction of the church is noted by Downs (1967, 13): "the Earl's courage in building the church before the income producing houses were constructed, was soon appreciated by [all] the new residents of Covent Garden."

Operation and Maintenance of the Public Realm

Although many early developers laid out streets as they subdivided their lands, and some provided central squares, there was often a lack of continued responsibility for their operation and maintenance. As many squares, such as Henry Jermyn's St James's Square and Nicholas Barbon's Red Lion Square, fell into disrepair, the residents on leases from a fragmentation of landowners, or those with freeholds, eventually rallied to press for private legislation to impose neighborhood fees to fund the repair and maintenance of the open space. This model was later adopted by most of the squares developed in the late 17th century and early 18th century, though it also provided the economic argument supporting the resident's attempt to restrict access to those squares during Georgian times. The communal structure for funding neighborhood amenities continues today in various formats, even in commercial precincts through the Business Improvement Districts (BIDs) as organizing entities.

However, as the 4th Earl of Bedford's home adjoined the piazza and he intended to continue to enjoy its view from his garden, he established a method for ongoing maintenance of its condition. He pledged the rental revenues from three of the residences around the piazza to the financial support of the parish church of St Paul's, in consideration for which its vestry accepted responsibility for the condition of the piazza. By most reports this arrangement worked effectively, though changing urban conditions and deterioration of the broader area during the following century probably strained it. At this time, however, the Bedford estate made an additional contribution directly to major capital improvements of the piazza, market stalls and streets.

Similarly, on the Bloomsbury estate, the 4th Earl of Southampton resided in a grand mansion overlooking the original square, and he is reported to have assumed responsibility for the maintenance of that public space. Although this arrangement gradually changed into one which corresponded with that of other squares, especially when the landlord's residence was demolished in 1800, Olsen reports that on the Bloomsbury estate the residents "tended to turn to the ground landlord whenever any extraordinary works were required ... [such as] rebuilding the iron railings, re-graveling the walks, or re-landscaping the gardens" (1982, 152–153). He also concludes that the well-managed Bedford Office, that assumed governance when the family estates were combined, had itself initiated improvements, being aware of both its responsibility to the community and the positive impact on the economic value of the residences.

Principles for Development and the Public Realm

There are numerous intersections of the private development activity and the public realm, and the symbiotic relationship has been presented as invaluable to both. Though the physical requirements for development projects and the financial expectations change, those changes are usually definable through building specifications and financial metrics. However, the relationship between development projects and the public is difficult to describe at any one time and subject to substantial and surprising changes even during the delivery of a project. To manage for an optimal outcome for the public realm requires flexibility in the procedures used; however, certain key principles gleaned from observing the initial projects and their changing circumstances are fundamental and will drive the process suitably. These are:

- Interaction with statutory and municipal authorities is necessary and continuous, with the influences and benefits being mutual.
- Urban projects occur within a political context that facilitates their success, and engagement in that dynamic is critical.

- By their existence within a community, development projects effect that context and should provide a positive impact, which establishes a cycle of mutual benefits.
- Physical contributions to the public realm require the consideration of their ongoing maintenance costs and management.

Definition of Real Estate Development

This model of private real estate development came into existence in 17th-century London and expanded rapidly in response to a critical housing need as the city flourished in trade and commerce. Its earliest manifestation in the works of the Earl of Bedford at Covent Garden was copied, though with some variations, by the Earl of Southampton, the Earl of St Albans, and Nicholas Barbon, amongst others. By the end of the century, it was adopted to meet urban expansion throughout Britain and in early colonial settlements. In the following centuries, its place has been further consolidated as the common business practice for privately producing the growing urban environment.

Summerson (2003, 27) does not acknowledge Covent Garden as the first innovative step in this private business practice, but rather presents Southampton's and St Albans's projects as the pioneering ventures. From these, nevertheless, he derives three important features of the development activity:

> These two great building schemes [Bloomsbury Square and St James's Square] had three features in common. First: the idea of an aristocratic lead – the presence of the landowner's own house in the square. Second: the concept of a complete unit of development, comprising square, secondary streets, market and, perhaps, church. Third: the function of the speculative builder operating as a middleman and either building the houses himself or subletting the sites to individual builders.

The principles he suggested are indeed pertinent to the appearance and growth of development activity, but the first two are overly specific to that time and place, and the third relegates it to the level of simplistic mass-building. The physical construction was certainly an extension of the housing schemes of master builders, who had practiced on various scales. However, even in its earliest manifestations, the innovative private activity involved much more than just construction, and its underlying actions were driven by deeper entrepreneurial and social principles that drove the first two features nominated by Summerson.

The historical tracing of more detail about the formulation of the real estate development model, rather than just Summerson's focus on the physical outcome, elucidates the significant new features in its practices. It reveals the complex process to have three other dimensions, with one pertaining to the mechanics of the production process, and the others concerning the invention of investment products for funding such production, and the advantage and desirability of making a contribution, not just physically but also socially and economically, to the broader community. Though this is given as an initial exposition, and its total nature is still to be fully defined and will be hopefully subject to ongoing modification, the ideal characteristics of a successful urban project achieved by a private developer are:

- The project should be substantial in some manner, usually scale, but it might consist of radically satisfying a critical community need, such as providing affordable housing and employment opportunities.
- There should be a discernible vision that goes beyond merely filling in the urban context with more of the same.
- There will be a change of use or variation in use of the land.
- The site should be spatially and coherently planned, with appropriate integration and sensitive response to the neighborhood.
- The buildings should be designed to enhance the experience of the intended inhabitants.
- The building and site should contribute positively to the public realm, aesthetically, economically, and socially.
- A long-term strategy for the management and maintenance of the whole project, including public spaces, should be put in place.
- It should provide a competitive market rate of risk-adjusted return on capital.

To achieve these objectives comprehensively requires a developer's commitment to high standards of vision, analytical rigor, diligence, management, and integrity, which together would qualify it as a professional discipline in which standards are set and universally adopted.

Development Process as a Business Model

The strategically organized approach to planning, funding, constructing, and selling a large-scale, multi-unit urban development scheme for unknown occupants had rarely been seen in the Western world as a private venture, broadly accepted and replicated, until the described projects were undertaken in 17th-century London. While the commercial activities of trading had emerged in Italy and the Low Countries and some other places globally, the application of the merchant business principles had not been applied to real property. However, as the commercial activities of rising capitalism expanded from the time of Elizabeth I, the traditional methods of land management were blended with the new financial and production structures of modern business. Faced with a compelling demand for housing, a new method of producing the urban built fabric and its attendant financial vehicles, though begun as individually courageous pursuits, were successively tried and tested, modified and modulated, and consolidated into an efficient and organized process that was recognized as a new business model.

To be described as a business, this activity transformed from comprising varied and unique approaches to single projects, as typical of "cottage industry," to a larger-scale undertaking with a defined set of principles, structures, and processes. During its emergence in early modern London, these business components were sufficiently simple to be observable, but also adequately structured for the application to a variety of situations and therefore able to be extensively deployed. Moreover, while they included some innovations, there were also advances on older methods, such as estate management and building construction, though these were modified in response to the new commercially minded conditions.

This new business of private urban development was observed to be a practice in which numerous different activities are performed and integrated to achieve an optimal outcome.

The objective of an "optimal outcome" was established to include the dimensions of economic return, urban topography, and social impact.

Towards Model Formulation

The earliest developers did not intentionally set out to create development firms, but rather applied their business acumen to delivering the product, with this product being financial returns as well as housing and community amenities. For them, an application of Porter's (1996) essential business strategy was how to best create a housing precinct such that the highest, long-term financial returns could be derived from it. It was not how to create a business entity that achieved long-term liquidity and capitalization, though, of course, the family estates as a whole were managed by such a strategy. Unfortunately, small developers without estates often did not survive a failed project and applied their labor to other activities, and the demands of development projects continue to overshadow the objectives of business survival today.

The emergence of the project management activity for the delivery of the various schemes has been discussed, but it was shown to be overly focused on its product and without sufficient consideration of an organizational model for the business itself. For the private urban development process to function as an ongoing business, the new developer also needed to function as a general business manager. By this consideration of the practice, it would take its place amongst other commercial activities that were forming in London at the time, and the measure of the outcome would be that of a viable business structure with sustainable economic returns to continue to employ its practitioners. This did not occur to any substantial degree.

As also seen in the formulation of the financial aspects of this new practice, the traditional role of landed estate management and the rising activities of merchants provided the foundations for the early attempts to form property development businesses. Those managers, whether the nobleman or an employed agent, quickly learnt from the merchants, adopting their accounting system, financial return metrics, methods of resource allocation, and understanding of supply and demand dynamics. However, these techniques were applied to each project, almost as a stand-alone entity, without strategic planning of the developer's own business and its operating activities.

For the maintenance of an ongoing business, the developer would additionally need to consider new projects as the completion of another was approaching. To do this, like a merchant, he viewed the market for the products he was able to offer and also noted if his products might need to be modified to meet new demand. He also noted what his competitors were doing – the details of the product, their customers, the pricing, and the quantum of their production. Instances of this business planning are evident in Southampton's providing a range of small and large sites though with co-terminal leases facilitating possible future changes to Bloomsbury Square.

In seeking successive projects, Barbon was exemplary, often selling leases on buildings under construction to fund new site acquisitions, though again, with each project funds were fully distributed, new capital sought, and new building teams engaged. His strategic planning was not for an operating enterprise but rather to achieve command of a succession of deals. Many developers continue to hold such a strategy for their activities.

With these general management shortcomings, the business of private urban development had lagged behind the evolution of other commercial practices. However, certain common features of structure and organization became apparent in the early activities and these established a partial framework of business management.

Organization and Strategy Features

Family Ownership

For centuries the English economy had been structured around family estates which were interwoven with the local community through agrarian production and distributed governance, as the nobles dispensed justice and imposed order. In this era personal contact within and between communities was critical to economic survival and social harmony. Such a construct of organization through community relationships continued to be fundamental to the evolution of economic activities even as the country moved from maintaining self-sufficiency to seeking profits and wealth accumulation. Kirby and Rose (1994, 5) describe this consequence for business structure: "In terms of finance, partners and information, the boundaries of the eighteenth-century and early nineteenth-century British family firm extended to embrace the local community."

Even as the composition of firms began to be other than derived from a family basis, this notion of strong interrelationships remained embedded in the business organization, even as industrial firms grew to substantial sizes: "The importance of community and personal contact was not, however, confined to family firms between 1780 and 1830 [the period of the Industrial Revolution]. The courts of the chartered trading companies and the insurance companies ... were filled by members of the City of London's commercial and financial communities" (Kirby and Rose 1994, 5).

For capital-intensive projects such as private urban development, this incorporation of an interwoven community was most evident in the take-up of residences in familial and social clusters. The experience of the aristocratic developers on their rural estates had been with infrastructure projects such as canals and drainage systems, where the necessary funding was raised from interested parties within localities. There was an understanding that those who were to benefit from the infrastructure work would be those most likely to invest in it, even though at times, like with Bedford's fens project, additional capital was raised more broadly.

In this way, the tight connection between physical projects, capital funding, and community benefits was inherent in the early development activities, particularly those of the gentry but also others by commoners such as with Seven Dials and Lincoln's Inn Fields. Even with the use of external capital, though mostly as debt, many development entities continued to be organized as structures with tight interpersonal relationships in their ownership and production activities. As a result, despite the global expansion of capital markets, family companies continued to be a dominant form for large-scale urban real estate holdings from the early development activities in London to the present day globally.

In broad business history in fact, it seems that for the enterprises that both required large amounts of equity capital and were not easily formalized as business activities, such as private urban development, the family company structure has been regularly adopted. However, extensive scholarship has compared the family firm with businesses that moved to a less personal structure, with the assessment that the survival of this "personalized capitalism" was a burden to economic growth (Rose 1994, 61). In his review of European business, Chandler (1990) found its growth to be less efficient than its American (non-family) counterparts; and Landes (1949) sees the relatively poor performance of the French economy later on in the 19th century being due to the conservatism of the family-based businesses.

In recent decades, large institutions have taken on ownership of large real estate portfolios (Clark 2000), also applying conservative investment strategies, though, as for many family holdings, that has helped stabilize prices to a certain degree during volatile times. Further empirical studies are following Clark's identification of the dynamic, and the effect on real estate asset performance over the long term will be of importance to the industry. However, for the property development activity, these entities are not usually participants, though their presence as buyers upon completion is providing an economic "pull" through development.

Therefore, if the completed development properties or land continued to be held indefinitely, the concept of the English long-term land estate provided a suitable model for extension to the urban context. By the economic strategy of such an entity, extensive infrastructure and community amenities were provided with an understanding of the mutual benefit derived. Also, with the financial focus on stabilized long-lasting annual revenues the quality of housing, and of tenants, was afforded more attention, with the responsibilities of the relationship clarified within leases. The survival of the early projects, and the success of later applications of the model, in London and globally, underscores the suitability of this ownership structure for the development business model.

The Entrepreneur

London's unprecedented increase in housing needs with statutorily suppressed supply was an economic situation of volatile demand and erratic supply. It is precisely such conditions that are best suited to the rise of the entrepreneur. As Casson et al. (2006, 9) write:

> [T]he demand for entrepreneurship derives not from the overall level of product demand, but rather from the volatility of such demand. Similarly, it also derives from volatility in supply conditions, such as technological change. Volatility generates novel and complex situations that call for improvised decisions.

The behavior of the early developers appears to be that of risk-taking entrepreneurs rather than managers of established, ongoing enterprises. The products they created – new formats of housing and, more importantly, a new process for the delivery of housing – came at a time when the concept of the entrepreneur did not exist. In this, their objective of economic gain makes them exemplary of William Baumol's (1993, 2) definition of the entrepreneur as "the individual willing to embark on adventure in pursuit of economic goals." But they ascribe even more faithfully to his more detailed description of one who "pursued through a variety of means, all of which have had an enormous impact on society" since they used financial, political, and social resources to create a new economic and topographical format for urban building. Additionally, he recognized that such entrepreneurs "struggled with the more entrenched aspects of society," just as the early developers defied building restrictions and social challenges on their projects.

Because of their perceived risk-taking they were often called "adventurers" along with sea-faring explorers, mining explorers, trading joint-stock enterprises, and other new commercial undertakings. Additionally, when they presented investment schemes, such as Barbon's varied offerings, they were often referred to as "promoters."

The modern idea of the entrepreneur only arose in the 18th century as "the product of a modern post-Enlightenment world in which continual change is the norm, where 'progress' (technical, social and economic) has become expected and where notions of liberal individualism predominate" (Ricketts 2006, 33–34). However, the actions of the private urban developers in London in the 17th century can importantly be seen as forerunners of the defined role of the entrepreneur. In observing their new mode of practice, these key components of the definition, "continual change" and "liberal individualism" are very applicable, and continue as embedded characteristics.

There has long been an interest in the traits or characteristics of personality attributed to the entrepreneur, among them risk-propensity, achievement-craving, creativity, self-motivation, and confidence. Real estate developers are often regarded as having this personality profile, and the earliest practitioners are notable in their origins at the cutting edge of commercial enterprise, whether working with Thomas Cromwell in building Henry's VIII's treasury as did Southampton and Bedford, or contributing to new economic thought as did Barbon. Many were known for their ambition and confidence, often self-proclaimed, as may be observed in practitioners today.

Although a generality, the prevalence of these entrepreneurial characteristics indicates a management mode that substantially influences the performance of urban development activity. A more detailed investigation by the economist Nigel Wadeson (2006) of the cognitive aspects in processes of information collection has revealed that the entrepreneur distinctly economizes on information costs, significantly employing heuristics to contain information load and yield quick decisions. This is often referred to by developers, being confidently proud of their speed and simplicity in decision-making, as "gut instinct."

Social Networks and Cooperation

Additionally characteristic of the real estate developer are entrepreneurial activities with respect to gathering and distributing information in order to advance a new idea. The successful entrepreneur is seen to utilize social and professional networks, though the extent of this has been difficult to observe and quantify, their predominant location in metropolitan areas indicates that personal networks spatially aggregated are important to the entrepreneur. For developers, cities are not only places where, like entrepreneurs, they find a variety of information sources, a number of potential collaborators, and a concentration of capital, but also usually the strongest demand for their buildings.

London, therefore, with its rising agglomeration of migrants, flourishing intellectual activities, variety of skills and capabilities, and focus of financial transactions, was ideal for the emergence of the early real estate developers. Barbon specifically made great use of the active intellectual scene, being a member of the Royal Society (Academy), though, as a postscript, his failure to meet his membership dues resulted in his house being used as the domicile of the organization after his death. To extend his network and range of influence, as well as protect him from prosecution, he also bought a seat in Parliament.

For the aristocrat developers, their social and political networks were of substantial assistance in obtaining approvals for their development projects. They also encouraged their friends to become residents in their projects, thus establishing desired neighborhood demographics. Also on offer to friends and colleagues were opportunities for investment and development partnerships, with this close network of investors being typical of all the new commercial enterprises at the time. Rabb (1967, 97) describes the dynamic for a specific instance of the trading and exploration adventurers, many of which both the Bedfords and Southamptons were a part:

> Personal relations among the investors were so close that it would be safe to estimate that at most 10 percent of the people in the list [of stockholders of the Bermuda Company] had no close relative elsewhere among company members ... [T]he leadership [was] a honeycomb of intermarriage and kinship (Smith linked to Warwick, Sandys to Southampton, and nearly all the great merchant families to one another).

Indeed, the social and economic network of just the few early developers observed in this book was complex and intertwined, but a very effective structure within which the new model became known and replicated. The use of a network has proceeded to be crucial for so many aspects of urban development, from finding sites to knowing markets, planning layouts, obtaining statutory approvals, gaining financing, managing construction, and marketing the completed projects. The network might possibly be the most distinguishing feature of the urban development business model!

Chapter 10: The Theoretical Schism in Urban Development Scholarship

Though this model of private urban development originated in the 17th century, it has not undergone significant advancement or alteration despite its practice having been broadly adopted throughout the Anglo-American world of capitalist economics and democratic governance. Further, in more recent times, with only the slightest legal and economic modifications, it has been embraced by formerly non-capitalist economies and other governmental systems. Given its persistent pace of adoption and general success, it has not been subjected to rigorous critical evaluation or to a search for substantial improvements in its principles and procedures.

Certainly, the resultant urban built form receives significant attention from a variety of scholarly disciplines which apply their respective frameworks of assessment and evaluation. As an economic product, real estate is rigorously examined as an investment asset, a vehicle for complex financial structures, and as a component of the macroeconomic system. As physical form, it is judged according to its aesthetic characteristics, its functional role in housing humans and their varied activities, and its manifestation of social symbolism. In its role of accommodating a community and its aspirations, it is assessed as a sociopolitical undertaking governed by policy and urban ideology. Numerous other areas of scholarship – anthropological, cultural, and technological – also address the city and its issues.

The scholarship and research on the development process itself, however, has been brief and meager. The related areas mentioned above are important and useful in understanding much of the urban condition, and various pertinent aspects of their scholarship contribute to a framework for exploring the private development model, particularly with respect to its broad socio-economic impact. However, this array of viewpoints represents the fractionalized or siloed approaches of a distinct, separated discipline. Since this has been the only continuing manner of its scholarly interrogation, the private development activity can be seen as "falling through the cracks" of academic coverage.

The contributions of the main related disciplines do establish significant assessment points for the outcome of the development process. Teasing out and clarifying these are therefore helpful for understanding the process and the various demands upon its performance, though their limitations with respect to knowing and engaging the actual process should also be noted. The predominant scholarship therefore includes the mainstream economic discipline, urban planning theory and policy, and economic activities in general.

Mainstream Economics

Notable scholarship in the broader area of urban economics has explored either the area of housing economics, predominantly within neoclassical theory, or the area of real estate finance and investment. The dominant body of this scholarship deals with urban development activity as a mechanistic, rational process by which the "utility-maximizers" undertake the production of the asset in response to supply/demand dynamics formulated by neoclassical economics, followed by detailed analysis of the outcome as an investment asset. It specifically applies the tools of property finance as derived from the capital asset pricing model (CAPM) used by corporate finance. Theoretical evolution within this paradigm has provided the almost globally adopted form of investment return analysis that supports transactions related to the $27 trillion of investment properties, and also has delivered the core textbooks in real estate educational programs worldwide (Baum 2015; Brueggeman and Fisher 2015; Geltner and Miller 2001). Unfortunately, its interest in the *production process* inherent in the business model has been relegated to consideration of management procedures by the engineering discipline without significant intersection with notions of economic value. This often subordinates the operational dynamics of the business model to external financial objectives to the detriment of organizational sustainability.

It has also been noted that the techniques of financial analysis currently applied to property development activity are as yet relatively undeveloped and possibly misleading for capital allocation decisions (Derrington 2020). The current capital sources for development projects are presented as relatively simplistic: homeowner/occupiers versus investors in commercial properties. As the financial crisis of 2008 demonstrated, however, the economics of homeownership are interwoven with sophisticated global financial instruments. Secondly, the capital structure for development projects today are complex, incorporating many sources and conflicting objectives, and are subject to displacement themselves during the process as it proceeds from pre-development to construction and on to operational start-up. Therefore, the need to identify the objectives of all the capital sources and monitoring their changing metrics and altering hierarchies, all within the framework of mainstream financial analysis, is a challenge to the methodology. Resolving this complexity requires a deeper comprehension of the multidimensional production model of urban development that can more effectively interface with mainstream financial theory.

Urban Theory

David Harvey (1978; 1989) approached urban development within the most comprehensive dimensionality of the economic, the social, and the spatial. He examined the process through the Marxian lens of economic production, but he also exposed significant politico-economic conflicts at the heart of the socially and spatially dysfunctional outcomes that had frequently occurred during the accelerated urban expansion of the 1970s and 1980s. Significantly, his model emphasized capital flows and the potential for substantial variation in their timing and quantum in relation to "general tendencies in financial investment, the role of an urban region within international patterns of economic competition, the effects of this on the economic and spatial structure within a region, and the role of public policy in creating and impeding investment opportunities" (Healey 1991, 234). However, other than referring to the economic surplus of production and the labor involved in construction, he did not dissect the production process itself.

Writing specifically on the intersection between real estate and the economy and formation of cities, Fainstein (2001, 17–18) appreciated that the private, speculative model, driven as it is by funding sources, could be harnessed to deliver the physical needs of the city while being better controlled in terms of equity distribution – not just pure financial equity, but also social ramifications. She said:

> My own position is that incentives to investors do make a difference and that growth can be combined with greater equity than has typically been the outcome of redevelopment programs. But perhaps the farthest one can go in addressing the issue is to identify areas of [production] indeterminacy that can be seized locally within the overall capitalist economic structure—that is, to identify courses of action that can produce lesser or greater growth, more or less progressive social policies.

Also addressing the creation of cities, Clark (2000, 17) asks: "What are the prospects for urban infrastructure and development funding given, on the one hand, the retreat of the state and on the other hand, the rise of pension fund capitalism?" He sees that while the latter institution gains financial heft, it is caught between an "exclusive benefit view" of satisfying its own economic performance, or a "reciprocal benefit view" by which a conception of social purposes extends to providing community benefits such as infrastructure or affordable housing (Clark 2000, 270). This acknowledges the realities of contemporary capitalism, but it also raises questions about how to achieve a more equitable outcome in both financial and social terms. Real estate development is similarly so dependent on society's facilitation of its activity, in terms of land use, law, governance, and municipal services that some beneficial reciprocity might be expected. The framing of this dialectic is an important scholarly linkage between urban form and private development, and proposes both parameters for its detailed evaluation, that is, not one to the neglect of the other.

In the 21st century, the impact of property development activities on urban environments is regarded as a global concern, affecting both developed and developing countries. While we needed the formation or enlargement of cities to provide the centers of scientific, cultural, economic, and social innovation (Glaeser 2011), this surge in urban growth also resulted in concentrated poverty, ethnic and social conflict, ecological crises, unaffordable housing, and homelessness (Storper and Scott 2016). This increased the challenge for an effective urban theory.

Within the debate among urban theorists, attention to the development activity itself was loosely attached to various formulations of the process. First, assemblage theory with its rhizomatic networks and detailed relationship structures (Latour 2005; Farías and Bender 2010; Simone 2011) accommodated the earlier structuralist formulations of Healey (1991) and Guy and Henneberry (2000). Its core principle of tenuous hierarchical structures, vulnerable to collapse, and decomposition and/or reformation (DeLanda 2006), provides a useful structural framework for a more granular examination of the real estate development process.

A second paradigm, postcolonial theory (Robinson 2011; Roy 2009; Sheppard 2014), evolved with its refutation of "Global North" foundations, and was useful to understanding rapid development of urban centers in the "Global South." Importantly, it laid the ground for incisive studies of globally diverse, specific situations of urban property development, with predominant attention given to gentrification by Mukhija and Loukaitou-Sideris (2014), Myers (2014), and Haila (2017). However, this approach examines the results of development or macro-scale urban decisions regarding development, rather than the detailed process of production itself.

Observing the "hyper-capitalized" activities of the new century, the urbanist Rachel Weber (2002) focused on the perception of real estate development as one of the "contemporary processes of spatialized capital accumulation." Concerned with the manner in which urban policies are often required to support the evolution of the built environment, but also with the ways those incentives and processes might be subjugated to the financial objectives of capital markets at the expense of the public interest, she regarded development activities as a process whereby compelling financial motivations, including a tussle between use (by residents) and exchange value (as represented by investment transactions) are established in "[t]he very materiality of the built environment." Subsequently, she provided a detailed description of how new flows of capital became the determinants of the topological development of Chicago in the late 20th and early 21st century (Weber 2015).

This exposure of the overarching influence of financial forces in the formation of the contemporary city usefully raised the perception of how substantial they can be. This implicitly demands an investigation of the development process under such conditions – its production mechanism, all its agents in addition to financiers, and the structural relationships involved in delivering the built form, once funded. To achieve this, however, requires a deep evaluation of the financial calculations that facilitate the influences, particularly underlying the rising dominance of financial objectives. By interrogating the calculative practices, the specific manner in which the agency of those practices achieves its objectives and impacts the outcome of the development project can be revealed. That is the point of this work.

While Weber and others such as Sagalyn (2016) continue to critique the financial engine behind urban development decisions specifically, others challenge the premise that decisions were made on the assumption that all resources were available, and all alternatives were possible. The urban scholar Beauregard (2005) postulated that the entities undertaking development are often also constrained by matters outside the capital-based context of the process, such as a developer's area of specialization, the lack of an existing track record within a region, or the relationships which may have formed amongst the agents involved in the delivery of the project. Pushing the theoretical construct to incorporate these more detailed frictions and "micro-logics," he further built on the socio-economic framework of Harvey (1978), Ball (1986), and Guy and Henneberry (2000) to challenge the reductionist and functionalist approach to property markets that leads to the collapse of all property sectors, housing, office, hotel, industrial, retail, and so on, into a market logic of supply demand relationships (Beauregard 2005, 2432). Specifically addressing downtown housing initiatives which became popular in the late 20th century, he incisively noted that a significant factor in the success of such projects was the synchronic delivery of necessary complementary activities such as retail, work, entertainment, public services, and amenities, and exposed the inadequacy of the neoclassical model of demand, supply, and market signals underlying the most prominent research in urban development in recent times, which typically excludes these urban functionalities (Bateman 1985; DiPasquale and Wheaton 1996; Thrall 2002).

This refocus on the functional dimension of an unfolding urban development activity neglected by contemporary economic analysis, but having severe financial consequences for the buildings produced, provides an additional layer to Fainstein's (2001) evaluation of urban outcomes that reinforces the need for a deeper and more rigorous understanding of the process.

Models of Economic Activities

As theoretical constructs form around urban development, there is a complementary approach to gaining a better understanding of private activity, and that is to examine the practice itself, then structure it within the most suitable theoretical frameworks. Clark and Monk (2017, 1) approached the practices of institutional financial managers in this manner and were successful in delivering "a stylized representation of institutional investment, the relationships between institutional investors and intermediaries, and the logic and principles underpinning the production of investment returns."

In many ways, the real estate development process resembles that of financial managers in that capital is received from investors and lenders with the expectation of financial returns. That the development process produces these financial returns through simultaneously producing the building product is a complication addressed within this book, but does not detract from the essential similarity of the process. The description of the production of investment returns provided by Clark and Monk (2017, 59) is applicable to the production process, dual in its products though it is, of real estate development: "Producing returns depends upon managing systems, motivating employees, and facilitating coordination with and between institutions in relation to market risk and uncertainty."

A further important similarity of the real estate development process and financial management processes is the extent of uncertainty inherent to the context in which they function, and the outcome of decisions made. Due to these features, the skepticism with which Clark and Monk (2017) view the use of "learning by doing" as the method of knowledge management is applicable to real estate development. Regarded in this book as a challenge for its effective performance has been the traditional mode of learning the practice by joining a development firm and learning on the job. This is unsuitable since such a method of "trade" learning, as discussed elsewhere, requires three conditions: (1) that the process is replicable time after time, (2) performance variations can be detected because effects are directly measurable, and (3) innovations are incremental not disruptive (Clark and Monk 2017, 9–10). Real estate development is distinctly lacking in these features and therefore requires another form of managing the essential knowledge of the process.

With the objective of their book being "to remind investors of their core function," Clark and Monk have an intent similar to that adopted from an alternative discipline, that of formulating a business model based on management theory and microeconomics. In the context of emerging capitalism and the particular business interests of its first practitioners, it is not surprising that the format for real estate development resembled the structure of its companion commercial undertakings. It had reference to the advancing mode of mechanized production and financial arrangements that were evolving in Europe and continue at the heart of Western capitalism today. As a consequence, although variant in some details such as the general absence of uniformity of product, the tension between its consumption and asset values and its unavoidable public impact, the private development of urban real estate can be viewed within the fundamental construct of the modern business model.

This is not contrary to Clark and Monk's description of the financial management process, but rather is complementary to it, in that in addition to elucidating that process as it performs for external interests, the business model sets out the process by which the operating entity survives. Or, as Haslam et al. (2013, 4) discuss "how focal firms, within their respective business models, have a strategic imperative to generate cash surplus (for liquidity) and secure ongoing capitalization (for solvency) where both conditions establish a 'going concern.'" Though seeming to be more about self-interest than serving the customers, or investors, this aspect of real estate development practice has received little attention, with the usual mode of practice being that of project to project. This book's exploration of the process serves to explain why this mode has been so prevalent and questions if it might be detrimental to performance.

Though this is not the full extent of a business model and in arriving at an understanding of the development process as a business model, the objective is to

> define the business's characteristics and its activities in a remarkably concise way … in a way that matches the generic level that defines a kind or type of behavior, but also suggests *why* it works, because it embodies the essential elements and how they are to be combined to make them work. (Baden-Fuller and Morgan 2010, 167)

In performing such work, this book serves a number of purposes, including classifying the business activity within the context of commerce, providing a description that can be subjected to research and investigation, and act as a "recipe" for creative managers (Baden-Fuller and Morgan 2010, 156). The better performance of private development would benefit from attention in all these three respects.

All these three approaches provide valid frameworks with objectives and evaluative structures that provide facets for exploring the private development process. The research specific to the process itself that has been accomplished to date shows the pertinent touchpoints with those disciplines, and will now be reviewed.

Current Practice and its Theoretical Formulation

The activity of private real estate development is conducted overall on a large-scale, globally dominating the production of the built environment in most urban centers. Consequently, academic programs that train young professionals in this discipline are becoming more prevalent and popular by providing a complementary educational approach to real estate practice. This stimulates discussion and research on the unique pedagogical challenges of promoting the acquisition of the skills and knowledge to manage the development process.

In addition to guiding specific improvement in the process and its professionalism, this expanding enquiry and education demands a basic intellectual framework for the process and its principles – not just its content but also the form of its principles. The industry must move from a standard of performing as a trade, that is, doing it "as it has always been done," to that of a professional discipline – that is, done in accordance with a praxis that refers to a theoretical construct of its activity and includes self-criticism, external performance evaluation, and constant readjustment. This book proposes the theoretical framework to move it in that direction.

Review of Real Estate Development Theory

Seeking the direction of theoretical exploration in real estate activity during the last decades of the 20th century and during the early 21st century, Breuer and Nadler (2012) conducted a citation-based review of the most influential journals from 1986 to 2010. Their conclusion was that two distinct perspectives emerged: urban planning and a greater management orientation. For its development sector, this represents a bifurcation of information and critical thinking, with development's impact on the urban environment on the one hand, and economic and financial outcomes on the other. Such investigations and incisive evaluations have lessons for developers, but they generally emanate from opposing ideologies, a conflict which challenges a developer's reconciliation of principles and insights. Further, there continues to be difficulty in applying these principles, usually intellectually framed, to the seemingly pedestrian actions and ad hoc decisions of a developer in constructing a new building (Drane 2013).

For the development process itself there has been some substantial scholarship during these decades, though it tends to veer towards or emanate from one of the two dominant perspectives. Nevertheless, there is a search afoot to understand the fundamentals of the process by which the built environment is delivered by private developers, and this has uncovered important dynamics and features that assist in the formulation of a theoretical model. Some scholars have also been able to make links between the two ideologies.

General Categories of Theoretical Models

It is necessary first to say that it is virtually impossible to construct a single general model that would be a theory of everything. The process under study is too complex and diverse in its features and contextual circumstances to afford the possibility of being contained within a singular perspective. For this reason, various important studies have directed their respective attention to limited areas of the process or to limited aspects of theorization concerning its functions, though in making those limitations such studies do not predicate any criticism with respect to the broader theoretical exposition. Therefore, essential to the valid pursuit of a theoretical construct for the activity is that it be sufficiently multifaceted to accommodate the diverse features, as well as enabling its subject to be fluid and constantly reconfigured.

The first steps towards the formulation of a robust theoretical model of current Western development practice were made in Europe and the USA during the second half of the 20th century, as post-war cities were rebuilt and communities expanded. Gore and Nicholson (1991) provided an insightful review of it, and classified land development models into five groups: neoclassical equilibrium models, event-sequence models, cyclical models, agency models, and structural models. Their express assessment criteria were clarity of exposition, internal consistency, comprehensiveness, and extent of applicability to the process. From a viewpoint slightly more focused on agency relationships and negotiations within the development process, Patsy Healey (1991) reviewed the models within four modified categories consisting of equilibrium (of supply and demand), event-sequence (inclusive of cyclical arrangements of events), agency, and structural models. Both reviews referred to respective theoretical underpinnings, though this is done in order to place each within its historical philosophical spectrum.

Healey (1991, 220) also went further back in time to acknowledge the "pioneers in the study of the development process," starting with William Form (1954) and his work that promoted the notion of the real estate market – specifically with respect to housing projects – as an area that was highly organized and influenced by certain large and powerful entities or connected groups, including real estate and land development companies, corporate America, government at various levels, and the increasing population. Form also described the economic and social forces working in conjunction with those entities to shape land use in the post-war United States. This progressive concept of land use patterns and associated development as a source of a social struggle was probably a decade before its time, and was quickly eclipsed by his compatriot scholars who embraced popular neoclassical economics and regarded participants within the development process as rational actors who worked in a solely economic context with little concern for social relations or consequences.

Economic Models

The two most prominent ideological frameworks applied to real estate fall within the economic domain. Currently, the private development sector is directed by and contributes to a capitalist macroeconomy that is largely global in its reach. This was the context in which the private real estate development business model was historically formulated and for which much of its underlying purpose was established. Therefore, its practice employs analytical tools that connect it with the necessary resources of land, capital in capital markets, materials and labor, with the use of its product by occupants, and with the community. However, even as it was formed within the nascent capitalist economy of 17th-century London, alternative ideological concepts regarding the urban community and the built environment exerted some influence on its model. Subsequently, further consideration of both the building product and its mode of production was given from various perspectives. Of these additions, the predominant and most durable was that of the Marxist framework.

As both these economic constructs, the neoclassical and the Marxist, continue to promote important functions for the development of urban real estate and offer helpful commentary on its performance, they must be taken into account in seeking a comprehensive theory.

Neoclassical Equilibrium Models and Financial Analysis

In work by Kaiser and Weiss (1970) in the USA, and Hall et al. (1973) in Britain, the fundamental laws of supply and demand were posited as driving the development process. Developers were seen to make their most important decisions on perceived and interpreted market signals, and the process, once begun, proceeded in a relatively self-organized manner. By the 1980s, a smoother process of construction was facilitated by a new agent in the process, the construction manager, who worked as an extension to other engineering functions on the project. Consistently with the perception of development decisions as fundamentally economic, the industry attracted many new entrants with sophisticated investment analysis skills, though with little aptitude or experience in development. The substantial ebb and flow of speculative capital and regular booms and busts of property markets in the following decades are evidence of the broad adoption of this model, particularly in the capital markets.

Research was also directed to the "stocks and flows" principle of land availability. It spawned an extensive academic field of real estate finance theory by adopting the corporate finance capital asset pricing model (CAPM) and extensively applying the discounted cash flow (DCF) analysis to operating properties. Strict analytical models were established for the valuation of property and calculating returns on real estate investment. See, for example, the works of Brueggeman and Fisher (2015), Geltner and Miller (2001), DiPasquale and Wheaton (1996), and Thrall (2002).

However, with a focus on development activity, Healey (1991, 222–223) pointed out that this model failed to address key aspects, which she listed, and which is expanded upon, as follows:

(1) "Diverse forms of demand, particularly the difference between [property] user and investor demand." In recent decades, this difference has resulted in the allocation of capital flows to meet short-term, high-return objectives, with its consequent diversion from more utilitarian development, such as workforce housing.

(2) "The non ooonomic interests of [some of] those involved in development." These "interests" are typically those concerned with qualitative objectives such as environmental, social or political issues. Within a strict economic evaluation of development decisions, these interests are neglected.

(3) "The very considerable uncertainty in assessing future gain due to the timescale of the development process and the limited number of transactions in land and property markets." This lack of predictability of development economic outcomes due to the protracted production process, the uniqueness of each project and the relatively small volume of comparable transactions continues to add risk to development activity. In recent times, however, investment analysis has adopted a herd mentality to counter these uncertainties which has led to persistent overbuilding for markets such as luxury condominiums.

(4) "The distortions produced by the valuation and appraisal methods used to assess risk and reward, for example … the different approaches to calculating property investment yields." This concern incorporates the stark differences in risk/reward metrics applied in the development phase compared with those of the operating phase of a property investment.

Dasso and Woodward's Financial Management Approach (1980) proposed a stronger focus on financial management in real estate research. Appreciating the importance that Milton Friedman (1970) placed on the shareholder wealth maximization norm for American corporations, they emphasized that real estate management should strive to maximize investor value. The risk of this emphasis for a developer is that it distracts attention from the detailed management of the production process in that respect. (The operating performance of the completed building might be adversely affected by a focus on short-term investment returns.) Additionally, in the development process, many activities pertaining to qualitative physical aspects, community sentiment, and municipal politics are not easily attended to within a strict view of maximum financial outcome for investors. By dismissing the pragmatic and logistical realities of the process by which the financial asset is delivered, this approach risks missing identifiable value that is created but difficult to represent solely in the abstracted financial evaluation.

Scholarly counterpoints to this mainstream economic theory were made by urban theorists in the late 19th and early 20th century. Beauregard (1994), Fainstein (2001), and Weber (2015) confronted with the adverse influence on urban development by aggressive speculative capital that caused egregious urban inequality, decried the contemporary capitalist framework as a whole. Particularly with respect to housing, Smith (1984) dissected the neoclassical definition of land value to demonstrate that it produced a starkly unequal "rent gap" in urban development decisions. Scholarship in global urban theory by Fraser (1984) and Soja (1989) made the mainstream economic model as the core object of its criticism and proposed a more socialist-based framework for urban development.

The mainstream neoclassical economic context for real estate development which was present at its birth and influenced its formation continues to be the backdrop of most private urban development undertaken globally today, even in countries with alternative economic ideologies. Its acceptance, however, can be moderated through a deep understanding of the calculative practices involved, and interrogation of or engage with them to elucidate the details of its influence and how this might be modified if necessary. Derrington (2020) focuses on the lacuna of the capitalization rate usage for investment analysis to show the specific manner by which capital markets are able to direct capital to specific property types. Miller and Geltner (1994) described the three dimensions of calculative practices as (1) technology (or techniques and procedures), (2) rationales, and (3) the relationship of (1) and (2) with the broad economic and social context. Crosby and Henneberry (2017) examine the pervasively used techniques such as the DCF method, and the rationale by which investors use it to make decisions, and their justification by it, to describe its continued elaboration and distribution. They conclude: "By these means, calculative practices (re)constitute the economic domain" (Crosby and Henneberry 2017, 187).

To this may be added the (re)constitution of the physical and social domains, if not moderated within the neoclassical calculative techniques. Similarly in seeking to understand decision-making in corporate finance, Baskin and Miranti (1997, 6) warned that "there is the very real danger that the regnant model biases the approach of analysts and restricts the degree to which they are willing to incorporate or recognize relevant variables." These additional variables of social and environmental impacts continue to gain importance in the 21st century, but remain impotent in being considered since they cannot be represented adequately within the commonly used financial models.

Neo-Marxist Economic Model

Continuing within an economic framework but overlaying an alternative ideology, Boddy (1981) applied the Marxist thesis with direct reference to struggles between landowner, production capital and labor, and devolves the development process into three "circuits of capital": (1) "industrial capital" that is created by the basic construction/production activity, (2) "commercial capital" that is produced by the various transactional activities of buying, selling and even renting of the land, materials and completed building, and (3) "interest-bearing capital" which is inherent in the funding structures of the process. By imposing the dynamics between these three forms of capital on an event-sequence model, he established a theoretical construct that regards the outcome for the built environment to be directly consequential to the capital-based relationships that exist within, evolve throughout, and ultimately dominate the delivery of developed property.

His focus on the physical process of construction funded by the circuit of industrial capital is appropriate for the object of his interest, that is, the rapid and extensive construction of office and industrial properties in post-war Britain. In subsequent periods when the pressures of his "interest-bearing capital" or property investment capital, or even more potently, the varying return objectives of the owners/agents of that capital, have driven development cycles, construction activity is less the instrument of capital than is the developer who arranges all its capital commitments.

However, Weber (2015) was of an opinion that capital's influence expands to operate additionally through urban policy pertaining to and supporting urban development. She earlier had established clarity in directly connecting real estate development to the macroeconomic context, describing it as one of the "contemporary processes of spatialized capital accumulation" (Weber 2002). In an important contribution to understanding the pervasiveness of its impact on the urban dweller, she has described the dynamic whereby compelling financial motivations, including a tussle between use (by residents) and exchange value (as represented by investment transactions) are established in "[t]he very materiality of the built environment." Consequences of this conflict and the dominance of investment capital were the mortgage defaults which were at the heart of the global financial crisis of 2008, and persistent global housing unaffordability in urban centers. Adding to an explanation of the method by which capital wins this conflict, Weber (2015) reviewed the physical evolution of inner Chicago in the early 20th century to reveal how urban policies are often subjugated to capital objectives at the expense of the public interest.

Adding to Weber's concept of the use of property, Derrington (2018) extended the theoretical dynamic of that use by adjusting the perception of consumption, of no economic value, to be viewed as a defined component of broad economic production, which enhances its overall value. People's use of a building, home, office, place of recreation, is necessary for the restoration of their working capability, or labor capacity, which is to be contributed to some part of the macroeconomy. To provide this use, the building can be seen to "labor," that is, deplete itself in providing this service which makes a non-material contribution of value to the socio-economic state. This productive activity is valued according to the usual allocation of habitation costs by workers, that is, a third of their earnings. Applying this economic component of housing use to Weber's description of the inequality of outcome due to urban policies facilitates an economic estimation of its detriment.

This extension of Weber's "use" concept to the earlier description of Boddy's capital circuits adds a fourth circuit, that it has value as "labor restoration capital." This addition also rectifies the implication in Boddy's three circuits that once the building is constructed its interaction with human labor and economic production is completed. Rather, buildings continue to have Weber's "use" value, and its acceptance as capitals allows its importance to be more easily measured and compared with its exchange value, or use by capital sources.

This reasoning that seeks a comprehensive dimensionality comprising the economic, the social, and the spatial, makes strong references to the seminal work of David Harvey (1978, 1985). He examined the process through the Marxian construct of economic production, parsing the components relating to labor and capital, from which Boddy (1981) further categorized the latter as being for the purpose of funding or investment. He also exposed the significant politico-economic conflicts at the heart of the socially and spatially dysfunctional outcomes that occurred during the accelerated urban expansion of the 1970s and 1980s, to which Weber (2015) has added contemporary detail.

Harvey's theoretical model provides an important foundation for laying out the economic context and capital dynamics of development fully, and it significantly contributes to it in a number of ways. If this conceptual framework can be fleshed out with detailed financial calculations, as commenced by Derrington (2020), its social evaluation can be expressed in financial terms and the manner in which financial calculations obfuscate social assumptions can be demonstrated.

As it can be seen in Harvey's model (Figure 10.1), his starting point is the "primary circuit of capital" which encompasses all capital sources and uses in the system of production and

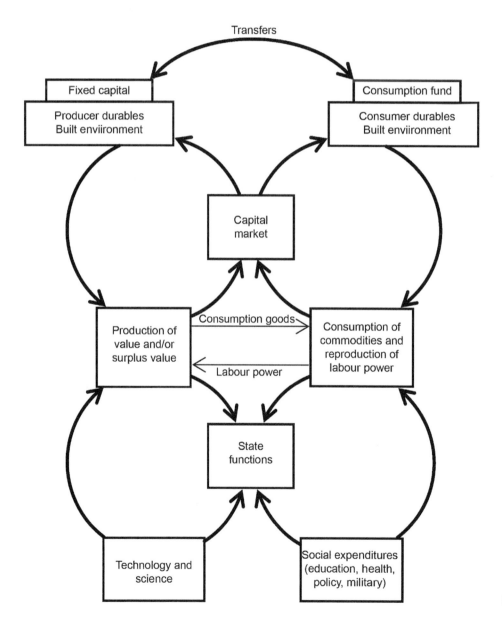

10.1

Harvey's circuit of capital.

consumption, and he underscores the importance of the dual role of labor in both. In the construction of the built environment, he divides the use of capital in the production process to deliver "Fixed capital" in the form of completed buildings that are traded as capital items, and as a "Consumption fund" that represents the employment of the buildings as commodities.

He further proposed that "surplus" value or capital is generated within these circuits of production, though he does not explicitly describe where and how it is generated and accounted for during the development process, but implies by his terminology that these things are within the province of capital providers. As a normative suggestion, in his model Harvey channeled some "surplus value" via the "State function" into "technology and science," and though perhaps not precisely applied, this represents taxation revenues at municipal and state levels. In the context of the increasing influence of capital markets in the production of urban environments, his explicit placement of "surplus value" into an independent category sustains attention to its newly recognized existence and invites further investigation as to its distribution, since it is broadly thought that households share in the economic benefits of property ownership and development. Certainly significant in his model was the emphasis on capital flows, which have a potential for substantial variation in their timing and quantum.

Healey (1991, 234) incorporated this construct in her model which elucidated "[the] general tendencies in financial investment, the role of an urban region within international patterns of economic competition, the effects of this on the economic and spatial structure within a region, and the role of public policy in creating and impeding investment opportunities." Weber (2015) showed the interconnections of all of these and described the physical consequences as they were played out in Chicago.

These theoretical views from the neo-Marxist perspective raise the importance of private urban development's evaluation both in its economic value, and in broader socio-economic conditions. Rather than just a form of analysis of financial performance and production outcomes, these features are presented as interacting dynamics, from both ideological frameworks which, in the formulation of development theory, will ensure that it balances investment of capital with building for societal use in its production process. It will continually assess the impact of new development on both the property investment market and the community's quality of life. Persistent overbuilding by the industry in its pursuit to capture capital and the discontent voiced loudly by urban communities make a rigorous evaluation by both ideological positions necessary.

Globalization and Capital Quantum

There has been a recent identification of another mechanism whereby real estate is influenced by capital markets. It pertains to the very powerful presence of global real estate funds, and though "not new, they currently are not only much larger in number but also manage much larger portfolios, often for large investors" (Aalbers 2019, 379).

Financialization Model

The nature of these investment funds and their allocation to urban development projects has also changed in response to "impatient capital" (Van Loon 2016). They promote short-term profit maximization as their dominant mandate. Their investors have required the transformation of illiquid, spatially fixed property with protracted returns into more liquid and uniformly measured financial investments. This has been achieved through "a range of regulatory and socio-technical changes and constructions," including "the invention of mortgage securities and real estate investment trusts, but also the development and use of advanced real estate valuation, benchmarking, categorization, market signals, rating, calculative practices and conventions that help translate between scales and sectors" (Aalbers 2019, 379–380). This phenomenon has been given the neologism of "financialization," and has permeated scholarship in urban economics and planning and in economic geography.

As a mechanism of the capital accumulation regime, it extends that regime's adverse impact on the built environment. Though this was long since warned against by Lefebvre (1991 [1974]), Harvey (1978; 1989), Ball (1986), and others, their concern has received recent reinforcement by Aalbers (2008; 2016), Christophers (2011), Gotham (2012), and many others. Financialized real estate, described as "feeding financial markets, on the one hand, and supporting private consumption on the other, is clearly not a formula for stability" (Aalbers 2019, 381–382). For the potential scale of financialization's consequences, it has been recommended "that the spatial causes and consequences of this circularity or flow of funds be subject to more critical attention" (French et al. 2011).

Its impact on the design and delivery of the built environment has been found in homogeneity of the building form (Henneberry, 1988; Crosby and Henneberry, 2016), and in some strange urban landscapes and perverse city expansions (Reiner de Graaf, 2017). Frequent poor decision-making has also been attributed to it: "That the objectives of the developer lean towards the maximization of sale price rather than long-term operational efficiency or occupant satisfaction are evidenced by the predominant use of images of form, finishes and façade, rather than functional or environmental efficiency, in the marketing materials" (Derrington 2019, 42).

Just as in mainstream economics, financialization has attained its current dominance by the perpetuation and dissemination of calculative practices, such as valuation methods and capitalized return analysis. Christopherson et al. (2013) point out that the long history of these methods, including their earliest formalizations in the history of real estate development as revealed in this work, would defeat any overstatement of the degree to which financialization is so different from prior investment behavior during times of excessive capital supply. Historically aware applied economists immersed in the field, Crosby and Henneberry (2016, 1426) suggest that "it represents the latest chapter in a much longer story and many of its supposedly new and different features are neither."

The recognition of this pervasive phenomenon in its recent guise is critical to the awareness of those involved in producing the urban built environment. To be cognizant of the power of its influence, even through public structures (Weber 2015), is to be capable of moderating decision-making to take account of its imbalances. Of importance is that this action be supported by analysis whereby evidence of financialization is not regarded as unknowable, unbeatable, and cringingly accepted. Rather, it is to be met through the details of monetary calculations and by an understanding of how they specifically affect property development decisions (Crosby and Henneberry 2016, 1425).

Action Models

A shortcoming of a purely economic view of private development is that it neglects consideration of the logistical complexity and variability of the inherent actions. Although the built form's spatial dimension is of interest to urban economists, more attention is given to the specifically transactional activities of site selection, land use approval, financial structure, and leasing or selling than the production activities by which the physical product is created. However, the procedural method by which land for development is resourced, managed, and rectified by human agents will have an impact on those transactions and, in turn, on the economic outcomes.

The Sequential Process Model

The sequential or action-descriptive approach, first adopted by Cadman and Austin-Crowe (1978), seemed sufficiently flexible to cover the whole range of development activities and the variety of stakeholders in one of Britain's most active periods. It tracked production events along the path a singular project might take from fallow site to completed building; that is, through the steps of (1) Evaluation, (2) Preparation, (3) Implementation, and (4) Disposal. Having grown out of post-war thinking which focused on engineering processes for temporal coonomic matters, including the controversial time–motion measurement of office workers, this procedural approach was initially impervious to feedback from the field or to flexibility of implementation.

Expanded formulations of the flow diagram were presented by Ratcliffe (1978), Punter (1986), and Goodchild and Munton (1985), and their use spread to the specific management of the design activities in the development process by Derrington (1981). However, the effectiveness of more detailed coverage was limited given the need to retain sufficient simplicity for comprehension despite the challenges of including the specifics of a complex development process. These models unfortunately presented a process isolated from how the broader socio-economic context of urban development might influence its sequence, including the influence of political, demographic, or financial changes. They were also not formulated to take into account the consequences and outcomes of its delivery as they might impact local economic conditions or quality of life.

The Provision Model

Michael Ball (1986) took an approach that adopted a production process metatheory but also examined the workings of the entities involved in development activities. It is particularly exemplified by his model of housing development. He studied the production and consumption of housing as an activity of "provision" – that is, one which goes beyond mere physical delivery with its attendant economic transactions to include social interaction. This dimension, additional to physical production, included socio-economic concerns such as affordability and physical aspects of aesthetic quality and societal symbolism. To incorporate this into his model, he expanded the number and nature of institutions, agencies, and entities involved in his survey. As a result, he saw a housing development as "a structure of housing provision [that] describes an historically given process of providing and reproducing the physical entity, housing, focusing on the social agents essential to that process and the relations between them" (Ball 1986, 158).

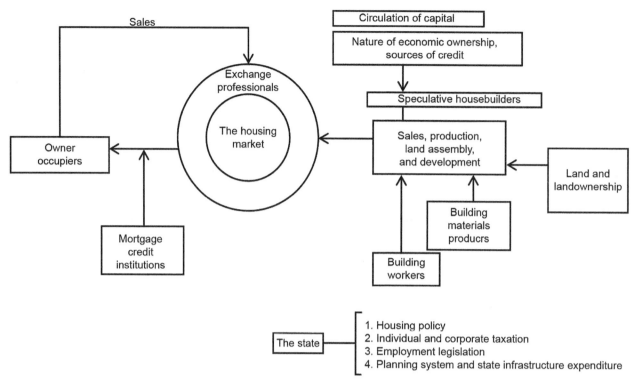

10.2

Ball's model of production.

Within his larger provision model (Figure 10.2), he embedded theoretical sub-propositions derived from production/consumption Marxist theory. These mid-level propositions are effective in interrogating key aspects of the development process through their address of the following:

- the social, legal, and financial relationships that produce the physical form;
- the economic relationships that arise in the production, transaction, and utilization of the resulting buildings;
- the emergent definition of aligned social agents with economic relationships for a specific mode of building provision, or property type;
- the evaluation of the roles, activities, and accomplishments of those social agents according to empirical evidence; and
- the interdependence of conflicts and collaborations with the socio-economic context at the macro level, each being an influencer of and influenced by the other.

Although he proposed that his "structure-of-provision" (SOP) model could be generally applied to most forms of development, he devised its application only to owner-occupied housing with its relatively simple associated economic transactions, and to British council housing with its formalized social relationships. Unfortunately, no further models for specific applications were developed to achieve what he had hoped would be "a means of ordering [development process] material so that it may be investigated" (Ball 1986, 462). This hope is as yet unconsummated in the search for a comprehensive development theory.

Ball (1998, 1502) also noted a further failing of such institutionally based models in that they often treated "mainstream economics … as the straw enemy," though he also spared no criticism for the Marxist theoretical constructs, pointing out that "[r]adicals can be as institutionally blind as the mainstream" (Ball 1998, 1506), as explicitly demonstrated in their tendency towards "conflict institutionalism," which assumed that conflict between the community and any developer was prima facie fundamental to the paradigm. His Structures of Provision (SOP) model connects the dynamics of the agency model with the structures of economic analysis: "Examining a structure of building provision involves specifying the *economic* roles of particular *social* agents" (Ball 1986, 455, emphasis added). And following his warning regarding ideologies, such specification must cut across both predominant economic theories.

As has been mentioned, such a necessary advance was made in 2005 by Beauregard in his judgmental consideration of the development process through the lens of urban political economy – specifically, in this instance, in relation to city revitalization. He proposed and incorporated an agency and relationship granularity, simplified but essentially in line with Healey's 1992 model and with reference to Harvey's circuits of capital (see also Beauregard 1994) and the production/consumption dynamic. This combination provides a more nuanced framework for testing urban development in the socio-economic context and evaluating the outcomes so derived.

Gore and Nicholson (1991, 729) strongly promoted Ball's model as the most promising of their four categories, for it provided for the "detailed investigations of the organizations, operations, financial mechanisms, personnel, and hardware involved, of the operating frameworks in which they work, and of the ways in which all these fit together … [and] the necessary theoretical basis for such investigations." In other words, it came closest to being a comprehensive and usable theoretical model. From this accolade, it should have seemed worthwhile for researchers in urban development to explore his theory's application to various property sectors. However, rising speculative real estate activity in most capitalist economies in the mid-1980s, combined with a retreat of social politics as took place, for instance, under the Thatcher and Reagan regimes, diverted the socially oriented sub-propositions of his model while the objective of broad "provision" was honed to one of focused maximized investment returns. It was therefore left to lie fallow as a framework which was no longer pertinent to contemporary economic conditions.

The Cyclical Model

The cyclical form of representing the development process was first put forward in the "development-pipeline" model of Barrett et al. (1978) and provided a triangulated arrangement of grouped events as follows:

1. Development pressures and prospects.
2. Development feasibility.
3. Implementation, or the building of the project.

This construct provided for varying influences and constraints of the physical and economic form, and incorporated feedback on new patterns at the end of every project cycle. Noticing that this private sector model was quarantined from local politics and socio-economic concerns as expressed in community resistance, Gore and Nicholson (1985) contributed an important enhancement by adding a fourth touchpoint in the cycle. It related to public sector activities, which provided a wider context for the theoretical project.

This addition of the public policy dimension kept the model useful for many decades of urban development across many countries, but its shortcomings arose from a lack of dynamism represented by its touchpoints. As structured, they acted as givens, or a "'black-box' approach to external variables" (Gore and Nicholson, 1991, 711) rather than as constantly and rapidly changing influencers also influenced by the project itself.

Further demonstrating that the model failed to respond to the dynamics of its touchpoints, the continued addition of luxury residences to their ongoing surfeit and falling pricing did not fully impact upon the feasibility evaluations within the process. Unfortunately, the sequential or cyclical models still broadly used by developers act in this way as "closed" systems with respect to dynamic economic conditions and societal trends. Consequently, they deliver an urban environment potentially at odds, physically, socially, and economically with the needs apparent in and expressed by its community.

Agency Models

The third broad category of development models identified by Healey (1991) and Gore and Nicholson (1991) comprises those which focus on the actors in the process. They define the actors' roles and describe their relationships that are present at the outset or are formed and modified in the process. These models consider human behavioral or activist aspects of the undertaking, conceding that the actors are driven by diverging interests and that decision-making may vary extensively and frequently from the process described by the event-based sequential models.

Individualist Approach

An early exponent of this focus on and definition of roles, concentrating particularly on the leadership of the developer, was Craven (1969), who endowed that actor with the skills of key-coordinator. Because of the centralized dependency on the developer, Gore and Nicholson (1991, 713) call this an "individualist approach," and Carlen (2016) notes it as being a key feature of the entrepreneur.

Addressing specifically the extensive activity in England of converting rural land to private residential use in the decades following World War II, Roy Drewett (Hall et al. 1973, 163) concentrates decision-making in this individualist role of the developer who "acts as a link man for perceiving the social and economic determinants of housing demand and supply, and having purchased land he has to anticipate consumer needs and to satisfy them." While this action by the developer, as a person or entity, can be commended for initiating specific projects, there are other numerous participants in identifying, gathering, and responding in various ways to establish the context in which that developer can proceed. These include municipal authorities, market analysts, financial and legal systems and political support.

Both of these approaches, while identifying roles and describing linkages between the actors together with their allocation to stages, imply almost unfettered authority for the developer without the significant constraint by, influence of, or support by other entities. Even in the days of substantial political and social enthusiasm for new urban and suburban development, the developer required the engagement of the community, the public authorities, funding sources, and so forth.

Hybrid Agency and Sequence Model
Forming a hybrid model by incorporating the influence of all actors into the sequential models, Kaiser and Weiss (1970) reduced the complexity of the numerous activities involved by assigning them to decision agents. While the activities that come under consideration in such analysis have social, policy, and logistical dimensions, financial considerations are ignored. Gore and Nicholson (1991, 713) highlight the strength of this model in "the way that it relates the decisions and events of the development process to the actors responsible or roles involved at each stage," achieving that important combination of necessary actions with the identification of skills, capabilities, and objectives in people who will perform them. But their review of the model criticizes its structure as "merely interpolating the position of actors at relevant points within an otherwise sequential flow," while the actors, despite their intentions and abilities are unable to influence the process. This outcome is often present in models that have a dominant prescriptive process with which to evaluate progress on achieving stages in the process rather than on the satisfactory completion of a participant's action. This is a common vulnerability of models derived from the framework of engineering operations if they are not sufficiently modified to accommodate the presence of the numerous actors and varied levels of skills necessary to the development process.

Multiple Actors Models
An expansion of the agency model was made by Bryant et al. (1982) by including the financial actors and their decisions, though they defined them explicitly in the land conversion process as "secondary decision agents" without explaining such subordination of the contribution of financial input by the farmer, land dealer, developer, and builder. Though in specifically addressing "urban fringe land markets" as the subject of their study, the theorists proposed a very comprehensive model of the agents which expanded the range of concerns and decisions applied beyond the development process to include "public intervention" and "pressures for change" in response to demographic, civic, or infrastructure changes, and to encompass "secondary agents" which included not just financiers but also "planners, politicians, institutions, realtors, [and] lawyers."

This extension of the model to the social, political, and economic context was a very useful advance, but although it expanded the potential reach of all relevant concerns, it does not advance any proposal for a process whereby these external inputs are sought and taken into account in the actions of "primary actors."

Making their first appearance in a development model, the notions of "response" and "impacts" were included. This afforded an opportunity for inherent critical evaluation of the process. Once again, however, the details of how these features are observed, measured, and judged – and specifically by whom and for the benefit of whom – are not proposed, nor is any method suggested for the provision of evaluative feedback during the process. Facilitating dynamic feedback during the process is of equal importance to directing actions in development theory, and has yet to be successfully achieved.

Moving beyond the individualistic notion of the all-powerful developer and focusing on the process of land management by local authorities in England, Barrett and Whitting (1983) proposed a more interactive approach that incorporated bargaining and negotiating between various actors. As their efforts necessarily had reference to a politically volatile time, the late 1960s and early 1970s, their elucidation of the identity of numerous stakeholders, their respective needs and demands, and potential conflicts among them are again relevant as urban turmoil in the 2020s continues to unfold. Their understanding of the broad array of people impacted by urban development also resonates with relevance for the surge in public attention from a variety of quarters ranging from the Crown to the common man, similar to that which private developers received in their early undertakings in 17th-century London.

Barrett and Whitting's (1983) model incorporates five principal actors: the developer, funder, builder, professional advisors, and the public sector. It then places them in a development-pipeline sequential model. This structured the process as a series of activities which brought together the necessary actors and their respective resources. Under this dynamic "resource exchange," the behavior of the agents representing each resource could be observed, and an assessment made of their motivations, bargaining power, and success in achieving desired outcomes. The model's broad definition of responsibilities and evaluative standards enables it to be comprehensive, flexible, and applicable to many project types. For this reason, it forms the theoretical underpinnings of most property development textbooks, especially that of Peiser and Hamilton (2012), Harvard (2008), and Millington (2014). But it stands in isolation from the socio-economic context that would map value systems onto responsibilities and performance requirements. As a result, an assessment of the outcomes of the resource exchange, while being important to the participants, is irrelevant in the community context, which fortifies the continued criticism of industry disregard for this aspect.

With a useful simplicity, Goodchild and Munton (1985) also incorporated multiple agents into their model and related them to two fundamental but distinct decision points: (1) the identification, analysis and preparation of the development site, and (2) the commencement of construction activity on that land. Stage (1) of the activity proceeds along six alternative routes, with appropriate agents responsible for go/no-go decisions on each path. Along each route, the three principal actors – planners, developers, and landowners – are nominated for various decision nodes, which contain the integrity of the process to some degree but enable flexibility in terms of roles, progress, and outcomes. Though this model suitably takes cognizance of social concerns, it fully places on planners the responsibility for exploring the details of the issues, proposing solutions and directing the implementation. As a result, the developer and landowner are required to respond to community concerns only in accordance with those formulated by the planner.

Peter Ambrose (1986) further incorporated the larger societal context by proposing what he termed the "development system" comprising three interrelated "fields": the construction industry, the financial sector, and the public authorities, the last being the vehicle for input and influence by the community. As his complex model presented a wide variety of potential interactions, it facilitated the possibility of many different outcomes, physically or economically. However, he also indicated that the consequences of the interactions are manifest in the final built form and therefore discernible. By this model, he almost provided the necessary means for evaluating how an urban development project works for its community, performed as it would be in the post-construction phase. Unfortunately, a developer is sometimes from neither the construction nor the financial sector, and although possibly influenced by the objectives of those "fields," may inject additional intentions and ambitions into the process. Not accommodating the admittedly difficult-to-predict consequences of this actor's presence reduces the application of the model.

Paul McNamara (1983) applied the framework of social concerns to the roles of participants, irrespective of how they are categorized by other models. He built upon Massey and Catalano's (1978) proposition that landholders' interests were derived from their broader socio-economic standing, and presented the development activity as a production process in which the participants further their existing interests within society. As Healey (1991, 231) pointed out, this approach is in harmony with that of Form (1954) from decades prior, which she saw as appropriately addressing "the alliance of production-based landowners, a residential development company, and the representatives of a local community as the 'social congery' which controlled the development process." McNamara's (1983) conclusion is also more recently underscored by Polanyi's (1957, 48) premise that "man's economy, as a rule, is submerged in his social relationships."

This tendency of agency models to include a broader societal context justifies their "challenge [to] simple divisions into 'public' and 'private' sector activity" (Healey 1991, 231). However, Healey detected what she believed to be a limitation of agency models in that they do not incorporate a means of assessment of what "agents, or roles, or interests, or certain networks of relationships [are] critical to a successful development", nor how the machinations of the process "related to the wider power relations of the economy and society" (ibid.). She found them simultaneously inclusive of all participants, almost always placed on the same level of potential influence, which is unrealistic, and yet often lacking in effective dynamic engagement with the broader socio-economic context. While commending these models as conscientiously detailed and comprehensive in describing the actors and relationships in the development process, she regretted their inability to expose fully the objectives of the actors and the purposes of their relationships and to evaluate how they play out.

Production or Structural Models

More inclusive of societal factors and motivations of actors, but still adhering in part to the application of the economic framework, are the models described as either "Structure Models" by Healey (1991, 232) or "Production-based Approaches" by Gore and Nicholson (1991, 721). Typically they refer to Marxist principles of production, which, however, pertain only to the construction activity, regarding it as similar to any commodity production. Generally, these models can be improved by treating the performance of completed buildings as economic production, as they perform the valuable social function of accommodating occupants (Derrington 2018).

These models are aptly described by Gore and Nicholson (1991, 721) in this way:

[The] production-based approach starts from a set of first principles which may be applied first to the particular characteristics of property development, and then to specific situations ... [P]roduction-based approaches focus exclusively on the flow of money or other forms of capital as the generating current of the system.

Despite the suggested centrality of capital, this approach moves beyond the neoclassical economic evaluation of the process to add a social objective, usually through the Marxist reference mentioned earlier. It also attempts to encapsulate the sequence-based approach in a structured framework that defines and observes the activities of participants in terms of their power or influence in decision-making. The point here is that it is an attempt to embed a socio-economic assessment as part of the production mechanism of the activity.

Healey (1992) supports Harvey's "general theorization of the flows of material resources, and most notably finance capital, through property" (Harvey, 1978; 1989, as cited by Healey 1992, 35), in that it provided a politico-economic metatheory by which a development process can be assessed in its social failings, even if these are to be blamed on its inherently capitalist formulation as currently practiced. She agrees with some aspects of the neoclassical economic model, such as its engagement of development in the broader economy, but highlights its shortcomings with respect to the economic tension between property users and investors; neglect of important non-quantitative aspects such as social and community concerns; lack of rigorous risk assessment; and continued distortions and misuse of calculations and metrics (Healey 1991, 232). Ideally, these neglected areas in each economic model would be satisfied by actions and procedures that can be structured according to the Marxist model at the same time as they are accommodated in the capitalist economic context.

Plainly aware of those ideological challenges, Healey (1992, 33) focused instead on "the complexity of the events and agencies involved in the process and the diversity of forms the process may take under different conditions." She proposed a comprehensively descriptive institutional model that avoids socio-economic or geographical context-dependency, but still includes attention to both economic and social concerns (see Figure 10.3). In its comprehensiveness and inclusion of different paradigms, she described her model as

> the link between structure [Ball, Boddy, and Harvey] and agency [Barrett et al. 1978; McNamara 1988; Massey and Catalano 1978; Lauria, 1982] empirically through relating the construction of roles, and the strategies and interests of agencies, to the material resources, institutional rules and organizing ideas which agents acknowledge implicitly and explicitly in what they do. (Healey 1992, 35)

In forming her model around the analytical use of resources and rules, she referred to Anthony Giddens's (1981, 1984) structuration theory. At the time, it was an important factor to include in development theory since it provided a framework for observing the continually shifting negotiations and bargaining that occurs between agents in possession of resources – such as land, capital, labor, and expertise – and those imposing authoritative rules, be they state-based, societal, economic, or legal.

Healey's robust model (Figure 10.3) is most effective in encompassing various levels of analysis rather than a singular definition of agents and their interests, and the events in which they participate in the process. These levels of analysis include (1) an initial description of the process as a series of specific events involving identified agents in pursuit of a defined outcome; (2) an identification of roles assigned to or adopted by agents, and of relationships to power over decisions from the starting point to their evolution and conclusion; (3) an assessment of the interests of agents and how they develop strategies based on given resources, and rules existing and applied, with respect to their relationships and realization of those

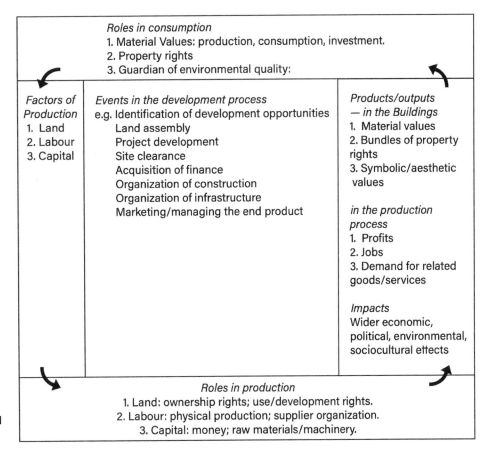

Roles in consumption
1. Material Values: production, consumption, investment.
2. Property rights
3. Guardian of environmental quality:

Factors of Production
1. Land
2. Labour
3. Capital

Events in the development process
e.g. Identification of development opportunities
  Land assembly
  Project development
  Site clearance
  Acquisition of finance
  Organization of construction
  Organization of infrastructure
  Marketing/managing the end product

Products/outputs
— in the Buildings
1. Material values
2. Bundles of property rights
3. Symbolic/aesthetic values

in the production process
1. Profits
2. Jobs
3. Demand for related goods/services

Impacts
Wider economic, political, environmental, sociocultural effects

Roles in production
1. Land: ownership rights; use/development rights.
2. Labour: physical production; supplier organization.
3. Capital: money; raw materials/machinery.

10.3

Healey's institutional model of development.

interests; and (4) a final observation within the overarching societal ideology or prevalent narratives underlying the mode of production. Such an approach was termed institutional, which meant that it was "understood as a methodological impulse to unpack these competing ways of seeing and acting [by various agents], by contextualizing them in terms of their 'frames of reference' (Werlen 1993, 112)" (Guy and Henneberry 2000, 2400).

Healey very rigorously detailed and developed the first three layers of her model in collaboration with Barrett as they extensively investigated and critiqued development projects within the strongly focused agency paradigm (Healey and Barrett 1990). However, the link which their research makes with the broader macroeconomic, social, and political structure, the fourth layer of her model, is more purely descriptive than explanatory. While this non-value-laden approach provided the flexibility "to explore, for example, the extent to which development processes have different forms" (Healey 1992, 37) pertaining to production processes, and to "be capable of application under different economic and political regimes," its non-evaluative approach is strikingly in contrast to the inherently critical function of the other analytical layers. So, while the model "made a significant contribution to research into property development" (Guy and Henneberry 2000, 2402) and is very effective in evaluating specific component features of the development process, the agents, and the relationships involved, it omitted to make a pertinent judgment on the projects' impacts on the broader community and economy, including the capital markets in which they played a substantial role, either upon completion or over subsequent years.

Alan Hooper (1992) felt that there were some difficulties in Healey's model, particularly with respect to the conflict between a proposed grand theory of an institutional model that covers all possible situations and the very local specificity of real estate development activities. Moreover, he was uneasy with the weak, purely sociological link she established between her dynamics of agencies and relationships and the theoretical economic construct, particularly related to the work of David Harvey, in which she placed her model. This latter problem in particular arises because Harvey's construct is difficult to reconcile with the mainstream format for incorporating the financial drivers and economic processes that are so obviously implicated in the urban development activity (Guy and Henneberry 2000; Derrington 2018).

Drawing on their prior work, Guy and Henneberry suggest that "the crucial influence on developers' decisions was the way in which they formulated their expectations of development values and costs, and hence profitability." Their research's discovery of three strategies for determining profit expectations were identified as (1) current price taking, (2) formal forecasting, and (3) habit-persistence based on past experience, the last being the most robust indicator (Antwi and Henneberry 1995). Guy and Henneberry (2000, 2408) concluded that "[p]rices and price elasticities are a reductionist measure of the many influences on the relations between demand and supply: this is particularly so when investors intermediate between producers and consumers."

Although empirical examinations of the phenomenon are yet to be carried out, there is evidence of "a huge herd mentality to stay in specific markets and on-brand" (Sperance 2019) that results in overcrowding and reduced profits in the most expensive markets (Beauregard 2005). Antwi and Henneberry's "habit-persistence" is not confined to individual habits or investment strategies. Sperance (2019) noted that this behavior is undertaken within a range of responsive acts for professional recognition or reputation, and he cited the remarks of a president of a real estate private equity firm: "It just sounds good. Who doesn't want to be in the top 10 [markets]?" As Derrington (2021 forthcoming) posits, this results in the direction of capital towards high-priced property types, despite their lower and less-attractive yields.

Delving further into the vagaries of decision-making, Guy and Henneberry (2000, 2408) sought to discover "how the actions of development actors are both framed by contextual factors, and serve to reshape contextual structures," and to build their exploration on the earlier work of Werlen (1993, 6), who saw "human action ... [as] an expression of sociocultural, subjective and material conditions." Viewing the development process through this lens, they incisively observed that the details of specifying materials and methods for a project are significantly influenced by the objectives of the source of capital, and that selections by homeowners are different from those of international investors.

They also addressed the demand side of the neoclassical equation by advertising to the general understanding that detailed development decisions are also influenced by the "increased awareness of the value of the workplace both as a financial cost and a source of organizational benefit" (Guy and Henneberry 2000, 2409). This emphasis on the notion of economic value to an organization in the quality of its workplace is an important reminder that development includes delivering a completed product which has a use value, and not just as a financial commodity. The recent race to enhance the work environment for creative, millennial workers is forcing developers to attend more carefully to the programmatic and design details of the white-collar workplaces they are producing. This detailed positive response to occupant needs will be shown to be an important component of the development process that was unfortunately discarded too soon after it was successfully applied in the earliest developments.

That the relational feature of the social and economic aspects of development activity raises a methodological challenge was noticed in the earlier work of Giddens's structuration theory (Giddens 1984). There is necessarily a duality of structure which links the two levels of analysis, that of agents and that of the socio-economic context within which they operate, but they should not be dichotomized since the actions of the agents also serve to change the knowledge inherent in the context itself. Later work by Steen et al. (2006) particularly focuses on the manner in which social actions of individuals will modify structures. By drawing on the strong methodological constructs of interpretative sociology, commentators incorporate a solution proposed by Jessop (1996) to study recursively the structure in its selective "strategic-relational" aspects, and the actions or behavior of agents in relation to the "structural orientation" which is adopted strategically to achieve their objectives. As a result, Guy and Henneberry (2000, 2413) posited a view of the property process as "dynamic, deeply contextual and contingent, both on the particular aims and objectives of development actors, and on a shifting market framework which may enable or constrain development strategies."

Restoring the momentum for formulating a model of the development process, Squires and Heurkens (2015) proposed a conceptual model that refers to the many formal and informal institutional formations that are involved as real estate development decisions are made. Following the suggestion of Adams and Tiesdell (2013) that an ideal model would "combine the various modal perspectives" of those previously formulated, and while admiring Healey's (1992) comprehensive model, they propose a new one with this objective. Elaborating a model proposed by Keogh and D'Arcy (1999), they sought to "embed and relate the principles of real estate development models" that have gone before, but as a comprehensive representation (Figure 10.4).

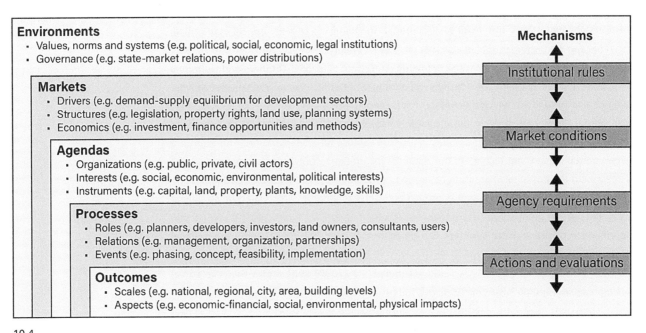

10.4

Squires and Heurkens's conceptual model for real estate development.

Squires and Heurkens (2015) relied heavily on institutional theory by regarding behavior in a group of people as being determined by regulative, normative and cognitive structures, not necessarily as a formal institution. In a way, they saw the independent acts of agency as being constrained by these structures since they are not merely formal and broadly held, but may be localized and even pertain to an individual, and therefore a wide range and nature of agency acts could influence action. Therefore, rather than considering whether the actions of agents are either conforming or non-conforming to the process's structures, they regard the many and various structures used in it as dynamically inclusive of agents' actions. As seen in the historical narrative of the beginnings of the private development process, in order to have his plans for the Covent Garden development approved, the Earl of Bedford engaged the Royal Architect, Inigo Jones, to perform the planning and design of buildings. By this, Jones established architectural features that became formal requirements for new London buildings, and the earl had acted according to the structure of moving business arrangements forward in London's political context, with which he had had prior experience.

In this model, Squires and Heurkens (2015, 578) echo Giddens's (1984) structuration theory whereby the power of the structure to enable or constrain action varies as it is altered by successful or repetitive actions that did not initially conform to it. They present their model to show "that understanding the [changes within the] institutional context of real estate development in specific territories is key to explaining how real estate development markets work." Their layered construct incorporates prior models that more definitively focused on structures and agents, often mixing the two, for example when "Agencies" incorporate "Organizations" that comprise public, private and civil actors. For this, the agent/structure interaction no longer has primacy in their description. Squires and Heurkens (2015) also describe certain dynamic "mechanisms" that work between the layers and that "determine the way real estate development is constrained (institutional rules), conditioned (market conditions), organized (agency requirements), delivered (actions), and perceived (evaluations)." These mechanisms were not those pricing/market mechanisms of neoclassical economics, but rather were arranged in such a way that each mechanism "offers opportunities to identify which institutional entities explain real estate development activities" (Squires and Heurkens 2015, 578), and this expands the possibility of adding other objectives such as the social well-being of a community in which a development is placed.

In comprehensively drawing upon earlier perspectives of the real estate development process, their work lays out in summary important factors for consideration. The idea of a dynamic mechanism that highlights the potential for influence between the layers is useful in describing the complex interaction of so many aspects of the markets, authorities, actors, and organizations. Further research might tease out the manner in which such mechanisms work, and spread them across more than just adjacent layers, for example by showing that the influence of the investor segment can be so compelling that it modulates the political environment.

Emily Ward (2018) built on Guy and Henneberry's (2000) suggestion that the social and economic aspects of property development are fundamentally interconnected, and framed her own model by interlinking structure and agency as proposed by Ball (1998) and Healey (1992), among others. Following the use of actor-network theory (ANT) by Doak and Karadimitriou (2007, 225) for interlinking political and cultural factors with social actions, Ward (2018) applied that theory to the property development process. Her model follows an iterative process through which a development project proceeds from Site Identification through to Construction and Marketing and Leasing, performed within four structures – Economic, Cultural, Legal, and Political – which both influence and are influenced by the process. On this tableau, she maps the very complex network between actors, human and non-human, on a project. Plainly, the developer is at the center of this network, which revives the Individualist Approach to the process's management as proposed by Craven (1969) and Drewett (Hall et al. 1973) and described above. Whether it is conceptually suitable for all development projects or just for a specific one is not clear, though it would appear that some actors, such as the "Rights to Light Expert," may not always be needed.

From this model and her earlier work, Ward (2016; 2018, 258) observed: "By viewing structure as comprised of human and non-human actants through an ANT lens, it is understandable why the development process is characterised by continuous change." To respond to this change, she did not necessarily propose specific guidance for actors but rather suggested that structures will be changed by actions: "It can be concluded that where structural changes cause disruption for the production-based network, sub-networks must be created so that the interests of actors can be re-aligned and solutions can be punctualised into the production-based network" (Ward 2018, 258). By this model, development projects are to be judged as to whether or not they "can adequately deal with constant change," and the developer is instructed to "measure the extent to which the interests of actors area are successfully aligned … in addition to a developments [*sic*] financial success" (Ward 2018, 258).

Perhaps because of the influence of structuralist theory on this model, it represents the social, governmental, and planning entities located within the layers as inherent "minders" or stewards of the socio-economic–environmental–physical outcomes. As in agency model of Goodchild and Munton (1985) these responsibilities are placed within the remit of legislative authorities and fail to assign any social responsibility for the outcome to the developer. It seems to be assumed that, logistically and tactically, a developer working to this model has a good understanding of its process and dynamics, and by engaging productively with local authorities can make the most suitable contributions to the public realm. To establish this productive engagement more securely, Henneberry and Parris (2013) applied a theoretical framework of "project ecologies" to complex local developments. Though adopting the given institutional structure and agency perspectives through this approach, they were able to "accommodate the heterogeneity of developers and development" (Henneberry and Parris 2013, 227). This was achieved by an empirical interrogation of the nature and quality, or "thickness," of the contacts between property developers and the many stakeholders. As a further advance for a theoretical construct of private development, their analysis through project ecologies provides an observation of the feedback or reverse impact that a development project has on the institutional forms and relationships of its milieu.

A Production Process within a Business System

This re-acknowledgment of the importance of the developer's management of the process results in a different perception, one that returns to the essential production activity. In contrast to the early approaches of sequence modeling which were sometimes devoid of connection to social or even economic contexts, Ball (1986, 158) formulated the "structure-of-provision" (SOP) model that incorporated social, legal, economic concerns, various agents, and their interdependencies as "theoretical sub-propositions."

Although this model was applauded by many scholars, unfortunately it was not extended beyond owner-occupied housing. The rising dominance of investment interests reduced attention to social concerns in the mainstream economy since there was no way of representing them in the financial models' increasingly guiding development decisions. As later models have shown, the social concern was restricted to models that emanated from a Marxist economic framework but did not have an analytical hook into the decision-making of mainstream participants.

Not only did social objectives diminish in importance, but financial drivers also pushed aside other aspects of the process, two of which are components of its production dimension. The first is attendance to the details of the product, that is, the physical features of the building. That attendance comes with a deep and rigorous understanding of its intended use. As demonstrated by Steve Jobs's extraordinary attention to endless details for the production of the iPhone, as well as with many other successful products, an investigation that leads to very specific product descriptions is fundamental to a production process. For development, this includes market research and neighborhood analysis, and the fashioning of the project's functional program and specification of spaces, layouts, amenities, and finishes. On the first private urban developments, the developers had excellent knowledge and understanding of their potential residents, since they were their social peers, and they planned their projects accordingly.

However, in the late 17th century, as in the second half of the 20th century, London and many other cities globally experienced accelerated development activity in response to overwhelming demand. With overly eager buyers, developers were relieved of the need to hone their designs or to advance the built environments of their users. "Cookie cutter" apartment buildings and bland office structures could be successful for the purpose. Additionally, the challenges to an accurate evaluation of innovative design, as described by Crosby and Henneberry (2016, 196), resulted in a reliance on "tried and trusted designs." Neither a developer, investor, nor lender will assume the additional risk of a novel design when more of the same currently popular product will suffice.

Following the boom came the bust, and developers ceased to undertake projects. As a result of that experience the financial analysis used for assessing development feasibility, or the "go/no-go" decision as it is often termed, advanced its method of calculations. A "rule of thumb" was taken up whereby the valuation on new properties was required to exceed replacement costs on a comparable property before new development would be feasible. Consequently, development activity typically does not commence until demand for space is strong, and in such conditions, it is often not necessary to give detailed attention to the quality of the product. As supply increases, a need for competitive details in the physical features of the building arises, but unfortunately this may lead to overspending on amenities and development failures. There continues to be a need for disciplined user analysis and rigorous cost-benefit analysis of building features with respect to long-term lifecycle performance in the planning stages rather than a simple response to immediate market fads.

The second important component of development activity that was neglected as a result of financial return priorities was the management of the process. The complete process is often acknowledged to be exceptionally complex and subject to continuous change as Ward (2018) described earlier. It has defied the formation of optimal organizational structures and procedural directions that have evolved for industrial corporations and professional firms, and even for the construction component of development. Management of parts of the process has adopted some practices of general project management, though generally this is rigorously undertaken only by large sophisticated entities. Often the project is guided by an entrepreneurial individual who works informally with a team, which may or may not have worked together before, and the management is rarely systematic and often subject to dissolution in weak markets.

Both of these neglected features have economic implications, but their benefit goes beyond an immediate return on investment. They require the intervention of disciplines other than finance, though there also remains a need to convert the evaluation of them into a form that can be integrated in the financial analysis. The development of buildings within the capitalist economy competes for necessary capital. It produces physical shelter that has a role in the broader economy, and it delivers financial assets for the capital markets. Fundamentally, it adds economic value to the resources of land, capital, materials, and labor, and its central analysis remains economic, so these features must have economic relevance.

In addition to economic analysis, other important aspects of the process were addressed by Graaskamp (1981). He introduced a comprehensive concept of real estate as a financial asset the value of which is derived from its essentially physical nature in a time-use dimension:

> Real estate can be defined as space delineated by man, relative to a fixed geography, intended to contain an activity for a specific period of time. To the three dimensions of space (length, width, and height), then, real estate has a fourth dimension – time for possession and benefit. This can be referred to as a space-time characteristic. The space-time concept is illustrated by the terms, apartment per month, motel rooms per night, square footage per year, and tennis courts per hour. A fundamental element in real estate is that any space-time unit has a corresponding monetary value. (Graaskamp 1981, 1)

Although he adopted political and social contexts similarly to the practice of other scholars of his time, he differed from them by regarding the economic aspects as centered on the development enterprise, or business. He embedded the financial interests of capital markets, real estate markets, municipal fees, and taxes within the interactions of three groups as they play out in the production of improvements to a site. The three interacting groups, presumably pursuing their own objectives, are the Space Consumer Group, the Public Infrastructure Group, or public realm, and the Space Production Group, that is, the developer (1981, 3). Importantly, he treated them as all deserving of what he termed economic "liquidity," and their financial inter-dynamics should be optimized to achieve a balanced outcome through the use of fees, capital transfers, taxes, and rents in response to the provision of services and "net benefits" (Figure 10.5).

Around this model he began to construct an evaluative framework that sought an optimization of the economic and social objectives pursued by the three groups. For example, and necessary to a scholarly framework, he formulated a modification of the traditional land use analysis of "highest and best use" to one of determining "best and most probable use." This advance was based on his evolving theory that recognizing development as a business activity required, beyond an analysis of a project's self-contained economic sustainability, social and public considerations that had external economic repercussions for the development project. Sadly, his progress in reformulating the model of private development practice in this more socio-economically balanced way was terminated by his untimely death, but his legacy of intellectual and progressive thinking remains compelling.

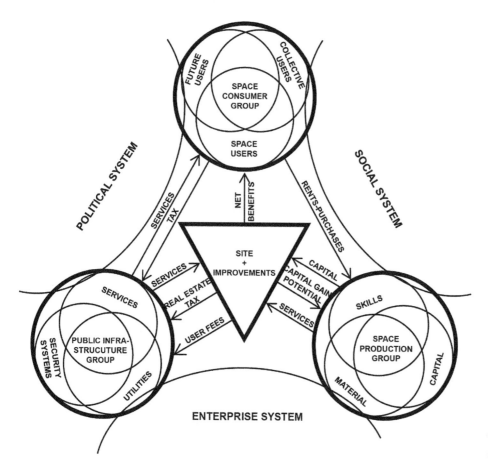

10.5

Graaskamp's model of the real estate process.

In Graaskamp's model it is not difficult to detect an overlay of Weber's (2015) view as to an excessive influence by capital markets on all three groups, or to project the possible addition of a fourth group, the Capital Markets Group, particularly given the changes in financial activities in the decades since Graaskamp's formulation. What continues to be very pertinent is that his model represents a mechanism by which all three groups are involved in the production of improvements to a site and receive benefits as a result. A Capital Markets Group would contribute the needed funds and receive the financial assets by which it does its trade.

As a mechanism for production, therefore, a development activity can recognize and respond to the "product" specifications of all the groups. The analysis focuses the process towards determining the specific features suited to users, the infrastructure (hard and soft) and revenue needs of the public realm, the financial and reputational wishes of the developer, and the competitive debt and equity products in capital markets. An efficient exercise of this analysis requires more than financial capabilities alone, and Graaskamp promoted a broader formulation of the discipline.

In the review of real estate research by Breuer and Nadler (2012), described earlier, Graaskamp (1976) was acknowledged as the first author, scholar, and teacher to produce an intordicciplinary approach to real estate. He reasoned that the body of real estate knowledge should be derived from physical sciences (architecture, soils and environmental science), behavioral sciences (sociology, demography, planning, political science, and psychology), and business administration (finance, accounting, marketing, organizational theory, management information systems, and law). These have yet to be functionally integrated, and instead remain discrete reference points for the development process.

In summary, of key importance is Guy and Henneberry's challenge to the simplistic mapping of the economic and the social by pointing out that economic behavior, while impacting social activities, is also itself molded by social constructions. This dynamic is described by Beauregard (2005) as the "thick" functional interactions in urban development in contrast to the simplistic and often erroneous "thin" market logic. Aiming to incorporate social constructions into their model, Squires and Heurkens (2015) made reference to the numerous informal and formal institutional formations, the composition of the "thickness" as development decisions are made, and identified the mechanisms by which these interact. And, seeking to construct theoretical dimensions around this understanding of the inherent relations by which the "thickness" is maintained, Henneberry and Parris (2017) apply project ecology theory.

Reframing Scholarship on the Real Estate Development Process

While research on the real estate development process is focused on formulating comprehensive production models, the field of urban theory and its associated policy implementation have observed and evaluated the results or consequences of the production process as they have materialized. However, much of urban theory study has severed connection with the mainstream economic context in which development takes place. Conversely, predominant models of development practice do not seek input from urban study other than that delivered by formal or informal institutions, and even some of the representations of those entities are not fully reflective of community feeling. This could be remedied by reference to the critical interweaving of concerns for urban form and social conditions with those of commercial interests revealed in this exploration of the origins of the private development activity. Through this, a comprehensive multifaceted theory of the development process can be constructed, one sufficiently aligned with its macroeconomic context for implementation in practice and yet adequately porous to changing insights regarding urban issues.

Chapter 11: Critique of the Private Urban Development Process

In the discussion of any established model, the element of evaluation is important even in the earliest instances of innovative activities that led to the model's establishment. Though noticeably lacking in private development activity as it continues to be practiced today, rather than merely accepting that solutions were fully formed as they evolved in early practice it is necessary to include an assessment of the processes by which needs and challenges were met, room for the possibility of alternatives, and an assessment of the consequences of adopted modes.

Towards a Framework of Evaluation

For the model of a typical economic process, such an evaluation primarily considers the product or outcome of the process. For real estate development, beyond a completed building, a critical analysis therefore focuses on the satisfaction of the occupants, the investment return metrics and also the sentiment of the community.

But an additional evaluation is required of the nature of the process itself as a socio-economic practice, not just as measured by product outcomes. For example, general development practice has been observed as being of a mode that proceeds from project to project. This may or may not affect the quality of the outcome substantially, though some variation in impact might result from the lack of operational continuity. But this approach often results in development entities not being sustained over the long term and thereby incurring the loss of corporate knowledge, the refinement of their functionality and the building of reputation. While the quality of projects may suffer to a degree, this short-termism of entities leaves a vacuum for the education and advancement of young professionals. It also misses the opportunity for the profession to consolidate best practices, to experiment with variations, and to deliver improvements to the model.

In evaluating urban real estate development activity as it is presently performed and what it produces, there are many measures. As described in the previous chapter, there are two principal categories of scholarly assessment, one made by urbanists according to social and topographical consequences, and the other by mainstream economists in terms of financial structuring and investment profitability. It appears from an examination of the process in its original emerging formulation that while these categories are seen distinctly, there was much more interdependency between them. It would be a serious error to ignore that symbiosis in achieving a full understanding of how each decision or action was compelled by the mixed objectives of both, and had consequences for both.

To achieve such an evaluation, it is proposed that a feature that has been omitted in the current dispersed ideological approaches, the production of needed functional space, be included as a relevant factor. This is not the building of square footage that is sought as speculative and iconic assets by global capital sources, nor the aesthetic triumphs of demonstrative wealth, nor the provision of community facilities that lie unused and unmaintained and only serve to remove marginal groups from integration into broader urban activity. The purpose that needs to be acknowledged is the fundamental action of producing occupiable space for use within an urban habitat.

The question as to how well, by its specific mode of practice, the real estate development activity produces the necessary settings for prosaic but fundamental urban activities is rarely raised, and the economic and social agendas that are embedded in the process's decisions and actions do not supportively advert to it. An ideologically structured assessment may be directed to issues of whether a certain space provision may disrupt an existing socio-economic group or provide particular social amenities, or to the extent of the investment return it may achieve; but it is done without any profound scrutiny of the actual production of the space by which are delivered the attendant communal consequences or financial assets. To be suitably comprehensive in the role of private development, it must be remembered that just as the objective of the government is to provide the connection for communal use, the urban developer's primary purpose is to provide usable space for urban centers to function.

That the current private development model first emerged when there was a shortage of housing providers to meet the rapidly growing demand in 17th-century London was not a coincidence: it arose in response to that compelling functional need. This predicates that the production of shelter for essential activity was a significant purpose for early activity, though it may have been ancillary to even the earliest developers' motives. Wealth creation was the driving force behind their innovative activities, but in support of that, the production of the urgently needed residential space was the content of the activity, its objective, and the process by which the motive was satisfied. The significance of this production objective, however, has been diminished in scholarly discussion and evaluation, and also remains neglected in any rigorous process of professional self-assessment by developers themselves.

This establishes the basic fact that the total worth of a development project includes a functional benefit for the urban community, if pragmatically and not just ideologically understood, though that may not have been the motivation or even the conscious intention of the stakeholders involved. At the same time, this does not substitute for other features of social benefit, or necessarily match needs such as housing equity, community retention, and educational advancement similar in nature if not in kind, that similarly rate as significant elements in an evaluation of the worth of a development project. Nor should it disadvantage the investment value, if the asset is properly considered within its broad economic context of the functioning community. Assessing the fulfillment of those various objectives for urban development is not subsumed and lost within this framework of the real estate production process. Rather, with the elucidation of a production process previously opaque and seemingly arcane, the intentions for this project are provided with valid structures for clarifying expected details, tracing and monitoring their creation, and evaluating their successful accomplishment alongside each other, within an optimal resolution of the whole.

The Objectives of the Real Estate Development Process

The objectives recognizable as fundamental to urban development activity by the end of the 17th century were three: achieving a competitive economic return on assets comprising land and capital, producing habitation suitable to the needs of intended occupants, and attending to the public realm of the project. Their pursuit may have been driven by different motivations, and the degree of interest afforded each may have varied, but all three objectives were present.

Fundamental to the origins and definition of these objectives was the dynamic of emergent capitalism that drove the flow of population to London, created a voracious appetite for the accumulation of financial assets, and imbued urban shelter with economic and social implications. This occurred within the historical context of England's solid foundations of governance and property law being advanced within a period of philosophical and scientific explorations. As a result, strong social traditions melded with rising democracy and tempered the formulation of the objectives to be ideologically composite, similar to the men who pursued them and the populace they served and satisfied.

A Hierarchy in the Importance of Objectives

Significantly, in the early process of urban development its objectives were not seen as having equal importance. They had, and have continued to have, a distinct hierarchy. The first in rank, the financial objective, was substantially the most compelling as the appetite for the accumulation of investment assets rose, and it persists because capital markets substantially influence urban decisions. The second objective in degree, the production of shelter, was met with some important innovations of architectural form, though mostly implemented by the unevaluated adoption of traditional construction techniques, and surprisingly little advancement in methods or management. The last, the social objective, although it was inspiringly if also pragmatically addressed at the outset, diminished significantly in importance over following centuries.

These categories bear some relation to the three groups identified by Graaskamp (1981) as fundamental to contemporary real estate development: Space Consumer Group (#1 users), Space Production Group (#2 creators of the asset/s) and Public Infrastructure Group (#3 urban impact). Contrastingly, Graaskamp places the "Consumer" or utilitarian function first, possibly due to the adoption of the demand-driven rationale in neoclassical economics. Certainly, the production of habitation is the most physical and obvious outcome, and has served the community's needs well. But history has shown that even the earliest instances of private urban development were primarily driven by the economic objective of maximizing the financial returns on land and capital resources, and the provision of habitation was merely the vehicle to that end.

Both resources, land and capital, have a history of subjection to human employment, land to produce goods by which to live, and capital to transfer economic value efficiently. In the Middle Ages, housing was created through a combination of both, whereby capital supported improvements to land to provide the shelter necessary to work the land and produce more capital. While this interaction served the utilitarian function of agrarian production by housing communities, its economic and social concerns were balanced. However, in the transforming metropolis of 16th- and 17th-century London, the concept of capital accumulation took hold and land was then considered in terms of its potential for contribution to that new goal. The objective of building shelter altered from merely satisfying a utilitarian need to that of maximizing the economic potential of the land on which it stood. From that time on, the results of urban development tended more towards assessment in terms of capital achievement rather than the provision of built form.

Through this and other forms of application of the new capitalism, it was understood that capital, including land, was no longer merely a means of transferring economic value but was a resource needed by many for a variety of activities. In its own right it could command recompense for its use by way of debt interest or investment return. When it was interwoven with land use, the objectives were extended from its utilitarian use to financial use, not just as a component of broad economic production but also as a capital asset.

Thus, within the economic climate of that time, maximizing land resources meant not only using them as they were but also actively changing land's use to what would achieve its highest economic return. Further, when capital was needed for improvements to land, not only was the maximum economic use of the land an objective, but that capital was also required to achieve a maximum return for its diversion from other investments. This doubly charged economic objective of land development therefore dominates the process and subordinates the utilitarian value of the mere production of shelter.

This economic driver of real estate development is still dominant, and is even thought to have become exacerbated since the middle of the 20th century (Piketty 2014) so that it has inhibited other important objectives of urban development (Weber 2015; Derrington 2019). Access to both resources, urban land and development capital, has been competitive and only those urban projects that extract the highest economic return from both have succeeded. In this way, maximizing financial returns constitutes the most important objective of private real estate development and remains so while this economic context continues unmodified.

Developers place some importance on Graaskamp's first group, the users. This is of necessity to enable maximum revenues from this primary source through fees, rental rates, or sales prices. However, other than this they generally do not give full attention to understanding and providing for the needs of users beyond immediately known solutions. This became apparent very early in the history of the industry, when typically developers were most active in times of overwhelming demand and the nuances of product details were overlooked by desperate residents.

It was not always so. The Earl of Bedford and the Earl of Southampton knew well their intended neighbors of their Covent Garden and Bloomsbury schemes within which they themselves resided, and they sought to provide adequately for those neighbors' needs both initially and over the life of their buildings. Later, developers built their new houses and moved on, unconcerned as to how their residences fared other than insofar as they might attract the initial tenants or buyers. Their interest in the functional needs of potential residents was superficial, and their programmatic formats followed readily duplicated solutions. The early importance given by Bedford and his architect Inigo Jones to exploring improvements in the built environment to accommodate shifting domestic needs and lifestyles, and thereby producing better shelter, was demoted in the hierarchy of private developers' considerations.

In much the same way, the objective of contributing positively to the public realm was initially important, but it was soon allocated an inferior third place in the model. At first, the impact upon the public realm was not a matter of choice but was fundamental to the placement of a project within an urban system of streets, infrastructure, and social amenities. Some early developers made much needed and delightful contributions through the construction of piazzas, gardens, and churches. Their motives may have been mixed, for although some did so through their sense of social responsibility, others complied with social *desiderata* in order to obtain necessary approvals for their projects. The Covent Garden project was a successful combination of both.

There were a few other contributions to the public realm on later developments, though they were usually driven to maximize revenue potential. An example was Barbon's attractive arch at the end of his Essex Street project which, for its upper-middle class residents, blocked the view of untidy wharves. But most developers built as much saleable square footage as they could, and were unwilling to sacrifice any space to public amenity other than when required by the municipal authorities. When it was imposed, such a requirement was regarded by the developer as a cost without any apparent offsetting economic benefit, and the opportunity to make a positive contribution to the community was relegated to a low-level objective, if not ignored altogether.

Therefore, in the persisting formulation of the private development model, there is little rigorous consideration of economic benefits that might result for the project, and investor returns, from the provision of amenities in the public realm. There is no inclusion of such attributes in the financial evaluation or the calculative processes commonly used in development feasibility decisions. The justification for including these features is usually made in qualitative terms, with little influence over the "cold, hard numbers." The question therefore arises: were the earliest developers, such as Bedford who delivered Covent Garden, incorrect in their assessment of the economic importance of contributing to the public interest? Or, as will be further discussed in this critique of the model, was the persisting formulation that diminishes this aspect the result of its jostling with other features such as the optimal holding period, the distance of financial interests, mistaken assessments of buildings' economic life cycles, and other complexities of the process?

With the economic interests of investors subordinating consideration of the product quality for occupants and the positive contribution to the public realm, the model's hierarchy of objectives was crystallized within decades of the beginning of private real estate development activity and extensively adopted. The imbalance is a formative flaw in the model and requires rectification if the activity is to satisfy the broad array of stakeholders, particularly urban residents and neighborhood communities, who are voicing their dissatisfaction to some political effect. Developers themselves would also like to deliver commendable projects, but need a useful, comprehensive, and reliable framework for evaluation of their projects and guidance for improvement.

Satisfying Objectives

The extant hierarchy of objectives will be useful for narrative direction, though such direction will forgo a commitment to that hierarchy's inherent value system. While the broad categories of financial return, shelter production, and community impact set the conceptual frame, arising within each are various components or sub-objectives that more substantially draw the attention of the process, depending upon the circumstantial context. For example, engagement with the public realm in respect of community impact might be critical in a residential neighborhood but less important in a CBD area. Security for debt products might be more critical in strained economic conditions. Similarly, the processes employed to meet objectives will vary. However, this evaluation will have broad application since it seeks to establish not a prescriptive framework for development activity, but rather a theoretical construct within which a developer takes responsibility for a detailed definition of intentions and procedures appropriate to the circumstances, which will always be unique for real estate.

Financial Objectives

The financial objectives of the process have multiple dimensions. The first developers sought to maximize the economic return of their resources by putting their land and capital together in a production designed to derive more than the sum of its parts. Craftsmen contributed their building skills with the objective of being compensated satisfactorily. Others who were confident in their business skill cast about for land and capital for a production that compensated for both and rewarded the dealmaker. Alternatively, those with capital pursued investment assets as part of the built form in the hope of returns that exceeded alternative opportunities. For a community that was intent on improving its conditions, its financial aim was the development's contribution of some components towards that better outcome.

These were all facets of the production of an economic good and the investment asset that coalesced as financially based objectives in the early decades of the private development process, and remain relevant today. An evaluation must consider the model's performance with respect to these objectives at that time, and also in the model's continuance.

With reference to various scholarly models of the financial dynamic, and cutting across various theoretical perspectives, the most common components of the financial objectives are funding of the production activity and the creation of tradable assets, which together draw from both debt and equity. Added to this, it is necessary to recall that development activity is performed by a business entity, as included in Graaskamp's (1981) model, and consideration must be given to its liquidity, its profitability on each project, and its ongoing viability as an enterprise. Satisfaction of financial objectives entails accomplishing the required outcomes in these three dimensions, the product, the asset and the developing entity.

Funding the Development Process

Examination of even the earliest attempts to obtain control of urban land reveals the inherent economic complexity in this initial step of the process. Except in cases of inheritance, the purchase of a developable site usually required a large capital sum or a commitment to a lengthy ground lease. The costs of constructing improvements also required a commitment of a large capital sum in advance. As such sums were usually beyond the resources of an intended user, a developer would take responsibility for upfront funding. However, since that was usually also beyond even the developer's personal resources, for even the Earl of Bedford's resources were strained on his Covent Garden project, external investments were usually needed.

When development funds are sought in the capital marketplace, the compensation that must be paid, in terms of interest rate or investment returns, is determined in accordance with the competitive cost of capital. Importantly, and not always fully appreciated, is that the funding requirement is not necessarily related to the product, though its economic proposition tries to be competitive with alternative investments. Many developers of the earliest times, and developers today, propose a funding need derived from their vision for a project, such as an architectural icon, without taking into account the required investment returns of capital markets. Urbanists, meanwhile, decry the influence of capital markets when funded development is not able to achieve the urban outcome they desire. For an urban project, therefore, it is incumbent upon the developer to resolve this tension between the capital needs to produce a satisfactory outcome for the inhabitants and community and the prevailing demands of the capital sources.

An additional friction in the model in meeting its financial objectives is that the built structure itself is not the actual investment asset, since, as it has been explained, it is the lease commitment and/or the sale that provides the investment return. It is the appeal to tenants or purchasers that is critical to meeting the financial objectives. The task of the developer is to sufficiently explore and understand the features of the building that will most appeal to the intended occupants or owners, though these are not usually fully identified at the outset. Usually, the developer resorts to broad market averages and the use of existing comparable solutions, rather than seeking more specific details and improving upon prior solutions. From this, the project's functional specifications are communicated to architects and other consultants and contractors, and the building is constructed. By doing this, the developer has focused on reproducing a recognizable physical form rather than fully examining the value proposition sought by tenants or buyers. Recently, this fracture between the physical form and allocation of financial value to attributes of their desired spatial construct is being bridged by rigorous data collection and analysis of occupants and their behavior. Google, for example, continually tweaks its internal spatial arrangements and features to seek optimal occupant behavior. The co-working entrepreneur, WeWork, also employed technology to provide feedback and direction on the details of its workplaces.

Further, urban development delivers a product that comprises a lasting asset, the land, and a consumption product, the building, that is occupied. With time and use it inevitably depreciates to be no longer habitable and therefore of no consumption value. In early developments, the lease of the building had a term equivalent to the ground lease, so that all that remained at the end was the ground, ready for a new building and new leases. But because building materials and structure became more resilient, and the term of their habitability extended beyond the ground lease period, rather than be rebuilt many structures were substantially upgraded, and were offered on a new lease. This introduced a confusion about real estate: the building was regarded as a long-lasting asset, not particularly distinguished from the non-depreciating land. The financial analysis allocated a reversionary value to the building as well as the land, and when ownership of land and building is combined, the reversionary value is a composite. This has led to a calculative method of unrealistically and incessantly extending the life of the building, in which the anticipated capital expenditure is estimated only for upgrading and some structural rectification. However, the recent admission of obsolescence in some high-rise office buildings, and the surprising decisions to fully replace them, challenges that presumed infinite life. Ultimately, the fundamental understanding in the earliest development activity, and the economic calculations that regarded buildings as deteriorating products, holds true.

The early funding of these privately built structures adopted some of the new capitalist methods for producing other consumption goods: the construction costs were covered by capital amounts that were recovered and rewarded by the rental payments of occupants through the period of consumption. However, rather than merely producing identical goods, the uniqueness of each building, even if just in terms of its fixed location, and the substantial variation in pricing, added the requirement for constant and rigorous evaluation of the changing needs and financial decisions of consumers. Further, the different economic features of the lasting value of the land and the temporal nature of the building upon it result in a complex and often obfuscated analytic process when combined in single ownership. And finally, the source of the new capital for private development projects extended from being that of the landowner and/or developer to include uninvolved, passive investors participating in the capital market with its own dynamic usually unrelated to urban building. As a composite funding structure of various commercial intentions, it has sufficed through the centuries, though the inherent frictions often result in problems that might be overcome with a more fully resolved funding construct.

Debt

The form of mortgage loan used for completed property was unsuitable in its support security for debt on a development project, and so such a lender required other forms of security than one that was attached to the building under production. Therefore, the loans on early developments were made on a personal basis, as for other nascent commercial activities in early modern London. This placed full liability on that developer and all his other assets, rather than generally being restricted to the property asset itself through the incorporation of the borrowing entity and shielding of beneficiaries. This practice of bearing personal liability during development, in contrast to its effective replacement by the mortgage security on an operating property, continues today, practically without relief for smaller entities.

Sometimes executed leases were offered as collateral for construction funding, and if the land was owned it could be mortgaged as security. Barbon often amassed necessary development funds by having building leases signed early by potential residents and then using them as security for a loan. In this he was a forerunner of the current practice of using the commitment by a major or "anchor" tenant in a proposed development to provide a construction lender with some assurance of debt repayment. The quality of the project over the long term was still at risk, however, since this funding structure enabled the developer to contractually transfer economic responsibility for the building onto the new owner of the lease, and thereby immediately be released from adverse consequences. The regularity of lawsuits against Barbon for his poor-quality workmanship, though usually dismissed by the application of contract law, provide evidence of the development model's inability to suitably bind decision-makers in the process to responsibility for enduring outcomes.

Equity

Within the funding of the new development projects, the evolution of the structure of equity versus debt was complex. Because of many features of its production, its uniqueness, its protracted time period, the quantum of capital needed, and the deferral of the crystallization of any value until completion, even the risk taken on solely by equity during the construction period was difficult to ascertain. Aligning with that equity the potential change of ownership and profits between the development and operating phases was also new and commercially unique. Consequently, the process of resolving the role of equity in the private development model resulted in certain embedded features that might be questioned today.

The concept of external equity capital was just in formation in 16th- and 17th-century London as ownership structures changed from that of sole proprietorship to include partnerships and eventually joint-stock companies. The extension of these concepts to the ownership of a project under development was challenging, given the lack of investor engagement in the production activity that would be typical of a partnership structure. Specifically the dynamic of its production process, in contrast to other traditionally long-term investments, required real estate development funding to conform to two principles: first, all the capital and earnings on it were to be distributed at the end of the venture, catalyzed by the sale to an occupant or subsequent investor; and secondly, in the absence of any interim income, the sooner the projected return of capital and its earnings through monetization of the completed project could be made, the more attractive was the investment. This established the foundational economic arrangement of equity in the private development model such that it typically be recouped as a lump sum upon construction completion, or shortly thereafter, rather than over a protracted operating period, and thereby qualified it as a short-term investment rather than one having the strategic nature of longer-term options.

In these features, for investors at the time, real estate development differed substantially from alternatives such as joint-stock companies, trading, mining, and proto-industrial production. However, some aspects, such as the short-term expectation of a singular repayment and reward, were embraced by rising financial entrepreneurs such as Barbon who made the most of the rapid recycling of capital. For traditional landowners and investors in real property, on the other hand, while accepting the interim lack of liquidity, the speculative risk of relying on an ultimate transaction with an unknown party for repayment of capital probably defied their full understanding and economic evaluation given analytical methods of the time. Fortunately for development projects towards the end of the 17th century, London's vibrant commercial markets had cycles where excess capital was available. There was also widespread enthusiasm for new ventures, and funding was easily obtained. Unfortunately, however, when capital was not so plentiful, the allocation to property development was rapidly curtailed. This above-average vulnerability to capital markets continues for development financing today.

Within this dynamic of production and associated capital features, in turn, equity capital affected decision-making regarding many aspects of the physical product and its place in the neighborhood. For example, both the speedy exit of capital, and its dependency on a speculative market-based transaction, tended to direct expenditure to physical features which made a compelling first impression, though may not perform well over the building's lifecycle. In an example of this, a number of Barbon's houses presented well for immediate leasing and sale of the lease, but quickly exhibited structural failures for the occupants. A modern example is the choice of building cladding that is striking when new but may require expensive mainte-nance. In addition to the resultant operational flaws, these development decisions may also impact successive financial interests such that equity returns for the long-term investor in the completed building will be diminished by structural deterioration or high maintenance costs. So, even the respective equity investors in the sequence of development and operation of the building may have conflicting ambitions in this complex process of creating and maintaining the urban built fabric.

Particularly caught in these trade-offs to serve differing equity objectives is the developer. The "promote" reward offered by the equity that funds the production process is greatest if the costs are minimized and the sale price upon completion is maximized. However, the incentives for a developer who intends to continue to engage in the industry after completion of a project are based on longer-term assessments. The developer's reputation suffers and there is a threat to the continuity of the general enterprise in any failure in meeting the objec-tives of both equity investors.

Further, since equity investors usually depart quickly from association with the project, there is no value to them by contributing to the betterment of the community. Barbon's lack of long-term participation in physical contribution or funding for maintenance at Red Lion Square was an example. For an urban project, the provision of a street frontage and public interface that offers amenities and advances the neighborhood will benefit the pro-ject itself over the longer term. These may seem to be relatively minor considerations, but they are examples of the unresolved complexities for the equity component of the private development model.

In summary, the most difficult challenges for the early developers was obtaining the fund-ing critical for the construction phase, ensuring that it was sufficient despite site and process unknowns, and relying on its continuance as capital markets changed. That these continue to be so indicates the need for further refinement of the business model.

Further, it provokes the question as to why the industry has not yet adequately resolved the funding problem, given the sophisticated advances in capital structuring for other indus-tries, and even new capital structures for real estate such as securitized debt and REITs usu-ally only applicable to operating buildings. The risks for both the developer and any lender or capital provider during the period of construction remain surprisingly unmitigated, with many failures on development projects relating to funding. Improvement of insurance coverage against the risks, or the more egregious forms of risks, might offer some solution, particu-larly if provided on an industry-wide, co-operative basis. But the production process and its management procedures might also benefit by the application of advances in operations management enhanced by technology. The capital structure is at the heart of the private development model but remains in need of improvement for the objectives of both equity and debt sources.

Funding the Longer-term Investment Asset
Though raising capital for their projects was challenging for the early developers, the pros-perity of London's commercial activity in the later part of the 17th century led to widespread

enthusiasm for the ownership of rental real estate. As at least two historians, Baer (2011) and Harding (2007), have discovered, those who became building landlords came from a broad range of society, including aristocrats, gentry, lawyers, merchants, and many enterprising commoners, and the prospect of a more egalitarian ownership of buildings, in contrast to land, seemed possible.

Once a building was constructed and fit for income production through occupancy, it became a favored target for the investment of capital. The acquisition was often funded from a variety of sources, usually through a combination of equity and debt, though sometimes with many tiers of risk exposure, and this formed the total funding package, also known as the capital stack. Though this financial structuring occurred after the development project was complete, its extensive activity and resulting market information regarding property valuations had an important impact on the funding of the development activity.

The loss of many records on early projects such as Covent Garden, and a less rigorous summation and analysis of expenditure at that time, make it difficult to compare total development costs with the market value of completed buildings, as profitability would be assessed today. The performance metrics of investments were recorded and discussed in terms of total revenues, as they competed with alternative income producing assets. Immediate revenue from completed and successful urban development projects has been described as substantial by Beckett (1986, 281): "In the 1660s the Bedford's Covent Garden property brought in ground rents of £1,500 a year." When capital was contributed to the construction activity, there would also be a comparison of returns on that capital with returns from other lending activities at interest rates of 4% or 5%, or the anticipated dividends from company stocks that were traditionally in the range of 5%–6%.

Critical to the formulation of this model had been an advance of real estate from just its primitive functional role as shelter to include its historical role as a repository of wealth, but which in modern times was reconstituted as a liquid and tradable investment asset. To describe this within current economic concepts, the financial value expressed in its price extended beyond its use as habitation in the macroeconomic production system to include its value as a wealth measurement and as enabling speculative trading. The added dimension of being a recognized, tradable and relatively safe investment asset provided an overlay of economic utility. This enlarged its array of potential capital sources beyond those interested only in its rental stream in order to include those who sought valuation arbitrage and speculation in changing economic conditions. This was advantageous to developers then, and still is, in channeling more capital to the purchase of the completed buildings, enabling retrospective payment of development costs.

In a further distancing of its value according to its functional use as habitation, in the buoyant investment trading markets of late 17th-century London real estate offered the unusual bifurcated return components of annual income and speculative value appreciation upon sale. Since investments in real estate could be compared in a variety of dimensions, such as annual income, annual return, and capital gains or profits from appreciation, with many other investment possibilities, and because these composite return metrics were estimated with optimism, real estate performed very attractively in the new capital markets. Its capability in this respect continues, and as noted by Weber (2015, 62): "Given the [historical] barriers to liquidity in real estate markets, the extensive and global integration of the financial and property sectors should be viewed as a tremendous accomplishment that reconciles fast-moving financial flows with locally situated built environments."

While offering a competitive advantage within capital markets, very early in the development process these high-level investment features substantially influenced the form of analytical decision-making, particularly with respect to returns for investors through speculative appreciation. Investment capital sources applied two separate and unique criteria to real estate evaluation, and these influenced the nature, capital structure, and profitability outcome of development projects:

1. According to market cycles, they favored certain asset types, which at one time was housing for the upper and middle classes and today are iconic office buildings and luxury condominiums (Derrington 2019).
2. They applied a form of asset valuation, based on trading markets, to the anticipated completed building and, based on that form of spot pricing, determined the amount of capital, debt, and equity which would be made available to the developer. Estimations of anticipated value over a longer period, such as made for proto-industrial or mining companies, were not calculated.

Earlier sources of debt and equity had been more simply focused on the completed building's contractual rental revenue stream, which not only provided the cash to repay the loan and its capital costs but also could be used as security for it. As calculative methods advanced within the emerging capitalist economy, the analysis of a property's value for a transaction or as security collateral incorporated concepts used in the asset trading market, and the trend of value determination relative to a specific trading instance became pervasive. And, the real estate industry continues to favor so-called short-cut methods, such as Income Capitalization, in the general discussion of valuation.

Further advances, much later in the 19th century, in the valuation of commercial enterprises produced the discounted cash flow (DCF) model and the analytic methods of real estate also adopted this construct for its valuation as an investment asset. Often, it is used as a longer method of value determination, proposed as a more rigorous alternative to the income capitalization calculation, though the two continue in regular parlance. Though the DCF model does overcome the fallibility of the spot pricing nature of the latter, it presents a further weakness that continues to be accepted probably as a result of the early complexities of real estate values as the first development projects occurred.

This questionable methodological feature pertains to the DCF component called the residual value. For goods production since the Industrial Revolution, this related specifically to the ongoing productivity of the company's assets, that is the production equipment, with the expectation that it would eventually wear out and have a residual value of zero or as scrap metal. Though well suited to the industrial era, this concept is now being challenged in its use for technology companies where the life cycle of assets, usually technology patents, is more complex. And, as this historical exploration has shown, the life cycle of real estate assets was complicated by the combination of the deteriorating asset of the building with the everlasting asset of the land. The presentation of the development model in the prior chapter pointed out that when the DCF model is applied to real estate it assumes an ongoing life if not appreciation of the building structure, as well as the land, as it proceeds through transactions. The ease with which the diminishing returns on development improvements could be masked by land appreciation resulted in the broad adoption of this mode of pricing justification by private urban developers touting the value of their projects.

Despite recent challenges arising from the increasing obsolescence of even 20th-century buildings, the presumption of a building's eternal life, with some expenditure of capital on upgrading, continues to be relied on as a rigorous calculative concept. Further, the residual valuation that is estimated at the end of a holding period to which the DCF calculation is applied, is based on the short-cut income capitalization method often using an overly optimistic *capitalization rate*. That this residual valuation has even more impact on the valuation estimation for shorter holding periods, has exacerbated the potential for error with respect to this component. In turn, this has encouraged the higher investment returns achieved by short holding periods, and as a further consequence, has enabled entities traditionally with longer-term strategies to participate in development projects. An example of this is the calculation that can be made by an institutional fund to offset the high risk of the development phase with the high return, though more moderate risk, of a short, stabilized post-development holding period of only 5–7 years, with numerous transactions of this nature occurring between 2017 and 2020.

As an additional consequence of adopted calculative practices, the formulation of the capital contributions to development projects are impacted by unresolved issues regarding capital returns on operating properties. Specifically, the controversy pertains to when the return *of* the investment capital, including additional amounts contributed for capital expenditure in building upgrades, is achieved, as distinct from receiving the investment return *on* capital. Technically it is understood that the latter returns occur after the contributed capital is returned. However, common discussion of the investment performance of operating properties includes metrics such as yield or cash-on-cash. These metrics are based on the comparison of annual net income to the capital base, either as a composite or just for the equity portion. From the net income, there is no priority given to the return of capital, or clarification as to which portion of the yield or cash-on-cash should be apportioned to return *of* capital and which to the investment return *on* the capital. The general use of the metric treats income as fully allocated to the measurement of the latter, and neglects consideration of the former. The underlying and mistaken assumption, or presumption, is that the return of capital occurs upon sale at the end of the investment period.

This conceptual error has arisen probably for many reasons; however, this historical exploration of the origins of the development activity has elucidated complexities that may have laid the foundation for mistaken assessments that were embedded in the calculative methodology. Initially, there was a clear distinction between the lasting value of land and the deteriorating building. Retaining its value, or even gaining, the capital used to acquire land could generally be retrieved upon its subsequent sale, with the rental revenues of a ground lease providing the annual investment return or yield. In contrast, the capital invested in the construction of a building must be recouped, along with an investment return, from the rent paid by residents, in protracted annual amounts through the life of the building. However, as buildings lasted longer, shorter supply often increased their rents and values during their life, therefore adding an element of price appreciation through transactions against the depreciation from age and wear. Therefore, the anticipated amortization of construction costs was achieved more rapidly, and additional profits were provided by the longevity. Additionally, the ownership of real estate altered from being the often-distinct ownership of land versus the structure in early modern London to that of a composite ownership of land and building. This negated the need to distinguish between the value of land and building upon sale, and the appreciating worth of the land might mask the deterioration of the building and provide the full return of capital contributed for both land and building. This removed the need to amortize the cost of construction during the holding period and presented the annual cash flow as fully attributable to investment returns.

For the development process, this analytical approach to determining real estate returns enhances the investment appeal of the projects. The valuation of a completed project, at its stabilized occupancy, is calculated according to the application of the capitalization rate, a return metric derived from the marketplace and not clearly inclusive of construction cost amortization. As such, the outcome is higher than it would be if cost amortization were taken into account, and the excess over development cost results in more profits. However, undertaking a longer-term valuation that included market fluctuations as well as building deterioration, necessary capital cost, and ultimate obsolescence or uninhabitability, would probably reveal a lower worth of the completed development project. This, of course, is not encouraged by private urban developers.

The concepts of financial analysis that have been employed by the evolving private urban development model have provided a gradual advancement in complexity, though they fundamentally continue the early combination of well-located land leveraged in value by improvements. The calculative practices adopted successive financial tools of the broad commercial markets facilitated the acceptance of real estate as an investment asset, but some mistaken concepts persist unchallenged, as yet.

Developer Liquidity

Although development's driving economic aim was always to maximize the return on resources such as land and investment capital, when the process was underway even the earliest developers realized the overriding importance of retaining the financial liquidity of their own business. For the completion of a project, access to sufficient capital at the appropriate times is a basic requirement, especially given the risks associated with expending large amounts of capital and the possibility of underestimation and poor cash management during the production process. A critical shortfall of funds at the moment of need was the most common reason for the financial failure of development projects during the 17th century, as it is today. Bedford soon knew that he did not have the necessary capital resources to fund all of the buildings in his project, so he included other developers. Southampton elected to follow a less capital-intensive approach by offering ground leases to developers and for residents to fund their own construction, and St Albans monetized his asset as soon as possible, preferring to avoid the risks of illiquidity during the risky construction phase. In contrast, Barbon provided numerous examples of project failure due to illiquidity. Graaskamp has identified liquidity as a requirement of principal concern, not just for a developer but also for other participants – including consultants, the construction contractor and subcontractors, sales or leasing agents, the long-term building owner, and the eventual occupants.

As will be seen later, the methods for monitoring construction performance were improved as the private development process expanded, but sometimes these had the unfortunate consequence of overlooking the liquidity of entities supplying the materials or performing the building work. This want of focus on liquidity throughout the operational network and across the entire production period has surprisingly remained a flaw in the business model.

Financial contingency is fundamentally present in human enterprise within a capitalist economy, but the more advanced processes of economic activity have developed detailed methodologies for estimating it and arranging for its economic accommodation. In recent times, the production of Apple iPhones has not been hindered by any want of funding, for example. Statistically rigorous models of prediction, coupled with the complex allocation of financial responsibility, will substantially ensure a continuation of funding. It is to be acknowledged that urban development is not a standardized, repeated process, as in the production of iPhones, and its vulnerability to external and novel circumstances tends more to resemble that of agrarian production. However, much of the process is performed traditionally and has substantial precedent, and with improved data collection there is the potential for better prediction of the incidence and quantum of costs and project delays.

Some larger development firms have internally set up these tools, but the industry in general resists sharing information, which would make rigorous management more broadly possible. At present, only insurance companies have sufficient access to information for such a system, and, sound and efficient though the insurance industry may be, it seems ineffective and unnecessarily expensive to leave such risks to be calculated and protected by that conglomerate. Although the methods of insurance actuaries and the nature of their subject may not be the same as the urban development activity, the degree of complexity and contingency that they can accommodate shows what can be done. The development financial model needs to be extended beyond its "rule of thumb" allowance for contingencies and plan for and meet budgets more accurately.

These observations do not imply that the liquidity of a development project is just a matter of financial analysis or project management, which will be discussed later. It also involves relationships between various participants in the process, particularly the developer and external sources of capital.

The Social Aspects of the Financial Needs

In accordance with the evaluative framework established, to achieve a better integration of the social and economic concerns of urban real estate development the "social roles of these economic agents" should be considered.

Real estate development is often viewed as one of the more unfortunate consequences or engines of capitalism, bringing with it a variety of social ills such as egregious profit-making, physical destruction of a community as a cohesive social entity, or urban economic inequality, to name just some. Although it is often coincident with these problematic conditions, it does not necessarily mean that it is directly causal of them. More often, they result from many contemporaneous urban factors and socio-economic dynamics such as urban policy and planning, social mores, legal structures, and the vagaries of global capital markets. In an examination of urban conditions, Storper and Scott (2016, 1117) warned that "... we must distinguish between phenomena that occur in cities but are not generated by urbanization processes as such, and phenomena that are legitimately elements of cities in the sense that they play an active role in defining the shape and logic of urban outcomes." Though undoubtedly playing a role in these outcomes, the development process should not be regarded as either the harbinger or the pure manifestation of capitalism.

Rather, through this examination, the formulation of its business model is shown to be inherent in the flourishing of Western commercial enterprise at the time of its birth, and assisted that economic growth by providing occupiable space in urban centers and also introducing new investment products. It has also been shown that some of the earliest developers gave priority to social concerns and contributed important amenities such as open space, churches, water and drainage systems and streets, as well as attempting newfound attention to socio-economic composition. Urban real estate continues to be a productive and critical component of the broader socio-economic system, and a considerable amount of neoclassical economic theory holds that social concerns are integral to its objectives, though the persisting debate involves how to address those social concerns and their weighting versus financial aspects. Recent attention by corporations to this dimension, often referred to as environment, social and governance (ESG) issues, and increasing research on its quantifying factors indicate that it is gaining attention.

Reviewing 17th-century London society from a hundred years later, Adam Smith rarely used the term "capitalism." Rather, he discussed the division of labor, improvements in the efficiency and quality of production, transactional pricing, and the minimization of costs, all as part of an economic system for a society in which the developer's creation of habitation played a part. He also considered that economic gains from real estate were partly due to good national and municipal governance, which justified taxation proportional to such gains, in effect, a giving-back to the society that facilitated the benefit. In *The Wealth of Nations*, he wrote:

> Ground-rents, so far as they exceed the ordinary rent of land, are altogether owing to the good government of the sovereign, which, by protecting the industry either of the whole people, or of the inhabitants of some particular place, enables them to pay so much more than its real value for the ground which they build their houses upon ... (Smith 1994, 909)

From another important socio-economic perspective, Karl Marx, also reflecting on the new face of modern London, considered the workers' alienation from land that occurred with increasing agrarian production to be at the heart of its changed mode, and saw it as capitalistic exploitation by those with capital which extended to problems in urban London. From his viewpoint, the ownership of the means of production, in this case, land, became the nexus between the society and its capital flows. The general concept of land ownership, usage and access rights did change in 16th- and 17th-century England, and particularly in metropolitan London. But, as it has been explained with respect to the use of ground leases by aristocrats who were committed to continuing ownership of their land, housing was more affordable than it might have been if only freehold land were available. Moreover, some of those landowners demonstrated an innate responsibility to the public realm that has not persisted in times of a more democratic distribution of land, such as in America. Some adverse impacts of new economic structures on social conditions will be discussed in more detail in the review later of the community impact of the new model.

At the nub of his investigation of socio-economic interrelationships within real estate development activities in growing London, Grassby (1999, 7) noted: "Since urbanization is virtually synonymous with civilization and with the market, capitalism has long been associated with towns rather than the countryside. The high population density and the social fluidity of cities is thought by some to have favored the division of labor and economic individualism." Certainly, the economic advances and social fluidity of London in those times caused more people to seek and afford housing, and created the demand that was addressed by early developers. In their innovative activities, these private developers were also driven by a sense of "economic individualism" which flourished at the time. Further, the more free and rapid circulation of capital that was critical to the funding of new houses was present. The dynamic urban socio-economic context was fertile ground for an inventive development model, and it was also the milieu in which its interwoven social and economic consequences were played out. However, despite these social concerns of some early developers and the nuanced benefits of the commercial context in which the new model evolved, the positive role that urban real estate might play in a more fluid socio-economic context was supplanted by its appropriation for competitive wealth building.

The Production of Shelter

Creating shelter of some kind is obviously fundamental to the development process as the vehicle for its profit-making purpose. In the simple form of building houses, it began long ago. What was changed by the modern developer was that the constrained distribution of skills, the limitation on the availability of land, and the growing costs of constructing buildings meant that the shelter needs in rapidly growing urban areas could not be filled effectively by the occupants themselves. As London's population grew to accommodate a half a million or more by the late 17th century, the demand for housing was unprecedented and required new methods of delivery (Beckett 1986, 262). As modern London progressed during that century with increasing sophistication and specialization in professions and skills, the need for focused production was met by entrepreneurial individuals who willingly took to the speculative culture of the times.

This journey of urban development activity began with traditional building practices, but soon adopted a chameleon response to changing commercial demands for the product and the investment demands of the new capital markets. At the same time, changing social attitudes required different solutions, and the rising interest in the aesthetics of urban form probably provided an impetus to the most substantial innovations in the process of producing shelter.

Building Trades

At the outset, urban development was simply an extension of the activity of the building trades from constructing client-led individual properties to successive projects on a few neighboring sites as land became available. The activity of lead tradesmen sometimes advanced to establishing and managing multiple projects. To finance this production, they generally used trade credit or personal loans, and for as long as they were not over-extended and were able to sell their products profitably, this form of master building was broadly practiced and still continues.

This traditional format for the provision of housing, however, contributed some fundamental principles of production that were to become part of modern development schemes. First, physical production was structured as an integration of different trades each of which performed defined work. For example, a bathroom was not a distinct item of production: it combined construction of the bare space, plumbing work, tiling work, partition work, and so forth. This production methodology aligned with what was being adopted for the production of other goods and would be played out more fully as industrialization got underway in the following century.

Secondly, the financing of this production was very specifically structured around the final delivery of the finished building, not as partial contributions during production. This was important conceptually since it gave rise to the perception that a building under construction has little value, which focused funding on the end product. This is different from the way in which industrial production often comprised a system of component parts which in themselves were recognized as goods of economic value. It is probable that because the parts of a building under construction are not easily removed and used elsewhere, they are perceived to be of little value separately. This continues to be a flaw in the business model, though it may be rectified in the future if financial analysis can evolve around the use of more modular and standardized components in development projects.

Also as a result of the focus on the completed product, the management of the building activity was structured around an individual's administration of that singular project. Even if a project manager were to be responsible for a series of buildings, the work would be defined, evaluated, and paid for in relation to the completion of each individual building. This resulted in the manager's focus on achieving completion, sometimes at the expense of other aspects such as the property's lifecycle, the impact on the neighborhood during construction, and the like. Today, the role of the individual manager might be played by an entity responsible for the delivery of the building. That this somewhat insular focus is also taken by financial interests in the project will be discussed later, but it is sufficient to note here that this conceptual construct may contribute to some consequences that are broadly condemned, such as short-term criteria regarding the quality of the building, and the local physical disruption caused by the building activity.

The Need for Scale
One of the notable features of the modern development model was that it responded to a larger demand and was based on a larger-scale building project than its predecessors. The larger dimensions of the site were advantageous for flexibility of layout, greater efficiency of land usage, and the possibility of a more attractive arrangement of the buildings. The amount of construction undertaken probably facilitated efficiencies, such as keeping disparate trades on site with a variety of buildings in progress and the provision of materials in bulk. It transformed the project from a mere continuation of surrounding form, such as the construction of a row of houses on an existing street, to a blank canvas that invited the developer to envisage a new urban typology, with aspirations of distinction from the norm.

The development potential of scale and the opportunity to produce a special urban precinct through an entrepreneurial developer's imaginative talents seem to have been operative for development activity to depart from simply building within an urban environment. To exploit the broad possibilities of the site, a developer often needed to obtain approval for changes of use in at least parts of the whole scheme, and their typical large scale more easily accommodated changes in layout that such change of use might require. Though this distinction was not always mentioned in commentary on the production of housing at that time, the term "developer" was applied differently from that of builder and indicated a conceptual difference in practice.

Although the history of the earliest developers focused on those who undertook larger schemes, and although their scale was in many ways necessary to support their provision of the attractive amenities and public spaces that defined their precincts, the model was also successfully adopted for smaller projects. Some of these, such as Golden Square and Temple Court, were situated amongst the larger projects in London's West End. There were certain components of the new model to be found in these smaller schemes. First, non-rentable spaces such as open public areas or gardens, though much reduced in size, were often incorporated in their plans, making them noticeably different from the crowded, compact and uniform surrounding row houses. Perhaps an apt description is that they were something different from what was expected of even a modest house. A further difference was that more consideration was given to architectural cohesion or composition of both the individual buildings and the spaces between. In this comprehensive approach, both the small and large developers regarded their projects as more than the production of individual lots and structures, and this primarily distinguished them from the builders.

Complex Development Schemes

Another important aspect of the early formulation of development practice was that it extended beyond merely building predetermined structures on given lots. It was both his financial ambitions and inspired estate management that enabled the 4th Earl of Bedford to envisage changing the use of his fields for higher economic potential, and further, for that to be an upmarket residential precinct rather than just a line of common houses. From its earliest spatial plan, the authorship of which was anonymous but very indicative of his concept, he decided upon the layout of the site as residences around three sides of a courtyard of substantial importance with his own house and garden on the fourth side. This notion was extended and embellished in Inigo Jones's plans, and was imitated in Bloomsbury Square, St James's Square, Red Lion Square, and many other London squares of the next century.

It was soon noticed that the most successful entrepreneurs approached their schemes with a more advanced concern for the comprehensive layout and arrangement of buildings, and also the provision of public space and amenities. Bedford had his piazza designed specifically to enhance the environment for his houses, making an economic calculation that the loss of financial return from this land contribution would be compensated through a higher value in residences in the proximity of this amenity. He also provided the parish church of St Paul's for the benefit of his intended residents and the community, though it also served in his obtaining approval for the scheme. Judging from the lack of recorded evidence, it appears that an explicit assessment in numerical terms of the benefits of providing amenities and an attractive layout was not made at the time, nor is it fully evaluated financially today.

However, the consideration of site layout and optimization of built form and open spaces became important principles of production for successful urban development projects.

In addition to planning the precinct, and having undertaken a change of use analysis by which the best economic use was determined to be housing, Bedford also provided for some commercial activities. By this variation, he extended the physical use of his site and its financial construct to be what is today termed mixed-use. Notably, this was not only to make the area more interesting and vibrant, it was a well-reasoned economic decision that the dour critic James Ralph described in 1734 as follows: "The piazza is grand and noble, and the superstructure it supports light and elegant. The market in the middle may be a matter of much profit to the ground-landlord."

In a similar intertwining of the production process with other aspects of development activity, in Barbon's development of the former Essex estate between the Strand and the Thames, he acted as a financial advisor by performing a very complex analysis of the ownership structure of chambers, or barristers' offices, in an existing adjacent building known as the Temple chambers. In rebuilding their accommodation, not only did he plan and construct one of the first privately developed office buildings but he also provided a mechanism for determining space allocations to the purchasers in accordance with their respective financial interests in the property. He insightfully structured the funding of the project in accordance with the complex partnership arrangement that lawyers establish for their chambers. In this way, Barbon extended the nascent development business model to include the analysis and, by different economic structures, the flexibility needed to produce buildings for a variety of uses and ownership. In this, the model was progressed to be suitable for the growing complexity of early modern cities, more so than the more restricted methods of traditional builders.

Because the properties that were developed in Covent Garden, Bloomsbury Square, Red Lion Square, and even Essex Street each comprised a single private holding, the necessary infrastructure such as streets, water supply, and sewerage was provided by the developer. This amounted to contributing to what would become the public realm, and often the more broadly used neighborhood infrastructure, while also supporting the success of the project. The example was followed by 18th-century developers of the London squares, and in other countries. William Ogden, a public leader and one of Chicago's founders, applied this strategy, mostly in his dealings on the north side:

> Over the years, a vast amount of real estate passed through his hands as the city grew … He built, at his own expense, more than one hundred miles of public streets upon which he planted shade trees, and a number of bridges, and he poured millions more into the infrastructure of the city. He was also among the most vocal advocates for public parks. (Harpster 2009, 90)

Although actions of this general kind may not be so direct today, a connection with and need for contribution to infrastructure remains an important part of the business model. Examples today can be found in Lee Tung Street in Hong Kong, where the developer has created, and funded, a composite urban environment. This mixed-use precinct interweaves private residential units, senior housing, and community care within a public pedestrian boulevard lined with 94,000 square ft of stores and entertainment (Figure 11.1). It also

11.1
**Lee Tung Street,
Hong Kong.**

completes the pedestrian linkage from the thoroughfare of Kennedy Road to the Wan Chai waterfront and includes an underground walkway to the Wan Chai subway train station. As a joint venture between two private developers, Sino Land and Hopewell Holdings, and the Hong Kong Urban Renewal Authority, it exemplifies the successful combination of private enterprise and the provision of public amenities.

In New York City, the office skyscraper at One Vanderbilt Avenue funded and integrated a $200 million commuter access network for the adjacent Grand Central Station (Figure 11.2). Through the contribution of additional access points and a pedestrian environment at the west side of the station, this development by the corporate entities SL Green and Hines delivers much needed upgrades to the public space unaffordable to municipal and state authorities. That the private development was able to expand its rentable space beyond the prior legislative restrictions enabled the project to achieve financial feasibility.

11.2
One Vanderbilt Avenue,
New York.

11.2
(Continued).

Numerous other examples can be found globally, particularly in Europe, such as the Hekla Paris development by Hines, where the dynamic of including private enterprise in the provision of public amenities has become necessary to meet budgetary constraints. Therefore, it is becoming more frequently found that although sometimes necessary for a project's progression, and at other times merely assisting with approvals of an intended development, the private contribution of public benefits is a key element for the success of urban development generally. That the economic dynamic was not formalized and its financial aspects incorporated into the analytical model for investment capital at the outset, and continues to be mostly discretionary, is a shortcoming of the business model as it stands.

Production Organization and Management
The essential aspects of this complex production process include organizational structure, efficiency of its procedures, innovation and aesthetics in product design, customer satisfaction, and the product's place in the urban context. Despite the early developers' extensive financial and social skills that were fortuitously suitable to the occasion, when project management's responsibilities increased for large schemes there was a surprising lack of advancement in formulating its place within the new model.

Although the production activity on a development scheme was much more complex than the building activity from which it was partially derived, the earliest developers seemed to manage it as they went by combining their experience with their landed estates, their skills in financial management, and possibly even the authority and preference inherent in their social standing. Their expertise was often taxed beyond their ability in the oversight of their complex schemes, and there were many examples then, and many today, where the complexity of the production overwhelmed the developer's project management skills.

Surprisingly, this important commercial activity did not provide for training in professional skills in infrastructure and mining activities, which were similarly large capital productions. As development entities grew and the size of their projects increased, it was assumed that the project management procedures of small schemes were scalable, as were many proto-industrial and trading activities, or that the larger-scale activities would naturally attract the most skilled people. However, this did not eventuate for the private development model. Rather, as the management scholar, Pollard (1965, 10) notes:

> It is by no means certain that larger size was always considered desirable, or could even theoretically be defended as being superior. On the contrary, organization theory itself suggests that while there may be technical, financial, or marketing advantages in growth, management difficulties tend to work in the opposite direction, towards a lower optimum size.

The organizational structure and scale of the managerial activities in the development model continue to be ad hoc in their formulation, and may be suitable for improvement by the application of new concepts in engineering and operations management.

On top of the general lack of specific formulation for management of the new urban projects, two specific and important aspects were neglected:

- Although the management of costs is a key issue on a project, the need for knowledge regarding the offsetting valuation of completed work, either as part or as the whole of the construction, was not addressed. Rather than making decisions within a cost/benefit construct, a project manager usually pursued a cost target that was set by the architect, engineer, or owner.
- As observed by Pollard (1965, 121), for general managerial capability, but particularly critical for labor-intensive development projects: "The greatest failure of all, the failure to deal adequately, or even sensibly in terms of long-term low cost, with labour, was paralleled by the complete absence of any science or teaching on the subject of labour management, apart from some *a priori* reasoning of the philosophers and political economists."

The first of these defects placed the responsibility for making more economic decisions, in contrast to sheer cost decisions, to the owner-developer, who was only sometimes advised by the architect or engineer. The developer would estimate what level of value was to be achieved in the completed building according to its anticipated rent, and then from a suitably adjusted budget would specify the size, layout, amenities, and quality of finishes suitable for the anticipated lessee. The general contractor then estimated and spent according to that specification. There is no indication that the early developer established any systematic method for seeking this important market information on rental rates and associated specifications, though the aristocrat developers would have had some general knowledge of both since they built for tenants of akin wealth and taste. Nor was such information provided by the developer's consultants such as the surveyor, or the architect who might have managed the translation of economic value to physical design specifications, and it remains a problematically ill-attended part of the private urban development process today.

The lack of overarching management of this fundamental economic dynamic of the cost/benefit decisions and monitoring on development projects resulted in some general production management failures noted by Pollard (1965, 122):

- Wasting capital on non-productive, ostentatious and costly infrastructure, such as hiring support staff and establishing elaborate company headquarters, or by engaging in excessive promotional activity ahead of supply processes.
- Overestimating the pace of production, or the extent of sales and the anticipated level of profits.
- Underestimating the cost of input materials and labor and/or their availability, with the result that production is either too expensive or disrupted in output.

To overcome these issues the management structure, or task organization, of a developer's operation has not been formulated in a manner that seems specifically appropriate for its production activities. Many developers start and continue as a project-focused activity, organized as such with teams that see the scheme through to completion, and then start on the next.

> Despite the size and omnipresence of a few full-service global companies, the most common type of development firm operates in smaller regional markets … They maintain their flexibility by keeping a low profile and low overhead, making up-front commitments to contractors and service providers outside the firm (e.g., architects, builders) that come due as each phase of development is completed. (Weber 2015, 40–41)

Though this may seem pragmatically efficient for a single project, and also the uniqueness of each development project requires that teams be arranged accordingly, more efficiency, continuity of team dynamic, and maintenance of a form of corporate intellectual property might be gained by a regularity of arrangements. Other team-based professional and commercial activities, even doctors in surgery for instance, appreciate the carry-over effect in the way of a developed understanding and reduced costs of consultation of standing arrangements. Some successful developers proceed informally in this manner, though the practice would benefit from more research.

In a similar way, general contractor skill in labor management, although much more advanced in recent centuries in response to legislation and trade union activity, remains, from the developer's broader perspective, problematically under-attended. Although typically the developer does not manage construction workers for a development project, coordination, logistical arrangement and personal relationships of the numerous subcontractors, consultants and their workforces present a major and critical task. This project management role was poorly handled in the beginning and generally continues to be undertaken without much strategic consideration. Its lack of structure and want of formalization with respect to the impact on the outcome of a project should be improved in the business model.

Production Efficiency

Much as the early developers applied existing modes of property management that had been used by their estate managers, and did not introduce a new professional class for the purpose, they similarly did not attempt to vary substantially the traditional process of construction. Distinct building trades, often performing under the authority of their guilds, were used, and the costing, scheduling, and management of the production process was organized within their production framework that retained traditional methods. In London's western suburbs beyond the authority of the guilds, some non-apprenticed tradesmen worked, but even they performed the same tasks in the same general way.

This perseverance with outdated methods might be considered surprising in the light of the enthusiasm for science and innovation prevalent in the later part of the 17th century. Some engineering advances were made for large infrastructure, and Christopher Wren, an astronomer, applied his scientific talent to the reconstruction of St Paul's Cathedral, but not much attention was paid to the more pedestrian practice of erecting housing, even dense urban housing. House building had advanced in the late Middle Ages through the use of timber construction which enabled it to rise to two, three or even four storeys, and this had spawned a large carpentry trade that progressed to specialize in framing, cladding and cabinetry. So it was that, in the early stages of increased housing development in the London metropolis, the lead tradesman was often a carpenter, and some of those undertook small-scale development projects themselves.

However, the Stuart kings promoted the use of masonry, primarily for aesthetic reasons and in competition with the fabric of the Continental cities, and the building trades adjusted to this with the rise of the stonemason and bricklayer just as the Covent Garden and Bloomsbury Square projects were conceived. Though these newly flourishing trades were also controlled by traditional guilds and, although novel architectural forms were envisioned for the innovative urban projects, they were constructed through the adaptation of vernacular methods.

Some advances in construction techniques were achieved by Barbon in order to reduce costs and increase his profits. Since much of the framing of his houses was timber, even if required stone cladding was used in part, he reduced on-site labor costs by having timber members pre-cut to required lengths before delivery. He made this even more efficient by using standard housing designs with no fundamental distinctions and establishing a prefabrication workshop for such production. Component prefabrication was extant in the coach and carriage building industry, and it might be asked why it was not used more in housing construction. Still, the challenges for prefabrication of buildings continue through until today for various reasons, not only those of technical feasibility but also funding practices. The challenges for the production and cost of urban structures around this production avenue are still apparent.

Design Innovation and Quality

The success of the courageous steps taken by the Earl of Bedford in his new development process at Covent Garden is to be applauded for the quality of his urban built form and his integration of good design with good economics. His project was also exemplary in its architectural innovations, for which it may even be more widely known. The reasons for this satisfactory outcome were numerous and sometimes due to serendipity, though still instructive. Some observers such as Summerson (1991a, 19) assigned credit to the patronage of the Crown and the Royal Architect. He said, "... Once the appropriate aesthetic guidelines were established ... it was Bedford who extended the innovation through production to meet the excessive need for housing at the time." Nor to be overlooked was the willingness of Inigo Jones, held in such high esteem, to work with the private developer and join with him in achieving his financial objectives. Together they worked to arrive at a design for a residential building that would appeal to the intended residents, was economically feasible in its production, and received praise as a new and refreshing "classical statement of the form which a London house-front should take."

But despite his primary enthusiasm for aesthetic features of the built environment, Summerson was also cognizant and accepting, if not admiring, of the private developer's role in adopting these new forms. He hailed Jones's designs for the developers, including Bedford and Newton, and regarded them as "strictly and artistically Palladian in character ... [and to be] the foundation stones of two centuries of London [aesthetic] taste" (Summerson 2003, 20).

The Covent Garden and Lincoln's Inn Fields projects were successful in respect of their innovative designs that improved the functional quality of the residences and at the same time were suitably socially symbolic for their occupants. However, the work of many contemporary developers was neither true to the quality of traditional building forms and methods nor concerned with improving the living conditions of intended inhabitants, but rather repeated patterns, and cut costs where possible. Unfortunately, in the rebuilding after the Great Fire, further design explorations were also constrained by statutory prescriptions to only four variations of house form.

The development of an urban aesthetic was also complicated by the realities of socio-economic conditions. Baer (2007, 313) found that

> [t]he often-cited, inferior quality of 'spec-built' housing (sometimes turning into slums) has been a constant complaint. 'Jerry-built' housing is not always a premeditated slighting of materials by a crafty builder. Sometimes it is simply employing inexperienced or inept workers when skilled labor is in short supply. But slum housing is also due to low incomes and the simple dynamics stemming from urban inhabitants with decidedly unequal incomes and wealth interacting in the housing market over decidedly different sized and quality units. Commentators who decry slums are really offended that society's resources are so unevenly distributed; that so many people are poor; and that the deplorable result from this inequality is made so highly visible in the case of housing.

Many of these conditions continue and remain unresolved by the private development model.

That the emerging development practice consolidated into a tight form in the context of such challenges to innovation might partially be the cause of its persistently herd-like approach to design. Fainstein (2010, 71) reflects on other causes to explain how this occurs today, not just for individual buildings but for whole development precincts:

> Although in the past market-driven development produced highly differentiated land-scapes as a consequence of local custom, small-plot ownership, minimal regulation, and incremental development, today's large developers, enmeshed within a globalized architectural and property market, build on a grand scale and repeat the successful formulas of everywhere else. The paradox is that the internally diverse character of festival marketplaces, entertainment districts, and live/work environments replicates itself, so that places lose their individuality just as much as had been the case under high modernism.

Though the specifics of the replicated features are different, this tendency was apparent in the early historical times with the use of the open square and colonnades as urban centers grew.

Alternatively, the fundamental economic restraints on changing building formats have been exposed by Crosby and Henneberry (2017, 185) who observed "that the emergence, diffusion and acceptance of new uses and built forms is a long, contested process." With particular attention to how those innovations are financially valued within the extant context of real estate's calculative practices, they found that "[t]hrough our elaboration of the calculative regime for comparative valuation, we have begun to indicate the difficulties that must be overcome for novel uses and buildings to become accepted elements of that regime" (Crosby and Henneberry 2017, 195). Even when putting aside the use of comparable valuations and applying the DCF method of valuation, the inputs of rents or sale prices, if not yet contractually committed, are determined with reference to those metrics of the most closely comparable properties. In conclusion, the authors conclude that "[t]his reproduces [and perpetuates] an environment antipathetic to the evolution of innovative land uses and developments" (Crosby and Henneberry 2017, 196).

The debate on design advances and innovation in development projects still rages. Some urbanists and urban dwellers, appreciative of orderly repetition of the Georgian era productions of residential squares, crescents, and terraces, look for similar solutions today. Others desire exciting new designs and the prevalence, or perhaps over-saturation, of self-nominated iconic buildings is noticeable in many urban topographies. Irrespective of the presence of surrounding external form, however, humans change their habits and lifestyles, and the arrival of new functional formats such as the shared workspace is indicative of a need for innovative and continual advancement in the development of the built environment, and this is a key responsibility of the private developer.

The Rise of the Architect

In England, the concept of the profession of architecture did not exist prior to Inigo Jones's rise to fame in that role, in which he practiced both for the court and on private commissions. But by the end of the century, architects of varying levels of education were drafting plans for commercial buildings. In the *London Tradesman* of 1747, the architect was recognized as having a fully established role. Architecture was described as "the Art of building, Houses,

Palaces, and other Edifices," though this possibly leaves unresolved the distinction between designing the building and erecting it, for the latter might also have been considered an "Art" by a competent master builder. However, it seems that by then architecture was widely known, and it was further acknowledged that "[i]ts Use is universal, and the Profits arising from it are very considerable" (Campbell 1747, 155).

A more specific definition was given to the architect, who was described as:

the Person who draws the Design and Plan of a Palace, or other Edifice; where he describes, in Profile, the whole Building, in all its proportional Dimensions; every Member of the Building is exactly delineated; all its Ornaments ranged in their proper Order; and every Part of the Edifice appears to the Eye in Miniature in the same Disposition as they are intended in the real Work. (Campbell 1747, 155)

And a further financial function seems to have been given to the architect of the time:

When the Employer has fixed upon a Plan, they then agree upon the Price, and the Architect either underwrites the whole Work, for a certain Sum, or is paid for superintending the Work only: in either case all the Workmen are generally of his own choosing, and such as he believes capable of executing their several Branches [trades] in the proposed Work. (Campbell 1747, 155)

That the first English architect was engaged in the first new format of private urban development at Covent Garden is important to the concept of the private urban development process and its inherent objectives. With the involvement of the architect, the design quality of the buildings and their frontage to the public realm was a specific aesthetic quality for which the earliest developers strove, and it was also regarded as critical to the project's economic success. It is notable that this first English architect also mixed his objectives for his design by a commitment to the project's economic feasibility as well as its beauty. The reasons for his elevation of this objective have been found in this exploration to be complex and associated with his social intentions, personal aspirations, and innate business sense. Unfortunately, a factor encouraging this high level of attention to design was not solidly formulated in the development model and is often lacking in current practice.

Integration in the Urban Context
When the early developments took their place within the growing London metropolis, their production and presence had a substantial impact in a number of ways. While their social consequences and contributions to the community were significant, as will be shown later, the scale of their physical addition to the urban typography was new and its impact palpable.

First, despite the critical population growth in London at that time the erection of more housing was generally contested. In providing new housing in an area that had previously been predominantly fields within large estates, both the Covent Garden and Bloomsbury Square developments were criticized just because they were built on pastoral land.

However, many recognized the need for more housing, though the complex perception of the urban fabric that continues to be voiced in the discussion of urban development remained.

"Successful cities must build in order to accommodate the rising demand for space, but that doesn't mean that building creates success" (Glaeser 2011, 53). The notion of what might have constituted successful urban additions at that early modern time is gleaned from commentary from a variety of sources: "As humankind becomes wealthier, more people will choose their locations on the basis of pleasure as well as productivity. To understand why cities are succeeding and whether they will continue to thrive in the future, we must understand how urban amenities work and how consumer cities succeed," writes Glaeser (2011, 119).

It was accepted that some early developers substantially contributed to the urban context by providing the public with open spaces such as the piazza at Covent Garden and the various squares. And in order to also enable their residential precincts to be accommodated logistically into the existing urban layout, they also made streets for traffic flow. In Barbon's Essex Street development, he cleverly constructed a connection with the wharves, though its intersection at the other end with the Strand was narrow and probably caused problems as the population of the area grew. By that time, of course, he had sold out and was gone.

From this beginning, the development model has included a partial interest in the physical integration of the project into the neighborhood, particularly when it was important for access to or use of the precinct, or when the integrating features were driven by legislation. However, though attention is paid to finding and using the appropriate form of building for a scheme, within its process of analysis and production the model does not substantially consider the surrounding urban form and movement for satisfactory integration. The fundamental financial analysis does not formally include the impact of changing economic conditions, positive or negative, in the surrounding area. Some derivation is achieved through estimates of rental rates and occupancy, though these are usually according to backward-looking reviews, and the possibilities of substantial alterations are not typically envisioned and analyzed. For this it has often been the subject of blanket criticism and condemnation, and the failure to do it has often resulted in the longer-term failure of the project.

It was not universally thus. Although Summerson (2003, 21) would say that "the basic principles of taste, which prevailed in Georgian London became recognizable somewhat before the basic principles of speculative development," from his own description of the entrepreneurship and financial success of the speculative developments of Covent Garden, Great Queen Street and Lincoln's Inn Fields, the sentence should be turned around. Rather, it could be said that the earliest, "basic principles of [good] speculative development," as distinct from merely repetitive building, included adherence to "the basic principles of taste". Following this combination of development and aesthetic quality, with the advice of his Surveyor of Works, Christopher Wren, Charles II issued the 1671 Proclamation that "required that houses be 'built Firmly and Regularly, according to such Design and Order as may best suit With the Public Benefit and Convenience'" (Baer 2007b, 273). The understanding that each building was to make an aesthetic contribution to the urban environment for the good of the community had been established.

Attention to design did not demand high-profile or expensive architecture. Although Covent Garden was something of a showpiece for Inigo Jones, after his first Portico Buildings many later ones of aesthetic merit were designed by lesser-known architects, though their plans were often reviewed by Jones to ensure a suitable quality of design, even if not of an extravagant nature or taste. This standard of design quality, where aesthetic objectives were met by economical means, was followed for some developments in the USA. As Krinsky (1978, 9–10) observed:

> Unquestionably, Rockefeller Center [in New York] has reminded developers both good and bad that the architecture of individual buildings need not be exquisite to be functional and an improvement to the city; that the open spaces do not have to be very large if they are well designed; that people seldom complain about uninteresting side streets if there are compensating amenities close by. The creation of an area which is active day and night is another legacy of Rockefeller Center to its own city and to other building projects designed to become essential parts of downtown areas.

She continued, "[i]t gives people the sense of the best that money could buy for a city, which is not the same as seeing expensive buildings."

By these actions, a concern for aesthetic achievement and social contribution may be directly engaged in the economic feasibility of the project despite its unprecedented novelty in many dimensions. Developers should understand that it is the full network of connections, including aesthetic and functional appeal, that renders their projects successful.

Satisfying Customers

As the development production process was speculative and not just a task of meeting a customized order for a resident, it did not include the preliminary time and process to define the eventual occupants, comprehend their needs, formulate their requirements, and engage someone to design the building. Rather, a speculative developer proceeded immediately to produce buildings to satisfy a perceived general need without its specific articulation. It was a new, rapid approach to providing a product to society, and given the crisis in supply, it could be seen to have afforded a developer much latitude as to the buildings delivered.

However, providing a product for an end-user, tenant, or purchaser whose particular needs and preferences would be somewhat unknown, established some production challenges for the development model from the outset. First, in those historical times, ascertaining the potential demand could be effected only by hearsay or general reports of housing shortages. Even today, rigorous estimates of demand volume are often difficult because of a potential offsetting supply by other developers, either underway or in the pipeline. The developers at that time knew the threat of competing supply, and this was behind Southampton's attempt to forestall the development of St James's Square.

These difficulties in prediction applied not only to the volume of demand but also to the nature of the shelter which would be required – that is, specific details of what features prospective residents would want and what they would be willing to buy. The aristocrat developers very strategically built for those whom they wished to have as their neighbors, people just like themselves. They well knew in detail the lifestyle, the format of house layout, the quality of space and finishes, and even the required land lot that would be desired by their customers. This knowledge was very useful, and it seems that their products were well received. Cleverly, the Earl of Southampton varied the size of his lots to provide for a slightly broader spread of economic standing of his potential residents.

For a developer such as Barbon who built for a different target market, including the "middling sort," anticipating the specifics of the product to be delivered would have been more difficult. Markets and lifestyles of all social levels were changing. Fortunately for these early developers, various pattern books were soon produced to present standard house designs, which had features that those intended residents would generally desire or at least expect. Because of Barbon's usual focus on a more economically constrained market, his consideration of the wants of future occupiers of his houses was not profound and he focused on efficiencies by standardizing construction and a strategy of speedy exit from his projects. Numerous later developers have proceeded in this manner by producing what is often called cookie-cutter houses or apartments, which are often accepted by the public as an affordable option. But the incidence of failure of such projects is not insignificant, and the blame may be placed on the developer's negligence in considering in more substantial detail the future occupants' needs and seeking to improve upon solutions.

Then, as now, the absence of precise market demand measurement and the details of physical requirements, or the misreading of them, is a weakness in the model that often resulted in oversupply, unsatisfactory and therefore unsalable properties, and financial loss for their developers.

Advancing the Theoretical Model of Production

Though development's complexity and its management are still not adequately handled by its business model, as mentioned previously some scholars have sought to understand and describe the production process more finely, and with a view to its better organization. For example, Ball (1986, 455) focused on the identification of human agents in the process and their interactions when he posited:

> Creating and using built structures involves particular sets of social agents defined by their economic relation to the physical process of provision itself. Each historically specific set of social agents can be defined as a structure of building provision. By provision is meant the production, exchange, distribution, and use of a built structure. Involved may be a landowner, a developer, a building firm, building workers, financiers, building owners, and final users.

Incorporating this interweaving of the social and economic dimensions and the entities involved in the process, which is people-intensive, was a central objective of this historical exploration. In a search for examples to support Ball's "economic roles of particular social agents," the complementary social roles of the economic agents were found present in the Earls of Bedford and Southampton. They had a sense of responsibility regarding the suitability of the buildings they produced, they phased production to organically integrate with the surrounding urban network, and they provided infrastructure of quality and maintained its physical condition, which, incidentally, Barbon did not do. This attitude should not be attributed to their aristocratic status. Rather, the idea of seizing opportunities to make contributions to the urban built fabric and the benefits of doing so were owed to traditions of land ownership tracing back to early English history, supported by philosophical thought and religious convictions, and facilitated by advanced property law. Unfortunately, without its formalization in the model, and when its use was appropriated by landowners and entities lacking these contextual features, the important intersection of social and economic concerns in the production process was lost.

However, this idea of social agency in the creation of the urban built environment is again rising in scholarly and corporate thought. Beauregard (2015, 541) noted that

> buildings, technologies and materials have agency, as do architects, their consultants, and clients. As philosopher and historian of science Bruno Latour wrote, 'all designs are *collaborative* designs—even if in some cases the *collaborators* are not all visible, welcomed or willing.' The agencies of humans and non-humans, however, are different, particularly when we consider what it means to be responsible.

Collaboration requires proximity, however, and even in the time of early development projects there were many activities not or only infrequently performed on site, including the arrangement of financing and legal contracts, and the promotion and selling of the project, much of which was undertaken by consultants or external contractors. Similarly, the funding structures for development projects often require an extension beyond internal resources and intimate relationships, as Weber (2015, 40) pertinently describes:

> Developers' reliance on external sources of finance stems partly from the fact that real estate is too expensive, complex, and long-lived to be paid for in cash up front. Their dependence also derives from the organizational structure of their firms. The field of development comprises a range of differently sized corporations; most are loosely conjoined operations that alter their legal and organizational form to about their current projects.

Though Weber continued with an investigation into some larger, vertically integrated firms where all activities were relatively contained, these were exceptional rather than the norm for the industry.

Although the larger socio-economic context in which the typical developer works is more fractured and less able to influence directly and efficiently decision-making around social and economic aspects of the production process, Henneberry and Parris (2013, 235) have proposed that the benefits of those larger organizational structures might be achieved at a smaller scale. They find that

> [l]ocal development milieus consist of a mix of latent and actual project networks. They are shaped and driven by 'the practise of episodic project collaboration.' Each project is born out of enduring but loose pre-project social networks. The pursuit of a project reinforces the ties between some of its network members but may weaken relations between others if they do not perform their roles well. Consequently, wider social networks mutate in response to project experience, with subsequent effects on future projects and the wider development sector.

If these sustained relationships are able to facilitate decisions that integrate economic concerns with the social network in which they and their professionally networked teams are engaged, the social results of projects within such a context should improve. This also would benefit from the strategy of team continuation beyond individual projects, as proposed earlier. There are advantages and disadvantages to this, though the trend seems to be growing.

The production activity in urban development is also becoming more conflicted as broader considerations, such as the connection or contribution of infrastructure and the provision of the public realm, are incorporated. The modeling of its complex decision-making has defied human skills, but hopefully advances in technology will provide for a more detailed understanding that can lead to better management. Once again, scholarship in the engineering and operations management area could inform some improvement in the technical structure of this dimension of the model. Further, connecting this technical advance in the integration of social and economic concerns in the production activity with the adoption of new socio-economic thinking, such as Sayer's (2000) proposed business model for a more moral economy, provides a framework within which to formulate this theoretical dimension of the development process.

Community Impact

The development activity that began in 17th-century London had a substantial impact on its community beyond its provision of shelter and creation of a new financial asset. This plainly occurred because of new developments' substantial physical presence in their neighborhoods' built environments, but was also related to developments' uses, occupants, social history, and involved economic activity. Weber (2002, 520) posits these factors as interrelated: "The very materiality of the built environment sets off struggles between use and exchange values, between those with emotional attachments to place and those without such attachments."

Observing the dynamic of that community impact and assessing the model's performance in this dimension is more complex than the same exercise for the production of shelter and financial products. It concerns the ideological fracture between urban social studies and mainstream economics in evaluating the outcomes of property development, and this complicates an understanding of real estate development as a comprehensive discipline with an agreed array of objectives and performance measures – a scholarly challenge acknowledged from the outset of this study. It is particularly complex when, in considering the impact of urban development on a community, an analysis selects one framework or the other, with the result that there is little common area of assessment and often widely divergent results. A simple example is the urban economist's observation of the benefits of growth through development in contrast to the social urban scholar's condemnation of the resultant displacement of lower economic groups.

Though a solution to the ideological divide has yet to be found, through this study's elucidation of the origins of the model by which the urban form came to be delivered through private production, it becomes apparent that these defined economic concerns and more qualitative social issues are interwoven within the development process. For example, in the funding necessary to construct buildings, the objectives of capital markets, sometimes including the demands of distant profit-maximizing investors, must be met, and these often override other socio/economic objectives such as affordability for local residents. This influences decisions as to land use and the functional program for projects. It also comes into consideration in respect of target occupants such as potential buyers of luxury condominiums in an improving neighborhood because that form of development would achieve the land's highest economic potential as soon as possible, irrespective of its disruption to the local community. That capital should be entitled to do this is justified in a widely accepted method of real estate financial analysis. However, at the same time, this exploration has revealed that some calculative practices inherent in that financial analysis are problematic, causing it to fail in incorporating the powerful, symbiotic dynamic of neighborhood externalities. Paradoxically, although so heavily relied on in the pursuit of maximum potential outcome, the fundamental economic methodology so commonly used has evolved to ignore the original potential of development to provide attractive financial returns that coexist with, if not mutually benefit from, improving community conditions.

There can be no reasonable criticism of the industry's profit motive, which is its *raison d'être* and provides the city with a valuable commodity provided through the undertaking of serious risk. However, a reasonable complaint can be made against profit's excessive precedence over community welfare. If there is not a more granular and transparent trading of costs and benefits between developers and the community, irrespective of funding sources, the interactions between developments and the urban context will substantially and adversely impact the success of projects over the long term. Bedford's provision of a parish church as part of his Covent Garden development demonstrated such granularity, since it was an unanticipated but eventually necessary component for the success of the project.

Even with respect to the production of needed shelter, which might be considered ideologically neutral, the decisions of early developers were progressive in their more nuanced evaluation of building form and spatial use as a means of both achieving economic potential and making a social contribution. The Earls of Bedford and Southampton both sacrificed valuable land in their contribution to the public realm, and provided for its maintenance, because they were aware of the need for balancing their business objectives with their obligations to society. Their layout of residences around open squares and the type of houses that would add to their desirability and value were parts of a decision that included contributing scarce recreational space for all social classes.

Unfortunately, only a short time later, these decisions lost their socio-economic intent as the development activity was harnessed by unfolding capitalism. The more purist profit-maximizing and less socially concerned Barbon made only a token contribution of public space at Red Lion Square in order to achieve higher rents that would be attracted by its format, and he also neglected to resource its maintenance, which led to its ultimate demise.

From these examples and others in this exploration, it follows that the objective of providing a positive community impact, in which the project will financially flourish, requires a deliberate business strategy which more carefully and rigorously integrates this concern with its other objectives of producing shelter and creating financial assets. The task of improving a neighborhood through a development is not best performed as a disparate undertaking, such as the recent imposition of community or infrastructure fees by municipalities or the allocation of often unwanted and under-used community spaces in projects. Its effectiveness requires the extension and improvement of the decision-making and procedures for shelter production and funding structures, as explained in the prior sections of the critique of the model. In addition, it requires a melding of the socio-economic perspectives that have developed as two separate theoretical strands in their evaluation of the activity, and that is the focus of this section.

The Intertwined Social and Economic Urban Context

Drawing on the experience of the early developers, the first step towards an ideological reconciliation is an admission that capital and the social dimension inevitably need each other to function. From one side, the most constant critic of capitalism, David Harvey (1989, 185), concedes that:

> It takes money ... to construct any alternative to the society predicated on the community of money. This is the essential truth that all social movements have to confront; otherwise, it confronts and destroys them. Money may be, as the moralists have it, the root of all evil, yet it appears also as the unique means of doing good.

For a developer of pure capitalist intent, the commonly used financial analysis of highest economic use, termed the highest and best use, and minimization of costs does not take into account a project's social context. But, as raised earlier, in recent decades general business is broadening its objectives, such as through Environmental, Social and Governance (ESG) mandates which require some deduction from profit while remaining valid within the capitalist economy. If, like broader businesses, the development process includes socially oriented objectives in its core decision-making, it can make social contributions that are relevant to its essential operations and of true benefit to the urban context. Some social historians such as Polanyi (1957, 46) have maintained an even more nuanced backdrop to the capitalist economy, saying:

> The outstanding discovery of recent historical and anthropological research is that man's economy, as a rule, is submerged in his social relationships ... Neither the process of production nor that of distribution is linked to specific economic interests attached to the possession of goods; but every single step in that process is geared to a number of social interests which eventually ensure that the required step be taken.

In examining where objectives and decision processes could more strategically integrate economic and social considerations, it is helpful to observe how and why both dimensions were important in the context which gave rise to this activity.

Governance: Early Planning Approvals and Restrictions

In even the earliest development activities the societal instruments of law and government were important to the economics of land control through their organization of property grants and their attendant obligations, such as leasing and other transactions, both of which are at the core of the industry and protect individual financial interests. Private property rights, both legally enforced and socially recognized, gave rise to the concept of real estate as an asset and a component of the capitalist economy. Then as now, although the distribution was often regarded as inequitable in certain respects, the array of stakeholders from tenants through financiers to builders and developers relied on the security and continuation of these rights.

The other critical feature of this order for development projects was the legislative system of planning constraints and the related process for obtaining project approvals. Development activity in the early metropolis was constrained by the restriction on increased building imposed by both the Crown and municipal authorities. And despite the desperate need for habitation, public opinion at the time also supported these curtailments since it resulted in overcrowding and loss of open space.

Unfortunately, at this early stage in its formation, the activity was perceived and evaluated by authorities in absolute terms of go or no-go decisions. Building activity in urban areas in Europe during the Middle Ages had little democratic planning except in some northern communities, and was achieved under the direction of monarchs or aristocrats. Although classical Roman cities, and their derivatives such as early London, were planned and controlled, in the 16th and 17th century neither the monarch nor the municipality had strategically managed the dramatic relocation of England's population in that metropolis. As in rapidly growing urban communities today, those already there resented the impact caused by new arrivals, including the necessary sharing of resources, and this objection was easily aroused by the blunt manifestation of new building construction. The London authorities saw the position as a choice of being overwhelmed by new buildings or prohibiting any building at all. Today the threat often underlies the controversy over building height: aside from the oft-cited problematic shadows from skyscrapers, greater height represents greater density and higher demand on local resources. This is troubling to existing residents, and therefore a development project's height, scale or bulk may be a catalyst for opposition. Such it was for any new building in early London.

The resolution of these constraints in 17th-century London began with the Proclamations of James I, which changed the law from prohibiting new buildings to establishing guidelines in terms of density, quality of construction and aesthetic standards. Under the administration of Inigo Jones as Surveyor to the King, a practical modification of the building ban resulted in the prescription of building materials, structure, function, and form that were necessary for a new building. These were regarded, especially by architectural historians such as Summerson (2000), as having been driven by aesthetic and topological objectives, as has been previously discussed. Jones's activities at Covent Garden and Lincoln Square, as well as reputedly in some other contemporary projects, are shown in this broader exploration of urban development to include an interest in the project's financial feasibility so that profits could be realized by the developers.

Additionally, Jones's design for residential buildings at Covent Garden allowed for a wide variety of functional arrangements behind its uniform façade, and indicates a solid understanding of what his anticipated tenants made by way of their domestic arrangements.

Reporting on this alteration in the criteria for building approval set by the early metropolitan authorities, Baer (2007, 273) noted concessions on both sides:

> The result was that now builders and building trades recognised the legitimacy of this government role, while government itself recognised the need for more building, retreating from prohibitions, now believing that informed guidance was the better policy and achieved better results. This attitude continued well into the eighteenth century for all kinds of housing.

This established framework of governance facilitated and encouraged new development activity and the proscriptive direction of the authorities established an important dynamic with the new entrepreneurs. Although it is often simplistically thought that it is the whole picture that developers build in response to market demand, the stimulus for economic activity at the source of that demand has been revealed by urban scholars to be substantially a result of governmental action. Speaking of American cities, Fainstein (2001, 220) suggested that:

> Public redevelopment programs and assistance to the private sector can form part of a sensible program for long-term economic growth. They need, however, to be within the context of economic planning. A good economic plan for a city would set levels of desired space for each market sector and each part of the city, with subsidies and regulatory relief geared to these objectives. The aim of policy should not simply be to create more space but rather to ensure that there is enough space to support industry without glutting the market.

Though this state allocation of land use to selected property types and its impact on real estate pricing might concern private developers and raise the specter of centralized state planning, the current market approach that results in successive booms and busts cannot continue to be accepted as efficient and broadly satisfactory either.

While such government policies can create a macroeconomic contest that is favorable or not for urban development, on another plane their implementation in respect to resource allocation and public services also substantially assists the process in achieving a positive social impact. Glaeser (2011, 88) noted that this is most obvious when the state delivers infrastructure and public services: "The case for federal action is strongest when that action is reducing the artificial separation of rich and poor created by the government itself. Whenever public services are radically different in two adjacent areas, those differences will influence where people choose to live." Such state direction can be complex at the topographical level, but, as Weber (2002, 524) has found, it is not entirely satisfactory in some instances as its influence penetrates to deeper levels of building economics:

> States discursively constitute, code, and order the meaning of place through policies and practices that are often advantageous to capital. Because the presence or absence of value is far from straightforward, states attempt to create a convergence of thinking around such critical issues as the economic life of buildings, the priority given to different components of value, the sources of devaluation, and interrelationships between buildings and neighborhoods.

Fainstein points out that when governments apply these levers with respect to property values, unintended consequences can occur:

> Initially, public intervention was intended to prevent inflation in land prices from making property unaffordable to businesses and residents. Rather than moderating price increases, however, it first inflamed speculation that produced leaps in land values

greatly exceeding the average rise in living costs; eventually, it contributed to the over-supply that caused rapid and damaging devaluation and a corresponding reduction in the value of the public's investment. (Fainstein 2001, 77–78)

And, Beauregard (2005, 2435) added, "to the extent that civic boosters and elected officials designate an area—for example, Wall Street—as 'defining the city,' this favours reinvestment beyond when it makes economic sense."

Even when it is not harmful, the relationship between the legislative authorities and private developers is not unilaterally beneficial to those private interests, since many governments from the earliest times have relied on the private sector to deliver much of the urban form in the various buildings necessary to sustain a community and its production activities. Government has increasingly used the private sector to develop buildings once provided by the state, such as social amenities and affordable housing. With restrictive tax policies incidental to a desire for re-election, federal, state and, municipal authorities do not have the capital resources to provide these important community components and are setting up incentive structures that can make these undertakings feasible for developers. Some initiatives are successful, others not. Inadequacies flowing from this entry of the private sector into the satisfaction of social needs are an offset to the lower taxes. However, as with other areas of privatized public services, those benefiting from the reduced taxes are often not those who are adversely impacted by any reduction in public amenities.

There is another socio-economic factor. From the earliest times, the state has been able to capture some of the economic benefits of real estate production through taxes and fees. In the historical case of London, a system to this purpose was first formally established in 1086 with William I's compilation in the Domesday Book of the economic production of all the nation's land so that it might be shared with the Crown. Later, when English land was put to a higher productive use, even that of housing the aristocracy or a more highly paid urban worker, the taxes payable to the authorities increased. In maximizing revenues for Henry VIII, Thomas Cromwell's strategy for distributing the ecclesiastical lands was aimed at higher economic production, and later monarchs and the London authorities continued this ambition, even if it was sometimes veiled by aesthetic and spatial requirements such as in the early 17th century. So, from the beginning of development the governing authority's financial revenues have been intertwined, if not almost perfectly correlated, with the maximization of the development potential of land. The economic and social functioning of the modern city and the model of urban development as it was formulated during early modern London are strongly symbiotic.

To close the socio-economic loop, it must be understood that such taxes, though often resented by property owners and developers, are a valuable contribution to maintain necessary legal and governmental communal services. Even the notable proponent of capitalism, Adam Smith (1994, 909), remarked on the necessity of this symbiosis:

Ground-rents so far as they exceed the ordinary rent of land, are altogether owing to the good government of the sovereign, which, by protecting the industry either of the whole people, or of the inhabitants of some particular place, enables them to pay so much more than its real value for the ground which they build their houses upon; or to make to its owner so much more than compensation for the loss which he might sustain by this use of it. Nothing can be more reasonable than that a fund which owes its existence to the good government of the state, should be taxed peculiarly, or should contribute something more than the greater part of other funds, towards the support of that government.

Though his comment was made in the 18th century on the issue of property tax, its method of calculation, its potential for discouraging development, and the often unequal burden of its allocation has since advanced in sociological scholarship, though only rather sporadically. There are many instances of attempts to restrict it. The notable California Proposition 13, which placed legislative restrictions on property tax increases, irrespective of municipal needs, has been examined in terms of consequences of housing unaffordability and reduced urban services. Though a discourse on property tax is beyond the scope of this book, its dynamic of supporting the improvement of real estate values and sharing of benefits throughout the community has been shown to be present at the historical origins of the private urban development process.

Public Needs in Urban Development

The 17th-century London formulation of development practice established a mutually beneficial dynamic between municipal authorities who establish the context for urban development and developers who deliver the built fabric. Although since then the relationship has often been more contentious, recent projects globally indicate that it may advance to a more effective level. Specific areas where that early potential might be extended are:

- Private delivery and maintenance of public infrastructure and amenities to include:
    - Funding to maintain the public realm.
    - More granular and temporally dynamic allocation of land uses to achieve functional interdependence.
- Social considerations including:
    - Maintaining social equity in the public realm.
    - Community engagement in development projects.
- New and creative formats of urban topology.
- Improved financial analysis that captures contextual impacts of neighborhood and community.

With the benefit of analysis of the efforts of the early developers, some directions for developing these parts of the model may now be suggested in detail.

Private Provision of Public Amenities

Although the earliest developers do not seem to have made an explicit evaluation of the economic benefits to their developments by their provision of amenities and the attractive public realm that was achieved, their actions and expenditures on these features indicated their belief in this dynamic. Further, it was found that successive attractive developments in the neighborhood could mutually increase the value of all properties, creating a virtuous cycle. Smyth (1985, 42) explains this:

> A site can be made prime if sufficient capital is invested on that site so that it will draw other users into the area, making successive capital investments on neighbouring sites. Therefore, investment on one site can induce investment on other sites giving rise to differential building rent II [as a result of development] by successive investments in the area.

One explicit component in which this occurs is infrastructure, whether the hard physical structures of bridges and roads or the soft forms of hospitals, schools, safety and social services. While development may improve the economic activity of a neighborhood, it usually results in additional usage of the infrastructure and some offset to that increased burden is necessary. Conversely, the economic success of urban development has persistently been dependent on the quality of the local infrastructure.

As those earliest developers of outer London areas were converting large agrarian fields into residential schemes, such sites required substantial infrastructure, even at the most basic level of roads and sewers. Sometimes they performed and executed these tasks well and significantly benefited their schemes, like in Covent Garden and Bloomsbury Square; or, they sometimes did so less well, as was the case at Red Lion Square and even St James's Square where the public realm deteriorated as a result. As the modern business model of development began its formation, its early practitioners undoubtedly understood to at least some degree the higher potential economic value of their residential schemes from attendant public amenities which contributed positively to the neighborhood.

The example of the larger projects was followed on smaller building projects during the latter part of that century, and Bowers Isaacson (1992, 143–144) has found that:

> at least for the years 1681 to 1720, the tradesmen and women of the middling sort to a significant extent controlled the building process which transformed the fields and lanes west of the City into streets and neighbourhoods. These builders created the infrastructure of sewers and paved streets and oversaw their maintenance. They built the outward structures of the houses and sometimes the insides, too. After construction, the builders negotiated their houses' tenancies among all levels of society.

In another instance, in the east of London, Thomas Neale, although a master builder of houses, followed the example of Bedford at Covent Garden and provided a church and marketplace to meet social and economic needs of the residents he sought to house. Power (1978, 43) credits Neale with creating the broad neighborhood: "Shadwell presents an interesting pattern of development; it grew rapidly into an amorphous suburb in the half-century before 1656; then, by the end of the century, helped by an enterprising speculator, it developed into an identifiable and unified suburban centre."

For the social dynamics of these amenities to be more social than superficial, the amenities had to be functional for all members of the community. They did not always have to be recreational spaces and might instead provide needed social services or aesthetic improvements in the urban topography. Commenting on this breadth of provision, however, the benefits have not always been universally admired. Glaeser (2011, 260) has condemned some:

> As much as I appreciate urban culture, aesthetic interventions can never substitute for the urban basics. A sexier public space won't bring many jobs if it isn't safe. All the cafés in Paris won't entice parents to put their kids in a bad public-school system. If commuting into the city is a lengthy torment, then companies will head for the suburbs, no matter how many cool museums the city has.

Though this somewhat misses the point that the two features are not mutually exclusive and that both are desirable, it is valuable as a reminder that balance and proportionality are necessary, in both directions.

The right balance was usually achieved when a developer remained involved in the community beyond mere production of the building for realization of a short-term profit. For instance, an important factor differentiating the Covent Garden and Bloomsbury developments from others was that the sponsors remained and were to remain financially and in other ways involved in the project for a protracted period of time. The value proposition of both these developments was substantially structured through ground leases, and both developers were not only the landlords who collected rents and made repairs. They also lived within their new precincts. By comparison, in two other residential square developments, St James's Square and Red Lion Square, their developers departed entirely from them upon completion. Although St Albans built his own house in St James's Square, he sold most of the remaining sites in fee simple to other developers or residents, and consequently retained little financial interest in maintaining its infrastructure. The greater deterioration of the public spaces of the latter developments by comparison with the former has been remarked upon earlier in relation to capital expenditure on the public realm.

A similar experience in the history of American development took place in William Ogden's development of Chicago. He built one of the state's first major rail lines which brought wealth into the area and stimulated its self-sufficiency, and then his work on public provision as the city's first mayor and later in his other contributions to municipal government helped make the city a site that was not only lived in, but livable. Harpster (2009, 61) provided confirmation of this:

> Economic historian Gates's charge that speculators did nothing to enhance the Midwestern land they purchased was true in the case of most of the Eastern moneymen, but it did not apply to Ogden. He improved the Chicago land he purchased in almost every case before reselling it, contributing significantly to the growth and betterment of the community.

While the provision of public amenities by some developers, the government, and other actors might seem to be a partial solution to urban needs, it has been pointed out that such a spatial fixity of amenities might not be an optimal long-term solution for a growing and changing metropolis. As it became possible for municipalities to offer economic incentives to specific developers to deliver these amenities, it was also regarded as a sacrifice of broader urban economic control and flexibility. Fainstein (2001, 77) warned:

> The property-led strategy for economic development has meant that public resources that might have been used elsewhere became embedded in real estate … In reality, public subsidy [to a land developer] represents a taxpayer investment in a leading industry – the property industry itself; ironically, the failure of the public sector to moderate expansion during the '80s destabilized the property sector.

Similarly problematic at times have been the efforts of municipalities to leverage their relationship with developers to achieve affordable housing solutions. This was specifically criticized by Schuetz et al. (2011, 298) in regard to recent actions by city authorities of providing private incentives to produce necessary housing, with nuanced results:

> In brief, our empirical analysis suggests that the ideological debate over Inclusionary Zoning (IZ) has greatly exaggerated both the benefits and the dangers of IZ: any negative effects on housing prices and production have been relatively slight, but only modest amounts of affordable housing have been produced through IZ programmes. We also find that IZ has different impacts on local housing markets, depending on the condition of regional housing prices.

Aside from the political winds concerning financial incentives for developers, the need for their positive contribution to the public needs of the areas in which their projects are located is an important principle of the development model. The potential financial benefits for them can be seen to have been present from the beginning. But it remains necessary for those initiatives to be part of a coordinated process in municipal planning to provide the best outcome for all: "However, based on such an understanding, urban planning and the management of the municipal typography is conceived of as area based rather than site based, and therefore is concerned with fostering the possible mutual reinforcement of good development in urban areas" (Smyth 1985, 47).

Funding to Maintain the Public Realm
Though developers sometimes participate, mostly involuntarily, in infrastructure contributions, development fees, arrangements, community contributions and the like, when cities have experienced periods of rapid growth many local governments were not able to extract sufficient revenues from them to meet local needs: "Public investments also had to be organized on an increasing scale and on a more and more long-term basis and in such a way as to compensate for individual capitalists' underproducing collective infrastructures" (Harvey 1989, 30).

This underlying need to fund the maintenance of public amenities was also an early problem that failed to be satisfactorily incorporated in the model as it formed, even in its early decades. There were notable exceptions. Understanding the dynamic as it was handled on their rural estates, Southampton and Bedford, now third- and fourth-generation nobility, established sources of funds for the maintenance of their developed public spaces. Most significantly for Covent Garden, where Bedford built the parish church of St Paul's, he formally invested the church as beneficiary with the rents from two of the surrounding residences on the condition that the church would maintain the piazza onto which it fronted. For the most part this arrangement worked efficiently, though his estate found it necessary to make larger infrastructure expenditures in subsequent centuries.

With his mansion fronting onto the public square, Southampton also accepted responsibility for its maintenance, as the family estate continues to do today. The absence of such an arrangement for the newly appointed Earl of St Albans's development of St James's Square, Barbon's Red Lion Square, and many others since has demonstrated the inadequacy of a mere provision of a physical contribution to the public realm without establishing its economic sustainability. Fortunately, it appears that this understanding is gaining hold once again with developers when providing public amenities: the recent development of the historic Domino Sugar site in New York, where the private developer, Two Trees, created six acres of public parkland spanning a quarter-mile along the East River in front of its mixed-use towers (Figure 11.3), and also established a trust-like financial structure to meet the maintenance costs of approximately $0.9 million each year.

11.3

Privately provided and maintained public Domino Park in Williamsburg, Brooklyn.

Furthermore, it is believed by the developers who have created such projects that the investment performance of the project as a whole would benefit by the continued maintenance of the neighborhood. It remains for financial analysis to provide a rigorous evaluation of the cost proposition as it pertains to both the economic and social benefits, and therefore facilitating decisions of optimal feasibility for both private and public stakeholders.

Functional Interdependence in Urban Development
While municipal authorities acknowledge that economic prosperity is supported by private development in the provision of necessary urban fabric and as a source of substantial tax revenues, their strategic planning does not always optimize the delivery of the most useful urban space as it is needed by their residents. Many use their city plans to combat noxious land uses and undesirable living conditions, and their objectives are predominantly topological, macroeconomic, infrastructural, and social. While these are important, more consideration of the detailed needs of communities for specific public amenities and complementary land uses in neighborhoods would better enable them to direct the private development projects to contribute to their city's functioning and social conditions. An example today of missed opportunities in functionally suitable development is the plethora of unoccupied luxury condominiums as well as an oversupply of unused space given to meet developers' statutory obligations of community contributions.

This shortcoming of land use policy has been demonstrated in various urban studies of the late 20th century. In particular, Beauregard's (2005) detailed study of inner-city rebuilding revealed the problems when private development was allowed to proceed by the municipal authorities to meet certain needs of intended residents while neglecting others. In particular, he revealed where residential uses were increasingly satisfied by apartment projects the necessary stores and social amenities were not planned for or sufficiently encouraged in private development. His consideration of urban renewal projects revealed a necessary action in municipal management:

> Functional interdependence, though, is not automatic—a fact that partly explains the need for governments to manage redevelopment efforts—and numerous urban redevelopment projects have floundered on the failure or delay in investment in complementary activities. Little attention, though, has been given to these functional and temporal discrepancies and the spatial dynamics in which they are embedded. (Beauregard 2005, 2432)

Importantly, this notable urban scholar did not place responsibility for managing this dynamic on either municipal land use policy or the private developer, since neither could proceed without the other. Rather, within the context of suitable municipal policy, he presents it as a challenge to the socio-economic framework of urban development:

> ... since the relative mix of land uses is being transformed in any downtown housing initiative, functional interdependence becomes more likely as developers and investors switch from one sector to another ... [but] [s]ynergistic timing and sectoral switching

are hindered by three 'thick' aspects of property markets: sectorial differentiation, the drive for stability in property relations and the local contingencies of property investment decisions. (Beauregard 2005, 2433)

In real estate terms and for the practice of private property development, the hindrance of balanced functionality in the urban composition of a project represents the inability of developers to perform across a variety of property sectors with specialization growing more prevalent, the herd mentality of real estate investors that is supported by market analysis dependent on comparability and past performance, and the constant local variation in economic performance which is not adequately incorporated in financial calculations.

Today, this problem of sectoral specialization by developers combined with the blunt instrument of land use policy is challenging the nuancing of urban space production necessitated by rapidly changing lifestyles and the obsolescence of traditional property types. Although Weber (2015, 205) sees that governmental direction might serve well here, she suggests it behooves the developer to anticipate changes in the building use and format in future years:

Most property owners already plan for the future on an ad hoc basis; for example, their building engineers consider the longevity of building systems to estimate when fixtures will have to be replaced. Formalizing future thinking through life cycle and reuse planning before a new building breaks ground could help stave off obsolescence. Planning, Lynch reminds us, involves seeing 'the spatio-temporal whole.'

Further, professional developers must be trained to be more knowledgeable across property types and more willing to explore new spatial and functional formats. To manage the decisions with respect to real estate markets and economic contexts better requires an application of technology that not only gathers data but also applies the analytical processing that makes that material informational.

A better functional operation of the built environment through more rigorous management of development initiatives would be beneficial not just to developers but also to individual city dwellers on whom their works have a deeper impact. For them, the balance of use and exchange values is fundamental to a viable household within a neighborhood:

The city is the setting for the achievement of both exchange values and use values; and the neighborhood is the meeting place of the two forces, where each resident faces the challenge of making a life on a real estate commodity. From the point of view of residents, this creation and defense of the use values of neighborhood is the central urban question. (Logan and Molotch 1987, 99)

That dynamic, the relation between the larger and the local, forms the nexus between exchange and social use values which are conflated and confused amid the financialization of a utility-based product such as the urban fabric.

Social Considerations

Development does not just add new shelter and new economic production activities but also alters the existing social opportunities and activities. Paradoxically, new development will often adjust the foundation upon which it initially attempts to capitalize. This is seen when upscale residences emerge in neighborhoods that are sought out for their vibrancy and social diversity, but which also gradually lose those characteristics as residents are replaced and economic conditions altered.

In the urban development of 17th-century London, this phenomenon was most strongly experienced in the loss of recreational fields and open space for a community who did not have the resources to travel far from their urban residences. The struggle for public access to open lands had continued since the enclosures of pastures by landowners for grazing in the 15th century, but in the urban areas, the loss of open space was mainly due to housing developments. Both Bedford and Southampton sought to moderate this loss as they developed their suburban lands by providing the open public realm, and included activities and markets that supported the economic transactions across classes.

Other early developers were shown to be less accommodating to existing communities and many were displaced to allow for new upscale housing. Avoiding this destruction to communities while enabling urban areas to be sustained and advanced continues to be a challenge for developers. Though the details are beyond the scope of this discussion, the historical exploration has indicated that the real estate development process is contingent on its social context and potential impact in terms just as rigorous as that of functional demands and the economic markets.

This attention to social needs informs decisions about built form. As Lynch (1960, 119) so pertinently reminded those involved in the large urban developments of the mid-20th century:

> True enough, we need an environment which is not simply well organized, but poetic and symbolic as well. It should speak of the individuals and their complex society, of their aspirations and their historical tradition, of the natural setting, and of the complicated functions and movements of the city world. But clarity of structure and vividness of identity are first steps to the development of strong symbols. By appearing as a remarkable and well-knit place, the city could provide a ground for the clustering and organization of these meanings and associations.

This is more highly aspirational than pragmatic, but it steers progress in the right direction.

Of course, social concerns are not all external to the process. The social relations between its numerous participants also have been found to be important to effective and efficient performance. Building on his extensive scholarship on development theory noted in the literature review, Henneberry explored with Parris (2013, 235) the dynamic of these relations:

> Local development milieus consist of a mix of latent and actual project networks. They are shaped and driven by 'the practice of episodic project collaboration.' Each project is born out of enduring but loose pre-project social networks. The pursuit of a project reinforces the ties between some of its network members but may weaken relations

between others if they do not perform their roles well. Consequently, wider social networks mutate in response to project experience, with subsequent effects on future projects and the wider development sector.

These concerns about the social context and the social process of urban production are further integrated by Ball in his search for a theoretical description of the development process. Having identified the pertinence of their dynamic, he fears for their subordination to the concerns of capitalist economic theory:

> The relative neglect of the social relations of building provision in these [economic] and other urban theories has arisen because the built environment is usually seen in functionalist terms, with emphasis placed on the *uses* to which built structures are put ... Attempts to produce general theories of the role of urban areas in advanced capitalist societies, or aspects of them (such as the existence of urban land rents), have led to this neglect. (Ball 1986, 448)

As the real estate development model adapts to these pressures by more serious inclusion of external needs and concerns, fragile social conditions must be factored in and improvement made with the assistance of social scientists, as to how it may be done.

Social Equity in the Public Realm
Even as cities redevelop their urban environments, they tend towards a solution that attracts a higher socio-economic level of resident:

> Overall, business interests have dominated the negotiations among government, community, and the private sector on the content of redevelopment. They have been supported by elite and middle-class consumers seeking downtown 'improvements' and attractive, centrally located housing. Neighborhood and lower-income groups have received some gains in some places from redevelopment. Generally, however, the urban poor, ethnic communities, and small businesses have suffered increased economic and locational marginalization as a consequence. (Fainstein 2001, 5)

Arising from this tendency is the question of the social dynamics layered onto private and public space. In the urban fabric, they can provoke disorder or prove unifying. Harding (2001, 550) has described the complexity at the time of the growing metropolis of London:

> The interface between public and private was by no means a decisive cleavage: There was a continuum from one to the other, and an area of interaction between the two. Public and private were constantly pushing into one another. Private uses invaded the public space, and the public interest restrained private owners' freedom to act on, and modify, the space that they considered their own.

Although the new elegant residential squares introduced the concept of exclusive housing precincts, the alley-front street dynamic of developed neighborhoods continued and, importantly, generated some spatial socio-economic mixing in ways generally beneficial for all classes, though also problematic in times of plague and social unrest. While there were limitations to social contact among classes, when spatially juxtaposed, the alley-front proximity bred a small form of collective efficacy (Sampson 2012) that benefited the entire community, such as during the Great Fire of 1666.

That collective efficacy was also manifest in the private and public interface, such as the street frontage, that was inherent in a development project. The earliest developers recognized and embraced it and responsibly ensured that it was aesthetically and functionally suitable. The first housing in Covent Garden provided a contiguous arcade to provide a "soft" transition between the private house and the public piazza. Even when houses were built as independent units throughout the project, the developer applied restrictions and direction regarding the form and aesthetics of their façades. This attention to the quality of the edges of the public realm was acclaimed at the time, and is still well received in similar projects. Although in later developments, and in the American version of the residential square, the open area was often enclosed in a way that restricted access, original versions had been modeled on the open plazas of the Continent. These had been created by governing authorities as places for the public to gather, even if often employed for the self-interested purpose of corralling them and providing stately proclamations.

Community Engagement

Whether the amenable public realm and improved neighborhood conditions result from effective municipal administration or private development initiatives, neglect of these aspects results in the most contentious dimension of urban projects. Here, community engagement can benefit all actors.

By increasing information and balancing ideas of imageability, flexibility, and fixity using the input of stakeholders, not only is the physical outcome improved but acceptance by the community is more probable. Indeed, the act of engagement is probably the first important step in meeting community needs. This should be a process that is sincerely receptive to local input and not merely the collection of comments on established proposals. In this respect, Freeman (2006, 184) describes a proactive dynamic:

> Effective community mobilization … might be the surest antidote to expressions of cynicism expressed herein. This tact generally entails focusing on community organizing first. Rather than first developing specific solutions to the problems confronting the neighborhood the goal is to get residents organized and thinking about what they can and want to do to improve the quality of life in their neighborhood.

Substantial scholarship on community engagement presents it as more complex than the usual cursory gathering of community members for the presentation of proposed development plans. Logan and Molotch (1987, 10) describe the deeply functional and social value of urban place: "Geographical communities are not mere containers of activities, some of which happen to have price results or respond to price cues. Rather, community is accomplished through concrete, practical activities of individuals, who, regardless of where they live, work, or invest, see place as the vehicle for meeting significant needs." Private development therefore must thoroughly understand, and neither underestimate nor overestimate, the needs of the communities in which they build.

There are, of course, limitations to community involvement, which must be taken into account when leveraging that input in decision-making. Glaeser (2011, 162) provides cautionary advice: "Ordinary citizens, rather than the planners in City Hall, should have more say over what happens next to them, but community control must unfortunately be limited, because local communities often fail to consider the adverse citywide consequences of banning building." Fainstein (2010, 175) suggests that a broad consultation is therefore necessary: "Plans should be developed in consultation with the target population if the area is already developed. The existing population, however, should not be the sole arbiter of the future of an area. Citywide considerations must also apply."

The determination of the most effective and satisfactory processes of community engagement is an area requiring substantial investigation in the continued refinement of the model for private development. The necessary breadth and complexity of community engagement should not be regarded as detrimental to achieving a satisfactory balance of social concerns with financial interests. The increasing use of technology for this process, such as the CoUrbanize application, widely used by the larger developers in the US, will advance the efficiency of the process and may even provide for surprises in terms of the type of policies and practices that such attention can engender. Similarly, with a more detailed understanding of how individuals navigate their locational decisions and how developers balance market prices with public amenities, municipal governments can more strategically evaluate the ensuing socio-economic order that results from their direction for development, beyond just the singular land use decision for a site.

Urban Topography

A development's provision of infrastructure and distinct amenities are not the only issues relevant to its impact on a city. Though a city is "a composite social, political, cultural and economic phenomenon ... that is very much greater than the sum of its parts," it also contains in its various quarters and neighborhoods "distinctive and idiosyncratic spatial articulations" (Storper and Scott 2016, 1129–1130). It is these built environments of various features of use and appeal that the private developer delivers. Also, as has been shown, from their early beginnings private development initiatives were required to comply with local planning authorities and even public opinion on matters of physical changes of density, height, and bulk in the neighborhood.

The façade of a development is usually important in the presentation of the property for commercial purposes, its street appeal, and in the projection of the nature of its intended inhabitants and how they wish to present themselves, but its interface with the public realm is not usually considered beyond such objectives. As a result, some developments will display ill-considered and unattractive edges when a better path does not advance their commercial purposes, and they may impose unfortunate influences upon the neighboring community. If the message delivered by the street frontage is one of exclusion, it does not foster a sense of social integration into the community. Not only is this alienation detrimental to the neighborhood, but over time this inability to fit within the local social and economic context will often have adverse consequences for the economic success of the development itself. Further empirical research of this symbiosis might reveal direction for the improved weaving of projects into the urban environment.

Urbanists and architects have viewed the aesthetic detriments of urban development with some specific concerns, namely, the impacts of height, bulk, non-contextual architecture, and impermeable boundaries. While many of these undesirable features result from satisfying other objectives of the activity, such as maximizing site usage and containing construction costs, what is noticeable about these design decisions is how minimally they consider their impacts. As formulated, the model gives only a cursory and superficial consideration to this important dimension, often merely limiting it to a response to municipal direction and constraint.

Lynch (1960, 3) has pointed out additional physical details at the smaller scale of the resident navigating the city and which provide the necessary personal, social, and even economic dimensions to the relationship between people and place. He describes how these functions occur:

> Although clarity or legibility is by no means the only important property of a beautiful city, it is of special importance when considering environments at the urban scale of size, time, and complexity. To understand this, we must consider not just the city as a thing in itself, but the city being perceived by its inhabitants.

The earliest developers such as Bedford and Southampton were very concerned with the integration of their projects with the neighborhood, both physically and aesthetically, and they often established size and aesthetic conditions for houses which might be built by third parties.

Some American developers too, such as the Rockefellers, were alive to the positive effect of the aesthetic quality of their projects on the proximate neighborhood, and included privately owned public space in their urban complexes. Rockefeller Center in New York, among them, was particularly exemplary. A similar example can be found in the investment of Pittsburgh Plate and Glass (PPG) in their downtown Pittsburgh headquarters. Toker (2009, 54) explains the corporation's strategy:

> The creation of PPG Place in 1984 was an American corporation's outstanding act of generosity toward its home city ... When the company considered building a headquarters tower near its birthplace on Market Street, it knew that it would be relatively easy to buy only the half acre it needed. But what PPG really wanted was to upgrade the whole district in the manner of Rockefeller Center, so it purchased an area ten times larger than needed for its own building.

Though it benefited economically as its holdings around its new headquarters improved in value, its expressed intention was appropriate to the condition and needs of the city. However, such a strategy is usually based on an intuitive understanding of the matter rather than rigorous analysis. It also involves expansive sites in order to accommodate such gestures, sites often unavailable in urban settings.

Aesthetic enhancement may also be achieved by placing art forms in urban settings, both public and private. In recent times, this method has grown through the presentation of cultural activities in privately owned public spaces. In atrophied urban areas of former manufacturing activities, these interventions are bringing people back and reviving environments. For example, Katsikos (2012, 22) describes this emergence in Miami, Florida:

> Wynwood Walls is ... another creation of [developer Tony] Goldman's, that brought more 'legal' graffiti to the exterior space just outside the Wynwood Kitchen and Bar. The Wynwood Walls is a series of 12 murals showcasing the work of graffiti artist Sheperd Fairey, Aiko and others ... Goldman's approach of highlighting the 'trendy' graffiti movement as a public attraction done by such well-known graffiti artists makes it a hip and 'high profile' piece to be seen by anyone walking by. Goldman seems to truly have an understanding of what will awe the people right from the street. Acting as a 'town center,' the Wynwood Walls and Wynwood Kitchen and Bar command attention with their edgy graffiti walls and clean modern design aesthetic.

This type of locally invested developmental model, and especially its special use of engagement to ensure an "imageable" neighborhood may well be traced back to Bedford's and Southampton's long-term residences and the enhanced features of their respective developments in early modern London. Although local authorities may impose certain conditions on size, setback, site coverage, and some aesthetic features, the thorough evaluation of the external impact of the physical nature of a project should be key considerations of the private development activity itself.

Real Estate Financial Analysis to Include the Community Context
The three basic features of community impact evaluation within the model that would achieve a constructive coalescing of social and economic objectives are:

1. The effect of the development on economic conditions in the neighborhood.
2. The physical changes to the neighborhood typography resulting from the development.
3. The impact of the project on the social dynamics of the community.

The commonly used analytical method for real estate valuation, with its adoption of the corporate finance's discounted cash flow (DCF) model and capitalized valuation technique, has been shown to be relevant to the English concept of land value formed over many centuries. Though this historical exploration has also presented the origins of various persistent shortcomings such as the inadequate determination of calculative inputs, misused assumptions such as in the calculation of residual values, and a general lack of analytical rigor in forecasting the conditions of the holding period. Other factors that have long bedeviled the way to a true knowledge of property values include inaccurate or unreliable market data, misleading sales pitches by many sources of information, and the easy manipulation of analytical outputs. To add to this, recent macroeconomic research has revealed a growing influence of global capital flows on the pricing of real estate assets, including those directed by institutional capitalism (Clark 2000). It has also indicated toward the insidious manner in which typical methods of investment analysis are able to direct capital flows to luxury developments rather than more modest buildings, despite the favorable return yields of the latter (Derrington 2018).

Urbanists who see a symbiotic relationship of real estate and government as an aberrant factor distorting rational market behavior have found further complications. Rachel Weber (2015, 9) noticed that governments have achieved a very detailed manipulation of fiscal matters to achieve their political objectives, often with adverse consequences for developers who are so enticed:

> City governments ... function as critical market makers during construction booms. They welcome speculative building. Hungry for tax revenues and eager to take credit for new trophy towers, municipalities loosen building restrictions, offer subsidies and infrastructure, and promote new submarkets. Overbuilding then forces cities to intervene at the bottom of the food chain, using tax dollars to reposition or demolish buildings at below-market values to reduce the supply of 'blighted' building stock. Dampening supply in this way eliminates some of the competition for tenants and serves to bolster the property values of new construction. These practices, paradoxically, can create even more incentive to overbuild as markets appear tauter and less imbalanced than they really are.

Often, the government is seen as being too restrictive with respect to urban development, but taking into account its participation in directing capital flows for real estate, it may also be seen as doing too much. As stated earlier in discussing the speculative dimension of real estate, it might even be suggested that the financialization of real estate is facilitated by the action of public authorities as they seek necessary budgetary support in the face of reduced tax revenues. Their participation in broader capital markets provides a forum in which land values are put in play as part of economic speculation, but whilst doing this they do not seek, or perhaps do not know how to moderate market results which may be excessive due to this effective subsidization of risky investments.

Irrespective of what forces are directing capital flows and influencing real estate values, what is most noticeable is the inadequacy of the commonly used method of financial analysis to incorporate important aspects involving community context. It is not merely a matter of improving the determination of inputs, though that would certainly help, but rather that the analytical model is so insular in its range of inputs and calculations. As this exploration has revealed that from its historic origins, the two most notably neglected considerations in the model are the sources and objectives of capital, and the context and the neighborhood conditions initially present, then altered, by the development project. While these inadequacies are shown to adversely affect investment returns, those risks are often offset by the liquidity of their transactional markets as buyers and sellers provide resolutions to miscalculations. The physical nature of urban form, however, is not so easily relieved of mistakes as development projects will remain as a problematic presence within a community despite the financial exit of the developer and original investors.

Certainly, a significant reason for the inadequacy of financial analysis and its adverse consequences for urban environments, particularly at the development phase, has been derived from the model's early adoption of the developer's possible exit from a project upon completion. The early developers who retained land ownership beyond the initial development phase appear to have invested more in infrastructure and community amenities, and also in funding ongoing maintenance of the public realm, though further empirical analysis is required to confirm this observation. Additionally of interest is the relative performance of their projects as investments over time, which should also be rigorously investigated.

This reason for inadequate financial analysis in the development model has also been shown to be supplemented by other factors prevalent at the model's early formulation. The rapid domination of investment returns as the reason for asset ownership, of all asset types, was a feature of rising capitalism in London and Europe, just as the private model of urban housing production was born. Perhaps, as history indicates, it may have been catalyzed by it. This pursuit of wealth, the demonstration of its achievement, and the collective enthusiasm of all social levels in London at the time, pushed aside traditional attitudes that bound social responsibility with land ownership. Without the inclusion of a social objective in development projects, the evaluation methodology did not seek to incorporate such factors.

Further, as mainstream corporate financial analysis advanced over subsequent centuries as a result of scholarship, real estate models have remained relatively neglected, particularly in application to the urban development activity. For example, although economists have performed rigorous analysis on positive and negative externalities, and various components of the economy have benefited from their inclusion, real estate calculative methods have not progressed with such an inclusion. This has continued despite increasing information from social scientists and urban economists regarding the compelling dynamic between a property and its urban context. The urban economists, Logan and Molotch (1987, 24) explicitly describe this impact: "Rent levels are based on the location of a property vis-à-vis other places, on its 'particularity' … In economists' language, each property use 'spills over' to other parcels, and, as part of these 'externality effects,' crucially determines what every other property will be."

With extended consequences for society generally also, if the value of amenities and external factors are not taken into account as the city evolves, social inequality can be entrenched. Storper and Scott (2016, 1117) note the potential for social conflict if these aspects are not fully known and equitably distributed:

The tensions created by competition for land uses, the urge to secure access to positive externalities and to avoid the effects of negative externalities, the rent-seeking behaviour of property owners and the need to protect or enhance certain kinds of urban commons (such as agglomeration economies), among other frictions, all create constantly shifting circles of urban social collisions.

Such exogenous impacts must be studied in a manner that enables their structural inclusion in the financial analysis used in private property development decision-making. The analytical model should account for the benefits, or non-existence, of the real estate developer contributing positively to the public context of their project. This would include the potential of that contribution in improving the social and economic conditions of the neighborhood, but also of improving the economic value of the project itself in future years. The early developers of Covent Garden and Bloomsbury Square understood these benefits to their projects over and above their personal benefits through their residential enjoyment of the ambience, but many modern developers are ignorant of the economic potential since it cannot be demonstrated in the financial model. As real estate professionals become more aware of the full context of their projects and its evaluation becomes more efficient through technology, the model should advance to a more dynamic state and reflect a broader array of influences on the internal financial mechanism.

Symbiosis of the Community, the Public Realm, and Private Property

The historical exploration of early private development and an assessment of how it occurs indicate that no governmental or private action is inherently good or bad, but that their functional interdependence is of highest importance. A private developer's considerations should be expanded beyond site boundaries to the larger neighborhood, and not just to provide better for that community but also to achieve the best long-term economic outcome for the project. In some cases and to some extent developers and governments have succeeded in capitalizing upon this synergy, but occasions of misdirected resources, unsuitable engagement with the community, and developers' continued inability to take account of their financial benefit from making investments in the community show that there are still areas for realizing the potential of this symbiosis.

Much as private development may learn something from the evaluation of its model in this book, so may government stand to learn more about the workings of development and the detailed ways in which it can impact communities at site level. If it is more fully conscious of the more micro-level process by which developers make land use decisions, and their market context, it would see the strategic opportunity to assist in obtaining the best economic outcomes of urban projects that also benefit the city. Specifically in respect of urban redevelopment, the scholar Beauregard has pointed out the necessarily functional or programmatic activities of reviving urban areas, and on this subject the development of complementary land uses should be considered in much the same way as the scaling up of the functions of a building or even the scaling down of the functions of a city.

In the meantime, for the suitable efficiency of the private development model, the industry, in partnership with government and the community, needs to address its own dimensions, economic, physical production, and community impact, and to make all participants cognizant of those dimensions for participation in the decisions.

Critique of the Business Format

Although the essence of real estate development lies in its component activities of producing shelter, creating a financial asset or assets (debt and equity), and contributing to the public context, as a new mode of production formulated in the 17th century it was distinguishable as a business model. With respect to the key components of a business model, objectives, actors, and analytics, it exhibited consistent, abstracted feature – such as gathering the necessary resources of land, capital and construction trades (outsourced) – and specific decisions based on analytical tools, as well as presenting a noticeable entrepreneurial spirit in its practitioners.

An understanding of abstract business models has benefited from substantial research and analysis over the past several decades, but private real estate development activity has not received the same attention as others such as industrial production. Given its increasing role in the production of urban environments, in addition to further explorations of the details of its process, it is hoped that subjecting it to observation and scrutiny through such a theoretical framework will improve its performance as a commercial enterprise as well as the quality of its products.

Although an extensive evaluation of the business model of private urban development is beyond the scope of this book, the features that were identified are evaluated briefly. However, more important to this launch of further investigation into the development process is to note the absence of the usual key features of business models.

Business Activities

In the context of emerging capitalism and the particular business interests of its first practitioners, it is not surprising that the format for real estate development resembled the structure of its companion commercial undertakings. It had reference to the advancing mode of mechanized production and financial arrangements that were evolving in Europe, and which continue at the heart of Western capitalism today. As a consequence, although variant in some details, such as the general absence of uniformity of product, the tension between its consumption and asset values, and its unavoidable public impact, the private development of urban real estate took the fundamental construct of the modern business model.

The formulation of this new business of private urban development has shown itself to be a composite practice in which numerous different activities are performed and integrated to achieve an optimal outcome. Though the definition of an "optimal outcome" in the production process reviewed above comprises the dimensions of topography, aesthetics, social impact, and other product-related features, in consideration of the practice specifically as a business model, the measure of the outcome is that of a viable business with sustainable economic returns. There is rarely any discussion of whether a development entity is maintaining its viability, but rather all performance evaluation is focused on the projects undertaken. Further, this assessment approach does not reveal the quality of the management processes of the development entity, as Jedamus and Frame (1969, 2) argue: "But can we really characterize a particular decision as 'good' or 'bad' depending solely on how things finally worked out?" The authors proceed to direct an assessment of business performance, specifically with respect to decision-making, "to be sure that the method used to make the decision was the best available." This analysis of the development entity is yet to be done.

Though not indicative of strategic action to this enterprise-related objective, the early activities included some features of structure and organization that can be evaluated.

Market Management

For the maintenance of an ongoing business, the developer would need to be considering new projects as the completion of one was approaching. To do this, like a merchant, he viewed the market for the products he was able to offer and also noted if his products might need to be modified to meet new demand. He also noted what his competitors were doing – the details of the product, their customers, the pricing and the quantum of their production. In this way, the emergent businessman undertook a simplistic market analysis which compared demand with supply to reveal unmet demand. Although that market analysis has grown in complexity today, the supply demand analysis continues to be regarded as a necessary part of the fundamental process of a development project. Many would say that this is the main driver of private urban development: developers respond to supply demand imbalances.

In this reactive position, however, the business of private urban development has lagged behind the evolution of general business practice. As the noted business historian Chandler has stated emphatically, "the modern business enterprise took the place of market mechanisms in coordinating the activities of the economy and allocating its resources" (Chandler 1977, 1). Though Chandler notes this did not occur during England's Industrial Revolution, it was achieved in America as the nation established extensive transportation networks which made efficient and profitable business coordination possible, and followed this with a structured delegation of management that could administer the very large-scale and diverse activities of modern businesses.

In this way, the modern American business was able to at least partially mitigate its vulnerability to fluctuations in demand as a result of the broader economy, and it did so by expanding or constraining production. Additionally, by utilizing structured middle management, industrial organizations were able to receive detailed reports on divisional performance and thereby alter their allocation of capital and resources accordingly.

Unfortunately, the smaller early development enterprises were, often disastrously, vulnerable to market changes in the demand for housing. Although they benefited enormously from disasters such as the Great Fire in 1666, they also fared badly in response to the economic downturn in the last decade of the century. They were seen to be at the mercy of demand resulting from conditions beyond their control, and this remains a feature of real estate development today. In fact, it is regarded as a tenet of the practice that it *responds* to market demand, which may seem somewhat passive in an era where products such as the iPhone create demand.

On the other hand, the area in which development is implicitly influential is that of supply. Responding to the demand frenzy, once underway many entrepreneurs took control of as many sites as possible and rushed to deliver completed buildings irrespective of what other supply was underway by competitors. In the battles for project success, there were instances where competing projects were delayed or destroyed through building crews being "bought off" with higher pay on other projects. At a more sophisticated level, also, the astute 4th Earl of Southampton appealed to the court and Parliament not to grant the Earl of St Albans the authority to develop St James's Place. St Albans's influence was greater and he was successful, but the awareness of risks inherent in competing supply was all too rarely apparent. When the political and economic troubles of the 1680s dampened demand, supply continued unabated until, like Barbon, they were bankrupt in the last decade.

Another example of advancing trade practice ignored by the early developers was the government-backed monopolistic or oligopolistic trading companies of the English and Dutch. In restricting competition, the trade guilds also provided industry structures, while being challenged by capitalism continued to be influential. The real estate developers, though surely becoming cognizant of their valuable provision of urban housing to the prosperous metropolis, did not gather together and strategically manage the production of housing to avoid the damages of oversupply. They were aware of each other, and copied techniques, product details and building processes, regularly touring competing schemes. Although not condoning the practice of collusion here, it seems unusual that these new practitioners did not make an attempt to coordinate activities, establish a trade organization such as were forming for other new professions and activities.

Industry Affiliations

This relative lack of professional association or regulation of practitioners for the development activity continues today. There is the adoption in some instances of related associations such as with the Royal Institute of Certified Surveyors (RICS), based in London and stretching across Europe, and the Council of Real Estate Advisors (CREA) and the Urban Land Institute (ULI) in America. There are also property councils and municipal real estate boards in many countries, though these are predominantly for professionals involved in brokerage and transactions, not typically development. The lack of collaboration has continued the dog-eat-dog competition of developers in urban areas with the recurring and detrimental oversupply evident in each economic cycle. Additionally, the lack of self-regulation has resulted in a wide variation in performance within the property development industry. With the instances of poor performance so visible in urban settings, and with no concerted effort to influence public opinion, the practice as a whole is regularly condemned.

General Management versus Entrepreneurial Leadership

Early developers, too, did not have or establish a structured management system for covering their expanding operations. There would have been many instances of projects stalling for want of attention to a problem but lacking the presence of an authorized or capable manager. There were many instances described in the Chancery Records of unsupervised trades abandoning projects when lured to competing schemes. The emergence of the project management activity for the delivery of various schemes has been discussed, and noted as being less than satisfactorily formulated. However, to oversee project managers and to direct the entire enterprise on a course of disciplined production activity and sustainable profitability a general business manager was also required.

An evaluation of the real estate development process as business practice, however, shows it to be substantially under-developed. This probably relates to the lack of importance given to the sustainability of the development enterprise, and the continued practice of the activity as entrepreneurial, led by an individual and defying organizational structure.

Although as a process of vision and creation real estate development will continue to be performed in this manner, the scale of projects, the increased responsibility, and accountability and the identification of distinct professional skills and standards will press the industry into more organized structures. Some very large and global organizations already have evolved, and that formation seems to have helped their production rather than inhibited it. Further research in determining optimal organizational formats for the activity would serve the industry in terms of its own survival and also its ability to best deliver the built environment.

Unfortunately, it is often found that entrepreneurs successful in the innovative thinking necessary to launch innovations are not so capable in broader managerial roles. Casson et al. (2006, 28) pointed out that "although self-confidence and pragmatic problem-solving are widely recognized as entrepreneurial attributes, the way that entrepreneurs frame decisions and deploy heuristics requires further investigation." Though diplomatically stated, there is generally noted to be lack of "fit" to general organizational structures of management.

Enterprise management, however, is a necessary capability even within an entrepreneurial undertaking. It is sometimes performed by a different person in the organization, though understanding that managing an entrepreneurial activity requires more structural flexibility and creative problem-solving processes than traditional production management. Often for private urban development businesses, two partners successfully divide the responsibilities so that the individual with more managerial capability performs this role though both are engaged, and financially immersed, in the development activity.

As a general business model, the private urban development activity was born of entrepreneurial spirit and continues largely to be managed as such. However, larger firms, more globalized corporations, and some sophisticated smaller entities determined to survive economic cycles are establishing some features of the normative business model. These enterprises formulate a strategy relevant to their function as ongoing businesses, not just pertaining to each project they undertake. This might involve retaining some properties to provide sustaining cash flow or extending capability to adaptive reuse and repositioning. Additionally, within this advanced business model is an organizational structure, which, though still appropriate to the creative task of development, also provides the clarity of responsibilities and the ability to retain human capital and corporate knowledge. And finally, and possibly most importantly, such enterprises refine and perpetuate an ethical and cooperative culture, as well as being relentless in strengthening their professional networks.

Conclusion

Globally, urban environments are criticized as over-built, unaffordable, and fostering social inequality, and the developer is held accountable.

> Out of sentiments such as these, many a movement of revulsion and revolt can build against the monstrous figure of the developer, the speculator, the urban renewer, and the highway builder who, like Robert Moses, takes a 'meat-axe' to living communities. The evil inherent in such figures has become legendary. They are the centerpieces of what Berman defines as 'the tragedy of development' whose epitome is Goethe's Faust, raging on the hilltop as he contemplates the one small piece of space, occupied by a venerable old couple, that has yet to be integrated into the rationalized and produced space appropriate for modern capitalist forms of development. (Harvey 1989, 192–193)

Perhaps a little melodramatic in its metaphor, but the sentiment is widely held by urban scholars such as Harvey and much of the general public.

Despite that, governments have retreated from governing to ensure the quality of built environment needed by growing urban populations. As Clark (2000, 17) has observed, "[t]he state is in retreat on many fronts, from providing the most obvious forms of infrastructure like bridges, roads, etc., through to the less obvious forms of urban development, including employment, housing, etc." Who then, is to envision a suitable level of built form, consolidate the ideas of its specification, secure a reliable source of funding, invest one's own equity, effort and reputation, and ensure that the occupants of the result are satisfied and happy, so far as should reasonably be expected? This falls on the private developer, who undertakes the larger part of urban building in most cities today.

Portentously, this was the situation when the population of 17th-century London almost doubled, and the response of both the royal court and London's municipal government was to restrict building rather than to provide a range of housing appropriate to the socio-economic mix of the unrelenting tide of urban immigrants. It was by stepping into this breach that the strategic urban development process emerged as a business practice to meet the housing crisis of the times, and it continues to deliver the essential urban fabric.

This book has explored this process. Although many are aware of this role, and often criticize the quality of the activity's output, very few know the details of what is involved in undertaking the development of an urban site. Practitioners proceed through a sequence of steps, and make decisions and perform tasks based on analysis and protocols that have long been the industry norm. It is complex and risky, and sometimes defies simplistic descriptions. Even some of those in the industry are hard pressed to describe exactly what they do, why they do it, and how it may be done better.

Three questions have arisen:

1. How and why did such a model of production emerge when it did, and become the dominant mode of urban growth?
2. Why does it take the form it does, and what exactly is that form?
3. Why is this form of economic production so poorly regarded and charged with responsibility for so many urban ills? And where might improvements be made?

The answers are interrelated. The format by which it is undertaken is not perfect and its flaws lead to unsatisfactory outcomes. A common example is the want of contribution or sensitivity to the needs of the community in which development takes place. An examination of such shortcomings, based on an analysis of the history of the process, can enable the opportunity for their rectification, such as through improved forms of community engagement and advances in financial analysis. Such an examination also has the beneficial effect that the commendable aspects of the model can be understood for their fundamental first principles and the manner in which they achieve its objectives. An example of this is to be found in the provision of stabilized yielding assets that suit the needs and tenure of retirement funds. An elucidation of the reasons for its proficiency in delivering this investment vehicle seeks and reveals the driving factors in its original formulation. This virtuous dynamic of understanding and evaluation can then be extended to its other areas yet to be fully and precisely formulated, such as its organizational structure for production, its comprehensive calculation of building lifecycles, and its integration of the social and economic dynamic of urban externalities.

Examining the current mode of practice in this way, however, encounters an intellectual barrier in the form of a conditioned reflex which responds that this is the way it has always been done, and is therefore accepted as right. If asked if it is the best way, the answer is to query what other way is possible or better with respect to what alternatives. This absence of an evaluative framework is indicative of what is called trade practice rather than a professional discipline. For the activity to be regarded as a professional discipline, a formulation of its theoretical construct around what it does, why and how it does it, and how well it is done, is required.

Some early scholarship on the process was undertaken in the latter half of the 20th century, and various models were devised to represent the actors, the actions, the context, and the influences. As it was adumbrated in Chapter 10, the intellectual construct that seems most appropriate for the 21st century integrates economic, physical, and social concerns. How this is to be achieved is a work in progress, but it requires a more granular knowledge of the process which must go beyond merely describing what steps are taken and expand the analytical construct to include understanding its detailed objectives and first principles as manifested in its steps and decisions. It must also reveal the embedded assumptions, and identify the changing external context and influences upon the activity. Such searches have been successfully applied to other complex economic practices including corporate finance, pension fund management, and venture capital.

To the present time, viewing current practice has resulted in overly complex graphic representations, or it has been confined to a specific property type or development activity. For the observation of the fundamentals of the process in a more simple and essential format, this investigation has sought, described, and evaluated its historical origins. Although there is much more to discover, this exploration has found its key principles and the essential dynamics, which may be employed as a skeletal framework for establishing a theoretical construct of it. These may be summarized as follows.

Why It Exists: Its Objectives

A starting point for seeking key principles lies in the question of why this activity is undertaken at all. Robert Hooke, the 17th-century scientist and surveyor of London, sought theoretical foundations for the New Philosophy of the time, saying, "There ought to be some End and Aim, some predesigned Module and theory, some Purpose in our Experiments" (Hooke 1969, 15). There are numerous and complex "End[s] and Aim[s]", and while still conceding an inter-relational dynamic, the objectives of the development activity are broadly threefold:

1. Provision of shelter for occupants and the community as a whole.
2. Creation of financial assets for the capital markets.
3. Contribution to urban topography and provision of public amenities.

Within each of these, additionally, the purpose and potential achievements of the process are complex and interwoven.

Providing Shelter

Human settlements by nature need shelter, but the manner in which this protected space was provided has varied with civilizations and cultures. In an Amish community, the erection of a family's house or a community hall is undertaken by all. But specialization in building has been a more common method, and in many societies tradesmen were engaged by the intended occupant, who paid for their services. This burden of payment was often a challenge. Some could afford to have a building constructed for their own home. Others would lease it to tenants and receive a return on their capital over a period of time with a moderate financial reward for their efforts, a commercial venture which is not unique to buildings, though it differs from some other consumables that are commonly limited to self-use. Societies have attempted for centuries to deter greed in this activity, with only moderate success.

The capital needed to pay for the materials and labor purchased to produce shelter is itself a resource, just as the materials and labor and the land upon which the building is erected. Capital is critical in the building process, where resources are combined through organized actions to deliver the completed structure. The development of a property is therefore essentially the productive combination of the physical elements of land, materials, labor, and capital.

Though the making of profit might be a personal motivating factor for the participants, the activity's primary purpose and societal justification is to provide necessary shelter for the community, and for this reason it should focus on that product, its suitability, quality, and value to its users both economically and socially, the price it commands, and its costs. In contemporary development activity, these aspects receive attention through a variety of analyses, including market research, neighborhood analysis, demographic investigations, consideration of existing products, and possible innovative solutions. Sometimes these are extensive, with resort to the services of consultants, but others are superficial. This disparity in analytical effort and rigor raises concern because of the importance of the answers to the substantial economic and social decisions inherent in the development process. Often, decisions are expediently made, rarely interrogated, and outcomes are decided by reference to existing solutions whether entirely suitable or not. A comparison of the process' standards with those of contemporary product design indicates that this feature is an under-formulated, unresolved, and weak component of the urban property production process.

In the historical exploration that has been conducted here, it was observed that the earliest developers gave substantial consideration to the details of their product and its suitability for the intended occupants, though those persons were so similar to themselves that formulating the necessary specifications was intuitive. In contrast, development of premises for the "middling sort" of occupant such as undertaken by Nicholas Barbon was achieved through formulated standardized solutions that were often described as "mean." Nonetheless, his houses were affordable to them, and in this way he was addressing that specific need. This demonstrated that the specification of the product is complex because of countervailing costs and benefits, and it was also seen that close attention to these factors should continue throughout production. But from its earliest formation, the industry failed to establish a structured procedure by which all proper details of the intended building might be fully explored and rigorously determined, and it remains ad hoc and under-informed despite the substantial data that is being collected by technology. Once again, general production management processes and operations theory could provide guidance to the industry on these matters.

As an act of creation, the development process is fertile ground for creativity. Unusually for production, the unique nature of each particular property requires extensive searches for solutions across an array of concerns. Admirably innovative ones were found by the earliest developers in Bedford's piazza which addressed spatial layout, Southampton's varied lot size which was devised to meet market diversity, and Barbon's lease capitalizations which were formulated to answer funding needs. Further, in Covent Garden, with the architectural assistance of Inigo Jones, Bedford created what was broadly applauded as a new format for the English urban residence, and influenced it for centuries. The combination of aesthetic and functional innovation and the economic success of the project demonstrated the exemplary dynamic of developer and architect to advance production of the urban environment.

Unfortunately, sometimes due to circumstances such as regulated building form and misleading market information, developers have not pursued innovation for the benefit of their contemplated occupants. "Iconic" designs for the building form and façade often conceal traditional internal layouts that are losing relevance for changing lifestyles. Discouragement to innovation in the physical form also has been shown to stem from real estate calculative practices whereby the valuation of a proposed development, necessary for obtaining capital commitments, uses metrics associated with existing buildings that are considered to be comparable. Scholarship has revealed that the valuations of innovative solutions are discounted because of the lack of market comparables, and therefore they cannot compete with the projected financial returns of traditional formats. However, if Steve Jobs had continued the production of the flip-phone because of the many comparable versions, contemporary life would be significantly different.

Providing Investment Assets

Continuing the master builders' tradition, and that of some noted large-scale developers in ancient Rome and 16th-century Antwerp, the English developer too might have continued to produce these necessary consumption goods in conventional form, and with satisfactory profits. However, and possibly contributing to its role as the dominant mode of delivery, the 17th-century London development industry found new contextual features that critically provided its new production model with the large amounts of capital needed, and in turn, directed the reformulation of the activity to suit those needs.

The central feature of this milieu was the rise of capitalism with its modern commercial practices. Within this new economic thinking, resources such as capital and land were to be put to work to maximize the financial return on their use. The advent of private real estate development was brought about by the Earls of Bedford and Southampton who drove to maximize the economic potential of their landholdings, which were, due to their ancestors' wealth strategies, fortuitously located proximate to the expanding London metropolis. These two progressed from the traditional aristocratic concept of relatively passive land management, and although themselves of that leisured class, had a lineage of business acumen which they applied innovatively. The developments of Covent Garden and Bloomsbury Square were driven primarily by the new concept of *highest and best use* of land for its economic maximization. That this comprised the production of houses added a challenge to their skill sets, but one which they met with creativity and enthusiasm.

From the beginning, private development of the urban fabric required substantial capital. Although they used their own financial resources for their two earliest developments, Bedford and Southampton outsourced the production of some buildings, thereby introducing external capital into the economic dynamic. Although they did not substantially benefit from it, since the rent from the houses constructed by other parties went to those builders, the outsourcers retained ownership of the land and received improved ground rent as a result of its "higher use," so that this also included a form of capital leverage.

Later developers who were without their own capital resources followed the business practices of other industries and directly raised external capital in the form of both equity and debt. However, the diversion of this capital away from the many other new and competitive offerings in the vibrant investment market required that the compensation offered for its use should be competitive. Though difficult to understand in today's climate of widespread real estate investing fervor, in the England of those centuries real estate was not a tradable asset. The Crown had restrained aristocratic land divestment since the time of William the

Conqueror, and as an investment of indefinite life its economic returns were very moderate, being typically the result of rent from tenant farmers. Though early foreign trading and mercantile activities attracted substantial investment capital, it is claimed that real property investing became of alternative interest only as a result of Elizabeth I's restrictions on the growth of trade.

However, once financial success through property development was noticed, real estate was launched as an attractive investment asset. There was an initial reluctance to invest before or during construction, but enthusiasm for the completed product created an economic "pull" through that process. Methods of investment analysis and metrics were adopted to enable comparisons of performance with other industries, and real estate became an identifiable and respectable asset class in the new capitalist economy.

Thus, in the overall picture, in addition to physical shelter, the production process of urban real estate development delivers financial products, both by way of equity investment opportunities and debt vehicles. Their users are generally very different from the users of the shelter, that is, both the specific occupants and the surrounding community. Although some property owner-occupiers enjoy both product types, it is very common that even equity ownership is complemented by external debt. Just as in the provision of shelter, in this asset creation process the developer is responsible for formulating products which are attractive to consumers, these being investment products that must appeal to the capital markets. This is also a purpose for the private development process, though of course inter-dependent with the production of shelter.

The Urban Topography and Community Amenities

As is evident from the protests against its intrusion in neighborhoods, development alters the urban topography and is fundamental to its nature. The question is not whether a new project will impact upon existing urban conditions, but rather to what extent it will do so and whether it will be adverse or positive. A significant impact was found in earliest productions and, as observed in substantial scholarship, the scope of its effect was broad and varied, ranging from physical features and aesthetic qualities to economic and social consequences.

Inherent in the actions of the earliest developers was a sense of responsibility to the community, partially emanating from their cultural and social background, but also personal to them. They understood and contributed to the new urban aesthetic and attended to the connection of their projects with the neighborhood through strategic spatial layouts and enhanced infrastructure. Later developers, however, perhaps having less extensive spatial control, became more inward-looking as to the physical aspects of their projects within the urban composition. Although Barbon demonstrated his understanding of the economic benefits of positive externalities and provided comprehensively attractive environments such as Essex Street, he ignored them when he developed some tightly packed and untidy housing. Although the issue was not formalized in economic expression by himself or others at the time, the attributes of urban space were being discussed by cultural commentators such as he. By Barbon's choice of actions, it would seem that he was aware of an economic dimension to the aesthetic relationship between a building and its context, but often took a simpler and more financially expedient route when he could get away with it.

That this relationship generally remains a vague and anecdotal consideration in the development process when it is not imposed by statutory authorities or overwhelming community demands requires rectification in its business model. It was shown that within decades of the birth of the development process the increasing demands of the capital markets diminished this purpose for the activity, both by introducing a more short-termist attitude and, even more importantly, by its chosen method of performance evaluation, that is, the commonly used investment return analysis, which does not allow for inclusion of this feature. Recent scholarship discussed in Chapter 10 has traced this adverse effect on 20th-century city growth and form. What remains necessary is the modification of performance measurement to include these externalities within investment returns, and not just immediately upon delivery but throughout the cycle of mutual impact that generally occurs over time. Some research is underway with respect to parks and recreational conditions, but the application of technology to more granular comparisons of the physical and economic aspects of properties can extend this exercise to obtain more input data and more informative analysis.

A further dimension of the inter-relational dynamic between the private development process and the endowment of public benefit is how the provision of shelter for particular occupants also benefits the community as a whole. The context of its first appearance was 17th-century London, crowded and overwhelmed by its population explosion, but without public leadership to produce a solution in the way that the French monarchs and Italian nobles had done. The English Crown was dependent upon the City of London for much of its funding, which was constantly depleted by military actions. The City's municipal authority was challenged beyond its resources and sought to prevent more housing in the hope that its scarcity would deter immigrants. Living conditions in the whole of London and nearby Westminster were deteriorating and traditional master builders were unable to obtain suitable sites or produce housing in the volume that was necessary. It fell to the private developers to make use of their landholdings, take the financial risk, and create a model of real estate development with a production of the necessary scale, but with attention to spatial order and control of the quality of built form that resolved this community need. It is true that they were paid for it, handsomely at times, but that does not detract from the value of their satisfaction of this need as a broad social benefit.

The contribution which a development makes to an urban community need not be confined to that which will happen existentially. In their urban schemes Bedford and Southampton provided attractive open public places that they ensured would be well maintained. Bedford also built an expensive parish church for the community. Though their motivation for these contributions was in part to obtain necessary building approvals, the quality of the amenities they provided and the personal responsibility they undertook for them indicated a conscious normative decision related to their activity. Unfortunately, the provision of these community benefits suffered the same fate as concern for the impact on the urban topography, abandonment, mostly as a result of the same imbalanced focus on financial aspects, and today both are typically addressed only when the developer is pressed to do so. However, the economic structure is the same, and an understanding of the feedback of financial value to a development by the amenities it provides for the public is being seriously explored.

Contribution to the composition of the urban topography, and positive contributions to the community needs and the public realm add a social purpose to the urban development process.

Management of the Development Process

Within these three categories of purpose, for each project more detailed and more specific components are identified anew. This need for constant reformulation presents a challenge in honing the developer's performance, but it is also an opportunity to consider new options. Thus, the process will be never formulaic but rather a continued exploration of creative and improved solutions to meet its multiple purposes.

General management strategy provides guidance for economic processes such as this, though real estate development's range and complexity of purposes and the uniqueness of its attributes, such as scale, timing, and stakeholder dominance for each project, makes it more difficult to organize and administer than usual. Many development companies commence their activities with one or two successful projects, but are then challenged to the point of insolvency on the next. With managerial attention spread over so many aspects of the process and projects continually requiring new solutions, the administration of the development entity itself is often neglected.

An additional objective for the development process therefore is the management of the business enterprise itself to ensure its economic sustainability, as posited by Graaskamp (1981). Although he extended the objective of economic sustainability to apply to all stakeholders in urban development, Graaskamp importantly pointed out that frequently, with the critical attention given to a project's success, the developer's own economic survival is not strategically managed. For example, perhaps with too much optimism in believing a project will achieve high investment returns, to attract capital a developer often offers benchmark returns to external investors that are not realistically achievable, with the result that the developer is adversely subordinated in profit distribution. More empirical research might result in an adjustment to this practice, though there is a difficulty in that underperformance is always under-reported in the industry.

This book's investigation and analysis has also shown that the project-to-project organizational strategy which is the most commonly adopted involves the distribution of all proceeds from each completed building without amassing any corporate reserves like other businesses. Developers often neglect the retention of corporate capacity in respect of financial resources, team capability, and corporate knowledge. This then should be a fourth key objective of the private development process: economic sustainability, and the associated retention of internal resources and capability.

Hierarchy of Objectives

While the objectives have been described with the understanding that they vary considerably from project to project, their hierarchy of importance may be given a normative evaluation as a result of this historical exploration and certain scholarship presented in Chapter 10.

Although all four objectives are essential dimensions of this activity, it has been seen in historical experience, and is vociferously noted today, that certain of them are accorded dominance to the neglect of others. On the Covent Garden project, the Earl of Bedford achieved a balance of all four: the provision of popular residences, a satisfactory financial return on his land and capital (with modifications of expenditure from time to time), the aesthetic improvement of the urban landscape and contribution of public amenities in the piazza and St Paul's church, and his family's continued presence in development activities on the Bedford estate in the centuries since.

It is important that while the driving force behind the project was his interest in maximizing the economic potential of his land resource, the other objectives were not heavily overshadowed. The critical housing shortage of the time was a catalyst for the birth of this new business, but once commenced the process engaged all four dimensions for the successful completion of the production. Objectives will vary in the initial impetus they give to a project and their relative importance will often vary during its process. However, as the scholars Graaskamp (1981), Guy and Henneberry (2000), and Ball (1986) have demonstrated, generally essential to the successful dynamic of a development process is the balancing and optimizing of all objectives in a relatively equal hierarchy.

This historical exploration has also shown the jostling for hierarchical ascendancy by enthusiastic and demanding capital markets as the attractiveness of real estate investments was noticed. The Earl of St Albans's development of St James's Square did not include protracted ownership and continued real estate activity within the site, and his sale of freehold resulted in exceptional financial rewards for himself and co-investors but poorly maintained public space and an absence of an aesthetic composition in the buildings, although many individual residences were architecturally commendable. Thus, the dominance of one objective over the others resulted in a partial failure of the project as urban development. Similarly, developers such as Nicholas Barbon, who were intent on a speedy and lucrative exit, were infamous for their poor-quality housing and disregard for public amenity, and in this they failed to contribute to the comprehensive needs of the urban built fabric.

Although it frequently occurs that some objectives may validly be given more importance in the final outcome, there is a need to be able to evaluate fully the trade-offs that must take place in achieving this, both at the beginning and throughout the process. For example, community amenities can be provided for, though the cost should be known and assessed, and the actual provision altered as conditions change. As the objectives are assessed for hierarchical position on projects, the cost-benefit analysis should be performed with the comprehensive task of urban development in mind.

The continued dominance of today's capital markets has been discussed. A suggested correction of the imbalance is in adjusting the methods of financial analysis to include all stakeholder objectives and their contextual facets more comprehensively, even if the more qualitative ones are difficult to quantify. Additionally, the overly conservative mode of valuation of innovative physical space should be rectified, especially as new social models and lifestyles demand changes to the functional program of the built environment. And, even respite from the dominance of certain financial strategies, such as the short-termist regard of asset appreciation, over others such as longer-term operating yields, could be gained through the rigorous calibration of real risks and returns beyond the narratives led by capital markets.

How it Works: The Process

If these objectives may be regarded as established, though flexible, it is necessary to consider the processes by which they can be achieved. Typically for business, these are the usual protocols and procedures by which decisions are made and actions taken. For more institutional businesses they are codified, and for more creative or innovative enterprises they are more loosely constructed.

As it has been explained, research of property development's procedures and decisions encountered the same challenge as when formulating objectives because of the complexity of influences, actors and their capacity for action, and again the uniqueness of each project. Graphically presented models are either too complex to be useful or too specific to a property type or institutional context. However, it may be posited that it need not be modeled in such a definitive and graphic form in order to convey fundamental protocols. Rather, a theoretical framework of the production process might be established from first principles relating to achieving identified objectives, such as is emerging in the field of engineering operations. Within this framework, the developer can devise and modify analytical tools, allocate human responsibility and actions, include the participation of other stakeholders and incorporate a mechanism of oversight, evaluation, and feedback.

Even in its early and most basic formulation, real estate development activity defied codification. Bedford was exceptionally innovative and intent on close management of his project, even proceeding to build three model houses as defined options for potential residents as well as being prescriptions for the building trades undertaking the work. This step was key in introducing a new and aesthetically advanced building form to the market, and though there are no specific records, it was probably accomplished through an effective collaboration of architect and developer to create and refine the intended built form while also maintaining financial feasibility.

However, Bedford's conscientious innovation and detailed management of the product quality was not formalized within the model of urban development that was adopted broadly by others. Perhaps this approach required skill and commitment beyond many who were able to undertake development and meet the urgent need for housing at the time, and the financial success, also assured by the excessive demand, enabled continuance of the general method during the 17th and 18th centuries with this significant procedural exception. It was discarded without adverse implications for the surviving business model, though an evaluation of its loss might be instructive as to the quality of product delivered and the challenges of innovation in urban topology.

Other procedural features were added to the process during the early decades without derailing its essential nature and perhaps enhancing its success. One example was Nicholas Barbon's early form of property "pre-sale." He adroitly leased an intended structure and, by making an early sale of that lease, he funded the construction without committing any of his equity. This materialization of a useful financial asset out of an expectation of revenues, secured by a contracted financial obligation in the form of a lease, became the basic strategy of his business. Although obviously open to abuse, and many instances of it are evidenced in Chancery Records, this might be seen as the converse of Bedford's model houses. Although seemingly not capable of logistical combination, these alternative courses in the process have persisted and can be expected to do so. What a suitable theoretical model of the process might achieve is to allow for each but, with the use of technological innovations such as virtual reality and machine learning for cost-benefit analysis, mitigate the adverse consequences of each.

Despite these added and subtracted features, the process retains the fundamental principles and protocols, tools and participants established at its 17th-century origins.

Principles of Production

In evaluating the model as it was originally formulated, and as it is now applied globally, its first principles have in some degree been teased out. Though not definitive, since that requires further scholarship and empirical analysis, they were found to be essential in guiding the processes to achieve the objectives of the early developers, and they remain relevant to the four objectives noted earlier.

By definition, principles are fundamental, and therefore mandatory as far as they go. Their importance stems from their establishment of norms, though also enabling variation in procedural features to achieve a better response to new challenges or contextual changes. They are usually identified and applied in the formulation of societal practices and traditional processes, and the result is often a set mode of operation that is conducted according to specified and clearly communicated steps and actions which are learnt through experience and training. However, this codified procedure, clearly observed in many trade practices, does not allow for deviation and is often challenged by novel or unknown circumstances. Principles must form a more flexible theoretical structure than just normative procedures. With similar origins as the development activity, structural engineering practice is shown by Straub (1952, xvii) to have evolved from being a mere experienced-based capability for producing major structures prior to the 18th century, to gaining significantly higher potential with its theoretical framework of building statics that "signified the birth of modern structural engineering; it revolutionized the entire art of building; it opened up possibilities previously undreamt of."

In the same way, the real estate development activity must evolve beyond its traditional mode of practice which, though proven helpful in keeping track of the many aspects to be incorporated and the multitude of actions to be taken, does not support its practitioners in the necessary deviations from prescriptive process to achieve more creative and profitable solutions. Within the theoretical framework of principles this book seeks to compel, procedures could be submitted to critical evaluation, flexibility could be incorporated to enable responses to changing socio-economic needs and unforeseen circumstances, and improvements made to the model of practice.

The exploration of its origins and the rapid formulation of its model have revealed several key principles which are set out in the summary of the model in Chapter 9, and will not be repeated here. What should be raised at this point is a reminder of some of their central tenets:

- Efficient and economic land management requires certainty of control and maximization of use, though its use may be modified according to statutory and community requirements and by what is best suited to long-term market conditions.
- The statutory and community context of a project may facilitate its success or ensure its demise, and constructive interaction with authorities promotes mutual influences and benefits.

- Planning and design require extensive and rigorous analysis of user and community needs, neighborhood conditions, real estate markets, capital markets, and construction modes, and such an analysis should continue throughout a project.
- Physical details should be adjusted to achieve an optimal product by continually subjecting the process to granular cost-benefit analyses.
- While traditional construction processes can be efficient, the prospect of a better result through innovative solutions will require that they be challenged.
- Equity provides funding for the riskiest art of the development process but in doing so it exerts the strongest influence in achieving its specific objectives on a project.
- Land typically retains some value forever, but a building deteriorates, and its production costs should be strategically amortized over a reasonable life cycle. Obsolescence is increasing with changing lifestyles and that life cycle is reducing.
- Price appreciation is speculative and largely reliant on external conditions, and this appreciation in value is recognized only upon sale or other form of equity extraction.
- A building's residual value is distinguishable from that of the land on which it stands. For assessing the residual value of land and building comprehensively, any appreciation due to market demand and change of use is predominantly to be found within the value of tho land.
- Early community engagement makes for the higher probability of a project's acceptance and often provides useful information on important neighborhood details.
- Throughout a development project, management should have feedback loops to inform the process and to build knowledge for subsequent ones.

These are mere starting points for the complex construction of a theoretical framework by which they spawn other principles and direct the process. As Adams et al. (2012, 2579) see as a continuing challenge to the industry: "The substantive academic account of what typifies the property developer has still to be written."

Evaluations and Feedback

What also remains lacking for the protocols of development activity is an evaluative structure, or more specifically, an internalized system of self-assessment of the process as it is underway and also as it is performed comprehensively by the real estate industry.

Evaluation during the Process

While other industrial modes of production employ strict quality control evaluations, the process of constructing a building on an open site is subjected to only initial comprehensive evaluations followed by irregular partial assessments in terms of satisfaction of an often-limited range of objectives. Though structural criteria and construction regulations are monitored, the optimal accommodation of user needs is regarded as fixed and modified only through exceptional procedures and cost. These restrictions are, however, being challenged by new partnerships in development where the occupant is directly involved in not just initial programmatic formulation but also ongoing refinement during construction, such as at Oxford Properties' rebuilding of the historic St John's Terminal, New York, for its progressive and demanding new tenant, Google. Generally, a project is fixed in many of its features by the time evaluations are made by the occupants, official authorities or community, and the traditional development procedures resist any impactful influence.

Close scrutiny of the early developments reveals, in a number of different aspects, the importance of continued oversight and evaluation throughout the process. Of course, a project's fundamental financial feasibility requires early analysis for the project to proceed, but the investment success also requires the ongoing assessment of that criteria. Some developers with sophisticated project management procedures are successful in monitoring and adjusting for financial objectives despite the continual change in circumstances, resources, capabilities, and other factors. But for many developers, the process is usually formulated merely as a cost-management activity such that, even if budgets are carefully watched, there is little optimization of costs with the changing valuation of the completed project.

Learning from general production management techniques, particularly new methods of using technology emerging from the field of operations and engineering research (OER) could provide the real estate industry with more suitable mechanisms of oversight and evaluation during the development process.

Industry Self-evaluation

The purpose of this book is to seed the formulation of a theoretical construct within which the development activity can evaluate itself and improve its mechanisms as needed. Such frameworks for self-evaluation are broadly used elsewhere, for example, in advances of legal and medical practice, scientific research and, in recent decades, business and commercial management. If it is to be respected as a professional discipline, the private urban development model must have core key principles and practice standards by which its performance can be continually tested. By examination, evaluation, and detailed attendance to the principles of practice, a professional discipline continues to define itself, refine its processes, and perform at its best.

Contributing to, or perhaps even a result of, this lack of examination and assessment of its essential processes is a paucity of scholarship and academic research. There is substantial commentary and solid empirical analysis in the area of real estate, but this is usually directed towards, on the one hand, its resultant social impact, economically and politically, and on the other, its finance and investment components. As well, there is much research on construction techniques and materials, and on technological advances in data gathering of property markets. However, all of this is either about the consequences of or just a component of the process. The comprehensive urban development process and how it functions as a totality have received little attention. An early start was made in Europe during post-war rebuilding, and the advances by British scholars in understanding and describing the model have been noted above. In the US, a few scholars such as James Graaskamp carried out some early interrogations of the process, but within the nation's fervent capital markets particularly in recent decades, academic analysis has mostly been directed to the financial outcomes that the trading of properties produces.

While the capital markets continue to dominate the real estate industry, there is an increasing need for consideration of social impact in the pursuit of commerce. Property development, with its delivery of goods necessary for human survival, society's prosperity, and an imposing presence in the urban public realm, is an economic production process of physical, economic, and social dimensions. By adopting and adapting emerging methods by which commercial enterprises may contribute to the public benefit, it can improve its procedural model to achieve its economic objectives while also satisfying the demands of its social context.

But these benevolent results cannot be successfully dictated by legislation and formulated as costly assessments on urban projects. Rather, they must be explored and rigorously understood as part of product specification, their costs and benefits rigorously evaluated, and their inclusion justified and practical. If the activity is to be modified and improved to meet its responsibility for delivering the bulk of the urban fabric, a continuous examination and assessment of its principles and processes must be undertaken. If it is to be a discipline, it must subject itself to this self-evaluation, and its scholarship should incorporate this critical methodology. Incorporating this within the complex process is the task of a more comprehensive framework for the private development activity, and this is where professionalism born of critical thinking and scholarship will do its work.

A Discipline and its Education

For the education of the future real estate developer, this book hopes to challenge a traditional view that the development process, or even the real estate industry comprehensively, is not a discipline in itself, but merely a confluence of multidisciplinary activities. Rather, it seeks to show that the central production process of creating the modern urban environment was formulated in such a way that it generated compelling first principles which guided decisions and structured processes that sought to optimize its financial, physical, social, and enterprise objectives. In its broadest sense, the ideal theory of real estate development would provide a framework for understanding how the process functions at the level of first principles, which would guide its practice and then enable evaluation of the process, indicating what actions may be necessary for an improvement in meeting its objectives.

Such a theoretical framework would underpin the education of real estate professionals so that they would not be superficially presented as trade practitioners, but rather as having a learning experience of critical exploration in all the wide and varied aspects, such as partially suggested by Adams et al. (2012, 2582):

> In reality ... the developer's expertise is often seen to lie in knowing the local market (product), spotting opportunities (location) and resolving constraints to make things happen when required (timing). So, successful development is not solely about the old adage of 'location, location and location,' but instead relies on broader knowledge of 'product, location and timing'.

From Past Achievements to Future Progress

Was it a coincidence that the history of the long-lasting and much applauded London square coincides with the history of the first private urban developer? This new format of urban residential precinct came about through a confluence of several factors: a demand for fine residences in suburban London, the availability of developable land, the financial capacity and administrative capability of an entrepreneur to take on a project of such scale, a landowner concerned with the welfare of the neighboring community, the leadership of the first

English architect substantially supported by a monarch, and a general public enthusiasm for this derivation of the Continental format. The case is made here that such a combination of factors was essential for the new process by which a private entity could undertake the siting, funding, and delivery of urban development on a scale that enabled its spatial layout to be strategically planned and achieve an improvement in the quality of habitation, the substantial enhancement of the site's economic value, and a positive contribution to the public realm.

Thus, the development of Covent Garden was a radical change in the way the modern city would be built. That commendable project established the architect as a commissioned professional to provide creative designs for buildings, advancing from the vernacular and traditional patterns of tradesmen, so as to be integral to the requirements of future citizens. It provided a breakout for both that emerging profession and the development process, by engaging that architect in development projects for a wide range of speculative residences beyond royal and government projects and designs for wealthy clients. Further, as the work preceded the advent of urban planners, that architect was required to design both the urban public realm and the specific private buildings of the entire project, which formed a physical manifestation of the important symbiotic relationship between a building and its public context in a modern urban setting. Cognizant of his social responsibility and of the amenities' addition of economic value to his commercial buildings, the private developer collaborated with the architect to deliver the first significant private urban development that incorporated substantial public amenities.

All of these were coincident with and integral to the first strategic and significant activity whereby a private entrepreneur envisioned a substantial change to an urban setting, evaluated its economic feasibility, established control of the land, engaged the necessary consultants to specify the details, organized the required capital, obtained necessary legal approval, engaged construction trades, managed the project, marketed and sold off the completed residences. Adopting some emerging commercial methods of other industries, though also incorporating old approaches where necessary, but most of all with vision and courage, a few capable entrepreneurs introduced a new method of providing an urban environment that suited the needs and spirit of the times. The leading contributors and their projects have been described, complemented by a running commentary on the features, processes, and consequences of the model as it evolved. As with many advances made in the civilization of mankind, the persons involved, the dramatic events which formed the backdrop, and some surprising turns of history are at their most vivid in this story of real estate!

References

Primary Sources

Archives of Alnwick Castle.

Barbon, Nicholas. 1685. *An Apology for the Builder: Or A Discourse Shewing the Cause and Effects of the Increase of Building*. London: Printed for Cave Pullen.

—— 1689. *An Apology for the Builder: Or a Discourse Shewing the Cause and Effects of the Increase of Building*. London: [s n]

—— 1690. *A Discourse of Trade*. London: Printed by Tho. Milbourn.

—— 1696. *A Discourse Concerning Coining the New Money Lighter.* London: Printed for Richard Chiswell.

Bedford Archives, Woburn Abbey, 4th Earl of Bedford's *Commonplace Book No. 25*, 1639.

Bruce, John. 1853 [1634]. "XV. — Observations on the Lease of Two Houses in the Piazza, Covent Garden, granted to Sir Edmund Verney." *Archaeologia: Or Miscellaneous Tracts Relating to Antiquity, 1770–1992* 35: 194–201.

Chancery Inquisitions postmortem: land ownership and inheritance in the medieval and early modern periods. The National Archives, Kew, UK. https://www.nationalarchives.gov.uk/help-with-your-research/research-guides/inquisitions-post-mortem/.

Clarendon State Papers.

Defoe, Daniel. 1745. *The Complete English Tradesman*. 5th ed. London: Printed for J. Rivington.

D.S.S.P. James xciv 93, Nov. to Dec. 1917.

Domesday Boke. 1783 [1086]. Edited by Abraham Farley and Henry Ellis. London: Published by the Record Commission.

Dyson, Humfrey. 1618. *A booke containing all such proclamations as were published during the raigne of the late Queene Elizabeth collected together by the industry of Humfrey Dyson, England and Wales*. Sovereign (1558–1603: Elizabeth I). London: Bonham Norton and Iohn Bill, Deputie Printers for the Kings most Excellent Maiestie.

Evelyn, John. 1906 [1677–1706]. *The Diary of John Evelyn*. 3 vols. Edited by Austin Dobson. London: Macmillan.

—— 1995a [1661]. "Fumifugium, or the Inconveniencie of the Aer and Smoak of London Dissipated." In *The Writings of John Evelyn*, edited by Guy de la Bédoyère, 127–156. New York: Boydell Press.

—— 1995b [1666]. "London Redivivium." In *The Writings of John Evelyn*, edited by Guy de la Bédoyère, 335–345. New York: Boydell Press.

References

Fortescue, Sir John. 1869 [c.1460]. A Thesis Concerning the Nature of the Law of Nature and Its Judgment upon the Succession of Sovereign Kingdoms, translated by C. Fortescue. In *The Works of Sir John Fortescue*, Vol. 1, edited by Thomas Lord Claremont, 187–336. London: Printed for private distribution.

—— 1997 [c. 1470]. *On the Laws and Governance of England*. Cambridge: Cambridge University Press.

Garrard, George. 1739 [1634]. George Garrard to Thomas Wentworth, Lord of Strafford. June 3, 1634. In *The Earl of Strafforde's Letters and Dispatches*, Vol. 1, edited by William Knowler, 261–263. London: Printed by William Bowyer.

Graunt, J. 1899 [1662]. "Natural and Political Observations Made upon the Bills of Mortality." In *The Economic Writings of Sir William Petty*, vol. 2, edited by C.H. Hull, 315–435. Cambridge: Cambridge University Press.

Grotius, Hugo. 1925 [1625]. *De Jure Belli Ac Pacis*. Translated by F.W. Kelley. Oxford: Clarendon Press.

Guildhall MSS, Guildhall Library Manuscripts, The National Archives, Kew, UK.

Hayes, Richard. 1789. *A New Method for Valuing of Annuities upon Lives and Leaseholds, or Leasehold Estates*. Dublin: Printed for H. Templeton.

Hobbes, Thomas. 1968 [1651]. *Leviathan*. London: Penguin.

Hooke, Robert. 1969 [1705]. *The Posthumous Works of Robert Hooke*. New York: Johnson Reprint Corporation.

Letters Patent, The National Archives, Kew, UK.

Locke, John. 1692. *Some Considerations of the Consequences of the Lowering of Interest, and Raising the Value of Money*. London: Printed for Awnsham and John Churchill.

—— 1970 [1690]. *Two Treatises of Government, and a Letter Concerning Toleration*. Cambridge: Cambridge University Press.

—— 2003 [1690]. *Two Treatises of Government, and a Letter Concerning Toleration*. New Haven, CT: Yale University Press.

London Metropolitan Archives (LMA), 40 Northampton Road, London, EC1R 0HB.

Luttrell, N. (1972). *The Parliamentary Diary of Narcissus Luttrell, 1691–1693*. Oxford: Clarendon Press.

Magna Carta. 1963 [1215]. Translated by G.R.C. Davis. London: British Library. Published online. https://www.bl.uk/magna-carta/articles/magna-carta-english-translation.

Morisyne, Richard. 1551. Richard Morisyne to the Marquis of Northampton, Grand Chamberlain, November 18. In *Calendar of State Papers Foreign: Edward IV, 1549–1553*, edited by William B. Trumbull, 196. Found online at British History Online. https://www.british-history.ac.uk/cal-state-papers/foreign/edw-vi/pp188-200.

Mun, Thomas. 1664–1718 [1623]. *England's treasure by foreign trade: or the ballance [sic] of our foreign trade is the rule of our treasure*. London: Printed for Thomas Horne.

Neve, Richard. 1736. *The City and Country Purchaser's and Builder's Dictionary: Or, the Complete Builder's Guide*. London: Printed for B. Sprint, D. Browne, J. Osborn, S. Birt, H. Lintot, and A. Wilde.

Noorthouck, John. 1773. *A New History of London, Including Westminster and Southwark*. London: Printed for R. Baldwin.

Norden, John. 1593. *Speculum Britanniae*. London: Printed at Eliot's Court Press.

—— 1618. *The Surveiors Dialogue*. London: Printed by Thomas Snodham.

North, Roger. 1887 [c. 1690-1734]. *The Autobiography of the Hon. Roger North*. Edited by Augustus Jessop. London: D. Nutt.

—— 1981. *Of Building: Roger North's Writing on Architecture*. Edited by Howard Colvin and John Newman. Oxford: Clarendon Press.

Pennant, Thomas. 1813 [1790]. *Some Account of London*. 5th ed. London: Printed for J. Paulder [and 13 others].

Pepys, Samuel. 1900 [c. 1660–1669]. *The Diary of Samuel Pepys*. 8 vols. Edited by Henry B. Wheatley. New York: Croscup & Sterling Company.

Petty, Sir William. 1689. *A Discourse of Taxes and Contributions: Shewing the Nature and Measures of Crown-Lands, Assessments, Customs, Poll-Moneys, Lotteries, Benevolence*. London: Printed for Edward Poole.

—— 1690. *Political Arithmetick*. London: R. Clavel.

Phillips, Henry. 1654. *The Purchaser's Pattern ... The Second Edition, Corrected and Enlarged*. London: Printed by R. & W. Leybourn for T. Pierrepont.

—— 1719. *The Purchaser's Pattern in Two Parts*. London: Printed for Edw. Symon.

Primatt, Stephen. 1680. *The City and Country Purchaser and Builder*. London: Printed for John Wright, and the Assigns of Sam Speed.

Privy Council Registers, The National Archives Series PC 2, Kew, UK.

Pufendorf, Samuel. 1994 [1660–1672]. *The Political Writings of Samuel Pufendorf*. Edited by Craig L. Carr and translated by Michael J. Seidler. New York: Oxford University Press.

Ralph, James. 1734. *A Critical Review of the Public Buildings, Statues, and Ornaments, In and About London and Westminster*. London: Printed for John Wallis.

Rugge, *Diurnal*, 1665. British Museum, MSS Dept., Additional MSS. 10,117.

Russell, Edward, 3rd Earl of Bedford. 1610. Edward 3rd Earl of Bedford to Lord Salisbury. April 27. In *Calendar of State Papers Domestic: James I, Volume 53, March-April 1610*. https://www.british-history.ac.uk/cal-state-papers/domestic/jas1/1603-10.

Russell, Frances, 4th Earl of Bedford. 1639. Commonplace Book No. 25. In State Papers Series, Foreign and Domestic, Public Records Office, The National Archives, Kew, UK: State Papers 7, Henry VIII: Wriothesley Papers, 1536–1540 (one vol.).

St. German, Christopher. 1974 [c. 1518]. *St German's Doctor and Student*. Edited by T.F.T. Plunkett and J.L. Barton. London: Published by the Seldon Society.

Stow, John. 1956 [1598–1603]. *Survey of London*. Edited by Henry B. Wheatley. London: J.M. Dent.

Strype, John, ed. 1720. *A Survey of the Cities of London and Westminster Containing the Original, Antiquity, Increase, Modern Estate, and Government of Those Cities*. London: Printed for A. Churchill [and 9 others].

Survey of London: Volume III, St Giles-in-The-Fields, Pt I: Lincoln's Inn Fields. Edited by W. Edward Riley and Laurence Gomme. London: London County Council, 1912, British History Online. www.british-history.ac.uk/survey-london/vol3/pt1/plate-3.

Survey of London, Volume 5: St Giles-in-The-Fields, Part II. 1914. Edited by W. Edward Riley and Laurence Gomme. London: Published by the London County Council. https://www.british-history.ac.uk/survey-london/vol5/pt2.

Survey of London, Volumes 33 and 34: St Anne, Soho. 1966. Edited by F.H.W. Sheppard. London: Published by the London County Council. https://www.british-history.ac.uk/survey-london/vols33-4.

Survey of London, Volume 36: Covent Garden. 1970. Edited by F.H.W. Sheppard. London: Published by the London County Council. https://www.british-history.ac.uk/survey-london/vol36.

References

Town Holdings (1886–1892): Reports of Select Committee on Town Holdings, House of Commons, Great Britain.

Woburn Abbey Archives.

Wriothesley, Henry VIII. 1540. "Letters Addressed to Sir Thomas Wriothesley, 1st Baron Wriothesley of Titchfield and 2nd Earl of Southampton, c 1500-1550." In State Papers 7: State Papers, Foreign and Domestic, Henry VIII: Wriothesley Papers, 1536–1540 (one vol.).

Secondary Sources

Aalbers, Manuel. 2008. "The Financialization of Home and the Mortgage Market Crisis." *Competition & Change* 12, no. 2: 148–166.

—— 2016. *The Financialization of Housing: A Political Economy Approach*. New York: Routledge.

—— 2019. "Financial Geography II: Financial Geographies of Housing and Real Estate." *Progress in Human Geography* 43, no. 2: 376–387.

Adams, David, Robert Croudace, and Steve Tiesdell. 2012. "Exploring the 'Notional Property Developer' as a Policy Construct." *Urban Studies* 49, no. 12: 2577–2596.

Adams, David and Steve Tiesdell. 2013. *Shaping Places: Urban Planning, Design and Development*. London: Routledge.

Akrigg, G.P.V. 1968. *Shakespeare and the Earl of Southampton*. Cambridge, MA: Harvard University Press.

Ambrose, Peter J. 1986. *Whatever Happened to Planning?* London: Methuen.

Antwi, Adarkwah and John Henneberry. 1995. "Developers, Non-Linearity, and Asymmetry in the Development Cycle." *Journal of Property Research* 12, no. 3: 217–239.

Appleby, Joyce Oldham. 1978. *Economic Thought and Ideology in Seventeenth-Century England*. Princeton, NJ: Princeton University Press.

Aquinas, Saint Thomas. 1964–1980 [1266–1273]. *Summa Theologiae*. 7 vols. Translated by Thomas Gilby. Cambridge: Blackfriars.

Archer, Ian W. 2008. "City and Court Connected: The Material Dimensions of Royal Ceremonial, ca. 1480–1625." *Huntington Library Quarterly* 71, no. 1: 157–179.

Aristotle. 350 BC. *The Athenian Constitution*. Available on MIT's Internet Classics Archive. http://classics.mit.edu/Aristotle/athenian_const.1.1.html.

—— 1991. *The Art of Rhetoric*. Translated and edited by H.C. Lawson-Tancred. Harmondsworth: Penguin.

Baden-Fuller, Charles and Mary S. Morgan. 2010. "Business Models as Models." *Long Range Planning* 43, nos. 2–3: 156–171.

Baer, William C. 2002. "The Institution of Residential Investment in Seventeenth-Century London." *The Business History Review* 76, no. 3: 515–551.

—— 2007a. "Is Speculative Building Underappreciated in Urban History?" *Urban History* 34, no. 2: 296–316.

—— 2007b. "Planning for Growth and Growth Controls in Early Modern Northern Europe, Part 2: The Evolution of London's Practice from 1580 to 1680." *The Town Planning Review* 78, no. 3: 257–277.

—— 2011. "Landlords and Tenants in London, 1550–1700." *Urban History* 38, no. 2: 234–255.

—— 2012. "The House-Building Sector of London's Economy, 1550–1650." *Urban History* 39, no. 3: 409–430.

Ball, Michael. 1986. "The Built Environment and the Urban Question." *Environment and Planning D: Society and Space* 4: 447–464.

——— 1998. "Institutions in British Property Research: A Review." *Urban Studies* 35, no. 9: 1501–1517.

Ballon, Hilary. 1991. *The Paris of Henri IV: Architecture and Urbanism*. Cambridge, MA: MIT Press.

Barber, William J. 1975. *British Economic Thought and India, 1600–1858: A Study in the History of Development Economics*. Oxford: Clarendon Press.

Barnes, Thomas. 1971. "The Prerogative and Environmental Control of London Building in the Early Seventeenth Century: The Lost Opportunity." *Ecology Law Quarterly* 1, no. 1: 62–93.

Barrett, Susan and Gill Whitting. 1983. *Local Authorities and Land Supply: Final Report of Research on the Role of local Authorities In the Supply of Development Land to the Private Sector*. OP-10, School for Advanced Urban Studies, University of Bristol, Bristol.

Barrett, Susan, Murray Stewart, and Jacky Underwood. 1978. *The Land Market and Development Process: A Review of Research and Policy*. Occasional Paper 2. School for Advanced Urban Studies, University of Bristol.

Baskin, Jonathan Barron and Paul J. Miranti, Jr. 1997. *A History of Corporate Finance*. Cambridge: Cambridge University Press.

Bateman, Michael. 1985. *Office Development: A Geographical Analysis*. New York: St. Martin's Press.

Baum, Andrew. 2015. *Real Estate Investment: A Strategic Approach*. Abingdon: Routledge.

Baumol, William J. 1993. *Entrepreneurship, Management, and the Structure of Payoffs*. Cambridge, MA: MIT Press.

Beauregard, Robert A. 1994. "Capital Switching and the Built Environment: United States, 1970–1989." *Environment and Planning A: Economy and Space* 26: 715–732.

——— 2005. "The Textures of Property Markets: Downtown Housing and Office Conversions in New York City." *Urban Studies* 42, no. 13: 2431–2445.

——— 2015. "We Blame the Building! The Architecture of Distributed Responsibility." *International Journal of Urban and Regional Research* 39, no. 3: 533–549.

Beckett, J.V. 1986. *The Aristocracy in England, 1660–1914*. Oxford: Blackwell.

Bedeian, Arthur G. 1998. "Exploring the Past." *Journal of Management History* 4, no. 1: 4–15.

Beier, A.L. and Roger Finlay. 1986. "Introduction: The Significance of the Metropolis." In *London 1500–1700: The Making of the Metropolis*, edited by A.L. Beier and Roger Finlay, 1–33. London: Longman.

Bell, Walter G. 1920. *The Great Fire of London in 1666*. London: John Lane.

——— 1924. *The Great Plague in London in 1665*. London: John Lane.

Beresford, Maurice W. 1967. *New Towns of the Middle Ages: Town Plantation in England, Wales, and Gascony*. New York: Praeger.

Bernard, G.W. 2011. "The Dissolution of the Monasteries." *History* 96, no. 4: 390–409.

Blackstone, William. 1765. *Commentaries on the Laws of England, Book the First*. Oxford: Clarendon Press.

——— 2016. *Commentaries on the Laws of England, Book II: Of the Rights of Things*. Edited by Simon Stern. Oxford: Oxford University Press.

Boddy, Martin. 1981. "The Property Sector in Late Capitalism: The Case of Britain." In *Urbanization and Urban Planning in Capitalist Society*, edited by Michael Dear and Allen J. Scott, chapter 11. London: Methuen.

References

Boulton, Jeremy. 1987. *Neighbourhood and Society: A London Suburb in the Seventeenth Century*. Cambridge: Cambridge University Press, 1987.

—— 2008. "London 1540–1700." In *The Cambridge Urban History of Britain*, edited by Peter Clark, 315–346. Cambridge: Cambridge University Press.

Bowers Isaacson, Lisa Margaret. 1992. "The Buildings Society: Speculative Building in the West End of London, 1660–1760." Ph.D. Dissertation. Princeton University.

Brett-James, Norman G. 1929. "A Speculative Builder of the Seventeenth Century, Dr. Nicholas Barbon." *Transactions of the London and Middlesex Historical Society* 6: 110–145.

—— 1935. *The Growth of Stuart London*. London: George Allen & Unwin.

Breuer, Wolfgang and Claudia Nadler. 2012. "Real Estate and Real Estate Finance as a Research Field— An International Overview." *Zeitschrift für Betriebswirtschaft* 82, no.1: 5–52.

Brewer, John and Susan Staves. 1996. Introduction. In *Early Modern Conceptions of Property*, edited by John Brewer and Susan Staves, 1–20. London: Routledge.

Britnell, R.H. 1993. *The Commercialisation of English Society, 1000–1500*. Cambridge: Cambridge University Press.

Brueggeman, William B. and Jeff D. Fisher. 2015. *Real Estate Finance and Investments*. 15th ed. New York: McGraw-Hill Education. (First published 1977.)

Bryant, C.R., L.G. Russwurm, and A.G. McLellan. 1982. *The City's Countryside: Land and Its Management in the Rural-Urban Fringe*. London: Longman.

Bujak, Edward. 2007. *England's Rural Realms: Landholding and the Agricultural Revolution*. London: Tauris Academic Studies.

Cadman, David and Leslie Austin-Crowe. 1978. *Property Development*. London: Spon.

Carlen, Joe. 2016. *A Brief History of Entrepreneurship: The Pioneers, Profiteers, and Racketeers Who Shaped Our World*. New York: Columbia University Press.

Casson, Mark and Catherine Casson. 2013. *The Entrepreneur in History: From Medieval Merchant to Modern Business Leader*. Basingstoke: Palgrave Macmillan.

Casson, Mark, Bernard Yeung, Anuradha Basu, and Nigel Wadeson. 2006. Introduction. In *The Oxford Handbook of Entrepreneurship*, edited by Mark Casson, Bernard Yeung, Anuradha Basu, and Nigel Wadeson, 1–32. Oxford: Oxford University Press.

Chancellor, Edwin Beresford. 1907. *The History of the Squares of London Topographical and Historical*, London: Kegan Paul, Trench, Trubner & Co.

—— 1930. *The Annals of Covent Garden and its Neighbourhood*. London: Hutchinson & Co.

—— 1932. *The Romance of Lincoln's Inn Fields and its Neighbourhood*. London: Richards Press.

—— 2012. *A History of the Squares and Palaces of London*. 2 vols. London: I.B. Tauris (First published 1907–1908.)

Chandler, Alfred D., Jr. 1962. *Strategy and Structure: Chapters in the History of the American Industrial Enterprise*. Cambridge, MA: MIT Press.

—— 1977. *The Visible Hand: The Managerial Revolution in American Business*. Cambridge, MA: Belknap Press.

—— 1990. *Scale and Scope: The Dynamics of Industrial Capitalism*. Cambridge, MA: Belknap Press.

Chisholm, Hugh. 1911. "Earl of Southampton." In *Encyclopædia Britannica*, vol. 11, edited by Hugh Chisholm, 489–490. Cambridge: Cambridge University Press.

Christophers, Brett. 2011. "Revisiting the Urbanization of Capital." *Annals of the Association of American Geographers* 101, no. 6: 1347–1364.

Christopherson, Susan, Ron Martin, and Jane Pollard. 2013. "Financialisation: Roots and Repercussions." *Cambridge Journal of Regions, Economy, and Society* 6, no. 3: 351–357.

Clark, Gordon L. 2000. *Pension Fund Capitalism*. Oxford: Oxford University Press.

Clark, Gordon L. and Ashby H.B. Monk. 2017. *Institutional Investors in Global Markets*. Oxford: Oxford University Press, 2017.

Clark, Gordon L., Adam B. Dixon, and Ashby H.B. Monk. 2013. *Sovereign Wealth Funds: Legitimacy, Governance, and Global Power*. Princeton, NJ: Princeton University Press.

Clark, Gregory and Anthony Clark. 2001. "Common Rights to Land in England, 1475–1839." *The Journal of Economic History* 61, no. 4: 1009–1036.

Coulter, John. 2016. *Squares of London*. Stroud, UK: The History Press.

Crafts, N.F.R. 1985. *British Economic Growth during the Industrial Revolution*. Oxford: Clarendon Press.

Craven, Edward. 1969. "Private Residential Development in Kent 1956–64: A Study of Pattern and Process in Urban Growth." *Urban Studies* 6, no. 1: 1–16.

Crosby, Neil and John Henneberry. 2016. "Financialisation, the Valuation of Investment Property, and the Urban Built Form in the UK." *Urban Studies* 53, no. 7: 1424–1441.

—— 2017. "Valuation and the Evolution of New Uses and Buildings." In *Transience and Permanence in Urban Development*, edited by John Henneberry, 185–198. Hoboken, N.J.: John Wiley & Sons.

Cummins, Neil, Morgan Kelly, and Cormac Ó Gráda. 2016. "Living Standards and Plague in London, 1560–1665," *The Economic History Review* 69, no. 1: 3–34.

Cunningham, William. 1890. *The Growth of English Industry and Commerce during the Early and Middle Ages. Vol. 1.* London: C.J. Clay & Sons.

Darby, Henry Clifford. 1940. *The Draining of the Fens*. Cambridge: Cambridge University Press.

Dasent, Arthur Irwin. 1895. *The History of St James's Square and the Foundation of the West End of London, with a Glimpse of Whitehall in the Reign of Charles the Second*. London: Macmillan.

Dasso, Jerome and Lynn Woodward. 1980. "Real Estate Education: Past, Present, and Future—The Search for a Discipline." *Real Estate Economics* 8, no. 4: 404–416.

de Graaf, Reinier. 2017. *Four Walls and a Roof: The Complex Nature of a Simple Profession*. Cambridge, MA: Harvard University Press.

DeLanda, Manuel. 2006. *A New Philosophy of Society: Assemblage Theory and Social Complexity*. London: Continuum.

Derrington, Patrice. 1981. "Controlling the Quality of Professional Performance in Architectural Practice." Ph.D. Dissertation. University of California, Berkeley.

—— 2017. "Real Estate Speculation in the Highest Office: George Washington, and Then, Donald Trump." *Journal of Business and Economics* 8, no. 11: 912–925.

—— 2018. "Property and Thomas Piketty: Casting the Lens of Thomas Piketty's *Capital in the Twenty-First Century* on Inequality in the Built Environment."*Journal of Contemporary Urban Affairs* 2, no. 2: 90–105.

—— 2019. "Creation, Calculation, Speculation— A Short History of Real Estate Development." *Baumeister* 116, no. 6: 34–42.

—— 2021, forthcoming. "Rethinking the Private Urban Development Process: Its History and Ideologies." *Environment & Planning A*.

DiPasquale, Denise and William C. Wheaton. 1996. *Urban Economics and Real Estate Markets*. Englewood Cliffs, NJ: Prentice Hall.

References

Doak, Joe and Nikos Karadimitriou. 2007. "(Re)development, Complexity, and Networks: A Framework for Research." *Urban Studies* 44, no. 2: 209–229.

Downs, Arthur Channing, Jr. 1967. "Inigo Jones's Covent Garden: The First Seventy-Five Years." *Journal of the Society of Architectural Historians* 26, no. 1: 8–33.

Drane, Jonathan. 2013. "The State of Contemporary Property Development Theory." Presented at the 19th Annual Pacific-Rim Real Estate Society Conference, Melbourne, Australia, January 13–16.

Duggan, Dianne. 2001. "The Architectural Patronage of the 4th Earl of Bedford, 1587–1641." Ph.D. Dissertation. Courtauld Institute of Art, University of London.

Dyer, Christopher. 1995. "How Urbanized Was Medieval England?" In *Peasants and Townsmen in Medieval Europe*, edited by J.M. Duvosquel and E. Thoen, 102–125. Leuven: Belgisch Centrum voor Landelijke Geschiedenis.

—— 2005. *An Age of Transition?: Economy and Society in England in the Later Middle Ages*. Oxford: Oxford University Press.

Eliassen, Finn-Einar and Geir Alte Ersland. 1996. Introduction. In *Power, Profit, and Urban Land: Landownership in Medieval and Early Modern Northern European Towns*. Aldershot: Scolar Press.

Everitt, Alan. 1966. "Social Mobility in Early Modern England." *Past & Present* no. 33: 56–73.

Fainstein, Susan. 2001. *The City Builders: Property Development in New York and London, 1980–2000*. Lawrence, KS: University Press of Kansas.

—— 2010. *The Just City*. Ithaca, NY: Cornell University Press.

Farías, Ignacio and Thomas Bender, eds. 2010. *Urban Assemblages: How Actor-Network Theory Changes Urban Studies*. London: Routledge.

Feinstein, C.H. 1978. "Capital Formation in Great Britain." In *The Cambridge Economic History of Europe*, edited by Peter Mathias and M.M. Postan, 28–96. Cambridge: Cambridge University Press.

Finlay, Roger and Beatrice Shearer. 1986. "Population Growth and Suburban Expansion." In *London 1500–1700: The Making of the Metropolis*, edited by A.L. Beier and Roger Finlay, 37–59. London: Longman.

Fisher, William Richard and John Mason Lightwood. 1977 [1852]. *Fisher and Lightwood's Law of Mortgages*. Edited by E.L.G Tyler. London: Butterworth.

Form, William H. 1954. "The Place of Social Structure in the Determination of Land Use: Some Implications for a Theory of Urban Ecology." *Social Forces* 32, no. 4: 317–323.

Foucault, Michel. 1977. *Discipline and Punish: The Birth of the Prison*. Translated by Alan Sheridan. New York: Vintage Books.

Fraser, W.D. 1984. *Principles of Property Investment and Pricing*. Basingstoke: Macmillan.

Freeman, Lance. 2006. *There Goes the 'Hood: Views of Gentrification from the Ground Up*. Philadelphia, PA: Temple University Press.

French, Shaun, Andrew Leyshon, and Thomas Wainwright. 2011. "Financializing Space, Spacing Financialization." *Progress in Human Geography* 35, no. 6: 798–819.

Friedman, Milton. 1970. "The Social Responsibility of a Business is to Increase Its Profits." *New York Times Magazine*, 13 September. https://www.nytimes.com/1970/09/13/archives/a-friedman-doctrine-the-social-responsibility-of-business-is-to.html.

Galsworthy, John. 1906. *The Man of Property*. New York: Grosset & Dunlap.

Geltner, David and Norman G. Miller. 2001. *Commercial Real Estate Analysis and Investments*. Cincinnati, MN: South-Western Publishing.

Gerhold, Dorian. 2016. *London Plotted: Plans of London Buildings, c. 1450–1720*. Edited by Sheila O'Connell. London: Published by the London Topographical Society.

Giddens, Anthony. 1981. *A Contemporary Critique of Historical Materialism*. London: Macmillan.

—— 1984. *The Constitution of Society: Outline of the Theory of Structuration*. Berkeley, CA: University of California Press.

—— 1995. *A Contemporary Critique of Historical Materialism*. 2nd ed. Basingstoke: Macmillan.

Glaeser, Edward L. 2011. *The Triumph of the City: How Our Greatest Invention Makes Us Richer, Smarter, Greener, Healthier, and Happier*. New York: Penguin Press.

Goetzmann, William N. 2016. *Money Changes Everything: How Finance Made Civilization Possible*. Princeton, NJ: Princeton University Press.

Gomme, Sir George Laurence. 1912. *The Making of London*. Oxford: Clarendon Press.

Goodchild, Robin N. and Richard Munton. 1985. *Development and the Landowner: An Analysis of the British Experience*. London: George Allen & Unwin.

Gore, T. and D. Nicholson. 1985. "Alternative Frameworks for the Analysis of Public Sector Land Ownership and Development." In *Land Policy: Problems and Alternatives*, edited by Susan Barrett and Patsy Healey, 179–202. Aldershot: Gower.

—— 1991. "Models of the Land Development Process: A Critical Review." *Environment and Planning A: Economy and Space* 23, no. 12: 705–730.

Gotham, Kevin F. 2012. "Creating Liquidity out of Spatial Fixity: The Secondary Circuit of Capital and the Subprime Mortgage Crisis." In *Subprime Cities: The Political Economy of Mortgage Markets*, edited by Manuel Aalbers, 25–52. Malden, MA: Wiley-Blackwell.

Graaskamp, James A. 1972. "A Rational Approach to Feasibility Analysis." *The Appraisal Journal* 40, no. 4: 513–521.

—— 1976. "Redefining the Role of University Education in Real Estate and Urban Land Economics." *Real Estate Appraiser*, March–April, 24–28; and May–June, 17–18.

—— 1981. *Fundamentals of Real Estate Development*. Washington, DC: Published by the Urban Land Institute.

Grassby, Richard. 1994. *The English Gentleman in Trade: The Life and Works of Sir Dudley North, 1641–1691*. Oxford: Clarendon Press.

—— 1999. *The Idea of Capitalism before the Industrial Revolution*. Lanham, MD: Rowman & Littlefield.

Green, Judith A. 2017. *Forging the Kingdom: Power in English Society, 973–1189*. Cambridge: Cambridge University Press.

Guy, Simon and John Henneberry. 2000. "Understanding Urban Development Processes: Integrating the Economic and the Social in Property Research." *Urban Studies* 37, no. 13: 2399–2416.

Habakkuk, H.J. 1940. "English Landownership, 1680–1740." *The Economic History Review* 10, no. 1: 2–17.

—— 1958. "The Market for Monastic Property, 1539–1603." *The Economic History Review* 10, no. 3: 362–380.

Haila, Anne. 2017. "Institutionalization of 'The Property Mind.'" *International Journal of Urban and Regional Research* 41, no. 3: 500–507.

References

Hall, Peter, Ray Thomas, Harry Gracey, and Roy Drewett. 1973. *The Containment of Urban England*. 2 vols. London: George Allen & Unwin.

Hardin, Garrett. 1968. "The Tragedy of the Commons." *Science* 162: 1243–1248.

Harding, Vanessa. 1989. Review of Jeremy Boulton "Neighbourhood and Society: A London Suburb in the Seventeenth Century." *Urban History Yearbook* 16: 206–208.

—— 2001. "City, Capital, and Metropolis: The Changing Shape of Seventeenth-Century London." In *Imagining Early Modern London: Perceptions and Portrayals of the City from Stow to Strype*, edited by J.F. Merritt, 117–143. Cambridge: Cambridge University Press.

—— 2002. "Space, Property, and Proprietary in Urban England." *Journal of Interdisciplinary History* 32, no. 4: 549–569.

—— 2007. "Families and Housing in Seventeenth-Century London." *Parergon* 24, no. 2: 115–138.

Hare, John. 2003. "Recycling the Monastic Buildings: The Dissolution in Southern England." *Historian* no. 39: 22–27.

—— 2013. "Inns, Innkeepers and the Society of Later Medieval England, 1350–1600." *Journal of Medieval History* 39, no. 4: 477–497.

Harpster, Jack. 2009. *The Railroad Tycoon Who Built Chicago: A Biography of William B. Ogden*. Carbondale, IL: Southern Illinois University Press.

Harris, John, Stephen Orgel and Roy Strong. 1973. *The King's Arcadia: Inigo Jones and the Stuart Court*. London: Published by the Arts Council of Great Britain.

Harvard, Timothy F. 2008. *Contemporary Property Development*. 2nd ed. London: RIBA.

Harvey, Barbara F. 1977. *Westminster and Its Estates in the Middle Ages*. Oxford: Clarendon Press.

Harvey, David. 1978. "The Urban Process under Capitalism: A Framework for Analysis." *Journal of Urban and Regional Research* 2, no. 1: 101–131.

—— 1989. *The Urban Experience*. Baltimore, MD: Johns Hopkins University Press.

Haslam, Colin, Tord Andersson, Nick Tsitsianis, and Ya Ping Yin. 2013. *Redefining Business Models: Strategies for a Financialized World*. New York: Routledge.

Healey, Patsy. 1991. "Models of the Development Process: A Review." *Journal of Property Research* 8, no. 3: 219–238.

—— 1992. "An Institutional Model of the Development Process." *Journal of Property Research* 9, no. 1: 33–44.

Healey, Patsy and Susan Barrett. 1990. "Structure and Agency in Land and Property Development Processes: Some Ideas for Research." *Urban Studies* 27, no. 1: 89–104.

Heinemann, Margaret. 1993. "Rebel Lords, Popular Playwrights, and Political Culture: Notes on the Jacobean Patronage of the Earl of Southampton." In *Patronage, Politics, and Literary Traditions in England, 1558–1658*, 135–158. Detroit, MI: Wayne State University Press.

Henneberry, John. 1988. "Conflict in the Industrial Property Market." *Town Planning Review* 59, no. 3: 241–262.

Henneberry, John and Simon Parris. 2013. "The Embedded Developer: Using Project Ecologies to Analyse Local Property Development Networks." *The Town Planning Review* 84, no. 2: 227–249.

Hollis, Leo. 2008. *The Phoenix: The Men Who Made Modern London*. London: Weidenfeld and Nicolson.

Honoré, A.M. 1961. "Ownership." In *Oxford Essays in Jurisprudence*, edited by A.G. Guest, 107–147. London: Oxford University Press.

Hooper, Alan J. 1992. "The Construction of Theory: A Comment." *Journal of Property Research* 9, no. 1: 45–48.

Hoppit, Julian, ed. 1997. *Failed Legislation, 1660–1800: Extracted from the Commons and Lords Journals*. London: Hambledon Press.

Hunter, John. 1834. Introduction to *Valor Ecclesiasticus*, edited by John Caley, i–viii. London: Published by the Records Commission.

Inwood, Stephen. 2005. *City of Cities: The Birth of Modern London*. London: Macmillan.

Jedamus, Paul and Robert Frame. 1969. *Business Decision Theory*. New York: McGraw-Hill.

Jessop, Bob. 1996. "Interpretive Sociology and the Dialectic of Structure and Agency." *Theory, Culture & Society* 13, no. 1: 119–128.

Johnson, B.H. 1952. *Berkeley Square to Bond Street: The Early History of the Neighbourhood*. London: Murray.

Jones, Geoffrey. 2002. *Merchants to Multinationals: British Trading Companies in the Nineteenth and Twentieth Centuries*. Oxford: Oxford University Press.

Jones, S.R.H. 1994. "The Origins of the Factory System in Great Britain: Technology, Transaction Costs, or Exploitation?" In *Business Enterprise in Modern Britain: From the Eighteenth to the Twentieth Century*, edited by Maurice W. Kirby and Mary B. Rose, 31–60. London: Routledge.

Kaiser, Edward J. and Shirley F. Weiss. 1970. "Public Policy and the Residential Development Process." *Journal of the American Institute of Planners* 36, no. 1: 30–37.

Kalsell, Frank and Timothy Walker. Forthcoming book on Nicholas Barbon.

Katsikos, Jacquelyn K. 2012. "Wynwood Rising: A Study of the Development of Miami's Arts District." M.A. Thesis. Sotheby's Institute of Art.

Keene, Derek. 1996. "Landlords, the Property Market and Urban Development in Medieval England." In *Power, Profit, and Urban Land: Landownership in Medieval and Early Modern Northern European Towns*, edited by Finn-Einar Eliassen and Gier Atle Ersland, chapter 6. Aldershot: Scolar Press.

Keogh, Geoffrey and Eamonn D'Arcy. 1999. "Property Market Efficiency: An Institutional Economics Perspective." *Urban Studies* 36, no. 13: 2401–2414.

Kilduff, Martin and Deborah Dougherty. 2000. "Change and Development in a Pluralistic World: The View from the Classics." *The Academy of Management Review* 25, no. 4: 777–782.

Kipping, Matthias, Marcelo Bucheli, and R. Daniel Wadhwani. 2014. "Analyzing and Interpreting Historical Sources: A Basic Methodology." In *Organizations in Time: History, Theory, Methods*, edited by Marcelo Bucheli and R. Daniel Wadhwani, 305–327. Oxford: Oxford University Press.

Kirby, Maurice W. and Mary B. Rose. 1994. Introduction. *Business Enterprise in Modern Britain: From the Eighteenth to the Twentieth Century*, edited by Maurice W. Kirby and Mary B. Rose. London: Routledge.

Krinsky, Carol Herselle. 1978. *Rockefeller Center*. New York: Oxford University Press.

Kuhn, Thomas. 1970. *The Structure of Scientific Revolutions*. Chicago, IL: University of Chicago Press.

Landes, David S. 1949. "French Entrepreneurship and Industrial Growth in the 19th Century." *The Journal of Economic History* 9, no. 1: 45–61.

Latour, Bruno. 2005. *Reassembling the Social: An Introduction to Actor-Network Theory*. Oxford and New York: Oxford University Press.

Lauria, M. 1982. "Selective urban redevelopment: a political economic perspective." *Urban Geography*, Vol. 3: 224–239.

References

Lees-Milne, James. 1953. *The Age of Inigo Jones*. London: Batsford.

Lefebvre, Henri. 1991. *The Production of Space*. Translated by Donald Nicholson-Smith. Oxford: Blackwell.

Le Patourel, John. 1976. *The Norman Empire*. Oxford: Clarendon Press.

Letourneau, Charles. 1896. *Property: Its Origin and Development*. London: Charles Scribner's Sons.

Letwin, William. 1963. *The Origins of Scientific Economics: English Economic Thought 1660–1776*. London: Methuen.

Linklater, Andro. 2013. *Owning the Earth: The Transforming History of Land Ownership*. New York: Bloomsbury.

Logan, John and Harvey Molotch. 1987. *Urban Fortunes: The Political Economy of Place*. Berkeley, CA: University of California Press.

Lynch, Kevin. 1960. *The Image of the City*. Cambridge, MA: MIT Press.

Maclean, S.G. 2015. *The Seeker*. London: Quercus.

Maitland, Frederic William. 1913. *The Constitutional History of England: A Course of Lectures Delivered by F.W. Maitland, L.L.D.* Cambridge: Cambridge University Press.

Margetson, Stella. 1967. "London's Old Auction Rooms." *Country Life*, November 16, 1267–1268, 1270.

Marriott, Sir John Arthur Ransome. 1914. *The English Land System: A Sketch of Its Historical Evolution in Its Bearing upon National Welfare*. London: J. Murray.

Marshall, William. 1804. *On the Landed Property of England*. London: Printed for G. and W. Nicol, G. and J. Robinson, R. Paulder, Longman and Reds, Cadell and Davies, and J. Hatchard.

Marx, Karl. 1976a. *Capital*, Vol. 2: *The Process and Accumulation of Capital*. New York: International Publishers Co. (First published 1885.)

—— 1976b. *Capital*, Vol. 3: *The Process of Capitalist Production as a Whole*. New York: International Publishers Co. (First published 1894.)

—— 1977. *Capital*, Vol. 1: *A Critique of Political Economy*. New York: Vintage Books. (First published 1867.)

Massey, Doreen and Alejandrina Catalano. 1978. *Capital and Land: Landownership by Capital in Great Britain*. London: E. Arnold.

McKellar, Elizabeth. 1999. *The Birth of Modern London: The Development and Design of the City, 1660–1720*. Manchester: Manchester University Press.

McNamara, Paul. 1983. "Towards a Classification of Land Developers." *Urban Land and Policy* 6: 87–94.

McRae, Andrew. 1993. "To Know One's Own: Estate Surveying and the Representation of the Land in Early Modern England." *Huntington Library Quarterly* 56, no. 4: 333–357.

Middendorf II, William. 2011. *Potomac Fever: A Memoir of Politics and Public Service*. Annapolis, MD: Naval Institute Press.

Miller, Fred D., Jr. 1991. "Aristotle on Property Rights." In *Essays in Ancient Greek Philosophy*, Vol. 4: *Aristotle's Ethics*, edited by John P. Anton and George L. Kustas, 227–247. Albany, NY: State University of New York Press.

Miller, Norman G. and David M. Geltner. 1994. *Real Estate Principles for the New Economy*. Cincinnati, MN: South-Western Publishing.

Millington, Alan F. 2014. *Property Development*. London: Routledge. (First published 1994.)

Milne, Gustav. 1992. *Timber Building Techniques in London c. 900–1400: An Archaeological Study of the Waterfront*. London: Published by the London and Middlesex Archaeological Society.

Monecke, S., Monecke, H., and Monecke, J. 2009. "Modelling the Black Death: A Historical Case Study and Implications for the Epidemiology of Bubonic Plague." *International Journal of Medical Microbiology*, 299: 582–593.

Mukhija, Vinit and Anastasia Loukaitou-Sideris, eds. 2014. *The Informal American City: Beyond Taco Trucks and Day Labor*. Cambridge, MA: MIT Press.

Muldrew, Craig. 1998. *The Economy of Obligation: The Culture of Credit and Social Relations in Early Modern England*. New York: St. Martin's Press.

Myers, Garth. 2014. "From Unexpected to Expected Comparisons: Changing the Flows of Ideas about Cities in a Postcolonial Urban World." *Singapore Journal of Tropical Geography* 35, no. 1: 104–118.

Needleman, Lionel. 1969. "The Comparative Economics of Improvement and New Building." *Urban Studies* 6, no. 2: 196–209.

Norwich, John Julius. 2017. "The Cadogan Estate: A History." In *Cadogan & Chelsea: The Making of a Modern Estate*, edited by Anjali Bulley, 10–35. London: Unicorn.

Novicevic, Milorad M., Jason Owen, Jennifer Palar, Ifeoluwa Tobi Popooola, and David Marshall. 2015. "Management and Organizational History: Extending the State-of-the-Art to Historical Interpretivism." In *Management History: Its Global Past and Present*, edited by Bradley Bowden and David Lamond, 157–172. Charlotte, NC: Information Age Publishing.

Offer, Avner. 1981. *Property and Politics 1870–1914: Landownership, Law, Ideology and Urban Development*. Cambridge: Cambridge University Press.

Olsen, Donald J. 1982. *Town Planning in London: The Eighteenth and Nineteenth Centuries*. 2nd ed. New Haven, CT: Yale University Press.

O'Sullivan, Mary. 2016. *Dividends of Development: Securities Markets in the History of U.S. Capitalism*. Oxford: Oxford University Press.

Palgrave, Francis. 1831. *History of England*, Vol. 1: *The Anglo-Saxon Period*. London: J. Murray.

Parsons, Malcolm. 2012. "Nicholas Barbon (1637–98): FRCP, Property Developer." *Journal of Medical Biography* 20, no. 2: 62–64.

Peiser, Richard and David Hamilton. 2012. *Professional Real Estate Development: The ULI Guide to Business*. 3rd ed. Washington, DC: Published by the Urban Land Institute.

Pierson, Christopher. 2013. *Just Property: A History in the Latin West*, Vol. 1: *Wealth, Virtue and the Law*. Oxford: Oxford University Press.

Piketty, Thomas. 2014. *Capital in the Twenty-First Century*. Cambridge, MA: Belknap Press.

Plato. 1998. *The Republic*. Translated and edited by R. Waterfield. Oxford: Oxford University Press.

Polanyi, Karl. 1957. *The Great Transformation*. Boston, MA: Beacon Press. (First published 1944.)

Pollard, Sidney. 1965. *The Genesis of Modern Management: A Study of the Industrial Revolution of Great Britain*. Cambridge, MA: Harvard University Press.

Porter, Michael E. 1996. "What is Strategy?" *Harvard Business Review* 71 (November–December): 61–78.

Porter, Ron. 1994. *London: A Social History*. Cambridge, MA: Harvard University Press.

Power, Michael J. 1978. "Shadwell: The Development of a London Suburb in the Seventeenth Century." *London Journal* 4, no. 1: 29–46.

Punter, John V. 1986. "Aesthetic Control within the Development Process: A Case Study." *Land Development Studies* 3: 197–212.

Rabb, Theodore K. 1967. *Enterprise & Empire: Merchant and Gentry Investment in the Expansion of England, 1575–1630*. Cambridge, MA: Harvard University Press.

References

Ratcliffe, John. 1978. *An Introduction to Urban Land Administration*. London: Hutchinson.

Reddaway, T.F. 1951. *The Rebuilding of London after the Great Fire*. London: Edward Arnold & Co.

Ricketts, Martin. 2006. "Theories of Entrepreneurship: Historical Development and Critical Assessment." In *The Oxford Handbook of Entrepreneurship*, edited by Mark Casson, Bernard Yeung, Anuradha Basu, and Nigel Wadeson, 33–58. Princeton, NJ: Princeton University Press.

Rigby, S.H. 1995. *English Society in the Later Middle Ages: Class, Status and Gender*. New York: St. Martin's Press.

Robinson, Jennifer. 2011. "Cities in a World of Cities: The Comparative Gesture." *International Journal of Urban and Regional Research* 35, no. 1: 1–23.

Rose, Mary B. 1994. "The Family Firm in British Business, 1780–1914." In *Business Enterprise in Modern Britain: From the Eighteenth to the Twentieth Century*, edited by Maurice W. Kirby and Mary B. Rose, 61–87. London: Routledge.

—— 2000. *Firms, Networks, and Business Values: The British and American Cotton Industries since 1750*. Cambridge: Cambridge University Press.

Rowlinson, Michael, John Hassard, and Stephanie Decker. 2014. "Research Strategies for Organizational History: A Dialogue between Historical Theory and Organization Theory." *Academy of Management Review* 39, no. 3: 250–274.

Rowse, Alfred L. 1965a. *Shakespeare's Southampton, Patron of Virginia*. New York: Harper & Row.

—— 1965b. "Thomas Wriothesley, First Earl of Southampton." *Huntington Library Quarterly* 28, no. 2: 105–129.

Roy, Ananya. 2009. "The 21st-Century Metropolis: New Geographies of Theory." *Regional Studies* 43, no. 6: 819–830.

Sagalyn, Lynne B. 2016. *Power at Ground Zero: Politics, Money, and the Remaking of Lower Manhattan*. New York: Oxford University Press.

Sampson, Robert J. 2012. *Great American City: Chicago and the Enduring Neighborhood Effect*. Chicago, IL: University of Chicago Press.

Sayer, Andrew. 2000. "Moral Economy and Political Economy." *Studies in Political Economy* 61: 79–103.

Schlatter, Richard. 1951. *Private Property: The History of an Idea*. New Brunswick, NJ: Rutgers University Press.

Schofield, John. 1984. *The Building of London: From the Conquest to the Great Fire*. London: Published by the British Museum.

Schuetz, Jenny, Rachel Meltzer, and Vicki Been. 2011. "Silver Bullet or Trojan Horse? The Effects of Inclusionary Zoning on Local Housing Markets in the United States." *Urban Studies* 48, no. 2: 297–329.

Schumpeter, Joseph A. 1954. *History of Economic Analysis*. New York: Oxford University Press.

Shapiro, Ian. 1996. "Resource, Capacities, and Ownership: The Workmanship Ideal and Distributive Justice." In *Early Modern Conceptions of Property*, edited by John Brewer and Susan Staves, 21–42. London: Routledge.

Sheppard, Eric. 2014. "Globalizing Capital and Southern Urbanization." In *The Routledge Handbook on Cities of the Global South*, edited by Susan Parnell and Sophie Oldfield, 143–154. London: Routledge.

Sheppard, Francis. 1998. *London: A History*. Oxford: Oxford University Press.

Simone, AbdouMaliq. 2011. "The Surfacing of Urban Life." *City* 15, nos. 3–4: 355–364.

Smith, Adam. 1994. *An Inquiry into the Nature and Causes of the Wealth of Nations*. Edited by Edwin Cannan. New York: Modern Library. (First published 1776.)

Smith, Neil. 1984. *Uneven Development: Nature, Capital, and the Production of Space*. New York: Blackwell.

Smuts, R. Malcolm. 1991. "The Court and Its Neighborhood: Royal Policy and Urban Growth in the Early Stuart West End." *Journal of British Studies* 30, no. 2: 117–149.

Smyth, Hedley. 1985. *Property Companies and the Construction Industry in Britain*. Cambridge: Cambridge University Press.

Soja, Edward W. 1989. *Postmodern Geographies: The Reassertion of Space in Critical Theory*. New York: Verso.

Somers, Margaret R. 1996. "The 'Misteries' of Property: Relationality, Rural-Industrialization, and Community in Chartist Narratives of Political Rights." In *Early Modern Conceptions of Property*, edited by John Brewer and Susan Staves, 62–92. London: Routledge.

Sperance, Cameron. 2019. " 'It Just Sounds Good': Why Some Investors Ignore the Data and Stick to the Priciest Markets." *Bisnow*, 30 October 2019. www.bisnow.com/national/news/economic-development/the-haves-and-have-nots-smaller-us-cities-look-to-tip-the-scales-on-economic-fortune-101340/.

Squires, Graham and Erwin Heurkens. 2015. *International Approaches to Real Estate Development*. Abingdon: Routledge.

Steen, John, Catelinje Coopmans, and Jennifer Whyte. 2006. "Structure and Agency? Actor-Network Theory and Strategic Organization." *Strategic Organization* 4, no. 3: 303–312.

Stenton, Frank Merry. 1908. *William the Conqueror and the Rule of the Normans*. New York: G.P. Putnam's Sons.

Stevenson, Christine. 2013. *The City and the King: Architecture and Politics in Restoration London*. New Haven, CT: Yale University Press.

Stone, Lawrence. 1966. "Social Mobility in England, 1500–1700." *Past & Present* no. 33: 16–55.

Stopes, Charlotte Carmichael. 1922. *The Life of Henry, Third Earl of Southampton: Shakespeare's Patron*. Cambridge: Cambridge University Press.

Storper, Michael and Allen J. Scott. 2016. "Current Debates in Urban Theory: A Critical Assessment." *Urban Studies* 53, no. 6: 1114–1136.

Straub, Hans. 1952. *A History of Civil Engineering: An Outline from Ancient to Modern Times*. Translated by E. Rockwell. London: Leonard Hill.

Sugarman, David and Ronnie Warrington. 1996. "Land Law, Citizenship, and the Invention of 'Englishness': The Strange World of the Equity of Redemption." In *Early Modern Conceptions of Property*, edited by John Brewer and Susan Staves, 111–143. London: Routledge.

Summerson, John. 1964. "Inigo Jones: Lecture on a Master Mind." *Proceedings of the British Academy* 1: 169–192.

—— 1991a. *Architecture in Britain, 1530 to 1830*. London: Penguin.

—— 1991b. *Introduction. 50 Years of National Buildings Record, 1941–1991*. London: Published by the Royal Commission on the Historical Monuments of England.

—— 2000. *Inigo Jones*. New Haven, CT: Published for the Paul Mellon Centre for Studies in British Art by Yale University Press. (First published 1966.)

—— 2003. *Georgian London*. New Haven, CT: Yale University Press. (First published 1945.)

References

Symes, J.E. 1903. "Economic Practice and Theory." In *Social England: A Record of the Progress of the People in Religion, Laws, Learning, Arts, Industry, Commerce, Science, Literature and Manners, from the Earliest to the Present Day*, Vol. 4, edited by H.D. Traill and J.S. Mann, 621–629. London: Cassell & Company.

Tawney, R.H. 1941. "The Rise of the Gentry, 1558–1640." *The Economic History Review* 11, no. 1: 1–38.

Tawney, R.H. and Elizabeth Power, eds. 1953. *Tudor Economic Documents: Being Select Documents Illustrating the Economic and Social History of Tudor England*. London: Longmans, Green and Co.

Thomson, Gladys Scott. 1937. *Life in a Noble Household, 1641–1700*. London: J. Cape.

—— 1940. *The Russells in Bloomsbury: 1669–1771*. London: J. Cape.

Thornton, A.P. 1966. *The Habit of Authority: Paternalism in British History*. London: Allen & Unwin.

Thrall, Grant Ian. 2002. *Business Geography and New Real Estate Market Analysis*. Oxford: Oxford University Press.

Toker, Franklin. 2009. *Pittsburgh: A New Portrait*. Pittsburgh, PA: University of Pittsburgh Press.

Ullmer, James H. 2009. "William Petty, Nicholas Barbon, Multiples, and a New Hypothesis of Inevitable Discovery." *Journal of the History of Economic Thought* 31, no. 3: 341–359.

Van Loon, Jannes. 2016. "Patient versus Impatient Capital: The (Non-)Financialization of Real Estate Developers in the Low Countries." *Socio-Economic Review* 14, no. 4: 709–728.

Wadeson, Nigel. 2006. "Cognitive Aspects of Entrepreneurship: Decision-Making and Attitudes to Risk." In *The Oxford Handbook of Entrepreneurship*, edited by Mark Casson, Bernard Yeung, Anuradha Basu, and Nigel Wadeson, 91–113. Oxford: Oxford University Press.

Walford, Lord Edward. 1878. *Old and New London*. Vol. 3. London: Cassell, Peter & Galpin.

Ward, Emily. 2016. "Modeling the Property Development Process: An Actor-Network Theory Perspective." Master's Dissertation. University of Sheffield.

—— 2018. "An Actor-Network Theory of Property Development." *Journal of European Real Estate Research* 11, no. 2: 246–262.

Ward, Joseph. 1997. *Metropolitan Communities: Trade Guilds, Identity, and Change in Early Modern London*. Stanford, CA: Stanford University Press.

Watson, Alan. 1971. *Roman Private Law around 200 B.C.* Edinburgh: Edinburgh University Press.

—— 1975. *Rome of the XII Tables: Persons and Property*. Princeton, NJ: Princeton University Press.

Weber, Max. 1930. *The Protestant Ethic and the Spirit of Capitalism*. Translated by Talcott Parsons. London: George Allen & Unwin.

Weber, Rachel. 2002. "Extracting Value from the City: Neoliberalism and Urban Redevelopment." *Antipode* 34, no. 3: 519–540.

—— 2015. *From Boom to Bubble: How Finance Built the New Chicago*. Chicago, IL: University of Chicago Press.

Weir, Alison. 2001. *Henry VIII: The King and His Court*. New York: Ballantine Books.

Werlen, Benno. 1993. *Society, Action and Space: An Alternative Human Geography*. London: Routledge.

Whitelock, Dorothy, ed. 1979. *English Historical Documents*, Vol. 1: *500–1042*. General editor, David C. Douglas. London: Methuen.

Williams, Elgin. 1944. "Nicholas Barbon: An Early Economic Realist." *Southern Economic Journal* 11, no. 1: 45–55.

Williams, Laura. 2001. "'To Recreate and Refresh Their Dulled Spirites in the Sweet and Wholesome Ayre': Green Space and the Growth of the City." In *Imagining Early Modern London: Portrayals of the City from Stow to Strype*, edited by J.F. Merritt, 185–213. Cambridge: Cambridge University Press.

Willson, David Harris. 1956. *King James VI and I.* New York: Holt.

Wood, Andy. 1997. "The Place of Custom in Plebeian Political Culture: England, 1550–1800." *Social History* 22, no.1: 46–60.

Youings, Joyce A. 1971. *The Dissolution of the Monasteries*. London: Allen & Unwin.

Reference of Figures

1.1   After his appointment as Justice of the King's Bench, by Thomas Gainsborough (1727–1788). Digital photograph: Reproduced with kind permission of the Tate, UK

1.2   Artist unknown (1597–1618). Digital photograph: Reproduced with the kind permission of the National Portrait Gallery, UK

1.3   Tudor Binding for Domesday Book. Digital photograph © The National Archives image library, UK and reproduced with kind permission

1.4   *The Old Parish Church and Village, Hampton-on-Thames, Middlesex*, 18th century by unknown artist of the 19th century, oil on panel. Image reproduced with the kind permission of the Yale Center for British Art, Paul Mellon Collection

2.1   Original copy of Thomas Cromwell's 99-lease lease of his property at Austin Friars, June 1532. Reproduced with the kind permission of the Drapers' Company of the City of London

2.2   Extract from Primatt (1680) *The City and Country Purchaser and Builder showing interest rate tables used in valuation*. Referenced above

3.1   Author

3.2   Extract from Brett-James (1935) *The Growth of Stuart London*. Referenced above. Original map in London Archives, UK and reproduced with their kind permission

3.3   *Portrait of Inigo Jones* c. 1650 by Sir Anthony Van Dyck (1599–1641). Line Engraving by Robert van Voerst. Published by Gillis Hendricx c. 1650 *Icones principum virorum*, Antwerp. Reproduced with the kind permission of the Royal Academy of Arts, UK

3.4   Cummins et al. (2016, 24) "Living Standards and Plague in London, 1560–1665", p. 24. Referenced above.

3.5   *A street during the plague in London with a death cart and mourners*. Color wood engraving by Edmund Evans (1826–1905) Wellcome Collection gallery, London, UK. Permission granted under Creative Commons Attribution 4.0 International Public License

4.1   Excerpt from Hayes (1789) *Tables and Method for determining the valuation of a building, inclusive of the opportunity cost of capital*, p. 69. Referenced above

4.2   Detail from *Morgan's Map of the Whole of London in 1682*. Survey of the City of London and the surrounding built-up area (including Westminster and part of Southwark), on a scale of 300 feet to the inch, completed in 1682 by William Morgan. From a facsimile published by Harry Margary in association with the Guildhall Library in 1977. Reproduced with the kind permission of British History Online http://www.british-history.ac.uk/no-series/london-map-morgan/1682/map

4.3   Excerpt from Walford, Lord Edward (1878) *Old and New London*, Vol. 3, chapter XXVII. Referenced above

5.1 *John Russell, 1st Earl of Bedford, 1468(?)–1555* by John Henry Robinson after Hans Holbein the Younger, stipple engraving on paper, published 1832, 13.03x10.79cm. Reproduced with kind permission of the Scottish National Portrait Gallery

5.2 Author

5.3 Illustration of Francis Sheppard (1998) *London: A History*. Fig. 19, p. 178. Referenced above

5.4 Detail from *Agas Map of London 1561*. Produced in c. 1633, depicting the City of London in the 1560s. Probably derived from the original 'Copperplate' map of c. 1560 of which three sheets are extant. Published in c. 1633. Reproduced with the kind permission of British History Online. www.british-history.ac.uk/no-series/london-map-agas/1561/map

5.5 Extract from plan-view of Westminster published in John Norden's, *Speculum Britanniae*, London 1593. Reproduced with the kind permission of the British Library Online Gallery

5.6 *Portrait of Frans Lord Russell of Thornbaugh, 4th Earl of Bedford (1587–1641), c. 1636*, by Anthony van Dyck (1599–1641). Digital Photograph: https://commons.wikimedia.org/wiki/File:Van_Dyck_-_Portrait_of_Frans_Lord_Russell_of_Thornbaugh,_4th_Earl_of_Bedford_(1587-1641),_1636_gedateerd.jpg. Reproduction permitted under Creative Commons Attribution 4.0 International Public License

5.7 Anonymous. Reproduced with the kind permission of the Archives of Alnwick Castle

5.8 Banner of Leghorn Merchants by Anonymous. (Inventory: 111 257 of the Collection of Minutel-SL, Cassettiera 01, Cassetto 010, N. 023) Reproduced with the kind permission of the Leghorn Merchants' Network, Livorno, Italy

5.9 *Design of the pomp and magnificence of the carousel made in the Place Royale in Paris on the 5th, 6th and 7th of April 1612*, engraving by Claude Chastillon (1560?–1616?) and published by Gabriel Tavernier (1520?–1614), Etching and burin, 39.5x50.4cm. Reproduced under Open License by Library of the National Institute of Art History, Jacques Doucet collections, Paris. (Atlas historique de Paris, Michel Huard, IPTC Photo Metadata)

5.10 Anon. c. 1627–29. Ink on paper, 27x20cm. Syon Y III 2, B3E3, Alnwick Castle archives. (Duggan 2001, Fig. 41)

5.11 Ink on paper, 28x31cm. Syon Y III 2 B3, E5, Alnwick Castle archives. (Duggan 2001, Fig. 42)

5.12 Detail from Bird's-eye plan of the west central district of London c. 1660, etching by Wenceslaus Hollar (1607–1677), London. Digital Image: 22302 LUNA: Folger Digital Image Collection, Folger Shakespeare Library. Reproduction permitted under Creative Commons Attribution-ShareAlike 4.0 International Public License

5.13 Detail of St Paul's, Covent Garden, London: elevations of the east and west prospects of the church and Grand Piazza. Inigo Jones (1573–1652) architect. Image by Colen Campbell (1676–1729), *Vitruvius Britannicus*, (London, 1717) vol. II, pp. 21–22. Reproduced with the king permission of the RIBA Collections

5.14 *View of the square in Covent Garden, with St Paul's Church at the end of the square. Without obelisk* c. 1644, by Wenceslaus Hollar (1607–1677), etching, (P.909). Reproduced with the kind permission of the Royal Collection Trust. Royal Collection Trust / © Her Majesty Queen Elizabeth II 2021.

5.15 *View of St Paul's Church in Covent Garden; figures strolling in foreground*. Etching by Thomas Malton, May 21st, 1774, London (19.4x29.9cm). Reproduced with the kind permission of The British Museum (Registration Number G,6.11). Also published by James Lees-Milne (1953) *The Age of Inigo Jones*, referenced above.

5.16 General view of Covent Garden looking north, circa 1720. Engraving by Sutton Nicholls. First published in *London Described of the most noted Regular Buildings both Public and Private, with the Views of several squares in the Liberties of London and Westminster*. Image: Photomechanical print. Digital Id: ppmsca 12670 //hdl.loc.gov/loc.pnp/ppmsca.12670, Library of Congress Control Number 2006686206, Reproduction Number LC-DIG-ppmsca-12670 (digital file from original print). No known restrictions on publication in the US.

5.17 Fragment retained in the North Arcade of Covent Garden

5.18 Detail of St Paul's, Covent Garden, London: elevations of the east and west prospects of the church and Grand Piazza. Inigo Jones (1573–1652) architect. Image by Colen Campbell (1676–1729), *Vitruvius Britannicus*, (London, 1717) vol. II, pp. 21–22. © RIBA Collections

5.19 Detail of General view of Covent Garden looking north, circa 1720. Engraving by Sutton Nicholls. First published in *London Described of the most noted Regular Buildings both Public and Private, with the Views of several squares in the Liberties of London and Westminster*. Image: Photomechanical print. Digital Id: ppmsca 12670 //hdl.loc.gov/loc.pnp/ppmsca.12670, Library of Congress Control Number 2006686206, Reproduction Number LC-DIG-ppmsca-12670 (digital file from original print). No known restrictions on publication in the US.

5.20 Extract from W. Edward Riley and Laurence Gomme (eds.) (1912) *Survey of London: Volume V, St Giles-in-The-Fields, Pt II*. Referenced above.

5.21 *A view of Covent Garden Piazza, London, looking west, with Saint Paul's, Covent Garden, the so-called 'Actor's Church'* (London c. 1702–1772 Bath), oil on canvas 22½x377/8in. (57.2x96.2cm), by Samuel Scott (1702–1772). Author's print.

5.22 (Duggan 2001, Fig. 57b, from Archives, Alnwick Castle)

5.23 (Duggan 2001, Fig. 57a, from Archives, Alnwick Castle)

5.24 (Duggan 2001)

5.25 Detail from *Morgan's Map of the Whole of London in 1682*. Survey of the City of London and the surrounding built-up area (including Westminster and part of Southwark), on a scale of 300 feet to the inch, completed in 1682 by William Morgan. From a facsimile published by Harry Margary in association with the Guildhall Library in 1977. Reproduced with the kind permission of British History Online http://www.british-history.ac.uk/no-series/london-map-morgan/1682/map

5.26 The House of Lord Archer in Covent Garden c. 1725, engraving attributed to Sutton Nichols (32.6x45.4cm), Bequeathed by John Charles Crowle (1811). Reproduced with the kind permission of The British Museum (Registration Number G,6.32).

5.27 Author

5.28 Crowle's Plan. Anon. c. 1690. Ink, (32x45cm) From Crowle's extra-illustrated copy of *Pennant*, Vol. 6. Reproduced with the kind permission of The British Museum, UK

5.29 Author's photographic record of item in Box 552, London Metropolitan Archives. Background material for *Survey of London: Volume V, St Giles-in-The-Fields, Pt II*. Referenced above

5.30 Author's photographic record of item in Box 552, London Metropolitan Archives. Background material for *Survey of London: Volume III, St Giles-in-The-Fields, Pt I: Lincoln's Inn Fields*. Referenced above

5.31 Blome's Map of the parish of St. Paul, c. 1686, "Plate 6," in *Survey of London: Volume 36, Covent Garden*, ed. F H W Sheppard (London: London County Council, 1970), 6. Reproduced with the kind permission of *British History Online*, http://www.british-history.ac.uk/survey-london/vol36/plate-6.

5.32 The Four Times of Day: Morning c. 1736, oil on canvas by William Hogarth (1697–1764) (29x24in.). National Trust Images/John Hammond. Reproduced with the kind permission of Upton House, Warwickshire (NT 446681)

5.33 From Records Box 552 of *Survey of London. London: Metropolitan Archives. Survey of London: Volume 3, St Giles-in-The-Fields*, Pt I: Lincoln's Inn Fields, ed. W. Edward Riley and Laurence Gomme. London: London County Council, 1912. British History Online. www.british-history.ac.uk/survey-london/vol3/pt1/plate-3

Reference of Figures

6.12 Detail from *Morgan's Map of the Whole of London in 1682*. Survey of the City of London and the surrounding built-up area (including Westminster and part of Southwark), on a scale of 300 feet to the inch, completed in 1682 by William Morgan. From a facsimile published by Harry Margary in association with the Guildhall Library in 1977. Reproduced with the kind permission of British History Online http://www.british-history.ac.uk/no-series/london-map-morgan/1682/map

6.13 Author's markup of Google map in 2020

6.14 Portrait of *Thomas Wriothesley (1607–67), 4th Earl of Southampton*, wearing his Garter Star and holding his Staff of Office as Lord High Treasurer c.1660 by Sir Peter Lely (1618–1680), Oil on Canvas (50x40in.). Collection of the Trustees of the Western Park Foundation, UK. Image reproduced with the kind permission of Bridgeman Images, Philip Mould Ltd, London

6.15 Rachel de Ruvigny, Countess of Southampton (c. 1640) by Anthony Van Dyck (1599–1641), oil on canvas (222.4x131.6cm). Digital record made available on the NGV Collection Online through the generous support of Ms Carol Grigor through Metal Manufactures Limited. Reproduced with the kind permission of the National Gallery of Victoria, Australia

6.16 Detail from Hollar's c. Bird's-eye plan of London c. 1660. Etching. Image reproduced with the kind permission of The Trustees of the British Museum under a Creative Commons Attribution-NonCommercial-ShareAlike 4.0 International (CC BY-NC-SA 4.0) license https://www.britishmuseum.org/collection/object/P_Q-6-136

6.17 Detail from Hollar's c. Bird's-eye plan of London c. 1660. Etching. Image reproduced with the kind permission of The Trustees of the British Museum under a Creative Commons Attribution-NonCommercial-ShareAlike 4.0 International (CC BY-NC-SA 4.0) license https://www.britishmuseum.org/collection/object/P_Q-6-136

6.18 Etching of Southampton House. Image from author's 1834 print of an antique print held by the Bedford Estate

6.19 Map of London 1661 by Richard Newcourt and William Faithorne Snr., London. Reproduced with the kind permission of the London Topographical Society. https://londontopsoc.org/library/images/#gallery-15

6.20 Southampton or Bloomsbury Square, etching and engraving made by Sutton Nicholls and published by John Bowles c. 1720–1728. Bibliographic reference: Crace (1878) *A Catalogue of Maps, Plans and Views of London, Westminster and Southwark*, collected and arranged by Frederick Crace. Image reproduced with the kind permission of The Trustees of the British Museum under a Creative Commons Attribution-NonCommercial-ShareAlike 4.0 International (CC BY-NC-SA 4.0) license

6.21 Author's markup of detail from *Morgan's Map of the Whole of London in 1682*. Survey of the City of London and the surrounding built-up area (including Westminster and part of Southwark), on a scale of 300 feet to the inch, completed in 1682 by William Morgan. From a facsimile published by Harry Margary in association with the Guildhall Library in 1977. Reproduced with the kind permission of British History Online http://www.british-history.ac.uk/no-series/london-map-morgan/1682/map

6.22 Detail from *Morgan's Map of the Whole of London in 1682*. Survey of the City of London and the surrounding built-up area (including Westminster and part of Southwark), on a scale of 300 feet to the inch, completed in 1682 by William Morgan. From a facsimile published by Harry Margary in association with the Guildhall Library in 1977. Reproduced with the kind permission of British History Online http://www.british-history.ac.uk/no-series/london-map-morgan/1682/map

Reference of Figures

Index

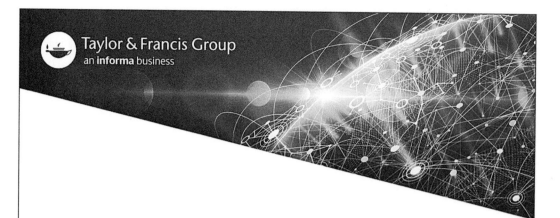